Agricultural Development Principles

The Johns Hopkins Studies in Development

Vernon W. Ruttan and T. Paul Schultz, Consulting Editors

Agricultural Development in the Third World
edited by Carl K. Eicher and John M. Staatz

Agricultural Development: An International Perspective,
revised and expanded edition
by Yujiro Hayami and Vernon W. Ruttan

Redesigning Rural Development: A Strategic Perspective
by Bruce F. Johnston and William C. Clark

The Agrarian Question and Reformism in Latin America
by Alain de Janvry

Basic Needs in Developing Countries
by Frances Stewart

Factories and Food Stamps: The Puerto Rico Model
of Development
by Richard Weiskoff

State and Countryside: Development Policy and Agrarian
Politics in Latin America
by Merilee S. Grindle

Neoconservative Economics in the Southern Cone
of Latin America, 1973–1983
by Joseph Ramos

Robert D. Stevens and Cathy L. Jabara

Agricultural Development Principles

Economic Theory and Empirical Evidence

The Johns Hopkins University Press
Baltimore and London

The Johns Hopkins University Press, 701 West 40th Street, Baltimore, Maryland 21211
The Johns Hopkins Press Ltd., London

The paper used in this publication meets the minimum requirements of American National Standard for Information Sciences—Permanence of Paper for Printed Library Materials, ANSI Z39.48-1984.

Library of Congress Cataloging-in-Publication Data

Stevens, Robert D., (Robert Dale), 1927–
  Agricultural development principles.

  (Johns Hopkins studies in development)
  Bibliography: p.
  Includes index.
  1. Agriculture—Economic aspects—Developing countries. I. Jabara, Cathy L.
II. Title. III. Series.
HD1417.S66 1988   338.1′8′091724   87-31076
ISBN 0-8018-3581-X (alk. paper)
ISBN 0-8018-3582-8 (pbk. : alk. paper)

For the hardworking, efficient, low-income farmers of the world—that through increasing understanding of the theory and practice of agricultural development they may escape their cycle of poverty.

Contents

List of Figures   *xvii*

List of Tables   *xxi*

Foreword by G. Edward Schuh   *xxv*

Preface   *xxvii*

List of Abbreviations   *xxxi*

1   Introduction: Social Learning, Development Goals, and Political Systems   *1*

Agricultural Development in the Perspective of World History   *2*
Development as Social Learning: Increasing Control over Technological, Institutional, Economic, and Social Variables   *4*
The Goals of Development   *5*
Political Systems and Agricultural Development   *6*
Important Concepts   *6*
Sample Questions   *7*

I   Agricultural Progress and Structural Transformation in Less Developed Nations

Introduction to Part I   *11*

2   Population, Resources, and Agricultural Development   *13*

Population Growth   *13*
   The Malthusian Model   *13*
   The Demographic Transition Model   *14*
   Prospects for Population Growth   *16*
Physical Resources for Agriculture in Less Developed Nations   *18*
   Climate, Water, Soils, and Biological Environment   *18*
   Arable Land Availability   *19*
   Size of the Farming Unit   *21*
   Implications of Physical Resources for Agricultural Development   *21*

Growth and Declines in Food and Agricultural Production   *21*
    The Demand and Supply Framework   *21*
    Real and Nominal Price and Income Changes   *23*
    Total and per Capita Food and Agricultural Production   *24*
Food Grain Prices, Stocks, and Trade   *26*
    The Gradually Declining Real Cost of Food Grains   *26*
    Comfortable Levels of World Cereal Stocks   *26*
    Historic Increases in Grain Exports from More Developed Nations   *27*
Summary and Conclusions   *28*
Important Concepts   *29*
Sample Questions   *29*

3   The Role of Agriculture in Economic Development   *31*
Development: Its Meaning and Measurement   *31*
    Meanings of Development   *31*
    Measures of Economic Growth   *32*
    Measures of Development   *33*
Growth and Variability in World Income   *36*
    Per Capita Income and National Economic Growth   *36*
    World Concentration of Income and Human Productivity   *37*
    Inequality in Personal Income Distribution   *38*
Changing Consumer Demand and Income Growth   *41*
    Gradual Growth of Personal Savings   *41*
    Patterns of Consumption with Economic Growth   *41*
    Nutritional Need and the Economic Demand for Food   *43*
The Growing Demand for Food and Agricultural Products   *46*
    The Rate of Population Growth and Food Demand   *46*
    Effect of Income on Food Demand   *47*
    Rate of Growth in Food Demand   *48*
The Structural Transformation of Less Developed Economies   *49*
    Measurement of Changes in Economic Structure   *49*
    Forces Causing Changes in Economic Structure   *49*
    Increasing Functional Specialization and Uneven Regional Growth   *50*
The Role of Agriculture in Economic Development   *52*
    Contributions of Agriculture to Other Sectors   *53*
    Contributions of Other Sectors to Agriculture   *53*
Important Concepts   *53*
Sample Questions   *54*

II   **The Economic and Social Theory of Agricultural Development**
Introduction to Part II   *57*

4   Economics of Traditional Agriculture   *59*

Traditional Agriculture: Definitions and Hypotheses   *59*
  What Is Traditional Agriculture?   *60*
  The Importance of the Study of Low-Income Farming Areas   *61*
  Five Hypotheses About the Economics of Traditional Agriculture   *61*
Empirical Findings About Traditional Agriculture   *62*
  The Productivity of Land, Livestock, and Labor   *63*
  The Price Responsiveness of Traditional Farmers   *65*
  Productivity and Farm Size   *67*
  Uncertainty and Variability in Traditional Agriculture   *69*
The Economic Equilibrium Model of Traditional Agriculture   *70*
  Little Change in Technological, Institutional, Economic, and Cultural Variables   *70*
  Equilibrium in Supply and Demand   *72*
  Efficient Allocation of Resources by Traditional Farmers   *73*
  Low Return on Investment in Traditional Agriculture   *77*
Growth in Traditional Agriculture   *79*
  The Neoclassical Model of Economic Growth   *79*
  Greater Use of Traditional Agricultural Inputs   *79*
Program Failures, Economic Theory, and Agricultural Development Strategies   *82*
  Development Program Failure Due to Wrong Theory   *82*
  The Implications for Development Strategy   *83*
  Conclusions   *84*
Important Concepts   *85*
Sample Questions   *85*

5   Theories of Socioeconomic Change, Cultural Variables, and Agricultural Growth   *88*

Social System Change and Agricultural Development   *88*
  Introduction and Objectives   *88*
  Pecuniary Variables Insufficient to Explain Economic Actions   *90*
Theories of Socioeconomic Development   *91*
  Evolutionary Modernization Theories   *92*
  Conflict and Marxist Theories   *97*
Cultural Variables and Agricultural Development   *99*
  The Components of Cultural Systems   *99*
  Institutions, Organizations, and Change   *100*
  Institutions and Agricultural Development   *102*
  Institutions and Economic Behavior   *103*
  Organizations and Institutions in Agriculture   *107*
Conclusions   *109*
Important Concepts   *111*
Sample Questions   *111*

6   Agricultural Development Theory   *113*

Introduction   *113*
  The Value of Economic Theory for Practitioners   *113*
  Investment Concepts   *114*
  Classical and Modern Agricultural Production Functions   *117*
Partial Theories of Economic and Agricultural Development   *119*
  The Conservation Model   *119*
  The Industrial Fundamentalism Model   *121*
  The Urban-Industrial Impact Model   *123*
  The Diffusion Model   *123*
  The Cultural-Change-First Model and the Community Development
  Movement   *125*
  The Neo-Marxist and Dependency Models   *127*
  Growth-Stage Theories   *130*
  The Schultz High-Payoff Input Model   *132*
The Induced Innovation Model of Agricultural Development   *134*
  The Four Elements of the Induced Innovation Model   *135*
  The Central Concepts of Induced Technological Innovation   *136*
  Induced Institutional Innovation   *143*
  Induced Innovation in the Public Sector   *146*
  Criticisms and Conclusions About the Induced Innovation Model   *148*
Income Distribution and Agricultural Development   *151*
  Economic and Social Theory of Personal Income Distribution   *151*
  Four Economic Factors That Influence Income Equity   *152*
  Government Strategies to Reduce Income Disparities   *158*
Important Concepts   *159*
Sample Questions   *160*

7   Land Expansion and Labor Supply   *161*

Introduction   *161*
Land in Agricultural Development   *163*
  Economic Evaluation of Land Development   *164*
  Higher Returns to Investment in Currently Farmed Land   *167*
  New Land Development and Technological, Institutional, and Economic
  Change   *167*
  Alternative Arrangements for Investment in New Land   *169*
  Criteria and Policies for Land Development   *175*
Labor in Agricultural Development   *175*
  Economics of Household Labor Allocation   *176*
  Female Labor in Agricultural Development   *178*
  Labor Supply   *182*
  Labor Demand   *185*

Labor Productivity, Employment, and Wages   *190*
Policies for Increased Employment, Productivity, and Equity   *194*
Important Concepts   *195*
Sample Questions   *195*

III Sources of Accelerated Change in Agriculture: Investment in Technology, Institutions, and Human Capital

Introduction to Part III   *199*

8   Economics of Change in Biological and Chemical Technologies   *203*

Increasing Crop Productivity on Currently Farmed Lands   *203*
Guidelines from Economic Theory   *204*
Large Shifts to More Productive Inputs   *206*
Economics of the Seed and Fertilizer (Green) Revolution   *207*
Farm Level Effects   *207*
National Effects   *209*
Future Prospects   *211*
Demand for Other Complementary Inputs   *216*
Increasing Animal Productivity   *219*
Characteristics of Animal Production in Less Developed Nations   *219*
Limited Increases in Animal Productivity   *221*
Strategies for Increasing Animal Productivity   *222*
Conclusions   *223*
Important Concepts   *224*
Sample Questions   *224*

9   Economics of Change in Mechanical Technologies   *226*

Introduction   *226*
Agricultural Mechanization in Less Developed Nations   *226*
The Isoquant Framework for Analyzing the Economics of Mechanization   *227*
New Hand Tools for Agriculture   *230*
Animal-Powered Mechanization   *231*
Increasing the Productivity of Animal-Powered Mechanization   *232*
Introducing Animal Power in New Areas   *232*
Stationary and Wheeled Motorized Power   *234*
Stationary and Hand-Carried Motorized Machinery   *234*
Tractor-Powered Machinery   *235*
Irrigation and Drainage   *239*
The Importance and Potential of Irrigation   *239*
Large Gravity-Flow and Pump Irrigation Projects   *240*
Economic Issues in Managing and Servicing Agricultural Machinery   *242*
Policy Issues in Agricultural Mechanization   *243*

Research, Development, and Supply   *245*
Import Controls, Taxes, and Subsidies   *246*
Employment and Income Distribution   *247*
Important Concepts   *247*
Sample Questions   *247*

10   Economics of Change in Institutions   *249*

Institutional Change, Technology, and the Role of the Social Sciences   *250*
The Role of Governing Institutions   *250*
Externalities   *250*
Technology and Institutional Change   *251*
The Social Sciences and Institutional Change   *251*
Improving Rural Financial Markets and Farm Credit   *252*
The Expanding Demand for Financial Services   *253*
Empirical Studies of Rural Financial Markets   *254*
Augmenting the Supply of Savings and Credit   *260*
Policies for Improved Rural Financial Markets   *263*
Cooperative Institutions and Agricultural Development   *265*
The Principles of Member-Controlled Cooperatives   *266*
The Example of the Comilla Village Cooperatives   *267*
Cooperatives and Development   *268*
Changes in Rights to the Use of Land: Land Reforms, Collective Farming, and Communes   *269*
The Wide Range of Landholding Arrangements   *270*
The Great Variability in Farm Size, Tenancy, and Landlessness   *272*
Land Reform, Tenure Reform, and Agricultural Productivity   *274*
Experiences with Agrarian Reform Programs   *277*
Conclusions About Changes in Landholding Arrangements   *282*
Important Concepts   *283*
Sample Questions   *283*

11   Investing in Research, Education, Extension, and Communications   *285*

The History of Agricultural Productivity Growth   *286*
Slow Increases in Agricultural Productivity in Human History   *286*
The Transition to a Science-Based Agriculture   *289*
High Total Agricultural Productivity Growth Rates in More Developed Nations   *290*
Accelerating Agricultural Research in Less Developed Nations   *291*
The Complexity of Technological and Socioeconomic Constraints   *292*
The Agricultural Research Gap   *292*
Economics of the Demand and Supply of Agricultural Research   *295*
The Dependency of Research Demand upon Expected Returns   *296*
High Social Returns of Much Agricultural Research   *296*

Demand for Social Science Knowledge *297*
Price Elasticity of Agricultural Products and the Demand for Research *298*
Increasing the Supply of Agricultural and Institutional Research and Technology Transfer *300*
Future Prospects for Agricultural Research: The New Genetics and Other Breakthroughs *306*
School Education for Increased Agricultural Productivity *308*
Education as an Investment in Human Capital *308*
The Demand for School Education *309*
Supplying School Education for Agricultural Development *311*
Agricultural Extension, Nonformal Education, and Communication Investments *313*
Demand and Supply of Nonformal Education *313*
Returns to Investment in Nonformal Education *314*
Agricultural Extension: Problems and a Model *315*
Economics of Communication Services *316*
Complementarities and Substitutions in Agricultural Research, Education, and Communication Investments *317*
Important Concepts *318*
Sample Questions *318*

IV National Policies and Programs for Agricultural Development
Introduction to Part IV *323*

12 Transforming Traditional Agricultural Marketing *325*
Marketing Problems, Functions, and Models *325*
Marketing Problems *325*
The Economic Functions of Marketing *326*
Marketing Models *327*
Marketing and Economic Growth *331*
Factors Causing Growth in Marketing *331*
The Role of Marketing in Development *334*
Evaluating Market System Performance *336*
Limitations of the Perfect Competition Model of Marketing *336*
The Environment-Behavior-Performance Model *336*
Facilitating Agricultural Input Marketing *338*
Biological Inputs *339*
Chemical Inputs *340*
Mechanical Inputs *343*
Aiding Agricultural Product Marketing *346*
Increasing Marketing Performance *346*
Increasing the Productivity of Urban Food Marketing *349*
Government Roles and Policies to Increase Marketing Performance *352*

Institutional Arrangements for Market Intervention *352*
Activities to Increase Marketing Performance *354*
Summary *358*
Important Concepts *359*
Sample Questions *359*

13 Changing Comparative Advantage and Trade Policies in Agricultural Development *360*

The Role of Trade in Agricultural Development *361*
The Theory of Comparative Advantage *362*
Changing Comparative Advantage *366*
The Trade Experiences and Opportunities of Less Developed Countries *368*
The Changing Structure of Trade *368*
Shares of Different Products in Less Developed Countries' Agricultural Exports and Imports *369*
Conditions Under Which International Trade Contributes to Economic Growth *371*
Managing Agricultural Input and Product Trade *373*
Import Substitution *373*
Balance of Payments Controls *374*
Inflation Controls *374*
Government Revenues *375*
Measures for Trade Intervention *375*
Price Measures *375*
Nonprice Measures *376*
Economics of Trade Intervention *377*
Arguments Against Trade Intervention *377*
Arguments for Trade Intervention *378*
Alternative Trade Strategies for Economic and Agricultural Development *382*
Important Concepts *382*
Sample Questions *383*

14 Price Policies and Planning for Agricultural Development *384*

The Role of Government in Planning for Agricultural Development *384*
Introduction *384*
The Economic Functions of Markets and Prices *385*
The Causes and Range of Government Intervention *386*
Private and Social Valuation and the Role of Government *386*
The Range of Government Intervention *388*
The Role of Agricultural Prices in Economic Development *389*
Methods of Agricultural Price Intervention *392*
The Objectives of Pricing Policy *392*

The Instruments of Price Intervention   *393*
The Effects of Price Interventions on Agricultural Development   *401*
Conclusions   *402*
Important Concepts   *403*
Sample Questions   *403*

V   Accelerating Agricultural Development
Introduction to Part V   *407*

15   Agricultural Development Strategies   *409*
Accelerating the Economic and Social Transformation of Agriculture   *410*
The Need for a National Consensus on the Goals of Development   *411*
The Importance of Understanding How Economic and Social Systems Can Be Changed   *412*
The Central Role of Agriculture in Economic Growth   *413*
The Government as Facilitator of Development   *413*
Core Strategic Elements for Rapid Growth in Agriculture   *415*
Investment in High-Return Activities   *415*
Investment in Applied Research   *415*
Investment in Human Capital   *416*
Complementarity Among Investments   *417*
Domestic Prices that Reflect Resource Costs   *418*
Maximizing the Limited Contributions of International Aid   *418*
Moderating Undesirable Income Distribution Effects   *419*
Enhancing Government Performance   *421*
Three Strategies for Agricultural Development   *422*
The High-Payoff Input Strategy   *422*
The Improved-Income-Distribution-with-Growth Strategy   *423*
The Regional, Total-Resource-Focused Strategy   *423*
Summary   *425*
The Different Paths of Agricultural Development in the Twenty-first Century   *425*
Important Concepts   *426*
Sample Questions   *427*

References   *429*
Index   *463*

Figures

1.1. World Population Growth, 8000 B.C. to 5000 A.D.   *3*

2.1. The Demographic Transition in More Developed and Less Developed Nations, 1800–2000   *15*

2.2. Rising and Falling Population Growth Rates in More Developed and Less Developed Nations, 1950–2020   *18*

2.3. Food Problems and Farm Problems Caused by the Relative Rate of Movement of the Supply and Demand Curves   *22*

2.4. Growth in Total and per Capita Agricultural Production in More Developed and Less Developed Nations, 1969–1984   *24*

3.1. Relations Between Standard of Living, Level of Living, Standard of Consumption, and Level of Consumption   *34*

3.2. Income per Capita: India, Kenya, Colombia, Japan, and the United States, 1950–1981, with Projections to 2010   *38*

3.3. Lorenz Curves of Income Distribution: India, Peru, Brazil, Japan, Sweden, and the United States   *40*

3.4. Engel Curves for Food: Declining Shares and Increasing Expenditures   *44*

3.5. Nutritional Need and Economic Demand for Food   *45*

4.1. A Traditional Humid, Upland, Farming System in Asia   *62*

4.2. Long-Term Rice Yields: The Philippines, Thailand, and Taiwan, 1900–1960   *65*

4.3. Farm Size and Production per Unit of Land in Less Developed Nations   *68*

4.4. Stable Demand and Fluctuating Supply for Staple Food Crops in Traditional Agriculture   *73*

4.5. Economic Equilibrium and Economic Efficiency: The Single-Variable Input Example   *74*

4.6. Allocative Efficiency with One Variable Input and Two Crops   *75*

4.7. Economic Equilibrium in Production with Two Inputs and One Product   *76*

4.8. Increased Labor Use in Traditional Agriculture and per Capita Farm Income *81*

5.1. Interrelations Between the Four Elements of the Hayami-Ruttan Induced Innovation Model of Development *89*

5.2. Effects of Owner-Operator and Share Tenant Landholding on Input Use and Agricultural Production *104*

6.1. Stages of Agricultural Development *131*

6.2. Effect of More Productive Technology on Agricultural Output and Costs of Inputs *133*

6.3. Induced Technological Change and Labor-Using and Labor-Saving Technological Change, Shown with Isoquants *136*

6.4. The Relative Prices of Capital and Labor and Types of Technology Developed and Adopted *139*

6.5. Agricultural Labor and Land Productivities and Paths of Technological Change, Selected Nations, 1960–1980 *142*

6.6. Long-Run Path of Induced Technological Development: From Labor Intensive to Capital Intensive Technology *143*

6.7. Decline in the Income Share of Labor with Increases in Population and No Change in Technology *154*

6.8. Relations of Share of Labor in Production to Labor-Using and Labor-Saving Technology *155*

6.9. Price Elasticity of the Demand Curve and Farmers' Income Gains or Losses from Increases in Supply *156*

6.10. Decreasing Food Crop Price and Income of Subsistence Farmers *157*

7.1. Benefit-Cost Analysis of an Investment Project and the Rest of the Economy *165*

7.2. Effect of More Productive Agricultural Technology Adapted to Currently Farmed Lands on Investment in New Land Development *168*

7.3. Agricultural Population Growth During the Economic Transformation *185*

7.4. Demand for Labor on New High-Yielding Crops *186*

7.5. The Movement of Labor Demand and Supply Curves and Changes in Wages *187*

7.6. Human Labor Availability and Use of New Watershed-Based Technology in the South Indian Humid Tropics *191*

7.7. Low or Zero Marginal Product of Labor in Agriculture *192*

III.1. Changes in Input and Product Flows During the Agricultural Transformation *200*

8.1. Decline in Relative Costs of Chemical Fertilizers and Farm Machinery in the United States and Japan, 1880–1960 *205*

8.2. The Greater Response of Modern Rice Varieties to Nitrogen Fertilizer: Experiment Station Yields in the United States and India, 1964 *208*

8.3. Profitable Nitrogen Applications for Irrigated Rice, with Traditional and Modern Varieties, the Philippines *212*

8.4. Resource Complementarity and Resource Substitution *213*

8.5. The Complementary Demand for Pesticide with Modern Crop Varieties *217*

9.1. Identifying Appropriate, Low-Cost Agricultural Technologies: An All-Technology Isoquant with Two Different Ratios of the Cost of Capital to Labor *228*

9.2. Capital and Labor Costs for Land Preparation: Hand, Animal, and Motor Tiller Power *233*

9.3. Cost of Operating Small and Large Machines with Different Amounts of Farmland *239*

9.4. Initial Capital Costs and Required High Annual Benefits for an Irrigation Project *241*

9.5. Changing Cost of Labor and the Shift to Motorized Agricultural Power *245*

10.1. Shifts Caused by Development in the Demand and Supply of Commercial Agricultural Credit *254*

10.2. Effects of a Government Interest Rate Ceiling on the Quantity of Agricultural Credit Borrowed *264*

10.3. Effect of Subsidized Credit on the Supply and Cost of Credit *265*

10.4. Unimodal and Bimodal Farm-Size Distributions in Taiwan, India, and Colombia *273*

10.5. Lorenz Curves of Agricultural Land Distribution, Seven Nations *274*

10.6. Adoption Curves of Modern Rice Varieties on Three Sizes of Farms in Thirty Villages in Asia *277*

10.7. Net Income for the Tenant Under Different Rent Terms in Taiwan, 1948–1960 *279*

11.1. Relations Between Accelerators of Social Learning and Elements of the Hayami-Ruttan Model of Induced Innovation *286*

11.2. Historical Trends in Rice and Wheat Yields, 750–1959 *289*

11.3. Variability Due to Weather and the Economic Optimum Level of Nitrogen for Two Rice Varieties, Mallgaya, the Philippines *293*

11.4. Spatial Distribution of Crops Planted in Mounds in a Farmer's Field, Abakaliki, Anambra State, Nigeria *294*

11.5. Yield Gaps Between Experiment Stations and Farmers' Fields Due to Biological and Socioeconomic Constraints *295*

11.6. Effect of the Elasticity of Demand for an Agricultural Product on Pressure for Government Agricultural Research *298*

11.7. Interrelations Between Farm-Level and Experiment-Station-Level Agricultural Research *305*

11.8. Average World Yields, Maximum Yields in Selected Tropical Experiment Stations, and Estimated Potential Yields *307*

11.9. Visit and Training System Model for Agricultural Extension *316*

IV.1. Principal Components in Agricultural Production-Distribution Systems *323*

12.1. Marketing Margins for Rice and Meat, Selected Countries *328*

12.2. Components of National Food Consumption *333*

12.3. Retail Food as Percentage of Total Food and per Capita Income *333*

12.4. Rates of Growth in Retail Food and Marketing Services with Increases in per Capita Income *334*

12.5. Alternative Farm Input Supply Channels *345*

12.6. Changes in Food Retailing and Wholesaling in Urban Areas of Less Developed Nations During Economic Development *351*

12.7. Potential Economic Gains and Losses from Marketing Monopolies *355*

13.1. Comparative Advantage and Gains from Trade in Less Developed Nations *364*

13.2. Immiserizing Growth with Free Trade *372*

13.3. Impact of a Tariff on Income and Trade *378*

14.1. Economics of Administered Prices *395*

15.1. Dual Organizational Needs of Each Agricultural Support Activity *425*

Tables

1.1. The Two Great Transitions in History: The Agricultural and the Scientific-Industrial (Modernization) *3*

2.1. Population Growth Rates, Percentage of World Population, 1975 and 2000, Fifteen Selected Nations *17*

2.2. Cultivated and Potential Arable Land, World Regions, 1965 *20*

2.3. Changes in per Capita Food Production, World Regions, 1968–1983 *25*

2.4. Declining Real Cost of Food Grains, 1970–1986 *27*

2.5. Changing Pattern of Net World Grain Trade, 1934–1986 *28*

3.1. Gross National Product per Capita and Real Rates of Growth, Selected Nations *37*

3.2. Variability in Household Income Distribution in Less Developed and More Developed Nations *39*

3.3. Changing Shares of Disposable Personal Income, Personal Savings, and Personal Consumption Expenditures, with per Capita Income Increases, Thirty-two Selected Nations *42*

3.4. Changing Personal Consumption and Expenditure Patterns as Income Increases, Thirty-two Selected Nations *44*

3.5. Changing Structure of National Economies with Income Growth, as Measured by Sector Income Shares *50*

3.6. Changing Structure of National Economies with Income Growth, as Measured by the Labor Force in the Agricultural, Industrial, and Service Sectors *50*

4.1. Average Yields for Maize, 1981–1984, Selected Nations *64*

4.2. Average Yields for Potatoes, 1982–1984, Selected Nations *64*

4.3. Average Yields for Unhulled Paddy Rice, 1981–1984, Selected Nations *64*

4.4. Average Yields for Wheat, 1981–1984, Selected Nations *64*

A4.1. Topics for Study of an Agricultural System *86*

A4.2. An Exercise to Determine How Much of a Resource (Input) to Use to Obtain the Greatest Return (Profit) in a Production Process *87*

5.1. The Great Number of Organizations Serving Agriculture in More Developed Nations: The Example of a County in Michigan *108*

5.2. Characteristics of Organizations Serving Agriculture in Less Developed and More Developed Nations *108*

6.1. Investment: How Income and Capital Stock Are Increased, an Illustration *116*

6.2. Large Increases in Agricultural Production with Little Change in Land Farmed: the United States, Japan, and France *121*

6.3. Changes in Relative Costs of Labor, Land, Fertilizer, and Machinery: Japan and the United States, 1880–1960 *141*

7.1. Rates of Change in Productivity per Agricultural Laborer, Land per Laborer, and Yield: Japan, Taiwan, and the United States, 1876–1967 *163*

7.2. Contributions of Area and Yield to Increases in World Grain Production, 1948–1971 *170*

7.3. Performance Ratings, Twenty-four Tropical Land Development Projects *174*

7.4. Female Labor in Agriculture in Six Less Developed African Nations *180*

7.5. Comparisons of Labor Use and Productivity in Rice Farming: West Bengal, India, and the Kinki District, Japan *188*

8.1. Changing Factor Shares of Agricultural Inputs in U.S. Agriculture, 1870–1958 *207*

8.2. An Illustration of Input Complementarity: Maize Yield in Western Iowa with Different Levels of Nitrogen and Phosphorus Fertilizer *214*

8.3. Fertilizer Use, 1970 and 1983, Selected Nations *216*

8.4. Annual Yields of Traditional and Modern Livestock Production Systems *220*

9.1. Importance of Hand, Animal, and Mechanical Power in Agriculture, Three Less Developed Nations *227*

9.2. An Illustrative Estimate of Optimum Tractor Size for Different Farm Sizes *238*

10.1. Farm Household Indebtedness by Type of Lender, Six Less Developed Nations *255*

10.2. Example of the Distribution of Loans by Real Interest Rates, Rural Areas in Chile *258*

10.3. Landholding Arrangements Arrayed by Extent of Social Control of Production and Consumption *271*

10.4. Tenancy and Sharecropping, Thirteen Less Developed Nations *275*

11.1. Population Densities that Can Be Supported by Different Agricultural Systems *287*

11.2. Rates of Change in Agricultural Output, Input, and Productivity, Japan, 1880–1975 *291*

11.3. Rates of Change in Agricultural Output, Input, and Productivity, the United States, 1870–1982 *291*

12.1. Income Elasticity of Demand for Retail Food and Marketing Services with Increasing per Capita Income *334*

12.2. Environment-Behavior-Performance Framework for Analysis of Food System Organization and Performance *337*

12.3. Optimum Rice-Processing Facilities, Employment, and Income: An Example from Sierra Leone *350*

13.1. Production Possibilities for Two-Country Trade Example *363*

13.2. Absolute Advantage in the Cost of Producing Wheat and Steel *365*

13.3. Less Developed Countries' Exports and Share Imported by More Developed Countries, 1955–1980 *368*

13.4. Less Developed Countries' Imports and Share Exported by More Developed Countries, 1955–1980 *369*

13.5. Less Developed Countries' Shares of World Exports and Imports of Basic Agricultural Commodities, 1960 and 1981 *370*

Foreword

There is probably no greater challenge facing national political leaders worldwide than the problem of agricultural development. The bulk of the world's population earns its living from employment in agriculture. A majority of these people, especially in the developing countries, are also poor—living on the bare edge of subsistence. Even in developed countries, a disproportionate share of the poor earn their living in agriculture.

The tragedy as we enter the final years of the twentieth century is that the knowledge is at hand to lift these people from their desperate state of poverty. We know what it takes to obtain successful agricultural development, and there are many successful demonstrations in both the developed and developing countries. Yet policy makers in the developing countries fail to use the knowledge at hand to improve the welfare and incomes of the bulk of their population. Often, instead, they cater to their politically volatile urban consumers, or concentrate on *symbols* of development such as steel mills and manufacturing plants that produce goods for political elites rather than for the broad masses.

One of the important ironies of this situation is that strengthening agriculture would provide both the basis and means for a broader and more rapid rate of industrialization in these countries. A productive agriculture would not only generate the "surplus" needed to finance a more rapid rate of economic development, it would also broaden the domestic market to absorb the output of a rapidly growing manufacturing sector.

This issue is not just a problem of national governments and their people, however. It is now a problem of the global community. A major share of the world's agricultural output is produced in the wrong place. Too much of global agricultural output is produced at high cost in the developed countries of the United States, the European Economic Community, and Japan, where it consumes huge government expenditures in the form of subsidies. Far too little of global output is produced in the low-cost developing countries, and this because governments in those countries discriminate severely against farmers with their economic policies. The result is a global loss of resource efficiency, with a loss in global income the logical consequence. In addition, there is the waste of public resources that are used to subsidize high-cost producers. These resources have alternative uses that could do much to further improve the lot of the poor and to advance economic development.

This book pulls together the best thinking of the brightest minds who have addressed the problem of agricultural development. It is comprehensive in its treatment of the problem and optimistic in its perspective on what can be done. Its audience includes advanced undergraduates and graduate students in the field of economic development and in schools of agriculture, as well as policy makers in all countries.

A distinguishing feature of the book is its emphasis on the use of neoclassical economics as the basis for both analysis and prescription. These are powerful analytical tools. Their use in no way depreciates the importance of political forces as factors holding back agricultural development, or as the source of pressures that constrain the choices policy makers can make. Economics is a key part of the development problem, and if we don't understand what the economic choices are there is little hope for getting the development process moving in the right direction.

Knowledge is a powerful source of economic growth. That is why new production technology and new institutions—the output of agricultural research—are such powerful sources of economic growth. It is also why formal schooling and other forms of education and training are inevitably associated with high levels of per capita income. This book, by synthesizing what is known about agricultural development and making it available as a cohesive whole, promises to be a source of economic growth in its own right.

G. Edward Schuh
The World Bank

Preface

Much empirical research on the agriculture of less developed nations has been carried out during the last thirty years, and great strides have been made in constructing a useful, coherent economic theory of agricultural development. However, knowledge of these advances has not been easily accessible. The objective of this book is to present to those interested in agricultural development an integrated theory that provides the intellectual tools needed to direct research and action programs into more productive forms.

A beginning text presenting current knowledge of the economic principles of agricultural development is not now available. This volume has been designed for a first college course in agricultural development. In U.S. universities, the junior or senior undergraduate year, or the first year of graduate studies, has been the usual place in the curriculum for beginning study of the economics of agricultural development. Other books currently available on agricultural development at this level of difficulty are either out of date (Mellor 1966), incomplete in their coverage of the economic theory of agricultural development (Wortman and Cummings 1978; Arnon 1981), or lacking in sufficient material from representative empirical studies (Ghatak and Ingersent 1984). Other texts (Hayami and Ruttan 1971 and 1985) have been written primarily for graduate students and assume much greater knowledge of economics. The material in this volume is drawn from twenty-five years of research and teaching in agricultural development in the United States and in less developed nations by the senior author and from domestic and overseas research by the junior author.

The Theoretical Underpinnings and Design

A central hypothesis of this work is that neoclassical economic analysis can lead to more effective strategies and programs for increasing agricultural production, income, and employment in all less developed nations. By drawing on empirical research in many of these nations over the last three decades, we have demonstrated the great power of neoclassical economic theory to clarify agricultural development problems. If skillfully used, it can increase an understanding of agricultural development, whether the rural areas are dominated by tribal organizations, smallholders, tenant farmers, large landholders, rural laborers, cooperatives, collectives, or communes. In addition, economic research on agricultural development problems in one part of the world can often elucidate problems in another part of the world; for example, Africans might find that economic studies of land tenure reforms in Latin America provide them with knowledge that can help them make better decisions about land tenure changes in their own countries.

We have used the Hayami-Ruttan model of induced development (Hayami and Ruttan 1971 and 1985) to integrate our theory, because it has advanced our understanding of agricultural development in several ways. First, it incorporates institutional change into the development process instead of assuming that institutions do not change or that change is exogenous to the economic system and is unpredictable. Second, it explicitly recognizes the interactions between cultural variables and the other important variables—resources, technology, and institutions. Third, it illuminates the development process through its focus on the relative prices of inputs and the effect of these changing price ratios on the different paths of agricultural development, both in more developed and less developed nations.

The three major sections of this book focus on the following general questions. (1) What is the nature and scope of the agricultural development problems facing less developed nations? (part 1). (2) Does current theory of agricultural development and of general socioeconomic development provide an economically rigorous and consistent guide for the acceleration of agricultural development? (part 2). (3) To what extent can the application of this theory in less developed nations improve the design and implementation of sound programs, projects, and policies for agricultural development? We largely take the micro point of view in part 3 and the national, or macro, point of view in part 4. A synthesis of strategies for agricultural development follows in part 5.

Those who believe in Marxist theory of development have written a considerable amount about the problems of less developed nations during the last two decades. Economic instruction in some of these nations is often largely limited by national ideology to Marxist and socialist teachings about development. As Marxist literature employs a different terminology than that employed in mainstream neoclassical economics, study of these writings and contact with students who use this terminology often creates great difficulties of communication with those who use standard neoclassical economic tools and terminology. For these reasons, we attempt in chapters 5 and 6 to clarify some of the basic tenets and terminology used in current neo-Marxist theory of economic development.

The Intended Audience

The text has been written so that students can understand the needed principles of economic theory without much previous course work in economics or agricultural economics. Technical jargon and mathematical formulations have been kept to a minimum. A knowledge of calculus is not needed.

However, the reader's understanding will be greatly enhanced if previous study has included a first undergraduate course in neoclassical microeconomics or its equivalent, in which the mysteries of supply and demand curves have been explored and the use of production functions examined. For classroom use of this text, such a basic economics course is recommended as a prerequisite. We suggest that readers without an understanding of this theory study these microeconomics topics in a beginning college text. Previous study of production functions and production surfaces, with one factor and two factors varying, will also greatly facilitate the understanding of the economic theory of development. Basic production theory is found in many beginning farm management or production economics texts.

We have kept three specific groups of readers in mind while writing: (1) advanced undergraduates in the fields of economics and agricultural economics from the more developed and urbanized world; (2) graduate students in the many agricultural, other professional, and social science disciplines, whether from less developed or more developed nations; and (3) administrators and practitioners of international, national, and private aid organizations who seek to accelerate agricultural development. The third group includes those who have responsibilities and backgrounds in national politics, international administration, and private and public development and aid organizations. It includes members of such groups as the Peace Corps and missionaries.

Classroom Use

In teaching with these materials, we have found that case studies can complement theoretical learning by helping students comprehend the realities of development problems and the sometimes intricate interactions of cultural, institutional, technological, and economic factors in low-income agriculture. Materials of this kind are provided in some anthropological and agricultural economics monographs or in collections of case studies that have an economic focus. (Examples of these materials are found in note 1 of chapter 4.) The appendix to chapter 4 contains a list of questions about farms and communities that can help the student focus on important questions while reading case materials.

More depth in discussion of any topic can be obtained by drawing on materials in the reference list or from articles in journals. Alternatively, collections of articles such as the excellent one assembled by Eicher and Staatz (1984) may be used. Students' interest can be increased by a classroom focus on a given country and assignment of papers on aspects of its agricultural development. Another suggestion is to require each student to choose a country or an agricultural development problem on which he or she will write a paper and perhaps report the findings to the class.

Credits and Editorial Matters

We wish to acknowledge our debt and to thank many colleagues, fellow professionals, and the pioneering researchers in agricultural development upon whose work we have drawn. They include particularly five leaders in the field: T. W. Schultz, John W. Mellor, Bruce F. Johnston, Yujiro Hayami, and Vernon Ruttan. Their contributions to agricultural development theory will be seen throughout this work.

Throughout the task of writing, Vernon Ruttan and Anders Richter, senior editor at the Johns Hopkins University Press, have provided the encouragement crucial to completion. The development of the initial outline for the text was aided by Robert L. Thompson, who also provided valuable comments on a number of draft chapters. We have been particularly helped by John Staatz, who provided very useful detailed comments and suggestions on the substance and phraseology of a complete draft. He also made important contributions to the first two paragraphs of chapter 14. We have also benefited from the advice received on outlines from Carl K. Eicher and on early drafts of chapters from Carl Liedholm, Harry Schwarzweller, Jay Artis, Allan Schmid, James Shaffer, Vernon Ruttan, Subiah Kannappan, Merle Esmay, Dale Adams, Rick Bernsten, Peter Dorner, Harold Riley, Michael Weber, Warren Samuels, and Vernon Sorenson, as well as many students, including particularly Judy Stallman and Valerie Kelly, who read drafts of these chapters.

Nancy L. Stevens gave us valuable editorial assistance on the whole manuscript, adding gracefulness of expression and improving sentence structure, and punctuation. Johns Hopkins University Press editor Diane Hammond significantly improved the book's readability and visual attractiveness. Nicole Alderman helped in many ways with her secretarial skills, and Patricia Neumann contributed by entering bibliographic citations. Ellen R. White and Ronald D. Tiefenbach of the Center for Cartographic Research of the Michigan State University Department of Geography did the art work for the figures. We also thank the Computer Applications Section of the Office of Medical Education Research and Development of the College of Human Medicine for use of the Macintosh MacDraw program and laser printer in making many of the figures.

In drafting the material, the junior author had primary responsibility for chapters 13 and 14. Any prejudicial language with regard to sex, race, or national origin that escaped either author's scrutiny is entirely unintentional.

Abbreviations

AID   U.S. Agency for International Development
CIAT   Centro Internacional de Agricultura Tropical (International Institute for Tropical Agriculture)
CIMMYT   Centro Internacional de Mejoraminento de Maiz y Trigo (International Wheat and Maize Improvement Center)
FAO   Food and Agriculture Organization of the United Nations
ICRISAT International Crops Research Institute for the Semi-Arid Tropics
IITA   International Institute for Tropical Agriculture
ILO   International Labor Organization
IMF   International Monetary Fund
IRRI   International Rice Research Institute
UNCTAD United Nations Conference on Trade and Development
UNESCO   United Nations Education, Scientific, and Cultural Organization
USDA   United States Department of Agriculture

1

Introduction: Social Learning, Development Goals, and Political Systems

> *It is ironic that economics, long labeled the dismal science, is capable of showing that the bleak natural earth view for food is not compatible with economic history, that history demonstrates that we can augment resources by advances in knowledge. I agree with Margaret Mead: "The future of mankind is openended." Mankind's future is not foreordained by space, energy and cropland. It will be determined by the intelligent evolution of humanity.*
>
> *—T. W. Schultz 1980, p. 641*

We start an exploration to discover how to accelerate agricultural production in less developed nations. Many puzzles appear on this journey that have led to confusion and a jumble of contradictory agricultural development theories, programs, and policies. Some theorists have proposed the need for a new economics to understand how agricultural systems work in some of these nations, particularly in Africa, with its highly varied agricultural and social arrangements.

The economists who scouted the new domain of agricultural development theory in the 1950s and 1960s sought to understand the economics of the diverse agricultures in less developed nations. They attempted to construct a map of economic theory that could guide decisions that would lead to more rapid growth in food and agricultural production. We have found that the economic theory of induced innovation proposed by Hayami and Ruttan (1971 and 1985) provides a useful integrating framework for exploration of the important topics in agricultural development. After much searching in the wilderness of useless theory, we found it exciting to discover a solid economic framework for the analysis of agricultural development, a framework that can be applied to the agricultural development problems of all developing nations—less developed and more developed, market oriented and nonmarket, socialist, and capitalist.

This volume tests the usefulness of the induced innovation theory by using the economic data and the results of empirical research from developing nations

1

over the last three decades. To what extent can the theory explain the successes and failures of agricultural development? Can it map the varied and confusing agricultural development terrains of different parts of the world? Could it guide agricultural investment, price, and trade policies for more effective use of the scarce development resources in the nations of Asia, Africa, and Latin America?

Among the development puzzles examined are the following. How have some less developed nations increased agricultural production as rapidly as more developed nations, such as the United States? Have the nations that placed highest priority on industrialization had better economic performance? To what extent are institutional arrangements in less developed nations, such as high levels of tenancy or the absence of collective and cooperative farming, the cause of slow progress in agricultural development? How best can less developed nations obtain more productive agricultural technology—through transfer from more developed nations or through the development of indigenous technologies more attuned to their unique resource and social conditions? Has poor performance in agricultural input and product marketing presented significant barriers to more rapid agricultural growth? What about the effects of government foreign exchange, price, and international trade policies on agricultural development? These and many other fundamental questions about agricultural development are illuminated in this volume by employing the rigorous tools of economic analysis.

Agricultural Development in the Perspective of World History

The study of economic and agricultural development is concerned with understanding why economic variables change over long periods of time, such as five years, a decade, half a century, and longer. Development, therefore, is not concerned with annual price changes due to cropping cycles nor with random events, like weather, that may temporarily increase or decrease production. The focus is upon the fundamental underlying causes of growth in an economy.

First, we take a very long view. Two great transitions in human economic history have been identified: the agricultural and the scientific-industrial (Kahn 1979). For a significant portion of the world's population, the agricultural transition occurred in the centuries near 8000 B.C. (see table 1.1). Before that time, humans had spent some two million years in hunting bands and as food gatherers in tribelike social groups. The second great transition, the scientific-industrial transition, or modernization, has been occurring since about 1800.

The incredible change occurring now in human history is highlighted by two extraordinary events. The first is the immensely rapid increase in world population, from less than half a billion in 1600 to a projected stabilized world population in the eight to eleven billion range some centuries ahead (see figure 1.1). The second extraordinary event is the very great increase in world production of goods and services, from some two trillion dollars in 1950 to an esti-

Table 1.1. The Two Great Transitions in History: The Agricultural and the Scientific-Industrial (Modernization)

Era	Characteristics	
	Hunting and food gathering (preagricultural and usually primitive)	
8000 B.C.		
	Basically agricultural (preindustrial and usually civilized)	
A.D. 1800		
	Various states of industrialization (modern or technological)	
A.D. 2000		Modernization, or the great transition
	Various states of postindustrialization (but initially 3/4 of world still lives in poor, transitional, or industrial economies)	
A.D. 2200		
	Transition largely completed to a worldwide high-level affluent postindustrial economy	

Source: Adapted from Kahn 1979 (p. 19).

Figure 1.1. World Population Growth, 8000 B.C. to 5000 A.D.

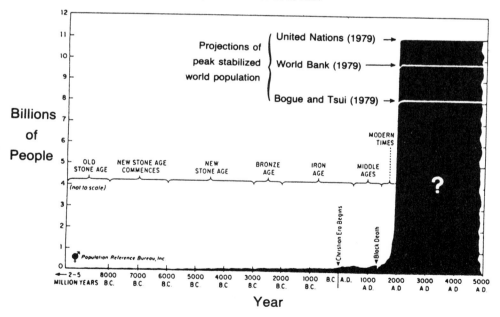

Source: Adapted from Population Reference Bureau 1979.

3

mated fifteen or twenty trillion dollars by the year 2000. During this period, the world's population will shift, barring a catastrophe, "from mostly poor to mostly middle income, or rich; from mostly rural to mostly urban; from mostly pre-industrial and illiterate to mostly industrial and literate; from mostly ill-fed, ill-housed, ill-clothed and short-lived to mostly well-fed, well-housed, well-clothed, and long-lived'' (Kahn 1979, p. 10).

To enable such rapid rates of economic growth in less developed nations, agriculture has to shift from dependence on mining the resources of the natural earth (as in traditional farming, food gathering, and hunting) to use of more productive, science-based methods. For the last several decades, such social and economic transformations of agriculture have been overtaking large areas of less developed nations. In some areas, the agricultural transformation began accelerating in the 1950s, while in more remote regions, agricultural change is only now beginning.

Development as Social Learning: Increasing Control over Technological, Institutional, Economic, and Social Variables

The design of development must be seen as a trial-and-error learning process. Contrary to the ambitions of the cerebral planners, there can be no trial without error. Contrary to the practice of let's-get-on-with-it activists, the poor should not be made to endure repeated trials from which nothing is learned. (Johnston and Clark 1982, p. 35)

Social learning is the process through which people and governments gain knowledge of economic and social processes and of how to influence them so as to better achieve human objectives. An overarching theme of this book is that social, economic, and agricultural development are processes that societies increasingly learn to influence more effectively in order to obtain desired goals. Social learning has been going on since man first learned to communicate, but the pace has increased greatly since the scientific-industrial transition began overtaking developing nations. Social learning is achieved in several ways: (1) by informal, careful, unstructured observation of the results of agricultural and social actions; (2) by learning from increasingly accurate scientific studies of the resources, the technology, and the economic and social conditions; and (3) by the elaboration of ever more powerful economic and social theory tools that illuminate how social systems operate and how they may be changed to improve social outcomes.

Dunn (1971) proposed that humans have passed three thresholds in human social evolution: (1) the emergence of learning in social groups; (2) the greatly increased ability for social organization, which enabled the rise of the great historic civilizations; and, (3) a threshold crossed quite recently

when man developed . . . the classical scientific method addressed to the understanding and design of deterministic systems. Man came to understand systematic empirical testing as a powerful method for advancing useful knowledge about the material universe.

Empirical experimental procedure emerged by fits and starts during the Middle Ages but became a widely understood and practiced procedure only during the last three hundred years. (Dunn 1971, p. 262)

The Goals of Development

Governments, political parties, and rural people in less developed nations usually seek to quicken the pace of development. The immense proliferation of communications in these nations, especially radio and more recently television, has enabled rural people everywhere to learn a great deal about more developed nations. Evidence is overwhelming that expectations and desires for material welfare have increased greatly and are pervasive in less developed nations. Most national leaders recognize that redividing the shares of a fixed national income can usually do relatively little to improve the welfare of a nation and that the need is to augment per capita income and food production.

It is important to be aware of the tendencies in goals and policies in less developed nations that slow agricultural development. Governments in these nations often become dominated by urban upper-class interests or other urban groups such as workers unions and then often (1) neglect and underinvest in agriculture relative to other, more "modern," sectors, such as the industrial; (2) neglect and underinvest in rural areas, and rural people generally, relative to urban areas and urban people; (3) neglect and underinvest in medium and smaller farms in favor of large farms; and, finally, (4) tend to be ignorant of or not greatly concerned about the increased disparities in income that often result from such government projects, programs, and policies. In view of these pervasive tendencies, we will attempt to highlight the economic and social advantages of increased investment in the agricultural sector, particularly in medium and small farms, and point out likely income distribution outcomes of different agricultural investments, programs, and policies.

As we developed this book, we have assumed the following goals for agriculture in developing nations:

1. Rapid growth in real per capita income
2. Increased food security
3. Reduction of the numbers of persons in poverty, with the poverty level defined by the local society
4. The least possible amount of disruption in cultural values, rural social life, and employment
5. A desired level of equity, as defined by the society, often involving decreased disparities in income and reduced unemployment
6. Economic incentive arrangements that encourage increased productivity, creativity, and enterprise
7. Increasing individual opportunities—economically and politically. This

implies free resource movement, including labor, and the choice of leaders and government through free elections.

We recognize, however, that people in each nation should define through their social, political, and cultural systems what they view as desired development.

Political Systems and Agricultural Development

National economic and political systems are often categorized in simplistic, overgeneralized terms, which communicate little useful information about how the economies operate. For example, those who praise "socialist" India may not recognize that in fact a much smaller part of its economy is in the public sector than "capitalist" United States. In all countries, capital is used to accelerate economic growth. More useful for solving development problems than general labels is a detailed study of the structure and performance of the different economic sectors. Some of them may be tightly controlled, monopolistic, or publicly owned, while others may be competitive and market oriented. Of much more use, therefore, than general labels is such information as (1) the extent to which the prices and quantities of goods and services produced and sold are determined by market forces; (2) the effects of any government price supports and subsidies; (3) the extent to which prices are controlled, or fixed, by monopolistic units or government organizations; and (4) how easy it is to enter or leave markets.

Despite widely varying political terminology and government systems, readers should recognize that the same central problems of agricultural development face all nations. Whether communist, dictatorial, free market, or variations of "socialist," nations have to make decisions about how to obtain the desired mix of goods and services with the scarce resources available. Specifically, the three central economic questions of all societies are what goods and services to produce, how to produce them, and how to distribute them. Major economic decisions can be largely centralized, as in command economies such as the U.S.S.R., China, and Cuba, or they can be decentralized, as in free-market economies. Some combination of centralized and decentralized economic decisionmaking is present in all societies.

Important Concepts

Agricultural transition   Goals of development
Scientific-industrial transition   Capitalist nations
Development as social learning   Socialist nations
Thresholds in human social evolution

Sample Questions

1. In the century from 1950 to 2050, in what ways will change in rural areas of less developed nations be extraordinary in world history?

2. Describe some of the important areas of social learning that occur as agricultural development proceeds.

3. What roles do economic theory and empirical studies play in social learning?

4. How would you describe the agricultural development goals of a particular less developed nation?

5. To what extent do political system labels, such as socialist, capitalist, and democratic, aid in understanding how the agricultural sector operates in a particular country?

I

Agricultural Progress and Structural Transformation in Less Developed Nations

Introduction to Part I

Less developed nations have experienced widely varying success in increasing food and agricultural production. In some regions, vast agricultural transformations have already taken place that have greatly increased agricultural productivity, so much so that agriculture in these areas has many of the characteristics of agriculture in more developed nations. Other regions remain little touched by change, continuing agricultural production in traditional ways at low levels of material welfare.

In chapter 2 we focus on population growth and agricultural resources, two crucial variables affecting the demand and supply of agricultural products. Population growth in combination with growth in per capita income greatly influences the demand for agricultural products, as is demonstrated in chapter 3. The quantity and quality of the soil and other resources available for agriculture greatly influence the scope for increasing supplies of agricultural products. In the last section of chapter 2, estimates of per capita food production changes in less developed nations are reviewed as a measure of success in agricultural development to date and as essential background for the rest of the book.

Chapter 3 explores both the changing interrelations in less developed nations between the agricultural sector and the other economic sectors as structural transformation accelerates, and the effect of the structural transformation on the demand for agricultural products. The chapter commences by clarifying the meaning of economic and other measures of increases in human welfare; it then examines the record of per capita income growth and variability in these nations, setting the stage for the exploration of changing personal expenditure patterns brought on by income growth and for estimating the rapid rates of growth in demand for food in these nations. An examination of the decades-long structural transformation of the economies of these nations and the essential role of agriculture in achieving rapid national economic growth concludes the chapter.

2

Population, Resources, and Agricultural Development

> *More than half the people of the world are living in conditions approaching misery. Their food is inadequate, they are victims of disease. Their economic life is primitive and stagnant. Their poverty is a handicap and a threat, both to them and to more prosperous areas.*
>
> *For the first time in history, humanity possesses the knowledge and the skill to relieve the suffering of these people.*
>
> —*President Harry S. Truman in the famous Point Four of his 1949 Inaugural Address*
>
> *The most important item on the agenda of development is to transform the food sector. If we can do this we will have a new international economic order.*
>
> —*Lewis 1978, p. 75*

Population Growth

The Malthusian Model

In 1798, when all nations were largely agricultural with low incomes, the parson Thomas R. Malthus set forth his well-known theory of development. This early economic theory stated that "the power of population is infinitely greater than the power in the earth to produce subsistence for man" (Malthus 1933, p. 13). Malthus proposed that men and animals have the ability to increase their numbers in a geometric ratio (i.e., $2^n = 2, 4, 8, 16, 32$, etc.), while subsistence (food production) can increase only in an arithmetic ratio (i.e., $2 \times n = 2, 4, 6, 8, 10$, etc.). Hence, if population always is able to increase more rapidly than food production, the number of persons in a society would be dependent upon increases in food.

Studies of population growth in low-income societies before they have been affected by modernizing influences support Malthus's model that population growth has been dependent upon increases in food production. In many countries, birth rates generally have been found to be in the range of thirty to

13

forty-five births per thousand persons per year, with death rates at approximately the same level. The equilibrating mechanism in Malthus's theory was the death rate. As population pressed on the food supply, death rates increased, and as the food supply became more abundant, the death rates fell, leading to population growth. Also note that, as population tends to outstrip the available subsistence, a low, relatively constant level of material living is likely, just high enough to sustain the society. The Malthusian model helps explain why throughout much of history most societies have had relatively stable populations with occasional slow growth—except, of course, when wars and epidemic diseases, such as the Black Death, caused sharp population declines (see figure 1.1).

Ironically, although Malthus's analysis was generally valid for much of the world he observed, during his life fundamental developments in human history were already under way that would result in a great change in economic conditions, so that food production capabilities would no longer be the primary determinant of population size. These developments were the rapid advance of modern science and the associated acceleration of industrial production in Europe. During the nineteenth and twentieth centuries, these historic changes helped accelerate industrial and agricultural production in many nations, resulting in continuing increases in food availability per capita. [1]

The Demographic Transition Model

Empirical research on population growth in all parts of the world has led to a model of population growth and economic development called the *demographic transition* (see, for example, figure 2.1). This model explains how nations that for long periods have had very slow population growth rates due to high birth and death rates generally pass through a period of rapid population growth associated with increased economic growth and then gradually return to lower population growth rates at much higher levels of population and per capita income. [2]

The rapid growth phase occurs when the death rate declines rapidly, to twenty per thousand, while the birth rate remains high, often at some forty per thousand per year. This large difference between birth rates and death rates causes high population growth rates. In this generalized figure, the population growth rate for less developed nations as a group was 2.35 percent per year during this phase. Thus, many less developed nations have found themselves faced with very high population growth rates. To appreciate the impact of these growth rates, note that a 3 percent rate would lead to a doubling of population in twenty four years, and a 2 percent rate a doubling in thirty six years, or about once every generation. With such extraordinary population growth rates and

1. A recent modified model and empirical study of Malthusian mechanisms is offered by T. P. Schultz (1981, chap. 2).
2. For discussions of population growth, more detailed examinations of the demographic transition model, and explorations of the factors affecting rates of population growth see T. P. Schultz 1981; World Bank, *World Development Report 1984* (pp. 51–206); and Boserup 1981.

Figure 2.1. The Demographic Transition in More Developed and Less Developed Nations, 1800–2000

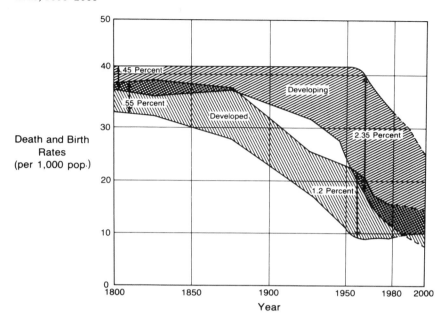

Source: Mahler 1980 (p. 75). Copyright © 1980 by Scientific American Inc. All rights reserved.
Note: The upper line is the birth rate, and the lower line is the death rate.

without increased capacity to produce and import food, the Malthusian equation would inexorably come into play, as it has in most of human history.

With increasing per capita income and urbanization, people in most societies reduce birth rates so they approach the new lower level of death rates of ten to twenty per thousand, leading to low population growth rates of less than 1 percent. This is projected to occur in many less developed nations in the next century. Note also that figure 2.1 shows that during their economic growth the currently more developed nations averaged lower population growth rates (1.2 percent) than many less developed nations are now experiencing. This is because the death rates in the more developed nations dropped more slowly and hence remained closer to their birth rates.

Two important causes of the reduction in birth rates are (1) increases in the number of surviving children per family due to fewer deaths, so that families decide that they do not need to produce as many children to have the same number survive; and (2) the increasing availability of less expensive birth control methods. Even before the availability of low-cost modern contraceptives, lower birth rates were achieved in many more developed nations through various means of social control, such as by postponing the age of marriage.

To summarize, many less developed nations today are in the rapid growth phase of the demographic transition, with high population growth rates in the 2 to 3 percent range (table 2.1). A large number of more developed, high-income, nations have shifted to a slow growth phase, with low rates of birth and death and relatively low rates of population growth, often under 1 percent. Among the less developed nations, China has apparently brought its population growth rate to 1.4 percent. This has been done through strong authoritarian measures of the central government, which decided to try to limit family size to one child.

Prospects for Population Growth

The number of persons on this planet in the next century will be determined largely by the rate at which the large, less developed nations pass through the demographic transition over the next few decades. The governments in many nations have programs to reduce birth rates. In addition to China, notable successes in reducing birth rates have occurred over the last few decades in other less developed nations. Some of these, with their 1970 to 1982 population growth rates, are South Korea (1.7), Colombia (1.9), and Indonesia (1.9) (World Bank 1984b, p. 254).

A historic turning point has recently occurred in human habitation of the earth due to the gradual movement of many less developed nations through the middle of the demographic transition. For the last five centuries, the rate of world population growth has generally been increasing. About 1970, the world population growth rate reached a peak and began to decline from a maximum rate of a little above 2 percent (see figure 2.2). Total world population by 2000, assuming no worldwide catastrophes, is estimated to be about 6.5 billion, as compared with a little more than 4.5 billion in 1980. In view of the shifts to declining rates of population growth in less developed nations, recent estimates of the maximum size of a likely stabilized world population now range between 8 to 11 billion (see figure 1.1).

Two additional facts about world population are important for those concerned with world food. First, in 1980, Asia supported more than half the world's population; Africa, 10 percent; Latin America, 8 percent; Europe, 13 percent; the U.S.S.R., 7 percent; and North America, 7 percent. And second, the proportion of the world's population living in nations now labeled less developed will increase, due to the differences in population growth rates between less developed and more developed nations. This proportion will grow from about three-fourths of the world's population in less developed nations in 1980 to about four-fifths in the year 2000.

With such population growth rates in less developed nations, can the "green revolution" remove the fear of a return of the Malthusian mechanism of population control in these countries? The recent famines demonstrate that the harsh Malthusian model relating population numbers to available subsistence is

Table 2.1. Population Growth Rates, Percentage of World Population, 1975 and 2000, Fifteen Selected Nations

Country	Total Population (millions)		Net Growth 1975 to 2000		Average Annual Growth Rate (percent)	Percent of World Population	
	1975	2000	Millions	Percent		1975	2000
People's Republic of China	935	1,329	394	42	1.4	22.9	20.9
India	618	1,021	402	65	2.0	15.1	16.1
Indonesia	135	226	91	68	2.1	3.3	3.6
Bangladesh	79	159	79	100	2.8	1.9	2.5
Pakistan	71	149	78	111	3.0	1.7	2.4
Philippines	43	73	30	71	2.2	1.0	1.2
Thailand	42	75	33	77	2.3	1.0	1.2
South Korea	37	57	20	55	1.7	0.9	0.9
Egypt	37	65	29	77	2.3	0.9	1.0
Nigeria	63	135	72	114	3.0	1.5	2.1
Brazil	109	226	117	108	2.9	2.7	3.6
Mexico	60	131	71	119	3.1	1.5	2.1
United States	214	248	35	16	0.6	5.2	3.9
U.S.S.R.	254	309	54	21	0.8	6.2	4.9
Japan	112	133	21	19	0.7	2.7	2.1

Source: Council on Environmental Quality (1980 (vol. 2, table 2.6).

Figure 2.2. Rising and Falling Population Growth Rates in More Developed and Less Developed Nations, 1950–2020

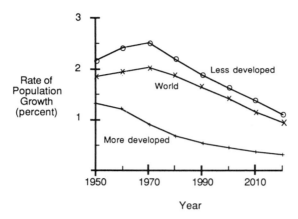

Source: Data from United Nations 1985 (p. 52).

still in operation in some areas. These famines have led to the death of an esti-mated 100 thousand people in Bangladesh in 1974 and a million in central Africa during the early 1970s. Local famines have continued to cause many deaths in some areas of Africa in the 1980s. Can humankind finally learn to produce enough food and income so that starvation will not determine who will survive? How can security of food supplies for all nations be assured? This is the subject of this text.

Physical Resources for Agriculture in Less Developed Nations

Climate, Water, Soils, and Biological Environment

The importance of the very great differences in climate, water availability, soils, and biological environment in the less developed nations is often not fully appreciated.[3] A large majority of these nations have subtropical and tropical climates. The wide variation in available water for agriculture ranges from moisture sufficient only for sparse livestock grazing in deserts to the very high precipitation in rain forests. In some areas, lack of rainfall can be compensated for by tapping rivers or underground water sources for irrigation.

Some tropical soils lack essential plant nutrients, including micronutrients such as magnesium. Day length is often unrecognized as an important climatic factor: as the equator is approached, day length becomes an almost constant

3. Climate maps in modern atlases such as *Goode's*, summarize the varied temperature and moisture conditions. For more on climate and farming conditions in less developed nations see Money 1976 and Slater and Levin 1981.

twelve hours throughout the year. Because many crops require longer days or changing day lengths to trigger flowering and fruiting for good crop yields, crop varieties from higher latitudes are often unproductive in these nations. Due to high temperatures and often high humidity, the biological environment for plant growth is very different from that in more temperate climates. Without winter freezes, more pest organisms remain in the soil. Fungus activity is also greatly encouraged in hot, humid areas.

Arable Land Availability

When population is small and a lot of arable land is available, farmers occupy the best agricultural lands they are able to cultivate. As population increases, the availability of additional agricultural land varies greatly. Potential arable land is that judged by soil scientists to be able to produce acceptable yields of locally adapted food crops. Estimates for some countries and continents is large compared to currently cultivated land (see table 2.2).

In Latin America, according to these estimates, only 11 percent of potential arable land is farmed, and in Africa, only 22 percent! The estimate for Asia, with its high population, is some 17 percent of arable land still uncultivated. Uncultivated land usually is of lower quality than that currently farmed, or it requires considerable investment to develop for farming. Much currently uncultivated land needs irrigation, drainage, stone or tree removal, or other investments before it can be farmed profitably. The large costs of putting potential arable land under cultivation are often not addressed in estimates of additional available arable land (for an exception see Chou et al. 1977, pp. 36–65). Under what circumstances might these uncultivated lands be used in less developed nations? What are the constraints? The cost of clearing? Labor shortage? Soils, disease, and pest problems? In other nations, with very limited amounts of additional arable land, how serious is the land constraint on increased production? These questions are addressed in chapters 4 and 7.[4]

Attempts have been made to examine whether limitations in the quantity of land available for world agriculture will limit future population growth. This question was explored by Chou et al. (1977, p. 37) under different assumptions about (1) the amounts of unused agricultural land available in different parts of the world; (2) the agricultural technology and inputs used and the yields achieved; and (3) the human food consumption standards to be met. Their lowest estimate of population that could be supported on a high-quality diet (including meat, protein, fruits, and vegetables), with current farming knowledge, was thirty-five billion. This number is well above the currently estimated stabilized world population of eight to eleven billion. The high estimate was some 146 billion persons with minimum-cost healthful diets.

---

4. For references on world resources for agricultural development, see Chou et al. 1977; Slater and Levin 1981; Simon and Kahn 1984; and Andreae 1981.

Table 2.2. Cultivated and Potential Arable Land, World Regions, 1965

Region	Area (million hectares)				Cultivated Land	
	Total	Potential Arable	Cultivated	Potential Arable, Not Cultivated	As Percent of Area Potential Arable	Per Person (hectares)
Africa	3,019	732	158	574	22	0.5
Asia	2,736	627	518	109	83	0.3
Oceana (Australia and New Zealand)	822	154	16	138	10	1.2
Europe	478	174	154	20	88	0.4
North America	2,108	465	239	226	51	0.9
South America	1,752	679	77	602	11	0.4
U.S.S.R.	2,234	356	227	129	64	1.0
World	13,149	3,189	1,388	1,801	44	0.4

Source: Wortman and Cummings 1978 (p. 59). Reprinted with permission.

Size of the Farming Unit

Farm size is a fundamental factor affecting strategies for increased agricultural production. In most of the less developed world, agricultural production is a family enterprise, except in plantation areas, where large labor crews are used, and in some socialist countries, where agriculture is organized on a large scale.

In most less developed nations, the size of the crop farm operating unit is largely determined by the amount of land an owner-operator or tenant family can handle, sometimes with the use of some hired labor. In highly productive soil areas where population may have increased toward its Malthusian limit, many farms may be smaller than could be handled by a farm family. Empirical studies in many less developed nations have shown that family farms often range from five to ten hectares in rain-fed areas, down to less than half a hectare in densely populated rain-fed or irrigated rice-growing areas. To achieve significant increases in agricultural income, quite different agricultural development strategies will be required for the farms in less developed nations than for those in more developed nations, with their large farms.

Implications of Physical Resources for Agricultural Development

Physical resource endowments set constraints on agricultural development, but they do not explain why some nations have been very successful in increasing farm productivity and agricultural production per capita while other nations have achieved little growth. With traditional agricultural technologies, farm production is almost completely dependent upon the natural resources available. But successful agricultural development is not dependent on large land resources per person, as illustrated by the achievements of Japan, Taiwan, and South Korea, as compared with land-rich nations, such as Thailand and various regions of Africa and Latin America, where agricultural productivity has increased more slowly.

Growth and Declines in Food and Agricultural Production

The Demand and Supply Framework

The economic theory of demand and supply provides a framework for judging the success of national agricultural development efforts. First, consider how the growth in food demand is shown by moving the demand curve to the right. The production of goods and services is a response to demand for desired goods and services. Examples of services are a haircut, food service in a restaurant, and the showing of a film in a cinema. In economics, an individual's demand refers specifically to a schedule of the amount of a good or service that person is willing to buy at a series of different prices. A market demand curve such as D_1 in figure 2.3, panel A, shows the quantities demanded at different prices by all the persons who participate in the market. The demand for a good or service in a market depends upon the number of purchasers in the market, the

Figure 2.3. Food Problems and Farm Problems Caused by the Relative Rate of Movement of the Supply and Demand Curves

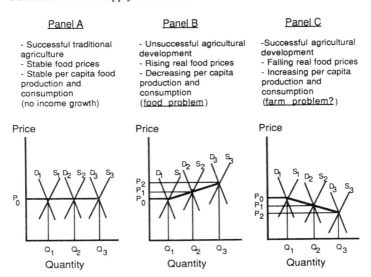

Panel A	Panel B	Panel C
- Successful traditional agriculture - Stable food prices - Stable per capita food production and consumption (no income growth)	- Unsuccessful agricultural development - Rising real food prices - Decreasing per capita production and consumption (food problem)	-Successful agricultural development - Falling real food prices - Increasing per capita production and consumption (farm problem?)

amount of income they have, and their decisions about how much to spend on each good or service available to them. In the national market for food, if per capita income does not fall, demand for food will increase at a rate equal to or greater than the population growth rate. This is illustrated in figure 2.3, panel A, by moving the demand curve to the right from D_1 to D_2 to D_3, so that the percentage increase in the quantity demanded at the same price, Q_1 to Q_2 to Q_3, is at least equal to the rate of population growth—say, 2.5 percent. As seen earlier in the chapter, many less developed nations have population growth rates in the 2 to 3 percent range, and some have even higher rates. In the next chapter, we examine how other factors, such as income, also affect the rate of growth in demand for food.

Now consider supply. Farmers and other entrepreneurs will attempt to produce certain quantities of products and services with the expectation of selling at prices that will cover the costs of production, including at least a small net return, or profit, for their effort. The higher the price farmers expect, the larger the quantity of agricultural goods and services they will supply to the market. If farmers succeed in moving the supply curves for food and agricultural products to the right as rapidly as demand, as indicated by supply curves S_1, S_2, and S_3 in panel A, the prices of food and agricultural products would remain about the same, P_0.

FOOD PROBLEMS

If, however, farmers cannot increase the supply of food at a rate equal to or greater than the rate of increase in demand, supply curves will shift more slowly to the right, and the price of food and agricultural products will increase, as indicated in panel *B* by prices P_1 and P_2. Rising food prices indicate that a nation has a "food problem." With higher food prices, per capita food consumption is likely to decline. As will be seen below, some less developed nations have great difficulty in moving the supply curve for food rapidly enough to the right to prevent declines in food consumption per capita.

FARM PROBLEMS

If farmers do succeed in increasing the supply of food more rapidly than growth in demand, prices will fall, as indicated in panel *C* of figure 2.3, by P_1 and P_2. Decline in the price of food and other agricultural products often causes a "farm problem," as more farmers have increased difficulty earning an acceptable income from agriculture. Farm problems, present in many more developed nations, signal the fundamental national achievement of successful agricultural development. Consumers benefit through lower food prices, as they have more money left over for other purchases after buying food. Nations should therefore applaud the success of gradual reductions in the real price of agricultural products. Farmers need to recognize that gradual declines in real prices for their products is a proof of their productivity gains, which are essential for increasing farm incomes, however paradoxical this may seem. Ways of achieving increases in the supply of agricultural products is the central topic of part 3 of this volume.

Real and Nominal Price and Income Changes

In studying economic change, it is essential to understand the difference between real price and income changes and nominal, or market, price changes. Prices of all products are affected by changes in the value of money, due to inflation or deflation. Thus, in order to obtain the real price changes, prices have to be adjusted for the changing value of money. So whenever, as in the preceding paragraph, the adjective *real* is used by economists (such as in "real price changes," "change in the real cost," or "real income changes"), the statement indicates that the prices, costs, or incomes have been adjusted for the changing value of money due to inflation or deflation. In many less developed nations, inflation rates of 10 or 20 percent or more per year continuously reduce the value of the currency, so that it buys less each year. The terms "current prices," "market prices," "nominal prices," and "income at current prices," or "nominal income" all refer to values that have not been adjusted for changes in the value of money. In the study of development, nominal income change is divided by an index of the rate of inflation in prices to obtain an adjusted estimate of real income change. Changes in prices, or income, that are simply due to alteration in the value of money can mask important economic changes.[5]

5. Two examples of how nominal income changes are adjusted to obtain estimates of real income change follow. Suppose income were observed to be $100 in the first year and $106 in the

Figure 2.4. Growth in Total and per Capita Agricultural Production in More Developed and Less Developed Nations, 1969–1984

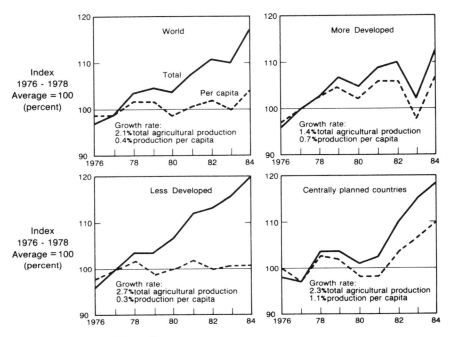

Source: U.S.D.A., 1985 (p. 67).

Total and per Capita Food and Agricultural Production

We now examine the success that less developed nations have had in meeting the needs of their populations by observing changes in per capita food production. The focus here is upon increases in the supply of food and agricultural products measured in physical quantities.

When growth in agricultural production in less developed nations is compared with growth in more developed nations, the average rate is greater in less developed nations (see figure 2.4). This is a great achievement.

However, the rate of growth in *per capita* agricultural production in less developed nations has generally been very slow, estimated at 0.3 percent over the last decade (figure 2.4). Imagine working thirty years in agriculture and achieving only a 10 to 12 percent increase in annual income! In more developed

second year. Example 1: The rate of inflation of the value of the money is 6 percent. Then $106/1.06 = $100, or no change in real income. Example 2: The rate of inflation is 3 percent. Then $106/1.03 = $102.9, and real income increased by $2.90.

Table 2.3. Changes in per Capita Food Production, World Regions, 1968–1983

Country Group	Index 1983 (1974–76 = 100)	Annual Rate of Change 1968–1983
Developing market economies	104	0.5
Africa	90	− 1.1
Far East	111	1.0
Latin America	104	0.9
Near East	97	0.3
Asian centrally planned economies	118	1.7
Total developing countries	108	0.9
Total developed countries	102	0.8
World	102	0.5
Low-income countries with per capita GNP up to $410 in 1982	111	0.9
Developing countries other than low income	102	0.7
Least developed countries	97	− 0.6
Developing oil exporters	102	0.3
Developing nonoil exporters	109	1.0

Source: FAO, *State of Food and Agriculture, 1983* (p. 9).

nations, more rapid increases in per capita agricultural production are regularly achieved (0.7 percent over the last decade; see figure 2.4). Part of this success is due to lower population growth rates.

In less developed nations, growth in *food* production per capita is a more useful measure of progress, for in these nations, food production represents a very large proportion of total agricultural production. For this reason the focus of this section is limited to growth in food production. We get a clearer view of the achievements and problems of food production in less developed nations from data disaggregated by continents (see table 2.3). Progress in per capita food production is strong in East Asia and in Latin America, generally, with much more uncertain progress in South Asia, due partly to the serious shortfalls in food crop harvests in 1965, 1972, and 1974, which caused serious famines. In Africa, in many countries south of the Sahara desert, decreases in per capita food production have caused widespread malnutrition and famine in some crop years since the late 1960s. The reader may wish to seek detailed per capita food and agricultural production data for countries of interest from standard sources, since statements about regional conditions often mask the variability in agricultural progress in particular less developed nations.[6]

6. The world agricultural situation is reviewed quarterly in USDA, *World Agriculture: Outlook and Situation Report*. An annual review is made by the FAO in *State of Food and Agriculture*. Some data on agricultural progress are also available annually in the World Bank's

When examining data on per capita food production, we should recognize that less developed nations with large foreign exchange earnings due to the export of oil or other products are able to import food and other agricultural products. Thus, declines in per capita agricultural production in these nations may not signal a significant national food problem. However, in all nations, slow growth in agricultural production may indicate a waste of national resources as well as low income growth and poverty in rural areas.

Two conclusions follow from the analysis in this section. First, success in moving the agricultural supply curve to the right more rapidly than the demand curve leads to larger quantities of food and other agricultural products consumed per capita at lower real prices. Second, the challenge for agricultural development theory is to explain how a nation can succeed in moving the agricultural supply curve more rapidly to the right than the demand curve. When social learning enables this achievement in all nations, the Malthusian threat will finally be banished from earth.

Food Grain Prices, Stocks, and Trade

The Gradually Declining Real Cost of Food Grains

Prices of the two dominant food grains in world trade, wheat and rice, indicate a gradually declining cost of production of food staples worldwide (see table 2.4). The wide fluctuations often seen in these prices are due to varied crop yields in major producing areas. However, when the prices of these food crops are deflated by the changing value of the dollar, the *real* prices of wheat and rice are seen to gradually decline.

This decline in prices for the important internationally traded food grains demonstrates that, at the world level, supplies have increased even more rapidly than the historically unprecedented increase in demand. These declining prices also show that the real cost of producing a unit of food has been reduced. Individual less developed nations, however, have had widely varying success in equaling demand. An examination of changes in real food costs by observing real market prices of food staples in a less developed nation provides an indicator of overall success in its economic development and trade policies.

Comfortable Levels of World Cereal Stocks

Estimates of world stocks of cereal grains, which include both food grains (wheat and rice) and coarse grains such as maize and sorghum, have increased since 1976, fluctuating at some 18 percent of the gradually increasing level of total world cereal consumption (FAO 1984, p. 45). Because a large proportion

World Development Report. Major studies of the world food situation include FAO 1979; the Presidential Commission on World Hunger 1980; Chou et al. 1977; Woods 1981; Winrock International 1983; Hanrahan, Urban, and Deaton 1984; FAO 1985b; and Council on Environmental Quality 1980.

Table 2.4. Declining Real Cost of Food Grains, 1970–1986

Year	World Consumer Price Index (1980 = 100)	Export Prices (dollars per 1,000 kg)			
		Wheat		Rice	
		Current	Deflated	Current	Deflated
1970	35.3	61	172	143	405
1971	37.4	60	160	129	345
1972	39.5	92	233	148	366
1973	43.3	178	411	274	633
1974	49.9	165	331	542	1086
1975	56.6	149	263	364	643
1976	62.4	117	186	255	405
1977	70.0	113	161	276	394
1978	76.8	131	170	369	516
1979	86.4	163	189	334	386
1980	100.0	164	164	433	433
1981	114.1	177	155	484	424
1982	128.1	161	126	294	230
1983	144.2	158	109	277	192
1984	164.5	153	93	253	154
1985	187.2	138	74	217	116
1986	201.7	115	57	210	104

Sources: FAO, *Production Yearbook* and FAO, *Monthly Bulletin of Statistics.*
Note: Current prices were deflated using the world consumer price index from IMF *International Financial Statistics.* Wheat is U.S. hard winter wheat, no. 2 ordinary protein, FOB Gulf ports; rice is Thai white rice, 5 percent brokens, FOB Bangkok.

of these cereals is fed to livestock, a food cushion is available for the world's human population—in case of food emergencies, a portion of the coarse grains could be diverted to human use.

These comfortable world grain stocks, however, do not assure sufficient food to poor nations, as conditions in many less developed nations demonstrate. Poor nations may not earn enough foreign exchange to buy sufficient food on the international market to avert famine. The poor in any nation may not have enough money to obtain food to prevent hunger. In these situations, international and domestic food aid can help moderate hunger.

Historic Increases in Grain Exports from More Developed Nations

Changes in the pattern of the world cereal grain trade over the last five decades illustrate the rapid progress in agricultural productivity and production per capita achieved in the more developed nations and the mixed progress in the less developed nations. In the 1930s, before population growth rates increased rapidly in the less developed nations, these nations were in general net exporters of grains, and Western Europe was the only large grain-importing region of the world (see table 2.5).

Table 2.5. Changing Pattern of Net World Grain Trade, 1934–1986

Region	1934–1938	1948–1952	1960	1970	1980	1986
North America (U.S. and Canada)	5	22	36	54	133	83
Central and South America	9	2	2	4	−15	−8
Western Europe	−24	−22	−25	−22	−11	18
Eastern Europe	5	0	−7	−6	−14	−4
U.S.S.R.	1	2	6	4	−29	−24
Africa (excluding South Africa)	1	0	−2	−5	−21	−25
South Africa	0	0	1	1	3	12
Asia	2	−6	−13	−37	−64	−59
Oceania (Australia and New Zealand)	3	3	4	8	19	22

Source: FAO, *Trade Yearbooks.*
Note: Measure is in million metric tons.

By 1980, however, this trade pattern was reversed, as Western Europe's net imports of grain had declined greatly, due partly to high import tariffs, and many areas of the less developed world had become net grain importers, with the United States, Canada, Australia, and New Zealand becoming the major world suppliers of grains. This global view masks the progress and problems of particular nations, such as the continuing net rice export status of Thailand and the considerable progress in meeting domestic grain needs that has been achieved by nations such as India over the last decade.

Summary and Conclusions

The material in this chapter leads to the following five conclusions. First, the world is passing through an unprecedented period of population explosion due to population growth of 2 to 3 percent in many less developed nations. However, the world population growth rate has recently passed its peak of about 2 percent. This population growth rate is unlikely to be approached again, due to the gradual lowering of birth rates in less developed nations as the demographic transition proceeds.

Second, agricultural resources available for food production in less developed nations are highly variable. However, the development experience of the more developed nations and of some less developed nations since World War II has demonstrated that nations with quite limited additional land and other physical resources for agriculture, such as Taiwan, South Korea, India, and China, can achieve strong growth in agricultural production. Thus, based on economic history and on the analysis in this text, land and other physical resource constraints may not be major impediments to large increases in agricultural production.

Third, two fundamental points about the world food situation are clear from the record of agricultural growth in less developed nations and the trends in world grain prices, stocks, and trade. Data show a continuing large availability of food at the world level, so that world food surpluses, rather than world food shortages, are likely to continue to require attention at the world level. However, despite very comfortable world food supplies, the agricultural experience of less developed nations indicates that, for some of them, growth in per capita food availability and the security of food supplies will continue to be very uncertain over the next few decades. Thus, serious domestic food shortages and famine may reappear from time to time in some nations, unless much more successful agricultural development and food security programs are completed.

Fourth, many less developed nations need to accelerate agricultural production to enable their citizens to obtain more income and food. By increasing agricultural production, especially of exportable products, and through greater economic growth in other sectors, less developed nations will be able to earn more foreign exchange. This will permit increased purchases of needed capital equipment from abroad to further economic growth and to increase food security, both for individuals and the nation.

And fifth, the challenges of agricultural development today in less developed nations range from managing serious food shortages and periodic famines to designing strategies to support the good performance in agriculture already achieved.

Despite general world success in agricultural development over the last three decades, the number of malnourished and poor persons in many less developed nations continues to grow. Periodic famines remain a threat to many people. The Malthusian model of development continues to operate in some areas of the world.[7] For how long?

Important Concepts

Malthusian model of population
Demographic transition
Physical resource conditions
Size of farm
Food problems
Farm problems

Nominal price change
Real income change
Per capita growth rates
Real world food prices
Trends in world grain trade

Sample Questions

1. Using the demographic transition model, explain why many less developed nations have higher population growth rates than more developed nations.

2. Explain the presence of much unused potentially arable land in many low-income nations.

3. In the perspective of world history, discuss the changing per capita

7. Paulino 1986 identified nations with the most severe food problems.

availability of food in the world as a whole, in a particular world region, or in a specific nation.

4. Over the past three decades, what has happened to the costs of producing the major world food grains? Explain.

5. What have been the trends in grain exports between more developed and less developed nations since 1950? Under what circumstances might there be significant changes in these trends?

6. In what parts of the world has there been famine since 1970? What have been the causes of these famines?

7. How is it possible for the world to have increasing stocks of food and, at the same time, famines in certain nations?

3

The Role of Agriculture in Economic Development

The next few decades will be extraordinarily dynamic in food production, consumption, and trade. Increased food production in both developing and mature economies will become more central to both growth and equity strategies.

—*Mellor 1982, p. 310*

Although a primary role of the agricultural sector is to produce food and agricultural products to support economic development, the agricultural sector makes other very important contributions to national growth. In this chapter we examine the interrelations between the agricultural sector and the rest of the economy. How dependent is the rest of the economy on agricultural growth? At what rate must food production increase to support national economic growth? What does the agricultural sector need from the rest of the economy?

Development: Its Meaning and Measurement

Before proceeding to the main topics of this chapter, we need to be clear about the meaning of economic development and to understand the different ways it can be measured. To estimate increases in demand for food, we also need data on income growth in less developed nations and on the variability in income distribution in these nations.

Meanings of Development

Economic growth is commonly measured by national income accounting. These calculations estimate the total amount of goods and services produced or consumed in a society. Such estimates clearly provide a limited measure of human development. Development is a broader concept than economic growth. Seers (1972, p. 21), for example, took a very comprehensive view: "development means creating the conditions for the realization of the human personality." Thus, some may judge that a nation may achieve economic growth (increase per capita production) without achieving a higher level of development.

The following are among the many proposed measures of changes in the human condition: (1) the proportion of persons below some defined poverty level; (2) the unemployment rate; (3) the extent of inequality in income; and (4) the extent to which the basic needs of nutrition, health, housing, and education have been met (Morawetz 1977, p. 44). [1] De Kant (1980) and the present writers believe that some progress in individual civil rights is also integral to development, as well as progress in the social rights represented by improved economic conditions. Most fundamentally, however, development is "an ideological concept; it implies goals of income distribution, justice and widespread participation in social and political institutions by all of the population, including the peasantry" (Barraclough 1969, p. 22). Thus, establishment of criteria for economic development requires value judgments about the nature of a good society. Each social group establishes its own view of the nature of development. Economic growth, by contrast, is measured by the goods and services a society decides to produce, which are determined to a great extent in most societies by the values of consumers through their myriad individual purchases. [2]

Measures of Economic Growth

Knowledge of five measures of economic growth is needed for our purposes:

1. Gross national product (GNP) equals total national consumption or production (C) of all final goods and services plus gross Investment (I_G).

$$GNP = C + I_G.$$

2. Net national product (NNP) equals GNP minus depreciation (D).

$$NNP = C + I_G - D.$$

(Depreciation is the loss in value of all equipment and buildings due to wearing out and from obsolescence during a time period, such as a year; it is subtracted from GNP to provide a more valid measure of economic growth.)
3. Per capita income equals GNP divided by population.
4. Disposable personal income equals NNP minus personal and corporate taxes and minor adjustments.
5. Personal consumption expenditure equals disposable personal income minus savings.

---

1. Other literature on Basic Needs includes Seers 1977; Streeten 1980; and Srinivasan 1977. Studies of poverty include Sen 1980 and Rao 1981.
2. Other literature on the meaning and measurement of development includes Morris 1979; Moss 1973; McGranahan et al. 1972; Scott, McGranahan, and Argalias 1973; and Seers 1977.

Gross national product is obtained by estimating for one year either all final goods and services produced in each sector or the total consumption of these goods and services by final purchasers, plus all investment (gross investment) made in each sector of the economy. Recall that the term investment refers to additions to the capital stock of an economy that are used to increase production and consumption in later time periods. Investment consists of such things as new machinery and equipment for farms and factories, and new buildings for industry and consumers.

Gross national product, although commonly used to estimate an economy's performance, overstates increases in production, for the value of the stock of national capital (past investment) declines as it becomes worn out. Therefore, an estimate of the annual depreciation in the value of the national capital stock is required to obtain a measure of net change in the stock of capital in a nation. When gross investment is adjusted for depreciation, net national product is obtained.

Per capita income is often calculated by dividing gross national product by population, because gross national product is a more commonly available figure. This rate of per capita income change is approximately the same as the rate of change of net national product per capita, a more accurate estimate of per capita income.

Both gross and net national product include consumption expenditures of government units and private citizens. To obtain an estimate of the resources controlled by individuals in the private sector, two measures are useful. One, disposable personal income, is an estimate of the resources controlled by private consumers. It is calculated by subtracting personal and corporate taxes and minor adjustments from net national product. Personal taxes plus corporate taxes in market economies provide a measure of the amount of resources used by the public sector for government functions such as social services, police, judicial services, defense, and transfers like old age pensions.

The fifth measure, personal consumption expenditure, estimates what individuals spend after they have put aside savings. [3]

Measures of Development

Many people are uncomfortable with measures of human welfare that are limited to the consumption of goods and services. "Ideally one would like some overall index (or measure) of human well-being which would overcome the weighting problem implicit in partial indexes" (Buchanan and Ellis 1955, p. 6). This measure would indicate the quality of life experienced. Davis (1945) has illuminated the issues in the measurement of human welfare by comparing two scales of measurement, one for the "level of living" and the other for the "level of consumption" (see figure 3.1).

---

3. Sources of information about national income accounts for many nations are found in the United Nations annual *National Accounts Statistics* and in national government documents.

Figure 3.1. Relations Between Standard of Living, Level of Living, Standard of Consumption, and Level of Consumption

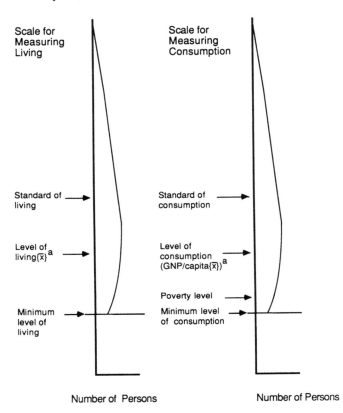

Source: Based on Davis 1945.
[a] The levels of consumption and living are averages of what is actually experienced. These measures can include a factor describing the shape of the distribution. Level of consumption is often estimated by GNP/capita, or by NNP/capita and similar measures.

Level of consumption is the amount of goods and services in the public and private sectors plus savings, which people experience as estimated by GNP or NNP per capita. The standard of consumption, in contrast, is the level of consumption earnestly desired and eagerly striven for by a social group, such as the consumption level achieved by the upper-middle class. This level can be considered a target of consumption of the society. The parallel scale measures quality of life. Hence level of living is the ideal that would provide an overall per capita index of "the whole of human activity as actually experienced by the individual or group" (Davis 1945, p. 11). In a similar fashion, standard of living is understood as the "content of living which an individual or group earnestly seeks and strives to obtain; . . . to preserve, if threatened; to regain, if lost" (Davis 1945, p. 11).

Three additional concepts are useful on these scales. The minimum level of consumption and the minimum level of living are levels below which individuals would have great difficulty in surviving due to a shortage of food and shelter or for social reasons, such as being an outcast. Those who have died of famine in South Asia and Africa were not able to achieve minimum levels of consumption—or living. Societies also have developed the concept of a poverty level of consumption, below which the society believes it is undesirable for any of its members to live. Poverty definitions can lead to a range of private and government activities that attempt to cut off the low end of the distribution of consumption in figure 3.1. A central point about the two parallel scales for measuring consumption and living is the assumption that movement on the two scales is usually in the same direction. People usually believe that an increase in consumption will increase human welfare, especially in low-income nations.

Shortcomings of monetary (national account) indicators of consumption include (1) poor coverage of household, subsistence, and female production, particularly in rural areas; (2) an exaggeration of differences in levels of living experienced in different countries, due to such factors as the exchange rates used in comparisons and the differences in prices of goods and services that are not traded, such as haircuts; (3) no indication of the amount of inequality of income; and (4) no adjustment for compensating variables, such as a warmer environment in some developing nations, which greatly reduces the real cost of housing and clothing.

Dissatisfaction with consumption and money measures of development has led to many efforts to construct nonmonetary indicators of the human condition. The physical quality of life index (PQLI), developed in the 1970s (Morris 1979), is an example. This index provides a good illustration of the problems inherent in the construction of all nonmonetary indexes. It includes three variables—infant mortality, life expectancy, and literacy—in a formula that gives each equal weight [PQLI $= (IM + LE + LR)/3$]. National rankings with this index are similar to those provided by per capita income for low and high per capita income nations, but among middle-income nations the income measures and PQLI measures cause quite different rankings. Is this a better ranking, or does it simply highlight certain variables in the development process? Or is the ranking an unimportant artifact of the method of constructing the PQLI index?

Two unresolved theoretical issues underlie the construction of nonmonetary indexes, such as the PQLI: (1) how to justify the choice of the particular variables used in the index; and (2) how to weigh the variables. In the case of the PQLI, why does the index have two health variables and one literacy variable? Is this just a health and literacy index? What is the justification for the equal weights of each variable in the index? Why not, for example, give life expectancy double weight, so it would represent 50 percent of the index? The PQLI also fails, as do the usual economic measures, to include any indication of inequality in the distribution of its variables.

To conclude, in contrast to most nonmonetary indicators of economic development, economic indexes are generally self-weighted by the myriad of purchasing decisions made by consumers, producers, and government officials in markets throughout the society. Thus, although economic indexes of human well-being have limitations, they provide the most comprehensive measures of economic development generally available. Nonmonetary measures may provide additional insight about particular aspects of the human condition.

Growth and Variability in World Income

Per Capita Income and National Economic Growth

Per capita income is extremely variable between countries, ranging in 1985 from an average of some $270 per year in low-income nations to over $11 thousand in high-income nations (see table 3.1).

The real rates of growth in per capita income have also varied greatly among nations over the last two decades, ranging from increases of 5 percent annually in Japan to decreases in Zaire and Ghana. During this period, nineteen industrial market economies averaged a 2.4 percent growth rate in real income per capita, while thirty-four low-income, thirty-seven lower-middle-income, and twelve upper-middle-income economies had average real per capita income growth rates of 2.9, 2.6, and 3.3, respectively.

The likely changes in per capita income in different nations over the next few decades can be readily envisaged by projecting per capita income growth rates (see figure 3.2). The figure indicates that wide income disparities among nations will continue for many decades. For example, at a growth rate of 2 percent a year, a populous, low-per-capita-income country such as India would have a per capita income of only about $460 per year by the year 2010, while the industrial market nations such as the United States and Japan would have average incomes above $20,000 per capita. A few nations, particularly Japan, have achieved such extraordinary economic performance that they have been closing the per capita income gap with the highest-income nations. The reason it is so difficult for many developing nations to close this gap is illustrated by the following calculation. With a 1 percent increase in income per year on a per capita income base of $5000, the increase in income is $50, while a 5 percent increase in income per year on a base of $200 provides an increase in income of only $10 per year. From the point of view of the low-income nation, however, a 5 percent annual increase in per capita income over a ten-year period would lead to a very significant 63 percent increase in per capita income. Rates of growth can be calculated using the formula

$$F \text{ (future amount)} = P \text{ (present amount)} \times (1 + i)^n,$$

Table 3.1. Gross National Product per Capita and Real Rates of Growth, Selected Nations

Type of Economy	1985 per Capita Gross National Product (dollars)	Average Annual Growth Rate, 1965–85 (percent)
Low-income economies	270	2.9
Ghana	380	−2.2
Zaire	170	−2.1
India	220	1.7
China	310	4.8
Lower middle-income economies	820	2.6
Indonesia	530	4.8
Philippines	580	2.3
Nigeria	800	2.2
Peru	1,010	0.2
Syrian Arab Republic	1,570	4.0
Upper middle-income economies	1,850	3.3
Brazil	1,640	4.3
Yugoslavia	2,070	4.1
Malaysia	2,000	4.4
Hungary	1,950	5.8
Poland	2,050	1.5[a]
High-income oil exporters	9,800	2.7
Industrial market economies	11,810	2.4
United Kingdom	8,460	1.6
France	9,540	2.8
United States	16,690	1.7
Japan	11,300	4.7

Source: Data from World Bank, *World Development Report 1987* (table 1).
[a] 1965–84

or, in the example of the low-income nation,

$$F = 200 \ (1 + 0.05)^{10} = 326.$$

Then the increase in income is

$$(326 - 200)/200 = 63\%.$$

World Concentration of Income and Human Productivity

Over the last few centuries, world income has become concentrated in the more developed nations and a few oil-exporting nations as a result of various economic, political, military, intellectual, religious, and other forces. In 1980, the more developed nations (including those in Europe, the United States, Ja-

Figure 3.2. Income per Capita: India, Kenya, Colombia, Japan, and the United States, 1950–1981, with Projections to 2010

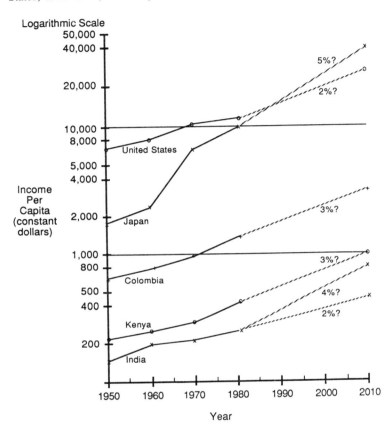

Source: Data from World Bank 1984b.
Note: Constant 1981 U.S. dollars on a semilogarithmic graph.

pan, and the U.S.S.R.), with 25 percent of the world's population, produced 79 percent of total world goods and services, due to much higher human productivity. At the same time, less developed nations, with 75 percent of the world's population, produced 21 percent of world income (World Bank, *World Development Report 1984,* p. 6).

Inequality in Personal Income Distribution

It is important for students of development to appreciate the considerable variability in the distribution of income among individuals in different nations.

Table 3.2. Variability in Household Income Distribution in Less Developed and More Developed Nations

Type of Economy	Percentage Share of Total National Household Income		
	Lowest 20% of Households	Middle 20% of Households	Highest 20% of Households
Low-income economies			
India	7.0	13.9	49.4
Kenya	2.6	11.5	60.4
Malawi	10.4	13.1	50.6
Middle-income economies			
Sudan	4.0	16.6	49.8
Indonesia	6.6	12.6	49.4
Peru	1.9	11.0	61.0
Malaysia	3.5	12.4	56.1
Brazil	2.0	9.4	66.6
Republic of Korea	5.7	15.4	45.3
Industrial market economies			
United Kingdom	7.0	17.0	39.7
France	5.3	16.0	45.8
United States	4.6	14.1	50.3
Japan	8.7	17.5	36.8
Sweden	7.2	17.4	37.2

Source: Data from World Bank, *World Development Report 1984* (table 28).

A common feature of many less developed nations is a highly skewed distribution of personal income. These societies, through centuries of cultural and economic change, have elaborated complex social structures and institutional arrangements that have produced these income distributions. In some of these societies, such highly skewed income distributions may have contributed to group survival.

The extent to which income distribution is skewed can be examined by observing the share of total national household income received by different groups in the population (see table 3.2). In India, the 20 percent of the households with the lowest income obtained 7 percent of all household income, while in the United States they received about 5 percent of all household income and in Brazil only 2 percent. Among all nations, the 20 percent of the households with the highest income are estimated to have had from a low of 37 percent of total household income in Japan and Sweden to a high of 67 percent in Brazil. In many countries, including the United States, this group is estimated to receive about 50 percent of total national household income. The middle 20 percent of

Figure 3.3. Lorenz Curves of Income Distribution: India, Peru, Brazil, Japan, Sweden, and the United States

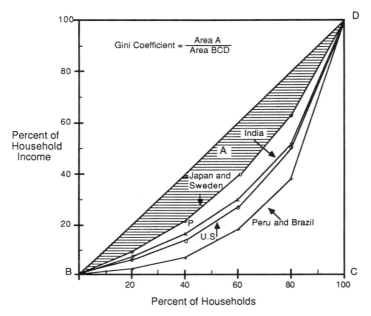

Source: Data from World Bank, *World Development Report 1984* (table 28).

the households in the industrialized market economies received a little higher proportion of total household income, some 14 to 17 percent, than in many low- and middle-income countries, where the share of this group ranged from 9 to 16 percent.

The Lorenz curve and the Gini concentration ratio summarize the extent of inequality in the distribution of income. The Lorenz curve in figure 3.3 shows, for example, that 40 percent of the households in Japan and Sweden receive about 22 percent of the total income in these societies (point *P*). The Gini concentration ratio, or Gini coefficient, is calculated by comparing area *A* in figure 3.3 with the total area of the triangle *BCD* (area *A*/area *BCD*). Thus the ratio varies from 0 to 1.0, and the closer the ratio is to 1.0, the less equal the distribution of income.

Ahluwalia found that developing societies have a wide range of Gini coefficients for income (see Todaro 1981, p. 129). Those with very unequal income distributions have Gini coefficients above .50, and those with more equal income distributions have Gini coefficients below .40. Most of the high-income market economies have Gini coefficients between .30 and .45, including the United States (.31), Japan (.31), and West Germany (.45).

How does economic development affect income disparities? Kuznets

(1963) proposed an inverted U-shaped hypothesis that, as nations achieve middle income, they experience greater inequality of income than low- or high-income nations. More recent work has raised questions about this thesis. [4]

To conclude, developing nations exhibit high variability in per capita income levels, in rates of income growth, and in the distribution of personal income. In many nations, regional disparities in income distribution are an important issue. These fundamental economic realities affect the feasibility and productivity of agricultural and economic development programs and policies in many ways. For example, nations with highly skewed income distributions will probably have somewhat lower rates of growth in demand for food.

Changing Consumer Demand and Income Growth

In order to estimate the rate at which agriculture has to grow to meet the increasing demand for food and other agricultural products, we need to know what consumers do with their money as per capita incomes increase. As their incomes increase, how much of the additional income is saved? If much of the increased income is saved, the demand for food and other goods and services will not increase very rapidly. Do consumers decrease purchases of some foods after they reach certain income levels? Or does the demand for all foods generally remain strong with income growth?

Gradual Growth of Personal Savings

In market economies, personal income (the net income obtained by individuals during a year) commonly ranges from 70 to 80 percent of gross national product (see table 3.3). Early studies by Nobel Prize winner Kuznets, confirmed later by Chenery and Syrquin (1975) and Chenery et al. (1979), demonstrated that consumers increase personal savings slowly as income increases. If most additions to personal income were saved, then savings would rise rapidly and expenditures for goods and services would rise little. Kuznets's studies of thirty-two countries at different levels of development showed the share of personal savings generally increasing from some 3 percent to 6 percent of income over very large (tenfold) increases in per capita income (see table 3.3). So the proportion of GNP for the purchase of goods and services declined only gradually. Thus, the rate of increase in expenditures for goods and services is likely to be only a little less than the rate of growth of income.

Patterns of Consumption with Economic Growth

After personal savings have been subtracted from personal income, the remaining income is labeled personal consumption expenditures, because this is the part of personal income that the consumer controls for purchases of goods

4. For additional discussion, see Hagen 1980 (pp. 55–62) and Yotopoulos and Nugent 1976 (pp. 237–41). Other useful sources on income distribution include Kuznets 1966, 1971; Adelman and Morris 1973; Fei, Ranis, and Kuo 1979; Chenery et al. 1979 (chap. 11); and Rostow 1980.

Table 3.3. Changing Shares of Disposable Personal Income, Personal Savings, and Personal Consumption Expenditures, with per Capita Income Increases, Thirty-two Selected Nations

Item	Low Income Nations		High-Income Nations	
Number of nations	11	8	6	7
Approximate per capita income (1952–54 dollars)	116	232	552	1,110
Share of gross national product (percent)				
Personal income	78.2	78.0	74.8	71.7
Personal savings	3.5	3.8	4.5	5.9
Personal (private) consumption expenditures	73.8	73.1	70.0	65.3

Source: Data adapted from Kuznets 1862 (p. 24).
Note: Percentage figures add only approximately due to various adjustments not included in this table.

and services. How do people change the allocation of personal consumption expenditures as per capita income increases? Shifts in consumer demand with income growth determine which sectors and subsectors of the economy will grow rapidly and which will decline. To explore this question, we first examine changes in the share of income spent on different groups of consumption items, such as food and clothing, as per capita income increases.

CHANGING SHARES OF FOOD AND CLOTHING AND OTHER EXPENDITURES

The relation between expenditures for particular goods or services and changes in per capita income is called an Engel curve. These curves may be shown either (1) as changing shares of income spent on consumer goods and services with income growth; or (2) as changing expenditure levels for these items with income growth. Engel curves provide an understanding of the general pattern of change in consumer spending for different goods and services as per capita income increases.

The changing shares of different groups of consumer items in personal consumption expenditures as income increases were first documented in Germany in 1857 by Ernst Engel. His study concluded that "the poorer a family is, the greater the proportion of the total expenditures which must be used to procure food" (Engel, as quoted in Schumpeter 1954, p. 961). Numerous studies in different countries since have confirmed, for example, the declining relation between the share of food in expenditures with increasing family income. Comparisons of countries at different levels of per capita income show this relation (table 3.4). Such international comparisons indicate that the food share of personal consumption expenditures is some 50 to 70 percent of these expenditures at low annual income levels of $100 to $300 per capita. At higher income levels, less than 30 percent of income is allocated for food. In a high-income country, such as the United States, only some 15 percent of personal income was spent for food in 1986 (USDA 1986, p. 31).

The clothing share of personal consumption expenditures appears to remain about the same, some 10 to 12 percent over a large range of incomes. The shares of other expenditure groups—such as things needed for housing like rent, water, fuel, light, and furniture—take an increasing share of income with economic growth. Personal care, health, transportation, communication, and amusements also increase their shares. Note that the data in this table are cross-section results based upon international comparisons at a certain time. Similar changes in consumption expenditure patterns have been observed in many time series studies of particular nations over long periods of time.

CHANGES IN EXPENDITURES FOR GOODS AND SERVICES

Despite the declining shares of income spent for food, per capita expenditures for food increase greatly, more than fourfold in our example, from $41 to $197 as per capita income increases nearly tenfold (tables 3.3 and 3.4). The relation between this increase in expenditures for food and the declining share of food in personal consumption expenditures can be seen more clearly in figure 3.4. For clothing, per capita expenditures increased at a faster rate than for food—from some $10 to nearly $84. Other consumer expenditures, such as for the house and for personal use, increased even more rapidly with income growth.

Expenditures for broad groups of consumer items like food and clothing are likely to remain more stable than expenditures for individual consumption items. This is because individual items are much more likely to have highly competitive substitutes, and hence the quantities sold will usually be quite sensitive to changes in the price of the substitutes. Therefore, expenditures for an individual food item may fluctuate considerably from year to year due to good or poor harvests, which change the price of one food relative to the price of a close substitute, leading consumers to shift to purchases of the lower-cost food. Although individual substitutions of consumer items occur in this way, the average expenditures for food as a whole by different income groups remain fairly stable.

Nutritional Need and the Economic Demand for Food

Finally, in considering increases in the demand for food, we need to be clear about the relation between the the physical concept of human nutritional need and the economic concept of the demand for food. Demand for food—or for any other good or service—refers to a demand curve, like D in figure 3.5, or to a point on a demand curve, like b. The curve indicates that a consumer will purchase the indicated quantities of food at the specified prices along the curve. In this example, the supply curve, S, shows that at the unit price of P_1, the quan-

Table 3.4. Changing Personal Consumption and Expenditure Patterns as Income Increases, Thirty-two Selected Nations

| Goods and Services | Changing Shares of Personal Consumption Expenditures (percent) | | | |
| | Low-Income Nations | | High-Income Nations | |
	11	8	6	7
Food, beverages, and tobacco	56.4	50.4	45.4	36.4
(Food)	(48.4)	(40.2)	(35.6)	(27.2)
Clothing	11.1	11.3	12.4	11.6
Rent, water, fuel, light, furniture, and household operations	18.5	18.2	20.1	25.2
Personal care and health, transportation, communication, amusements and miscellaneous	14.5	23.9	20.7	26.4
Adjustments	−0.5	−3.8	1.4	0.4
Total	100.0	100.0	100.0	100.0

Source: Data in first four columns from Kuznets 1962 (p. 24).
[a] Calculated from data in table 3.3.

Figure 3.4. Engel Curves for Food: Declining Shares and Increasing Expenditures

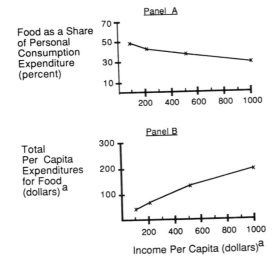

Source: Data from Kuznets (1962, p. 24).
[a] In 1952–54 dollars.

Changing per Capita Expenditures (dollars)[a]			
Low-Income Nations		High-Income Nations	
11	8	6	7
48	86	175	264
(41)	(68)	(137)	(197)
10	19	48	84
16	31	78	183
12	41	80	191
0	−7	5	3
86	170	386	725

Figure 3.5. Nutritional Need and Economic Demand for Food

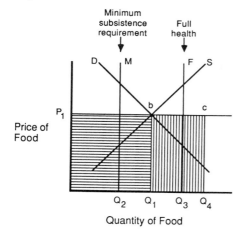

tity Q_1 of food will be purchased. The demand curve therefore reflects an assumption that the consumer has the money to buy the quantities of food indicated at the corresponding prices—it indicates his or her "effective" demand for food (the amount of food the consumer purchases at the different prices, not the amount of food the consumer might want if it were free). A hungry person may not have P_1 amount of money and would not be able to buy a unit of food. Therefore, although he may have nutritional need for it, he would not have an effective demand for it—he is not able to buy it.

Nutritional need for food is determined through studies in biochemistry and nutrition. The relation between this physical, quantitative concept of food need and the economic concept of effective demand for food is illustrated in figure 3.5. Suppose, on the basis of careful nutritional studies, line M and the quantity Q_2 indicate the quantity of food required for daily minimum survival, perhaps at lower levels of physical activity and at increased risk of poor health and disease. Line F and Q_3 indicate the daily quantity of food needed for full health. Suppose also that a laborer were able to earn only the daily income needed to purchase Q_1 amount of food (horizontally shaded area). With this money and a market price of P_1, the demand curve D would cross the supply curve at b, and hence the laborer could buy only Q_1 amount of food. This amount is greater than the minimum subsistence requirement, Q_2, but less than the amount needed for full health, Q_3. Another laborer who earned enough to buy a larger daily quantity of food, say Q_4, would be able to buy more food than needed to meet the requirements for full health. The quantity of food that can be produced by subsistence farming or earned by a laborer may or may not meet the nutritional requirements for full health. The effects on human nutrition of the new crop varieties are examined in chapter 8.

The Growing Demand for Food and Agricultural Products

Knowledge of the rates at which the effective demand for food and other goods and services will grow would enable government officials, farmers, and other entrepreneurs to better plan investments to increase production or to arrange for needed food imports. The long-term rate of growth in demand for consumer goods is largely dependent upon three variables: (1) population growth; (2) per capita income growth; and (3) the income elasticity of demand for the good or service.

The Rate of Population Growth and Food Demand

If per capita income did not change, the rate of growth in demand for food (d) would be equal to the growth rate of population (p), or $d = p$, assuming tastes do not change. Hence, to prevent food price increases, agricultural production or food imports would have to increase at least as rapidly as population.

The rate of growth in per capita income (g) also affects growth in food demand. The examination earlier in the chapter of changes in consumer purchasing behavior showed that expenditures for food increase as income increases. Thus income growth, as well as population growth, causes the demand curve for food to move further to the right.

Effect of Income on Food Demand

The income elasticity of demand (n) for any good or service indicates how changes in per capita income effect the demand for food or other products and services. Conceptually, the income elasticity of demand for a good or service is the proportionate, or percentage, change in expenditure for the item compared with the percentage change in per capita income ($\%\Delta C/\%\Delta I$) (Δ is the symbol for change in). As shown below, income elasticities can be estimated by calculating the arc elasticity (the slope of a line connecting two observed consumption levels) as income increases. Or a point income elasticity can be estimated by obtaining the slope at a particular income level of a mathematical function relating consumption to income:

A. Conceptually,

$$e \sim \frac{\%\Delta C}{\%\Delta I}.$$

B. Arc elasticities
   1. For easy approximations of arc elasticity over small changes in income, the following equation may be used:

$$e \sim \frac{C_2 - C_1}{(C_1 + C_2)/2} \Big/ \frac{I_2 - I_1}{(I_1 + I_2)/2} = \frac{C_2 - C_1}{I_2 - I_1} \times \frac{I_1 + I_2}{C_1 + C_2} = \frac{\Delta C}{\Delta I} \times \frac{I_1 + I_2}{C_1 + C_2}.$$

   For example; data from tables 3.3 and 3.4 for food would give

$$\frac{197 - 41}{41 + 197} \Big/ \frac{1110 - 116}{116 + 1110} = .81$$

   2. To estimate the arc elasticity exactly between specified points, the equation for the slope of a line in logarithms may be used.

$$e = \frac{\text{Log } C_2 - \text{Log } C_1}{\text{Log } I_2 - \text{Log } I_1} = \frac{\Delta \text{ Log } C}{\Delta \text{ Log } I}.$$

C. Point elasticities on a function are estimated as

$$e = \frac{d (\text{Log } C)}{d (\text{Log } I)} = \frac{d(C)}{C} \Big/ \frac{d(I)}{I} \text{ or } \frac{dC}{dI} \times \frac{I}{C}.$$

The following examples of long-run arc income elasticities of demand for the different groups of consumption goods were obtained from the data in table 3.4: food 0.81; clothing 0.97; rent and so on, 1.04; and personal care and so on, 1.09. These figures help demonstrate how elasticities work. Note particularly that, if the percentage increase in expenditures is the same as the percentage increase in income, the income elasticity is 1.00, and the share of the item in the expenditure pattern remains the same. Clothing is an example in this data set with an income elasticity close to 1.00 (0.97). Think also about the meanings of a 0.0 income elasticity and an elasticity that is negative (− 0.50).

Income elasticities enable economic definitions of two important categories of goods or services. Inferior goods and services are those that experience declining total consumer expenditures as income increases—they have a negative income elasticity. Such a good might be a time-consuming, hard-to-prepare, largely carbohydrate food. Or an inferior service might be animal transportation that completely drops out of the consumption pattern with economic development. In contrast, expenditures for luxury goods, such as meat, increase more than proportionately with income growth. Luxury goods and services are defined as those that have income elasticities greater than 1.00.

Finally, the income elasticity concept should not be confused with the price elasticity of demand. Price elasticity measures the slope of the demand curve that relates the quantities bought to the prices of a good or service. Conceptually, price elasticity is the percentage change in the quantity of the product bought in response to a percentage change in the price of the good or service ($\%\Delta Q/\%\Delta P$).

Finally, focusing on empirical estimates of income elasticity of demand for food, many studies of developing nations have shown that, over long periods of time, it is very likely to remain somewhere near 0.7, being somewhat higher at very low levels of income, while gradually declining at higher income levels. In higher income nations, the income elasticity of demand for food expenditures may drop below 0.4.

Rate of Growth in Food Demand

The relation among the three main factors that affect the rate of growth in demand for food (d) is $d = p + gn$ (see Ohkawa 1956; Stevens 1965). Using this equation with typical data for less developed nations, we find that the rates of growth in demand for food is likely to range from a low of perhaps 2.7 percent [2.0 + 1(.7)] to perhaps 5.1 percent [3.0 + 3(.7)] or more.

To conclude, the annual rates of growth in the demand for food in less developed nations are likely to range from 3 to 5 percent if the nation increases real per capita income at rates from 1 to 3 percent. Such a growth in food demand is a challenge for those concerned with food production. As seen in chapter 2, few nations have achieved a 4 percent rate of growth in food production over long periods. Nations that fail to achieve the rates of growth in food production required to meet demand at current prices have to either increase food imports or suffer increases in agricultural prices. Increases in food prices relative to other prices slow the rate of growth in per capita income. How can agricultural production be accelerated to meet this development challenge?

The Structural Transformation of Less Developed Economies

The structural transformation of an economy, also referred to as the economic transformation, is defined as a change in the relative importance of the different economic sectors associated with the shift from a predominantly agricultural economy to one dominated by the industrial and service sectors.

How do the changing demands for goods and services affect the structure of an economy? How does the structure of an economy change with economic growth, and what effects do these changes have on agriculture?

Measurement of Changes in Economic Structure

Two common measures of changes in economic structure are (1) the proportion of income produced in each sector; and (2) the proportion of the labor force in each sector. Studies of changes in the proportion of national income produced in each sector show that in very low-income nations almost half of the gross national product originates in the agricultural sector. For example, in Bangladesh in 1982, agriculture produced 47 percent of GNP, while industry produced only 14 percent (see table 3.5). However, in twenty eight low-income nations, the industrial sector generated an average of 32 percent of national income, while the service sectors produced about the same proportion (31 percent). In high-income industrial market economies, the importance of the farming sector becomes very small, creating an average of only 3 percent of national income, while service sectors increase in importance. One of the reasons for the decline in the size of agriculture is the increasing specialization of agricultural processing and marketing services, which are transferred off the farm into other sectors of the economy. Another reason is the greatly increased productivity of agriculture.

The changing proportion of the labor force in each sector of the economy is shown in table 3.6. In a low-income agricultural nation such as Bangladesh, some three-fourths of the labor force worked in the agricultural sector in 1982, with only 11 percent in the industrial sector (table 3.6). In the high-income market economies, the table shows an average of some 56 percent of the labor force in service sectors, with only 6 percent remaining in the agricultural sector. [5]

Forces Causing Changes in Economic Structure

What causes these vast changes in the structure of economies? Two causes are fundamental: (1) changes in consumer demand; and (2) the varied increases in productivity in the different sectors of the economy, due to specialization and

---

5. Important studies of changing economic structure with economic growth include Chenery et al. 1979; Mellor 1984; Johnston and Kilby 1975; Yotopoulos and Nugent 1976 (chap. 15).

Table 3.5. Changing Structure of National Economies with Income Growth, as Measured by Sector Income Shares

Measure	Bangladesh	Low-Income Economies
Average gross national product per capita (1982 dollars)	140	280
Proportion of gross domestic product by sector		
Agriculture	47	37
Industry	14	32
Services	39	31

Source: Data from World Bank, *World Development Report 1984* (tables 1 and 3).

Table 3.6. Changing Structure of National Economies with Income Growth, as Measured by the Labor Force in the Agricultural, Industrial, and Service Sectors

Measure	Bangladesh	Low-Income Economies
Average gross national product per capita (1982 dollars)	140	280
Proportion of labor force by sector (1980)		
Agriculture	74	72
Industry	11	13
Services	15	15

Source: Data from World Bank, *World Development Report 1984* (table 21).

division of labor associated with scientific and industrial advances. In an earlier section, studies of changing consumer expenditure patterns with economic growth demonstrated that, as per capita income increases, the need for some goods and services (those with high-income elasticity) will increase more rapidly than others. National economies respond to consumer demand through the myriad decisions by private and public decisionmakers who make investments to increase the productive capacity in sectors of the economy faced with increasing demand and who decrease the production of goods and services for which there is reduced demand.

Increasing Functional Specialization and Uneven Regional Growth

The way in which increased productivity is achieved through the industrial application of scientific advances with associated changes in industrial structure has been well stated by Johnston and Kilby (1975):

Lower Middle-Income Economies	Upper Middle-Income Economies	High-Income Industrial Market Economies
840	2,490	11,070
23	11	3
35	41	36
42	48	61

Lower Middle-Income Economies	Upper Middle-Income Economies	High-Income Industrial Market Economies
840	2,490	11,070
56	30	6
16	28	38
28	42	56

The mechanism of economic progress in farming is the same one that operates in every other sector of the economy. The mechanism is specialization. Not only is there specialization along specific crop lines among farmers, but a host of functions formerly carried out by the household is transferred to specialist producers. Increasing division of labor in all economic activity brings with it the opportunity for using machinery whose power, speed, and precision multiplies the yield of human effort. Specialization not only makes possible the introduction of capital equipment, it facilitates changes to better organization and more productive technologies. The result is to raise the productivity of land and capital as well as that of labor. As these processes get under way, individual productive units shift from self-sufficiency to dependence upon markets, both for the disposal of their production and for purchase of their raw materials and other services. (p. 34)

Changes in economic structure lead to increased geographic specialization and uneven growth in regional agricultural production. Major causes of uneven growth include the following four. First, the changing demand for different agricultural products increases prosperity in some regions and causes declines in others. Second, better agricultural resources and growing conditions in some areas enable more rapid increases in farm productivity and income. Where growing conditions are best, crop yields are high, and hence for the same input costs higher net returns are obtained per unit of land. Thus the production of many crops tends to concentrate in high-yield areas. However, some lower-yield areas may be major producing areas for certain crops due to the economic law of comparative advantage. (For an explanation of this term, see chapter 13.) In these areas, the income-earning potential of the lower yielding crops provides a higher income than other economic opportunities.

Third, the regional impacts of new agricultural technologies vary. Often they are more productive in areas with good soil. A side effect is decreased production—and agricultural income—in areas with poor soil. And fourth, the reduction in transportation costs and increased speed of delivery is uneven regionally. Johann Von Thuenen (1783–1850) long ago demonstrated that transportation costs affect the location of production of different agricultural products. As the real cost of transportation declines, it becomes profitable to grow crops further from major markets. Thus, in many more developed nations today, fruits and vegetables, which earlier had been produced close to large urban markets due to the costliness and slowness of transportation, have now shifted to areas where growing conditions enable high yields and profitable production despite very great distances to market.

The Role of Agriculture in Economic Development

How important a contribution does agriculture make to overall economic development? Because, as demonstrated earlier in the chapter, economic growth requires more rapid growth in the industrial and service sectors than in the agricultural sector, national development plans and investments often have been focused on nonagricultural sectors. Government development plans in the 1950s often assumed that increases in agricultural production would be forthcoming without much government policy attention and without much additional investment. The growth of the agricultural sector was assumed to be of low priority and hence could be neglected in an ambitious development program. Such industry-first strategies, however, often led to serious food shortages, as, for example, in the U.S.S.R. in the 1920s and in India in the 1960s, with resulting slower national growth. Why?

The essential interrelations between the agricultural and other sectors of the economy were not then well understood. These interrelations were illuminated by Johnston and Mellor (1961); Jorgenson (1961); Nicholls (1964); Ranis and Fei (1961); and Mellor (1984), who demonstrated the crucial importance of agricultural growth for rapid national economic development. Studies also showed that these linkages between the sectors increase with economic growth. Not only are increased flows of products from agriculture necessary to support growth in the other sectors, but agriculture in turn requires certain resources from other sectors for increased growth. These interactions can be summarized as follows.

Contributions of Agriculture to Other Sectors

The essential contributions of agriculture to the other sectors for accelerating economic growth are (1) increases in the production of food and other agricultural products for urban domestic use and for export; (2) the supply of additional labor to nonagricultural sectors; (3) a net outflow of capital for investment in other sectors; and (4) an increase in consumer demand in the agricultural sector for the goods and services produced in the other sectors.

Contributions of Other Sectors to Agriculture

More rapid growth in the agricultural sector requires the following contributions of other sectors to agriculture: (1) the industrial production of improved farm inputs, such as chemical fertilizer and pesticides and capital equipment, including farm machinery, pumps, and irrigation equipment; (2) an increased demand for food and other agricultural products from both increasing income and the shift of a greater proportion of the labor force to nonagricultural sectors; and (3) the provision of needed infrastructure, such as roads, transportation equipment, and communications, as well as education. Many of these economic flows among the sectors increase greatly with economic development. Shortages of more productive inputs and capital equipment slow agricultural growth, which in turn reduces the national rate of growth in per capita income. Slower growth in agriculture has an especially dampening effect on economic growth in those nations with a high proportion of income still originating in agriculture.[6]

What policies and programs of development can be pursued by less developed nations to enable the sectors of these nations to make increased contributions to other sectors and thereby accelerate growth?

Important Concepts

Economic growth
Economic development
Gross national product (GNP)
Net investment
Per capita income
Levels of consumption
Levels of living

Nonmonetary indicators of
   development
Physical quality of life index
   (PQLI)
Lorenz curve
Gini concentration ratio (Gini
   coefficient)

6. Additional references on the role of agriculture and about interrelations between the agricultural and other sectors include Nicholls 1964; Johnston and Mellor 1961; Johnston and Kilby 1975; Cheetham, Kelley, and Williamson 1974; Thorbecke 1969; Lee 1971; and Yotopoulos and Nugent 1976 (pp. 299–307).

Human nutritional need
Economic demand for food
Income elasticity of demand
Inferior goods
Luxury goods

Price elasticity of demand
Rate of growth in food demand
Structural transformation
Measures of economic structure

Sample Questions

1. What do you view as the meaning of development? And how might it ideally be measured?

2. Explain the nature of currently used monetary and nonmonetary measures of development. Comment on their usefulness.

3. What range of rates of growth in real per capita income have been achieved by less developed nations in the last two decades?

4. What analytic tools can be used to show changes in the distribution of income or of the control of agricultural resources, such as land? Explain how they are used.

5. Describe graphically, or in words, how the shares of food and clothing usually change when per capita incomes increase from $100 to $1,000.

6. What is the meaning of income elasticity of demand? How can it be written mathematically?

7. How can general estimates of needed rates of growth in food and agricultural production be obtained? What range of rates are usually found in less developed nations?

8. In a particular nation, what foods are likely to have high income elasticities (above 1.0), lower income elasticities (0.0–1.0), and negative income elasticities?

9. Explain the meaning of the structural transformation of an economy of a less developed nation. How is structural change measured?

10. What are the contributions of the agricultural sector to the growth of the national economy? And what contributions are required from other sectors for the development of agriculture?

II

The Economic and Social Theory of Agricultural Development

Introduction to Part II

Part II seeks a theory of economic and social development that will facilitate solving the immense economic and agricultural growth problems seen in part I. How can agricultural development be accelerated to enable more rapid economic progress in developing nations? Can agricultural development theory explain both the stagnation of traditional agricultural areas and the rapid growth of agriculture achieved in other regions? How do farmers become more productive? What economic forces influence the development of needed new agricultural technologies and institutions so that agricultural growth rates can be increased? Does currently available economic and social theory provide an integrated model of growth to guide the design of more effective programs and policies for agricultural development?

The interaction of many natural, economic, technological, institutional, social, and political variables determines the productivity of farmers throughout the world. The objective of this part of the text is to examine the extent to which current economic and social science theory can illuminate these interactions. Chapter 4 explores the results of theoretical and empirical research focused on traditional agriculture. It presents the equilibrium model of traditional agriculture offered by T. W. Schultz, which explains both the stagnation and the growth of agriculture during much of human history. Chapter 5 examines the interrelations between the agricultural sector and the broader rural environment—social, political, and cultural—in which economic life takes place. This analysis identifies important constraints and variables affecting agricultural development that stem from other parts of a social system. Chapter 6 presents the economic theory of agricultural development by first identifying the shortcomings of important partial theories of agricultural development and then by presenting the general economic model of induced innovation. This model provides the theoretical structure on which this text is built. Chapter 7, the final one in part II, examines two important parts of agricultural development theory, the economics of the historically important contributions of additional land to agricultural growth and the economic theory of labor productivity in agriculture.

4

Economics of Traditional Agriculture

King Sobhuza II of Swaziland officially celebrated his 71st birthday on July 22, 1970. . . . He is the leader in agricultural development in his country, and his own royal pastures set the example of modern farming methods for his people to follow. When the king plows, and not until then, everybody plows. When the king reaps, everybody reaps.

—*New York Times, 26 July, 1970*

We are all bound to be humble in the presence of the producers. . . . How many of us, who are so wise in international gatherings about what other people should do, could emulate them in winning subsistence, survival, dignity, and fortitude in the face of calamity from the meager resources of traditional rural society in tropical environments?

—*Bunting 1979, p. 8*

Traditional Agriculture: Definitions and Hypotheses

In the early 1950s economists were puzzled by the lack of progress over the last century in many agricultural areas of the less developed world, while rapid economic growth had occurred in many agricultural areas of more developed nations. To better understand this complex issue, economists have pursued many empirical and theoretical investigations in the last three decades. This research has enabled a cohesive economic theory of traditional agriculture and of ways to accelerate agricultural development.

The objective of this chapter is to examine how technological, economic, and institutional variables affect traditional farming. We need to understand both how these agricultural systems have succeeded over the centuries in sustaining many peoples and why they have generally had low productivity and slow growth. The chapter seeks to provide reasons for the vicious cycles of poverty and the economic equilibria encountered in much of traditional agriculture. It provides economic explanations for the continuing existence of traditional farming in some areas of less developed nations. One of the quotations at the beginning of the chapter provides an example of the highly integrated nature of some traditional agricultural systems: the king of Swaziland in 1970 still influenced farmers' decisions about when to plow and when to harvest.

This chapter focuses on farmers' decisionmaking at the micro, or farm, level and the economic realities of the traditional communities, where a limited economic pie can be increased only slowly. Linkages between farmers' individual production decisions and the national, or macro, effects of these choices on a country's economy are addressed later, particularly in chapters 13 and 14.

We now need to travel in our minds to traditional agricultural environments, where millions of people live on very low incomes. To learn which factors are most important in this new environment, we have to leave behind many assumptions about economic life that we unconsciously hold due to our experience of life in the more developed and urban world. What technological, economic, institutional, and other factors really do influence decisions by traditional farmers? And what criteria do they use in making these decisions?

Suppose tomorrow you were to arrive in a low-income agricultural area of a less developed nation about which you had little knowledge. How would you begin to analyze the agricultural problems of that area? What kinds of information should you seek to explain why the area remains so poor? This chapter identifies the important economic variables that affect the performance of traditional agricultural systems that would need to be focused upon. It also provides essential economic theory tools to explain economic equilibrium. This understanding is required to enable the development of useful economic theory that can aid acceleration of agricultural development.

What Is Traditional Agriculture?

Traditional agriculture can be defined as farming in which the technology used has been developed by keen observation of nature by people who lack knowledge of and access to science and industrial technology. Technology refers to any standardized means for attaining a desired objective (see, for example, Babbie 1980, p. 423). Traditional farming practices (technologies) have been developed without access either to knowledge of the sciences of biology, chemistry, and physics, or to industrially produced inputs. Traditional agricultural technology is the art of agriculture, which has been passed on verbally and by demonstration from one generation to the next, based upon much observation and experience in local farming areas over the years.

Until about 1850, most of world agriculture was traditional. Until 1950, most of the agriculture in Asia, Africa, and Latin America remained traditional. Today, millions of farmers in low-income nations have adopted some items of more productive, science-based, agricultural technology, but they continue to use many traditional agricultural methods.

The Importance of the Study of Low-Income Farming Areas

To understand the problems faced by traditional farmers in low-income agricultures, students whose experience is limited to more developed nations, often to urban areas, need to shed their preconceived ideas and learn to identify and be sensitive to the social and economic variables that affect a very different society. Such students might read in-depth studies or do field studies themselves. Readers from urban areas of less developed nations often have similarly limited understanding of the very different nature of agricultural life, particularly in the poorer areas of their countries—stereotypes abound among these urban intellectuals about farmers and peasants. Readers with considerable experience with one low-income agricultural area can benefit from intensive study of different farming areas, enabling them to understand the extent to which many complex development problems faced by their groups are general and which ones are in fact peculiar to the resource, economic, and social conditions of that area. To aid in in-depth study of an area through monographs or on-site study, an outline is offered in appendix table 4.1.[1]

The objective of in-depth study is to gain detailed knowledge of the social and economic problems that really confront traditional farmers, who often successfully manage a large number of different agricultural and other economic activities in difficult environments. The great complexity of many of these farms is illustrated by figure 4.1.

Five Hypotheses About the Economics of Traditional Agriculture

In 1964, T. W. Schultz presented a cohesive economic theory of traditional agriculture in his now classic book *Transforming Traditional Agriculture* (1964b). Five hypotheses from this theory guide our exploration of the economics of traditional agriculture.

1. Farmers in traditional agriculture respond to economic incentives (Schultz 1964a, p. 19).
2. Agricultural development "is not primarily a problem of the supply of capital. It is rather a problem of determining the forms this investment must take, forms that will make it profitable to invest in agriculture" (Schultz 1964b, p. 4).

---

1. Additional sources of information about the types of traditional agriculture include Spedding 1979; Morgan 1977; Grigg 1979; and about their prevalence Pryor 1977. Book-length materials that include case studies of traditional agricultures include Stevens 1977; and about Hacienda Vicos, Peru, Dobyns, Doughty, and Lasswell 1971; and these collections: Dalton 1967; McLoughlin 1970; Heyer, Roberts, and Williams 1981; Ruthenberg 1980; and Hall, Cannel, and Lawton 1979. For monographs see Hill 1977; Bliss and Stern 1982; Brush 1977; Hayami et al. 1978; Buck 1949; Geertz 1964; Sahlins 1972; and on shifting cultivation J. E. Spencer 1966.

Figure 4.1. A Traditional Humid, Upland, Farming System in Asia

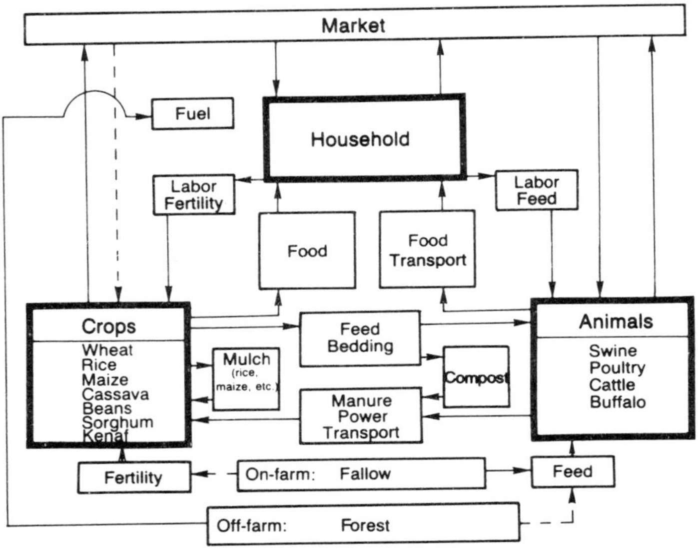

Source: McDowell and Hildebrand 1980 (p. 21).

3. "There are comparatively few significant inefficiencies in the allocation of the factors of production in traditional agriculture" (Schultz 1964b, p. 37).
4. "There is not much to be gained from imitating the best farmers in traditional agriculture" (Schultz 1964a, p. 19).
5. "The rate of return to capital is low in traditional agriculture" (Schultz 1964b, p. 84), or, in other words, "the price [cost] of increasing the [productive] capacity of traditional agriculture is high" (Schultz 1964a, p. 19).

We test these hypotheses about the economics of traditional agriculture by examining important empirical findings.

Empirical Findings About Traditional Agriculture

Since World War II, a large body of empirical information has become available about traditional agriculture, based on much research on farms in the low-income world. The following four central empirical findings about traditional agriculture are a base upon which economists have constructed a theory of traditional agriculture.

The Productivity of Land, Livestock, and Labor

The most general empirical finding in studies of traditional agriculture is that the average productivity of land, livestock, and labor is very low compared to farming in more developed nations, except in unusual circumstances. *Productivity* is measured by comparing the products obtained (output) with the resources used (inputs). Considering land productivity first, what average crop yields (product per unit of land) are achieved by farmers who employ traditional agricultural technologies? Have farmers using traditional technology been able to increase yields appreciably?

LOW LAND PRODUCTIVITY

National statistics (USDA *Agricultural Statistics*) on crop yields in the early 1980s demonstrate the low yields obtained in the still largely traditional agricultures of the less developed nations. Representative comparative national yield data for four major world crops (maize, potatoes, rice, and wheat) show that average crop yields in less developed nations are generally one-half to one-fourth those in the more developed nations (see tables 4.1 through 4.4). Part of the explanation for low income in traditional farming areas, then, is that yields are low, and hence land productivity is low.

Not only are yields low in traditional agriculture, but essentially no increases in yields are achieved. Of course, over very long periods of time, gradual yield increases have been achieved before science-based agricultural techniques were adopted. However, the rate of increase was so low that, when yearly yields are averaged over ten years to smooth the varying effects of weather and disease, yields in most agricultural areas of the less developed world have shown very little change until the last two decades. In some areas, during certain periods, yields have gradually declined for a variety of reasons, including soil exhaustion, slow changes in moisture, pests, and increasing population pressure.

To illustrate the very gradual rates of increase in yields achieved in traditional farming, yield growth rates from two sets of very long-term yield data were calculated. Wheat yields in England from the year 1250 to 1750 had an average annual compound rate of increase of 0.2 percent. In Japan, rice yields from 750 to 1885 increased at a rate of 0.05 percent per year (see figure 11.2). A more recent detailed analysis of rice yields in three less developed nations between 1900 and 1964 shows a slow decline in average rice yields in Thailand, a gradual rise in yields in the Philippines, and in Taiwan a very slow increase until the 1930s, when an acceleration in yield occurred following the introduction of new agricultural technologies by the Japanese (see figure 4.2). The decline in yield during World War II was followed by a more rapid yield increase due to the land reform and other changes in the early 1950s.

Table 4.1. Average Yields for Maize, 1981–1984, Selected Nations

Nation	Metric Tons per Hectare
Nigeria	0.9
India	1.1
Mexico	1.4
Brazil	1.7
U.S.S.R.	2.9
Argentina	3.1
Egypt	4.3
United States[a]	6.4
Iowa	6.9
Michigan	6.2
North Carolina[b]	4.9

Source: USDA, *Agricultural Statistics* 1984.
[a] Largest producer.
[b] North Carolina's yield was about 0.81 metric tons per hectare in 1900 (Cummings, p. 38).

Table 4.3. Average Yields for Unhulled Paddy Rice, 1981–1984, Selected Nations

Nation	Metric Tons per Hectare
Brazil	1.5
India	2.0
Pakistan	2.6
Indonesia	3.7
China (mainland)[a]	4.7
United States	5.3
California	7.7
Arkansas	4.9
Japan	5.7
Egypt	5.7

Source: USDA, *Agricultural Statistics* 1984.
[a] Largest producer.

Table 4.2. Average Yields for Potatoes, 1982–1984, Selected Nations

Nation	Metric Tons per Hectare
Kenya	7.1
Peru	8.2
U.S.S.R.[a]	12.0
China	12.5
Poland	15.9
Egypt	16.3
West Germany	28.8
United States	30.8
Maine[b]	27.9
Michigan[b]	28.2
Washington[b]	55.8

Source: FAO, *Production Yearbook* 1984.
[a] Largest producer.
[b] Data for 1981–83 calculated from USDA, *Agricultural Statistics* 1984. Fall yield.

Table 4.4. Average Yields for Wheat, 1981–1984, Selected Nations

Nation	Metric Tons per Hectare
Algeria	0.6
U.S.S.R.[a]	1.5
Turkey	1.6
India	1.7
Argentina	1.7
United States	2.4
Kansas	2.3
Michigan	3.2
China	2.5
Egypt	3.4
Mexico[b]	3.9
France	5.1

Source: USDA, *Agricultural Statistics* 1984.
[a] Largest producer.
[b] Mexico's yield was 0.7 metric tons in 1945.

Figure 4.2. Long-Term Rice Yields: The Philippines, Thailand, and Taiwan, 1900–1960

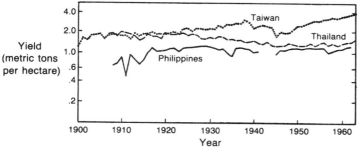

Source: Hsieh and Ruttan 1967 (p. 311). Reprinted with permission.

LOW LIVESTOCK PRODUCTIVITY

In traditional agriculture, livestock productivity is also very low. Average weights of animals at various ages are generally much lower in less developed nations than those in more developed nations; rates of weight gain of one-third as fast as modern livestock are common. Milk, egg, and draft power yields are also much lower.[2]

LOW LABOR PRODUCTIVITY

The labor productivity levels achieved in the traditional agricultures of developing nations are examined in detail in chapter 7. It is sufficient here to state that a great deal of data are available that show the small amounts of agricultural products produced per farmer per year. The income earned by agricultural laborers is also very low. Factors contributing to low labor productivity include limited amounts of land available per farmer, limits on other resources to use with hand and animal tools, and the low productivity of crop varieties and livestock.

The Price Responsiveness of Traditional Farmers

Of central importance in building an economic model of traditional agriculture is knowledge of the effect of price changes on the decisions of traditional farmers. It has often been asserted that farming decisions in traditional areas are largely determined by cultural factors, little influenced by economic variables. If this were so, a largely noneconomic approach would have to be undertaken to understand how farming decisions are made. The issue of the price responsiveness of traditional agriculturalists has two parts. First, do farmers produce different quantities of crops in response to changes in the relative price of one crop

2. See FAO *Production Yearbook* for information on livestock productivity in traditional agriculture. Also see references on livestock productivity and development in note 5 in chapter 8.

compared to another? Second, to what extent do farmers respond positively to increases in all agricultural prices relative to other prices?

Questions about price responsiveness are so fundamental that a large number of empirical studies have focused on this question in the last two decades. The almost unanimous conclusion of these studies is that farmers in less developed nations on all continents are price responsive in their production activities. Thus, when the price of one product they know how to produce increases relative to the prices of other products, farmers increase the production of the product with the price rise. They do this because it increases their net income. In economic terminology, these studies have investigated the price elasticity of supply of agricultural products. The price elasticity of supply is the percentage change in the quantity of the good produced compared with the percentage change in the price of the good, holding all other prices constant.

Krishna (1967) examined studies in less developed nations of the changes in land cultivated in each crop in response to relative price changes. He concluded that the acreage (land) price elasticities for staple food crops ranged from 0.0 to 0.4 and that the acreage price elasticities for two commercial fiber crops, cotton and jute, were higher, 0.4 to 0.7. In comparing these results with studies of acreage responses to price in more developed nations, he concluded that the responses of traditional and commercial farmers to price are of similar magnitude. A study by Behrman (1968) of four crops in Thailand over the 1937–63 period showed similar results. These largely traditional farmers demonstrated supply elasticities similar to those of modern farmers in the United States! A more recent survey of the large amount of econometric research on the supply response of farmers cites thousands of positive supply response estimates (Askari and Cummings 1976).

In spite of this evidence, two objections are sometimes raised. The first one concerns the fact that some traditional people use very little money. This argument implies therefore that relative price changes cannot be known when money is little used, and also that, without money, economic incentives cannot be present. We know, however, that in all traditional societies a considerable amount of barter occurs among families and between groups. Through these trades, the relative value, or price, of many products become known. Therefore, even in societies without money, the members of the group can often observe when there is a relative increase in the value of one product compared to others.

The second question points out that, in some more isolated traditional areas where money is present, it still may have relatively little value to farmers, as the things they desire are not obtainable with money. This is either because the desired products are customarily exchanged only for other products, or because desired goods for which money could be used are not available locally. Under these circumstances, it is possible that money offered for agricultural products would elicit little response. However, in these areas barter mechanisms may come into play to reflect the increased demand for agricultural products.

The second part of the price responsiveness question is whether traditional farmers as a group will increase total production when the prices of all agricultural products rise relative to all other prices. This question is important because, in national policy discussions, proposals are often made that food prices should be increased to encourage greater farm production. In the previous section, farmers were shown to be price responsive in switching between crops they know how to grow in response to relative changes in the prices of these crops. With a general increase in agricultural prices relative to other prices, farmers may have both limited incentive and limited capacity to respond. Research on this question requires estimates of the price elasticity of total agricultural production. For more traditional low-income agricultural areas, studies have shown that the aggregate price elasticity of supply is usually low (Herdt 1970).

The reasons why traditional farmers have a low response in total agricultural production to general price increases in crops include the following three. First, the limited marketing of crops by many low-income farmers would reduce this price incentive. In many areas of less developed nations, the average proportion of marketed agricultural products sold by farmers is less than half of total production. And as farmers purchase only limited amounts of nonagricultural products, the potential increase in total net farm income from increased prices for marketed crops would be relatively small. In spite of this, the marketed surplus of agricultural products could increase significantly in response to general agricultural price increases, as farmers shift somewhat further toward production for market.

Second, increased farm income may reduce incentives in traditional environments for more production. When farm prices increase, the farmers who do market significant amounts will have higher incomes, so the incentive to devote additional family labor and other resources to agriculture may diminish. The third and most important reason why farmers in many traditional agricultural areas have little ability to respond to a relative increase in the prices of all agricultural products is that additional land, labor, and other inputs are often quite limited. The high marginal costs for these additional resources make it unprofitable to increase agricultural production, even with higher prices. The price responsiveness of farmers during agricultural development is explored in chapter 14.

Productivity and Farm Size

A third very important finding based on many empirical studies in less developed nations is that increasing farm size is usually associated with decreasing land productivity and lower total productivity. This empirical result is contrary to the teaching of economists from the time of Adam Smith that, through economies of scale (or size) and division of labor, productivity is increased! *Economies of size* are defined as increases in output per unit of input (productivity increases) due to enlarging the size of a farm or business. The existence of economies of size in many economic activities is supported by experience in industri-

Figure 4.3. Farm Size and Production per Unit of Land in Less Developed Nations

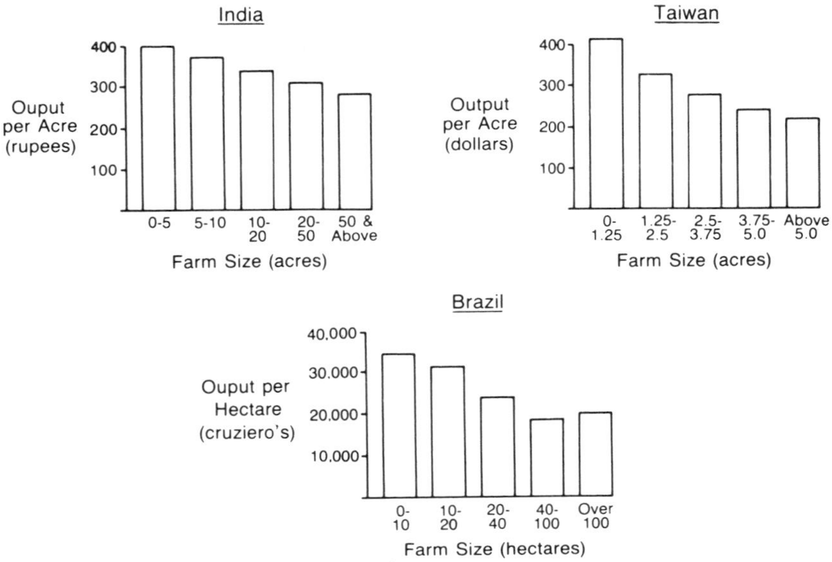

Source: Data from Christensen 1968 (p. 41) and Schmid 1969 (pp. 5 and 13).

alized societies, where large firms are very often more productive than small firms. This experience has led many to assume that larger farms in less developed countries would also have higher yields, and therefore that agricultural productivity would increase if farm size were increased.

The evidence for diseconomies of size in many agricultural areas of less developed nations is based on much empirical research. One of the more comprehensive studies included analyses of data from Brazil, Colombia, the Philippines, Pakistan, India, and Malaysia (Berry and Cline 1979). It reaffirmed the general negative relation between farm size and product per unit of land and between farm size and total resource use. Of particular interest is the finding that these relations held both in Latin America, where average farm size is large and population density is low, and in Asia, where average farm size is small and population densities are high. Earlier data from other sources have also shown this inverse relation between farm size and yields (see figure 4.3).

A detailed econometric study of Indian farms by Lau and Yotopoulos (1971) found that small farms (less than ten acres) had greater productivity. The explanation for these results is that agricultural productivity depends upon the increased quality and quantity of labor available when needed on small farms, associated with increased diligence, entrepreneurship, and better labor management (Yotopoulos and Nugent 1976, p. 102). The general finding of an inverse relation between agricultural productivity and size of farm in low-income nations provides a strong economic rationale for land reform in some countries, a topic examined in chapter 10.

Uncertainty and Variability in Traditional Agriculture

HIGHLY UNCERTAIN YIELDS

With little control over soil moisture, pests, and other crop-growing varia-bles in many agricultural areas of less developed nations, there is great uncer-tainty in traditional agriculture. Uncertainty is defined in economics as an event having more than one possible outcome, whose probabilities may not be known or inferred from experience. For example, rainfall is uncertain, and where few pest control techniques are available, pest destruction cannot be estimated.

Traditional farmers have developed many strategies to cope with yield un-certainty, sometimes very intricate procedures discovered through many years of trial and error. Common techniques include mixed cropping and intercrop-ping on the same field. Farmers who have successfully coped with uncertainty, especially low-income farmers, are rightly skeptical about any proposed agri-cultural practices that have not been extensively tested locally over several years, especially if they involve staple food crops. The new practices might in-crease yields considerably in a good year, but what about food for the family in a poor crop year or an insect-infested year? The importance of reducing uncer-tainty in agricultural production for people living close to minimum subsistence levels can hardly be exaggerated.[3]

HIGHLY VARIABLE FARMER PERFORMANCE

The wide range in individual farmers' performance due to health and skill increases the uncertainty of production. Great variability in farmers' perform-ance is due to (1) physical and mental handicaps; (2) varied access to local agri-cultural resources; (3) different values held about agricultural work; and (4) competing demands on farmers' resources. The wide variability of yields and of labor productivity in traditional agriculture in contrast to more developed agri-culture is explained in part by the greater variety of work opportunities available in more developed societies. In these societies, poorly performing agricultural workers usually find other work. In traditional agricultural areas, these individ-uals have little choice but to continue to try to produce, by farming, food needed for themselves and their families.

The many empirical studies of traditional and low-income agriculture now available provide a great deal of knowledge about the economic realities of these agricultural systems—how they operate, and how they perform economically. But these empirical studies do not explain why land and labor productivity has

---

3. Examples of strategies used by traditional farmers to reduce uncertainty have been explored by Norman 1977; Dillon and Anderson 1971; and Roumasset 1976. Other research on farmer decisionmaking in the face of uncertainty includes Binswanger 1980; Pope 1981; and University of Illinois 1978.

continued to remain so low. To understand this, we need a set of concepts, or a theory.

The Economic Equilibrium Model of Traditional Agriculture

A model, or theory, in economics or any other field, is a simplification or abstraction from reality to aid understanding of how complex systems operate. For example, the theory or law of gravity is useful because it helps us understand why an object falls at a certain rate. But near the earth, because of air friction, the actual rate of fall is slower than the rate predicted, because the Newtonian model of the law of gravity did not include the factor for air friction. So the Newtonian law of gravity and most theories or models are not perfect predictors. Hence, economic theories such as T. W. Schultz's economic model of traditional agriculture presented here is often limited by not including all the explanatory variables from the complex world. However, if the most important factors are included, theories can be very helpful tools in understanding the operation of systems.

We now ask whether the theory of traditional agriculture developed by T. W. Schultz (1964a, b) can explain how these economic systems operate and why they have continued to produce so little throughout history. This theory employs standard neoclassical tools of economic analysis. If these tools are not useful in explaining the stagnation of traditional agriculture, alternative theories should be sought. These might include ideas drawn from Marxist theory or proposals for the development of nonwestern, or indigenous, economics.[4] We examine Schultz's theory by focusing on four central economic concepts about traditional agriculture.

Little Change in Technological, Institutional, Economic, and Cultural Variables

An underlying fundamental concept in this theory is that traditional agriculture exhibits little change in key technological, institutional, economic, and cultural variables over long periods of time.

In this study traditional agriculture will be treated as a particular type of economic equilibrium. . . . The critical conditions underlying this type of equilibrium, either historically or in the future, are as follows: (1) the state of the arts remains constant, (2) the state of preference and motives for holding or acquiring sources of income remains constant,

---

4. Barlett (1980, pp. 7–8) reviewed the theoretical debates in the economic anthropology literature "between formalists, who argued that formal economic concepts derived from Western market economies can be applied to all cultures, and substantists, who argued that such concepts as rationality and maximization are culture-bound and distort the reality of non-Western nonmarket economies." She concluded, "Distinctions between 'primitives,' 'peasants,' and 'farmers' are now seen as stemming from different cultural adaptations based on different values of the same variables." Other material with pleas for and attempts to develop alternative new economics for traditional societies includes Hill 1966; Halperin and Dow 1977; and Reynolds 1971 (chaps. 8 and 9).

and (3) both of these states remain constant long enough . . . to arrive at an equilibrium. (Schultz 1964b)

Let's be clear about Schultz's terminology. First, "the state of the arts" refers to all the knowledge and technological equipment, such as tools, plants, and animals, available in a society for the production of goods and services. Knowledge of traditional agricultural and rural arts is passed down through the generations from elders to children verbally and by demonstration. This knowledge is combined with labor to produce the reproducible capital available in a society, such as the traditional farm implements, irrigation structures, houses, food, and equipment for making clothing. In this way, the knowledge is embodied in agricultural technology, and when combined with labor and other resources, determines the positions of the supply curves for agricultural products available to the society. If no new inventions of any significance appear in a rural area, and if there are no introductions from outside the community of more productive agricultural and rural techniques, the state of the arts remains constant, often over many generations. One example of the extraordinarily unchanging technology of traditional agriculture is a 1000 B.C. sculptor's image of a wooden stick plow drawn by cattle, which was placed in an Egyptian tomb. This same animal-drawn stick-plow technology continues to be used today in remote areas of the Middle East, thirty centuries later.

A second part of this theory is that, in traditional agriculture, the state of preferences and motives remains constant for long periods of time for holding or acquiring economic goods and services. We speak here of the whole range of cultural factors, such as beliefs, tastes, traditions, and institutions, that are unique in each culture but that set a cultural pattern that influences what things will be valued and desired. If preferences for goods and services do not change, demand curves have stable locations both on a per capita basis and also in a community as a whole if there is no growth in population. Since important cultural inventions are infrequent in a traditional society, and significant outside cultural changes have been infrequently introduced from other peoples throughout history, social systems have tended over time to have stable sets of preferences and motives for demanding goods and services. As there seldom are new products that consumers need information about, any information would have little effect on the stability of the locations of the demand curves.

The general issue of the rate of social change in traditional societies, and how significant these changes are for the economic activities in a society, is debated by anthropologists and historians. These disciplines often emphasize continuous change in society. Over long periods of time, very great social and economic changes do occur in many traditional agricultural areas. Hence, the time span of analysis is critical. The economic theory presented here is concerned with the short and medium term of several decades or less, during which only occasional significant economic changes typically have taken place in most traditional agricultures in history.

When an economically significant change does occur, either in the state of the arts that would augment supply or in the state of preferences and motives for demanding goods and services, such a change would work itself out through the economic system over a series of years. Then a new, relatively stable equilibrium arises until another significant change appears.

Although a stable, essentially unchanging cultural environment over a number of decades may be hard for modern readers to comprehend, the value for a society of cultural patterns that reinforce cultural stability to aid group survival is emphasized by the following passage.

A traditional agriculture tends to be dominated by an attitude which emphasizes survival and maintenance of position rather than improvement and advancement of position. Two features of a traditional agriculture encourage this attitude. First, there is high risk associated with innovation because of lack of systematic research and testing. Thus most new ideas in traditional agriculture turn out to be poor ideas which result in a loss of position rather than improvement. Second, there is a high penalty for error in innovation because the farmers' low income will not absorb a sharp drop before reaching minimal requirements for subsistence.

Over a period of time the economic advantage of conservatism often becomes institutionalized in religious strictures and other cultural traits. Once that has occurred it becomes difficult to change behavior toward innovation even when research reduces the risk of failure. (Mellor 1966, p. 244)

Equilibrium in Supply and Demand

If little change has occurred in the positions of the demand and supply curves in traditional agriculture over considerable periods of time, farmers will have been able to adjust the allocation of their resources so as to achieve maximum income, given the demand curves facing them, the resources available to them, and their knowledge of production arts. This economic equilibrium can be illustrated with supply and demand curves. In a traditional society, the demand curves for each good and service would on average remain in the same position because of the stable preferences and motives and because average per capita income remains approximately the same over the years. Hence, the proportions of the budget allocated to each good and service would remain about the same. Similarly, the average positions of the supply curves facing the community would be in the same position, except for random changes caused by uncontrollable variables, such as weather and pests, that move the supply curves to the right or left, resulting in lower prices in good crop years and higher prices in poor years (see figure 4.4). With a fixed demand curve and a fluctuating supply curve, a range of quantities and prices would be generated over time that would establish means for prices (P_A) and for quantities (Q_A).

To clearly understand this equilibrium, consider the decision farmers face about producing more agricultural products when the usual downward sloping demand curve is present. Extra effort to produce more becomes increasingly costly, and the supply curve for the crop would move to the right. The price

Figure 4.4. Stable Demand and Fluctuating Supply for Staple Food Crops in Traditional Agriculture

Usual Range in Quantity of Food Produced

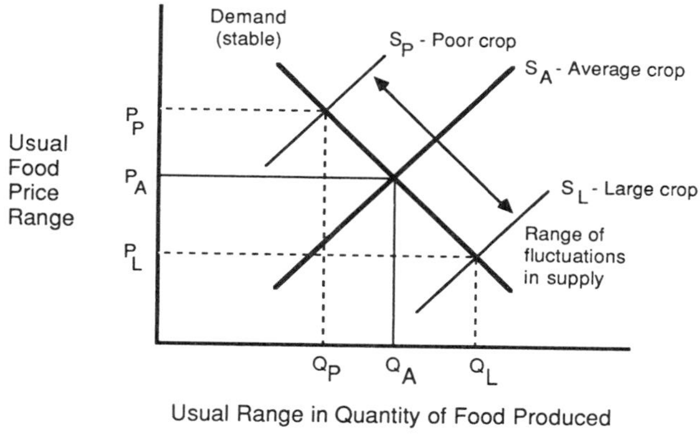

would decline, so that the returns received for the extra labor often decline. At some point, at least some farmers will conclude that the additional income is not worth the extra effort. Then the supply curve would move somewhat left, until it settled into a stable position. Hence farmers in traditional agriculture, once they have found at least their approximate equilibrium position, have no opportunity to significantly increase per capita income by increasing the supply of agricultural products with the resources available to them. Traditional farmers are thus accurately described as being in a low-level equilibrium trap, or a vicious circle of poverty.

Efficient Allocation of Resources by Traditional Farmers

The preceding discussion of equilibrium of supply and demand in traditional agriculture leads to the fundamental proposition that traditional farmers generally allocate their resources efficiently. In economic theory, efficient allocation of resources occurs when marginal (additional) costs are equated with marginal returns. The basic tools of production economics demonstrate this central economic proposition. For example, when one variable input, such as fertilizer, is combined with a fixed amount of other inputs, such as land and labor, to grow a crop, at Q_1 level of fertilizer, net income, or profit, is greatest (see figure 4.5, panel A). At this level of fertilizer use, the farmer is at an equilibrium point. The use of one more unit of fertilizer, at Q_2, would increase costs by three dollars but increase the value of the marginal product by only two dollars. If the farmer used one unit less of fertilizer at Q_3, he would obtain four dollars additional value of product at point b. Hence, it would make sense for him to use more fertilizer, Q_1, to increase his net income a little more. Thus it is irrational for the farmer to use more or less fertilizer than Q_1. At this level, he is allocating

Figure 4.5. Economic Equilibrium and Economic Efficiency: The Single-Variable Input Example

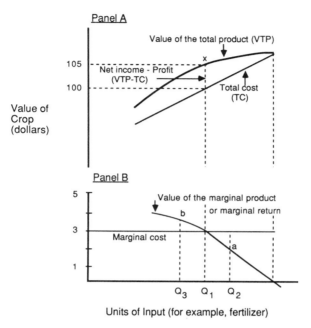

Note: The marginal cost is the cost of one additional unit of input. The value of the marginal product is the additional value of output obtained from using an additional unit of input.

fertilizer efficiently, because he can do nothing to increase his income by changing the amount of fertilizer used.

We can generalize this model. When farmers allocate all inputs at such levels that the additional gains, or marginal returns, are equal to the additional, or marginal, costs, they are allocating all their resources efficiently. They obtain the highest net return, or profit, possible. Only changes in other variables held constant in the analysis, such as the relative prices of the resources used, agricultural technology, or institutional arrangements, can upset this equilibrium. Readers who at this point do not understand the basic relations in economic production functions and the associated economic terminology are referred to the exercise in appendix table 4.2 and to beginning chapters in production economics textbooks.[5] We now illustrate the central proposition of allocative efficiency with two important additional examples.

5. See for example Langham 1979; Perrin et al. 1976; Osburn and Schneeberger 1983 (chap. 2); Harsh, Connor, and Schwab 1981 (chap. 3); and Nelson and Mach 1986.

Figure 4.6. Allocative Efficiency with One Variable Input and Two Crops

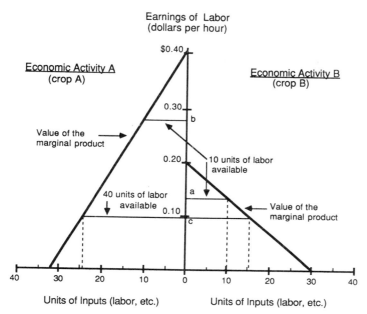

ALLOCATIVE EFFICIENCY WITH ONE VARIABLE INPUT AND TWO CROPS

Allocative efficiency and economic equilibrium in traditional agriculture can also be demonstrated where two alternative economic activities, such as crop A and crop B, are available to a farmer (see figure 4.6). Consider first how a farmer with ten units of labor would allocate them. If the farmer is limited to allocating them to crop B, a marginal return of $0.13 per hour (point a) for the tenth unit of labor would be obtained. Suppose instead, the farmer allocated all labor to crop A. He or she would then obtain a larger marginal return for the last unit of labor, $0.27 per hour (point b). Hence the farmer's net income would be greater if only crop A were grown.

Now suppose that the farmer had forty units of labor available to use. In this case, most income would be gained by splitting the use of the forty units of labor between the two crops, as indicated in figure 4.6. Then the marginal return to labor for crop A would be equal to the marginal return for labor from crop B, at about $0.09 per hour (point c). With this allocation of labor, the highest net income possible is obtained. Allocative efficiency is now present, because no increase in income is possible with alternative allocations of labor among these crops.

Figure 4.6 also illustrates how Malthus's law works. If population, and hence labor, were to increase in a farming area faced with a fixed set of two agricultural crop technologies such as these, the addition of, say, ten additional

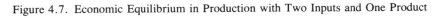

Figure 4.7. Economic Equilibrium in Production with Two Inputs and One Product

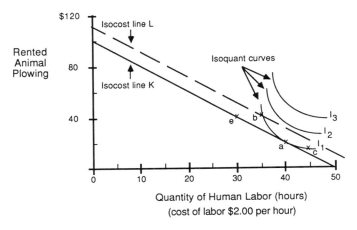

Quantity of Human Labor (hours)
(cost of labor $2.00 per hour)

units of labor, for a total of fifty units, would reduce the marginal earnings of labor below $0.09. This in turn would reduce the average earnings of each laborer. Thus, if population growth continues to press against fixed resources, a lower average income results. If this trend continues, some members of the society would obtain less than needed for survival. This Malthusian mechanism explains, when viewed over the centuries, the human experience of fairly stable population numbers with irregular fluctuations due largely to uncontrolled events, such as weather, crop pests, human disease, and wars.

ALLOCATIVE EFFICIENCY WITH TWO VARIABLE INPUTS

A different tool illustrates allocative efficiency by farmers when two variable inputs produce one product. This is an important economic tool that will be used to clarify many agricultural development issues later in the text. Suppose two variable resources, labor and rented animal plowing, are used for the production of a certain crop (see figure 4.7). In this example, a farmer has learned from experience that forty hours of labor and twenty dollars of animal use per hectare produce a certain yield, say one ton per hectare (point *a* in figure 4.7). He also has learned that he can produce the same yield using more animal services and a little less labor at point *b*, and that the same output is obtained with more labor and a little less animal services at point *c*. Thus any point on the curve I_1 produces the same yield per hectare, or quantity of product, with varying combinations of labor and animal services. This curve is termed an *isoquant*.

Before proceeding, note that this figure represents three dimensions. Two single-variable input production functions, one for labor and one for animal plowing, have been placed at right angles, as viewed from above. Output rises toward the reader. Thus, for example, on the labor axis, as more labor is used in moving to the right, crop output increases toward the reader. This viewpoint enables us to draw contour lines, or isoquants, such as curve I_1, which represents a constant level of output on a three-dimensional production surface. Isoquants I_2 and I_3 are higher crop output contour lines at increased constant levels of output.

Figure 4.7 also illustrates various combinations of labor and animal service inputs that would have the same cost. These combinations are represented by an isocost line such as K. At any point on this line, the farmer would incur the same costs of production. If a farmer could produce the same yield using the resource combination represented by point e (forty dollars of animal services and thirty hours of labor at a cost of two dollars per hour for labor) and point a, he would be indifferent as to whether he used one combination or the other, for his net income would be the same. To confirm your understanding of the isocost line, take any point on the line and see if the total cost of labor and animal services equals $100.

Now with these isoquant and isocost tools in mind, let's determine the most efficient allocation of the two variable resources and hence the point of highest net return, or economic equilibrium. Returning to isoquant curve I_1, at which point, a, b, or c, would a farmer gain more profit? To operate at points b and c, he would have to use more labor and animal services to obtain the same output as at a, and hence he would be on a higher isocost line. (Note: at b, \$41 of animal services and $35 \times \$2$ labor $= \$111$, the total cost of inputs.) Thus, point a is the equilibrium point that produces the most profit with these inputs. Given the technologies that determine isoquant curve I and the relative prices of animal services and labor indicated by the slope of the isocost lines, traditional farmers after reaching point a can do nothing to increase their income. Traditional farmers are economically efficient, doing the best they can, given their personal characteristics and their technological, cultural, resource, and institutional environment.

Schultz's economic model of traditional agriculture proposes that these states of economic equilibrium and allocative efficiency are generally accurate portrayals of the conditions that have prevailed in rural societies until recent times. Much empirical research in developing nations, reviewed earlier in the chapter, has shown that traditional farmers who have lived in an area for a long time become very skilled in allocating their resources to achieve these highest net return positions. Note that these conclusions include farmers' best judgments about any adjustments they should make for uncertainties in farming outcomes.

Low Return on Investment in Traditional Agriculture

The fourth important part of our economic model of traditional agriculture is that low rates of return on investment generally prevail. How is this consistent with our model of traditional agriculture?

First, let's be clear about economic terminology. Investing is the act of setting aside the use of resources, such as labor, land, machinery, or buildings, to aid in producing something at a later time, such as livestock, another building, fences, or an irrigation system. When a farmer's resources are invested, they are not available for use in other productive activities. Investments can also include allocating family labor to the production of different crops, buying labor for use in producing crops, buying fertilizer, using farm animals for tillage, buying tillage services from a neighbor, buying a farm, or renting machinery. Note especially that the term *investment* is often used in economic literature to refer to the purchase of durable items, such as farm machinery, buildings, and so forth, that provide services over a period of years before they are worn out. But the use of resources to produce a crop five months later is also an investment of resources in that production process, as the resources cannot be used for anything else. Resources that are invested in this way, such as seeds and fertilizer, that are used up during a crop production process are often labeled *current inputs,* or *farm expenses,* in agricultural economics literature.

A complex, multiyear analysis of farm investments may be required to determine the rates of return from the use of both current inputs and more fixed investments, for some investments are in land or farm equipment, which provide services over a period of years. The tool most generally used for evaluating the returns to investments that provide services over more than a year is benefit-cost analysis, which is presented in chapter 7.

A less complex illustration of the calculation of rates of return on investment is used here. The time frame is the usual crop period of less than twelve months. The rate of return on investment, in percent, is obtained by comparing the difference between gross output (benefits) and total costs (investment). This net return, or profit, is divided by the total costs (investment), multiplied by 100 or $[(VTP - TC)/TC]$ (100). The calculation is multiplied by 100 to provide the rate of return in the usual percentage form. In figure 4.5 the quantity of inputs used is at equilibrium where the value of the marginal product is equal to the marginal cost (price) of the input, so that maximum net return, or profit, is obtained. In this illustration, the value of the total product is 105 and the total cost is 100, so the rate of return on the investment is 5 percent. To conclude and generalize, farmers seek to gain the highest rate of return from all their investments. When the rates of return to all their investments are equal at the highest rate possible, they have obtained the highest income possible and are in equilibrium. They cannot do any better by reallocating resources.

This economic equilibrium theory proposes that traditional peoples have continued to invest more and more resources—largely labor in combination with other traditional inputs. This has led to lower rates of return from additional investment, after which it is not worth allocating additional resources to agricultural activities. The lowering rates of return are due to limited land and other resources, the unchanging levels of technology and institutional arrangements, and generally stable relative prices. Many empirical studies of the rates of return obtained in traditional agriculture, carried out during the last two decades, have provided a large body of evidence that supports the conclusion of this theory that returns to investment in traditional agriculture are low.[6]

Growth in Traditional Agriculture

The previous section focused on a theory of economic equilibrium in traditional agriculture in which we assumed a zero or very slow population growth, the experience of traditional societies much of the time. From time to time, and particularly in more recent decades, many low-income traditional agricultural areas have experienced rapid population growth. They also have succeeded in increasing agricultural production, often as fast as 2 or 3 percent per year, as shown by the data presented in chapter 2. As the long-term average level of real food prices has often not changed very much in these countries, the supply curves for food must have moved to the right about as fast the demand curves (see figure 2.3, panel *A*). Such rates of agricultural growth have been a real achievement of many less developed nations. How can we explain these increases in total agricultural production in traditional agriculture?

The Neoclassical Model of Economic Growth

Since the time of the first great economists, Adam Smith, David Ricardo, and others, economic growth has been explained primarily through the use of more of the same inputs already available: land and other physical resources (*R*), labor (*L*), and traditional tools and equipment, collectively labeled capital (*K*). In production function notation, output (*Y*) is some function of the amount of these inputs [$Y = f(R, L, K)$]. This model proposes that increases in agricultural production are obtained through the use of more of the inputs available in traditional farming communities, requiring movement further out on the agricultural production function already known to the community. Let's examine the nature of these traditional inputs in more detail and how they may be increased.

Greater Use of Traditional Agricultural Inputs

USE OF MORE LABOR

How is more labor obtained for use in agriculture? The population growth, which increases demand for agricultural products, at the same time provides more labor. And since labor represents such a large share, some 80 to 95 percent, of the value of the resources used in traditional agricultural production, growth in output depends largely upon the productivity of the additional labor.

It is often assumed that tradiational agriculture has reached situations in which decreasing marginal, and hence decreasing average, returns to labor are present. But many empirical studies of traditional agriculture, even in areas

6. Important references on the economics of smallholder decisionmaking include Helleiner 1975; Lipton 1968; Becker 1976; Barnum and Squire 1979; Fisk 1975; Bartlett 1980; and Dillon and Anderson 1971.

where little additional land is available, have shown that, as more labor becomes available, known technology has been able to increase production. The measures that have been used include better land preparation, terracing, and more weeding; and in some areas farmers have improved irrigation systems and practices or have increased multiple cropping. Increases in total agricultural output obtained in these and similar ways have often been sufficient to maintain average per capita agricultural production as population and total output increased. This implies that the marginal and average production of labor may not decline much in the currently relevant part of the labor production function. Of course, sooner or later, as more and more labor is combined with other fixed resources like land, the marginal and average per capita income will eventually decline.

Hence, at a particular time, for any community, the shape of the relevant section of the labor production function is an empirical question (see figure 4.8). If a farming community were at point x on its agricultural labor input production function, then which of the possible production functions, a through e, does the community currently face as its population grows? If it faces function a, the marginal return to the use of additional labor would be very low, and average incomes would decline quite rapidly until a minimum level of subsistence would increase the death rates and reduce the population—or migration occurred. But if any function b through d represented local conditions, average incomes would decline more slowly. Function e would enable maintenance of per capita income for considerable increases in population and labor use.

Empirical evidence about the shape of labor production functions in less developed nations has been gathered in many studies by historians, economists, and other social scientists. Boserup (1965) has even found that sometimes "population increase leads to the adoption of more intensive systems of agriculture in primitive communities and an increase in total output [which]—at least in some cases—can set off a genuine process of economic growth with rising output per man-hour" (p. 118).[7] Many other studies have found that, in agriculture with traditional technologies, population numbers have been constrained by available resources, especially land.

USE OF MORE LAND

In traditional agriculture, the cultivation of more land depends almost entirely upon the use of more labor. Our theory indicates that previously available labor has been fully allocated if known technology is used in its highest return activities. In world agricultural history, as more labor became available through population increase, expansion onto new lands has been a continuing phenomenon. In the last few decades, much additional agricultural land has been brought under cultivation in parts of Asia, Africa, and Latin America. Today, in Africa and Latin America particularly, large amounts of additional land may yet be brought into production. In more populated areas, however, increased crop

7. Other literature on population pressure in traditional agriculture includes Boserup 1981; Robinson and Schutjer 1984; Cleave and White 1969; and Grigg 1979.

Figure 4.8. Increased Labor Use in Traditional Agriculture and per Capita Farm Income

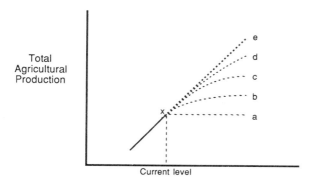

Labor Use in Agriculture by a Community

acreage has been obtained instead by increasing the intensity of multiple cropping. Analyses of the sources of expanded agricultural output in less developed nations over the last few decades, where relatively little change in agricultural technology has taken place, have shown both increases in the amount of land cropped and increases in the cropped area through higher multiple cropping rates.

USE OF MORE TRADITIONAL CAPITAL

The use of additional traditional agricultural capital, such as tools, animal equipment, and animal shelter, has contributed a small amount to increased agricultural production in traditional areas of developing nations.

Capital refers to physical and other things of value, such as hand tools, machinery and equipment, draft animals, farm buildings, and land, that are used in the production of other goods and services. These things of value are produced through investment of resources. Agricultural land (often identified separately from other capital) is also produced through investments of clearing and other activities that make it ready for cultivation. Capital can also refer to human capital—the accumulated stock of health, physical strength, and knowledge used in production. Human capital may be increased through formal or informal education and improved health services (see also p. 308). Capital used by farmers and other producers often provides services over a period of years, such as the farm power produced by draft animals and the shelter provided by buildings. The knowledge about crop production and about the allocation of farm resources learned by younger farmers from their elders, or in school, is human capital.

Capital is measured in two ways. One is as a stock of capital, which is the total quantity or value, of the capital—tools, equipment, buildings—used in production. The other measure of capital is a flow of capital services. Since many capital items are durable, lasting for more than a year or one production period (such as a crop season), many units of capital provide a flow of services over many production periods. The value of the flows of services provided by capital units is often measured by the rental or other payments required to obtain the use of the capital item. Thus payment for land preparation by animals, for custom machinery services, or for the rental of a structure provides an estimate of the value of the flow of these capital services. As measures of capital stock and the flow of capital services are usually of such different magnitudes, attention to which measure is used avoids confusion. The term current inputs (expenses) aids in distinguishing longer-lasting capital from other inputs used in production. Current inputs are resources used in a production process that disappear during that production cycle.

Many estimates are now available of the relatively small proportion of nonland capital in the total stock of capital used in traditional agriculture. For example, in the mid-1950s in a wheat area of Lebanon, nonland capital represented less than 10 percent of the stock of capital used in farming (Stevens 1959, p. 285). However, when the flow of the services from capital is examined, nonland capital is seen to be a much higher proportion of the capital used. An estimate for the United States in 1870, where relatively high use of nonland capital had already occurred, shows that the flow of inputs, other than land and buildings, was about half of the total capital flow (see table 8.1).

To conclude, in traditional agriculture increases in production are achieved by moving further out on the agricultural production function using traditional technological knowledge. As population has increased, average per capita incomes have often been maintained through the use of more labor and traditional capital combined with land. Occasional new inventions or introductions have also increased agricultural productivity. An example of an agricultural invention in Asian history that greatly increased land productivity is the technique for flooded (paddy) rice production. However, many traditional agricultural areas in much of history have faced declining marginal returns from the use of additional agricultural inputs. The resource constraints facing agriculture have often led, until recent times, to reduced real incomes, and from time to time to Malthusian mechanisms which increased death rates or caused migration.

Program Failures, Economic Theory, and Agricultural Development Strategies

Development Program Failure Due to Wrong Theory

Two illustrations of program failures that keep reappearing in less developed nations highlight the importance of (1) the use of a valid economic model; (2) a knowledge of the empirical realities of traditional agriculture; and (3) avoiding incorrect assumptions. False ideas about the economics of agricultural areas in less developed nations continue to be held in both national and international aid and development circles. These wrong mental images lead to the elaboration of many ineffective programs and much waste of development resources.

EXTENSION PROGRAMS FOR TRADITIONAL FARMERS

Often the objective of new programs is to aid all farmers to follow the practices of the best farmers. This development strategy has been used successfully in more developed nations by agricultural professionals for many decades, and it continues to provide valuable assistance to these farmers. To carry out this program, scientists study the more successful farmers and then advise other farmers on how to increase their incomes. In traditional agricultural areas, however, the model of economic equilibrium indicates that farm management research of this type will not provide much new information of use to other farmers, for all the villagers already know well the traditional technology and the local agricultural resources. Hence, there is very little new knowledge to be transferred from one farm to another. Such extension programs are costly and have usually led to little increase in agricultural production. Program decisions were made without an understanding of the economic function of extension in agricultural development. This function will be clarified in later chapters, especially chapter 11.

PROVISION OF LOW-COST CREDIT TO TRADITIONAL FARMERS

Many credit programs have been based on the empirical observation that moneylenders in traditional agricultural areas of less developed nations often charge real interest rates of 30 to 60 percent or more to small farmers. These high rates appear to indicate a shortage of credit. To provide credit, new institutions, such as cooperatives or government agricultural credit programs, are then often set up. But when low-cost credit is provided in these areas, the almost universal experience has been only small increases in agricultural production, with much of the program's loan funds lost. A lack of understanding of the low economic returns possible from investment in traditional agriculture has led to many of these failures. Chapter 10 explains why moneylenders' interest rates are so high and the circumstances in which agricultural credit programs can be successful.

The Implications for Development Strategy

What conclusions can we draw about development strategy from the findings of empirical research on traditional agriculture and the Schultzian economic equilibrium model? Four general implications follow.

1. The most general implication for agricultural development that follows from the equilibrium model of traditional agriculture is that little unused or new agricultural technology is available in these traditional, rural areas. Hence new and much more productive technology needs to be made available for agricultural areas of developing nations to accelerate growth.

2. The economic equilibrium usually found in traditional agricultural areas has two implications for development. First, if farmers are trapped in a low-level income economic equilibrium, the task of development is to discover how to break out of, or upset, the equilibrium so that farmers may have more opportunities to increase their productivity and incomes. Second, as traditional agricultures tend to achieve a dynamic equilibrium by moving the supply curve to the right to maintain the same real price for food and hence to secure the same real per capita income, the task of agricultural development is to reduce the real cost of producing food so that the supply curve can be moved to the right more rapidly than the demand curve. Real income would then be increased through food price decreases.

3. If farmers in low-income traditional communities are price-responsive and efficient in the allocation of their resources, then farmers are using their resources at the right levels to gain the highest income. Hence, an important implication is that there are usually good economic or other reasons why some resources, such as apparently idle land or idle farm workers, are not used. Additionally, we should have great respect for these farmers, who have achieved economic efficiency and the highest income possible given their limited resources and constrained economic, technological, and cultural environments.

4. The central conclusion for development strategy about the finding of low rates of returns to investment in traditional agricultural areas is that higher return investments need to be developed and made available to farmers in less developed areas of the world. How this can be achieved is the subject of part III.

Conclusions

An analysis of traditional agriculture leads to the following three conclusions. First, the Schultzian model of economic equilibrium in traditional agriculture is consistent with empirical research. Second, this neoclassical model is economically rigorous and a powerful tool in examining how traditional economies operate. It provides an explanation of both (1) the little change in per capita income experienced in most agriculture throughout history; and (2) how total agricultural output can be increased in traditional agriculture when population growth does occur. Third, we find that these neoclassical economic tools, if used in the right way, enable an understanding of how traditional agricultural systems work. And thus no special, or different, economic theory is required to explain the economics of agricultural systems in developing nations.

Empirical research and economic analysis have shown that traditional agriculture is a finely tuned economic system. In the next chapter we focus on the interrelations between agriculture and the socioeconomic system in which it is embedded.

Important Concepts

Traditional agriculture

Price responsiveness of farmers

Elasticity of supply of agricultural
products

Economic equilibrium

State of the arts

State of preferences

Efficient resource allocation

Isoquant

Isocost curve

Rate of return on investment

Neoclassical production function

Human capital

Flow of capital services

Sample Questions

1. How can traditional agriculture be defined?

2. Many false assumptions are made about agriculture in traditional areas of less developed nations. Give two examples.

3. Set out two important empirical findings about low-income, traditional agriculture.

4. What are three of the four central economic concepts about traditional agriculture?

5. Is there a relation between the concept of allocative efficiency and the concept of economic equilibrium? Explain.

6. Explain why a low rate of return on an investment also means that it is costly to expand output.

7. How can agricultural production be increased in traditional agriculture?

8. Set out two basic implications for a development strategy of the equilibrium model of traditional agriculture.

Appendix Table 4.1. Topics for Study of an Agricultural System

The Rural Community System	The Farm Production System[a]
1. Background conditions (physical features, climate, etc.)	1. Objectives of the members of the farming unit and relations with other producing units

2. Community's relation to rest of nation
  a. Communication, transport, and distances
  b. Central government influence
  c. Community imports
  d. Community exports (external demand for agricultural products)
	a. Problems as seen by the farming unit
	  b. Cooperation in agriculture in the community
	2. Agricultural resources available to the farming unit
	  a. Land
	  b. Labor

3. Social, political, and economic conditions
  a. Social and cultural matters
  b. Community world view
    • Religions
    • Purpose of economic activities
    • Attitudes toward work and labor
    • Problems as seen by community
  c. Political system
  d. Demographic situation
	c. Capital situation, loan availability, and terms
	  d. Technology used
	  e. Entrepreneurship, education (knowledge and skills)
	3. Institutional environment of the farming unit
	  a. Tenure
	  b. Marketing arrangements for inputs and products
	  c. Sources of new technology
	  d. Incentive environment for increased production

4. Agricultural support
  a. Supplies of conventional agricultural resources (land, labor, and capital)
  b. Education
  c. Agricultural research and technology sources
  d. Government and nongovernment institutions for marketing (products and inputs)
  e. Influence of government on price and other activities
	4. Production activities and farming results (input-output data)
	  a. Crops
	  b. Livestock
	  c. Income from agriculture
	  d. Income from other sources

5. Changes in agriculture (amounts and causes)	5. Changes in the farming unit (causes, particularly economic factors)

[a] Focus on the agricultural decisionmaking unit—usually a farm (microeconomic analysis).

Appendix Table 4.2. An Exercise to Determine How Much of a Resource (Input) to Use to Obtain the Greatest Return (Profit) in a Production Process

Instructions: 1. Carry out the calculations. 2. Prove that when highest net revenue is obtained, then VMP = MC.

Source of Variable	Empirical Data from an Experiment		Calculated Average and Marginal Physical Products		Calculated Production Values (assume price of a unit of product is $2)			Calculated Input Costs (assume cost of a unit of input is $10)		Calculated Net Return
Name of Variable	I (units of input)	TPP (total physical product)	APP (average physical product)	MPP (marginal physical product)	VTP (value of total product)	VAP (value of average product)	VMP (value of marginal product)	MC (marginal input cost)	TC (total input cost)	Profit
How Data is Obtained	Experiment	Experiment	TPP/I	ΔTPP	TPP × product price	VTP/I	ΔVTP (ΔMPP × price)	Δ Input cost	Inputs × cost of a unit of input	VTP − TC
Calculations	Units	Units	Units	Units	Dollars	Dollars	Dollars	Dollars	Dollars	Dollars
	0	0	___	___	___	___	___	___	___	___
	1	4	___	___	___	___	___	___	___	___
	2	20	___	___	___	___	___	___	___	___
	3	38	___	___	___	___	___	___	___	___
	4	50	___	___	___	___	___	___	___	___
	5	60	___	___	___	___	___	___	___	___
	6	66	___	___	___	___	___	___	___	___
	7	70	___	___	___	___	___	___	___	___
	8	72	___	___	___	___	___	___	___	___
	9	70	___	___	___	___	___	___	___	___

Note. This is the case of one-variable input, $y = f(x_1 \mid x_2 \ldots x_n)$.
Δ = change in.

5

Theories of Socioeconomic Change, Cultural Variables, and Agricultural Growth

> *Economics is readily adaptable to the recognition of the interdependence of "material" and "social" dimensions of behavior.*
> *—Joy 1967, p. 35*

> *All social sciences are studying essentially the same system, . . . this is the total sphere of all human beings, their inputs and outputs, their organizations, their images, behaviors and so on. The "econosphere" is an abstract segment of the sociosphere. . . .*
>
> *When one is giving advice, therefore, about a system that involves the total society, it is extremely dangerous to be overtrained in a certain abstract element of the total process. . . . It is my own view . . . that we must move towards a more integrated and perhaps even rearranged social science.*
> *—Boulding 1967, p. 307*

Social System Change and Agricultural Development

Introduction and Objectives

In this chapter, we seek to identify social and cultural, or "noneconomic," variables that have important influences on the rate of agricultural development. They usually originate in the nonagricultural sectors of social systems. How much agreement is there among different socioeconomic theories of modernization about the variables that have important influence on economic and agricultural growth? In what ways do cultural and social variables affect agricultural development? Those engaged in agricultural development would like to know which variables in other sectors of a social system require special attention to facilitate growth. Such knowledge would enable the incorporation of these variables in analysis and in the design of development programs. Then these variables could contribute to, rather than block, desired development.

More specifically, in this chapter we focus on (1) the role of agricultural development in the broader framework of socioeconomic change, by examining

Figure 5.1. Interrelations Between the Four Elements of the Hayami-Ruttan Induced Innovation Model of Development

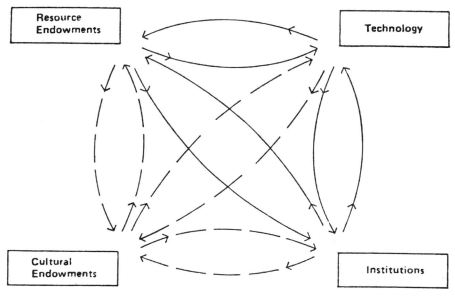

Source: Hayami and Ruttan 1985 (p. 111). Reprinted with permission.

prominent theories and hypotheses about social change; (2) those social science tools that can aid in understanding and implementing agricultural development; and (3) illustrations of how these social variables can affect agricultural development. We explore here the theory and empirical work of sociologists, anthropologists, the institutional and public choice schools of economics, and Marxists. Many topics in this chapter remain unsettled or are controversial areas in agricultural development. The examination of general socioeconomic growth and change in this chapter sets the stage for a sharp focus on economic theories of agricultural development in the following chapter.

The interrelations between cultural and social factors and other important sets of variables in the agricultural development process are illustrated by the four elements in the Hayami-Ruttan model of induced innovation (see figure 5.1). Cultural endowments (social and cultural variables) are seen in this model as influencing, and being influenced by, the other three elements, resource endowments, technology, and institutions. Hence, cultural endowments or variables are viewed as possible aids to, or brakes on, agricultural development. In much of the agricultural development literature, this set of variables is not recognized. In many instances, they may therefore place hidden constraints on programs and projects. Thus, knowledge of how these variables affect agricultural development can often be crucial in increasing agricultural production.

Numerous examples of the effect of cultural endowments on agricultural development could be provided; three follow. First, the effect of these variables on agricultural production systems is shown graphically by the large difference in the size of farm fields on the two sides of the United States–Mexican border in California. The Mexican side has many small fields and farms. The soil resources are the same, but the different social environments, as well as economic conditions, have led to quite different agricultural systems. Can we identify the cultural variables that led to the different paths of agricultural development? How much of the difference in these agricultures, including their yields and rate of increase in productivity, can be explained using economic analysis tools alone?

A second example is provided by the rapid increases in rice yields in Japan over the last century. When contrasted with the very slow growth of rice yields in India and Indonesia, this economic success appears to be due to a considerable extent to Japanese social and cultural variables, for the more usual economic variables, including the availability of land and other resources, appear to help little in explaining the much greater gains in Japan.

The third example is drawn from the work of a well-known Philippine sociologist Gelia Castillo, who found that women control the money in 93 percent of the rural households in the Philippines (Castillo et al. 1973, p. 223). How does this cultural practice affect the way decisions about farming and other activities are made in these families? She also reported that the families believe they should not incur debt. How much does this belief slow the use of credit to enable a more rapid adoption of high-yielding rice varieties, which require high-cost chemical fertilizer? Castillo also estimated that village fiestas often consume 10 percent of the annual village income. Do such cultural practices present a significant barrier to agricultural growth? How easily could some of this income be channeled into development activities?

Pecuniary Variables Insufficient to Explain Economic Actions

The importance of cultural variables in economic behavior is recognized and has been demonstrated in the economic theory of the personal utility function, a fundamental underlying postulate of economics. In this theory, people act so as to maximize their net benefits compared to costs. The utility function contains both pecuniary and nonpecuniary elements. Pecuniary elements are goods and services purchased or traded and that can be given a monetary value. Nonpecuniary elements are benefit- or cost-producing, elements that cannot generally be bought or sold, such as security, leisure, prestige, glory, and love. The maximization of utility involves equating marginal returns per unit cost for all elements in the utility function, both pecuniary and nonpecuniary. To quote from a concise exposition by Yotopoulos and Nugent (1976) from which this discussion is drawn:

The pecuniary elements can be readily homogenized and aggregated through the use of prices to give income. In this form, they are relatively easy to handle: if the cost of champagne increases, there is a readjustment that involves less champagne. . . . If there is an increase in the return of labor, the readjustment involves more labor, so that the equality of return per unit of cost at the margin is restored.

The convenience of handling the pecuniary elements in the utility function often leads to neglecting the nonpecuniary elements—to assuming that the nonpecuniary elements have zero weight. This at times can be done with impunity. But the more this assumption departs from reality, that is the greater the weight of nonpecuniary elements relative to pecuniary elements, the more likely we are to observe "strange" economic behavior, and the less satisfactory the concept of income becomes as a . . . proxy for the utility function. (p. 130)

Thus if pecuniary variables change and there is no response, this does not imply that the utility function does not exist or that the person is not maximizing his or her utility, but that adjustments were made in nonpecuniary elements of the utility function. In this case, the pecuniary part of the utility function was not a good proxy for the whole utility function. In order to understand this person's response, nonpecuniary elements would have to be examined. Conversely, a change in nonpecuniary elements could lead to changes in pecuniary behavior.

Instead of being useless in economic analysis, a knowledge of the nonpecuniary or cultural variables that affect behavior promises a more comprehensive analysis and a greater accuracy in predictions. Many believe that nonpecuniary elements are, in fact, dominant and assert that economic activities are derivative—used to maximize the utility obtained from nonpecuniary elements. Observe that chapter 4 focused on pecuniary elements, although the hypothesis of little cultural change implied equilibrium among nonpecuniary variables. In this chapter, the primary focus is upon identifying variables, often not considered explicitly in economic analysis, that can have significant effect on agricultural development.

Theories of Socioeconomic Development

In a recent sociology text Babbie (1980, p. 31) expressed the view held by most social scientists that no generally agreed upon comprehensive theory of social and economic development has as yet been constructed. Such a theory would explain the great stability of traditional societies through long periods of time and the rapid social and economic differentiation of dynamic societies. Dunn (1971, chap. 8) sees all social scientists—including historians, philosophers, psychologists, cyberneticists, general systems theorists, decision and organization specialists, economists, sociologists, political scientists, and Marxists—as entering the same socioeconomic theory domain through different doors. In spite of the nascent state of a general theory of social development, the approaches have identified a number of useful variables.

In examining the varied approaches to a general theory of social and economic development, space limits require selection of only the prominent groups of theories. Long (1977, p. 6) classified socioeconomic development theories into two groups: (1) those in the mainstream of modernization approaches, based generally on an evolutionary theme; and (2) those that emphasize social conflict, including Marxist-oriented theories.

Evolutionary Modernization Theories

Following the biological analogy, the theme of evolutionary theories of socioeconomic development is that of social differentiation balanced by necessary social integration. This is a "structural functionalist" approach, illustrated by the important work of Parsons (1951; Parsons and Shils 1966). We summarize Hoogvelt's (1976, p. 51ff) four basic methodological premises underlying these theories.

1. Society is a system that consists of interdependent parts.
2. The whole comes before the parts, so any part (that is, cultural beliefs, legal institutions, social patterns of family organization, political institutions, or economic-technological organizations) cannot be fully understood without reference to the whole society.
3. A part of the system, therefore, is seen as performing a function for the maintenance and equilibrium of the whole.
4. The interdependence of the parts is functional, since the parts are mutually supportive and serve to maintain the whole.

Although each culture defines progress and desired change for itself, Hoogvelt (1976, pp. 13–30) concluded that there is general consensus in these modernizing theories about criteria for judging social progress. These include "the proliferation of material elements, increase in the division of labor, the multiplication of social groups and subgroups, and the emergence of special means of integration" (p. 13).

Social differentiation is further described as consisting of an evolution from a primitive stage, exhibiting little functional differentiation among members of the society, to a modern stage where, according to Parsons,

the completed social differentiation of all functional spheres, including the economic/ occupational sphere, has created such a multi-stratified, plural system of society, that the effective exercise of political responsibilities can no longer be accomplished without the mediation of consensus, both in policy formation and in the exercise of power, on the part of all the differentiated subunits of society. Democratic association with its features of fully enfranchised membership and elected leadership is therefore a final evolutionary universal and belongs to the modern stage. It differentiates . . . power from leadership, giving the power to those who are led. (Hoogvelt 1976, p. 30)

Evolutionary modernizing theories can be usefully grouped on the basis of whether they focus on (1) the dominance of beliefs and values; (2) psychological and motivational variables; (3) political variables; (4) social structure variables;

or (5) social learning. To aid in the identification of important cultural variables, we examine these approaches briefly.

THEORIES EMPHASIZING BELIEFS AND VALUES

A number of important anthropologists have placed special emphasis on the role of beliefs and values in influencing the response of persons to economic opportunities. The theory of the limited good is one of the best-known hypotheses about the effect of beliefs on economic activities.

Foster (1967) proposed that much economic behavior in traditional societies can be explained by the concept of the limited good. His conclusions were based on field research, particularly in the Spanish-speaking village of Tzintzuntzan, 230 miles west of Mexico City, where per capita agricultural production had remained static through 1939. In describing the effect of beliefs and values on the economic activities of the villagers, Foster concluded that "in . . . peasant communities a great deal of behavior can best be explained if it is viewed as a function of the assumption that almost all good things in life, material and otherwise, exist in limited and unexpandable quantities" (p. 12). These things include wealth, friendship, love, masculinity, and power. When this view is held, one person's gain implies another's loss. Thus, "everyone sees himself, almost from birth to death, facing a hostile world in which access to a few good things in life to which one has a right is constantly threatened by hunger, illness, death, abuse by neighbors, and spoilation by powerful people outside the community" (p. 134).

In these circumstances, if cooperative endeavors are undertaken, a person who "takes nothing from his neighbors can gain nothing (limited good), but he risks, through participation, exploitation on the part of associates. Reluctance to cooperate is a highly rational behavior. . . . The good society . . . conforms to the equilibrium model: security and safety are achieved within the village by maintaining the status quo" (p. 136). Note that this is a cultural equilibrium model of a traditional society and is consistent with the economic equilibrium model presented in chapter 4.

In reviewing the analytical difficulties of the image of the limited good, Long (1977) pointed out that Foster's formulation tends to give causal priority to internal cultural (i.e., value and belief) phenomena. Long concluded that "in attempting to explain why in one situation peasants respond positively to new economic opportunities and in another respond negatively, one needs to consider the total complex of both internal and external factors—technical, economic, structural, and cultural. . . . Furthermore . . . individuals behave in such a way as to maximize satisfaction within a framework defined by change and opportunities as well as by social norms and cultural values" (pp. 46–52).[1]

---

1. Other references to social change theories emphasizing beliefs and values include Goldthorpe 1975 (pp. 228–50), in which he examines religion and economic development; and Wilber and Jameson 1983.

THEORIES EMPHASIZING PSYCHOLOGICAL VARIABLES, MOTIVATION, AND ENTREPRENEURSHIP

Theories of socioeconomic development that emphasize psychological variables include those of the economist Hagen (1962, pp. i–55). After work in Burma and research on theories of economic growth, he concluded that "economic theory has rather little to offer toward an explanation of economic growth, and that broader social and psychological considerations are pertinent." He asked, for example, why the accumulation of needed scientific and technical knowledge has been so slow in some societies. Is it due to values and beliefs, social organization, and the associated personality makeup of these largely traditional societies? Why has technological advance since the early nineteenth century been so spotty in different parts of the world? It occurred fairly rapidly in Japan, but in many other Asian, African, and Latin American countries it did not. Hagen (1962) proposed that the differences were due only to a small extent to economic obstacles, such as lack of information or lack of training. This led him to more general theories of social change. After extensive research in the social sciences, he concluded that "to understand why some traditional societies enter upon economic growth sooner than others, we must understand the internal structure and functioning of these societies. For both the barriers to growth and the causes of growth seem to be largely internal rather than external" (p. 55).

In searching for a useful theory, he dismissed as proven false earlier explanations based on race, climate, and geography. He also turned to the famous thesis of Max Weber (1956) that the personal values associated with Protestant Christians in Europe were fundamental contributors to Western economic development, and to McClelland's (1961) thesis that increased levels of achievement motivation are critical to increased economic productivity. These explanations led to a model of socioeconomic development that focused on personality development and the contrast between behavior in traditional and modern societies. "A society is traditional if ways of behavior in it continue with little change from generation to generation. . . . A traditional society, in short, tends to be custom-bound, hierarchical, ascriptive, and unproductive" (Hagen 1962, p. 56).

Hagen (p. 71) also proposed that authoritarian personalities tend to predominate in traditional societies and that they tend to discourage economic growth and change. He concluded, therefore, that more rapid development depends upon innovation, not emulation; hence, greater economic growth would require both increased numbers of innovative personalities and increased opportunities for individuals to earn status, instead of having status ascribed to them, as often occurs in traditional societies. Additionally, he concluded that

solving the technical problems is the easy aspect of technological progress for present-day low income countries. Technological advance requires doing new things; it requires also the creation of new economic, political, and social organizations and relationships, or the adaptation to new functions of old organizations and relationships. But the things one does in a traditional society are not merely means to the end of living, means which one can readily discard in favor of others. They are symbols of one's identity and place in the world. . . . It is demeaning for a professional man or a member of the landed gentry in a traditional society to turn his attention to tools or machinery or become the manager of a business enterprise. (p. 33)

Theories that emphasize psychological variables have also led to a focus on entrepreneurial activity in developing nations. In a review of studies of entrepreneurship Long (1977, pp. 105–43) concluded that, although a large literature has been produced, it has not led to the formulation of valid propositions of a general nature. Instead, he sees knowledge of anthropology leading to better understanding of the differential responses to change shown by different social categories in a population. Such analysis would focus on the transactions, networks, and decisionmaking processes associated with entrepreneurship. Long also proposed that researchers would make progress by shifting emphasis from identifying one or two so-called key factors, such as a particular value orientation or social background, to analyzing the processes entrepreneurs use in attempting to deal with problems. [2]

THEORIES EMPHASIZING POLITICAL VARIABLES

Social scientists trained in political science have also focused on development problems and the needed integration of the social sciences. Important representatives of this group include Uphoff and Ilchman (1972), who propose a "new political economy":

The political economy of which we speak is an integrated social science of public choice. It is political in that its subject matter is the exercise of authority and the competition for authority within a community. . . . It is economic in that it treats with the allocation and exchange of scarce resources, including political and social resources, as well as those generally dubbed economic. . . . As a supradisciplinary approach to social science, political economy is pertinent for the analysis of any issue or policy of public relevance. . . . For us, the continuous exchanges required for achieving public purposes, together with their consequences, whether called economic, social, or political, constitute the subject matter of political economy. (p. 17)

Note that this political economy approach to integrating the social sciences is limited to the public part of the social system. "Purely private aims and activities that do not impinge upon the use or possession of authority remain outside the purview of political economy" (Uphoff and Ilchman, p. 1). This limitation leads to confusion for economists, as the term *political economy* has historically been used by them to refer to all aspects of an economic system, whether public or private.

---

2. Other references to theories emphasizing psychological variables include a review article by Kunkel 1976; Kunkel 1970 (pp. 94–101); Lauterbach 1974; Chodak 1973 (pp. 147–87); McClelland 1961; and McClelland et al. 1969. For a critique of McClelland's achievement motivation thesis, see Eisenstadt 1963.

Uphoff and Ilchman (p. 101) also propose that, just as economic development can be measured by changes in such variables as gross national product, social development could be measured in terms that would express the aggregate productivity of social relations, and that political development could be measured by the productivity of political activity. More productive political activities would achieve identified objectives with less cost in time and other resources.[3]

THEORIES EMPHASIZING SOCIAL STRUCTURE AND BEHAVIOR

These theories emphasize the interrelations between social structure and the associated behavior, or social relations. In his review of mainstream structural theories of socioeconomic development, Kunkel (1970, p. 108) found that there are varied definitions of "social structure" but concluded that "the different conceptions of 'social structure' mentioned . . . appear to have enough common elements to indicate the direction of convergence of meanings and probable area of eventual agreement: 'social structure' consists of behavior and social relationships." There remains some confusion, however, as to whether social structure refers to actual behavior or the abstracted rules of behavior (or ideals of behavior), or both. Thus many studies appear in which "an institution or a community may be described without reference to any divergence between inferred rules and actual behavior."

Many social structures in a society can contribute to, or present barriers to, agricultural development. In order to understand how they may influence development, Kunkel (1970, p. 134) believes studying behavior and social relations, which would include specification of the conditions for the shaping, maintenance, and alteration of particular activities, would help an investigator to understand the multivariate character of social structure and the requirements of the socioeconomic progress. Much research by sociologists is carried out within this general structural-functional framework elaborated particularly by Parsons and Shils (1951). The material in this volume fits within the social structure, function, and behavior framework of socioeconomic development.[4]

THEORIES EMPHASIZING SOCIOECONOMIC DEVELOPMENT AS SOCIAL LEARNING

More recent social change theories have seen socioeconomic development as a process of social learning, or behavior modification. This approach is part of the social structure, function, and behavior framework considered above.

3. Additional references to theories emphasizing political variables include Eisenstadt 1966; Wilber 1984: Popkin 1979; Huntington 1969; Lenski and Lenski 1978; and sections of Myrdal 1968 on the "soft state." Also see a review of Rigg's prismatic society thesis by Hoogvelt (1976, pp. 112–22).

4. Overviews of mainstream theories that focus on social structure and behavior in socioeconomic change can be obtained from Kunkel 1970; Hoogvelt 1976; Goldthorpe 1975; Long 1977; Smelser 1968; and Lerner 1958.

Undergirding this approach is the progress achieved in learning theory by experimental psychologists over the last fifty years (Kunkel 1970; Dunn 1971).

Dunn, in presenting this approach to socioeconomic development, begins with biological evolution as a learning process and then examines social evolution and social learning as evolutionary experimentation. Kunkel (1970, p. 44), in a more detailed methodological exposition, shows how modern learning theory can guide behavior modification to achieve desired socioeconomic change. His behavioral model of humans indicates how the variables that impinge continuously on human behavior throughout life provide a learning process framework within which there is large potential for further useful research on how to facilitate socioeconomic and agricultural development. The major thesis of this model is that human behavior can be changed at any time by judiciously altering those aspects of the social environment that constitute sanctions (rewarding or punishing consequences) for specific activities: "the knowledge and application of behavioral principles makes the success of a development program possible, while ignorance guarantees its failure unless there is a generous portion of luck" (p. 315). Kunkel proposes that an agent of effective change needs the qualities of a physician—to diagnose and design development programs—and of an engineer—to assure completion of the program.

Conflict and Marxist Theories

Writers who adopt conflict and Marxist theories of development hypothesize that class conflict is the central cause of human progress. Among those employing conflict theories for study of socioeconomic development, neo-Marxists are the largest number. Non-Marxist social scientists who employed conflict theory include Mills (1956) and the Lynds (1937).

Karl Marx (1818–83) drew on the ideas of the German philosopher Georg Hegel and concluded that human progress was dialectical, based upon the movement from one idea (thesis) to a second, opposite idea (antithesis), which after a struggle would result in a synthesis. Marx proposed that the dialectical process involved not only ideas but economic conditions and relations, and thus his theory of development became known as dialectical materialism. Marx believed human progress could be explained by analyzing the struggles between two different economic classes, in particular between workers, who were assumed always to be oppressed, and the owners of property, who were assumed to be the oppressors (Babbie 1980, p. 50).

It is difficult to make an adequate summary of the large recent neo-Marxist literature, especially as there are many different interpretations, which vary considerably. The most well-known neo-Marxists who have addressed economic and agricultural development questions include Baran (1975), Stavenhagen (1975), Frank (1975), Griffin (1978), Magdoff (1969), Amin (1974 and 1977a), Roxborough (1979), and Wallerstein (1979). These writers employ theory derived from Marx to analyze current social, political, and economic development and to identify changes, usually revolutionary, that they view as required to improve the life of the working class—which is defined as the goal of development.[5]

Criticisms of Marxism and neo-Marxist theory are many. A useful perspective is provided by a sympathetic review of the social philosophy of the "young Marx" by Dunn (1971, p. 304), who concluded that "the truth is that he offered an evolutionary hypothesis that was untestable through social action because it contained insufficient operational detail." Other central criticisms are that Marxist theories are oversimplistic, unilinear, and too narrow to encompass the wide variety of human experience in less developed nations. Todaro (1981, p. 84) concluded, for example, that "at its core it is a rigid ideology and has an extremely demanding goal of economic development together with the brutal realization of its necessity. . . . Other . . . observers, however, while agreeing with much of neo-Marxist analysis (though disputing fundamental propositions) . . . point out that neo-Marxists have no prescriptions beyond revolution, and note that revolutionary movements have a tendency to substitute one kind of exploitation (political, religious, and social) for another kind (economic)."

To conclude this section, we believe the following statement provides a useful outline of a general theory of socioeconomic development.

Of the various attempts at formulating a model to depict this process, Neil Smelser's [1963], based on the idea of structural differentiation, is perhaps the most elegant. For him a developed economy and society is characterized as a highly differentiated structure and an underdeveloped one as relatively lacking in differentiation; hence change centers on the process of differentiation itself. By "differentiation" Smelser means the process by which more specialized and more autonomous social units are established. This he sees occurring in several different spheres: in the economy, the family, the political system, and religious institutions.

Economic development takes place through (a) the modernization of technology, leading to a change from simple traditional techniques to the application of scientific knowledge; (b) the commercialization of agriculture, which is characterized by the move from subsistence to commercial farming, leading to a specialization in cash-crop production and the development of wage labor; (c) urbanization which consists of changes in the ecological dimension and is the movement from farm and village towards the growth of large urban centers. These processes, he suggests, sometimes occur simultaneously and sometimes at different rates. (Long 1977, p. 9)

---

5. Concise expositions of the tenets of Marxism are provided by Chodak (1973, pp. 21–24); Todaro (1981, pp. 79–85); Dunn (1971, pp. 297–304); and Deere and de Janvry (1979). Long (1977, pp. 71–104) reviewed dependency theory. For additional references to Marxist, dependency, and radical studies on Africa, see Eicher and Baker 1982 (pp. 35–40). Collections of edited Marxist studies include Galli 1981: and, in anthropology, French micro-Marxist studies are included in Seddon 1978. For more a moderate analysis employing conflict theory, which recognizes the oversimplification of the worker-capitalist dichotomy, see Griffin 1974a.

Cultural Variables and Agricultural Development

The Components of Cultural Systems

The preceding sections, which examined different theoretical approaches to socioeconomic change, have indicated a range of fundamental cultural variables that affect social structure and human behavior. These in turn affect agricultural development. In order to better understand these variables and to work effectively with them, we need to be clear about basic terminology. The terminology set out below is drawn primarily from (1) the two disciplines that take as their domain the whole of social life—sociology and anthropology; and (2) the branch of economics that specializes in the interface between economics and general theory of social development.

The following summary of social science terms is drawn particularly from a basic text by the sociologist Babbie (1980, pp. 97–120). Culture (or social system) "is a general term sociologists, anthropologists, and others use to refer to the whole collection of agreements that the members of a particular society share. It includes the shared points of view that define what's true and what's good and what kinds of behavior people can expect of one another . . . but which might seem very strange to an outsider" (p. 97).

The components of culture are symbols, beliefs and values, status and role, norms (expectations) related to status and role, sanctions (rewards and punishments), and artifacts.

Symbols are shorthand representations of the shared knowledge and understandings of a group of people, such as national flags, the dove of peace, the Christian cross, the Islamic star and crescent, the Russian hammer and sickle, and such words as *democracy* and *communism.*

Beliefs are agreements about what is true, and *values* are agreements about what is preferred. They compose the overarching umbrella of agreements under which a society operates (Babble 1980, p. 116).

The term *status* is used to describe the social locations a person holds in an organization or social system. A person usually holds a number of different statuses at the same time, such as mother, wife, chief family food producer, and leader of the village women's group. Status positions may either be assigned (ascribed) without the person's doing anything, such as the status of woman or of an Asian; or they may be achieved (earned) by actions, such as the status of student, athlete, criminal, or physician. An individual is assigned a status by the members of the society. When a person puts the rights and duties associated with that status into effect, he or she performs the role. *Role* describes what a person does; thus a student's role is described as to go to class, study, take exams. Roles are agreed upon expectations of behavior by people who occupy given statuses.

Norms of behavior are the expectations or rules of behavior that the society agrees members holding different statuses should follow. A person concerned with development needs knowledge about whether the proposed development change would cause individuals to transgress behavioral norms and, if so, whether there are ways to modify the economic opportunity so that behavior that could lead to group sanctions would not be needed.

Sanctions are the elements of culture used by a group to attempt to assure that behavioral norms are followed. They can be either positive or negative. In a learning framework, positive sanctions or (rewards) reinforce or encourage behavior consistent with the norms. Negative sanctions (punishment) discourage socially undesirable behavior. Should a new economic opportunity, say for women, require behavior outside of accepted norms, those concerned with development need to know the severity of possible sanctions associated with the proposed change.

Artifacts refers to material things produced by a culture, such as its art, technology, furniture, and buildings.

Institutions, Organizations, and Change

THE CONCEPT OF AN INSTITUTION

Institutions, or social structures, are persistent patterns of social interactions with associated statuses, roles, norms of behavior, and sanctions. They develop from the interaction of past beliefs, values, statuses, and roles, influenced by norms of behavior and social sanctions and the new economic and social opportunities available. Institutions are agreement systems that often involve particular aspects of social life in the economic, political, or family spheres.

As with most terms in the social sciences, the term *institution* currently has varying meaning. However, the following definitions drawn from three major social sciences show the convergence in use. "Sociologists use the term 'institution' to refer to the agreement system that organizes some general aspects of group life," according to Babbie (1980, p. 15). "An institution is a relatively stable and integrated set of symbols, beliefs, values, norms, roles, and statuses relating to some aspect of social life" (p. 114). The behaviors analyzed may be the observed (actual) behavior or the ideal rules of behavior (Kunkel 1970, pp. 109 and 133). Economic institutions are thus agreement systems that organize the production and distribution of goods and services (Wolf 1955, p. 868, n.). For economists the term *institution* was clarified by Commons, one of the major figures in the institutional school of economics:

Sometimes an institution seems to be analogous to a building, a sort of framework of laws and regulations, within which individuals act like inmates. Sometimes it seems to mean the "behavior" of the inmates themselves. (Commons 1961, p. 69)

Collective action ranges all the way from unorganized Custom to the many organized Going Concerns, such as the family, the corporation, the holding company, the trade association, the trade union, the Federal Reserve System, the "group of affiliated interests," the State. (Commons 1961, p. 70)

Human beings are born into this process of collective action and become individualized by the rules of collective action. Thus an institution is collective action in control, liberation, and expansion of individual action. (Commons 1950, p. 21)

Economists Hayami and Ruttan in their 1985 study define institutions more specifically as

the rules of a society or of organizations that facilitate coordination among people by helping them form expectations which each person can reasonably hold in dealing with others. They reflect the conventions that have evolved in different societies regarding the behavior of individuals and groups relative to their own behavior and the behavior of others. In the area of economic relations they have a crucial role in establishing expectations about the rights to use resources in economic activities and about the partitioning of the income streams resulting from economic activity. (pp. 94–95)

THE CONCEPT OF AN ORGANIZATION

The concept of an organization is often confused with the concept of a social institution. An organization consists of any identifiable group of individuals who participate together regularly in attempting do something. An organization often has symbols, beliefs, values, statuses, roles, norms of behavior, and sanctions, and establishes many of its own institutions (rules or social structures) to aid its own operations. Any particular organization benefits from and is limited by the many social structures, or institutions, of the wider society in which it operates. Organizations are "going concerns, with the working rules that keep them agoing, all the way from the family, the corporation, the trade union, the trade association, up to the state itself. . . . The passive concept is a 'group'; the active is a 'going concern'" (Commons 1961, p. 69). Economic and business organizations include informal, regular, sharing activities among farmers and complex formal international corporate structures. A wide range of organizations have been present in the many societies throughout human history, and are related to religious, political, educational, or other domains of life.

INSTITUTIONAL CHANGE

"Institutional innovation or institutional development will be used to refer to a change (1) in behavior of a particular organization (a household, firm, association, bureaucracy), (2) in the relationship between such an organization and its environment, or (3) in the rules that govern behavior and relationships in an organization's environment" (Ruttan 1978, p. 329). Any of these changes are defined as institutional change.

To conclude, although definitions of an institution or social structure vary somewhat, three core components of the concept are present: institutions (1) influence the behavior of people, and hence have economic consequences; (2)

have continuity through time; and (3) arise, change, and disappear in fulfilling changing human economic, religious, social, or political goals.[6]

Institutions and Agricultural Development

The economist Brewster (1967), while examining "Traditional Social Structures as Barriers to Change" in Taiwan, concluded:

In most economically backward societies, the dominant units of collective action are the extended family, village, clan, or tribe. Such small social units are capable of producing and applying only very primitive farm (and other) technologies. This means that the requirements of economic progress are twofold. One is technological: the creation and widespread adoption of ever more effective gadgets for conquering nature. The other is the organizational requirements of the gadgets—the creation and operation of increasingly larger units of collective action, including progress-oriented stable governments, which are necessary for enabling a people to devise the more efficient gadgets they need for turning physical materials and forces into an ever faster flow of want-satisfying goods. The literature mainly focuses on barriers to meeting the gadget requirements of progress. To offset this imbalance, this paper has centered on the way in which the social structures of backward societies necessarily generate only primitive technologies, and also induce in people strong conviction concerning appropriate ways of life and work that commonly operate as formidable barriers to meeting the new organizational requirements of the gadget component of progress. (p. 862)

The pervasive influence of institutions on economic activities is illustrated by Dalton's (1967) conclusion that, in traditional African economies, "the question, what forces, institutions, or rules direct labor, land, and other resources to specific lines of production, can be answered only with reference to community social organization" (p. 68). Hence "neighboring societies sharing the same physical environment often produce markedly different ranges of output, with different technologies used within differently organized production groups. . . . Such economic and technical differences are largely attributable to differences in social organization" (p. 65).

In an African example, economist Helleiner (1975), in studying decisionmaking on small farms, found that social structures, or institutions, affected the specification of the appropriate decisionmaking unit for purposes of economic analysis. (A similar analysis was made by Cleave [1977].)

On the one hand, the sexual division of labor within the nuclear family at times suggests the need for more than one decision unit per household. Females may be engaged exclu-

6. For more discussion of institutions and structural analysis by anthropologists and sociologists see, for example, Cernea 1986, Dunn 1971 (pp. 204-20), and Kunkel 1970 (pp. 105-32). For economists' use of the term *institution,* see Binswanger and Ruttan 1978 (pp. 328-29); Bromley 1982b (p. 839); and Cohen 1978. Other important references providing greater understanding of cultural and institutional variables include Dalton 1967, 1971; Leagans and Loomis 1971; MacAndrews and Sien 1982; Olson 1982; Anthony et al. 1979; Scott 1976; and Schwarzweller 1984. See in addition Spicer 1952; Barlett 1980; and Cernea 1986 which provide a range of examples of the intermingling of technological, economic, and cultural variables as development activities are attempted.

sively in food production or marketing activities which are to a large extent independent of their husbands' economic activities. Analysis based on notions of using total household labor or maximizing household earnings may therefore be quite misleading. On the other hand, the extended family system and/or communal tenure systems may require units larger than the household, for analytical purposes. Relationships among family, household, or even community members are believed by many to be qualitatively different from those with outsiders, with the latter more narrowly economic in the sense that they are market based. (p. 46)

Institutions and Economic Behavior

In an important early paper, Wolf (1955) explored the interrelations between institutions and economic growth. To explain slow economic development, he proposed that

the inadequacy of technology and capital formation may be due less to a shortage of information about techniques or potential savings than to shortages of the right kinds of institutions—"right" implying those kinds of institutions which permit or stimulate rather than impede the adoption of new techniques and the formation of productive capital. In other words, institutions—as well as capital and technology—are productive; or more accurately, different institutions come to have differentially productive consequences. Growth-promoting institutions without themselves adding resources to the economy . . . may so restructure the environment in which factors of production meet that the rate at which combinations occur is accelerated. (p. 867)

Wolf provided examples of ways that institutional arrangements affect economic behavior. They include:

1. Institutional arrangements that affect the net income of producers
2. Institutions that affect the relations between production and the distribution of production
3. Institutions that encourage economic growth by sharing uncertainty
4. Institutional arrangements that influence economic activity by facilitating the flow of knowledge of new economic opportunities.

EFFECTS ON PRODUCERS' INCOME

Two examples of the ways institutional arrangements affect the net income of producers follow. (1) The establishment of tariff schedules for imported goods directly affects the net income of domestic producers. An increased level of tariffs will usually increase the profits of producers within the nation. (2) Tenure arrangements affect farmers' incomes. The long-run effects of land-to-the-tiller programs in land reforms are clear examples of how changes in institutional arrangements (tenure laws) have resulted in higher productivity. In the Japanese, Taiwanese, and other land-to-the-tiller programs, the institutional change did not itself provide more land resources but stimulated farmers to acquire and use more inputs and hence to increase productivity and output. Thus, institutions (social agreements, social rules) may stimulate increased productivity or, conversely, impede economic growth.

Figure 5.2. Effects of Owner-Operator and Share Tenant Landholding on Input Use and Agricultural Production

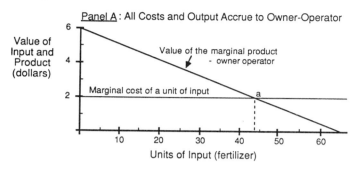

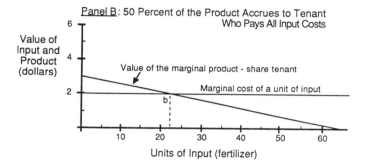

To illustrate the use of economic analysis of different institutional arrangements, we examine the likely effects of two land tenure arrangements on income and agricultural production (see figure 5.2). Using the production function concepts from the previous chapter, we observe that an owner-operator would apply chemical fertilizer on a unit of land at a level so that the marginal cost of the fertilizer equals the marginal return obtained from the crop in order to obtain maximum net income from his field (point *a*). In this example, forty four units of fertilizer would be applied.

What amount of fertilizer would share tenants apply if they pay a rent of 50 percent of the crop to the landowners (a common arrangement in traditional agricultures in many parts of the world, including Taiwan before the land reform)? These share-rental rules often require that tenants pay for all inputs, such as fertilizer. If tenants pay half of the crop to their landlords, their marginal product would be half as much at every level of fertilizer input (see figure 5.2, panel *B*). With the same unit cost of fertilizer as owner-operators, tenants would obtain highest net returns by applying fertilizer to a level where their marginal returns equaled marginal costs (point *b*), or only twenty-two units. Thus, if tenants are free to decide the amount of fertilizer to use, they will use less under this contract, and hence the field will have a lower yield and produce less net income. This analysis indicates that a community of tenants and landlords with these share-rental arrangements will produce less net income than if the farmers were owner-operators or if there were other tenure arrangements, such as fixed rent.

To test your understanding of this theory of the possible effects of different tenure arrangements on income and production, ask yourself under what tenure arrangements would a tenant be likely to apply forty-four units of fertilizer and hence obtain a total production as high as an owner operator? Hints: What other payment agreements might a tenant have? Would it be practical for the landlord to share input costs?

In the 1960s and 1970s, the conflict between the lowered productivity implications of the preceding economic analysis of share tenancy and its pervasiveness in traditional societies led to renewed empirical and theoretical work on tenure contracts. The result has been the development of a new land tenure economics. Findings of this research have identified risk and transaction costs, especially in the enforcement of tenure contracts, as important determinants of landholding arrangements—whether share tenancy, fixed rent, or land ownership. What the costs of tenure contract enforcement and risk are in a particular community is an empirical question depending upon local social and economic conditions. In traditional agricultural areas at subsistence levels, the costs to tenants of risk to their food supply are very high. The costs of tenure contract enforcement by resident landlords are, however, usually low in a small community, as everything is known by everyone. Hence, this theory proposes that, in traditional agriculture, both tenants and landlords may often be better off with share rental contracts.

As agriculture develops with an accelerating series of technological and market changes and as tenant incomes and alternative opportunities increase, the risk of a poor crop to a tenant becomes less and the transaction costs of share tenant contracts are likely to become greater for the landlord. Then fixed rent contracts and greater amounts of owner-operator farming are more likely to produce greater community income. "Thus the new land tenure economics . . . demolished the traditional doctrine that share tenancy is always inefficient [less productive] and thereby removed the rationale for its replacement by leasehold tenancy or owner-operatorship as a prerequisite to rapid productivity growth in agriculture" (Hayami and Ruttan 1985, p. 395).

For the purposes of this chapter, it is important to note the interrelations between (1) the preference for different tenure contracts implied by the new land tenure economics and (2) social and cultural variables. This theory highlights the relations in the village between tenants and owners as a crucial influence on tenure contract transaction costs and hence the productivity of the different possible tenure contracts. Thus, village values and beliefs, statuses and roles, and sanctions affect tenure arrangements and therefore yields.[7] In chapter 10, we consider in more detail experience with land tenure arrangements and land reform.

EFFECTS ON THE RELATIONS BETWEEN PRODUCTION AND DISTRIBUTION

Development literature has many illustrations of institutional arrangements that affect production decisions and the distribution of production. These institutional arrangements include any redistributive methods societies use, including gifts and taxes. For traditional peasant and tribal societies, the succinct statement of Raymond Firth (as quoted by Dalton 1967, p. 71) may often apply: "from each according to his status obligations, to each according to his rights in that system." Thus, decisions about what and how to produce may be made for the community by leaders, and the distribution of production may follow community rules. In some cases at least, the agricultural laborer may obtain little directly from his work on a particular field.

The customary rules in the joint or extended family in many cultures also illustrate varied relations between production and distribution, with possible positive or negative effects on production. In extended family systems, the cost ot the additional effort in production is borne by the individual carrying out that activity, but the economic fruits of the activity are usually shared by other family members and relatives. Although the individual making the effort may gain some benefits, including psychic income and prestige, the question remains about the effect of the distribution rules on his or her investment of labor and other resources and entrepreneurial effort. If the incentive to make extra effort is low, output may not increase.

In other circumstances, extended families may contribute to more rapid growth. For example, many Chinese and other merchant and shopkeeper groups distribute resources to younger members to enable them to establish new businesses, sometimes in remote locations. In these circumstances, the distribution of resources by the family to its members aids in expanding output and starting activities and enterprises.

In another example, effective patent and copyright institutions illustrate the relation between production and distribution. These laws provide increased incentives to creative individuals to make additional efforts, because their financial rewards are likely to be greater. Where these institutional arrangements are not present, there is less encouragement to individuals to produce useful new goods and services, because others may immediately copy them for their own economic benefit.

EFFECTS ON UNCERTAINTY

Uncertainty was defined in the previous chapter as events in which the probabilities of the outcomes are unknown. Examples of institutional activity

---

7. For more material on the new land tenure economics, see Hayami and Ruttan 1985 (pp. 389–96), from which this material was drawn.

that can reduce the number of uncertain events and the magnitude of their impact include the following three: (1) the establishment of limited liability business organizations that reduce the negative effects of business failure on entrepreneurs; (2) the development of public or private insurance arrangements to reduce losses from fire, accident, storm damage, or crop failure; and (3) the elaboration of consistent government decisionmaking procedures that reduce uncertainty about agricultural input and product prices. Shifts to more realistic agricultural and other government policies based on sound economic analysis can greatly decrease fluctuations in these prices and hence reduce uncertainty in farm decisions and variability in family and national agricultural incomes.

EFFECTS ON THE FLOW OF KNOWLEDGE

Institutions that facilitate the flow of information include laws and regulations that either encourage free speech or control communication through censorship. Such rules greatly affect the development of communications technologies and organizations in radio, television, and the press, as well as extension education systems. Wolf (1955) pointed out, however, that simply increasing the availability of information about new economic opportunities may not be sufficient to lead to change. In some cases, the perceptions of people may need to be altered about what can help them to achieve their own goals, before new economic opportunities will be seriously entertained—for beliefs and values cause people to filter out information they do not consider relevant to their lives.

Organizations and Institutions in Agriculture

A list of some of the organizations that serve an agricultural area in a more developed nation is instructive to indicate the scope and complexity of organizational and institutional change to be expected in traditional agricultural areas (see table 5.1). A review of the contrasting nature of organizations in traditional and dynamic agriculture leads to some generalizations about the development of agricultural organizations and institutions (see table 5.2).

In traditional areas, organizations serving agriculture can be characterized as being few in number, often little specialized, informal, of small scale, with family membership assumed. In contrast, in more modern agriculture the very many more organizations serving agriculture are characteristically very highly specialized, such as for the artificial insemination of milk cows, and much more complex, with extensive formal legal organizational arrangements. They often cover a wide geographic area, even spanning national boundaries, as illustrated by fertilizer and pesticide companies. Also, membership in these organizations is usually based on the individual farmer.

The elaboration of general and specialized agricultural organizations of the kinds indicated above depends upon the development of many general institutional arrangements that enable their productive operation. Important institutions affecting the productivity of agricultural organizations include reasonably

Table 5.1. The Great Number of Organizations Serving Agriculture in More Developed Nations: The Example of a County in Michigan

Nongovernment Organizations	Government Organizations

Farm input supply
  Farm machinery dealers
  Seed and plant dealers
  Fertilizer suppliers
  Custom field fertilizer applicators
  Animal feed suppliers
  Poultry and livestock suppliers
  Artificial insemination experts
  Veterinarians
	Farm input supply
	  Experiment stations
	    (more productive inputs)
	  Resource development and conservative
	    groups

Farm credit supply
  Banks
  Cooperatives
  Input services
	Farm credit supply
	
	Farm management services
	  Agricultural education (high school
	    and college extension information)
	  Accounting services
	  Price and regulatory information
	    services
	  Weather reporting services

Farm management services
  Accountants
  Advisors	

Agricultural product marketing
  Grain storage and sales
  Food processing
  Trucking
  Hedging and financing sales
	Agricultural product marketing
	  Price support
	
	Agricultural development and promotion
	  Experiment stations
	  Extension service

Agricultural development and promotion
  Farm bureaus
  Grange
	Judicial system
	
	Security system

Legal services Private law firms	Legislative system

Table 5.2. Characteristics of Organizations Serving Agriculture in Less Developed and More Developed Nations

Less Developed Nations	More Developed Nations
Few organizations	Many organizations
Unspecialized organizations	Highly specialized organizations
Informal organizations	Formal and complex organizations[a]
Small organizations	Unlimited size of organizations
Family-focused organizations	Individually focused organizations

Source: Based on McHale 1962 (pp. 30–55).

[a] Having written charters of organization, bylaws, and organizational and procedural rules.

stable government rules and regulations and an effective national legal system enabling timely enforcement of contracts.

In conclusion, institutions are an integral part of socioeconomic systems. They arise and change to serve social needs. They are influenced in their development by other elements of culture, including resources, technology, and beliefs and values. Institutions in turn influence the other elements of culture. In the many agricultural areas of the world, different types of organizations accomplish needed economic functions. Hence, the focus of analysis should be on the economic functions required for desired development in order to evaluate the present adequacy of local and national organizational and institutional environment and what changes may be desirable. If institutional arrangements and organizations do not exist to perform the needed functions, then modified or new institutions and organizations may be required to accelerate agricultural development. Much social science research has demonstrated that it is often easier to modify existing institutions and organizations to take on new functions than to establish entirely new ones.

Conclusions

Significant agricultural development cannot occur without cultural and institutional change. An immense shift is required from traditional ways of life, in which the same patterns of agricultural life are reinforced, to a social and cultural environment in which rural people will seek continuous change in cultural and institutional patterns to better serve them.

This chapter has shown that the economic equilibrium of traditional societies set out in chapter 4 is supported in many traditional societies by a more general cultural equilibrium. We have also emphasized the interrelated nature of socioeconomic change, especially with respect to institutions. This knowledge should help reduce discouragement if "obviously" profitable economic opportunities are rejected. In such cases, effective development aid may require social analysis of the impediments to growth to identify changes in cultural variables that could open up new economic opportunities. For example, in tribal areas with shifting cultivation, persons proposing ways to increase food production are likely to need considerable aid in understanding the broader social framework within which food production takes place. In particular, they are likely to need to know some of the beliefs and values held by the group, how rights to the use of fields are obtained, which work groups would be involved and how they are constituted, and who will have rights to the resulting crops.

The failure of a government project to provide well water to a desert village in Peru due to lack of attention to cultural and institutional variables is a clear example (Holmberg 1952, pp. 113–24). Involved in this case were cultural symbols, beliefs and values, norms and sanctions, and traditional political and social structures. In trying to provide well water (1) the government technicians ignored local village water experts; (2) the technicians did not discover or consult with the real leaders in the community, only the externally appointed nominal leaders; (3) the first well was drilled on the property of a large landowner, who the technicians later discovered was not liked; and (4) the well was not given the traditional, symbolic blessing by the priest. The drilled well had water but was not used, and the project could not be continued.

This case illustrates that success in a technological activity can be blocked by a failure to recognize the cultural and institutional variables involved. It also points out that the amount of time required to carry out the physical part of a technological change, such as drilling the well, may be small compared to the time required to discuss the plan with the people involved to assure that the new technology is acceptable and will be used by a community. Significant technological changes are likely to have large, often unseen, shadows of social and institutional change associated with them. Many have seen the artifacts of failed agricultural development projects scattered over the rural landscape in the form of unused buildings and rusty machinery. Often, a poor understanding of cultural and institutional variables has doomed the technological change. Hence, "noneconomic" factors can have a great influence on agricultural supply response.

Placing agricultural development in the wider framework of socioeconomic change

shifts the onus of poverty and slow development from the peasant, his culture and his society to the elite of his nation, to the planners and to the international technocrats. The slowness of economic development is not to be laid at the mythical conservatism of the peasant, or at the feet of his ignorance, or at his lack of receptivity to income-raising opportunities. The burden falls on the planners and administrators for not seeing the structure of economic opportunity through the lens of the peasants' real choices and possibilities, and hence failing to design, present, and offer meaningful economic options. . . . What is needed is the commitment of the nation's elite to the public welfare and the technocrats' willingness to relax the constraints of trained incompetence to encompass the capabilities, cultures and careers of the peasantry. (Nash 1966, p. 208)

From the exploration of how cultural and institutional variables affect agricultural development, we draw the following three conclusions. First, when new, more productive technology has been identified for introduction into an agricultural area, some analysis of the belief, value, and social structure dimensions of the rural social system that may be affected by the technological change will often enable more rapid and effective introduction, reduce negative consequences, and avoid social blocks. The more complex the innovation or technological change, the more likely social analysis will contribute to its early productivity by reducing the cost of the change and the likelihood of failure. The "happy technologists" who ignore the social environment in which they are working can do great unintended damage to a community by introducing technology that greatly increases conflicts or that markedly worsens income distribution. Hence, in many developmental situations, anthropologists, sociologists, and other social scientists often can enable agricultural development to proceed more rapidly in the desired directions at less financial and social cost.

Second, the exploration of alternative institutional arrangements needed to accelerate development is likely to be central to increasing farm productivity. Changes in land tenure arrangements, cooperative organizations, agricultural credit, input and product market changes, research, education, communications, and extension are as crucial to agricultural development as changes in farm technology, such as more fertilizer-responsive seeds and better farm machinery. As Commons asserted above, the right institutional changes and collective action can greatly expand the scope for individual action. As will be seen in chapter 11, one of the most fundamental institutional changes contributing to the acceleration of agricultural growth worldwide has been the development of national and international agricultural research systems, public and private.

Third, to be most effective, those who desire to accelerate agricultural development need to know how to use both social and economic analysis tools. They need as much knowledge as possible of the processes of both agricultural development and more general socioeconomic development. The latter includes cultural and institutional information about the rural society of concern and, in particular, knowledge of the income distribution objectives of the society. We hypothesize that economists working on problems of less developed nations who effectively employ social variables and analyses, such as those highlighted in this chapter, will in many instances be more effective in contributing to agricultural development than those who limit themselves to economic analysis tools alone.

Important Concepts

Noneconomic variables	Psychological variables
Cultural endowments	Political variables
Personal utility function	Social structure
Nonpecuniary elements of utility	Marxist theory
Evolutionary modernization	Components of culture
theories	Institution
Conflict modernization theories	Organization
Structural-functional framework	Institutional change
Social differentiation	New land tenure economics
Theory of the limited good	

Sample Questions

1. Does neoclassical economic theory assume that all human behavior is based on buying or selling (or bartering for) goods and services? Explain.

2. There are both evolutionary and conflict theories of the modernization

process that less developed nations are experiencing. Explain the basic concepts of the two groups of modernization theories.

3. The evolutionary modernization theories have different emphases, or approaches. Summarize three approaches.

4. How do beliefs and values affect economic activity? Give an example of each.

5. Explain the meaning of an institution, or social structure, and how it can affect economic activity. Include examples.

6. In what way do status, role, and norms relate to organizations?

7. Provide three examples of how institutions affect economic behavior in agriculture.

8. Explain the economic justification for economists concerned with agricultural development to do research on organizations and institutions.

6

Agricultural Development Theory

The model of agricultural and economic develop-
ment remains incomplete unless the process is specified by which collective
action, from the local community to the central government level, is organized
for the supply of public goods, including new technical knowledge and
institutional arrangements, in response to changes in economic conditions.
—Hayami and Ruttan 1985, p. 62

This chapter presents the core economic theory of agricultural development.
The subject of development is how to increase the size of the economic pie and
how to divide it up. The chapter first reviews basic investment concepts and
important partial theories of economic and agricultural development. Then it
examines the central ideas of the induced innovation model of agricultural development. This economic theory explains the development of agriculture in the
wide variety of economic conditions prevailing in both less and more developed
nations.

Introduction

The Value of Economic Theory for Practitioners

Some students and practitioners of agricultural development may question
the value of the effort required to understand economic theory of agricultural
development when they are impatient to get on with the formidable practical
tasks of helping low-income farmers to find better lives. The challenge of this
and the following chapters is to demonstrate that knowledge of economic theory
can enable practitioners to be much more productive than they currently are in
using scarce development resources as they design strategies and carry out programs to increase farm and national welfare.

The usefulness of economic theory in agricultural development may be

113

clarified by noting the great contribution that theoretical work in the biological sciences has made to solving practical agricultural problems. In the fields of crop and animal science, the study of genetic theory is concerned with developing knowledge about how different strains of plants and animals can be produced through manipulation of their genes. Geneticists are usually not much concerned about what biological material they work with or about the economic use of their experimental results. In contrast, plant and animal breeders, like the development practitioner, have the objective of obtaining increased plant and animal production on farms in particular agricultural areas. To succeed in their breeding objectives, these scientists have to know and draw on the work of geneticists.

In economics, the study of development theory is discipline oriented, as is the study of genetics. Development theory seeks to explain how economic growth is obtained and to understand the functional interrelations among the parts of economic systems. Applied economists and agricultural development practitioners who know the basic theory of their science, as plant breeders must, will be able to design more productive agricultural development policies and programs. In particular, a knowledge of economic and agricultural development theory can help one avoid wasting large amounts of development resources on low-productivity development projects and strategies. We now review the core investment concepts and classical and modern production functions, two essential parts of economic growth theory.

Investment Concepts

Economic growth is a process of investment, or capital accumulation. Why? As was seen in chapter 4, classical economists viewed agricultural output as dependent upon the amount of land, labor. and capital used in production. When these three variables are examined, the amount of land available is generally found to be limited, and the amount of labor in a society is increased only through population growth, so capital is the sole source of rapid growth. But what is the nature of output-augmenting capital? Of what does it consist? And how can more of it be obtained to accelerate growth? To increase capital, investment is required.

WHAT IS INVESTMENT?

Consider a farm. Each year annual operating expenses (variable inputs) are used for production purposes and a certain amount of fixed farm capital equipment has to be replaced or repaired as it is worn out. The value of the farm capital that has to be repaired or replaced each year to maintain the same amount (stock) of farm capital is labeled *depreciation,* as was pointed out in chapter 3. In order to maintain the stock of capital and to obtain the same farm production each year, the farmer either produces the needed replacement capital through repairs and construction or obtains the needed capital through purchase from others. The labor used in repairing or producing capital equipment, such as a tool, is "invested" in making that tool, for if the labor is used to make the tool, it cannot be used in directly productive activities, such as growing a crop. Hence, the income that would have resulted from applying the labor to current crop production activities was instead invested in making a tool to maintain future levels of crop output.

If the tool had been bought instead of made, some income would have been spent, and savings or consumption would be lower. For a household, the relation between investment and income is summarized in the equation Income = Consumption + Investment + Savings. Thus in general, for a given income, any use of income to replace or increase the capital stock necessitates a reduction in consumption or savings. If depreciated capital stock is not replaced, production will decline. At the macro, or national, level, income is largely allocated between consumption and investment, as net social savings are generally small. Thus, when national income is allocated, there is a trade-off between additional investment in output-increasing development projects to accelerate growth in future years and additional consumption in the current year, a choice of more future consumption versus more current consumption.

HOW DOES INVESTMENT INCREASE ECONOMIC GROWTH?

Production can generally be accelerated only if productive capital is also increased (see table 6.1). To increase investment, the gross investment (GI) each year has to be greater than depreciation (D). Thus the change in the amount of capital, or net annual investment (NI) = gross investment (GI) minus depreciation (D). If more productive capital is added to a farm, greater income will result in the next time period. With increased income, and the same proportion of capital invested in the next time period, a further increase in farm capital and income would result.

In the example in table 6.1, an initial capital stock of $500 was used, resulting in an annual income of $100, due to the not unreasonable assumption of a capital productivity (output) ratio of $5 in capital required to produce $1 worth of production during a year. In panel A, the gross investment in the first year was 20 percent of income, or $20, leaving $80 for consumption. Of the $20 gross investment, $10 was used for repairs and capital purchases to replace worn-out equipment, and $10 was added to the capital stock ($510) for use in year 2. This increased income in year 2 to $102. If the same 20 percent of income continues to be invested in this way, growth in both income and capital stock will continue. Note that the rate of return on the capital investment is 20 percent. Note also that an income growth rate of 2 percent per year is obtained.

In panel B of table 6.1, a higher proportion of income was invested (30 percent), limiting consumption to $70 in year 1 but enabling a higher rate of income growth—4 percent per year. After 9 years, consumption is greater ($95.80) due to the higher rate of investment. A fundamental development trade-off is seen here, between higher current consumption and higher invest-

Table 6.1. Investment: How Income and Capital Stock Are Increased, an Illustration

Year	Total Stock of Capital: K	Income: Y(0.2K)	Consumption: C	Gross Annual Investment: GI	Depreciation D(0.02K)	Net Annual Investment: NI(GI−D)	Rate of Growth Income (percent)
			Panel A: 10 Percent Net Investment				
1	500.0	100.0	80.0	20.0	−10.0	10.0	
2	510.0	102.0	81.6	20.4	−10.2	10.2	2
3	520.2	104.0	83.2	20.8	−10.4	10.4	2
8	574.3	114.6	91.1	23.0	−11.5	11.5	
9	585.8	117.2	93.8				2
			Panel B: 20 Percent Net Investment				
1	500.0	100.0	70.0	30.0	−10.0	20.0	
2	520.0	104.0	72.8	31.2	−10.4	20.8	4
3	540.8	108.2	75.7	32.5	−10.8	21.7	4
8	658.1	131.6	92.1	39.5	−13.2	26.3	
9	684.4	136.9	95.8				4

Note: This table includes the following assumptions. The capital to output ratio is 5 to 1, or a 20 percent gross return on capital investment. The overall average depreciation rate for all capital investment is 2 percent. In panel A, one tenth of income is added to the stock of capital each year, and in panel B, two tenths of income is added to the capital stock each year. The capital stock in any year equals the capital stock in the previous year plus net investment that year.

ment with lower initial consumption, which leads eventually to higher future consumption.

Observe that the productivity of the investment in each year affects the rate of growth in income. In table 6.1, all capital was assumed to have a continuous capital to output ratio of 5 to 1 throughout, or a rate of return on investment of 20 percent. Often, the productivity of additional capital inputs will decrease as more of one resource (capital in this case) is added to fixed amounts of other resources in production, unless at some point there is technological change. To prevent this, research and development is required to continuously find more productive capital. In chapter 11, we explore investment in research to increase productivity in agriculture.

OPTIMIZING SCARCE INVESTMENT RESOURCES

With limited capital resources to invest, how should decisions be made between different investments? Clearly, the resources available for investment should be allocated to those investments that would provide the most additional income (the highest returns). Note that returns to investment can include nonmonetary returns, such as improved health, which are obtained from public health programs and investments in medical training.

The most generally used investment methodology to estimate the rate of return available from development investments is benefit-cost analysis, presented in chapter 7. Once estimates of the rates of return are available from a series of investment projects, such as pump irrigation projects, expansion of fertilizer production, or increased research on high-yield plant materials, governments can first choose to allocate resources to the highest return investment, then sequentially choose lower and lower return investments, until all the capital available for investment has been committed. Using this approach, the highest returns, and hence the highest rate of growth, would be obtained from a given amount of investment resources. This procedure for choosing development investments at the national level is conceptually parallel to the economic framework farmers employ in the use of their resources, as presented in chapter 4. Farmers estimate their marginal increase in income from each alternate farming activity, then choose the set of activities that will provide the highest returns, and hence income, from their limited resources.

Classical and Modern Agricultural Production Functions

Chapter 4 presented the neoclassical production function of Adam Smith and David Ricardo $Y = f(R, L, K)$. It identified the determinants of growth as land and other physical resources (R), labor (L), and capital (K).[1] As researchers attempted to use this production function to explain the growth of national economies, controversy arose in the 1950s over the sources of economic growth. T. W. Schultz (1956), after examining research on agricultural growth

1. The growth theories of classical and neoclassical economists are summarized in Hagen 1980 (pp. 71–80).

using this production function, concluded that "the link between . . . conventional inputs and output is . . . too weak to bear the analytical burden of determining supply" (p. 756). His research identified two inputs neglected in the neoclassical production function: activities that improve the quality of people as productive agents, and activities that raise the level of the productive arts (technology). Later Hagen (1980, p. 207), in reviewing analyses of growth in the United States, northwestern Europe, and Japan, concluded that capital, land, and labor only explained from 19 to 37 percent of the increase in national income. He estimated that some 35 percent of the increase in national income in these nations was due to advances in knowledge and its application. Increases in the educational level of labor were also found to contribute significantly to increased national income, particularly in the United States.

Thus, the controversy about the sources of growth led to identification of two new, or nonconventional, factors of production that are now understood to be central to economic and agricultural growth: (1) the quality of labor as influenced particularly by education; and (2) the quality of capital due to technological change. Increasing the quality of labor and the quality of capital requires investment in education and in research and development.

This new understanding of the contribution of nontraditional inputs through investments in education and in research and development was incorporated in a useful reformulation of the aggregate production function by de Janvry (1973, p. 416),

$$Y = F[f(K_R, R), g(K_L, L)].$$

In this equation, output (Y) depends upon two subfunctions, one for land and other physical resources (R) and one for labor (L). Capital (K) is introduced as an augmenter of the productivity of both land and labor. This formulation of the agricultural production function places emphasis on the augmenting potential of capital investments through land saving and increased labor productivity. In the land subfunction, $f(K_R, R)$, capital, K_R, augments output through investment in the production of improved farm inputs, such as higher yielding seeds, more productive animal breeds, better chemical inputs, such as fertilizer and pesticides, as well as through improved mechanical equipment, such as soil drainage pipes and irrigation equipment.

Associated investments in institutional changes for improved input supply and product marketing also contribute. In the labor subfunction, $g(K_L, L)$, capital, K_L, augments labor productivity through such investments as tractor mechanization and the education and training of laborers and also through institutional changes that increase human productivity. This reformulation of the agricultural production function places emphasis on the likely substitutability of inputs within the subfunctions, say between fertilizer and land or between labor and mechanization, and also helps focus on the likelihood of low substitutability of the inputs between the two subfunctions for land and labor. This equation shows also that, if the supply of land were inelastic, investment emphasis should be placed on increasing land-augmenting capital, while if labor were in short supply, investment should be increased in labor-augmenting capital, such as farm machinery.

Partial Theories of Economic and Agricultural Development

In this section, we review briefly eight models of development that have limited explanatory power. They are the conservation, industrial fundamentalism, urban-industrial impact, diffusion, cultural-change-first, neo-Marxist, growth-stage, and high-payoff input models. It is important to know the limitations of these theories of development, since they reappear periodically in the literature, in development plans, and in field strategies. People involved in development who are unaware of the shortcomings of these models are likely to waste time and resources in rediscovering their inadequacies before seeking better theory. Each model, with its insights and limitations, is discussed below. Six of these discussions draw heavily on the excellent, more extended discussions by Hayami and Ruttan (1971, pp. 10–43; 1985, pp. 11–72).

The Conservation Model

The conservation model of agricultural development has a long history, beginning at least at the time of the English agricultural revolution of the eighteenth century. The model is based on two assumptions: (1) that land for agricultural production is scarce and becoming more so; and (2) that soil exhaustion is possible, and actions to prevent decreases in yields or to increase land productivity will have only slow effects at best. The conservation model as it developed was supported by the economic theories of the classical English economists Thomas Malthus, David Ricardo, and John Stuart Mill. These theories proposed that, as land scarcity increases, poorer land is used, causing the marginal productivity of labor and of land to decline. To forestall these declines, high priority was attached to maintaining soil productivity at its present level, or in the extreme conservation model, attempting to return the soil to its "original," presumedly more productive, level.

As England and much of Europe in the eighteenth century had largely traditional agricultures with only very slowly increasing yields, agricultural output was then, in fact, largely constrained by land availability. In England, these conditions led to specific measures to conserve or to increase the productivity of the soil, such as the Norfolk crop rotation system, which enabled increased cropping intensity through the addition of root crops in the rotation. In 1840, Justus von Liebig's discovery of the mineral nutrition of plants reinforced attempts to maintain plant nutrient levels in the soil to assure crop productivity. The conservation model was valid for the largely traditional agricultures of Europe in the eighteenth century and is relevant for the traditional agricultures analyzed in chapter 4. It indicates ways that slow increases in land productivity may be obtained.

For most areas of less developed nations today, however, the short-run and long-run implications of the model have different relevance. In the short run, when declines in land productivity can be later reversed by investment, alternative uses of land at different levels of productivity are often economically rational. In the long run, the conservation model retains relevance for some areas of less developed nations, for it warns nations in areas where farming is causing large and irreversible losses of productive land that they may be sacrificing future income if they do not stop the loss of this resource. Contemporary concern is focused by conservationists on three world areas: regions of Africa where large tracts of agricultural land have been lost to erosion and to the encroachment of the Sahara desert; some large irrigated areas, such as in Pakistan, where increasing salinity is destroying agricultural lands; and some areas in Latin America where forest clearing is exposing immense areas of tropical soils to harsh environmental conditions.

The weaknesses of the conservation model as a general guide for agricultural development in low-income nations today can be summarized under four points. First, in the last few decades the scope for increasing the productivity of land has become much greater than was foreseen by the classical economists. In the more developed nations, most of the large increases in agricultural production in the last fifty years have been due to yield increases, with little contribution provided by additional land (see table 6.2). This experience has greatly weakened the relevance of the conservation model for many agricultural areas. In the United States, for example, from 1940 to 1980 the index of total farmland has remained about the same, while agricultural output more than doubled. Other more developed nations, such as Japan and France, have had similar experience. Also, Boserup (1965; 1981) has provided a great deal of evidence that, even in traditional societies, soil productivity in some areas appears to be a dependent variable, responding to the intensity of farming at least within a certain range—rather than the soil's controlling yield. Second, the conservation model usually does not recognize the contribution of industrially produced inputs, such as chemical fertilizer, in greatly increasing agricultural production. Third, the conservation model has failed generally to recognize the past and potential impact of technological change on the demand for land in agriculture. Thus, soil in certain agricultural areas that might be conserved today at great cost may not be needed in the future for agriculture, due to expected technological changes that will greatly increase land productivity in the better farming areas.

And fourth, the greatest weakness of the conservation model is its noneconomic nature. Conservation models generally measure land and productivity only in physical units. Such exclusively technical orientation prevents these models from being used to weigh the net economic benefits of one conservation investment against another. For, as we saw in chapter 4, the use of marginal returns concepts is required to maximize the returns from limited resources. Proponents of conservation models tend to set high priority on certain conservation investments without a serious consideration of alternative uses of these re-

Table 6.2. Large Increases in Agricultural Production with Little Change in Land Farmed: the United States, Japan, and France

Country and Year	Agricultural Land Index	Agricultural Output (1960 = 100)
United States		
1880	46	29
1900	73	46
1920	83	53
1940	94	68
1960	100	100
1980	97	146
Japan		
1880	78	30
1900	86	41
1920	99	61
1940	101	71
1960	100	100
1980	90	146
France		
1880	100	43
1900	101	47
1920	104	54
1940	97	57
1960	100	100
1980	92	167

Source: Data from Hayami and Ruttan 1985 (pp. 467–70).

sources. Hence, economically rational farmers who ignore soil conservation practices are condemned, even when these investments would considerably reduce their incomes. To conclude, wise decisions about conservation activities can be made only when they are placed in an economic framework. Then the rate of return on these investments can be compared by farmers and by society with the returns from alternative uses of these resources. [2]

The Industrial Fundamentalism Model

The overwhelming impact of the industrial revolution on Europe, the United States, Japan, and other nations over the last two centuries, and particularly the success of the Soviet Union in industrializing rapidly after 1917, led to development theories that made industrial development the priority task. Other sectors were viewed as playing peripheral and derivative roles. Early quantitative general economic development models reinforced this industrial emphasis,

2. Useful book-length treatments focusing on scarcity of land resources and conservation issues include Spengler 1961; Held and Clawson 1965; Boserup 1965, 1981; and Barnett and Morse 1963.

seeking to identify how to increase economic growth most rapidly. With the assumptions made in these models, they showed that if investment focused on industrial development, rapid growth could be achieved. Further elaboration of this kind of model for India in the 1950s provided an elegant and mathematically consistent economic development plan for rapid growth of the nation, based on a strategy that gave industry priority. Investments were concentrated on the production of capital goods (machinery, steel, motors), with an effort made to save as much as possible of the profits from these enterprises for reinvestment in more capital goods industries to further accelerate growth. The key to the plan was a high level of savings and investment to prevent resources from escaping into consumption.

With industrial fundamentalism prevailing through the late 1950s, the agricultural sector was assumed to be of little importance in accelerating growth. Mellor (1976, p. 15) concluded that, for India in the 1950s, this assumption may have been valid—for during that period the largely traditional agricultural sector may have provided little opportunity for high-return investments as compared with investments in the industrial sector. Thus he viewed an industrially focused plan as "suitable to an economy presumed to have poor prospects for agricultural and export growth" (p. 2). The portfolio of loans made by the World Bank to less developed nations throughout the 1950s included little for investment in agriculture, providing witness to the prevailing development theory of industrial fundamentalism.

The shortcomings of industrial fundamentalism were highlighted in the early 1960s both by economic theory and by development experience. Jorgenson (1961) and Ranis and Fei (1961) produced rigorous two-sector economic models of growth that demonstrated that a lagging agricultural sector would slow economic growth. In the words of Fei and Ranis (1964) "any underdeveloped economy which attempts to force the pace of industrialization while disregarding the need for a prior—or at least simultaneous—revolution in its agricultural sector will . . . find the going most difficult" (p. 121).[3] Development experience in India and other countries where periods of spurts and poor performance in agriculture greatly slowed national economic growth highlighted the need for more attention to the development of agriculture.

The income distribution implications of industry-first models were also becoming more recognized, for both in theory and in practice, allocating high proportions of investment resources to a small industrial sector usually results in high incomes for the few and slower income growth for those in other sectors, particularly the very large agricultural sector. By the early 1970s, after the demonstration of the very high returns possible from investment in agriculture

---

3. The shortcomings of two-sector, or dual-economy, models for agricultural development policy and strategy are presented by Mellor (1967); and Hayami and Ruttan (1971, pp. 20–25; 1985, pp. 22–33). Dual-sector and other general development models were also examined by Yotopoulos and Nugent (1976, pp. 206–18); and Meier (1976).

shown during the early phases of the green revolution, the importance of balanced sectoral investment programs was recognized.

The Urban-Industrial Impact Model

In the conservation model, the productivity of agriculture is explained largely as a function of soil and the physical environment, augmented to some extent by farming and conservation activities. In the urban-industrial impact model, agricultural productivity is a function of distance from urban and industrial areas. This model drew on the Ricardian theory of rent and Johann Von Thuenen's demonstration that the distance from an urban market influences both the intensity of cultivation and the mix of crops grown. In the Von Thuenen model, the explanatory variable is the cost of transporting agricultural products to the urban market. Therefore, bulky or perishable agricultural products, such as some vegetables and milk, tend to be produced near urban and industrial areas on high-cost land. Less perishable staples, such as wheat and wool, tend to be produced further away on lower cost land, since little product loss occurs even over long time periods and transportation routes (see also Dunn 1954).

In 1953, T. W. Schultz built upon the Von Thuenen model to attempt to explain regional disparities in agricultural growth and development in the United States. The central hypothesis of his theory was that economic organization works best in agricultural areas located favorably in relation to urban industrial complexes (Schultz 1953, p. 147). In evaluating the urban-industrial impact model, Hayami and Ruttan (1971) concluded: ''Schultz presented a rationale for the urban industrial impact hypothesis in terms of more efficient functioning of factor and product markets in areas of rapid urban industrial development than in areas where the urban economy had not made a transition to the industrial stage. . . . Results of . . . studies have generally sustained the validity of Schultz's empirical generalizations with respect to the impact of urban industrial growth on geographic differentials in per capita and per farm worker income'' (p. 35).

Although the validity of this model has generally been sustained, to what extent can it provide a guide for actions to accelerate agricultural development? The conclusion that more rapid agricultural growth is dependent upon urban and industrial growth provides only modest help in identifying investments and other policies to accelerate agricultural production. There are a limited number of urban areas, and governments often have relatively little influence on the location and rate of urban and industrial growth, especially in the short run. However, an important general implication of this model is that a wider dispersal of urban and industrial centers over the land area of a nation would lead to more even and rapid growth in agriculture.

The Diffusion Model

The diffusion model of agricultural development, when applied internationally or domestically, is based upon the hypothesis that appreciable increases in agricultural production may be obtained by devoting considerable resources to (1) increasing the flow of information to farmers about new agricultural technology and new institutional arrangements, such as for credit; and (2) teaching tradition-bound farmers how to make more economically rational management decisions about the use of resources they have access to. Diffusion activities in agriculture have usually been carried out by extension workers, but other communications systems also contribute, such as newspapers and magazines, radio and, in some instances, television. *Diffusion,* as defined in the sociology and communications literature, "is the process by which innovations spread to the members of a social system" (Rogers 1971, p. 12). Diffusion studies focus largely on messages that contain new ideas.

The international model of diffusion is supported by much of world agricultural history, for the dispersion of plant and animal varieties throughout the world has led, from time to time, to large increases in agricultural production (Sauer 1969). After World War II, as aid to less developed nations expanded, the success of extension work in more developed nations led to the assumption that the international diffusion of the highly productive agricultural technologies available in more developed nations would result in rapid rates of agricultural growth in less developed nations. A primary initial focus of U.S. development aid was this kind of "technical assistance," as signaled by the beginning of aid to less developed nations in President Truman's famous Point Four of his Inaugural Address in 1948.

How useful has the diffusion model been in increasing farm production in less developed nations? In the 1950s, many effective, experienced U.S. agricultural extension agents went to these nations to establish and carry out extension work. However, after spending considerable effort and resources in many areas, they achieved relatively little increase in agricultural production. Why? In particular, the location-specific nature of agricultural technology has now become recognized as greatly limiting the diffusion of much agricultural technology from the more developed nations. The location-specific nature of agricultural technology has many dimensions, including (1) highly varied soil, pest, moisture, and other important plant growth variables, (2) the varied cost of capital relative to labor, and (3) the different social and institutionalized rules that affect the profitability of farming activities. Hence, in any area, agriculture usually requires much local adaptation of farming practices. Until the mid-1960s, most of the agricultural research in the world (some 95 percent of it) had been focused on crops in the temperate climate, where relatively large farms prevailed. Thus, relatively little modern agricultural technology had been produced that was profitable on small farms in less developed, tropical nations. In addition, development experts enthusiastic about diffusion did not appreciate the culturally specific nature of many institutional arrangements for agriculture, which had been developed in high-income nations. Thus, the vastly different social and institutional environments of less developed nations have prevented profitable diffusion to these nations of many institutional arrangements, such as landholding laws and credit arrangements.

To conclude, the diffusion model has four general limitations as a model of agricultural development. First, research has demonstrated that traditional farmers have good knowledge of available traditional technology and are efficient allocators of their resources (See chapter 4). Hence, extension efforts devoted to trying to teach these farmers how to improve the allocation of their traditional resources is wasted. Second, there has often been little new agricultural technology available in less developed nations that would be productive if diffused. Third, extension personnel have often not been well trained, and thus they have not been able to successfully transfer to farmers what useful knowledge was available. And fourth, these extension agents have generally lacked detailed personal knowledge of agricultural and social conditions in the areas they were supposed to improve, as they have often been outsiders—government appointees from urban or other parts of the nation.

The limitations of the diffusion model as a guide for agricultural development are highlighted by assuming that this model works. Suppose currently available technology were diffused and applied. Development would then come to a stop until new, more-productive agricultural knowledge was found. The diffusion model does not address the question of the source of more productive agricultural technologies and institutional arrangements. Thus, the model provides little guidance for agricultural development strategies. However, as part of a comprehensive theory of agricultural development, diffusion processes that focus on effective extension and communication to farmers of new, more productive, agricultural information can contribute greatly to accelerating growth (see chapter 11).

The Cultural-Change-First Model and the Community Development Movement

The thesis that significant social and cultural change had to occur before rapid agricultural growth could be achieved was also prevalent in the 1950s and early 1960s. It was advanced by anthropologists, sociologists, and some economists. The poor performance of the diffusion model during the 1950s supported this view.

The cultural-change-first model identifies values and institutions, as well as technology, as the fundamental variables affecting development. In the 1960s, Elder (1968), in reviewing the cultural-change-first model, stated, "it seemed possible to talk about the phenomenon 'traditionalism.' In those days, 'traditionalism' was seen as an interrelated collection of social institutions and cultural beliefs that blocked the path of progress" (p. 40). Elder pointed to Hagen's theses, discussed in the previous chapter, that traditional personalities and behaviors can be barriers to economic growth. He also reminded readers of Myrdal's (1968) belief that many traditional values held by both members of the elite and a majority of the people serve as obstacles to development (p. 73). The well-known sociologist Hoselitz (1960) also suggested that for less developed nations to become more developed, they must change their value orientations and some of their traditional institutions. Reports also appeared, such as those by Nair (1962, pp. 46–51), that provided illustrations of how cultural factors inhibit agricultural growth. For example, she reported that some Indian farmers, because of their values, refused to use available irrigation water on their land.

Strong positions were also taken by Hagen (1962), McClelland (1961), and Hoselitz (1960), who believed that the particularistic and ascriptive value orientations of traditional societies had to become universalistic and achievement oriented before rapid growth could be achieved. Other writers who emphasized the need for ideological changes before much economic growth could occur include Weber (1956) and Karl Marx. Weber believed in the necessity of a progressive ideology, such as the Protestant work ethic. Rostow (1960), in his growth-stage model, supported this thesis, stating: "Something like this group of sociological and psychological changes would now be agreed to be at the heart of the creation of the preconditions for take-off" (p. 26).

The widespread community development movement of the 1950s and 1960s was consistent with the cultural-change-first model. Holdcroft (1984), in reviewing the rise and fall of this movement, outlined the community development process as one in which the people of a community organized themselves for planning and action. He pointed out that community development "was described as rooted in the concept of the worth of the individual as a responsible, participating member of society and, as such, was concerned with human organization and the political process. Its keystones were seen as community organization, community education, and social action (p. 48). Thus, the movement tended to assume that village cultural and institutional change, aided by outsiders, could achieve significant economic and agricultural growth.

Village-level workers were thought able to aid villagers to better organize their resources and to help them change their beliefs, value systems, and social institutions to enable more rapid economic progress. Three underlying assumptions of this movement became apparent: (1) that village resources were not efficiently allocated, (2) that village-level community development workers would be able to significantly change village values and institutions, and (3) that the community development workers knew about and were able to bring to the villages relevant new technology and information, which would increase income. Could an urbanized, educated government worker, with little detailed knowledge of village resources, production activities, and socioeconomic life, succeed in this large task? A more important impediment to the success of this effort was the fact that community development workers were usually civil servants, who were likely to view a desk job in a city office as more appropriate to their education, status, and aspirations, than working daily in a poverty-bound village.

The cultural-change-first model and the community development movement both received crippling blows in the late 1960s from development experience. The most devastating blow was the agricultural growth due to the initial waves of the green revolution, as high-yielding varieties of wheat, corn, and rice were adopted rapidly by traditional people in many areas of less developed nations (see the discussion of the green revolution in chapter 8). In most places no appreciable cultural change was required to enable these very large increases in agricultural production.

By 1968, Elder had concluded,

the dictum that the removal of traditionalism is a necessary condition for economic development needs revision. . . . "Traditional institutions" (such as the joint family, traditional religion, caste, etc.) are not necessarily detrimental to increasing yields per acre. . . . The evidence is also ample that so-called "traditional attitudes" (strong ties to family members, concern over life after death, desire for conspicuous consumption, and expenditure at ritual occasions, etc.) are not necessarily detrimental to increasing yields per acre. (pp. 42 and 51)

After 1960, following a decade of considerable international aid effort in over sixty developing nations, support for community development waned rapidly. "Perhaps the most universal criticism of the community development movement was that its programs were inefficient in reaching their economic goals including food production" (Holdcroft 1984, p. 52). Community development activities were generally not able to alleviate food problems and poverty because of the unavailability of new, more productive agricultural technology for increased income.

Despite three decades of generally poor experience with the cultural-change-first and community development approaches, versions of these programs reappear from time to time. When resources are devoted to these activities in low-income, largely traditional environments, they are likely to divert resources from development activities that can provide much more rapid development.

The Neo-Marxist and Dependency Models

What help does neo-Marxist theory provide for agricultural development strategy? The general socioeconomic theory of Marxist writers was examined in the previous chapter. Here we focus on their economic development theory. As neo-Marxist writers are not in agreement among themselves about development and dependency theory, we have chosen the work of a few of the more influential. Because of the prevalence of Marxist teaching and economic thinking in many less developed nations, it is important that those concerned with development understand both basic Marxist economic terminology and the shortcomings of Marxist development theory. In this section, we have drawn on the review by Todaro (1981, pp. 79–85).

THE MARXIST GROWTH MODEL

The Marxist growth model is quite limited, because it assumes that the means of production, or technology, is the primary determinant of institutional change (Hayami and Ruttan 1985, p. 34). Hence other fundamental relations affecting economic performance (shown in figure 5.1) are largely ignored, such as between resource endowments and technology change and among resource endowments, cultural endowments, and institutional change.

VARIATIONS ON THE DEPENDENCY THESIS

Many neo-Marxists have placed heavy emphasis on dependency theory in the last two decades. This theory views the increasing interdependence of the economies of less developed and more developed nations as causing a drain of resources and income from the less developed periphery to the more developed center. Todaro (1981, p. 79) noted that Baran, Sweezy, and Magdoff held the extreme position that trade was such a drain of "surplus" that economic development in less developed nations was impossible. More recent neo-Marxists, such as Amin (1976), have rejected this view but have emphasized that trade and the associated dominance of more developed nations necessarily causes an "inappropriate" pattern of development in less developed nations. This view leads, for example, to rejection of investment in tourist industries as inappropriate, in spite of very great foreign exchange needs. Some recent neo-Marxists have taken the view that metropolitan centers of the more developed world control all less developed nations, even isolated agricultural workers in all parts of poor nations. Some of these writers also hypothesize that more developed nations are the major cause of low income in less developed societies. Griffin (1978, p. 38) for example, stated that "Europe did not 'discover' the underdeveloped countries; on the contrary, she created them." At the national level, this theory asserts that rural areas are dependent and controlled by the urban areas of a nation. Likewise, all rural peasants are viewed as controlled and dependent on a small minority of rural elite. In contrast to this theory, neoclassical economists point out that increasing economic interdependence and trade has to provide some benefit to all parties on the basis of comparative advantage; otherwise there would be no trade unless goods were extracted by military force or occupation (for the economics of comparative advantage, see chapter 13).

When applied within a nation, dependency theory proposes that local elites are trapped, tending to contribute to the further "exploitation" of the nation by responding to external trade demands and leading to wrong paths of local development. This thesis—that local elites are too impotent to make decisions that will achieve national growth—leads to the conclusion that state control is required to achieve desired development. State control is to be accomplished either through state-operated capitalist enterprises or by controlling loans to local industrialists. The latter approach, ironically for Marxists, supports the development of a class that "exploits" local labor. These writers are unclear about how shifting control of industry to the state would improve its performance. Experience in the last two decades with nationalization of industry in such less developed nations as Ghana, Bangladesh, and Tanzania has generally been associated with poorer industrial performance.

Finally, the logic of dependency theory leads to an emphasis on national self-sufficiency, with reductions in international trade and aid—whether bilateral or from international agencies—as the way to achieve desired economic growth. Although better control over the kinds of trade and aid in which a less developed nation participates may often be needed to achieve national goals, it is a puzzle how reduced aid and foreign investment, which dependency theory proposes, can accelerate growth.

Neo-Marxist dependency theory thus leads to a quandary. If trading relations between high-income nations and low-income nations (the U.S.S.R. and Eastern European nations also?) drain and distort the economies of low-income nations, reduction in trade would be the appropriate policy. Yet much empirical data since World War II has shown that growth in per capita income in less developed nations is associated with increasing trade and foreign investment. This in turn has enabled greater imports of capital equipment and technology. Fairly rapid economic growth with little trade may be possible for some very large nations, as occurred to a considerable extent in the Soviet Union. But as even China discovered in the late 1970s, a withdrawal from the world trading economy and international technology flows slows economic development. For most smaller nations, rapid economic growth with greatly reduced trade would be exceedingly difficult to achieve.

To conclude, neo-Marxist theory of development has a number of internal contradictions, has not been developed into a consistent model, and generally marshals little empirical research to support its theses. For example, Eicher and Baker (1982, p. 37), in reviewing the work of Amin, a currently prominent neo-Marxist, found that although he "has provided valuable insights into the development process . . . his prescriptions for agriculture have been naive and have changed over time." During the 1960s, he favored animal traction and industrial crops, believed traditional values were a serious constraint on development, and held that the transition to privately owned farms was a precondition to socialism. "By the mid-1970s, Amin had reversed himself, recommending the collectivization of agricultural production and abandoning support for animal traction and industrial crops. These shifts reflect, in our view, the weakness of deriving prescriptions for agricultural policy on the basis of global and abstract analyses of the world economy."[4]

4. See Amin 1976, 1977a, 1977b. Critical surveys of Amin's work are provided by S. Smith (1980). Other useful discussions on this topic include de Janvry 1984. Writings on dependency theory include Dos Santos 1970; Wallerstein 1979; T. Smith 1979; and Griffin and Gurley 1985.

Growth-Stage Theories

THE ROSTOW FIVE-STAGE GROWTH MODEL

The history of growth-stage theories of economic development were succinctly reviewed by Hayami and Ruttan (1971, pp. 10–17; 1985, pp. 15–21). The foremost authors of nineteenth century growth-stage literature included Friedrich List and other members of the German historical school and Marx and his followers. These writers proposed varied numbers of stages of economic growth based on different criteria. List used occupational distribution as the basis for his classification of five stages: savage, pastoral, agricultural, agricultural-manufacturing, and agricultural-manufacturing-commercial. Marx identified his stages by employing the type of production technology used, the system of property rights, and the ideology associated with the technology. His stages included primitive communism, ancient slavery, medieval feudalism, industrial capitalism, and socialism. He also proposed that society was composed of two classes: the class controlling the means of production and the class of laborers. He envisioned that the struggle between the two classes would cause economic systems to move through these economic stages. Two ideas contained in Marx's growth-stage model are relevant to current economic growth theory. They are (1) that the mode of production (technology) could influence the form of institutions in society; and (2) that institutional changes, such as those that facilitate larger scale farming, can sometimes lead to greater productivity.

More recent interest in growth-stage theory arose from Rostow's (1960) model based on the concept of leading sectors. With technological change, a certain economic sector forges ahead, causing increased growth in the whole economy. Growth in the leading sector then slows due to saturation of demand and other factors, while another sector moves ahead, further increasing national growth. Rostow saw agriculture as a leading sector in some nations during certain time periods. This point helped highlight the sometimes forgotten role that the agricultural sector often plays in accelerating economic growth.

The five sequential growth stages in Rostow's model are (1) traditional society; (2) the preconditions for take off; (3) the take off; (4) the drive to maturity; and (5) the age of high mass consumption. He believed it useful "to regard the process now going forward in Asia, the Middle East, Africa, and Latin America as analogous to the stages of preconditions and take-off of other societies in the late eighteenth, nineteenth, and twentieth centuries" (p. 139). All societies were expected to follow this linear sequence, which he judged had occurred in more developed nations.

STAGE MODELS OF AGRICULTURAL DEVELOPMENT

A number of agricultural economists elaborated stage models of agricultural development based on Rostow's general model and drew on theory from the dynamic dual-economy models of Jorgenson (1961) and Ranis and Fei (1961). These agricultural stage models were summarized by Wharton (1963, p. 1162) as consisting of essentially three stages—traditional (or static), transi-

Figure 6.1. Stages of Agricultural Development

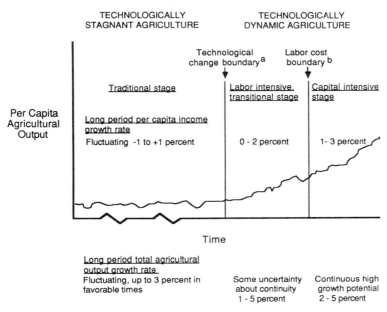

Source: Adapted from Mellor 1966 (pp. 223–43).
[a] This boundary identifies the beginning of a stream of new technology based on the application of modern science to agriculture, through either imports or domestic activity.
[b] The labor cost boundary represents a significant increase in labor costs compared to capital costs.

tional, and dynamic. Mellor's (1966) formulation of the agricultural stage model places emphasis on two boundaries (figure 6.1). The first is a technological-change boundary between the traditional and labor intensive stage, and the second boundary is identified by change in the cost of labor relative to capital.

The five characteristics of the labor intensive stage in Mellor's model accurately represent traditional agriculture. They are that (1) the agricultural sector remains a very large proportion of the economy; (2) the demand for agricultural products rises rapidly due to both population growth and per capita income growth (as shown in chapter 3); (3) capital is generally scarce and costly relative to labor; (4) average land area per farm is likely to decline due to increasing rural population densities; and (5) labor-saving agricultural machinery often cannot be used, because the value of the labor it saves is less than the additional cost of the machinery (Mellor 1966, p. 225). In the transitional stage, increases in agricultural output and productivity are seen as depending upon technological and institutional changes, which gradually gather momentum. And, because of the relative shortage of land, the emphasis is on increasing yields per unit of land and livestock.

The capital intensive stage of the model, in contrast, points to a fundamental economic change. Nonfarm sectors become larger and draw increasing quantities of labor out of agriculture, and hence agricultural labor becomes more costly relative to capital. Then, more labor-saving machinery is profitably used in agriculture. At some point in the capital intensive stage, the amount of farmland per agricultural laborer stops declining, and average farm size begins to increase.

This agricultural stage model assumes that less developed nations will pass in sequence from the traditional stage into a labor intensive transitional stage before the cost of labor rises appreciably relative to capital. Although this is the experience of many less developed nations, a few resource-rich less developed nations, such as Saudi Arabia, have experienced a very rapid rise in wages early in their agricultural development. In these cases, the transitional stage of low cost labor is hardly present.

Criticisms of stage theories of economic and agricultural development have been strong. They point out that they simply provide historical descriptions with little analytic power or value for policy guidance. Specifically, Ruttan (1965) judged that the technological alternatives becoming available to developing nations are likely to negate much of what has been learned about agricultural development from history. While recognizing the general validity of these criticisms, we believe the Mellor stage model of agricultural development aids in our understanding of two central agricultural development issues by focusing on the two fundamental variables: technological change and the price of labor relative to capital.

The Schultz High-Payoff Input Model

After observing years of poor results from attempts to transfer the highly productive agricultural technology of advanced nations to poor nations based on the diffusion model, T. W. Schultz (1964b) pointed out:

There are very few reproducible agricultural factors in technically advanced countries that are ready-made for most poor communities.

In general, what is available is a body of useful knowledge which has made it possible for the advanced countries to produce, for their own use, factors that are technologically superior to those employed elsewhere. This body of knowledge can be used to develop similar, and as a rule superior, new factors appropriate to the biological and other conditions that are specific to the agriculture of poor communities. (p. 147)

In the second half of this work, Schultz focused on the two central questions: (1) how to create and provide to farmers the new, higher-payoff technology embodied in capital equipment and other inputs; and (2) how to increase the productivity of labor.

Figure 6.2. Effect of More Productive Technology on Agricultural Output and Costs of Inputs

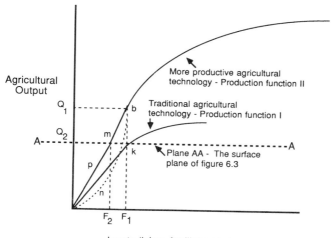

Inputs (labor, fertilizer, etc.)

INVESTMENTS IN AGRICULTURAL TECHNOLOGY DEVELOPMENT

With respect to investments in agricultural technology, Schultz (1964b) stated that "economic growth from the agricultural sector of a poor country depends predominantly upon the availability and price of modern (nontraditional) agricultural factors. The suppliers of these factors in a very real sense hold the key to such growth. When they succeed in producing and distributing these factors cheaply, investment in agriculture becomes profitable. . . . But the suppliers have received little attention" (p. 145). In viewing the technological progress of agriculture in more developed nations, he saw clearly that agricultural experiment stations and businesses that provided higher-productivity capital equipment and other inputs to farmers were the source of the new high-payoff, or high-return, inputs for agriculture.

The economics of the high-payoff input model are illustrated with single-variable production functions (see figure 6.2). On the traditional technology production function (*I*), output is increased by using more of the variable input, say, fertilizer. If resources had been invested successfully in creating a more productive agricultural technology (technology production function *II*), such as higher yielding seeds, greater output would be obtained at *b* with the same fertilizer input, F_1, for technology *II* is more profitable at most levels of fertilizer use. If a large number of farmers shifted to technology *II* by buying the more productive inputs, such as high-yielding seeds, the cost of the investment in the research to create technology *II* would probably be repaid many times over. Farmers would benefit from the new technology by increasing their total output, productivity, and income, which in turn would increase agricultural growth.

Two additional important points are shown in figure 6.2. First, note that the same output level achieved with technology I with fertilizer use F_1 could be obtained with technology II at m with much less fertilizer, F_2. In the next section, as the induced innovation model is presented, we focus on this fact—that the adoption of more productive technologies enables movement from point k to point m, where fewer resources are needed to achieve the same output. The second important point shown in figure 6.2 is that at the low end of the technology II production function, an alternative dotted line n is shown to indicate that, at low levels of input use, new agricultural technologies may or may not be more productive than traditional technologies. Thus, at low levels of fertilizer use, if technology II followed line n, this new technology would be less productive, and hence it would be more profitable for farmers to continue to use the traditional technology I.

INVESTMENTS IN HUMAN CAPACITY

In addressing investment in farm people (increasing the quality of labor) to increase agricultural productivity, Schultz (1964b, p. 175) said, "the next proposition has radical social and economic implications. It consists of two theses, namely, that the acquired capabilities of farm people are of primary importance in modernizing agriculture and that these capabilities, like capital goods, are produced means of production. . . . They are, in essence, an investment in human capital." He thus hypothesized that the right sort of education for farmers could provide high returns in increased income to farmers and the rest of society.

With the two hypotheses that high returns to investment in farming could be obtained by producing more productive technology and more productive farm people, Schultz provided the fundamental elements for a microeconomic theory that explains both the stability of agricultural production in traditional agricultural areas (presented in chapter 4) and how more rapid agricultural growth may be achieved. However, his high-payoff input model was largely limited to the microlevel. So, for example, it treats investment in experiment station capacity as exogenous, or outside the model. Also, the high-payoff input model did not attempt to explain how the variable economic environments of less developed nations would lead to the adoption of different agricultural technologies and institutions.

The Induced Innovation Model of Agricultural Development

The theories of development examined so far have contributed to an understanding of agricultural development, but each provides limited knowledge of how agricultural production can be accelerated. In 1971, Hayami and Ruttan proposed a theory of induced technological and institutional innovation in agriculture that provides a significant advance in economic understanding of how agricultural development is achieved. It incorporated the concepts of the Schultz high-payoff input model. [5]

The Four Elements of the Induced Innovation Model

Hayami and Ruttan (1985) proposed that a complete model of development includes four elements: resource endowments, cultural endowments, technology, and institutions (see figure 5.1). The four elements interact with one another, as indicated in the figure by the connecting lines. Hence, changes (or differences) in the levels of variables of any of the elements could induce changes, or account for differences, in the levels of the other variables in the other elements due to changed supply or demand conditions. Thus, for example, different resource endowments will influence the kinds of technologies and institutions used in an economy. Note also that technological change is seen as causing changes in resource endowments, institutions, and cultural variables. Likewise, institutional innovation can lead to technological change, change in resource availability, or change in cultural endowments.

With the addition of cultural endowments in the 1985 version of the model, the theory became a much more general socioeconomic change model, for cultural endowments were recognized to "both constrain and direct a nation's capacity for institutional and technical innovation" (Hayami and Ruttan 1985, p. 114). Thus values related to the pursuit of knowledge and science will influence resource allocation to, and the success of, science. When trade-offs between growth and equity or human disruption arise, social choices will also be influenced by the values held by a society.

We have explored resource endowments for agricultural development in chapter 2 and will do so more intensively in the next chapter, concerned with land and labor. Chapter 5 included an examination of the effect of values on economic decisions. We turn here to the remaining two elements of the model, technology and institutions, and how they are changed. The mathematically sophisticated dual sector growth models developed in the 1960s paid little attention to technological and institutional change and improvements in the quality of labor—or to how these were to be achieved. "With few exceptions, technical change was treated as exogenous to the economic system, and institutional change was not dealt with at all in formal growth theory" (Binswanger and Ruttan 1978, p. 2).

5. Major works on agricultural development that contain somewhat differing theories of agricultural development include the following: Mellor 1966, 1967, 1976; Arnon 1981; Harwood 1979; Clark and Haswell 1964; Griffin 1974a; T. W. Schultz 1978; Weitz 1971; Beckford 1972; Johnston and Kilby 1975; Wortman and Cummings 1978; and Ghatak and Ingersent 1984. See also chapters in Eicher and Staatz 1984.

Figure 6.3. Induced Technological Change and Labor-Using and Labor-Saving Technological Change, Shown with Isoquants

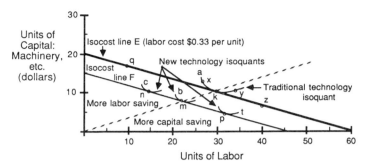

The Central Concepts of Induced Technological Innovation

Hayami and Ruttan (1985) pointed out that, since John R. Hicks' *Theory of Wages* was published in 1932, economists have generally accepted the view that changes, or differences in the relative prices of inputs, could affect the direction of technological change. The theory of induced technical change attempts to go further in "an effort to interpret the process of technical change as endogenous to the economic system. In this view technical change represents a dynamic response to changes in resource endowments and to growth in demand" (Hayami and Ruttan 1985, p. 84). We now examine the operation of the mechanism that induces technological change.

THE INDUCEMENT MECHANISM

The responsiveness of technological change to factor prices can be demonstrated by using an isoquant graph. Figure 6.3 shows a slice of a three-dimensional, two-input, one-product production surface when viewed from the top. This figure is in plane *AA* in figure 6.2. A production surface also enables demonstration of the extent to which a new technology is labor saving or capital saving. An isoquant is a line that indicates an equal quantity, output, or yield. In this figure, for example, the curved isoquant *a* shows the different amounts of labor and capital a traditional agricultural technology requires to produce the same level of output. Thus, points *x*, *k*, and *y* indicate the same level of output because they are on isoquant *a*. The equilibrium, or highest profit point, when this technology is employed is at point *k*, because it is on the lowest possible isocost line, given the ratio of the cost of labor relative to the cost of capital assumed in this example. An isocost line, such as *E*, simply indicates the location of all points that would have the same input cost. In this case, isocost line *E* represents a total input, or total resource cost, of $20, as indicated on the capital axis, if no labor were needed for production. Note that, on the labor axis, if no capital were required, sixty units of labor could be used at the same cost. Hence, the wage, or cost, of labor represented by isocost line *E* is $20 divided by sixty units of labor, or $0.33 per unit of labor. The cost of producing at any points *z*, *k*, or *q* on isocost line *E* is the same. This can be checked by adding the cost of labor and capital at any point. For example, the cost of production at *k* is

30 units of labor × $0.33 = $10.00 + $10.00 of capital, or $20.

And at *q*, the cost is $3.33 labor and $16.67 capital, or $20. Finally, note that the slope of the line indicates the ratio of the cost of labor relative to capital. So, for example, if labor became more expensive than $0.33 per unit, fewer than sixty units of labor could be obtained for $20.

Now suppose an improved technology is developed that provides the same level of output as the traditional technology but requires fewer resources. How can this be represented in figure 6.3? The new technology can be indicated by an isoquant such as *b*. It represents the same level of output as isoquant *a*, but it is located on a lower isocost line *F*, giving an equilibrium, or high-profit, point of *m* for this technology. The new isocost line *F* has been drawn parallel to the old isocost line *E* to indicate that the same relative price of labor to capital has been assumed as on line *E*. New technology *b* at equilibrium point *m* uses a combination of 22.7 units of labor at $0.33 per unit equals $7.50. This amount plus $7.50 of capital gives a total cost of $15, to produce the same output as with the traditional technology, which required $20 of input cost. Note that new technology *b* has the same ratio of the amount of labor to capital used in production as the traditional technology. Therefore, technology *b* is neither labor saving nor capital saving. It is factor neutral, saving both capital and labor because it requires proportionately less of each input to produce the same output as the traditional technology.

If, however, a new technology with the same level of output, such as that indicated by isoquant *c*, were used, it would be labor saving, for the amount of labor used would decrease proportionately more than the amount of capital when compared with traditional technology *a*. The opposite case of labor-using, capital-saving technology is represented by isoquant *t*, in which proportionately more capital is saved than labor. Observe that the equilibrium points *n*, *m*, and *p* of the three new technologies *c*, *b*, and *t* are on the same isocost line *F*. Therefore, each would use the same number of total inputs. In these circumstances, farmers would be indifferent as to which of the three technologies they used; all three would be equally profitable. We can now see why entrepreneurs and inventors are "induced" to develop new technologies, such as the three indicated in this figure. Farmers would buy these new more profitable technologies, if they were available, to reduce production costs.

Pay attention also to the income distribution implications of the different new technologies. All three would increase farm income by the same amount compared with the traditional technology *a*. However, if there were many unemployed agricultural laborers, use of labor intensive technology, *t*, would be likely to lead to a less skewed distribution of income than the more capital intensive technology, *c*, which would be likely to increase unemployment.

RELATIVE FACTOR COSTS AND TECHNOLOGY DEVELOPMENT

A fundamental question for a theory of agricultural development is, What economic mechanism induces agricultural experiment stations or private firms to develop the different types of more productive mechanical and biological technologies for agriculture in different nations and agricultural regions? Developers of agricultural technology seek to produce new technology that will provide a high return to farmers, for such technology would be in great demand. When large quantities of the new technology can be sold, research and development costs can often be recouped, and sometimes a large net income may be made.

The economic mechanism that induces different technologies to be developed in different economic environments can be more easily understood with the use of an innovation possibility isoquant (see figure 6.4). This isoquant indicates a range of possible technologies that use different combinations of capital and labor to obtain a given level of output. It assumes that specified amounts of resources devoted to agricultural research and development could lead to technologies tangent to it. Thus new technologies r, s, d, and t might be obtained for a less developed nation through local research or through technology imported from abroad. With the given local price ratio of the cost of capital to labor, as indicated by isocost lines E and F, technologies d and t would be adopted by farmers on the lower isocost, line F. Technologies r and s would not be popular, as they require more capital and labor than technologies d and t to obtain the same output, and hence would be less profitable.

Note particularly that the cost of using the most capital intensive technology, r, that might have been obtained from a more developed nation, would be greater than traditional technology a in this economic environment. Although technology r requires the least amount of labor, it requires so much capital that total resource costs for its use in this location would be high. Hence, if technology r were the only new one available, farmers would obtain higher income by continuing to use the traditional technology. How often have international and domestic development officials tried to convince low-income farmers to adopt cost-increasing capital intensive technologies such as represented by r? In some less developed nations today, large four-wheeled tractors represent such a farm-income-decreasing technology.

Also note that figure 6.4 shows that persons producing or importing agricultural technology have an incentive to focus their activities on that part of the innovation possibility curve closest to the tangent point with the isocost line F, such as technologies d and t. These technologies will be most profitable. Finally, it should be recognized that the shape of the innovation possibility curve can be very variable for the investment of a given amount of research and development resources, depending both upon the position of currently used technology and the ease with which knowledge of the relevant sciences can be incorporated in needed agricultural technologies during any particular time period.

Figure 6.4. The Relative Prices of Capital and Labor and Types of Technology Developed and Adopted

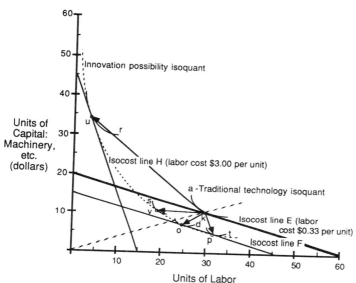

THE VARIED PATHS OF PRODUCTIVITY CHANGE IN AGRICULTURE

Now consider how different paths of technology development might be followed, as innovators respond to different economic environments. As the relative prices, or costs, of resources such as labor and capital vary greatly among nations, and different regions of a nation, they will induce a variety of agricultural technologies to be produced and adopted. In figure 6.4, a number of new technologies are shown, and two economic environments are illustrated by different ratios of the cost of capital to the cost of labor by isocost lines *H* and *F*. Isocost line *H* shows a relatively high cost of labor compared to capital, as in high-labor-cost nations such as the United States and some oil-exporting nations. In this illustration, wages are three dollars per unit of labor, or nine times the wage rate indicated by isocost lines *E* and *F*, which represent the much lower cost of labor relative to capital, as found in many less developed nations. With the high-cost labor represented by isocost line *H*, new technologies such as *r* or *s* would be induced, for in this economic environment the more labor intensive technologies represented by *d* and *t* would be less profitable, requiring more labor and capital to produce the same output. Hence with the theory of induced innovation, we can understand why a great variety of technologies have been developed in different parts of the world.

In order to test whether the different paths of productivity change, predicted by the induced development model, have been followed, Hayami and Ruttan studied changes in resource costs and changes in land and labor productivity in a large number of countries. For the 1880–1960 period, the different resource endowments of nations resulted in varied changes in the relative cost of land, labor, fertilizer, and machinery. Many nations, such as Japan, have had relatively inelastic supplies of land. In the case of Japan, the land to labor cost ratio increased from 1,559 in 1880 to 3,216 in 1960 (see table 6.3). Land in the United States, in contrast, has been more plentiful, and the supply of labor has been less elastic, leading to a decrease in the ratio of land to labor cost over this time period—from 181 to 107. Under these conditions, the induced innovation model predicts that agricultural research in Japan would have focused on technologies that would increase land productivity, while U.S. agricultural research would have attempted to increase labor productivity.

These changes in agricultural technology did occur. Estimates of land productivity in Japan in 1880 indicate an equivalent of 3.3 wheat units (tons) of agricultural output was produced on each hectare, while in the United States at the time, only about 0.5 wheat units were produced per hectare (Hayami and Ruttan 1985, pp. 467–68). Thus, agricultural land productivity in Japan was more than six times greater than in the United States. Labor productivity was quite different. In Japan in 1880, annual agricultural output per male agricultural laborer was estimated at 2.3 wheat units, while in the United States it was estimated at 13 wheat units, more than five times as great. By 1950, in Japan, because of the relatively high cost of agricultural land, land productivity had almost doubled to 5.9 wheat units per hectare, while in the United States, due to the relative decline in the cost of land to labor, land productivity increased by only 20 percent, to 0.6 wheat units per hectare. Agricultural labor productivity in Japan over the same period increased more than twice, to 5.5 wheat units, while in the United States, with a rapid increase in labor costs relative to capital, labor productivity increased more than threefold, to 46.5 wheat units per male worker.

Similar estimates for the 1960 to 1980 period of the varied labor and land productivity growth in the agriculture of selected nations are shown in figure 6.5. These data, calculated on a slightly different basis than the figures given above, support the thesis that the elasticity of supply of different agricultural inputs and their various relative prices in different nations greatly influence the technology paths followed in increasing productivity in agriculture.

THE LONG-RUN PATH OF INDUCED TECHNOLOGY DEVELOPMENT

Induced technology development may be summarized by focusing on the path such development can be expected to take in developing nations over the long run (see figure 6.6). During early decades of development in many nations, the cost of labor relative to capital remains low. This economic environment induces the development and use of a series of new, more productive, relatively labor intensive technologies in agriculture (isoquants *a*, *b*, and *c*). As development proceeds, the cost of labor relative to capital increases the slope of the

Table 6.3. Changes in Relative Costs of Labor, Land, Fertilizer, and Machinery: Japan and the United States, 1880–1960

Item	Japan (in yen)			United States (in dollars)		
	1880	1920	1960	1880	1925	1960
Cost						
Labor (farm wage per day)	0.22	1.39	440.00	0.90	2.35	6.60
Land (per hectare)	343.00	3,882.00	1,415,000.00	163.00	269.00	711.00
Fertilizer (per ton)	402.00	850.00	82,100.00	212.00	240.00	168.00
Machinery	66.00	160.00	37,000.00	146.00	152.00	356.00
Ratios						
Land price to labor cots (hundreds)	1,559.00	2,793.00	3,216.000	181.00	114.00	107.00
Fertilizer price to land price	1.17	0.22	0.002	1.30	0.89	0.24
Machine price to labor cost	300.00	115.00	84.000	162.00	65.00	54.00

Source: Hayami and Ruttan 1971 (table C-2). Reprinted with permission.

Figure 6.5. Agricultural Labor and Land Productivities and Paths of Technological Change, Selected Nations, 1960–1980

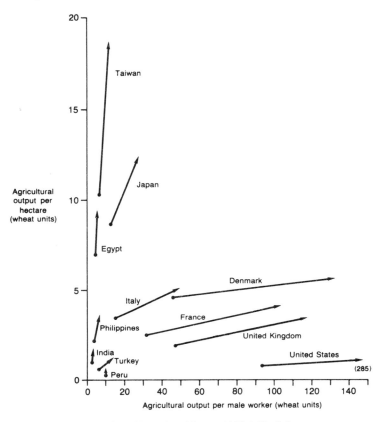

Source: Based on data from Hayami and Ruttan 1985 (table 5.1).

isocost curves, and gradually a series of more profitable technologies (*d* through *g*) will be developed, which are more and more capital intensive.

ENDOGENOUS AND EXOGENOUS TECHNOLOGY DEVELOPMENT

A final, very important point about the model of induced technological innovation is that Hayami and Ruttan (1985, p. 89) do not propose that all technological change in agriculture is endogenously caused by economic factors. Other causes, such as the general progress of basic science and technology, unrelated to a particular sector's factor prices, often appear. Clear examples of technological development exogenous to agricultural needs include the invention of the internal combustion engine and of microchips for computers. Although not induced by farmers' technological needs, these technologies have contributed and

Figure 6.6. Long-Run Path of Induced Technological Development: From Labor Intensive to Capital Intensive Technology

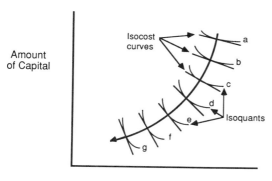

Amount of Capital

Quantity of Labor

Note: Isoquants move toward the origin, and the slopes of the isocost curves increase as labor becomes more costly relative to capital.

will contribute greatly to the development of much more productive farming technology.

Induced Institutional Innovation

The induced development model also hypothesizes that economic opportunities cause changes in institutions in the same way they induce changes in technologies. This enables institutional change to be incorporated as an endogenous part of an economic model of growth. As in the case of technological change, multiple paths of institutional change are expected, influenced by resource endowments, available technologies, and cultural endowments. Just as in the creation of new technologies, institutional change is understood to require resources and, hence, is viewed as an investment process. As agricultural development occurs, new and changed economic functions have to be carried out. New and modified organizations and institutional arrangements are therefore required. If we can identify the new functions that need to be performed as economic and social change occurs, we should be able to identify the organizational and institutional requirements. If there are no new economic functions to be performed, no economic organization or institution is likely to arise, succeed, or be needed.

Economic theory has usually excluded considerations of institutional change by assuming institutional arrangements as given. In some theories, institutional change has been treated as an exogenous variable, with little or no explanation of its causes. In their review of development theory, Hayami and Rut-tan (1985, p. 95ff.) found that institutional change had been treated very differently by historians and other social scientists. Hypotheses ranged from one position, held by Marxists, that institutional change is dependent upon technological change, to another extreme, that institutional change determines technological change.

THE DEMAND FOR INSTITUTIONAL INNOVATION

Two important sources of the demand for institutional change are technological change and shifts in relative resource availability.

Resource Availability and Institutional Innovation. Much historical information and some recent empirical research supports the thesis that, in many cases, institutional change is caused by changes in resource availability, generally indicated by changes in relative factor prices. In many nations, as agricultural population density has increased, institutional arrangements for the use and ownership of agricultural land have changed. There are many examples in less developed nations of agricultural groups with low population densities and shifting cultivation. Use rights to land prevailed without rental payment as long as the plot was cultivated. As population densities increased, permanent rights to land were established, with transfer of these rights to heirs. In the history of Western Europe, Douglas North and Robert Thomas viewed the cause of economic growth between 900 and 1700 as being due largely to changes in the rules that governed property rights. These changes, in turn, were caused by growing population pressure on increasingly scarce agricultural resources (see Ruttan, in Binswanger and Ruttan 1978, p. 334).

Another example of the effect of the relative availability of resources on social institutions was the shift between 1850 and 1950 in Thailand from property rights in people to property rights in land (Feeny 1982). In the 1850s slavery was prevalent in Thailand; there was a high land to person ratio, and hence labor was scarce (costly) relative to land. Gradually, from 1868 to 1915, slavery was abolished, as was a labor tax. Property rights in land in the 1850s in Thailand were not well defined. Gradually, titles to the rice lands of the central plain were made clearer, and in 1901 cadastral surveys and central land records were established. Feeny's thesis is that, as population increased, land prices increased relative to the value of labor. This made it easier to abolish slavery and also caused farmers to seek secure rights to agricultural land. These large changes in human and land property rights are viewed as induced by significant changes in the value of land relative to the value of labor.

Technological Change and Institutional Innovation. The demand for change in institutional arrangements caused by technological change has been seen often during the last twenty years. The introduction of high-yielding crop varieties has caused changes in the institutional arrangements for paying laborers and for determining land rent. In some cases, as more productive technology has become available, the initiatives for institutional change have come from governments in the form of land reform or other rule changes in an attempt to increase the income of cultivators and to reduce the rent obtained by landlords.

In other cases, the initiative has come from landowners seeking to reduce the wages that would have had to be paid under the prevailing institutional arrangements. An example of landlord actions to change harvest laborers' wage payment arrangements was documented in the Philippines by Hayami and Kikuchi (1982, pp 99–123). Over the twenty years ending in 1976, farm labor payment arrangements shifted as a result of technological changes that increased rice yields. In 1956, laborers who participated in the rice harvest received one-sixth of the rice harvested. As yields went up, this payment rule caused harvest laborers to receive considerably higher income, in spite of the fact that rural wages generally remained stationary. Farmers therefore sought to adjust payment downward so that the wage received by harvest laborers would more nearly approximate the local market rate for agricultural laborers. This was done by employing a different, locally recognized, wage payment arrangement, under which harvest laborers were required to weed also, without receiving additional wages. Estimates of the wage received under the latter arrangement resulted in pay about equal to the local market wage rate for agricultural laborers.

Another case of institutional change showed a shift in land-leasing arrangements associated with a dramatic rise in rice production per hectare, from 2,529 kilograms to 6,714 kilograms in the Philippines (Hayami and Kikuchi 1982). This yield increase was due to two technological innovations—installation of a gravity flow irrigation system and the introduction of high-yielding rice varieties. These technological changes led villagers to make considerable changes in landholding arrangements under land reform legislation, which gave tenants the right to initiate a shift from shares to fixed rents. Tenants acted on this opportunity, causing total village land farmed under share tenure arrangements to decline from 70 percent in 1966 to 30 percent by the mid-1970s. Second, tenants greatly increased the number of illegal subtenancy arrangements, which called for a fifty-fifty sharing of costs and output.

A different kind of example shows how a new technological opportunity induced institutional innovation in nineteenth-century Michigan agriculture. A law (institutional change) enacted by the Michigan legislature enabled accelerated increases in land productivity.

In 19th-century Michigan and other Great Lake states there was a great deal of poorly drained but otherwise productive land. At an early date we developed drainage technology. Research on the sources of growth might suggest that high returns would accrue to capital investments in education so that farmers would know of the great productive possibilities of drainage. But, do we have to wait until most of the populace are aware of these possibilities so that they will join together to construct drainage ditches in common? A rule change was developed in Michigan which speeded this development. Usually there were a few landowners who saw the opportunities in drainage. The law allowed a small percentage of landowners to initiate a petition to create a public drainage district. The proposed drainage was then investigated by a publicly elected commissioner and engineering experts. After a public hearing, the drain was constructed, if feasible, and the costs assessed to the benefitted parties. (Schmid 1965, p. 277)

In this case, an institutional change in the form of a new law was enacted by a state legislature to enable more rapid adoption of a technology to increase farm income. Since the productivity of new agricultural technology may depend upon new institutional arrangements, technological change is likely to induce institutional change. If institutions cannot be changed, agricultural growth will be slowed.

THE SOURCES OF SUPPLY OF INSTITUTIONAL INNOVATION

There is . . . a close analogy between the supply of institutional change and the supply of technical change. Just as the supply curve for technical change shifts to the right as a result of advances in knowledge in science and technology, the supply curve for institutional change shifts to the right as a result of advances in knowledge in the social sciences and related professions (law, administration, social service, and planning). . . . Advances in knowledge in the social sciences and professions should result in a reduction in the cost of institutional change just as advances in knowledge in the natural sciences and in engineering have reduced the cost of technical change.

For example, research leading to quantification of commodity supply and demand relationships can be expected to contribute toward more efficient functioning of supply management, food procurement, and food distribution programs. Research on the social and psychological factors affecting the diffusion of new technology is expected to lead to more effective performance by agricultural credit and extension services, or to more effective organization and implementation of commodity production campaigns.

This is not to argue that institutional change is entirely, or even primarily, dependent on formal research leading to new knowledge in the social sciences and professions. . . . institutional change may occur as a result of the exercise of innovative effort by politicians, bureaucrats, entrepreneurs, and others. . . . If we were satisfied with the slow pace of technical and institutional change which characterizes most of trial and error, there would be no need to institutionalize research capacity in either the natural or the social sciences. (Ruttan 1981, pp. 244–45)

A current example of a technological change that is increasing demand for social science research and new institutional arrangements is the growing flood of available information due to the communications and computer revolutions. These technological changes have opened up a wide array of new opportunities. They are likely to induce increased supplies of economic and other social science research that will enable more rapid and effective use and delivery to decision makers of a much greater array of information. These far-reaching technological changes will engender expansion of the supply of social science knowledge, leading to considerable institutional change.

Induced Innovation in the Public Sector

In the preceding presentation of the induced technological and institutional development model, primary emphasis has been placed either on private sector actors seeking changes in response to economic opportunities, or on individuals influencing government to change technology and institutional arrangements to facilitate more rapid growth. In this section the focus is on public sector actors.

In less developed nations, the public sector undertakes varying amounts of economic activity, with some socialist economies incorporating high proportions of national economic activity within the public sector. Is the induced development model applicable to public sector economic decisions? Does it provide policy guidance for public sector development in agriculture? Hayami and Ruttan (1985, p. 87) found no economic theory of induced innovation for the public sector, although they did find a growing literature on public research policy. This literature cites three reasons for public sector research: (1) when the public interest is believed to transcend private incentives, such as in health and aviation; (2) when in some sectors of the economy individual firms are too small to carry out research and development and hence are not able to produce or capture the benefits from research, such as in agriculture and housing; and (3) when support for needed basic research and science education is not being provided by the private sectors (Nelson, Peck, and Kalachek 1967, pp. 151–211).

What is the mechanism that induces technological innovation in the public sector? "We hypothesize that technical change is guided along an efficient path by price signals in the market, provided that the prices efficiently reflect changes in the demand and supply of products and factors and that there exists effective interaction among farmers, public research institutions, and private agricultural supply firms" (Hayami and Ruttan 1985, p. 88). Hayami and Ruttan propose that two conditions will increase the effectiveness of the interaction among farmers, scientists, and administrators: (1) effective local and regional farm organizations; and (2) a public agricultural research system that is decentralized. The responsiveness of scientists and research administrators to changing relative prices of agricultural inputs and the technological needs of farmers in the different regions of a nation is a critical link in the inducement of productive agricultural research in the public sector. The recent elaboration of farming systems research (see chapter 11) has had as one of its objectives increasing the effectiveness of links between farmers' technology needs and agricultural researchers.

Public sector institutional innovation is usefully explored by examining the demand for, and supply of, institutional change. Two important examples of the demand for public institutional innovation are the demand for changes in property rights and for changes in marketing institutions. In chapters 10 and 12, institutional innovations related to land and marketing are explored.

The costs of supplying institutional innovation have not been examined much by economists and other social scientists. Much public institutional innovation is carried out in government and political arenas. Major public institutional changes, such as land reforms, require the mobilization of large amounts of political resources. The supply of an institutional innovation will depend upon the judgment of politicians or government officials about whether the expected return from an institutional innovation will exceed the political and other costs of mobilizing the necessary resources to achieve the change.

The supply of institutional innovations in both the private and public sectors can be increased through social science research. "Advances in social sciences that improve knowledge relevant to the design of institutional innovations that are capable of generating new income streams or that reduce the cost of conflict resolution act to shift the supply of institutional change to the right'' (Hayami and Ruttan 1985, p. 109–10). In the past, institutional change has been achieved mostly through trial and error, as was the case earlier with technological change. Currently, the growth of research in the social sciences enables institutional innovation to be achieved at less cost, for social scientists can use their skills and knowledge to develop, analyze, and estimate the benefits and costs of alternative institutional arrangements before they are proposed or implemented. In our view, a major task of social science research is to go beyond attempts to understand the historical origins of social institutions and to contribute to the design of more effective social institutions to serve contemporary needs. Through this investment process, at least some institutional changes that would have reduced growth would be prevented from being implemented and futilely absorbing large amounts of public resources. Specific investments to increase the supply of agricultural and institutional research are addressed in chapter 11.[6]

The historical record in more developed nations shows that much of the increase in agricultural productivity has been due to public sector research and development. Useful agricultural development models, therefore, must include an explanation of the role of the public sector in finding ways around constraints imposed by inelastic supplies of certain inputs.

We also recognize that socially undesirable institutional innovations are often carried out by political entrepreneurs and authoritarians of the right and the left who succeed in gaining control of police and military power. These leaders often undertake a whole range of institutional changes to increase their control and power to benefit them, their party, or their families. Common economic tactics include the use of licenses, quotas, rationing, and price controls that provide monopoly profits for the group in power. Institutional changes used in this way usually reduce national economic performance, lower national income, and thus waste scarce national resources.

Criticisms and Conclusions About the Induced Innovation Model

CRITICISMS

The three strongest criticisms of the induced innovation model have focused on (1) the institutional rigidities in less developed nations that have maintained price distortions; (2) the lack of emphasis on ''improved'' distributional outcomes with growth; and (3) the implication that the ''invisible hand'' of prices will automatically lead to efficient growth paths.

The institutional rigidity criticism was made early by Beckford (1984). He hypothesized ''that the economic and social situation of underdeveloped countries today is significantly different from those that obtained for present-day ad-

6. A more extended discussion on induced institutional innovation in the public sector is found in Hayami and Ruttan 1985 (pp. 87–90 and 97–110).

vanced countries in the nineteenth century. The social order that existed in the latter countries was of a kind that permitted the emergence of economic institutions and behavioral patterns that fit the neo-classical marginalist framework of economic analysis'' (p. 150). Less developed countries ''are for the most part characterized by imperfect market conditions and social institutional arrangements that create artificial rigidities in the flow of factor supplies and inflexibilities in the patterns of resource use'' (Beckford 1972, p. 334). This echoed Myrdal's (1968) earlier views of greater institutional and cultural rigidity in South Asia compared to Europe. The rigidities in less developed nations often support highly uneven income distributions and fragmented labor markets, with continuing socially undesirable consequences (see also de Janvry 1978, chap. 11).

The reality of institutional rigidity in less developed nations does not, however, negate the usefulness of the induced development model, for the inducement mechanism does not depend upon the speed of response or the presence of undistorted prices. In fact, when price distortions are present, the model aids in illuminating the less productive development path that the constrained prices induce the economy to follow. Through research on the magnitude of the effects of institutional constraints that distort prices and slow economic growth, the costs of current institutional arrangements can be evaluated, and the size of the possible net benefits of institutional changes can be investigated. In this way, pressure for change can be increased.

The criticism that the induced development model provides little direct guidance about income distribution outcomes is valid. This void is present in most economic development theories. Beckford (1972) proposed that, to be complete, ''any model of induced institutional reform must explain how the existing institutional arrangements affect different groups in the society, how change will affect these groups, and the balance of power between these groups. This calls for a political, social, and psychological analysis'' (p. 152). Some of the known effects of agricultural development on income distribution are explored in the next section.

The criticism that suggests that the invisible hand of price incentives does not lead to the most desired growth paths misses the central point of the model. All socioeconomic systems have resource constraints and institutional rules that limit possible growth paths due to the way their particular price or other resource allocation systems operate. The reality of persistent institutional rigidities and possibly large price distortions does not change the incentives provided by high economic returns. The invisible hand operates no matter how constrained the economic system, as demonstrated by recent failed national experiments in China and Cuba, which attempted to eliminate the invisible hand of price and investment incentives.

And finally, with respect to the importance of the public sector in any nation, the induced development model does not prescribe the amount of private or public sector activity. The analytic task is to identify economic activities that need to be supported by government either because the needed economic incentives are not present in the private sector or because the tasks would be more productively carried out in the public sector. The economic rationale for government support for agricultural research is examined in chapter 11. Hayami and Ruttan see government as having a very active role in attempting to modify policies and institutions, so that the invisible hand will produce socially desirable outcomes.

CONCLUSIONS

The induced development model has enabled an enormous step forward in our understanding of agricultural and economic development. It offers a comprehensive economic theory of how agricultural growth is achieved. Thus, it provides guidance for policies and programs that can accelerate growth in different resource and institutional environments. The model incorporates Schultz's concept that high-payoff investments in technology and the human agent are core strategies for more rapid growth. This model has six particularly significant characteristics.

1. Investment in technological and institutional change plays a central role in the induced innovation model, in contrast to the classical models of economic growth, which were concerned with land, labor, and more capital resources. Farmers in rapidly developing economies operate in a dynamic economic and institutional environment and are thrust onto a technology treadmill, with changes occurring more and more rapidly. If they do not adopt lower cost production techniques from the stream of technologies or do not respond to institutional and policy changes affecting farming, they will earn less income and may have to leave farming.

2. The induced development model reemphasizes the classical economists' central focus on the role of resource scarcities and hence prices in influencing not only entrepreneurs' decisions but the even more important decisions by private innovators, government researchers, and administrators in their development efforts.

3. The central role of prices in guiding efficient development places emphasis on the importance of high performance in agricultural input and product marketing. Marketing systems that reflect rapid changes in the real costs of resources to farmers and consumers will lead to production and consumption decisions that produce higher rates of income growth. More competitive marketing systems usually quickly indicate changes in the real costs of inputs and products. In contrast, monopolistic marketing and other constraints on marketing generally cause prices to vary widely from real costs, slowing adjustments to economic changes and reducing income growth.

4. The induced development model is particularly useful in providing an economic explanation for the varied paths of agricultural development followed in different countries and regions, and especially the changing rates of growth in land and labor productivity. The model therefore points to the

technologies and institutions most likely to accelerate agricultural growth in particular regions of less developed nations.

5. The integration of institutional change into economic growth theory is the most significant advance achieved by this model. No longer will institutional arrangements be assumed constant and excluded from growth theory. The mechanism of induced institutional change aids an understanding of past institutional changes and enables us to identify needed institutional innovations, to facilitate better resource use, and to increase agricultural productivity. And as de Janvry (1973) demonstrated in research on Argentine agricultural development, the political and social structure of a nation can cause agricultural institutions to be very rigid and thus can slow national economic growth.

6. The model indicates important roles for government. Hayami and Ruttan (1972) judge that government has important roles in the early stages of development when the "socialization of much of biological research in agriculture is essential if the potential gains from biological technology are to be realized. The potential gains from public sector investment in other areas of the institutional infrastructure which are characterized by substantial spillover effects are also large. This includes the modernization of the marketing system through the establishment of the information and communication linkages necessary for the efficient functioning of factor and product markets" (p. 143). Other areas where government activity is essential for accelerated growth include the development of a legal system that enables speedy and evenhanded enforcement of contracts and sufficient public security.

Income Distribution and Agricultural Development

Economic and Social Theory of Personal Income Distribution

A comprehensive model of socioeconomic development would include an explanation of how the distribution of personal income would change with increases in agricultural production. Such an income distribution model as Beckford (1972) pointed out would be a comprehensive political economy or socioeconomic analysis that would include the cultural and institutional variables considered in chapter 5. The more limited economic model of induced innovation presented in this chapter does recognize that a full knowledge of agricultural and economic development requires understanding of the interaction between cultural endowments and the other three more strictly economic groups of factors: resource endowments, technology, and institutions (figure 5.1).

Neoclassical economics has not yet succeeded in providing an integrated set of tools for analyzing how economic growth affects the distribution of personal income. Yotopoulos and Nugent (1976) concluded that the economic theory of personal income distribution was almost nonexistent.

Neoclassical equilibrium theory . . . relies on pure production relationships and factor supply conditions that generate competitive market equilibrium solutions, with the reward of the (functional) factors being determined by marginal productivity. At the other extreme is . . . Marxist wage theory, with fixed real wages and a capitalist class that appropriates all surplus value.

Neither extreme position is consonant with reality. Had the Marxian thesis been correct, the observed income distribution would have been bimodal, one for the capitalists and one for the workers, with the latter being more or less flat at the subsistence wage rate. The neoclassical theory, on the other hand, is uninformative as far as personal income distribution is concerned. (p. 247)

Models of personal income distribution are difficult to construct because many factors affect the income-earning opportunities of individuals, including access to resources, new technology, and the productivity of institutional arrangements. The cultural endowments of a society may also limit certain individuals from certain occupations, and some institutional arrangements may favor certain persons over others. For example, values and beliefs may reduce social and economic mobility due to discrimination on the basis of caste, race, culture, language, color, sex, or religion. Thus, a particular individual's opportunity to increase income and personal assets may often be limited.

Four Economic Factors That Influence Income Equity

The four factors affecting income equity examined here are (1) economic growth; (2) personal assets; (3) the capital intensity of technology; and (4) product market demand.

ECONOMIC GROWTH

Neoclassical economic theory indicates that, in general, with unrestrained competition and free markets, wage and income differentials should decrease over time due to market forces. International comparisons have generally shown higher equality of income in more developed nations than in low-income nations. Time-series studies have also shown that inequality of income has decreased in more developed countries (Yotopoulos and Nugent 1976, p. 248). However, the detailed studies of national economic growth in many countries by Kuznets (1966, chap. 4) indicated that over shorter periods of time, in some less developed countries, increases in income inequality have occurred. He concluded, therefore, that as growth is accelerated in a low-income nation an inverted U relation may be common between the level of per capita income and the inequality of income distribution. In this model, personal income disparities increase in early stages of economic growth. This relation is disputed by others. Whether income distribution is due primarily to market forces or is greatly affected by government policies and institutions and social and cultural patterns is unclear.

PERSONAL ASSETS

Economic theory shows that, generally, the assets controlled by an individual in the form of physical and human capital largely determine personal income. Thus, income is affected by the amount of land, business equipment, or financial assets a person controls, and by the amount of human capital he or she obtains in the form of knowledge and skills valued by society. Hence, changes in personal income distribution will occur (1) if the distribution of productive capital controlled by individuals is changed, either through redistribution or by investing to increase the physical capital controlled by particular groups; or (2) if investment in human capital through education and training focuses on certain income groups, so that they would command higher wages. For example, laborers who may have little opportunity to gain control of productive physical capital can often increase their income through education and by learning skills.

CAPITAL INTENSITY OF TECHNOLOGICAL CHANGE

The capital intensity of technological change affects the share of income received by the different factors of production, including the share received by labor (Hayami and Kikuchi 1982). To comprehend this, consider three cases.

Case 1: No Technological Change, Increased Labor Supply. If, as population increases there is no progress in agricultural technology, the wage rate of labor will decline as a community moves further out on the labor production function (see figure 6.7). If we assume in traditional agriculture that only two resources are used in production—land and labor—Hayami and Kikuchi (1982, p. 50) demonstrated that the share received by labor from production will decline as more labor is added while other inputs are held constant. This is seen by noting in figure 6.7 (lower panel) that the ratio of the lower wage rate, W_1, to the production per unit of labor, q_1, is smaller than the ratio of the earlier higher wage rate, W_0, is to the previous lower product per unit of labor, q_0. At the same time, the share of rent for land increases from r_0 to r_1.

If agricultural lands were largely owned by one group and labor provided by another, as population increased the distribution of income between the two groups would become more skewed in favor of landholders. This case, in which no technological change occurs, illustrates the immiserization of agricultural laborers as their real income declines, a result predicted by the classical economists, including particularly Ricardo. If more labor continues to be applied long enough to a fixed agricultural production function, malnutrition and extreme poverty would reduce the growth rate of laboring families until a new equilibrium occurred.

Case 2: Labor-Using Technological Change. If a new technology that was more labor intensive than the traditional technology was adopted, it would increase the proportion of labor to other resources and increase the amounts of labor employed (production function T_1 in figure 6.8). Assuming no change in the wage rate, equilibrium on the two production functions, T_0 and T_1, would occur at points A and B, with L_0 and L_1 labor applied, respectively. Whether the

Figure 6.7. Decline in the Income Share of Labor with Increases in Population and
No Change in Technology

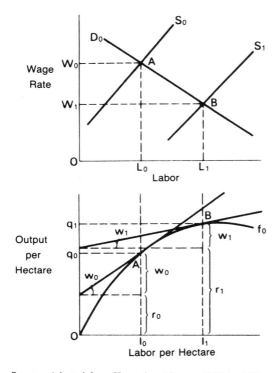

Source: Adapted from Hayami and Ruttan 1985 (p. 355).

income of labor would increase or decrease when the new function, T_1, is used
depends upon two factors: (1) the changes in the wage rate due to the net effect
of changes in the supply and demand for labor, generally; and (2) the increase in
labor demand caused by the new technology, $L_1 - L_0$.

Case 3: Labor-Saving Technological Change. If new agricultural technology
has been developed that requires proportionately less labor (production function
T_2 in figure 6.8), labor used would decrease compared to the amount used with
the original technology, T_0. When a labor-saving technology is used, the share
of labor in the income produced is likely to decline unless wage rates rise rapidly. It is very important to note, however, that a narrow analysis of the effect of
a particular labor-saving agricultural technology, such as a tractor, on labor requirements can lead to the wrong income distribution conclusions. A wider
(whole-farm, or regional) analysis may show that the use of such a technology in
an agricultural area enables more crops to be grown or enables labor to be used

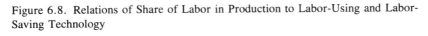

Figure 6.8. Relations of Share of Labor in Production to Labor-Using and Labor-Saving Technology

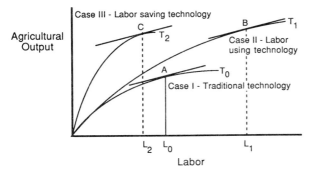

in other more productive enterprises and therefore may cause either little net change or even an increase in labor use and the income of laborers. [7]

Thus the distribution of income between the factors of production, particularly the income of labor, will be determined by the rate of growth in the supply of labor relative to the rate of growth in the demand for labor. The demand for labor will be influenced by the amounts and kinds of technological change occurring in agriculture. A clear policy implication of this analysis is that government activities that reduce the cost of capital below market rates, such as subsidies for capital intensive agricultural technologies like farm machinery, will tend to encourage the adoption of labor-displacing technologies and slow the growth in the demand for labor, or reduce it, resulting in a worsened income distribution.

PRODUCT MARKET DEMAND

Technological change in agriculture, interacting with market demand conditions, affects income distribution. The question is how increases in the supply of agricultural products, due to technological change, affect the incomes of different groups, such as agricultural producers and consumers. To illustrate these complex relations Hayami and Herdt (1977) considered two farming situations common in less developed nations: first, an agricultural area where farmers sell most of their products (figure 6.9). With a downward sloping demand curve for agricultural products, D_0, an increase in the supply of agricultural products due to technological change represented by the shift from supply curve S_1 to S_2 would, in a competitive market, result in a reduction in price received by producers from P_1 to P_2 and an increase in the quantity sold to Q_2.

Whether producers or consumers would gain more is determined by the price elasticity of the demand curve. If we consider an inelastic demand curve,

7. A more detailed exploration of these issues is provided by Hayami and Ruttan (1985, p. 336) and by Hayami and Kikuchi (1982, p. 50).

Figure 6.9. Price Elasticity of the Demand Curve and Farmers' Income Gains or Losses from Increases in Supply

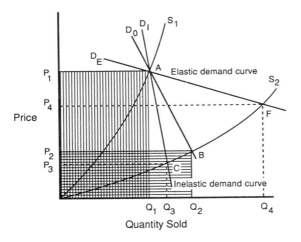

D_1, the price farmers would receive would decrease more to P_3, with little increase in quantity sold, Q_3, at the market equilibrium point, C. In contrast, if there were an elastic demand for the product, curve D_E, the price farmers received would drop only a little, to P_4 at the market equilibrium point F, while the quantity sold would increase greatly to Q_4. Hence, with an inelastic demand for their products, farmers are likely to lose income relative to consumers, but with an elastic demand for their products, farmers are likely to see increased incomes relative to consumers.

Thus, for any group of farmers in any region at any particular time it is a complex empirical question of how the following three factors will work themselves out and hence affect relative incomes. The factors are (1) the elasticity of the demand curve for the particular products farmers sell; (2) the rate at which the demand curve for the products is moving to the right; and (3) the rate at which the supply curve for these farm products is moving to the right. The interaction of these economic forces will determine whether the income of a particular group of farmers increases or decreases relative to consumers, or to other farmers (see also Hayami and Ruttan 1985, pp. 352–58).

In the second farming situation, consider, the more usual farm and rural community condition in many less developed nations, where a considerable proportion of agricultural production is retained on the farm for home consumption. Production retained for home consumption is indicated in figure 6.10 by the vertical demand curve D_H. The quantity H of the total amount of the product produced (supply) is retained for subsistence—not sold for cash in the market. When technological change increases production, as indicated by the shift from supply curve S_0 to S_1, although the price received by farmers declines to P_1, two

Figure 6.10. Decreasing Food Crop Price and Income of Subsistence Farmers

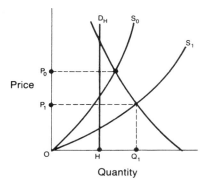

Source: Hayami and Herdt 1978 (p. 246).

offsetting changes occur: (1) the real cost in time and resources of producing the home-consumed portion of production declines, so the farmer gets more subsistence product (retained income) for a given amount of resource use; and (2) the farmer may obtain more or less income from the portion of the product Q_1-H sold at the new lower market price, P_1, depending on the price elasticity of demand. Additional local benefits of a price-decreasing technological change for staple products include lower food prices for local consumers, including the farmer's nonfarm relatives and laborers. These groups would experience increases in real income, because they would then pay less for food. Thus, farmers who produce a high proportion of farm products for home consumption and adopt new technologies are likely to experience real income increases due to a cost-reducing technological change, although their cash income may or may not increase.

Empirical estimates of the gains of producers from technological change relative to consumers and of the gains of large farmers compared to small farmers in a developing nation were made by Hayami and Herdt (1978, pp. 283–302) from studies of changes in rice farming in the Philippines. These estimates indicated that the technological changes that increased rice production (1) led to a net loss for rice farmers who sold all their crop, usually the large farmers; (2) provided a small net gain in income to semisubsistence producers who sold only 40 percent of their crop; and (3) gave consumers significant real income gains. A review of the many studies of the impact of green revolution technology in Asia is provided by I. Singh (1985) and by Barker, Herdt, and Rose (1985, chap. 13). In the following chapter, additional examination of distributional impacts of new technologies in agriculture is provided. [8]

8. Of the very large literature on the impacts of the green revolution on income distribution, the following additional sources provide a sample: Scobie and Posada 1984; Farmer 1977; Bayliss-Smith and Wanmali 1984; Pearse 1980; Griffin 1974b; Cline 1975; and Maunder and Ohkawa 1983.

To conclude the examination of this farming situation, technological changes in major food crops that cause price reductions provide significant income increases to consumers. Farmers as a whole may gain or lose, but small farmers with a high proportion of subsistence production are likely to increase their real income. Thus, this mechanism of technological change in agriculture tends to reduce income disparities between large and small farmers. Although economic theory cannot yet provide a general explanation of the relations between agricultural growth and income distribution, some aspects are understood.

The examination in this section of economic growth and equity leads to the following two general conclusions. First, the assumption that growth and increasing income disparities are associated is very often wrong (Hayami 1983). Both economic theory and empirical studies in less developed nations show that rapid agricultural growth is associated in many instances with increased equity. The use of agricultural technology with the highest rates of return will often increase the demand for labor, as will be shown in chapter 8, and hence can often at least maintain labor's relative income. Also, in less developed nations many of the new biological and chemical technologies that increase agricultural yields most are often more productively used on small rather than large farms, leading to reduced income inequalities.

Second, to achieve greater equity of personal income and to accelerate growth in income for all groups, more productive agricultural technology must be produced that is profitable under the relative-factor price conditions that exist in less developed nations. Slow technological progress in agriculture will reduce rates of income growth. A lack of agricultural growth is likely to cause greater income disparities.

Government Strategies to Reduce Income Disparities

Three general strategies are available to governments to reduce income disparities and poverty: (1) make structural and institutional changes; (2) transfer income; and (3) carry out investment programs that improve the employment opportunities and human capital of low-income groups. Effort and resources can be focused on different mixes of these somewhat interlinked strategies.

The structural and institutional change strategy attempts to shift income flows from higher income groups to lower income groups. Three examples of these strategies are (1) agricultural rent reduction programs that cause a larger share of agricultural production to go to the person who works the soil; (2) agricultural land reforms that transfer land assets, and therefore farm income, from large landholders to small farmers; and (3) the establishment of government-sponsored, low-price, food shops in urban areas restricted to the poor. The attempts to carry out these changes often face great political and social obstacles, and because these changes are often difficult to implement successfully, they can have undesirable long-run economic effects. Consider two examples. Poorly implemented land reforms have, in some cases, led to the eviction of many tenants from lands they farmed (land reform is examined in chapter 10). Programs that establish low-price food shops in urban areas that force farmers to sell food grains at low prices to government can have the following three undesirable outcomes: (1) food subsidies for high-income urban consumers; (2) migration of the rural poor to overcrowded urban slums because of lower food prices in the cities; and (3) low farm prices for agricultural products, which further reduce poor farmers' incomes, slowing the rate of agricultural development and lowering the rate of national income growth.

Some governments in less developed nations such as China, Cuba, and other socialist states have carried out large land reforms and other structural changes. These have often included the establishment of large state farms and required membership by farmers in cooperative farms. To what extent these very different agricultural structures have increased income and improved equity, especially in the longer run, remains unclear, largely due to tight restrictions on independent research about the economic performance of these units. Thus, structural and institutional changes can increase equity and may be carried out with this objective either due to forces exogenous to the economic system, because of major political or social changes in the socioeconomic system, or because they are induced by changes in resources, other institutions, or technology.

The income transfer strategy that uses taxation is common in more developed nations. Lower income groups are given financial and other aid from resources obtained by taxing higher income groups. Programs providing minimum income for the poor and aged and free health care for the poor are examples. In most less developed nations, however, two realities usually prevent significant transfers of income through taxation: (1) the tax system in many less developed market economies is very little developed; and (2) the number of the poor is so great that, even if much larger amounts of taxes were collected and distributed, these resources would be small in relation to the number of persons in need. Thus, in most less developed nations, government transfers usually alleviate only a small amount of the most severe poverty.

The investment strategy focusing on increasing the physical and human capital controlled by lower income groups, is consistent with the objective of rapid economic growth when high-return investments of this kind are identified. Examples of such investments include irrigation programs in poorer agricultural areas that have high productivity potentials and technical training of lower income groups in a wide range of applied fields through nonformal and technical secondary school classes.

Important Concepts

Investment
Depreciation
Nontraditional inputs

Modern agricultural production
function
Growth-stage theories

Conservation model

Industrial fundamentalism model

Urban-industrial impact model

Diffusion model

Location-specific agricultural
  technology

Cultural-change-first model

Community development

Marxist growth model

Dependency model

Stages of agricultural development

High-payoff input model

Induced innovation model

Induced technical innovation

Innovation possibility isoquant

Labor intensive technologies

Paths of productivity change in
  agriculture

Induced institutional innovation

Induced innovation in the public sector

Sample Questions

1. Explain why a focus on optimizing the use of scarce investment resources is at the core of agricultural development theory.

2. Summarize three partial development theories and indicate their shortcomings.

3. Show, using an isoquant diagram, how innovation is induced.

4. Using the induced innovation model, explain why agricultural technology produced in a more developed nation often is not profitable in less developed nations.

5. Identify two kinds of changes that can induce institutional change. Give an example of each kind.

6. How can accelerated technological and institutional change be achieved?

7. How does the induced development model explain the different paths of development followed in different less developed nations?

8. We have some understanding of the effects of agricultural development on income distribution among different groups in society. Explain one effect. Be specific about the groups being considered and your assumptions.

7

Land Expansion and Labor Supply

The impact of technical innovation is a highly complex affair and technological policy a difficult business with many traps for crop production, engineering and other specialists promoting simple solutions. The currently fashionable emphasis on maximization of employment creation could become one such trap unless one appreciates that it is the overall impact of technical change that is critical, and that without appropriate institutional structures, employment creation may guarantee labour a share of the work but not of the benefits.

—*Clay 1975, p. 74*

Introduction

How can the two economic resources, land and labor, be best used to accelerate agricultural production? Two centuries ago, Adam Smith, David Ricardo, and other early economists viewed land, labor, and capital as the three fundamental resources that would increase agricultural production. The amount of capital at that time could not be increased very rapidly; the amount of labor is dependent upon population growth, which can be little influenced; thus the addition of new land for agriculture was seen as the avenue to more rapid growth in production. However, many theories of economic development have viewed labor as an underutilized resource, which if better employed could accelerate economic growth.

This chapter focuses on the economics of the land (R) and labor (L) variables. These variables are fundamental in modern agricultural production theory, as indicated by the function $Y = F[f(K_R, R), g(K_L, L)]$ discussed in the last chapter. An examination of the most important variable, capital (K), follows in chapters 8 to 11. As emphasized by the equation, capital is now understood to be the most important resource for increasing the productivity of both land and labor. This is achieved through investment in technological and institutional change and in human capital.

A clarification of the interrelations between increased quantities of land and labor in agriculture and the productivity of these resources is provided by the following identity:

$$\frac{\text{Agricultural production } (Y)}{\text{Agricultural laborers } (L)} =$$

$$\frac{\text{Area of land } (R)}{\text{Agricultural laborers } (L)} \times \frac{\text{Agricultural production } (Y)}{\text{Area of land } (R)} \; .$$

The first term of the equation indicates that the productivity of agricultural labor (Y/L) is dependent upon the amount of land (and other resources) available per laborer (R/L) multiplied by the productivity of the land, or yield (Y/R). These relations between growth in land and labor productivity and land area per laborer provide perspective on how resource conditions may induce different agricultural development strategies. For example, in traditional agricultures where there is little possibility of increasing yields, if rapid population growth occurs, leading to an increase in the labor force, increases in the amount of land under cultivation are essential to prevent declines in production per laborer and, hence, income. However, if the amount of productive land available is greatly constrained in a particular area, the equation shows that increasing yields becomes essential to maintaining or raising labor productivity in agriculture and, hence, the incomes of farmers.

The changes in labor productivity experienced in three nations over a number of decades illustrate the varied patterns of land and labor productivity induced by different resource conditions (see table 7.1). Japan, since 1876—with limited additional land for agriculture and high rural population—succeeded in increasing yields. Increases in land area per agricultural laborer were achieved only after World War II. Then, a greatly accelerated shift of laborers out of agriculture into higher paying employment in other sectors of the economy resulted in increases in agricultural land per laborer. This rapid shift, enabled by more productive agricultural technology, contributed greatly to the high annual growth rate of 5.8 percent in output per agricultural laborer during this later period.

In Taiwan, available land and labor during the first few decades of this century were similar to Japan's, and about the same success was achieved in increasing productivity. However, after 1952, as population growth continued, until the mid-1960s, opportunities for agricultural laborers in other sectors did not grow rapidly, so a decline in land area per agricultural laborer occurred. Fortunately, large increases in yields were achieved during this period, more than offsetting reductions in land per worker, enabling a 3.3 annual growth rate in agricultural labor productivity. More recently, rapid industrialization in Taiwan has led to increased land per agricultural laborer.

The contrasting experience of the United States illustrates the working out of the economic inducement mechanism under very different resource availa-

Table 7.1. Rates of Change in Productivity per Agricultural Laborer, Land per Laborer, and Yield: Japan, Taiwan, and the United States, 1876–1967 (percent)

Country and Period Measured	Production per Laborer	Land per Laborer	Yield per Acre
Japan			
1876–1920	1.82	0.72	1.10
1920–40	0.71	0.19	0.52
1952–67	5.80	2.90	2.90
Taiwan			
1901–50	1.20	0.40	0.80
1952–66	3.30	−0.80	4.10
United States			
1880–1900	1.10	1.20	−0.10
1900–20	0.60	0.50	0.10
1920–40	2.20	1.50	0.70
1940–60	5.80	4.20	1.60

Source: Johnston and Kilby 1975 (p. 143). Reprinted with permission

bilities and relative costs. These consisted of (1) low initial rural population density; (2) early rapid expansion of employment opportunities in other sectors; and (3) the availability of large amounts of productive agricultural land. These conditions led to high rates of increase in land area per agricultural worker during all periods. Annual yield increases, however, rose above the 1 percent rate only after 1940.

This analysis demonstrates that in less developed nations with high rural population growth rates, and hence high rural labor force growth, new land development could be a significant contributor to maintaining or even increasing labor productivity and thus to increasing national per capita agricultural production. The data presented in table 7.1 also indicate the productivity increases that may be achieved in the coming decades in less developed nations if they have effective agricultural development programs. The importance of yield increases as a central contributor to the growth in labor productivity in agriculture is highlighted in all three examples. This is the topic of chapter 8.

Land in Agricultural Development

Ownership and control of land have many values for rural people. Land, and improvements in land, often represent a high proportion of invested capital in traditional and developing agricultures. Land ownership provides some security of income and food supply. Investment in land can also serve as a bank for accumulated savings in nations where uncertain financial institutions and high inflation rates prevail. Hence, in many areas of less developed nations, the price of land is very high in relation to the net value of agricultural products harvested, leading to low real rates of return to the owner from agricultural activities, ranging up to perhaps 4 or 5 percent.

How can economic theory guide more productive decisions about the use of land resources to accelerate agricultural production? Many view the varied amounts of extensively used and uncultivated lands indicated in table 2.2 as large untapped agricultural resources with high potential for increasing total agricultural production. Under what circumstances could investment in such potentially arable lands provide high returns to the use of scarce resources? Can such land investments significantly expand national agricultural production? An associated question is, What types of land development projects and policies will facilitate socially desirable agricultural development: state farms, plantations, government settlements, spontaneous family farm settlements, or other land development activities?

Economic Evaluation of Land Development

Most land development projects, such as for the expansion of irrigation or plantations, produce increases in income many years after the investments have been made, whether they are carried out by farming families or by large public or private organizations. To evaluate these investments in land, a specialized economic methodology, benefit-cost analysis, is very often used. Benefit-cost (or cost-benefit) methodology was developed in the 1930s and has become an almost universally accepted tool for estimating the net returns from multiyear development projects.

Benefit-cost analysis is a form of multiyear budgeting. Three measures of project worth are generally estimated with this tool—project net return (net present value, or worth), the benefit-cost (B/C) ratio, and the internal rate of return (IRR). In budgeting, costs are subtracted from expected gross income to estimate net income. In benefit-cost analyses, the sum of the expected change in gross income (or benefits) resulting from the project over the life of the investment is subtracted from the sum of the costs of the project over its life, to obtain a project net return. When benefits are divided by costs, a benefit-cost ratio is obtained. The benefits and costs of a project are identified by focusing on estimates of gross income and costs "with" and "without" the project. The estimated increases in gross income each year are the benefits of the project, and the increases in the costs are the project costs. The relation between an investment project and the rest of the economy is clarified by figure 7.1.

To use a numerical example for a one-year period, a change in gross income (or benefits $[B]$) of $120 million minus project costs (C) of $100 million leaves a project net return of $20 million. The benefit-cost ratio for the same data would be 1.2. Clearly, the larger the ratio of gross income to costs, the more desirable the investment project.

As land development projects and other investment projects generally produce a stream of benefits (gross income) over a series of years into the future and usually incur a series of costs in future years, the benefits and costs for all years

Figure 7.1. Benefit-Cost Analysis of an Investment Project and the Rest of the Economy

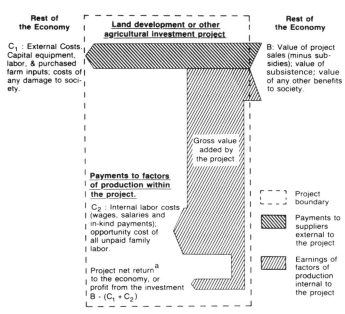

Source: Modified from Gittinger 1982 (p. 295).
Note: The benefit-cost ratio $(B/C) = B/(C_1 + C_2)$.
[a] The net value added by the project after all resource and other costs have been paid.

are summed for comparison to obtain a multiyear benefit-cost ratio for the project life, or the period of analysis, which may be five, ten, twenty-five, or more years, depending upon how many years the project benefits are expected to be received. Future benefits and costs present an analytical problem. For people in all parts of the world, the value of a unit of money, or income, received in the future is less than if it were received today. For this reason, income received from an investment project in a future year (and future costs) are discounted or decreased by an appropriate time discount (or interest) rate to reflect this economic reality of human behavior. This discounting is carried out as indicated in the full benefit-cost equation shown here:

$$\begin{array}{cccc} \text{Year 1} & \text{Year 2} & \text{Year 3} & \text{etc.} \end{array}$$

$$\frac{B}{C} = \frac{B_n/(1+h)^n}{C_n/(1+h)^n} = \frac{B_1/(1+h)}{C_1/(1+h)} = \frac{B_2/(1+h)^2}{C_2/(1+h)^2} + \frac{B_3/(1+h)^3}{C_3/(1+h)^3} + \cdots + \frac{B_n/(1+h)^n}{C_n/(1+h)^n}$$

where h is the interest (discount) rate and n is years.

Note that benefits (B_n) and costs (C_n) are estimated, then divided by the discount factor $(1 + h)^n$ for each year of the life of the investment project, and then summed to obtain the B/C ratio. The benefit-cost ratio is simply a comparison of the sum of discounted benefits and costs. The internal rate of return in multiyear projects is equal to the interest rate (h) that makes summed benefits and costs equal. Although benefit-cost calculations may appear difficult, hand calculators and recently developed microcomputer programs enable rapid estimations of these three measures of project worth.

The economically soundest way to make decisions about the use of scarce development resources is to have many projects evaluated and then to rank them by their benefit-cost ratios. In general, if projects are chosen starting with the highest B/C ratios until the investment funds are exhausted, the highest rate of return for the use of the limited investment funds would be obtained, and income would be increased most rapidly. In practice, governments may set a certain benefit-cost ratio, such as 1.2, or an internal rate of return of 15 percent, as a minimum against which projects are tested for inclusion in a government development program. Note that valid comparisons of benefit-cost ratios from different projects are possible only if the same discount, or interest, rate (h) has been used in analysis. Benefit-cost analysis is of particular value in exploring the possible effect of changes in important output or cost variables on project worth. A government agency might want to know, for example, by how much a project worth would be decreased if yield, or product price, decreased by 10 percent. Such tests of project worth with different data or assumptions are called sensitivity analyses.

Benefit-cost analysis is valuable also because estimates of project worth can be made from different points of view, such as that of the operating unit (a farm, a firm, or government agency), or that of society as a whole. The former analysis is usually labeled *financial* benefit-cost analysis, because the focus of the study is upon the financial impact of the project on the operating unit. When the point of view of society is taken, the evaluation is labeled *economic* benefit-cost analysis. Different costs and benefits are included, depending upon the point of view taken.

Benefit-cost analysis can be used in both market economies and socialist nations to improve the allocation of scarce resources among alternative proposed development projects. These analyses can aid in discarding proposed projects that would incur large losses to operating units or to society. Project benefit-cost analysis has properly been labeled the cutting edge of development, for it sharpens the focus on careful project design and on the collection of sufficient quality data on variables likely to significantly affect the productivity of the investment. Significant increments in social learning about resource use is obtained through project analysis. The World Bank, regional development banks, and many national aid organizations require benefit-cost analysis of proposed land development and of most large agricultural projects before they consider grants or loans. [1]

Higher Returns to Investment in Currently Farmed Land

In largely traditional agricultures, expansion of cultivation onto new land has been a continuing significant source of increased agricultural production, as was seen in chapter 4. Farmers making economically rational decisions invest labor and other resources to bring additional land under cultivation when such returns would be greater than the returns from further intensification of production on their cultivated land. When the amount of land under cultivation expands, the costs of bringing additional, increasingly poorer quality, land into cultivation increase, and the benefits decrease. Hence, in largely traditional areas, a low, approximately equal, marginal return can be expected from additional investment in currently farmed land and from investment in new land. Therefore, uncultivated land in less developed nations is likely to be uneconomic to cultivate or to provide very low returns to investment, given no change in technology, institutional arrangements, and economic conditions.

The choice between investment in new land and in currently farmed land can be illuminated by a production function analysis, which shows why, in many largely traditional agricultural areas, investment in new land has continued, while in more rapidly developing agricultural areas, relatively little investment has been made in new land (see figure 7.2).

In largely traditional environments, the marginal returns to investment in both farmed land and new land are generally low and have had long periods of time to become adjusted, so that the returns are approximately equal from investing in the two possibilities (point *a*). In the circumstances in our example, with, say, five units of investment resources available, three would be invested in the development of new land and two would be allocated to increasing output on farmed land. Thus, in traditional farming areas, some continued land expansion often occurs, despite the low returns.

New Land Development and Technological, Institutional, and Economic Change

The development of new, more productive technology for agriculture usually greatly increases the productivity of the better agricultural areas of currently farmed land and has a variable impact on the returns to investment in new land. Thus, in our example, when yields can be doubled profitably on currently farmed land due to new seed and fertilizer technologies, greater returns to investment may often be obtained by allocating a much higher proportion, or all,

1. Gittinger 1982 is a standard work for the analysis of agricultural projects. Many calculation programs are now available to facilitate benefit-cost analysis. For example Crawford, Ting-Ing, and Schmid (1983) developed a template for microcomputer spreadsheets.

Figure 7.2. Effect of More Productive Agricultural Technology Adapted to
Currently Farmed Lands on Investment in New Land Development

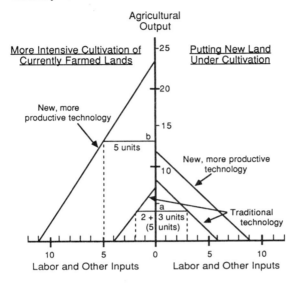

of investment resources for intensification of production on this land (figure 7.2,
point *b*).

During the last thirty years, new high-yielding agricultural technologies
have led to intensified use of currently farmed land and reductions in new land
development. Estimates for the years 1948 to 1971 illustrate the shift to an increased contribution of yield as compared to area in total grain production as
nations develop (see table 7.2).

Total grain production increased up to 100 percent during this period in
some areas. The contribution of additional land in the less developed nations of
Asia, Africa, and Latin America ranged from 42 to 57 percent in the 1960–71
period. But the more developed nations, such as those in Eastern Europe and the
U.S.S.R., had only a 3 percent increase in grain crop area. In Western Europe,
land area declined by 3 percent. These shifts to proportionately much greater
investment in currently farmed areas as development proceeded demonstrate
that changes in technological, institutional, and economic variables usually open
many high-return agricultural investment opportunities in this land and relatively few in new land. In spite of this general trend, some changes in technology
may positively affect certain uncultivated land areas and provide opportunities
for high-return investments in new land. As indicated in a subsequent section,
high-intensity plantation development for certain crops is one example.

Changes that could enable profitable land development include the following: (1) changes in agricultural technology (seeds, plant materials, and fertilizers); (2) changes in nonagricultural technology (transportation, processing,

and disease control); (3) changes in institutional, social, and political arrangements (affecting security, tenure, and the operation of plantations, government settlement programs, and family settlement of new lands); and (4) changes in economic variables (reducing input costs, increasing product prices, and changing the relative cost of inputs or their availability). Any of these changes can either increase or decrease the returns to new land development relative to further investment in farmed lands.

Alternative Arrangements for Investment in New Land

The institutional arrangements and other dimensions of projects for the cultivation of both idle and extensively used land are of endless variety, from tightly controlled projects to incremental cropland additions to current farms to family-based spontaneous colonizations. We examine three of the most important institutional arrangements for new land development.

PLANTATIONS AND OTHER HIGH-TECHNOLOGY LAND INVESTMENT PROJECTS

Plantations were defined by Wolf and Mintz (1957, p. 380) as agricultural estates, usually organized into corporations, that often have a dependent labor force and that seek to supply large-scale markets, using large amounts of capital investment per unit of land. Commercial, profit-oriented, land development projects in Africa, Asia, and Latin America fit this definition, whether operated privately or by a government. These units generally have produced a limited number of export crops, particularly rubber, coffee, tea, bananas, cocoa, sugar, ground nuts, cotton, and more recently, palm oil. Plantations on agricultural estates have been developed on both previously unused and extensively used land. The economic opportunities provided by intensive farming have induced nations to establish the necessary legal structures, including particularly the institutional arrangement of the limited liability company.

Courtenay (1980) provided a perspective on the evolution of plantations over the last four centuries. He pointed out that, due to the association of plantations with colonialism, it was often assumed in the 1950s and 1960s that the plantation sectors of less developed nations would decline rapidly as the new, independent governments became established. However, in many less developed nations, plantations have not been abolished, although control has often been shifted to citizens or governments. Plantations have been found to have technological and economic advantages that bring high foreign exchange earnings, high productivity, and high income. These advantages are partly due to their ability to successfully recruit skilled technical, marketing, and management personnel. But they are also due to economies of scale in the production and marketing of certain crops, especially for export markets.

Despite the general economic and technological success of plantations in less developed nations, they have had mixed social and political influence. Sometimes pay scales are low, or living conditions are poor, or health and edu-

Table 7.2. Contributions of Area and Yield to Increases in World Grain Production, 1948–1971

Region	Grain Production (million tons)		Annual Change (percent)
	1948–1950	1969–1971	
Western Europe	72	137	3.1
Eastern Europe and U.S.S.R.	107	230	3.7
North America	162	244	2.0
Latin America	31	69	3.9
Near East	22	42	3.0
Far East	135	249	2.9
Africa	28	52	2.9
China	104	202	3.2
Oceania (Australia and New Zealand)	7	15	3.7
World	669	1,238	3.0

Source: Adapted from FAO, *State of Food and Agriculture 1972* (p. 12).

cation services are lacking. The political influence of plantation operators can be great, particularly if plantations provide a significant proportion of foreign exchange earnings or taxes. If large amounts of foreign capital are involved, especially in small countries, too much unwanted foreign influence can lead to undesired international political involvement. Thus, primarily for social and political reasons, further plantation development by private individuals, especially foreign corporations, has often been viewed as not in the interest of a less developed nation. In these circumstances, to reduce foreign influence and to attempt to capture the profits, governments may take control of plantations; or in socialist nations, plantations may become state or collective farms. However, with the scarcity of managerial and technical talent available to most less developed nations, this strategy has led often to higher costs and lower productivity, with reduced income or losses, even with subsidies from the government. Successful government plantation programs have, however, been carried out in some nations, particularly in Malaysia.

To conclude, plantations in their many guises are now playing a bigger role in national agricultural development in many nations than they have for many decades (Courtenay 1980, p. 205). Some further expansion of capital intensive plantations and corporate farms will likely continue to provide high returns from development resources. Such expansion can increase the productivity of some crops in particular regions, increase foreign capital inflows, and increase foreign exchange earnings.

| Change (percent) | | | |
| 1948–1971 | | 1960–1971 | |
Area	Yield	Area	Yield
3	97	− 3	103
11	89	3	97
− 50	150	− 35	135
69	31	57	43
78	22	36	64
50	50	42	58
48	52	43	57
28	72	21	79
73	27	118	− 18
28	72	20	80

GOVERNMENT SETTLEMENT PROJECTS

Government settlement projects usually have to surmount formidable obstacles to become profitable, including (1) the creation of a considerable minimum infrastructure, such as land clearing, roads, communications, clean water, health services, education, and police, judicial, and other government functions; (2) the testing and adaptation of agricultural technologies in new areas; (3) the establishment of input and product marketing systems; and (4) the development of an effective management organization.

Solutions to housing problems in settlement projects sometimes are humorous. For example, Paris-trained government architects with urban backgrounds may provide designs that do not incorporate local knowledge of and preferences for temperature, orientation, and air currents. "Improved" houses have been built all lined up neatly in a row, but settlers refused to live in them, preferring instead their own "untidy" houses, built in a seemingly helter-skelter pattern. Thus, building houses for the settlers usually simply increases costs while producing undesired structures, however "modern" they may look. The provision of house-building materials for settlers may, however, be a necessary project cost.

The objectives of a government settlement project throw considerable light on its economic potential. Some settlement projects are undertaken for defense purposes, or to pay off exsoldiers, or to settle refugees. When objectives such as these are primary, often little analysis has been undertaken to estimate expected settler income and project costs. However, when increased agricultural growth is the primary goal of a settlement project, it should meet the usual criterion of at least a reasonable benefit-cost ratio or an internal rate of return for use of private or government resources.

Government settlement programs often face particular problems in attempting to become productive. One problem arises in the settler selection process. Settlers most likely to contribute to project success include better-than-average farmers and those with farming experience in a similar ecological area. Often, however, the settlers chosen are inexperienced in the ecological area of the project, or have weak farming ability, such as retirees from government service. Problems of social integration may arise when settlers with different backgrounds are given nearby plots. The development of a sufficiently harmonious group life may take considerable time, and in the meantime, social conflicts can reduce crop production and cause some settlers to leave.

High government costs often arise because settlement projects generally require whole new agricultural and social systems. A review of ten settlement projects aided by the World Bank, located in Brazil, Colombia, Ethiopia, Kenya, Malawi, and Malaysia, showed an average cost per family settled was greater than $5,000, ranging from $1,327 in Kenya to more than $13,000 in Malaysia (World Bank 1974, p. 40). In view of the large number of very poor and unemployed persons in most less developed nations, where average per capita incomes are in the $200 to $500 range, it is hard to justify such high investments in, or transfers to, a relatively few families. Hence, government settlement projects often result in a highly skewed allocation of scarce government development resources (see also Lewis 1964).

The following five conclusions based on the history of government settlement projects need to be kept in mind to aid in improving the allocation of scarce government investment resources. First, it is very difficult for governments to carry out high-return land settlement projects. Second, informed decisions about investments in settlement projects require data from several years of farming trials in the area, which will allow estimates of performance made in a benefit-cost analysis framework. In particular, data are needed on crop and livestock productivity in representative parts of the proposed settlement area, based upon the levels of technology and other resources that the settlers are expected to use. Third, as benefits are normally discounted at rates of 5 to 10 percent annually in real terms, to obtain high net project returns and to assure early income to settlers, settlers will need a staple annual cash crop on part of their land. A high-value crop, perhaps for export, is also likely to be necessary if the costs, including interest of 5 or 10 percent, are to be paid for by the settlers. Fourth, choosing settlers experienced in the farming conditions of the area can contribute greatly to achieving early high productivity. An alternative is to employ potential settlers as laborers so they may acquire local farming information and increase their cooperation, responsibility, and pride in the settlement. And fifth, the need for sufficient social cohesion in a settlement area suggests that efforts be made to choose groups of families who already know each other or are of the same cultural group. They will be more likely to provide social support to each other when needed.[2]

SPONTANEOUS FAMILY SETTLEMENTS

From the point of view of the best use of scarce social resources, government support for spontaneous settlements and colonizations is likely to enable low-cost expansion of land under cultivation (see Nelson 1973, pp. 108–16). From an economic point of view, the question is what low-cost actions government might take that would increase settlers' incomes sufficiently so that farmers would be induced to settle in the desired areas. Road building alone may sufficiently reduce agricultural input costs and increase product prices to achieve this objective, as has been the case recently in areas of the Amazon River basin in Brazil. The Malaysian government did not even have to provide feeder roads—it required loggers to build feeder roads as a part of the tax on logging operations.

Another example of government action relates to changes in the rules of settlement. In the United States in the last century, the Homestead Act made an institutional change that was sufficient to encourage spontaneous settlement of very large tracts of land in the central and western states. Under this act, a settler could obtain the rights to 160 acres (about 60 hectares) if he or she lived on the land for five years, made improvements, such as building a house, and paid twenty-six dollars. Later, arrangements were made to provide loans to homesteaders to further encourage settlement. In developing nations today, assuring input availability and a market for certain crops might provide sufficient incentive to accelerate settlement in some areas. In other areas, certain social services, such as disease control, health services, or improved communications, might be required.

Programs undertaken to encourage spontaneous settlement, if not made too lucrative for settlers, will tend to attract the healthier, abler farmers who are more likely to be successful in new areas, for only those who believe they have the minimum amount of resources required for settlement will undertake the risk. This strategy, in addition, has the advantage of encouraging the use of private savings of farming and other families in new land investment. Also, the results of any losses will be absorbed to a considerable extent by the private sector, instead of causing reductions in scarce government development funds. However, spontaneous settlement projects may not be able to help the poorest farmers or landless laborers, for these people will usually not be able to obtain the minimum resources needed to establish themselves productively in a new settlement area.

In conclusion, human history has a long record of spontaneous agricultural settlement of large areas of land. Spontaneous settlements continue in some ar-

2. References to government settlement projects include Peacock 1981 and, for Africa, Chambers 1969.

Table 7.3. Performance Ratings, Twenty-four Tropical Land Development Projects

Level of Government Participation	Project Performance and Expectation of Economic Viability[a]		
	Dynamic	Acceptable	Poor
Directed colonization		Nuevo Ixcatlan (low) Cihaultepec (low) La Chontalpa (low)	La Joya (low) Bataan (low) Alto Beni I (low) Alto Beni II (medium) Chimore (low) Yapacani (medium)
Semidirected colonization	Santo Domingo de los Colorados (high) Puerte Presidente Stroessner (high)	Upano (high) Tingo Maria (medium)	
Spontaneous colonization	Caqueta (high) Caranavi (high) Puyo-Tena (high)		Chapare (low)
Private subdivision	Ivinheima (high) CMNP (high)		Gleba-Arinos (medium) Tournavista (low)
Foreign colonization	Filadelfia (high)	San Juan (high) Okinawa (high)	

Source: Nelson 1973 (p. 246). Reprinted with permission.
[a] Expectation of economic viability: high, medium, low.

eas with or without government aid. In many sparsely settled areas, governments of less developed nations may undertake a wide variety of relatively low-cost, incremental actions, of a technological, institutional, or economic nature, that would induce spontaneous settlement. Care is required to prevent activities that would cause serious negative ecological consequences, but in countries with significant areas of uncultivated arable land, it is likely that encouraging spontaneous settlement will be a high-return approach to increasing the amount of land under cultivation.

AN EVALUATION OF THREE TYPES OF LAND DEVELOPMENT

An evaluation of twenty four land development projects in Latin America provides empirical support to the preceding analysis (see table 7.3). Five of the eight semidirected and spontaneous land development projects studied were judged to have dynamic performance, with high expectation for economic viability. However, all nine of the government-directed colonization projects in this study had only acceptable or poor performance. Seven of these had low economic viability expectations, and two had medium economic viability expectations.

Criteria and Policies for Land Development

This examination of the economics of land development programs and world experience with land expansion leads to the following two general conclusions. First, in areas where little or no new, more productive, agricultural technology is available, and where little institutional and economic change is taking place, few opportunities for high-return new land development projects are likely. Under these conditions, land development is likely to provide low returns on investment. Second, in areas of less developed nations where significant changes are occurring or very likely, some high-return land development opportunities may arise. However, in these circumstances, it is even more likely that many high-return investment opportunities will be found in currently farmed areas.

To conclude, land development programs will continue to attract some development resources. In some less developed nations, significant high-return investment opportunities in new land development will continue to be found, such as in some areas of Africa and Central America, where significant areas of arable land remain uncultivated. But as agricultural development proceeds in most nations, the number of new land investment opportunities that will offer higher returns than those on currently farmed lands are expected to decline. Also, it should be recognized that, in most cases, new land development is likely to contribute only a small, one-time, increase in national agricultural output. For these reasons, the focus of the remaining chapters is placed on increasing the productivity of currently farmed lands. The economic analysis in these chapters is, however, applicable to the development of new agricultural lands.

Labor in Agricultural Development

We do not view what has come to be called "the employment problem" as unimportant. Rather . . . that the term is a misnomer because it conjures up the image of labor market failure. The slow rate of growth of workers' income at the bottom of the distribution, despite quite high aggregate rates of growth of output . . . is better termed a poverty or distribution problem. . . . The most important factors influencing the dynamics of supply and demand for labour—population growth, educational opportunities, the levels of investment, technology—are themselves only moderately influenced by aberrations in the interaction of suppliers and employers of labour services. (Berry and Sabot 1978, p. 1232)

Labor represents more than half to almost all of the value of nonland resources used in agricultural production in most less developed nations. Generally, only small amounts of low cost equipment and hand tools are used. Exceptions to the predominant value of labor in agricultural inputs include livestock raising and other very specialized farming systems, in which animals, or other productive inputs of high value such as large irrigation structures, are used. As labor is the predominant agricultural input beside land, traditional societies are poor because their labor productivity is low. Throughout human history until about 150 years ago, agricultural labor productivity was able to be increased only very gradually.

Before the mid-1960s, models of economic development, such as the industrial fundamentalism and dual-sector models, assumed that most new high-return investment opportunities and associated higher productivity job opportunities would be created in the cities and the industrial sector. Hence, industry received priority in planned government investment. By the late 1960s, both agricultural research and the results of the first waves of the green revolution demonstrated that high private and social returns to investment could be obtained with new technologies in agriculture. The high returns justify allocating large proportions of scarce national development resources to agriculture. This section deals with the employment implications of investments in agriculture. In what ways does accelerated investment in agricultural development affect rural wages, employment levels, labor productivity, and equity?

Neoclassical and Marxist development theories predict very different changes in wages with agricultural development. Marxist theory hypothesizes that the owners of land and capital are able to hold wage rates down to subsistence levels. Then, when the real cost of producing food declines with increasing labor productivity and agricultural development, the wage will decline to the new lower subsistence level. This is supposed to occur even if the demand for rural labor increases more rapidly than supply, because of the assumed absolute control of capitalists over wages. In contrast, neoclassical economic theory indicates that when demand for labor increases more rapidly than supply, laborers will obtain increased wages. Empirical data from less developed nations over the last thirty years have provided overwhelming evidence of rising real wages for rural labor in areas where demand for labor has increased relative to supply, due to outmigration and accelerated rural and agricultural development. In other rural areas, where the supply of labor has increased more rapidly than the demand for labor, wages have not changed or have declined in real terms (see for example Bardhan 1984).

Economics of Household Labor Allocation

The economics of the allocation of resources in the household, the most basic social unit of production, is central to understanding the economics of agricultural labor. Recent developments in the analysis of household labor supply and demand have contributed to an increased understanding of labor markets and of the contribution of women's labor in less developed nations (Becker 1976 and 1981). The household labor model assumes that rural people make economically rational decisions about the allocation of their labor and other resources, given the constraints of their knowledge and social and institutional environments. Barnum and Squire (1979) explored the use of such a model by focusing on three sets of essential household decisions: (1) labor allocation; (2) farm and household production; and (3) household consumption.

Household labor allocation decisions were modeled by allocating all household labor among four activities: (1) on-farm agricultural production; (2) household production activities, usually predominantly carried out by women; (3) off-farm work; and (4) leisure. To maximize overall family utility, production theory as presented in chapter 4 indicates that the greatest net household income is obtained when the marginal utility (or marginal return) is equated from each of the four income sources. Thus, for example, if the marginal returns to off-farm labor increased significantly due to a rise in off-farm wages, some family labor time would be shifted to off-farm work from farm production, household production, or leisure.

Labor allocation between farm and household production would likewise depend upon any changes in utility of income obtained from them. If, for example, a higher yielding crop increased the income from farm work, more labor would be employed on the crop until the marginal returns to labor from this activity returned to a level equal to the marginal returns from the other uses of household labor. A different reallocation of labor would occur toward household production as a result of investment in, for example, a new profitable tailoring technology, such as a sewing machine. In the preceding discussion, the inclusion of all needed adjustments for risk in any allocation or production decisions are assumed.

Household consumption decisions are modeled in a similar fashion, so that household members obtain maximum satisfaction, given household time constraints and income. The operation of the consumption model hypothesizes that each individual seeks equal marginal satisfaction through three consumption possibilities: (1) goods and services produced by the family; (2) goods and services purchased from others; and (3) leisure. For maximum household satisfaction, time allocated between work (which increases consumption) and leisure is adjusted so that the satisfaction lost through the last unit of leisure sacrificed would be equal to the satisfaction gained from the added income (and consumption) obtained from labor.

Examples of specific changes in resource allocation that this model implies were explored, using farm data from a rural area of Malaysia. The econometric estimates obtained indicate, for example, that in an average-sized household a 10 percent increase in the price of rice sold by the farmer would be expected to cause the household to increase rice production 6 percent and to increase the consumption of purchased market goods 20 percent. To achieve the increase in rice production, the household would increase hired farm labor 16 percent, while at the same time it would reduce the amount of household labor on rice production 6 percent in order to increase leisure due to higher household income. Further development of household economic models holds considerable promise in better understanding the response of farm family labor supply to changes in the family's economic environment.

Female Labor in Agricultural Development

Much of the agricultural development literature has ignored the large contribution of women to agricultural production. This literature also has seldom examined the effect on women of agricultural development programs. Economic theory of the household and the induced innovation model both point to the central need for new higher return technologies for women to use so they may contribute more to increasing household income. A first step in understanding how women can increase their contribution to agricultural and rural development is to gain better knowledge of the existing contributions of women.

WOMEN'S CONTRIBUTIONS TO AGRICULTURAL PRODUCTION

Only recently has the development literature recognized that women (1) manage a very significant part of farm production; (2) provide a great deal of labor for crop and livestock production; (3) predominate in food processing and preparation; and (4) often devote large amounts of time in obtaining the fuel and water required to make food and other agricultural products ready for sale or home consumption.

The extent of women's participation has often not been recognized, in part due to the immense variability in women's activities in the different cultures and farming systems of the Third World. Boserup's (1970) data based on census information show that female labor as a share of total farm labor ranges from 2 percent to 50 percent, with, for example, less than 10 percent in Latin America:

Country	Female family labor as a Percentage of the Agricultural Labor Force
Africa south of the Sahara	
Sierra Leone	42
Liberia	42
Ghana	36
Region of Arab influence	
Algeria	37
Tunisia	38
Turkey	49
South and East Asia	
India	24
Thailand	50
Latin America	
Brazil	8
Colombia	3
Chile	2

To indicate the problems of census data on women's participation in agriculture, the Economic Commission for Latin America, in contrast, concluded that women compose as much as 40 percent of the agricultural labor force in Latin America. In Asia the proportion of women in the agricultural labor force has been estimated at 25 to 50 percent. In some areas of Asia, such as South India, poor women compose a high proportion of the hired agricultural labor force.

Boserup has pointed out that Africa south of the Sahara is a region of "female farming systems," in which women often provide the greater share of management and labor (see table 7.4). One-third of African farms have been estimated by the United Nations to be managed and worked by women, with higher estimates for Tanzania (54 percent) and Ghana (41 percent). The high female participation in agriculture in some areas is illustrated by a study of Yoruba women, which showed that one-fifth of the women received nothing from their husbands and therefore had to provide all their own food and income from their own farms, while in some cases also helping on their husbands' farms. In other areas of Africa, a high proportion of family farms are operated by women because their husbands are not present for long periods due to employment in mines or for other reasons.

The fact that women process a high proportion of agricultural products in much of the Third World is often overlooked. This may be largely due to an overly narrow definition of agriculture as simply consisting of field work in crop and livestock production. The contribution of women to family food production, processing, and preparation by providing fuel and water supply is also not often recognized. In some areas of Kenya, for example, women spend two to six hours per day per household obtaining water. Fuel gathering for food processing and preparation is often the women's task, sometimes requiring many hours per week.

To conclude, women in many less developed nations produce a large share of the income generated in rural households and in agriculture. These facts show that extension and other activities intended to increase agricultural and rural labor productivity will, in many areas, have to be programmed to reach women in order to be effective.

WAGE DISCRIMINATION

The difference in money earned by women and men for equivalent agricultural and other work is often large. Women may receive little remuneration for much of their labor in the fields or from processing food and agricultural products for sale and for family use. Lower pay for women is partly due to lighter and less skilled work, but it is also due to cultural values arising from the complex history of different peoples. A study in six villages in southern India found, for example, that female wages were 56 percent of male wages (Ryan, Ghodake, and Sarin 1979, p. 370). Standards for eliminating sex and racial discrimination in wages have been set by international labor codes and by the United Nations.

Table 7.4. Female labor in Agriculture in Six Less Developed African Nations

Country	Percentage of Women in Family Labor Force in Agriculture	Average Hours Worked per Week in Agriculture		Female Hours as Percentage of Male Hours	Percentage of Work on Farm Done by Women
		Active Females	Active Males		
Senegal	53	8	15	53	29
Gambia					
1944	51	19	11	168	64
1962	52	20	9	213	70
Cameroon	62	13	16	81	56
Central African Republic					
Traditional methods	55	15	15	99	55
Improved technology	58	20	13	150	68
Congo (Brazzaville)	57	24	15	160	68
Uganda					
Sample A	67	28	15	193	79
Sample B	61	20	15	136	68
Sample C	53	18	4	450	45

Source: Adapted from Boserup 1970 (pp. 21 and 27).

NEGATIVE IMPACTS OF AGRICULTURAL DEVELOPMENT ON WOMEN

Studies have shown that in some cases new agricultural technologies and machines have led to decreased opportunities for female wage earning, especially among poor women. New milling technology, for example, which usually replaces women's work, has often been acquired by men, leading to a transfer of income-earning opportunities from women to men. Such shifts in the income-earning opportunities of women may increase or decrease their welfare, depending upon the way income is allocated within households. Negative impacts on women can be due to the relative decline in the demand for female labor, the departure of men who provided labor and support, the lack of productivity increases in women's household and farm activities, and the perverse working out of culturally defined sex roles. Therefore, women's resistance to change may result from well-founded fears that proposed changes will cause loss of income and less control over their own lives (Tinker 1979, pp. 9–25).

As agricultural development proceeds, changes in the demand for sex-segregated activities will have varied impact on the demand for male and female labor. For example, in regions of South India, where a large proportion of the hired agricultural labor consists of poor females, technologies that displace this labor reduce the income of these already most disadvantaged persons. A number of studies in Africa that focused on the impact of development on women and children have found that, while new technology for cash crops has increased income, nutritional levels have fallen (Tinker 1979, p. 15). The cause is linked to conventions about sex roles. "The primary reason for this seemingly contradictory phenomenon is the fact that this income belongs to the man. Men use this money for improving homes, throwing 'prestige' feasts, buying transistor radios. In the Cameroons men do use their income to pay school fees, unlike Kenya." Research that has shown the negative impacts of rural development on women has led to concern that cultural traditions and decisions made mostly by men, often in the roles of international and national development officials, may result in more dependency for women, greater restrictions, and reduced economic and other opportunities.

INCREASING THE GAINS FOR WOMEN FROM AGRICULTURAL
DEVELOPMENT

Although women's levels of living have usually risen with increases in agricultural production, this result is not automatic. With equity objectives in mind, attention to the likely impacts on women is required when designing and promoting new agricultural technologies and institutional changes. This focus necessitates a knowledge of cultural endowments, particularly sex roles, income sources, and household distribution practices. Agricultural development programs specifically for women are needed in many areas, both to reduce discrimination and to increase women's contribution to agricultural development and levels of living. Because of past neglect, some programs for women will have a greater impact and higher marginal returns in increased income and health than current programs, which primarily benefit men.[3]

Labor Supply

FACTORS AFFECTING LABOR SUPPLY

The rate at which the rural labor supply curve moves to the right is dependent primarily upon three factors: (1) the rate of rural population growth; (2) changes in the proportion of the population participating in the labor force; and (3) the rate of net outmigration.

A preliminary indication of the rate of growth in the rural labor force is provided by national population growth rates, such as presented in table 2.1. However, as the number of children per family is usually higher in rural areas than in urban areas, the natural rate of increase in the rural population will usually be higher than the national rate.

International comparison studies of labor force participation rates have shown only a few percentage point differences over large increases in per capita income. The participation rate is the number of persons working compared with the number in the relevant population, expressed in percentage. Overall participation rates for males in less developed nations average 53 percent working, while in more developed nations these rates average 58 percent working (Turnham 1976, p. 24). The International Labour Office, in making projections of male labor force participation rates in less developed nations for the period 1980 to 2000, estimated that they would increase from 52 to 55 percent (Edwards 1974, p. 240). Female labor participation rates in these nations were estimated much lower, at 23 percent by Turnham, with only a four percentage point change between less developed and more developed countries. However, these participation rates for women are much more uncertain, due to the large number of unsolved theoretical and empirical problems related to how women's work has been, should be, and can be measured. In summary, empirical research indicates that participation rates usually change only slowly; thus they are unlikely to much influence rates of change in the agricultural and rural labor force.

The effect of net outmigration from rural areas is variable on rural labor supply. Both economic theory and economic history demonstrate an increasing demand for labor in urban areas as development proceeds. Empirical data on the structural transformation during economic development presented in table 3.6 show the large shift of labor out of agriculture; much of this shift is associated with urban migration.

---

3. Books on women and work in developing nations include Benerid 1982; Epstein and Watts 1981; Buvinic, Lycette, and McGreevey 1983; Tinker and Bramsen 1977; and Dixon-Mueller 1985. The growing literature on women and development includes the following important works: Presvelan and Spijkers-Zwart 1980; Boserup 1970; Dixon 1978; Charlton 1984; and Rihari 1978. Economic theory is applied to women's work by T. P. Schultz (1982) and Amsdan (1980).

A number of economic models have sought to explain the causes of urban labor migration. After reviewing them, Yotopoulos and Nugent (1976, pp. 226–36) concluded that empirical tests of these models show that people move in response to the probability of obtaining larger lifetime earnings in urban areas. This research has also demonstrated that young unmarried persons are more likely to migrate than other laborers, because (1) they can expect to gain a higher urban wage rate over a greater number of years; (2) they are usually poorer and have lower wages and hence will gain more from migration; and (3) with the same urban job prospects, younger persons without spouses are more mobile because they have weaker family links and fewer material possessions and psychic ties to an area.

Migrants also have been found to have higher educational levels than those remaining. More education increases the probability of greater lifetime earnings in urban areas. However, the departure to urban areas of the more educated young arouses concern that the complex tasks of agricultural development will have to be carried out by the less able left in rural areas, resulting in lower rates of national income growth.

Given high rates of natural population growth in rural areas, the rate of growth of the rural labor supply depends upon the rate of shift to urban employment. In lower income nations where the industrial sector is small relative to the agricultural sector, even rapid increases in industrial growth will cause little reduction in rural labor supply. In the 1960s and 1970s, the history of industrial employment growth in less developed nations was disappointingly slow. In India, for example, Krishna (1980, p. 169) estimated that, during the decade ending in 1978, the modern industrial sector provided jobs for less than 12 percent of the entrants into the labor force. The slow growth of employment in the modern industrial sector in the last two decades, coupled with the high personal and national costs associated with large flows of people to urban areas, has placed renewed focus on how employment opportunities can be increased more rapidly in the agricultural sector and rural areas.[4]

THE MAGNITUDE OF INCREASES IN AGRICULTURAL LABOR SUPPLY

Estimates of the growth of the agricultural labor force have been made by assuming it is a residual depending upon the rates of growth of the nonagricultural labor force and the total labor force. These estimates usually assume no changes in labor force participation rates. Mellor's (1966, p. 25) equation for this estimate is

$$r_A = \frac{r_T - r_N(L_N/L_T)}{1 - (L_N/L_T)} .$$

In it, the rate of growth of the agricultural labor force, r_A, is dependent upon the

---

4. Important references to the literature on the economics of migration include Todaro 1976, 1981 (pp. 225–46); Berry and Sabot 1978; and Mundlak 1979.

difference between the rates of growth of the total labor force, r_T, and the nonagricultural labor force, r_N, multiplied by the ratio of the nonagricultural labor force, L_N, to the total labor force, L_T, all divided by one minus the ratio of the nonagricultural labor force to the total labor force (see also Johnston and Kilby 1975, p. 83). Thus, if the total labor force grows at 3 percent and the nonagricultural labor force grows at 5 percent, with an initial 25 percent of the labor force in the nonagricultural sectors, the agricultural labor force will increase at a rate of 2.33 percent. Note that, due to the more rapid rate of growth of the nonagricultural labor force, in the next time period the ratio of nonagricultural labor to total labor will be greater, and hence the rate of growth of the agricultural labor force will decline.

Projections of total labor force growth rates for 1980–2000 indicate the following: China and India, 1.7; other low-income countries, 2.7; middle-income countries, 2.6; industrial market economies, 0.7; and nonmarket industrial economies, 0.6. Urban population growth rates in the 1970–80 decade were as follows: low-income countries, 4.1 (range 2.5–8.7); middle-income countries, 4.0 (range 2.5–8.6); industrial market economies, 1.4; nonmarket economies, 1.8 (World Bank, *World Development Report 1982,* pp. 146 and 148).

Dovring (1959) provided useful illustrations of the growth that could be expected in an agricultural population using a similar method (see figure 7.3). With a fixed ratio of agricultural labor to the agricultural population, the rate of growth in agricultural labor would be the same as the rate of growth of the agricultural population. In this example, if initially two-thirds of the population were in agriculture, the population growth rate were 2.5 percent, and the nonagricultural population growth rate were 3.9 percent, then the agricultural population would continue to grow for about four decades. And the agricultural population would double before it began to decline in absolute numbers. If national population growth rates were higher, or net rates of nonagricultural population growth were lower, additional decades would be required before an absolute decline in the agricultural population (or labor force) would begin. Because of the uniqueness of each rural area, regional estimates of this kind are needed to gain insight into the expected local population and labor supply.

Empirical estimates for less developed regions of the world indicate the following percentage increases in the agricultural population for the fifteen-year period 1970–85: East Africa, 31 percent; South Asia, 24 percent; and Latin America, 14 percent. Estimates of the year when peak agricultural populations will occur in Asia range up to the year 2052, with the year 2011 in the middle of the estimates (World Bank, *World Development Report 1972,* pp. 13 and 14). With continued high rates of growth in the agricultural population and labor force likely into the twenty-first century in many less developed nations, persistent downward pressure on agricultural and rural wages can be expected in these nations. In some less developed nations, however, particularly those in Latin America that have had high rural outmigration rates for a number of decades,

Figure 7.3. Agricultural Population Growth During the Economic Transformation

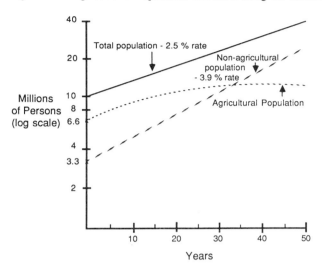

Source: Adapted from Dovring 1959 (p. 8).

the structural transformation is further along. In these nations, a much higher proportion of the total population is now in nonagricultural sectors, and therefore the agricultural labor force growth rate has decreased considerably.

Three conclusions follow from the preceding analysis of agricultural and rural labor supply. First, for less developed nations in the early phases of structural transformation, an increasing agricultural labor force can be expected for many years. Second, with an increasing agricultural population, farm size, as measured by land area, is likely to further decrease in less developed nations. Thus, increasing numbers of small farms are likely to be a central feature of agriculture in many of these nations for several decades to come. Third, the prospect of the continued existence of large numbers of small farms in many less developed nations has many implications for the kinds of agricultural technology and institutions that will be induced to be developed by researchers and entrepreneurs in biological, mechanical, and social science fields.

Labor Demand

As knowledge of more productive production processes becomes available and as per capita incomes rise, great structural changes are induced in national economies (see chapter 3). These changes greatly affect the demand for rural labor in three ways: (1) through increased direct demand for farm labor on farms; (2) through indirect off-farm demand for rural labor for work generated by agricultural development; and (3) through increases in the demand for the production of nonagricultural goods and services in rural areas.

Figure 7.4. Demand for Labor on New High-Yielding Crops

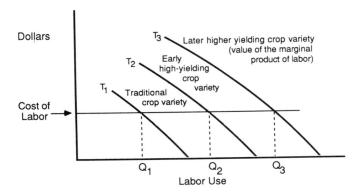

DIRECT LABOR DEMAND WITH NEW AGRICULTURAL TECHNOLOGY

The demonstration of increases in demand for labor in agriculture, associated with adoption of new more productive farming technology, is provided both by production theory and by empirical studies of agricultural development. Production theory gives a clear guide for the amount of labor a farmer should employ. As presented in chapter 4, the amount of labor needed to obtain the highest net return is determined by comparing the marginal cost of labor, or wage, with the marginal returns obtained from the use of the labor. As new high-yielding crop varieties or other yield-increasing agricultural technologies are adopted on farms in less developed nations, increased marginal returns to labor are very often found in such activities as hand weeding, fertilizer spreading, pesticide application, and harvesting larger crops. Thus, in many areas, as new agricultural technology is introduced, increased amounts of labor can be profitably employed, leading to increased demand for labor (see figure 7.4).

The sum of each farmer's demand, determined by the marginal return curves for labor, establishes over time a sequence of community labor demand curves D_1, D_2, and D_3 (see figure 7.5). As the supply of rural labor moves to the right through time (S_1, S_2, and S_3), the wage levels at which the labor supply and demand curves intersect will depend upon the relative rate of movement of the supply and demand curves. With low rates of introduction of labor demanding new technology, the demand curve for labor will move less rapidly to the right, resulting in a downward pressure or decline in the price (wage) of labor (panel *A*). Empirical examples of these declines include data from some of the poorer agricultural areas in India in the decade of the 1970s, where little productivity change was occurring. When a rapid series of more productive agricultural technologies is introduced, the marginal productivity of labor often increases rapidly; then the labor demand curves move rapidly to the right, and wages and rural incomes increase (panel *B*). Great increases in the demand for labor in

Figure 7.5. The Movement of Labor Demand and Supply Curves and Changes in Wages

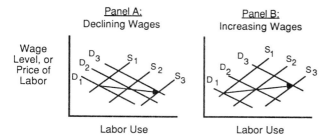

agriculture occurred for this reason in the 1970s in the Punjab area of India, for example.

Mellor explored the increase in employment that could be expected as small farms in favored agricultural areas of less developed nations became modernized (see table 7.5). He compared labor used on a traditional rice farm in India with labor used on a modernized rice farm in Japan. Both rice farms were typical in size, about 1.2 hectares (3 acres). On the Japanese farm, more labor was available per unit of land (12 months), but more than three times as much labor was used (7.2 months) per unit of land than on the Indian farm (1.9 months). Hence, in spite of the greater availability of labor per unit of land in Japan, a higher rate of utilization was achieved (58 percent). This was associated with a ten-times-larger gross output per unit of land on the Japanese farm, with an average gross agricultural production per unit of labor almost three times as great. These data suggest the magnitude of the increases in production that can be expected in many traditional irrigated rice farms in the better soil areas, as modern agricultural technology replaces traditional techniques.

National statistics from Taiwan support such farm-level estimates. Countrywide data that include all qualities of land indicate that over the forty-five-year period ending in 1960, labor use increased about 50 percent per unit of land, associated with increased cropping intensity and a tenfold increase in gross agricultural production (Johnston and Kilby 1975, p. 253).

As the green revolution got under way in the late 1960s, there was great concern that rural employment opportunities might decrease. To explore this question, Barker and Cordova (1978, p. 177) reviewed studies of labor utilization in rice production in seven Asian countries. They found that modern high-yielding rice varieties were associated with an increase of 10 to 44 percent in labor input per unit of land. In two of the most important rice-producing areas of the Philippines over the ten-year period (1966 to 1975), during which the first waves of high-yielding rice varieties were being introduced, labor input generally increased, with a fairly substantial gain in hired labor use and a tendency for the amount of family labor use to decline (Barker and Cordova 1978, p. 131).

Table 7.5. Comparisons of Labor Use and Productivity in Rice Farming: West Bengal, India, and the Kinki District, Japan

Measure	West Bengal	Kinki District
Average size of holding (acres)	2.90	3.00
Annual available labor per holding (man months)	24.00	37.00
Annual available labor per acre (man months)	8.00	12.00
Labor utilization per acre (man months)	1.90	7.20
Labor utilization as % of availability	23.00	58.00
Operating expenses per acre (dollars)	17.30	132.00
Value of fertilizer per acre (dollars)	2.70	34.90
Gross output per acre (dollars)	45.80	448.30
Gross output per month of labor (dollars)	24.00	62.00

Source: Modified from Mellor 1962 (p. 42). Reprinted with permission.

This result is consistent with the economic model of the household presented earlier.

To conclude, a moderate increase in labor input per unit of land has generally been associated with the introduction of more productive biological and chemical technologies, such as improved seeds and chemical fertilizers. However, due to the much higher yields, labor input per ton of crop has usually decreased significantly, resulting in higher labor productivity and a lower real cost of production. In the next chapter, additional evidence is presented on the positive effect on labor use of the new biological and chemical technologies. The potentially negative consequences on employment of the introduction of some new mechanical technologies are examined in chapter 9.

INDIRECT LABOR DEMAND THROUGH BACKWARD AND FORWARD LINKAGES

While in a particular region the direct impact of changes in agricultural production activities on agricultural labor may be positive or negative, the indirect, off-farm demand for labor with the shift to more productive agriculture is very often positive, for two reasons. First, as agricultural development accelerates, backward linkages grow as the flow of farm inputs produced in other sectors increases. These expanded marketing systems require more labor to supply such inputs as improved seeds, fertilizer, pesticides, and farm machinery (the great changes in input supply are shown in table 8.1, discussed in the next chapter). Second, forward linkages increase as agricultural product processing and marketing grow beyond the farm gate. Increases in both these linkages expand off-farm demand for labor.

Ahammed and Herdt (1983) provided an example of the magnitude of the direct and indirect impacts on employment through a study of changes in rice production technology in the Philippines. They found shifts to power tillage and power threshing and an increased use of gravity flow and pump irrigation. Using a national social accounting matrix for analysis, they estimated that the direct employment effects of mechanization were mostly negative, but the indirect effects were often positive. However, both the direct and indirect effects of increased irrigation were positive on employment. The combination of the changes indicated strong positive direct and indirect employment effects, because the positive effect of irrigation greatly outweighed the negative effect of mechanization. This research demonstrates the importance of including estimates of the direct and indirect off-farm employment effects of changes in agricultural technology.

LABOR DEMAND IN THE NONAGRICULTURAL SECTORS

The professional literature has for a long time assumed that the increased demand for nonagricultural labor originated primarily in urban areas. However, recent research on nonfarm rural economic activities led by Liedholm (Chuta and Liedholm 1984) and others has demonstrated the existence of large numbers of rural nonfarm economic activities and predicts that considerable expansion of employment in these sectors can be expected. Some of the expansion in rural nonfarm economic activity results from the increased input and product marketing demands of the agricultural sector, but much of it originates with demand for many high-income elasticity nonagricultural goods and services (examined in chapter 3).

Estimates of the proportion of the rural labor force with primary employment in nonfarm sectors in seventeen less developed nations ranged from 14 to 33 percent for the years between 1964 and 1972. In nine less developed nations, rural manufacturing was the most important source of nonfarm employment, followed by service sector activities, and then by trade and commerce, with smaller numbers employed in construction (Chuta and Liedholm 1984, pp. 4 and 9).

What are the prospects for increases in nonagricultural employment in rural areas as development accelerates? Some economists have viewed goods and services produced in rural areas as inferior, with negative income elasticities. If this were true, the demand for these goods and services would decrease with economic growth, and rural nonagricultural employment in these industries would decrease. Empirical research, however, has shown that the income elasticities of many rural nonfarm goods and services are positive—some above 1.0—due to both domestic and foreign demand. Hence, in many areas, increasing employment in these industries can be expected. Estimates of the annual percentage rates of growth of rural nonfarm employment over a recent ten-year interval in representative less developed nations are Taiwan, 9.4; Kenya, 8.8; the Gapan area of the Philippines, 8.5; India, 4.0; and South Korea, 3.2 (Chuta and Liedholm 1984, pp. 18 and 80).

Labor Productivity, Employment, and Wages

The preceding section has explored theory and empirical studies that identified the causes of changing supplies and demands for rural labor. This section focuses on labor productivity, employment, and wages.

THE ANNUAL CYCLE OF LABOR DEMAND

It is important to begin an examination of labor productivity by recognizing the variability of labor demand in agriculture. Agricultural labor shortages occur in peak labor demand periods, such as during land preparation, weeding, and harvest. Wages of agricultural laborers are often higher during these periods. Linear programming studies that examine labor use in short periods of time during an agricultural cycle also usually show high shadow prices for the value of labor during peak labor demand periods. Such results often indicate marginal returns to labor three or four times the wage rate. These studies highlight the point that annual farm income is often limited by the quantity of labor available at peak demand periods. However, during other parts of the year little productive agricultural employment may be available.

An example of labor demand peaks is provided by a study in southern central India (see figure 7.6). This figure shows both existing labor demand peaks and the much larger peaks in labor demand that would be generated with the introduction of proposed new crop technologies. The figure also illustrates a number of important problems in making estimates of labor productivity and unemployment.

First, the horizontal lines show estimates of the average amount of labor available in cultivator households and in all village households for all work, assuming seven hours of work is available per day all year, including holidays. However, not all of this time is available for agricultural labor, as these households engage in many other economic activities. Using the economic model of the household, with its assumption of economic rationality in the allocation of labor, the data in figure 7.6 suggest that the real availability of labor for agriculture is likely to be much closer to forty or fewer man-equivalent hours per hectare, for this is the observed peak level of labor use with current agricultural practices. Unless the marginal returns to labor in agriculture were to increase greatly, these observed peaks in agricultural labor use are likely to indicate periods of significant labor constraint for new agricultural activities due to existing high marginal returns to labor in agriculture and to competing opportunities for household members to earn income.

Second, the figure shows that the much larger labor demand peaks, projected to arise with the use of new agricultural technology, are likely to lead to severe labor shortages. Thus, additional forms of labor-substituting mechanization are likely to be required to moderate these labor bottlenecks and to increase total annual labor productivity and income. And finally, it is clear from the figure that what is important is the sum of the amounts of labor and wages of house-

Figure 7.6. Human Labor Availability and Use of New Watershed-Based Technology in the South Indian Humid Tropics

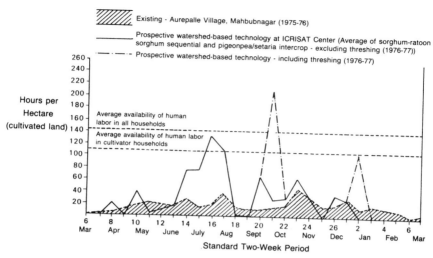

Source: ICRISAT 1979a (p. 364).
Note: Average labor available per working person was assumed as seven hours per day for 365 days per year.

hold members over the whole year. This determines income and levels of living. Thus, in some circumstances, increasing labor productivity and income through mechanization during peak labor demand periods could increase annual farm income sufficiently to offset some reduction in total annual days of employment. Note, however, that the income effect of mechanization on household labor is likely to vary greatly among households, depending on their land, labor, and other resources.

LABOR PRODUCTIVITY

The post–World War II models of economic development often assumed a sizable pool of largely unemployed labor in rural areas with very low or zero marginal productivity. If this "free" labor resource was available, it could be drawn into more productive industrial employment with little or no decrease in agricultural production. This hypothesis of the availability of large amounts of rural labor for transfer to other economic activities has engendered a great deal of empirical research on rural labor.

The circumstances in which zero or very low marginal returns to labor might exist were indicated by Mellor and Stevens (see figure 7.7). Farming families in many instances may attain a level of average annual product per family member, d, considerably above the subsistence level, g. In these circumstances, as more members are added to the family, a situation may arise in which the

Figure 7.7. Low or Zero Marginal Product of Labor in Agriculture

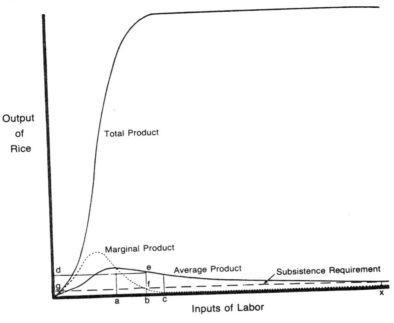

Source: Mellor and Stevens 1956 (p. 782). Reprinted with permission.

additional inputs of labor contribute very little or nothing to agricultural production at *c*. As long as the average product of family labor is above the subsistence level, the family can continue to share the work and food. In this way, in productive farming areas, considerable numbers of farm workers who produce little could be maintained for long periods. Many estimates have been made for different agricultures of the amounts of labor that might be withdrawn under various sets of assumptions without reducing agricultural production. However, despite the apparently unneeded labor indicated by these studies, the labor continues to be employed in agriculture.[5]

The presence of large numbers of apparently low-productivity laborers is partly explained by recent household economic theory. Becker (1976) and others have emphasized the value of leisure as an opportunity cost that would have to be forgone for work; hence, a zero opportunity cost for labor in agriculture appears unlikely, as laborers would have to produce more than the opportunity cost of leisure to engage rationally in work. However, very low marginal pro-

5. A review of the large number of studies of "surplus" agricultural labor that began before World War II was provided by Kao et al. (1964). Issues in defining kinds of unemployment are discussed by Todaro (1976, pp. 207–12); Meier (1976, pp. 180–82); and Yotopoulos and Nugent (1976, pp. 198–217).

ductivity of labor in agriculture is likely in some situations for significant numbers of family farm workers. Despite the very low marginal product from this labor, other nonmaterial benefits from work with the family, such as the enjoyment of working together and the escape from negative sanctions for not working, may explain considerable "excess" labor use in these agricultural areas.

EMPLOYMENT, UNEMPLOYMENT, AND UNDEREMPLOYMENT

The economics profession does not have generally accepted definitions for employment and unemployment. The definitional issues highlight and are intertwined with theoretical and empirical problems of labor measurement. These problems include the following three. First, the time frame used in data gathering: Is employment estimated for a particular day, for a month, or over the whole year? A rural laborer at harvesttime would be reported fully employed, although he or she might be unemployed much of the rest of the year. Second, the definition of productivity: some laborers reported as working full time may, because of handicaps, illness, or lack of complementary resources to work with, not produce enough for minimum subsistence. And third, the values and social rules that define and measure employment: for example, Christian monks and Indian holy men hold values such that they are voluntarily materially very poor but not "unemployed" in their view. The effect of social rules is illustrated by cultural prohibitions against female employment in some occupations. Such social rules often reduce income and increase unemployment.

Two other issues affect estimates of unemployment. First, who classifies employment status—the worker, based on his or her views about employment, or the data gatherer, based upon a set of productivity or other criteria? The second problem relates to the varying criteria for the range of ages to be included in the labor force, and particularly the way in which people in school are counted.[6]

The use of the term *underemployment* is particularly controversial because of the uncertainty of its meaning in a developmental context. Underemployment implies that changes can be made in government policies or the investment of government or private resources that could draw the underemployed into more productive employment. If, however, constraints in the government and private sectors prevent actions from being taken to more productively employ the underemployed, the concept and the associated labor estimates appear to have little value for development policy. In these circumstances, underemployed laborers are simply producing less than someone judges they could or should by some often undefined set of criteria, often under undefined circumstances.[7]

---

6. See also Edwards 1974; Todaro 1976 (pp. 207–12); Meier 1976 (pp. 180–82); and Yotopoulos and Nugent 1976 (pp. 198–217).

7. Of the many studies of labor productivity, wages, and employment in rural areas of less developed nations, the following are representative: Cleave 1974; Edwards 1974; Binswanger and Rosenzweig 1984; ILO 1977; and Krishna 1973, 1974, and 1980. The issue of the backward-bending supply curve of labor was examined by Miracle and Fetter (1970) and by G. Ellis (1981).

Policies for Increased Employment, Productivity, and Equity

Rural employment, labor productivity, and equity can be increased to some extent through action in seven policy areas (see also Squire 1981).

1. The modern agricultural production function presented at the beginning of this chapter demonstrates that growth in agricultural production is a function of the quantity and quality of physical (production equipment) and human (labor) resources employed in production. Hence, labor productivity is increased by the development and use of new, more productive technologies and the invention and the adoption of associated required changes in institutional arrangements that increase the marginal productivity of capital and labor.

2. Expanding nonagricultural employment opportunities in rural areas of less developed nations can contribute in many ways to increasing national income, for creating jobs reduces both the costs of finding other employment for people earning little in rural areas and the need for large additional resources in urban areas to provide migrants with minimal physical and social conditions.

3. The modern agricultural production function also shows that the quality of labor affects production. Hence, activities that increase the performance levels of labor, such as literacy and the ability to calculate, will increase the productivity of labor. Additional important human investment measures include mid-level technical educational experiences that include increasing knowledge of the sciences of crop and animal production, agricultural chemicals, mechanics and motor repair, electrical and electronic repair, plumbing, metal and plastic working, and machine woodworking.

4. A fundamental conclusion of the induced development model and of empirical studies in agricultural and rural employment is that the underpricing of capital inputs for farming usually leads to less employment. Whenever farmers and entrepreneurs can gain access to profitable labor-displacing technology at prices below market costs, employment is unnecessarily reduced. Specifically, underpricing capital through subsidies has two negative effects on labor: (1) it increases the optimum amount of capital relative to labor in farming; and (2), much more insidiously, it induces technological and institutional change to be biased in a labor-saving direction (see figure 6.4).

5. Among the kinds of barriers that reduce the optimum allocation of labor are the following two: (1) any actions that increase the segmentation of labor markets, including labor legislation that sets minimum wages too high and unions that push wages too high and limit access to occupations; and (2) discrimination in hiring and in wages based on noneconomic factors, such as race and sex. The reduction of labor market barriers will increase total

output and improve labor's earnings and, thus, income distribution. Particularly insidious are high minimum wages, for above-market wages cause management in both the public and private sectors to choose more capital intensive technology than they would otherwise. Reduced demand for labor follows, and the share of labor in total factor cost declines.

6. In some areas, there are opportunities for building labor-intensive infrastructure projects to increase agricultural productivity. These include projects in irrigation, drainage, roads, communications, and electric power. Experience with rural works programs in Bangladesh and the organization of rural labor in the People's Republic of China are instructive (see, for example, Thomas 1974).

7. Policies to reduce disparities in income between agricultural laborers and other workers include not only those that increase the demand for labor and labor's human capital but those that augment the physical capital and social services that laborers control or have access to. Specific programs include land reform, land-to-the-tiller programs, programs that help workers obtain improved housing, education, and health and other private and government services. This can occur if government brings service availability in rural areas up to the level in urban areas.

Important Concepts

Labor productivity	Household labor allocation model
Land productivity	Women in agricultural development
Benefit-cost analysis	Peak agricultural population
Benefit-cost ratio	Indirect labor demand
Internal rate of return	Backward and forward linkages
Sensitivity analysis	Peak labor demand and the annual
Financial and economic analysis	agricultural cycle
Plantations and agricultural estates	Marginal, average, and zero
Government settlement projects	productivity of labor
Spontaneous settlements and	Employment, unemployment, and
colonizations	underemployment

Sample Questions

1. Explain the relation between agricultural labor productivity, land productivity, and land area per agricultural laborer.

2. What is cost-benefit (benefit-cost) analysis? Why is it used to evaluate land development projects?

3. Explain in economic terms why farmers, in order to increase production in less developed nations, often increase the amount of land used in farming, while those in more developed nations do not.

4. Despite the political and social problems that have often been associated with plantation development, why have plantations and similar land development projects been increasing in less developed nations?

5. Why have government settlement projects often been so costly per settler as compared with spontaneous land development?

6. How does the economic model of the household aid in understanding the changes a farming family is likely to make in its use of labor resources? Specifically, what are the ways the adoption of a new, more productive agricultural technology could affect family labor allocation? Specify important assumptions.

7. In what ways can agricultural development negatively affect women?

8. Using a single input production function, show how new agricultural technology could increase or decrease the demand for labor.

9. What government policies are likely to increase employment opportunities in agriculture?

III

Sources of Accelerated Change in Agriculture: Investment in Technology, Institutions, and Human Capital

Introduction to Part III

Continuously increasing growth in agricultural productivity is achieved by shifting from a resource-based to a science-based agriculture. Productivity in traditional agriculture depends largely on the kinds of soil, seeds, and other resources farmers have been able to gain control of over the centuries. Continual search and selection of the best seeds have also contributed to gradual yield increases. In some areas, investment of labor in modifying soil and moisture, such as digging gravity-flow irrigation systems and terracing, has augmented crop productivity, as has the occasional invention of new agricultural technologies and institutional arrangements.

However, these methods of increasing agricultural productivity are not able to increase farm output rapidly enough to match either present population growth rates or increases in demand for agricultural products resulting from more rapid growth in per capita income. Hence, an immense transformation of traditional agriculture to scientific agriculture must occur, to achieve the growth rates required of agriculture. Over the last 150 years, the knowledge gained from the sciences of biology, chemistry, and physics has been increasingly applied to farming. In more developed countries, a great many resources have been used to produce new agricultural technology; to improve institutions for agriculture and aid farmers to improve their allocation of resources; and to invest in human capital through education. These investments have increased agricultural growth rates and productivity. Without the achievement of a science-based agriculture in the more developed nations over the last century, which has enabled the export of large food surpluses in the last three decades, many more less developed nations might have faced grim Malthusian food shortages.

The great scope of the transformation to scientific agriculture is seen by contrasting the sources of inputs and the amounts of agricultural product marketing required in traditional and science-based agricultures (see figure III.1). In traditional agriculture, essentially all of the agricultural inputs are obtained from within the village or from the surrounding area, including seeds, crop nutrients from natural soil regeneration and manure, tools (mostly handmade), and credit (solid lines on figure III.1). As new, higher return inputs, embodying modern

Figure III.1. Changes in Input and Product Flows During the Agricultural Transformation

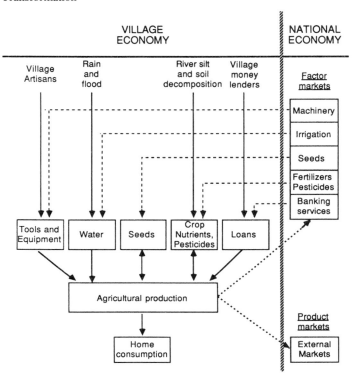

——— Major agricultural input and product flows in Traditional Agriculture

- - - - - New, or greatly enlarged, agricultural input and product flows due to a technologically and institutionally dynamic agriculture

scientific knowledge, become available, farmers obtain them from outside the village: high-yielding seeds, farm machinery, chemical fertilizers, pesticides, larger amounts of credit at lower costs, and so forth (dotted lines on figure III.1). To pay for the more productive inputs, farmers have to sell an increasingly greater proportion of their agricultural production. Increasing farm sales requires great expansion of agricultural product marketing services, also. In this agricultural transformation, farms become factories in the fields, requiring technological, social, and economic change in just about every aspect of farm and family life. This takes decades.

In the preceding chapter, which focused on the classical economist's production resources of land and labor, relatively little scope was found for rapidly increasing agricultural production. The following four chapters focus on the economics of the application of the biological, chemical, physical, and social sciences to agriculture. They are concerned with investment in technological and institutional change and in human capital to enable rapid increases in rates of agricultural growth. These chapters employ the microeconomic tools of the induced innovation model to provide guidance for improved decisions in the allocation of scarce investment resources by farmers and by society for increased farm productivity in the widely different economic, technological, institutional, social, and political environments of less developed nations.

In applying the theory of agricultural development presented in chapter 6, particular emphasis has been placed in these chapters on examining the results of empirical studies of agriculture development in emerging nations in order to test the usefulness of the induced innovation model and neoclassical economic tools, generally. In this way, we hope to demonstrate the use of economic theory in identifying better policy for improved use of agricultural and other resources in these nations.

Agricultural development implies change, the upsetting of equilibria. These chapters explore how the economic equilibrium of traditional agriculture is upset to obtain more rapid growth in agricultural production and income. The challenge of development is to create and manage the continuously shifting disequilibria in agriculture that enable greater productivity and higher levels of living. The four fundamental elements in this process are technological change, institutional change, investment in human capital, and investment in research and extension to accelerate technological and institutional change. The greater the rate of these changes, the greater the need for complementary investment in human capital to enable more productive management of increasingly complex farms and agribusinesses and the growing agricultural sector.

8

Economics of Change in Biological and Chemical Technologies

This transformation is dependent upon investing in agriculture. . . . But it is not primarily a problem of the supply of capital. It is rather a problem of determining the forms this investment must take, forms that will make it profitable to invest in agriculture.

—T. W. Schultz 1964b, p. 4

Mankind is in the midst of an agricultural food-production revolution, but has witnessed only the initial stages. Most of the dramatic developments in food production have occurred in this generation. Hybrid corn has been commercialized scarcely more than 40 years. . . . Most of the scientific achievements for increased agricultural food productivity have occurred since the 1950s, and many originated in the 1960s. Dramatic changes have occurred in many agricultural and food statistics since the early 1970s.

Modern food-production technology has touched only a few areas, primarily temperate-zone agriculture. Many major food crops—seed legumes, sweet potatoes, cassava, and the millets—have thus received only token attention. The sciences of home food gardening, small-scale agricultural and farming systems have scarcely been addressed.

—Sylvan H. Wittwer in Chou et al. 1977, p. 114

Increasing Crop Productivity on Currently Farmed Lands

This chapter focuses upon the economics of increasing agricultural productivity on currently farmed land. It is concerned with the economics of the green revolution (the seed and fertilizer revolution), which can be defined as the period of initial rapid spread to less developed nations of short-stature, high-yielding, fertilizer-responsive varieties of wheat, rice, and maize. The widespread adoption of these new varieties began about 1967 in many nations. Many of the early improved wheat and maize varieties were developed at the International Maize and Wheat Improvement Center (CIMMYT) near Mexico City, and many of the high-yielding rice varieties at the International Rice Research Institute (IRRI) in the Philippines (see also Hayami and Ruttan 1985, p. 61).

The increased yields of the green revolution were due largely to the use of modern seeds and chemical fertilizer. The economic gains that we expect from further application of the biological and chemical sciences to agriculture make possible a continuously evolving green revolution in less developed nations, if national resource allocation and policy decisions for agriculture are made that facilitate the growth of agriculture.

The analysis in this chapter aids in these decisions. It shows how increased use of more productive inputs, such as modern seeds and improved animals, augments the demand for complementary inputs, such as labor, irrigation water, pesticides, animal feeds, and veterinary services.

A focus upon land operated by millions of complicated small farms sometimes appears uninteresting compared to dramatic projects, such as large land development schemes. But the importance of this focus is highlighted by the reality that only relatively small additions to arable land by the year 2000 and beyond are possible in many less developed nations; even small yield increases achieved on the large areas of currently farmed land would have much greater impact on national agricultural output.

The development problem in currently farmed areas can be posed as follows. If no significant change in agricultural technology is taking place and the relative prices of inputs and agricultural products remain fairly stable, what government or private activities would yield high returns in increased agricultural growth? What activities does the induced innovation model point to as being most likely to lead to greater farm productivity? Can successes of the rapidly growing agricultures in some areas of less developed nations aid in identifying high-return strategies for agricultural growth?

Guidelines from Economic Theory

The induced innovation model presented in chapter 6 is based on neoclassical microeconomic theory. It indicates that farmers will increase their investments if one or more of the following three changes occurs: (1) increased yields from a given amount of resources (an increase in the productivity of agricultural technology); (2) a decline in resource (input) costs relative to product prices; or (3) an increase in product prices relative to the cost of inputs. How may these changes be achieved? The induced innovation model proposes that private and government innovators will seek to develop new agricultural technologies that either enable substitution of lower cost resources (inputs) in agricultural production or increase output with the same resource costs. Farmers will then buy these new inputs and technologies to increase their net return.

Changing relative prices of agricultural inputs are common. Many less developed nations have had increases in land costs relative to labor costs, as population grows on currently farmed land. A relative price change of this kind induces the development of innovations in agriculture that increase output per unit

Figure 8.1. Decline in Relative Costs of Chemical Fertilizers and Farm Machinery in the United States and Japan, 1880–1960

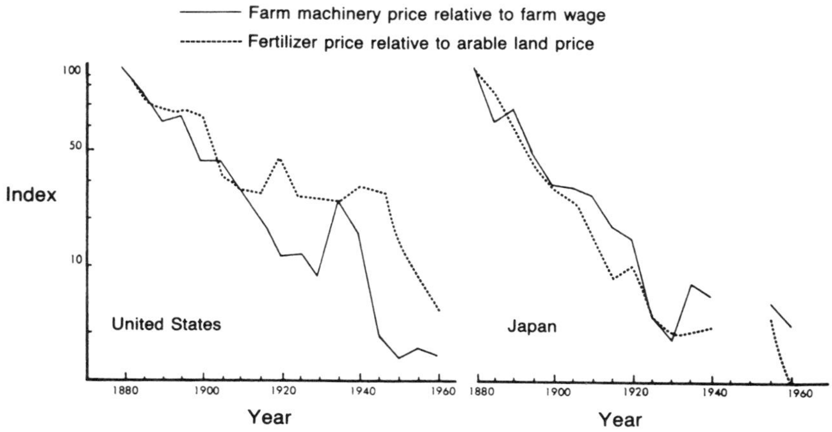

Source: Hayami and Ruttan 1971 (p. 123). Reprinted with permission.
Note: 1880 = 100.

of land, such as through greater crop yields or increased cropping intensity (more crops grown per year on a piece of land). Technologies and institutions that are more profitable under the new relative prices with higher land costs will be incorporated into agriculture.

Empirical examples of dramatic changes in the relative prices of two important agricultural inputs come from the United States and Japan over the last eighty years (see figure 8.1). The similar relative price changes experienced in these nations with such widely different land and labor resources are very instructive. In both nations over the period from 1880 to 1960, the price of fertilizer relative to the cost of land declined dramatically. In Japan, fertilizer prices relative to land declined continually, except during the two world wars. In the United States, fertilizer prices relative to land declined until 1910, held about steady until 1950, and then dropped further. The cost of agricultural machinery relative to agricultural labor declined almost continuously in both Japan and the United States over the eighty-year period, with the exception of the 1930s. For both fertilizer and agricultural machinery, the declines in relative prices were greater than 90 percent! According to the induced innovation model, price changes of such a magnitude would be expected to cause innovators in the two nations to develop agricultural methods that would use more fertilizer and more machinery. They did, and vast quantities of these inputs were used.

The desirability of substituting low-cost agricultural inputs for more costly ones during agricultural development can be seen another way, by focusing on input supply curves. Generally, the challenge is to replace farm inputs that have inelastic supply schedules with farm inputs that have elastic supply schedules.

An inelastic supply schedule leads to rapid increases in price, preventing profitable use of much more of this input. In contrast, increased use of an input with an elastic supply schedule leads to only small increases in price. Animal manure and chemical fertilizer illustrate these supply curves. The supply of plant nutrients from animal manure, once all local manure has been spread on the fields, becomes very inelastic. Obtaining more manure usually involves greatly increased production and transportation costs and hence much greater cost per unit spread on the field. In contrast, with large-scale chemical fertilizer plants or fertilizer imports, fertilizer supply curves are very elastic in less developed nations after initial distribution problems have been solved. Thus, the real cost of fertilizer to the nation and to farmers can remain about the same as the use of chemical fertilizer doubles, quadruples, or increases tenfold. And in many cases, as increasing volumes of chemical fertilizer are delivered to different areas, economies of scale in input marketing lead to real declines in fertilizer costs.

Large Shifts to More Productive Inputs

As a science-based agriculture develops with increasingly more productive technology and as changes in the relative prices of inputs occur, immense shifts in the use of farm inputs result. The shifts in the factor shares, or the proportions of the different inputs, in agricultural production are illustrated by U.S. data from 1870 to 1958 (see table 8.1). In 1870, 65 percent of the value of all inputs used in agriculture consisted of labor, while capital inputs were divided about evenly between the costs of fixed capital (18 percent), consisting of land and buildings, and other inputs (17 percent), which included seed, tools, animals, and other equipment. In many areas of less developed nations today, labor inputs represent a much larger share and capital inputs a smaller share than in the United States in 1870.

In the United States over the last hundred years, two major changes in factor shares in agriculture have taken place. First, as the relative cost of labor to all forms of capital increased, the share of labor in agricultural production declined, until in 1958 labor represented only 30 percent of the value of inputs in farm production. And second, a large shift occurred also in the shares of the different forms of agricultural capital. As the productivity of other capital goods increased and their relative cost declined, their share in total inputs increased from 17 percent in 1870 to 55 percent in 1958, becoming almost four times more important than fixed capital. Similar shifts in the proportions of agricultural inputs have taken place in other more developed nations. We expect even more rapid changes in the mix of inputs in less developed nations as agriculture becomes modernized. Thus, a central question of agricultural development is what technological forms these new inputs will take in each area. We only know they need to be in elastic supply and to provide high returns.

Table 8.1. Changing Factor Shares of Agricultural Inputs in U.S. Agriculture, 1870–1958 (percent)

Year	Labor	Capital	
		Land and Buildings (Fixed Capital)	Other Inputs
1870	65	18	17
1900	57	19	24
1920	50	18	32
1940	41	18	41
1940[a]	56	14	30[b]
1950	40	15	45
1958	30	15	55[b]

Source: Loomis and Barton 1961 (pp. 11–12).
[a] New series.
[b] Components of other inputs are shown in table below.

Year	Power and Machinery	Seed, Feed and Livestock (percent share)	Fertilizer and Lime	Other
1940	10	5	2	13
1958	22	11	5	17

Economics of the Seed and Fertilizer (Green) Revolution

Farm Level Effects

The development of fertilizer-responsive, high-yielding varieties of wheat, rice, and maize (corn) adapted to less developed nations provides a dramatic example of the use of more productive inputs with highly elastic supply. The increasing cost of land relative to the cost of seed and fertilizer has induced farmers to invest in these new high-return inputs. These choices by farmers caused the large spurt in agricultural production that occurred in South Asia after 1967. When first introduced in traditional agricultural areas, high-yielding varieties and more chemical fertilizer often increased yields by 50 to 100 percent—truly a green revolution for these farmers. Such yield increases have seldom been experienced in history, even by modern farmers in more developed nations!

The economics of the adoption of modern crop varieties was demonstrated in a classic paper by Herdt and Mellor (1964). It compared the rice to fertilizer production functions of two traditional varieties grown in India with two high-yielding varieties in the United States that had been developed through decades of research (see figure 8.2). The study illuminates two fundamental points about the yield revolution achieved by crop scientists in the last three decades. First,

Figure 8.2. The Greater Response of Modern Rice Varieties to Nitrogen Fertilizer: Experiment Station Yields in the United States and India, 1964

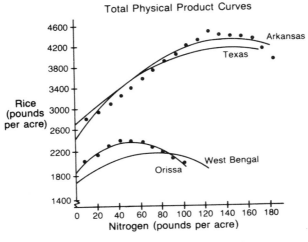

Source: Adapted from Herdt and Mellor 1964 (p. 152).

without additional fertilizer the modern varieties may or may not produce higher yields. In this particular study, without added nitrogen fertilizer, the modern U.S. varieties had a somewhat higher yield than the traditional Indian varieties, probably due to the higher nitrogen levels in the U.S. fields. This is often not the case, for in many areas of less developed nations modern crop seeds often do no better, and sometimes worse, than traditional varieties without additional fertilizer. Traditional varieties have been selected over the decades from plants that continue to produce even with low soil fertility. The second point is that the traditional varieties usually achieve maximum yields with less nitrogen, in this case at 60 to 100 pounds per acre (67 to 50 kilograms per hectare), while the maximum yields for the modern varieties were not reached until 140 to 160 pounds per acre (72 to 82 kilograms per hectare) were applied.

Unfortunately for many traditional agricultural areas in the less developed world, grain varieties have not been developed that can be grown profitably in areas with poor soil structure, difficult moisture conditions, water control problems, and other environmental constraints. In these areas, traditional crops may continue to be the most profitable for some time. Such farming areas remain challenging to agricultural scientists.

The greatly increased crop yields of recent decades have not been limited to grains. Agricultural scientists have achieved large yield increases in many other crops, including potatoes, sugar, cotton, rubber, and palm oil. Prospects for productivity increases in the decades ahead, through additional investment in the application of science to agriculture, are explored in chapter 11.

National Effects

THE ECONOMICS OF ADOPTION

What factors influence the rate and the extent of adoption of new technologies, such as the modern grain varieties? In path-breaking studies of the adoption of hybrid maize (corn) by farmers in the United States, Griliches (1957 and 1960) demonstrated that the rate of adoption by farmers of more productive hybrid seeds was largely a function of the amount of increase in income obtainable. In areas where high-yielding seeds were much more profitable than currently planted varieties, (1) the adoption rates of the new seeds were higher; and (2) the proportion of the area planted with the high-yielding seeds was greater. This research provides strong empirical support for the induced innovation model which proposes that farmers are responsive to the amount of economic incentive provided by new technology. Where large gains in income were possible, the adoption of new crop varieties has been rapid. By 1983, the percentages of the total areas planted to modern grain varieties had increased to the following levels: for wheat—Asia, 79 (excluding communist nations); China, 31; Near East, 31; Africa, 51; Latin America, 78; and for rice—Asia, 45 (excluding communist nations); communist Asia, 81; Near East, 8; Africa, 5; and Latin America, 33 (Dalrymple 1986a, b). Thus, after less than two decades in the three continents of the less developed world, an overall weighted average of more than 50 percent of the land in these crops has been seeded to modern grain varieties. The rapid adoption by farmers of these varieties was caused by the large increases in income they obtained. [1]

THE EFFECTS ON NATIONAL PRODUCTION

The impact of the modern grain varieties on national agricultural production in many nations was great, and in a number of less developed nations it was dramatic. For example, from 1967 to 1971, as modern wheat seeds produced in Mexico from varieties developed by CIMMYT were introduced into Pakistan, national average wheat yields increased by one-fourth, and national wheat production increased by approximately one-third (Eckert 1977, p. 155). In Colombia, total rice production doubled in a commercial, irrigated farm area between 1969 and 1974, as the modern rice varieties were being adopted (Wortman and Cummings 1978, p. 216). In Turkey, wheat yields increased about 40 percent over a ten-year period ending in 1976, while total production increased even more (Wortman and Cummings 1978, p. 214). In India, between 1966 and 1974 wheat yields almost doubled, and national wheat production more than doubled.

A dramatic untold story lies behind these great achievements. In the 1970s, how much famine and misery would have been suffered in less developed nations if the international research institutes had not produced the high-yielding

---

1. Economic appraisals of the new crop technologies are in Humphreys and Pearson 1979; Goodwin, Sanders, and De Hollanda 1980; and Thiam and Ong 1979.

wheat and rice seeds and if these nations had not organized effective programs for their importation, multiplication, and distribution to farmers?[2]

THE EFFECTS ON NUTRITION

The possible negative effects on human nutrition of the modern crop varieties were of concern to many. (1) How do the new varieties affect the quantity of calories and protein and other nutritional elements produced? (2) Has the quality of the protein and other nutrient elements for human consumption been affected? (3) What is the overall effect on family food consumption?

The first question requires estimates of total calories and protein produced per unit of land. As the calories, or food energy, produced per unit weight of grain are essentially the same in the modern varieties as in the traditional varieties, any increase in yield will increase the calories produced. With respect to protein, the grains of high-yielding varieties have been found to contain 5 to 10 percent less protein per unit of weight. But with the usual yield increases of 25 and 50 percent or more, a much greater total amount of protein is produced. Thus, a farm family would have more total protein available to eat or to exchange for other foods of higher protein value, such as meat, or to purchase other goods.

To the second question, concerning protein quality, an Indian study provides an answer. This study compared the weight gain produced in rats from two high-yielding rice varieties and a popular traditional variety from northern India. (Rats are used in studies of nutritional value for humans because their digestive system is similar to that of humans.) The new rice varieties caused weight gains and had protein efficiency ratios equal to or greater than the traditional rice variety (Mitra and Das 1971, p. 928). Many other studies have shown similar results. Explorations of nutrient values for other food elements in the modern grains generally lead to similar conclusions.

In addition, some new grain varieties have been bred for superior nutritional performance. Examples are high-lysine maize and sorghum. These varieties have increased levels of the amino acid, lysine, which provides increased protein nutrition value. Unfortunately, these varieties, to date, have had somewhat lower yields, and hence unless a higher price is paid for the high-lysine grains, they are less profitable to grow than other modern varieties.

In answer to question three, the overall effect of increased grain productivity per unit of land is an increase in grain and money income through grain sales. The increased farm income obtained in many areas from adoption of the new

---

2. Additional useful references on the impacts of the green revolution include Gotsch and Falcon 1975; Singh and Day 1975; Farmer 1977; IRRI 1978b; R. S. Anderson 1982; Dalrymple 1986a, b; Herdt and Capule 1983; Eckert 1977; Bernsten, Siwi, and Beachell 1982; Castillo et al. 1973; Randhawa 1974; Ladejinsky 1970; Ruttan and Binswanger 1978; Hayami 1984; Ruttan 1977; Falcon 1970; and Pinstrup-Andersen and Hazell 1987.

grain varieties has led to increased nutritional levels (see chapter 3 for the effect of income on food consumption). [3]

Future Prospects

The continuing expansion of the seed and fertilizer revolution and the increasing demand for these inputs result from their greater profitability. The increased return has been caused by (1) lower chemical fertilizer prices, especially in relation to other inputs; (2) more productive plant materials; (3) the high economic complementarity between the modern seeds and fertilizers; and (4) the elastic supplies of these inputs.

INCREASED DEMAND FOR MORE PRODUCTIVE PLANT MATERIALS AND FERTILIZER

Worldwide fertilizer use has increased greatly over the last several decades for two reasons: (1) a real decline in world fertilizer prices until 1974, and then, after a period of increased prices, a resumption of the decline (see figure 8.1); and (2) the decline in chemical fertilizer cost relative to the cost of other sources of greater agricultural production, such as land.

The economics of increased demand for chemical fertilizer are illustrated by production function analysis of the optimum levels of fertilizer use. Data in this example are drawn from fertilizer response curves of rice obtained from farm trials in the Philippines (see figure 8.3). First consider the effect of a decline in the cost of fertilizer on the quantity of fertilizer demanded by farmers. At the time of the world energy shortage in 1974, the farm-level price for nitrogen fertilizer in the Philippines was about forty cents per kilogram. With traditional rice varieties, using the estimate of the value of the marginal product, the highest profit point occurs when the farmer uses eight kilograms of nitrogen fertilizer per hectare (Q_1). Later, the real price of nitrogen declined to about one half the earlier level, affected by a variety of factors, including reduced fertilizer production costs and improved marketing arrangements. With the lower fertilizer price (P_2), much more nitrogen per hectare could be used profitably, some twenty-five kilograms (Q_2), a threefold increase.

How does the adoption of modern rice varieties affect the most profitable level of fertilizer use? With a higher marginal value product from the modern rice varieties, the most profitable level of nitrogen fertilizer use was about seventy-five kilograms per hectare (Q_3), assuming the lower farm fertilizer price (P_2). This is another threefold increase in nitrogen demand, assuming farmers could obtain the additional money needed to purchase this fertilizer.

---

3. References to the nutritional effect of high-yielding crop varieties include Berg 1981; FAO 1985b; Reutlinger and Selowski 1976; Kennedy and Pinstrup-Andersen 1983; and Timmer, Falcon, and Pearson 1983 (esp. chap. 2).

Figure 8.3. Profitable Nitrogen Applications for Irrigated Rice, with Traditional and Modern Varieties, the Philippines

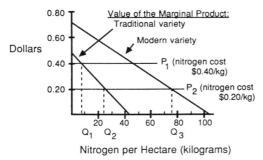

Source: Developed from data in David and Barker 1978 (pp. 183 and 332).
Note: Rice price was $0.044 per kilogram.

INCREASED DEMAND DUE TO SEED-FERTILIZER COMPLEMENTARITIES

In most agricultural and other production processes, there is considerable complementarity among many of the inputs. Economic complementarity occurs when the productivity of one input is influenced by the use of another input (see figure 8.4, panel A). The isoquants have three regions. In the center of curve 1 between points b and c, the quantity of one resource, such as seeds, can be substituted for another resource, such as phosphorous fertilizer. Thus, when moving from b to c on this isoquant in reasonably fertile soils, less fertilizer might be used with a higher seeding rate to achieve the same yield. In this region of this isoquant, seeds and fertilizer substitute for each other to achieve the same yield. However, in the part of isoquant 1 above point b, no additional amount of fertilizer can substitute for seeds; the minimum of Q_1 seeds is required to obtain this level of output. Hence, in the region a to b on the isoquant, the two resources are complementary. Obviously, with only Q_1 of seeds it would make no sense to add any more fertilizer than Q_2, because costs would simply be increased without additional yield. To increase output from point a, additional seed would have to be used to reach, say, point e on a higher isoquant.

The isoquants of inputs that are perfect complements are shown in panel B of figure 8.4. In this case, neither input can substitute under any circumstances for the other. An example could occur in a very low phosphorous soil. To have any level of yield, some phosphorous fertilizer would be required, as would some level of seeding. Another example of almost perfect complements is that of a tractor and its driver: neither can be used without the other. To move to a higher isoquant, such as isoquant 8, would require an additional driver and another tractor. More people per tractor or more tractors per person will usually not increase production much. Thus, the arrow indicates that when two or more inputs have high complementarity, combining them in the right proportions increases productivity and net returns to farmers and society.

Figure 8.4. Resource Complementarity and Resource Substitution

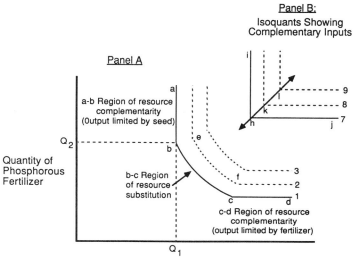

Quantity of Modern Seeds

An empirical illustration of complementarity is provided by different combinations of nitrogen and phosphate fertilizer used in maize production experiments in Iowa. Similar results are obtained in all parts of the the world. In this research, shown in table 8.2, the addition of 160 pounds per acre (180 kilograms per hectare) of nitrogen with no additional phosphate fertilizer increased the yield from 16.5 to 20.0 bushels (550 to 954 kilograms per hectare). Similarly, when phosphate fertilizer was increased to 160 pounds without additional nitrogen, yield increased to a maximum of only 26.8 bushels. However, when 160 pounds of both fertilizers were used the yield was 110.3 bushels (5,261 kilograms per hectare) of maize!

Suppose, instead, the 160 pounds of nitrogen were put on one maize field and the 160 pounds of phosphorous were put on another; the total yield of the two fields would be 20.0 plus 26.8, or 46.8, an increase of only 30 bushels over no fertilizer. This compares with the much larger yield of 110.3 bushels that would be obtained for the same input cost when both fertilizers were put on the same field. This production is 94 bushels more than with no fertilizer. Thus, complementarity between these inputs tripled the yield. Why? Growing plants require nitrogen and phosphorous in certain ratios; if these ratios are available to the plant, much greater growth occurs; otherwise, growth is limited by the lack of one of the complementary elements. Farmers continuously attempt to find complementarities in order to obtain greater productivity and higher net returns.

In planning development activities, professionals, government officials, and entrepreneurs also search for complementarities in the program elements to be included in a project or new production activity. In India, the term *package*

Table 8.2. An Illustration of Input Complementarity: Maize Yield (bushels per acre) in Western Iowa with Different Levels of Nitrogen and Phosphorus Fertilizer

Nitrogen (pounds per acre)	Phosphate (pounds per acre)				
	0	40	80	120	160
0	16.5	21.8	24.0	25.5	26.8
40	18.5	51.5	63.4	72.0	79.1
80	19.2	59.5	74.0	84.5	93.1
120	19.7	65.0	81.2	93.1	102.8
160	20.0	69.2	86.9	99.8	110.3

Source: Modified from Heady and Jensen 1954 (p. 194).

program was used for agricultural programs to indicate that using a complete package with a mix of inputs and agricultural practices at specified levels would achieve greater complementarity, and hence higher yields and net income, than if the inputs were used separately on different fields. One can hardly overemphasize the importance of assuring the availability of complementary inputs for increasing the productivity of agriculture. It should also be clear now that the shape of the isoproduct curve matters a great deal when different inputs are combined in production. Whenever significant complementarity is present, increasing the use of one resource without the other will yield much lower returns. Thus, the complementarity between seeds and fertilizer provides an additional incentive for using more of them.

ELASTIC SUPPLIES OF PLANT MATERIALS AND FERTILIZERS

The development of increasingly elastic supplies of more productive high-yielding plant materials and chemical fertilizers is fundamental to the transformation of traditional agriculture. World supplies of chemical fertilizers have been expanding more rapidly than demand, putting a downward pressure on real prices (see for example FAO, the *State of Food and Agriculture 1984,* p. 53). The source of continuous supplies of much more productive crop varieties is national and international agricultural research (see chapter 11). More elastic supplies of fertilizers to farmers depend both upon increasing the performance of input marketing (a topic of chapter 12) and the prospects for international mining and manufacturing of fertilizer.

Here we focus on government policies to facilitate more elastic supplies of fertilizer. Increases in fertilizer supplies to farmers are achieved by greater world fertilizer production and by appropriate national fertilizer policies. In a less developed nation, fertilizer prices are affected by (1) the extent to which low-cost fertilizer marketing has been developed in the different farming areas; and (2) government fertilizer policies that affect the price and supply of fertilizer. In farming areas where little fertilizer has been used to date, transportation and other marketing capacities may be poorly developed for this heavy and bulky farm input, so farm fertilizer prices may remain high. In these areas, the potential for large declines in fertilizer prices may be great if marketing costs can be reduced.

Government fertilizer policies range from those that restrict fertilizer production and marketing, causing higher prices, to those that augment supplies to farmers. National programs that support rapid expansion of fertilizer supplies have included aggressive action to facilitate fertilizer imports and marketing to farmers at the lowest prices possible. In most food deficit nations, policy changes that lower the cost of fertilizers but do not subsidize them will reduce net foreign exchange outflows, because each unit of fertilizer produces three to ten additional units of crop in areas where high-yielding fertilizer responsive seeds are used. The additional agricultural production either substitutes for costly food imports or, through the sale of some of the increased production abroad, provides a net gain in foreign exchange to the less developed nation.

The question of whether fertilizer subsidies should be given by governments to increase their use is important. Although the general topic of government price policies for agriculture is examined in chapter 14, a number of points are appropriate here. Subsidies for fertilizer have sometimes been used successfully in less developed nations to accelerate use, particularly in conjunction with programs to encourage adoption of modern varieties in new areas. Fertilizer and other input subsidies provide farmers with greater net returns from the adoption of new crops and practices. Pakistan in the early 1970s provides an example of this strategy (see for example, Eckert 1977).

The economic arguments against fertilizer and other input subsidies are strong, however. First, if particular crops are unprofitable without input subsidies, a shift of farmers to the production of otherwise unprofitable crops reduces national agricultural output. Second, as fertilizer sales become large, the subsidies provide increasing transfer payments to farmers and often become a large and increasing drain on the national treasury. In many cases, these funds would provide higher economic returns in other development activities, leading to greater growth. The transfer of scarce development resources to some group through subsidies almost always slows growth. Third, continued fertilizer subsidies provide farmers and innovators with a price below the real resource cost of fertilizer. This induces economically less appropriate and less productive technological and institutional innovations for agriculture. Thus, for most rapid acceleration of growth in the longer run, removal of significant subsidies is especially important. And fourth, fertilizer subsidies, once they have been in place for a period of time, usually become very difficult to remove for political reasons.

To conclude this part, the prospects are high for both (1) the further spread of high-yielding grains to less accessible farming regions with good agricultural resources; and (2) the continued development of profitable drought and pest resistant grains for a variety of ecological areas. Thus, the demand and supply curves for more productive, high-yielding crops and for chemical fertilizer are

Table 8.3. Fertilizer Use, 1970 and 1983, Selected Nations

Nations	Fertilizer Consumption (hundreds of grams of plant nutrient per hectare of arable land)	
	1970	1983
Low-income countries	184	661
India	114	394
China	418	1,806
Middle-income countries	206	443
Zimbabwe	466	576
Nigeria	3	87
Brazil	169	307
Argentina	24	35
Industrial market economies	985	1.233
Japan	3,849	4,370
United States	800	1,045
France	2,424	3,116
East European nonmarket economies	635	1,221

Source: Data from World Bank, *World Development Report 1984* (annex table 6).

expected to continue to move rapidly to the right over the next few decades in most less developed nations. The use of these inputs will increase greatly, even if some real increases in fertilizer prices should occur. The current low per hectare use of chemical fertilizers in most less developed nations, compared to more developed nations, suggests the scope of likely increases (see table 8.3). In some less developed nations, chemical fertilizer use may eventually surpass current use in more developed nations. More chemical fertilizer and new crop varieties are likely to offer farmers in less developed nations high-return investment opportunities well into the next century.

Finally, some people properly express concern about the possible negative ecological impacts of large increases in chemical fertilizer applications. Experience in more developed nations with high fertilizer use indicates that these impacts have been manageable in most areas. Whether the technological and social conditions in less developed nations pose more difficult ecological problems for such fertilizer use merits attention.

Demand for Other Complementary Inputs

How does the adoption of modern seeds affect the use of other farm resources? In the previous section, we demonstrated that fertilizer usually has high complementarity to modern crop varieties. In chapter 7, higher yielding crop varieties were shown generally to cause farmers to use more labor—another, although weaker, example of economic complementarity. What about the prof-

Figure 8.5. The Complementary Demand for Pesticide with Modern Crop Varieties

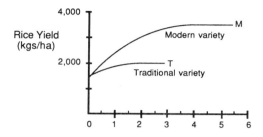

Panel A: Total Product

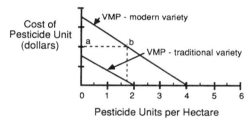

Panel B: Value of the Marginal Product

Pesticide Units per Hectare

itability of using greater amounts of other inputs, such as pesticides and irrigation water, with the new varieties?

Consider the effect on the yield of rice of applying a pesticide (see figure 8.5). Without the use of pesticides, yields of traditional varieties of rice in less developed nations have in many areas ranged around 1,500 kilograms per hectare (see chapter 4). Pesticides used with traditional crop varieties in high-infestation areas might increase yield to 1,800 kilograms (total product curve *T*, panel *A* in figure 8.5). High-yielding varieties may yield 1,500 to 2,000 kilograms without pesticides but reach 4,000 with pesticides (total product curve *M*). An examination of the value of the marginal products of these production functions shows that, for traditional varieties, the cost of pesticide applied to rice could be greater than the largest value of the marginal product obtainable (point *a*). If, in these circumstances, farmers with traditional varieties used the pesticide, they would reduce their income. Hence, it can be rational for farmers growing traditional rice varieties not to use high-cost pesticides. However, with modern varieties of rice, the increase in product from use of pesticides is greater. This is because the yield potential is much greater, and hence the potential losses to pests would be greater. In general, therefore, pesticide use is more likely to be profitable on higher yielding crops. In this example, when the modern variety is grown, the pesticide level with the highest returns is at point *b*, with 1.75 units of pesticide used per hectare.

The same reasoning follows, but even more strongly, when improved water control and irrigation is possible. With traditional varieties and little fertilizer use, the marginal returns to better water control and additional irrigation are often relatively small. With the much higher response potential of the newer grain varieties, the marginal return to better moisture control can be very large. In some wheat and rice areas, such as in Pakistan, the returns to increased irrigation water applied to the high-yielding varieties have been so great that thousands of large tube wells, sometimes seventy meters or more deep, have been profitably installed. In the Philippines, research supports the hypothesis that a major factor inducing large government investment in the expansion of irrigation programs was the increase in the returns that could be obtained from water if high-yielding rice varieties were introduced (Kikuchi and Hayami 1978, p.327). Water is such an important complementary input that the availability of more water and the possibility of better water control often determine whether modern crop varieties will be profitable to grow.

The impact of modern varieties on labor use can vary greatly, depending primarily upon the quality of land and other resources available to farmers. In farming areas with good soils and moisture conditions, modern varieties usually increase on-farm and off-farm employment, the latter due to expanding backward and forward marketing linkages to agriculture. Estimates of employment gains associated with the adoption of the modern crops were given in the preceding chapter. In farming regions with below average agricultural resources, labor demand may decrease.

In general, many inputs are complementary to modern seeds in areas with good growing conditions for that crop. Thus, a number of inputs will tend to be used at increased levels with the more productive crop varieties because of increases in their marginal returns. In some cases, as the demand for inputs increases, the prices for those with inelastic supplies will rise, such as for animal tillage. Then other inputs will be substituted, such as tractor-powered tillage. We will consider questions of input substitution, associated with accelerated development, in greater depth in the next chapter.

Because high productivity and high profits depend upon the right combinations of complementary inputs, which are to a considerable extent farm specific, continuously finding the most profitable mix and level of inputs generally requires much local experience and ongoing field trials by farmers and researchers. Also, as the complementary effects of inputs determine the profitability of new plant materials, rapid adoption in many agricultural areas may depend upon the availability of the required combination of inputs. If complementary inputs, such as chemical fertilizer and better moisture control, are not available, adoption of the currently available high-yielding plant materials may not be profitable. In drier farming areas of Asia, Africa, and Latin America, complementary moisture greatly constrains profitable use of these technologies.

Increasing Animal Productivity

Characteristics of Animal Production in Less Developed Nations

Animal production in less developed nations is characterized by (1) its widely varying importance; (2) the lack of modern production systems; (3) significant crop to livestock and other complementarities; and (4) the large scope for increases in productivity. The importance of livestock raising in farming areas of less developed nations varies greatly. For some, such as pastoral groups, livestock may provide a high proportion of household food and income. In many other areas, draft animals are crucial to maintaining farm income. Although globally, animal production is currently estimated to represent nearly 40 percent of the value of agricultural production (R. Levi, FAO, personal communication), in developing nations it is usually a much smaller percentage of total agricultural production.

Animal production in many less developed nations continues to be based on harvesting plant materials and using household food wastes that cannot be eaten by man. Animals also eat plant materials in hedgerows, wetlands, mountains, and other areas that cannot be cropped. For this purpose, a small flock of chickens, a pig or two, some goats or a few sheep, and perhaps a cow are typical livestock enterprises. Ruminants, including cattle, buffalo, sheep, and goats, which feed on otherwise unusable grasses and tree leaves, make an important contribution to farm income in some areas. Little supplemental grain or feed concentrates are fed in traditional livestock enterprises, except from time to time to milk-producing or heavily worked draft animals. Although animal production often represents only a small part of farm income, its contribution to family nutrition can be of considerable importance. Wider socioeconomic benefits of livestock raising for crop farmers include companionship, reduction in farm food and income variations due to poor crops, and the banking and social prestige functions of animals, considered below.

In contrast to the general picture of a few scavenging animals on predominantly crop farms in most areas of less developed nations, some regions are highly specialized in livestock raising. Nomadic herding peoples, such as the Middle Eastern Bedouin or the African animal herdsmen, are usually found in the drier, poorer, and less hospitable soil areas, where crops are difficult to grow. Through centuries-old herding practices, these pastoralists convert the vegetation of vast areas into milk and meat or, in the past, into transportation (by camels, horses, or llamas). Although pastoral groups often effectively controlled their herds, so that overgrazing was prevented, recent population growth and other changes have led to overgrazing in many areas and to serious declines in livestock production.

In addition to increasing farm income, livestock provide financial liquidity and wealth accumulation. Animals are a convenient store of liquid capital, a hedge against inflation and the risks of drought. With few other opportunities

Table 8.4. Annual Yields of Traditional and Modern Livestock Production Systems
(kilograms per head)

	Cow Milk		Beef and Veal	
Region	1961–65	1984	1961–65	1984
Subsaharan Africa	320	357	14	13
Latin America	938	948	30	26
Far East	406	526	4	4
U.S.S.R.	1,713	2,214	42	59
Europe	2,911	3,883	92	89
Oceania (Australia and New Zealand)	2,370	3,529	46	58
United States and Canada	3,417	5,386	107	94

Source: FAO, *Production Yearbook 1975* and *1985.*

for investment or savings in easily negotiable form, when cash accumulates, farmers and herding people can purchase animals for later sale. Like savings accounts, animal investments usually increase in value through growth and reproduction. For many pastoral groups, the wealth accumulation, prestige, and banking opportunities provided by livestock are central to their cultural life. [4]

Animal production over the centuries has evolved through processes of natural selection, influenced to some extent by humans, often under hard environmental conditions. In this way, farmers obtained environmentally resistant animals that were, however, not very productive compared to modern livestock breeds. Generations of experience with local livestock has led to economically efficient sizes of animals and traditional livestock management practices, sometimes of great complexity. For example, in the traditional Chinese system of hog and fish raising, hog manure is put in fish ponds to provide nutrition for algae, upon which the fish feed. In this way, two animal products are obtained at low cost from very small amounts of land and other resources. In many less developed nations, traditional breeds continue to be more productive than modern breeds, which cannot survive under local conditions.

Significant economic complementarities exist in many crop and livestock enterprises. Low-cost inputs that make livestock raising complementary to other farming activities include crop wastes for feed; naturally growing fodder; low-opportunity-cost labor (after the day's field work or when crop labor requirements are low); and child labor (for herding and feeding). The products of livestock include not only meat, other foods, and hides, but also inputs complementary to crop production in the form of draft power, transportation, and manure for plant fertilization. These animal products and services all contribute to higher family income.

Complementarities in inputs usually play a very important part in livestock

4. For further discussion of animals as a store of wealth, see Doran, Low, and Kemp 1979; Jarvis 1980; Sanford 1983; and Evangelou 1984.

Sheep Meat		Eggs	
1961–65	1984	1961–65	1984
3.4	3.5	1.1	1.3
2.6	2.4	2.5	2.7
2.7	4.7	1.1	2.8
7.5	5.6	3.4	3.9
7.2	9.2	5.3	6.4
5.0	5.4	7.5	4.8
12.1	14.8	9.1	9.2

development. More productive livestock technologies generally require the adoption of a package of practices to gain the most economic increases in animal productivity. The package is likely to include improved breeds, better nutrition, disease control, and improved animal environment.

The large scope for increased livestock productivity in less developed nations is indicated by comparing animal productivity in more developed nations with that obtained by livestock production systems in less developed nations (see table 8.4). These regional data comparing milk, meat, and egg production per total animal stock show the orders of magnitude of animal productivity differences in traditional and modern systems. The animal systems in the United States and Canada achieve sometimes ten times the national yield per animal of traditional systems.

Limited Increases in Animal Productivity

International work to increase animal productivity in less developed nations has evolved slowly. As late as 1970, an international animal expert could say, "The application of modern animal production technology is virtually confined to Western Europe, the North American continent, to Australia, New Zealand, and Japan," with poultry production the exception (McMeeken 1970, p. 5). The most prominent examples of modern animal production systems that have been transferred to less developed nations are large-scale, high-yielding broiler chicken and egg factories. These poultry production systems have been established in many parts of the less developed world in the last two decades, particularly near rapidly growing urban areas, often assisted by international feed and other input suppliers induced by profit opportunities.

Concerning larger animals, variable amounts of research have been carried out in less developed nations to attempt to increase productivity. Many young animals have been shipped to these nations. In the case of milk cows, the introduction of high-producing animals from more developed, temperate climate, nations has had mixed results, as high temperatures and local management practices often lead to low productivity. However, Holstein cows, for example, with sufficient feed, disease control, and shelter, offer opportunities to increase animal protein production and income in certain areas. But successful increases in milk production may depend even more on workable marketing arrangements. In many areas, including West Africa, significant constraints on livestock productivity are much clearer, such as diseases and the lack of forage in the dry season.

Strategies for Increasing Animal Productivity

An economic approach to technology transfer in livestock production would seek high-return investments in new animal production activities. Techniques that have high potential for significant increases in productivity include (1) improved feeding and feed supplements; (2) disease control; (3) better environments for animal growth, particularly shelter; and (4) better breeds (animal genetics). The potential of improved feeding practices associated with improved breeds and disease control is illustrated by the successes of small confined poultry flocks (two to three thousand birds) and large poultry factories. Low-cost veterinary services and disease control often require the training of "barefoot" veterinary technicians in the villages. The Western model of animal disease control through highly trained veterinarians is too costly for most low-income nations. Improved environmental conditions for animals, through better shelter and other changes that reduce heat stress and disease exposure, have considerable potential in many areas. These and other technologies and management practices can greatly increase animal yield. When combined with new, more productive breeds, these technologies and practices can provide high rates of return, due to complementarities in production.

Increasing animal productivity through breeding is a long-term and costly process, especially with the larger animals, because long gestation periods and a considerable number of animals are required. With large animals, decades may be required before sufficient research evidence can be gathered about the increases in productivity. Hence, most less developed nations should attempt to use livestock improvement resources for importing and testing the best available breeds. (These material and design transfers are examined in chapter 11).

It is often not recognized that small animals may be more productive than large animals on the small farms of less developed nations. For example, goats give more milk per unit of weight than cows. And under conditions of constrained feed, smaller animals of a particular breed can provide greater overall productivity than larger animals. These economic realities are contrary to the prestige big animals often provide and to the assumption that larger animals are always more productive. Farmers are very conservative, for good reason, about changes in animal production methods, since risks are high and the costs of error are often large relative to a farmer's total income. Therefore, proposers of new animal production systems need to demonstrate their superiority on typical farms.[5]

To conclude, animal production systems are a complex technology. Increases in the productivity of these systems can be obtained from two sources: (1) the international transfer of better animal technology and management practices, based on research in more developed nations; and (2) research in less developed nations. To date, relatively little animal production research has been mounted in less developed nations. Research in the foods and nutrition, the diseases, environments, and the performance of the breeds relevant to local farming conditions is likely to provide high private and social returns in many farming areas over the longer run. In the short run, more productive animal technology and production practices will be obtained from international sources. It should be recognized, however, that most livestock research in more developed nations has assumed temperate climates and high labor costs, so its applicability in subtropical and tropical nations with low labor costs requires extensive evaluation.[6]

Conclusions

Success in the transformation of traditional farming through the adoption of more productive crop and livestock systems is fundamental to national economic growth. The adoption of these new systems reduces the real costs of production and enables more rapid increases in per capita income.

The extent to which different nations will benefit from more productive agricultural technology will vary greatly. Nations with poor agricultural, technological, institutional, and human resources may be able to increase agricultural production only slowly. Nations that lag behind in developing and adopting more productive agricultural technologies will lose out relative to other nations in agricultural export opportunities, will have higher domestic prices for food, and will have to depend more on imports of agricultural products.

Within nations, regional changes in the location of different crops and livestock will be accelerated as more productive crop technologies are adopted. Crops and animals usually are concentrated in the better growing areas for that

5. References to integrated crop and animal production systems in less developed nations include McDowell and Hildebrand 1980 and DeBoer and Welsch 1977. References to livestock development in less developed nations include the bibliography for Africa by Eicher and Baker (1982, pp. 164–78); Crotty 1980; Baldwin 1980; J. A. Smith and Hays 1982; Williamson and Payne 1978; Simpson and Evangelou 1984; and Jarvis 1986.

6. Three international research institutes have recently been established with livestock development responsibilities: the International Livestock Center for Africa in Ethiopia (1974), the International Laboratory for Research on Animal Diseases in Kenya (1974), and the International Center for Agricultural Research in Dry Areas (ICARDA) in Syria (1976), which has responsibility for research on sheep productivity, as well as for a number of crops.

crop or animal. For some agricultural activities, however, the economics of comparative advantage (discussed in chapter 13) will lead to the concentration of a crop in certain less favorable agricultural areas. An example is provided by wheat. This crop is often concentrated in lower rainfall areas, where many other crops cannot be grown, such as in the western United States and western Canada. In these areas, much lower wheat yields prevail than in the moister, more productive areas further east. In all countries the locations of crop and livestock production illustrate the working out of the economic laws of regional comparative advantage. The most profitable locations for each activity change as technology and institutions change.

In general, programs to improve crop and animal productivity will continually modify the comparative advantage of different regions and countries. The breeding work for the early modern grain varieties in the 1960s put a great deal of emphasis on superior yield. More recently, many of these programs have shifted their focus to shorter time to maturity (to avoid droughts on rain-fed land), toxic soil tolerance, and greater disease and insect resistance. Success in these efforts will provide rain-fed areas with increased cropping opportunities. Thus, newer varieties continually change the boundaries of profitable growing areas. As agricultural development proceeds, farmers' incomes in the various agricultural areas of a country and the world will be affected differently.

Important Concepts

Resource-based agriculture
Science-based agriculture
Continuously shifting disequilibria
   in agriculture
Green revolution
Changing relative prices
Elastic input supply
Shifts in factor shares
Fertilizer-responsive varieties

Modern grain varieties
Protein quality
Seed-fertilizer revolution
Economic substitutes
Economic complementarity
Input subsidies
Demand for complementary inputs
Livestock productivity

Sample Questions

1. Contrast the sources of inputs for traditional and modern agriculture. Be as specific as you can.

2. Why do those concerned with agricultural development seek to replace inelastic with more elastic input supply curves?

3. Why have the high-yielding green revolution seeds of wheat, corn, and rice often induced increased fertilizer use? Explain, using graphics.

4. What have been the usual employment effects of the seed and fertilizer revolution in less developed nations? Explain in economic terms.

5. What prospects are there for a continuing green revolution?

6. What are the economic reasons for greater use of pesticides and irrigation water with the high-yielding crop varieties?

7. Discuss the potential for increasing animal productivity in less developed nations. What specific steps will be required?

8. Find, using figure 8.3, the most profitable level of nitrogen application for the traditional and modern crop varieties if fertilizer costs sixty cents per kilogram.

9. What was, or is, the green revolution?

9

Economics of Change in Mechanical Technologies

The . . . technology backlog . . . creates the possibility for late-developing countries to bypass the vast investment of time and resources that the accumulation of this knowledge involved. This opens the way for more rapid rates of economic growth.
—Johnston and Kilby 1975, p. 76

Introduction

The topic of agricultural mechanization in less developed nations brings forth a flood of views, ranging from enthusiastic certainty that rapid mechanization will be the salvation of poor farmers to an equal certainty that mechanization is the primary threat to the income of farm workers. Much has also been said about the need for "appropriate technology." Some propose banning the importation of much of the technology developed in higher income nations, as it is feared, sometimes correctly, that its use would cause much economic and social disruption. In some areas, agricultural machines become the symbol of all the forces that threaten to destroy the centuries-old economic stability and values of rural life. The opposing naive view is that rapid transfer of large amounts of agricultural machinery from more developed nations will assure a better life in less developed nations. How can the complex issues of agricultural mechanization be analyzed to guide public policy so that truly appropriate agricultural mechanization is facilitated?

Agricultural Mechanization in Less Developed Nations

Extremes of agricultural mechanization are present in less developed nations. Many people do not appreciate that hand planting and cultivation persists in large areas of the less developed world; in 1976, human-powered hand tools were estimated to represent 80 percent of the power in agriculture in Kenya and northeast Brazil. This contrasts with high levels of animal power in India (see table 9.1).

226

Table 9.1. Importance of Hand, Animal, and Mechanical Power in Agriculture, Three Less Developed Nations

Nation	Hand Tool Farming	Animal Power Cultivation	Mechanical Power Cultivation
Kenya (percent of area, 1977)	84	12	4
Northeast Brazil, three municipios (percent of use, 1976)	95–30	5–70	0
India (percent of use, 1966)		89	11
three southern semiarid, nonirrigated states		89, 96, 75	11, 4, 25

Sources: For Kenya and India, ICRISAT 1979b (pp. 199 and 231); for Brazil, Sanders and de Hollanda 1979 (p. 106).

Animal power in farming varies widely on the three continents of the less developed world. In Africa, little animal power was used before the beginning of this century, partly due to severe animal diseases (Le Moigne 1980, p. 213). Although some pastoral groups in Africa manage large numbers of animals, most of these animals are not used for draft, as these groups practice little crop agriculture. Hand hoe cultivation still dominates much of the African continent south of the Sahara. On smaller farms in Latin America, cattle, donkeys, and mules are a main source of power for land preparation and other agricultural activities, including transportation. In Asia, water buffaloes, in addition to cattle, are important sources of farm power, especially in rice areas. In the poorer areas of these two continents, however, hand cultivation remains important. [1]

The Isoquant Framework for Analyzing the Economics of Mechanization

The central issue of identifying socially desirable, cost-reducing, "appropriate" new agricultural technology can be most usefully viewed in an economic framework that relates the productivity of the technology to the cost of labor and capital (the latter includes all nonlabor resources used). The three variables—labor, capital, and level of output—indicate the productivity (and the relative profitability) of each technology. The relations between them are usefully analyzed with the isoquants presented in figures 6.3 and 6.4. Recall, in examining isoquants, we are looking down on a production, or output, surface. All points on an isoquant indicate the same level of output. Figure 9.1 shows that agricultural machines developed in high-income nations, where agricultural wages are

1. General references to agricultural mechanization in less developed nations include National Research Council 1981; A. U. Khan 1974, 1977; IRRI 1978a; Howes 1979; Binswanger 1984; and Cloud 1986. For Africa, see Eicher and Baker 1982 (pp. 140–49); for Asia, Morris and Anwar 1978; and for the Taiwanese experience, Johnston and Kilby 1975. Studies emphasizing employment impacts include Duff 1978a, b; IRRI 1978a; and FAO 1975; also see Esmay and Hall 1973.

Figure 9.1. Identifying Appropriate, Low-Cost Agricultural Technologies: An All-Technology Isoquant with Two Different Ratios of the Cost of Capital to Labor

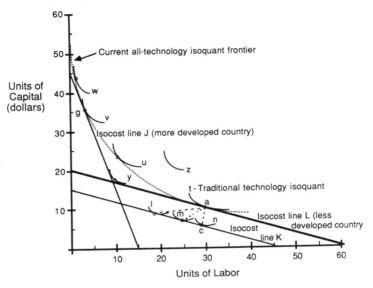

high relative to capital costs, are not likely to be profitable in less developed nations, where agricultural wages are much lower relative to the cost of capital. Traditional technology in a less developed nation is represented in this figure by isoquant *t* with equilibrium point *a* on isocost line *L*. This is the highest profit point for this technology, with the relative prices of labor and capital indicated by isocost line *L*. In a higher wage nation, the low relative cost of capital compared to labor is represented by isocost line *J*, which indicates more capital can be obtained for an equivalent amount of labor. In this case, equilibrium point *g* indicates that *v* is the least costly technology currently available. This technology uses less labor and more capital than traditional technology *t*. Note that each isoquant in figure 9.1 represents a different technological package, usually based on a particular fixed-capital investment. With each equipment package, output can be maintained with a relatively small variation in variable capital and labor inputs, as indicated by the locations on the individual technology isoquants.

Most agricultural mechanization research and development has been carried out in more developed nations. The agricultural equipment and machinery developed in these economic environments are shown in figure 9.1 by individual isoquants *u*, *v*, and *w*, representing capital intensive technologies. If a curve is drawn tangent to these individual technology isoquants and to the traditional technology isoquant, a current all-technology isoquant frontier is obtained. This frontier indicates the most productive technologies available at a given time for any ratio of labor to capital cost. Any specific technology represented by an isoquant to the right of this frontier, such as technology z, would be inferior (more costly) for all possible prices of capital and labor. Technology z would use more resources to produce the same output. And any technology to the left or below the all-technology isoquant would indicate a new, more productive, less costly technology.

Many technologies developed in higher income nations are unprofitable in agricultural areas with low labor costs relative to capital costs. This is illustrated by viewing isocost line L in figure 9.1. In the low-labor-cost environment, traditional technology, t, is the most profitable current technology, as shown by the tangency of this technology with isocost line L at a. If the agricultural machines and equipment, represented by isoquants u, v, and w, that are profitable in more developed nations were to be used in a low-labor-cost nation such as represented here, more capital and somewhat less labor would be required, with a higher total cost for the same output. Hence, if farmers in a low-income nation used technologies represented by u, v, or w, the higher machinery costs would reduce their net income. With the costs and technologies illustrated in this figure, transferring modern agricultural technologies u, v, and w from more to less developed nations would reduce agricultural productivity and reduce net income from agriculture in the less developed nations.

What kinds of technologies are needed to increase incomes in less developed nations with low labor costs? They are the technologies represented by isoquants l, m, and n, which have not yet been developed or made available to farmers. These isoquants represent more productive agricultural technologies, which would produce as much product (have as high an output) as the technologies on the current all-technology isoquant, but would use fewer total resources, as indicated by the lower isocost line K. These more profitable technologies are the appropriate technologies less developed nations require. Thus appropriate technology can be defined as technology that will be financially profitable for farmers to use in their economic environments. A more general definition is that technology is appropriate when it is profitable both from a private (the individual farmer's) point of view and also from a macro, or social, point of view (see also p. 303). The economic (or social) profitability of using a new technology has to be evaluated by adjusting for any subsidies and price supports—and any positive or negative social costs—to accurately reflect the real net costs to a nation.

Finally, isoquant y illustrates a technology of particular interest for equity reasons. This technology, if adopted in the low-labor-cost nation that currently uses technology t, would simply reduce the amount of labor used, without decreasing the cost of production (without increasing income). From time to time, such mechanization may become available to farmers who naturally take a private financial point of view in evaluating the profitability of the machines. Adoption of technology with these characteristics, however, would simply reduce the amount of labor, with no cost reduction or productivity gain. If alternative opportunities for labor were scarce, laborers' incomes would be greatly reduced by the adoption of this technology, leading to increased income dispari- ties. With few alternative employment opportunities from a national or social point of view, the real cost of labor would be much less than indicated by isocost line *L*. The line therefore should be rotated flatter. Then technology *y* would be seen as less profitable from a social point of view than traditional technology *t*.

New Hand Tools for Agriculture

The potential for use of more productive hand-powered technologies is of- ten neglected. Through the centuries, traditional peoples have fashioned the most productive hand tools they could devise, based on generations of experi- ence with the materials (wood, bronze, and sometimes iron) available to them. It is unlikely, therefore, that new, more productive, hand tools using these materi- als can be produced without incorporating new scientific or technological knowledge. Modern materials, as emphasized by A. U. Khan (1974), are thus more likely to provide scope for the development of improved hand tools and equipment. These materials include high-technology steels, aluminum, plastics, and other synthetic materials, some of which are difficult to work, and the incor- poration of small, complex, factory-made bearings, pumps, controls, and so on.

There are many examples of more productive human-powered tools that incorporate new knowledge and materials. Early examples include the foot- pedal rice thresher and the Japanese straw-weaving machine. Hand- and foot- operated water pumps incorporating modern materials and technology may still be new in some areas. Hand-powered pesticide dusters and sprayers are very productive. The expanding use of more complex hand tools in a less developed nation is illustrated by data from Taiwan. By the end of the 1950s, nearly every farmer seemed to have a foot-pedal rice thresher, and some 11 thousand hand dusters and 104 thousand hand sprayers were used in agriculture (*Taiwan Agri- cultural Yearbook 1962*). At that time there were fewer than 4 thousand power tillers (two-wheeled tractors) and 400 power sprayers in Taiwan. Hand carts and bicycles for transporting agricultural inputs and products illustrate other impor- tant human-powered equipment.

In Africa, the International Institute of Tropical Agriculture has developed several hand-powered tools and associated cultivation practices to help farmers in increasing their crop areas five- to tenfold. Many farmers using traditional hand tools can grow only about a half acre of crops. A spectacular, but perhaps not cost-effective, hand-carried crop sprayer developed at IITA runs either on batteries or from power produced by a solar panel the cultivator wears on his or her head as a hat, at the same time offering protection from the sun. The de- signer was thoughtful enough to provide an electrical outlet so that a transistor radio can be played while the farmer sprays the crops! Other IITA hand tools include a rolling seed-injection planter, a herbicide applicator, and an applicator that places a band of fertilizer in the soil.[2]

Animal-Powered Mechanization

Animal power in agriculture is highly variable throughout the less developed world. This complex technology has evolved slowly through the centuries, involving as it does the animals' care and feeding, their training for draft, and the development and effective use of animal equipment in the field. Cattle, mules, horses, donkeys, and water buffaloes are the principal sources of draft power for field operations and transportation.

We hypothesize, based on the model of induced agricultural development, that if prevailing constraints are lifted, additional scope may be present for profitable adoption of animal-powered technology. In areas where animal power is new, questions arise, however, about the costs and time lags involved in establishing animal-powered mechanization, especially compared to motorized power alternatives. To determine whether animal draft power will be productive in new areas, several years of research with local farmers under representative farming conditions will often be needed. The analysis of animal power costs and the increase in income draft animals could provide is especially complex due to the difficulty of correctly valuing all the products that are jointly produced with animal power and of valuing the costs of maintaining animals. The jointly produced products include the manure used as fuel or fertilizer, the meat, the hides, and sometimes the milk.

On the cost side, animals may increase competition for the use of scarce land to produce livestock feed. Hence, the net value of maintaining livestock for draft purposes includes any loss of crops or other income from land and labor (the opportunity cost of these resources) required to maintain the livestock. There is a high complementarity among the use of animal power, animal care, and driver labor. Direct maintenance costs may be low, as children and other low-productivity (low opportunity cost) laborers typically care for animals. However, if animal care deprives a child of an education, the indirect long-run costs to the family and society could be considerably greater. An additional important cost factor is the risk of animal losses, through disease, for example. Where knowledge of loss factors and how to reduce these risks has been gained over time, losses can often be kept low enough to keep these costs down. In the future, as the labor costs rise relative to the value of meat and of draft power, motorized draft power will become more attractive. Thus, animal power is more likely to remain profitable in areas where machine power costs are expected to remain high and labor costs low.

2. Reports from IITA contain information on improvements in hand tools. Also see, for example, Wijewardene 1980 and, for human-powered pumps, Islam 1980.

Increasing the Productivity of Animal-Powered Mechanization

The potential to increase animal-powered productivity depends upon the rate at which modern science and technology can be applied to animals and animal-powered equipment. The considerable increases in animal productivity achieved through better breeding, feeding, disease control, and environmental management were shown in table 8.4. As the development of animal tillage equipment in the more developed nations mostly ceased by the 1950s, more recent technologies may now be available that could be incorporated into new animal equipment, if sufficient research and development were undertaken.

Attempts to increase the productivity of animal tillage are illustrated by studies comparing the use of traditional animal cultivating equipment and a wheeled tool carrier for land preparation and weeding in the semiarid areas of South India (Binswanger et al. 1979). To be a high-return investment for farmers, this implement must increase production enough to pay for its cost. Increased production could arise from increased yields due to better land preparation and weeding or to increased double cropping enabled by the new equipment. Studies indicated that the new tool carrier, used with a new cultivation technique, greatly reduced the number of days of bullock labor, but that stronger than average animals were required. The research also showed that increases in yields on fields operated by ICRISAT were large enough to pay for the additional equipment costs. However, before conclusions are drawn, results from trials by farmers on their own fields are needed to determine if the tool and cultivation practices will be profitable for typical farmers. These trials also need to include comparisons with small motorized hand tractors and four-wheeled custom tractor services.

Introducing Animal Power in New Areas

Animal power is a complex technology. The daily and annual cycles of feeding and other animal reproduction and maintenance activities have to be mastered to control and maintain animal productivity. Farmers also have to learn the details of animal training and the use of tillage and other equipment in the fields. Farmers inexperienced in the use of animals for power usually incur high learning costs as they attempt to adopt animal traction on their farms. It takes several years before the costs of animal tillage decline to stable levels. Hence, the economic advantages of animal power for farmers must be large enough to pay for their investments in machines, animals, learning, early errors, and possible large losses.

Considerable experience has been gained in Africa in the 1960s and 1970s from programs attempting to introduce animal traction. A major study of government-subsidized animal traction projects over the 1975–80 period in the nation of Burkina Faso found that farmers adopting animal traction for the first time required about four years before they knew how to use the complete package of equipment (Barrett et al. 1982). Although there was a 25 percent reduc-

Figure 9.2. Capital and Labor Costs for Land Preparation: Hand, Animal, and Motor Tiller Power

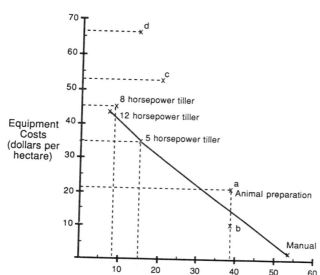

Source: Data from Morris and Anwar 1978 (p. 169).

tion in labor input when animal traction was used, little increase in sorghum or millet production occurred. Cash flow problems, animal losses, and the high cost of the initial investment to obtain the animal power relative to the small additional income discouraged adoption. Eicher and Baker (1982, pp. 139–50) concluded that African research on animal traction at the farm level is still largely impressionistic, due primarily to the fact that most of the research has been carried out on experiment stations. They also observed that successful use of animal traction in Africa has usually been associated with the production of commercial and export crops.

In Asia, research to determine the least-cost method of preparing one hectare of rice land compared manual, animal, and two-wheeled tractor systems. In this Indonesian study, labor and other variable costs of tillage were estimated. Figure 9.2 shows that manual methods can become too costly and how small motor-powered tillers can become profitable. The variable costs per hectare of land preparation were greater with animals (39 + 21 = $60) than with five-horsepower motor tillers (15 + 35 = $50) or with an eight-horsepower tiller (9 + 45 = $54). Land preparation using animals would be the lowest cost system only if the cost of animals were less, say, at point *b*, providing total costs of $49 (39 + 10). On the other hand, if equipment costs (due to, for example, tiller breakdowns) increased by 50 percent, to $52.50 at *c* and $67.50 at *d*, manual and animal land preparation would be more profitable for longer periods of time—until wages greatly increased or the cost of tillers declined.

The potential for expanding the use of animal power in agriculture in less developed nations is quite unclear. The large proportion of world agricultural land still tilled by hand suggests the very large potential for increasing human productivity through the use of animal or other modern power sources. But for animal traction to be profitable in many areas, significant changes in the productivity of animal-powered technologies, or significant changes in the prices of inputs or products, would be required. An important issue is the cost of animal power relative to the cost of mechanical power. Governments that seek to expand animal power will need to have long-range, consistent support policies, particularly to encourage veterinary services and research on animal technologies—including many trials on farmers' fields.

In the longer run of several decades, six factors are likely to increase the cost of animal power relative to machine power. First, the cost of the complementary use of fairly large amounts of human labor with animal power will cause animal power costs to rise as wages rise, relative to motor power costs. Second, increased competition for the use of land will increase animal feed costs. Third, diseases are an ever-present risk. Fourth, exogenous factors, such as prohibition on the use of irrigation channels to cool water buffaloes in some areas of Java, increase animal costs. Fifth, social factors, such as the increased social status associated with tractors, may affect power choices. And finally, even after the latest scientific technology has been incorporated into modern animal-powered equipment, it will always have distinct speed and power limits. In the longer run, field operations will be mechanized in most agricultural areas of less developed nations. The changing economics of motor power will determine the timing and rate at which the final shift to motor power occurs.[3]

Stationary and Wheeled Motorized Power

The issues in the expansion of motorized power for agriculture in less developed nations are examined under two headings: (1) the often unrecognized significant role of stationary and hand-carried motorized machinery; and (2) tractor mechanization.

Stationary and Hand-Carried Motorized Machinery

The extensive use of stationary and portable motorized machinery without powered wheels in agricultural development is often unrecognized, although considerable information on this part of agricultural mechanization is available for a number of East Asian countries. In 1969 in Taiwan, for example, an esti-

---

3. Additional illustrative references on animal power in agriculture include Goe and McDowell 1980 and Pagot 1977. For South Asia, see Binswanger et al. 1979; for animal use in paddy rice production, see Alviar 1979; for use of animals in Africa (Berkina Faso), see Barrett et al. 1982; and in francophone West Africa, see Sargent et al. 1981.

mated 15 thousand power sprayers and 52 thousand power pumps were in use in agriculture (*Taiwan Agricultural Yearbook 1970*), many more than the number of two-wheeled and four-wheeled tractors in the country. South Korea and the Philippines have had similar agricultural mechanization experiences. Widespread adoption of motorized pumps has occurred in many countries, because their water delivery costs are lower, even where wages are very low, as in Bangladesh. Backpack power sprayers reduce labor costs and increase yields. In many applications, stationary motors with belt-powered transfer become multiuse power sources, as they are easily shifted from one single-purpose machine to another.

Single-purpose motorized equipment that can reduce peak labor demand periods may provide a high return on investment. For example, in areas where weeding is the most important labor constraint, such as in some parts of Africa, hand or motorized herbicide sprayers might enable much larger harvests in spite of high herbicide costs, especially if the machines could be shared by a group of farmers. In conclusion, initial steps in agricultural mechanization with small motors on stationary and portable agricultural equipment are likely in many areas. Increased experience with these machines can reduce the costs of introducing tractor power when it becomes economically feasible.

Tractor-Powered Machinery

THE POTENTIAL CONTRIBUTIONS OF TRACTORS

Farmers are induced to adopt tractor mechanization if increased net financial returns are provided or if family utility is increased. Increased utility may be in the form of reduced drudgery, higher prestige, or other nonmaterial gains. New, shiny, and clean tractors have occasionally been observed in farming areas placed in prominent positions in front of farm houses, but seldom used!

When greatly expanded use of machines powered by internal combustion engines is contemplated, concern arises about the long-run availability of fuel. Since the energy crisis of 1974, a great deal of energy conservation has been undertaken to reduce the demand for petroleum-based fuel in more developed nations, and estimates of world petroleum reserves have greatly increased. Thus, for the next several decades, sufficient petroleum-based fuel is expected to be available. When these supplies dwindle, alcohol (produced from such crops as sugar and maize) and petroleum fuels (derived from the earth's vast shale oil and coal reserves) will be available to power agricultural machines.

Tractor mechanization has great potential over the long run to increase farm production and income in less developed areas. The potential contributions of tractor mechanization relate to three parts of the crop cycle: land preparation and planting, crop growing, and harvest and postharvest operations. Tractors may also increase cropping intensity.

Although many people concerned with development often assume that a positive relation exists between land preparation by tractors and yields due to better tillage, empirical research in less developed nations has generally shown small yield increases (Duff 1978a; Binswanger 1978). For example, studies of paddy rice production have shown few direct yield advantages from the use of mechanized land preparation, compared with traditional methods (Duff 1978a).

More timely land preparation through mechanization can reduce the risk of significant crop losses in some areas. For example, in 1971 IRRI studied rain-fed rice on upland fields, where soil moisture tends to be depleted during the later stages of the growing season. In that year at two sites, a seven-week delay in rice planting reduced yields by about 40 percent, while at two other sites, a six-week planting delay had little yield-reducing effect. In most areas, several years of research on farmers' fields will be needed to determine the extent to which tractors may increase yields through more timely operations.

The effect of tractor power on crop growing through weeding, fertilization, and pesticide application is also highly variable. With the adoption of higher yielding crops, if weeds become more of a problem, the marginal returns to weed control will increase. Where weeds significantly reduce yields and a shortage of weeding labor constrains the total area cropped by a farmer, as in some areas of Africa, motor-powered weeding could increase farm income. Yet, since the costs of tractor weeding are often high, animal-powered weeders or hand application of herbicides might be more cost effective. Duff (1978a, p. 153) believes that motor-powered equipment that can accurately meter and place fertilizers and pesticides at the optimum location in the root zone of the soil—particularly flooded rice soils—could reduce the application rates of costly chemicals by 50 percent or more without reducing yields. The effect on net farm income of mechanization that increases input productivity needs to be explored in the different farming systems of less developed nations.

The mechanization of harvest and postharvest operations appear to provide considerable gains in some areas of less developed nations. The gains are obtained through reductions in grain losses, primarily through reduced handling and more timely harvesting and processing. In a study of postproduction rice-handling systems, Toquero et al. (1977) showed that a shift from manual threshing to mechanical threshing reduced grain losses by as much as 9 percent. When mechanical drying was substituted for solar drying, grain losses were reduced by as much as 12 percent. These researchers also explored the effect of more timely postharvest operations on yield. They found that rice yield was appreciably decreased when a delay of more than five days occurred, and that milling quality decreased after a two-day delay. Overall, the study found that mechanical threshing and drying could reduce the time of all postproduction operations on these rice farms from more than four to less than two days. Although the increases in yields appear important, these studies did not examine the profitability of the mechanization steps. Detailed partial budgeting of the costs and additional revenues to be expected from the different mechanization steps is needed to estimate the net returns a farmer might obtain by investing in mechanical harvesting and improved postharvest operations.

Increased cropping intensity through tractor mechanization has particularly great potential in many productive agricultural areas with good rainfall or irrigation. When field power bottlenecks and labor shortages in peak periods are relieved, more timely field operations may be carried out. This is achieved in field preparation through such steps as early plowing on drier ground and an earlier harvest, which enables an additional crop. In this way, a family's annual cropped area may be increased on the land it controls. In many irrigated areas and under some rain-fed conditions in warmer climates, double and even triple cropping is possible. Tractor mechanization often spreads the demand for labor and, by enabling increased cropping intensity, can augment total demand for labor, thereby increasing the income of agricultural laborers. Mechanization increases the incentive for greater cropping intensity, so that machines can be used more hours per year to reduce the average cost of machine services for each crop.

THE ECONOMICS OF TRACTORS

Important design, management, and service criteria that achieve low-cost agricultural power in less developed nations are (1) designs that have low complexity and easy repair; (2) high annual machine use; and (3) sufficient repair service and assured parts supply. Economic issues involved in alternative arrangements for managing and repairing agricultural machinery are examined in a later section.

Much of the agricultural machinery produced in more developed nations today is high cost and highly complex. A. U. Khan (1977, p. 30), for example, found that most Japanese two-wheeled tractors were too complex for farms in low-income nations. Hence, IRRI developed simpler two-wheeled tractors and made the designs freely available to private manufacturers in less developed nations. For nations that lack the required scientific design and testing resources to respond to the economic inducement to produce less costly agricultural machines, the strategy of providing resources to the international research institutes, such as IRRI, can accelerate technology development and use.

Low-cost tractor services require high levels of machine utilization. Tractors and other large machines are "lumpy" units of capital, meaning their services often can be obtained only if a large investment is made. When farmers can arrange to rent agricultural machines or obtain their services through contracts or custom operations from a machine operator, the individual or organization that buys the machine has to earn sufficient income to repay the large capital investment to prevent losses.

Two types of costs are associated with all capital equipment. Fixed costs (purchase price, finance charges, taxes, and general maintenance) are incurred irrespective of the amount of use. Variable costs (fuel, servicing and repairs, and operator's labor) are a function of the amount of machine use. Since the fixed costs have to be added to the operating costs, unit costs of machine service, such as the cost of plowing a unit of land, are dependent upon the number of hours per year the machine is operated. Thus, hourly costs of operation = annual

Table 9.2. An Illustrative Estimate of Optimum Tractor Size for Different Farm Sizes

	Farm Size (hectares tilled)				
Item	4	8	16	32	64
Optimum tractor size (hp)	5.76	9.11	15.24	27.00	50.20
Annual tractor cost (per hectare dollars)	38.46	29.32	23.27	19.51	17.34
Annual use (hours)	191.00	241.00	289.00	325.00	351.00

Source: Adapted from Chancellor 1978 (p. 65).

fixed costs/annual hours of use + variable costs per hour. Tractors operated many months a year for several agricultural operations have lower hourly costs than the same units that are limited to one operation, such as land preparation for one crop during a short period.

The need for high annual use requires a consideration of machine size in relation to farm size. Illustrative estimates from studies of the use of small and large tractors provide a perspective on the farm sizes required for full tractor use and hence low tractor costs. In table 9.2, the high estimated cost of using small tractors (5.76 horsepower) is due largely to the limited hours of use per year on which the estimate was based. If farmers could sell additional tractor services to neighboring farmers, lower costs could be achieved. Custom operators are often able to operate small or large tractors a thousand hours or more per year, sometimes through the night in peak demand periods, to achieve lower unit costs. Obviously, many conditions related to local growing conditions, cropping intensity, alternative rental and ownership possibilities, and the varying resource costs in different countries will determine the most cost-effective tractor size for each farming area.

Understanding the relations between the amount of use and the unit cost of operating small and large machines is aided by figure 9.3. Here the unit costs of small-machine mechanization, such as with fifteen-horsepower tractors, are compared with larger machine mechanization, such as with thirty-five-horsepower tractors. The figure presents an example of the relation between the area farmed and the number and kind of machines that would be least costly.[4]

4. More information on tractor power for small farms may be obtained from Valdes, Scobie, and Dillon 1979; Crossley and Kilgour 1984; IRRI 1984; University of Illinois 1978; and Asian Productivity Organization 1983; and for an analytic review of tractor studies in Pakistan, India, and Nepal, see Binswanger 1978. Experience with large tractors in Pakistan was provided by Herring and Kennedy (1979); and in Bangladesh by Sarkar (1981). A review of the African experience was provided by Eicher and Baker (1982, pp. 146–50); and by Pingali, Bigot. and Binswanger (1986). An examination of custom operating arrangements and ownership patterns for tractors in Asia was presented by Chancellor (1978).

Figure 9.3. Cost of Operating Small and Large Machines with Different Amounts of Farmland

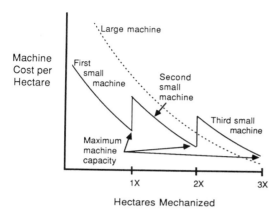

Hectares Mechanized

Source: Duff 1978a (p. 21). Reprinted with permission.

Irrigation and Drainage

The Importance and Potential of Irrigation

Increased control of soil moisture through irrigation and drainage is central to reducing yield variability and increasing crop productivity. The advent of higher yielding fertilizer responsive crop varieties has increased greatly the returns to investment in improved water control systems. Irrigation and drainage technology have been employed by farmers throughout the centuries. The development of large, intricate, gravity-flow irrigation systems supported the flowering of many great civilizations. Other types of irrigation employ hand watering, human-powered basket and treadle water lifting, stream-powered water wheels, and a range of animal-powered water-lifting devices. The water-lifting capacity of human and animal-powered methods provides relatively small amounts of water, often at high cost, even when wage rates are low. Due to their large water-lifting capacity during a twenty four-hour period, motorized water pumps can provide large quantities of irrigation water, often at very reasonable cost—in many cases below the cost of traditional methods.

The importance of irrigated land in the agriculture of less developed nations is variable, with an average of 14 percent of total arable land irrigated in 1983, with great variability among nations. The ratio ranges from an average of 2 percent in African nations south of the Sahara, 10 percent in Latin America, 18 percent in the Philippines, up to 73 percent of the arable land irrigated in Pakistan (FAO, *Production Year Book 1974*). Irrigation is very important also in

Egypt, the Indian Punjab, and on the island of Java. In less developed nations as a group, irrigated land has increased at the rate of 2.2 percent per year since 1960. By 1980, irrigated land in these nations was one-fifth of the harvested area, used about 60 percent of all fertilizer, and produced about 40 percent of all annual crops (World Bank, *World Development Report 1982,* p. 62).

Increased irrigation continues to offer large potentials for doubling and tripling yields during the main crop season and often makes possible a second or even a third crop in tropical climates. Large areas are potentially irrigable in many less developed nations, particularly in Africa, where only a small proportion of irrigable land currently has supplemental water.

The complementary nature of irrigation water and the new fertilizer responsive crops has increased the marginal returns to water and the private and social returns from pump and gravity-flow irrigation projects. Many irrigation projects have very high initial costs for dam and canal construction and, in the case of pump projects, for well digging, pump purchase, and pump installation (see figure 9.4). In this figure, note that the future benefits and costs were not discounted. If they had been, the levels of all the lines would continuously drop as they moved out on the horizontal time axis. By imagining this discounting, we see the central investment issue in these projects—for to be of net benefit to society, discounted benefits produced in later years would have to be sufficiently large so they would be greater than the large initial capital construction costs. This would achieve a benefit-cost ratio greater than one or (the same thing) an estimated internal rate of return on the investment greater than the interest rate.

Many large irrigation projects provide benefits to nonagricultural sectors, also, through electricity production, flood control, and improved navigation. When there are multiple benefits, irrigation water users are charged to recover an appropriate share of total project costs. When irrigation water is the only benefit, irrigation fees have to cover all capital construction and operating costs to be socially profitable.

Large Gravity-Flow and Pump Irrigation Projects

Where water, terrain, and soil conditions are favorable, large gravity-flow irrigation schemes that require large dams continue to be undertaken. The very large capital costs and long construction periods required by these projects, often ten or more years, have regularly resulted in high water costs per hectare. The capital costs alone in recent large canal schemes with storage reservoirs have ranged from $2 thousand to more than $10 thousand per hectare of agricultural land benefited (World Bank, *World Development Report 1982,* p. 62). Other factors that have increased the social and private costs of some large gravity-flow schemes include social disruptions due to forced moving of people, negative impacts on the local ecology, and elevated human disease rates (Hunter, Rey, and Scott 1982).

As the per hectare costs of large gravity-flow irrigation projects have in-

Figure 9.4. Initial Capital Costs and Required High Annual Benefits for an Irrigation Project

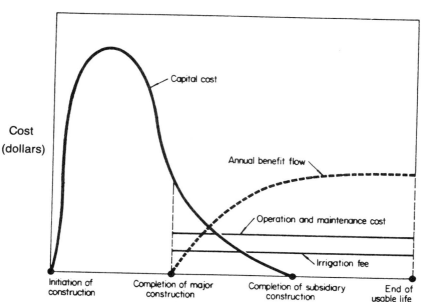

Source: Barker, Bennagen, and Hayami 1978 (p. 348).

creased, much greater attention has been paid to small perimeter, local, pump irrigation systems in areas where groundwater is available. The two types of pumping systems in use are low-lift centrifugal pumps, which can raise water as much as sixteen meters when operated in pairs, and electric or internal-combustion-powered tube wells, with turbine pumps placed down in the well. In waterlogged areas, drainage pumps can be important contributors to increased crop area and yields.

Already, pump irrigation has had a great impact in many areas of less developed nations. In poorer countries such as Bangladesh, power pumps have become very important for the food supply. By 1977, nearly 50 percent of the winter irrigated crop area was watered by low-lift pumps and tube wells (Bhuiyan 1980, p. 59).

To achieve low pump-operating costs, high annual hours of use are required. The need to minimize water costs highlights the importance of making physical and social arrangements that assure the flow of water from the pump head to a sufficiently large area. As water becomes scarce and hence more costly, it is profitable to shift from water-using crops, such as rice, to water-conserving crops, such as wheat and potatoes.

Social and institutional arrangements generally have a large effect on the cost of irrigation water in both large gravity-flow and pump irrigation systems. Coward (1980), among others, has explored many of the complex issues of irrigation organization. Barker, Herdt, and Rose (1985, p. 105) emphasized the importance of making sufficient "software" investment to complement the investment in irrigation hardware (dams, canals, and pumps), in order to assure that the needed institutional and management arrangements are made to provide incentives for the most profitable use of the irrigation water produced by the hardware.

Much of the reduced productivity of irrigation projects is due to inappropriate and unproductive institutional arrangements, which prevent greater production from available water. An important consideration in the design of the rules of payment for water from irrigation projects relates to incentives to encourage as much production as possible so that the costs of the capital invested can be repaid. Thus, in pump irrigation projects, physical and payment arrangements should be made so that there are incentives to use the system to capacity by producing as much as possible annually. For with a large total acreage, the annual cost of providing the irrigation water can be distributed over a larger area and a greater number of farmers, leading to lower unit water costs and to a greater likelihood that water payments will cover the cost of the irrigation system. For example, a lump sum charge to a cooperative or farmers' association would provide an incentive to the group leaders to arrange for sufficient land to have acceptable water charges. By contrast, selling water on an individual basis to farmers may provide little incentive for the system to be used to capacity, so the water payments received may not cover the cost of the project.[5]

Economic Issues in Managing and Servicing Agricultural Machinery

The unit cost of tool and machine services is greatly influenced by management and repair arrangements. Specific management and service factors affecting cost include machine control and operating arrangements, the skill and training of animal and machine operators, the speed and quality of repair, and the availability of low-cost spare parts. Important issues in the management and servicing of agricultural machinery relate to the role of government machinery stations and the nature of institutional arrangements that provide incentives for full use of increasingly complex farm machines.

In the earliest stages of agricultural mechanization, many less developed nations have controlled agricultural machinery introduction and use, especially nations with highly centralized authority and socialist nations. Government ma-

5. On the economics of irrigation, see Carruthers and Clark 1981; Bergmann and Boussard 1976; and Wang and Hagen 1981. For pump irrigation and groundwater use, see Carruthers and Clark 1981. General references on irrigation include Plusquellec and Wickham 1985 and, for Asia, Glasser 1981. Irrigation organization and policy issues are of primary interest in a bibliography on the socioeconomic aspects of irrigation in Asia in IRRI 1976. See also Coward 1980; Taylor and Wickham 1979; Radosevich 1974; and Bromley 1982a, b; and, for Asia, IRRI 1978c. For the Philippines, see Korten 1982 and IRRI 1980.

chinery stations have often been set up to provide agricultural machinery services through rentals, repair shops, and spare parts supply. These machinery stations generally have had difficulty keeping costs down. High costs often arise from disincentives for high rates of machine use, due to such factors as traditions of government service that discourage working outside regular government hours and on holidays, even in the busy season. Other productivity-reducing factors include cumbersome government administrative procedures, difficulties in scheduling services, delays in service, and insufficient attention to stocking spare parts. These factors result in diseconomies of scale in many government agricultural machine stations.

Local custom rental arrangements and joint and cooperative ownership provide alternative models for the provision of the services of large agricultural machines. In many parts of the world, once sufficient supplies of machinery and parts become available, farmers, local mechanics, small custom rental services, and sometimes local cooperatives find they can provide machine services at lower cost than government machine stations. For example, Chancellor (1978), in studying the provision of tractor services to small farms in Thailand and Malaysia, observed the shift to local private machine services from government tractor stations. Some private machine service suppliers are willing to accept less than the market wage to assure that their machines are paid for or that their neighbors succeed in getting a crop. Thus, it is likely that improved allocation of scarce government development resources will be achieved if government investment in machine station operations is minimized. Even in the centrally planned Eastern European countries, machinery stations have been discontinued, as farms and custom tractor service operators have provided needed services at lower cost.

Institutional arrangements can provide appropriate incentives for effective sales and maintenance of low-cost agricultural machinery services in rural areas. Chancellor (1978) pointed out that machinery dealer credit can facilitate successful machine use on farms: the sales organization, through the credit provided to the farmer for machine purchase, has a strong incentive to support good machine performance that will enable credit repayment. This incentive can cause the machinery dealer to provide the purchaser with sufficient training for proper machine operation and minor repairs and to assure the availability of needed parts and major repair services. As the demand for agricultural machines expands in less developed nations, and as farmers and other rural people gain experience in managing, operating, and repairing these machines, the real costs of machine services in agriculture will decline.

Policy Issues in Agricultural Mechanization

The mechanization of agriculture, whether by hand, animal, stationary machine, or tractor power, is one of the fundamental processes through which scientific knowledge is incorporated into agriculture to increase productivity. Vigorous support for appropriate agricultural mechanization can offer high social returns from investment of government development resources. Because most farms in less developed nations are small and in many nations are likely to decrease in size for a number of decades, inexpensive small machines that require low initial capital costs are more likely to be in demand in many areas, even if their unit costs of operation are somewhat greater than for larger machines. If a government desires both to facilitate technological change in agriculture through mechanization and to monitor possible serious negative impacts, minimal national data collection, research, and economic analysis of mechanization are required. Studies should enable an understanding of the changing impacts of mechanization and other technological, economic and institutional changes on different agricultural areas. Two issues of particular concern are the extent to which additional mechanization steps substitute for, or complement, labor and how mechanization developments affect regional farm income and employment.

Government policy for the mechanization of agriculture should be guided by an understanding of two fundamental factors that affect the productivity of agriculture: (1) the changing cost of capital relative to labor; and (2) the rate at which research, development, and machinery supply systems are able to provide farmers with new, more productive (lower cost) agricultural technologies. The capital and labor isoquant framework shows the effect of these two factors (see figure 9.5).

If there is a potential for a twofold, threefold, or greater increase in hand tool productivity as indicated by arrow *a*, as might be the case in some agricultural areas in Africa, government policies to encourage the development, production, and adoption of the needed hand-powered tools could quickly cause large increases in production at relatively low capital cost. In such areas, efforts to make the more difficult and costly shift to animal- or motor-powered agricultural equipment might be delayed until significant increases occur in the cost of labor relative to capital. If increases in the relative cost of labor to capital were occurring, as shown by rotation of isocost line *A* to the location indicated by isocost line *B*, then improved hand-powered tools would be less likely to be profitable.

If the productivity of animal-powered machinery could be increased, say, to *b*, policies to support animal mechanization might be wise. However, in areas where animal draft power costs are high (represented by isoquant *m*), there would be little reason for government to support this much-less-productive technology. Alternatively, if it were possible to reduce the costs of animal-powered or tractor mechanization, the shift to the power sources indicated by points *b*, *c*, and *d* would enable more rapid progress in agriculture. Where the costs of large-tractor mechanization can be reduced very greatly, as at *d*, programs and policies to aid small-tractor mechanization might be a less productive use of scarce government resources. Finally, where rural population densities are high, as in South Asia, and labor costs are likely to remain low for long periods

Figure 9.5. Changing Cost of Labor and the Shift to Motorized Agricultural Power

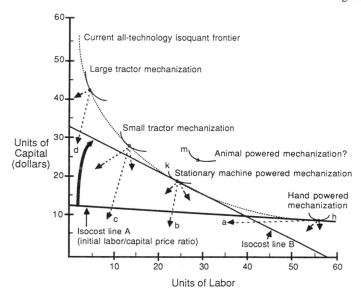

relative to the cost of capital, the figure shows that government should support labor intensive technologies to prevent adverse income distribution effects. Particularly important technologies for these economic conditions include hand equipment, animal power, and small-tractor power, to achieve the highest rates of return on the use of resources now in agriculture.

In a recent analytical review of the economics of tractors in the 1965–75 decade in the Indian subcontinent, Binswanger (1978, p. 73) concluded that the large number of studies he examined failed to show that tractors increased cropping intensity, yields, timeliness, or gross returns on farms, but that they were largely substitutes for labor and bullock power. He also found that most of the tractor investments were confined to the limited areas with rising wage rates. He concluded that only in labor-short areas should government mechanization policy focus on facilitating the substitution of tractors for labor.

Research, Development, and Supply

Governments can accelerate agricultural mechanization through the following four activities: (1) supporting research for the adaptation and development of hand, animal, and motorized tools to the different farming areas and agricultural production systems; (2) encouraging the importation or the production of profitable equipment; (3) facilitating the introduction of new machinery into the farming systems; and (4) encouraging an effective repair and parts supply system. Governments in many socialist and some less developed nations have decided that only the public sector will be permitted to carry out such activities. In market economies, many of these activities are carried out in the private sector, while government supports a certain amount of mechanization research in government-supported institutes and agricultural experiment stations, often coordinated with research on crops and livestock. Research and development activities of both government and the private sector illustrate induced agricultural machinery research, production, and marketing in response to the private and social profit opportunities opened up by scientific advances.

Import Controls, Taxes, and Subsidies

Government decisions influence agricultural mechanization through such institutional arrangements as import controls and taxes on agricultural machinery and the subsidization of machinery. What guidance does the induced innovation model provide for these policies? A fundamental tenet of this model is that development will be accelerated most if the costs of resources used in production reflect the real costs of obtaining them. If national currency is not significantly over- or undervalued, import barriers and taxes should be low in order to increase the profitability of mechanization and credit should be allotted to farmers at competitive interest rates to facilitate appropriate agricultural mechanization.

Government import controls to slow mechanization are sometimes justified for short periods. One justification is the infant industry argument, discussed in chapter 13. Another relates to the early phases of machinery introduction, when a government may limit adoption in an area to one make of a complex machine in order to increase the number of machines of the same make, thereby providing a greater incentive for adequate parts supply and service. Once machine use has been established in an area, however, it is equally important for the government to open the market to competitive machines so that suppliers will have an incentive to provide farmers with newer, lower cost, more productive equipment and better service. All interventions should be temporary, with termination dates written into the original legislation or government directives.

Seldom can subsidies of agricultural mechanization be justified, especially for tractor mechanization. Government decisionmakers often falsely assume that rapid agricultural development depends upon tractor mechanization. This leads to, for example, low interest rates for loans to buy tractors. These actions lower machine costs relative to labor costs and cause an artificial rotation of the isocost line toward isocost line *B* in figure 9.5 that does not reflect the real costs of labor and capital in the economy. A premature acceleration of agricultural mechanization results from such price distortions, leading to four undesirable effects: reduced employment, greater income disparities, attempts by those with tractors and other machines to increase farm size, and worst, increased incentives to inventors and manufacturers to develop and produce even more labor-saving agricultural machinery.

Employment and Income Distribution

The structural transformation of the economies of less developed nations requires the gradual displacement of labor by machinery. This process proceeds because the use of more productive tools and mechanical equipment is privately and socially profitable. Hence, the mechanization of agriculture in these nations will continue to accelerate. However, the pace and timing of shifts in the demand for labor, as affected by agricultural machinery, are crucial for the income of rural labor. Hence, the extent to which mechanization developments are complementary to, or substitute for, labor will greatly affect the wages, employment, and income of rural laborers. A reduction in employment usually worsens income distribution. In areas with large numbers of landless agricultural laborers, the effect of mechanization on rural employment is critical for rural welfare. It is often also important for social and political stability in urban areas, due to the possible excessive flows of rural labor to overcrowded cities. In cases where the social and private gain from mechanization is high but severe loss of employment for labor occurs, government action may be necessary to slow the impacts on labor. Steps to moderate this threat can include temporary import duties and taxes on machinery or compensatory actions to aid agricultural laborers who lose employment.

Important Concepts

All-technology isoquant frontier
Appropriate technology
Potential of animal-powered
  agriculture
Stationary motorized power in
  agriculture
Tractor land preparation and yields
Timeliness
Cropping intensity
Machine complexity
Machine-utilization levels

Fixed and variable machine costs
Potentials of irrigation and drainage
Gravity-flow and pump irrigation
Institutional arrangements and
  irrigation
Management arrangements for
  agricultural machinery
Servicing arrangements for
  agricultural machinery
Government machinery stations

Sample Questions

1. Using an all-technology isoquant on a graph with labor and capital, explain why the equilibrium (highest profit) technology would differ between a more developed and a less developed nation.

2. Explain under what circumstances in less developed nations new kinds of hand tools might greatly increase the productivity of agriculture.

3. In what economic environments is use of additional animal power in agriculture likely to be productive?

4. What problems have to be overcome for the successful introduction of animal power?

5. Why has stationary motorized agricultural machinery been so popular in early phases of agricultural development?

6. In less developed areas with low labor costs, under what circumstances might tractors make a significant contribution to the income of farm laborers?

7. Assuming that the use of large tractors becomes profitable in an area of a less developed nation, outline three ways the services of these tractors might be made available to small farmers.

8. When pump-powered irrigation water is delivered to farmers on small farms, an economist is likely to say that the group of farmers using the water should be charged a lump-sum cost for the season instead of each farmer being charged on the basis of the number of acres he or she irrigates. Why?

9. Under what circumstances might subsidies for tractors be economically and socially justified?

10

Economics of Change in Institutions

> The really tough part of economic development is not fabricating improved technologies but rather the organizational tasks of recombining human behavior under new rules that enable people to help each other in creating and putting to widespread use the more effective technologies.
>
> Unlike physical materials and forces, the rules that combine behaviors into mutually helpful ways of living and making a living are not lifeless affairs. They are very much alive because, at least, the most important ones are interlocked with deep-seated convictions (beliefs) which people hold concerning the kinds of rules which deserve their respect and allegiance, and the kinds that merit their distrust and opposition. . . .
>
> Economic development is thus far more than a mere technological or physical transformation of inputs into increasing outputs, it is more fundamentally an organizational transformation of old ways of life and work into new rules of impersonal behaviors. And this in turn is possible only to the extent that people are able to make revisions in their heritage of basic convictions concerning the kinds of interpersonal rules which do and do not deserve their respect and support.
>
> —Joint Commission on Rural Reconstruction in China,
> Taiwan, 1966, in Mosher 1971, p. x

The greater the changes in technology and in the relative prices of inputs and products, the larger the amount of institutional change that is likely to be induced. Institutional changes in rural areas will also be engendered by social and political forces exogenous to the economic system. Increased understanding of the productivity and income distribution consequences of different institutional arrangements in various parts of agriculture can enable better design and choice of institutions.

Institutional Change, Technology, and the Role of the Social Sciences

The Role of Governing Institutions

Common law, formal statutes, and official directives formalize the traditions, rules, and institutional arrangements agreed to by social groups for the use of land, credit, and other resources. In a development context, consumers, farmers, and other entrepreneurs depend upon government to aid in carrying out the thousands of social rule changes required for the creation and more productive use of new technologies and institutions for agricultural production and marketing. Governing institutions are needed also to manage any negative external effects of private farm and other business activity that may arise. In addition, individuals and groups depend upon political and government leaders to settle conflicts and to carry out social changes they are not able to make by themselves that would benefit a community or subgroups in communities.

An example of the central role of institutional change in responding to change in the relative cost of agricultural resources has been highlighted by a researcher with much experience in Asia:

A number of developing countries in Asia have only recently moved from a land-surplus to a labor-surplus condition. However, the social structure of these economies has been molded under centuries of land-surplus condition (particularly in Southeast Asia) and under a highly skewed farm-size distribution (particularly in South Asia). This social structure erects a formidable barrier to the investment of social-overhead capital at the optimum level.

To keep pace with food demand, public capital investments needed to maintain the growth in agricultural production should increase sharply over the next decade. There will be strong incentives for institutional reforms and other measures to raise the productivity of these investments. . . . but there is no clear understanding as to what organizational and institutional changes are needed and, under the existing social structure, what can be accomplished; social science research that comes to grip with these issues can accelerate the process of change toward a more optimum institutional structure. (Barker 1978, p. 157)

Externalities

Externality problems illustrate the role of government and the ongoing need for institutional change as development proceeds. Externalities are defined as negative or positive effects on others of actions by individuals or organizations that these actors do not have to take into account in making decisions. Pollution by farmers, industrialists, or the government is a common example of an externality. Producers often do not have to include the costs of preventing or cleaning up pollution in their estimates of profit. The reason they do not include these costs is because customs and laws that have been agreed to by the social group do not require them to halt—or to pay for cleaning up—the pollution. When negative external effects, such as pollution, increase, or when persons negatively affected gain more influence, government provides a mechanism for changing the social rules to moderate the negative external effects. Government can require producers to take these costs into account by enforcing fines for pollution or by taking other decisions, such as prohibiting pollution and increasing its monitoring. Changes in rules that affect the externalities of producers may be caused by factors endogenous to the economic system, or they may result from exogenous factors, such as changes in beliefs and tastes.

Technology and Institutional Change

The economic theory of induced innovation examined in chapter 6 proposes that, in order to productively respond to the new opportunities stemming from changes in relative prices or from new technologies, increasing numbers of social rule (institutional) changes will be required. Much of modern agriculture and industry in more developed nations could not operate nearly as productively without the succession of rule changes continuously worked out legislatively, administratively, and judicially among the various industries and the rest of society. Examples of these include import rules, grades and standards, worker protection laws, and product safety requirements. Government provides a central social mechanism for such institutional change. Much institutional change is also carried out in the private sector as entrepreneurs develop more productive arrangements for input and product marketing. Thus, the level of government performance in facilitating institutional change and in settling disputes has great influence on the rate of development. Effective public decision-making is critical for rapid social and economic progress.

The Social Sciences and Institutional Change

Administrators, political leaders, and social scientists have a great deal of knowledge about how institutions perform and the likely impact of changes in social rules on the various parts of society. Hence, the supply of experienced and knowledgeable administrators, responsible politicians, and social scientists can have considerable effect on the rate at which more effective institutions are developed and adopted—and thus can have considerable effect on the national rate of economic growth.

Throughout most of history, the social learning that has given rise to improvements in institutional performance and to institutional innovation has occurred primarily through the slow accumulation of successful precedent or as a by-product of administrative or managerial expertise or experience. Within the last century, advances in knowledge in the social sciences have opened up new possibilities for efficiency in institutional innovation. . . . Advances in knowledge in the social sciences can lead to more efficient performance by existing institutions and to innovations that promote the development of new and more effective institutions. (Binswanger and Ruttan 1978, p. 355)[1]

1. For more material on institutional change and agricultural development, refer to chapter 6; Blase 1971; Myrdal 1968; Esman and Uphoff 1984; and Binswanger and Ruttan 1978 (chaps. 12–14).

Improving Rural Financial Markets and Farm Credit

Rural financial markets and farm credit rules, agricultural cooperatives, and landholding arrangements are central institutions in agriculture. The greatly increased demand for farm loans during agricultural development arises from the much higher returns to investment obtainable from the new, more productive biological, chemical, and mechanical farm technologies explored in chapters 8 and 9. Increases in farm loans can greatly accelerate the use of these new agricultural technologies and hence the growth of agriculture. Increasing loans to farmers requires the transformation of rural financial markets from limited, informal, traditional, local savings and lending arrangements to an integrated, formal, national savings and credit system.

Improvements in rural financial markets facilitate economic growth in at least five ways. First, the rural financial markets provided by banks, for example, offer checking services that enable rural people to make payments from distant locations through the mail, so that money or farm goods do not have to be transported and exchanged in person to make payments. Second, loans in these markets enable improved resource allocation. This occurs when a farmer who has a high-return investment opportunity available is able to borrow from a local financial institution where savings have been deposited by farmers who happen to have surplus cash and only low-return investment opportunities available. Third, loans, by providing more flexible command over resources, enable farmers to better manage the common risks of farming, due to the vagaries of weather and price, by increasing debt during bad crop years and reducing it during good crop years.

Fourth, loans facilitate the purchase of large investments. And fifth, loans ameliorate life-cycle problems, in which the young need to acquire farm and household assets—often by borrowing from established persons in the community who have accumulated savings (Adams, Graham, and Von Pischke 1984, pp. 12–14). Normally, loans enable borrowers to use someone else's savings. Government credit provides borrowers with the forced savings collected through taxes or inflationary financing.

Abolish the money lenders! This is a prescription often heard from those who would improve rural financial markets. Both the very bad experiences and misfortunes of a few persons at the hands of some moneylenders and the lack of understanding of the important contributions informal rural financial arrangements provide have led to this view. In fact, if moneylenders could be abolished, credit costs would in most cases increase and the volume of loans decline.

Without informal credit, agricultural development would proceed more slowly. If informal credit was not available and formal credit difficult to get, the rate of investment in productive farm inputs would depend upon the savings accumulated by each farmer and his near relatives. However, in all societies there are individuals who accumulate considerable savings. They would like to loan their money if they could be paid a reasonable amount for its use. If borrowed money can be invested in agricultural activities that provide a high enough return, the borrower can pay an interest rate to the lender and at the same time increase the borrower's income. In this way, agricultural production is stimulated. For many types of financial needs, informal transactions are less costly, as in the case of many small and short-term loans, unsecured loans, and emergency loans. There will always be a role for some informal forms of finance.

Finally, note that loans have an important special economic characteristic; they are *fungible*. Loans are not agricultural inputs; rather, they increase a borrower's command over inputs for production or consumption. A fungible financial instrument has the characteristic that, once the loan is received, the additional command over resources can be allocated to any purpose. The fungibility of loans is shown in the economic model of the household that proposes that additional family resources will be allocated to highest return investments available, whether in agricultural or nonagricultural activities. Thus, although the stated purpose of a loan may be to purchase seeds and fertilizer, the farmer might have been planning to purchase these inputs anyway. As the loan is fungible, the additional physical inputs or funds may enable other funds to be used for other purposes, such as a child's schooling, or for consumption, or for other nonagricultural investment. The loan has simply increased the amount of resources over which the family has command. A rational family will use the additional resources in ways that will provide the highest returns.

The Expanding Demand for Financial Services

The need in agricultural development for much more credit from expanded and more efficiently operating rural financial markets is clearly shown by economic theory. The new agricultural inputs considered in the previous two chapters provide farmers with opportunities to invest greater resources in higher return opportunities. Technological change also introduces greater heterogeneity among farm and rural households, creating greater cash surpluses and savings in some and greater credit needs in others. Hence, the demand for savings opportunities and for credit increases the need for more financial intermediaries.

The transformation of rural financial markets involves a shift from the inelastic traditional demand and supply curves in the informal village credit market, which often intersect at a high real cost (see C_1 in figure 10.1), to a more elastic supply curve for loans, S_2, that will intersect with the much greater demand for loans at a lower real cost, C_2. To achieve this requires (1) greatly expanded supplies of financial services, (2) a broader range of services, and (3) technological and institutional changes in the rural financial markets themselves, to reduce the costs of financial transactions.

How is the loan supply curve to be shifted to the right? In traditional areas, credit supply is often limited to a small geographic area, such as the village. Thus, the local informal supply curve for loans is likely to be inelastic (S_T). Then increased demand (curve D_2) leads to much higher interest rates with only

Figure 10.1. Shifts Caused by Development in the Demand and Supply of Commercial Agricultural Credit

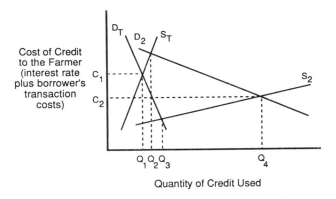

Quantity of Credit Used

small increases in credit supplied at Q_2. Such constrained availability of credit through informal sources often dampens increases in agricultural production, as more profitable agricultural technologies become available to farmers. Hence, the challenge for governments is to facilitate the growth of more integrated, efficient, and flexible rural financial markets so that much larger quantities of credit can be obtained at lower real interest rates from wider areas, including national financial markets.

The demand curve for loans shifts far to the right and becomes more elastic with agricultural development (D_2). This is because most of the more productive technologies are available only as purchased, off-farm inputs. Therefore, farmers are required to assemble more financial resources. Examples of two-, five-, and sometimes tenfold increases in the amounts of chemical fertilizer that could be profitably used were shown in chapter 8.

Empirical Studies of Rural Financial Markets

A detailed knowledge of existing credit supply and demand conditions and financial arrangements is useful in developing programs to increase rural financial services. The following empirical information illustrates agricultural credit conditions commonly found in less developed nations.

SOURCES, PURPOSES, SECURITY, AND TIME PERIODS OF LOANS

Credit sources are highly diverse in rural areas of less developed nations, but a large proportion of the credit provided to agriculture in many areas continues to come from noninstitutional sources, such as relatives, merchants, and moneylenders (table 10.1).

The reason villagers borrow from other villagers and local moneylenders is that the costs of making the transaction can be minimized for small loans. In the village, a farmer is known personally, so the information costs are low; little

Table 10.1. Farm Household Indebtedness by Type of Lender, Six Less Developed Nations (percent)

Item	Republic of China 1960	Republic of China 1977	Republic of Korea 1962	Republic of Korea 1977	Nepal 1976/77	Pakistan 1956	Pakistan 1970/71	Philippines 1953	Philippines 1978	Thailand 1976/77
Institutional lenders	56.7	36.6	68.6	64.7	42.9	28.6	40.0	17.4	61.4	63.0
Government		1.6				14.3	5.4	4.4		
Government-owned bank	32.6	5.5					27.9	13.0	24.8	39.2
Agricultural cooperatives or farmers' associations	24.1	29.5	66.0	63.8	29.5	14.3	4.9			16.4
Rural banks				0.6	7.0		1.9		36.6	
Commercial banks, etc.			2.6	0.3	6.4					7.5
Noninstitutional lenders	43.3	63.4	31.4	35.3	57.1	72.1	60.0	82.6	38.6	37.0
Landlords					2.1		7.5	7.8		0.2
Merchants		16.8			4.8	4.7	3.6	34.3		13.4
Professional moneylenders			22.8	1.7	5.0	1.1	1.9	18.6	23.3	13.4
Pawn shops							2.4			
Informal groups		22.1			24.9					
Individuals and others	43.3	24.5	8.6	33.6	20.4	66.3	44.5	21.9	15.3	23.3

Source: Adapted from Asian Productivity Organization 1984 (p. 10).

checking or paperwork is required to make a loan. Also, in these circumstances little or no collateral is needed by the creditor. The agreement is made in a few minutes and the money immediately provided. This contrasts with the time and travel costs incurred to complete complex institutional loan applications at a distant office and the uncertain wait for verification visits and approvals.

The examination of the stated purpose of a loan highlights the fungible nature of credit. In attempting to assure the ability to repay a loan, agricultural credit institutions usually try to target the use of loans for increased production. Empirical studies indicate the wide variety of purposes for which farmers borrow. Despite the stated purpose of the loan, because loans simply increase command over resources, it is difficult to be sure what the additional resources were used for. This fungible nature of loans places central focus on the importance of high-return investments for farmers. Without more productive investment opportunities, additional credit can only move farmers further out on currently available production functions, probably reducing the rate of return on investment in agriculture. A lower return often increases the risk of nonrepayment.

The security, or collateral, arrangements for loans are also highly variable, depending upon many local factors. Examples of these arrangements are illustrated by Lebanese data (Stevens 1959, pp. 213–22). In this area, about three-fourths of the randomly sampled farms reported one or more loans. Among 124 loans to farmers, 26 percent of them were not secured in any way, 18 percent included a signed written statement of debt to the creditor, 41 percent had a written statement of debt guaranteed by the signature of another local person, while only 15 percent had land as security.

A reason for the few loans from formal credit sources in some nations is the common requirement that land be offered as security. Many farmers are exceedingly reluctant to mortgage their land. They would rather forgo using formal credit and pay higher interest rates for informal loans. Additionally, in many areas cadastral surveys have not been completed to register ownership of land, and even when land has been surveyed and registered, titles to land often are not kept up to date.

If transaction costs are approximately the same, the shorter the time period of the loan, the higher the transaction costs per loan and per period of time, for both the borrower and lender. In the case of the credit study in Lebanese villages, 80 percent of the loans were for twelve months or less. These loans represented two-thirds of the total value of all loans.

To summarize, many agricultural loans in less developed nations are small, mostly extended for short periods of time, with security based on the lender's personal knowledge of the borrower. Also, a significant proportion of the loans are used for purposes other than agricultural production, whether or not that is their stated purpose, due to the fungibility of credit. In some areas where farmers have become continuously indebted to landlords or moneylenders, a high level of loans may prevail in relation to annual income, and a considerable proportion of net farm income may be paid out in interest charges, although the average proportion of net income paid by all farmers may be much lower.

INTEREST RATES

As farm families who are able to save generally have a number of opportunities for investment of their savings, to attract these savings into agricultural investments usually requires payment of a certain real interest rate. In societies where charging interest is illegal, borrowers may be given less money than they agree to pay back, thereby providing an effective interest rate to their creditors for the use of their money.

Governments in many less developed nations often fix the nominal rate of interest permitted in formal financial markets at relatively low levels, such as between 6 and 12 percent. These rates very often do not cover the costs of providing loans, even when there is no inflation. When typical inflation rates of 10 or 20 percent occur, the real interest rates for these loans are often negative. Thus, farmers in less developed nations face exceedingly variable real interest rates on loans, from the negative rates in nations with significant inflation, to no nominal interest charged within families, to very high real rates charged to individuals in some monopolistic environments.

The variability in the real costs of farm credit is illustrated by a study in Chile, where almost a third of the loans were given with no interest charged (table 10.2). In this case, due to a 33 percent annual inflation rate, the borrowers returned at the end of the year a value in money of only 67 percent of the value they had borrowed. These borrowers had a net gain of 33 percent simply for borrowing the money for the year. The real interest rate received by the lender was − 33 percent (a loss of one-third of the capital). Another third of the farmers experienced a zero real rate of interest, as a nominal interest rate of 33 percent was paid. In these cases, borrowers had to pay back only a value equivalent to the money borrowed. Those who borrowed from moneylenders, traders, and village stores, however, paid a nominal interest rate of some 100 percent per year, leading to a real interest rate of about 67 percent per year. The following equation estimates the real interest rate:

$$\text{Real interest rate} = \frac{1+i}{1+p} - 1,$$

where i = the rate of interest paid (nominal rate), and p = the change in the price index.

In many less developed areas, much data indicate that real rates of interest charged by moneylenders in rural areas range widely, from 5 to 50 percent or more per year. Are these rates justified by the transaction and other costs of supplying credit in these areas, or do they represent monopoly profits and forced extractions?

The high interest rates charged on the many small loans lent in many areas of less developed nations are explained to a considerable extent by lending costs.

Table 10.2. Example of the Distribution of Loans by Real Interest Rates, Rural Areas in Chile

Type of Lender and Loan		Number of Loans at Each Real Interest Rate																Total
		-33	-22	-20	-13	-7	-3	0	18	27	30	33	40	46	60	75	90-360	
Friends:	Cash	4	1			1												6
	Kind							6	1										7
Neighbors:	Cash																		0
	Kind							4											4
Relatives:	Cash	3	1																4
	Kind							7											7
Patrones:	Cash	16																	16
	Kind							3											3
Village stores:	Cash	1	1	1	2	1	1							2			1	10
	Kind							9								1	1	11
Itinerant traders:	Cash																		0
	Kind										1		1		1	1		4
Moneylenders:	Cash									1				1			1	3
	Kind							2				1	1		5	3	3	15
Total		24	3	1	2	2	1	31	1	1	1	1	2	3	6	5	6	90

Source: Slightly modified from Nisbet 1967 (p. 77). Reprinted with permission.
Note: Interest rates are on actual loans for the agricultural year May 1964 through May 1965; rates were deflated.

What are the components of these costs? Bottomley (1975) identified the three most important costs as the opportunity cost of the money, transaction and administrative costs, and a risk premium. The opportunity cost of funds for agricultural loans depends upon the alternative investment opportunities available (say, in marketing or outside the village) that may provide, for example, a 10 percent return. Lenders with this return available would not be rational if they did not seek at least this real rate of interest.

Transaction and administrative costs for small loans can be high as a percentage of the money loaned, depending upon the amount of effort required to negotiate the loan. In the formal credit market, the paperwork and required verifications make small loans costly. The risk premium needed to cover average loan losses can be calculated with the following equation:

$$P = P(1 - d)(1 + r),$$

where P is the principal or amount lent, d is the default rate, and hence $P(1 - d)$ is the amount of the principal recovered, and r is the interest rate that has to be charged to cover the loss in principal. When reduced, the equation becomes

$$r = 1/(1 - d) - 1.$$

Thus a 10 percent default on loans would require

$$r = 1/(1 - .10) - 1,$$

or an 11 percent interest rate to cover the default risk. A 25 percent default experience would require a 33 percent interest rate just to cover the risk.[2]

In addition to the costs of providing informal credit, a monopoly profit may be added in some circumstances, increasing the interest rate further. When there are few barriers to entrance into the informal credit market, as is often the case, considerable local competition is likely, preventing much monopoly profit. In situations where a borrower is limited to one lender due to some kind of control over the borrower, such as in a tenancy situation, monopoly profit may be extracted.

When the three lending costs reviewed above are added, they can reach a real rate of 30 percent or more: an opportunity cost of money of 10 percent, administrative costs of 10 percent, and a risk premium of 10 percent. Hence, in villages in the informal market, a real interest rate of 40 percent on small loans may not be much above the rates required for the lenders to continue to make these loans. In high-income nations, where many competitive credit sources are available, consumers commonly pay real rates of interest of 15 percent or more for credit, as, for example, on credit card loans.

---

2. The equation was contributed by John M. Staatz through personal communication.

Augmenting the Supply of Savings and Credit

A growing literature indicates that a major departure in the approach to farm credit is required in many less developed nations to enable more rapid growth of self-sustained rural and agricultural credit. In the past, governments and donors have focused on channeling increasing amounts of loans to farmers at low interest rates, with the common assumption that the informal rural credit market is evil and antiquated and therefore should be destroyed. In the process, little attention has been paid to stimulating savings. Instead, the criterion for success has been the quantity of farm loans outstanding.

The new approach ''would mean learning from the informal lender, stressing savings-deposit services, downgrading the importance of agricultural credit, opening rural financial markets to nonfarm rural firms, creating a more healthy environment in rural areas for financial innovation, less loan targeting, and making major adjustments in the way external donors relate to these markets'' (Adams, Graham, and Von Pischke 1984, p. 231). The criterion for credit program success proposed by these authors is overall performance of the rural financial market, including the quantity of savings and loans. These points are explored in more detail below.

INCREASING INSTITUTIONAL SAVINGS IN RURAL AREAS

The poor people who make up the majority of rural inhabitants in developing countries are often viewed as being unable to save because of their poverty. In fact, they can and do save. The task of institutionalizing some of these rural savings is primarily a question of financial technology, that is, of finding ways to provide the financial services that rural savers want and will respond to. (Von Pischke, Adams, and Donald 1983, p. 414)

Savings in a society are generated by forced saving through government taxation, by inflation, by exchange rate distortions, and by voluntary personal savings. Funds for agricultural loans from government sources are usually limited, although in some countries considerable agricultural credit may also be available from time to time through international aid programs. In the long run, the development of savings institutions, which can accumulate large amounts of voluntary savings from rural people, is the soundest source of increased rural and agricultural credit.

There are four reasons to improve the savings performance of rural financial institutions. First, the greater availability of loans with realistic interest rates enables a more equal distribution of loans, leading to greater income-earning opportunities for small farmers. Loans at unsubsidized rates enable rural financial institutions to lend to small as well as large farmers, as subsidized credit mostly goes to large farmers (Gonzalez-Vega 1977). Second, the effective mobilization of savings by rural financial institutions enables more efficient and productive resource use, for savings placed in financial institutions draw funds from persons who have relatively low productivity investments directly available to them. These funds are loaned to farmers and others who are able to obtain much higher returns.

Third, the mobilization of savings increases the financial stability and health of financial institutions. A community has less stake in lending institutions that do not have its savings. Moreover, institutions without savings are more subject to cycles of high defaults and the vagaries of increases and decreases in their loan funds from other government institutions. And fourth, if the amount of credit a lending institution can obtain from other sources is tied to the amount of savings accumulated, the institution will try to attract savers by providing better services to them and will take more action to encourage high loan repayment rates. To succeed in a competitive environment, rural financial institutions with savings accounts have to become more responsive to local financial needs. Also, rural financial institutions that have been strengthened by local savings become less dependent upon government and more able to limit political intrusions into their financial affairs.

Three actions that can increase rural savings are (1) maintaining real interest rates through regular adjustments for changes in the rate of inflation, so that the returns to savings approach the returns these deposits could make in other investments; (2) reducing savers' transaction costs by reducing paperwork and waiting times, opening branches closer to residences, and establishing postal savings at nearby post offices; and (3) insuring individual savings accounts.

Building rural credit cooperatives can also contribute significantly to generating rural savings and augmentating rural credit supplies, as demonstrated by experience in more developed nations as well as in South Korea and Taiwan. In Comilla, Bangladesh, credit cooperatives were organized in a very low-income rice-producing area by requiring a small weekly deposit of savings equivalent to ten cents in U.S. currency. Farmers accumulated savings and shares in the cooperative until they equaled more than 50 percent of the large amounts of agricultural loans extended to them by the cooperative system (Stevens 1974, p. 411). In South Korea, the very large National Agricultural Cooperative Federation and other rural savings institutions succeeded in encouraging high levels of rural savings. Rural households were estimated to have saved an average of 12 percent of their income in 1963 and 33 percent in 1974 (Lee, Kim, and Adams 1983).

FACILITATING THE GROWTH AND DIVERSITY OF RURAL CREDIT ARRANGEMENTS

The types of institutional arrangements that have enabled greatly expanded agricultural credit in less developed nations are illustrated by cooperatives (discussed latter in this chapter), borrower groups, specialized farm credit institutions, and credit from input suppliers.

Successful group lending is illustrated by experience in Malawi, where borrowers' groups offered farmers an opportunity for lower interest rates, price discounts on inputs, and lower loan transaction costs. The principles of German Raiffeisen cooperatives (see below) were applied in the formation of these small groups based upon the initiative of farmers. These lending groups could disband and reform each year. The loan was managed by an elected member, without pay. Members were fully liable for individual defaults, and group security against default was achieved through an advance deposit of 10 percent of the value of the loan, which was refunded with interest after full repayment of the loan (Schaefer-Kehnert 1983).

Specialized Government Farm Credit Institutions. Many problems have arisen in establishing specialized government farm credit programs. Although some succeed, with relatively high repayment rates, many fail, with continuing large losses of government funds. Loan default rates can range from 10 or 20 percent to 60 percent or more. Large farmers often have default rates as high as small farmers, implying that the ability to repay is not a primary factor in defaults. Government credit programs fail because of a lack of skilled managers and because of farmers' belief that the program is political—and therefore that the loans are gifts to aid needy farmers.

The experience of the Agricultural Bank of Malaysia provides an example of the incorporation of private sector participants in a government agricultural credit program. This bank established local credit centers to offer competitive loans to farmers and made arrangements for participation by both public sector units (rural cooperatives and farmers' associations) and traditional rural private sector businesses (rice millers, licensed paddy buyers, merchants, and shop-keepers) who sell inputs and purchase paddy. Evaluations of these local credit centers showed that the private sector program participants used a higher proportion of the credit available to them and generally had greater repayment rates compared to the cooperative and farmer organization participants. This multi-channel credit system was of considerable value to farmers, as they had increased choice of credit sources from different suppliers. This system also encouraged credit suppliers to reduce transaction costs so they could compete better (Wells 1983, p. 220).

Credit from Input Suppliers and Marketing Organizations. In many situations, local agricultural input suppliers and product marketing firms provide significant opportunities to increase agricultural credit to small farmers. These firms have strong incentives to increase the amounts of inputs and products sold. Farmers also have an incentive to repay loans from agricultural input suppliers and product marketing firms in order to be able to borrow for the next agricultural season. Credit from machinery dealers has the advantage that the dealer has an added incentive to aid farmers in using the machines productively by providing training, repairs, and spare parts so they will be able to repay their loans. [3]

3. The section on rural financial markets draws on two state-of-the-art publications: Von Pischke, Adams, and Donald 1983 and Adams, Graham, and Von Pischke 1984. For a review of evidence on savings capacities in rural areas of less developed nations, see Adams 1978; and for a

Policies for Improved Rural Financial Markets

Farmers and lenders are now viewed as rational in their savings and credit behavior. Both institutional and informal lenders provide valuable financial services to agriculture, although there are always cases of bad performance. Therefore, if rural financial markets are to grow, savers and lenders have to receive sufficient economic reward from their savings and credit activities to make them worthwhile. The following four policies to strengthen rural financial markets are based, in part, on the important review of rural credit projects and policies by Adams and Graham (1984).

Identifying Financial Market Problems. Many misconceptions surround the operation of rural financial markets. With little empirical information about the performance of either institutional credit (public and private) or informal credit in the different rural areas, it has been easy for governments to make wrong assumptions about constraints on rural financial markets and to undertake unproductive and counterproductive programs intended to improve the performance of rural financial markets.

Assuring Interest Rate Flexibility to Attract Savings. In order for savings and credit institutions to operate without loss and for savers to earn positive real interest rates, the rates offered on savings accounts and on loans must be adjusted with inflation. Legislative fixing of interest rates unrelated to inflation almost always reduces real interest rates, often causing them to become negative.

Consider the effects of a fixed nominal interest rate (say, 10 percent) that is below the equilibrium cost (say, 23 percent) required to provide loans to small farms (see figure 10.2). With the ceiling rate of 10 percent imposed, less credit would be supplied to agriculture, Q_1, instead of Q_2, at the equilibrium rate. An even greater quantity of loans, Q_4, would be demanded at the ceiling interest rate. With many borrowers seeking the limited funds available, loans go to the larger farmers, because they offer increased security and reduced transaction costs.

Thus, with limited low-cost loan funds, political influence and graft are more likely to determine who receives the very profitable loans. Others are forced to turn to secret arrangements in an informal market at interest rates that are likely to be higher than equilibrium. Part of the higher cost on the informal credit market would be due to the additional risk premium needed by the lender to cover the costs of possible government prosecution. An additional adverse effect of unrealistically low interest rate ceilings is reduced institutional saving by rural people which, in turn, decreases the credit supply.

---

more extended discussion of approaches to increasing rural savings, see Von Pischke 1983. Other general studies of agricultural credit include Bathrick 1981; Donald 1978; and Howell 1980. See Singh 1983 and Harriss 1983 for discussion of monopoly profits and forced extractions. Eicher and Baker 1982 (pp. 198–204) reviewed agricultural credit literature on Africa.

Figure 10.2. Effects of a Government Interest Rate Ceiling on the Quantity of Agricultural Credit Borrowed

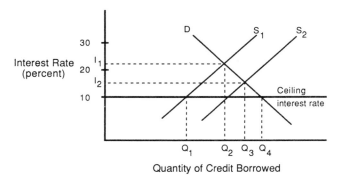

Quantity of Credit Borrowed

The fundamental point that rural credit expansion and lower interest rates require reductions in transaction and other costs of supplying credit is also illustrated in figure 10.2. When lending costs are reduced, the credit supply curve shifts to the right, S_2. Under competitive market conditions, this leads to a lower interest rate I_2 on loans and a larger quantity of credit, Q_3. Thus, fixing unrealistically low fixed interest rate ceilings on agricultural loans usually causes the perverse result of less credit availability to farmers. This occurs because government leaders have little social learning about rural financial markets.

Reducing Subsidized Credit for Agriculture. Subsidies for agricultural credit are often provided through government agricultural credit programs that charge low real interest rates. Observe the effect of the additional credit supplied to agriculture (see figure 10.3). The additional credit at lower than equilibrium rates shifts the upper part of the credit supply curve to the right, resulting in a segmented credit supply curve (*abcd*), with a new, lower equilibrium market interest rate of i_2. The length of the *bc* segment depends upon the amount of credit provided at the subsidized rate. Although the subsidized credit does increase the total amount of credit used, from Q_1 to Q_2, several negative outcomes follow. Credit received at a lower than equilibrium rate provides a net transfer of government resources from taxpayers and other sectors of the economy to the agricultural borrowers equal to the difference between the market interest rate and the subsidized rate. Whether this transfer can be justified depends upon who the taxpayers, the savers, and the borrowers are. If, as often happens, the largest and most influential farmers obtain most of the subsidized loans, the income transfer can be from the poorer persons in the society to the more wealthy.

Reducing Costs of Financial Intermediation. The successful expansion of institutional credit in rural areas depends on reducing the costs of credit and saving transactions both for the farmer and for the lending institution. Adams and Graham (1984, p. 318) concluded that there is an important inverse relation

Figure 10.3. Effect of Subsidized Credit on the Supply and Cost of Credit

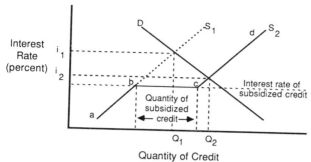

between the real interest rate on loans and transaction costs. When credit institutions are required to charge low interest rates, a flood of applications is received—which have to be processed. The institutions, in an attempt to reduce losses, increase the number of steps in the loan application process for nonpreferred borrowers. With more realistic interest rates, loan transaction costs will be reduced, especially for nonpreferred borrowers.

Cooperative Institutions and Agricultural Development

As resource costs and product prices change and as more productive technology becomes available, new and modified institutional arrangements will be demanded. One type of new institution that may facilitate increased productivity is the member-controlled cooperative. What is the nature of this institution? What roles should it undertake? And what are the criteria for the success of cooperatives?

In many cultures, traditional community cooperative activities are undertaken that benefit participants. These can lead to more formal cooperative organizations, which operate as economic enterprises to provide expanded amounts of goods and services to their members. Cooperatives can bring farmers new economic opportunities and increased control over their economic environment. Cooperatives can often lead to greater influence in political arenas, also.

Thousands of formally organized cooperatives are operating in Asia, Africa, and Latin America, with highly varied success. Programs to support further development of cooperatives in less developed nations have had extremely variable results also. Great success has been achieved by some cooperatives in India, such as the Anand Milk Cooperative. It has expanded many times since the 1950s and in 1981 had 300 thousand members in about 900 local societies (Anand Milk Cooperative 1982). However, large numbers of cooperatives in many less developed nations do little business and benefit only a few.

The Principles of Member-Controlled Cooperatives

The positive connotation of the word *cooperative* has led to a wide range of institutions that use this term, ranging from independent, democratic, member-controlled units to branches of a state-run centrally controlled administrative structure. Many quasi-cooperatives with some membership control have also been elaborated.

The institutional form of the member-controlled cooperative was developed by the Rochdale weavers in England in 1844 and by the Raiffeisen credit cooperatives in Germany about 1860 (Roy 1964, pp. 41–68). Three basic principles define these institutions: (1) control of the cooperative through one vote per member, with membership open; (2) a limit on the return retained by the cooperative from capital investment; and (3) the return to members of any savings, or surplus, on the basis of the volume of business engaged in by the members (Larson 1969, p. 31). Quasi-cooperatives incorporate at least one of these principles. In some less developed nations, Eastern Europe, and some socialist countries, cooperative organizations are often simply units of centrally controlled government ministries. For the individual, the economic inducement for participation in a member-controlled cooperative is that more benefits will be obtained, such as lower input prices, higher product prices, easier access to more productive technology, and increased availability of farm and consumer goods and credit.

Cooperatives are complex business organizations that include objectives, an organizational structure, and specified methods of operation and financing that require member accounts. The development of cooperatives requires much training and experience. A strong central cooperative organization is usually required to support local cooperatives. Thus, in judging the performance of a particular cooperative or a cooperative system, one needs to analyze the results in relation to the history of development over five- and ten-year periods. Cooperatives with a largely illiterate membership may take a long time to achieve strong business performance. The requirements of strong management performance and the costs of managing cooperatives may in many circumstances be too great to obtain the desired economic results, compared with other institutional arrangements—such as the private business firm.

Much effort has been spent in attempting to transfer to less developed nations the principles and organizational arrangements of cooperatives that originated in Europe. As less developed nations have very different cultural and institutional endowments, considerable testing and adapting is often required before a cooperative can succeed in the new environment. For example, in authoritarian societies, it is uncertain whether the votes of the members in a local cooperative will reflect their interests, as opposed to the interests of their social and political superiors. In other cultural environments, the prospects for independent, member-controlled cooperative organizations may be bleak due to values held, as illustrated by the case of Tzintzuntzan, Mexico, discussed in chapter 5, or due to political and government opposition to the development of local independent organizations in many socialist and authoritarian countries.

In less developed nations, cooperatives have often been sponsored by government departments. Government, if dedicated to the eventual establishment of member-controlled cooperatives, can greatly aid testing, modification, and training for expanded cooperative organization (see for example Spaeth 1969 concerning the Japanese and Taiwanese experience). However, for political and other reasons, other sponsoring governments and administrators may view cooperative units as just another part of government to be administered or may consider any increased independence and strength of these units as a threat. [4]

The Example of the Comilla Village Cooperatives

A new cooperative system that attracted much international attention was established in Comilla, Bangladesh, in the 1960s, among a largely illiterate, very low-income population. The development of these cooperatives was led by the Academy for Rural Development at Comilla, which began operating in 1959 with a staff of twelve faculty, most of whom had master's degrees. The objective of the academy was to improve the skills of civil servants to aid the development of rural areas. The first director of the academy, Akhter Hameed Khan, pointed out to the recently arrived, academically trained, instructors that they and others knew little about how to aid rural areas of their country. Hence, he proposed an activity not planned for the academy—that before much instruction was provided to the civil servants, research was to be undertaken to obtain information about nearby agricultural and rural conditions and what farmers and other villagers wanted help with.

In discussions with villagers, the faculty found out that help was wanted to increase rice production, control water, and obtain credit. Dr. Khan and the faculty decided that in order to provide instruction on how to improve rural areas they needed to undertake pilot rural development projects. They chose to try to organize a new type of cooperative, which would be based on the small social unit of the village. These cooperatives might provide a mechanism through which villagers could work with the academy. In this way, villagers would gain new resources, and the academy faculty would learn how to accelerate agricultural development in that environment.

These cooperatives were organized as follows. The village was told to choose a chairman for their cooperative society from among the elderly and respected persons and a younger, more active, person to be the organizer, or manager, of the cooperative. The younger man was to be responsible for the ac-

4. General works on cooperatives in less developed nations include Dulfer 1980; McGrath 1971, 1978; and Dorner 1977. Several reports are also available from the United Nations Research Institute for Social Development, including United Nations 1974; on Latin America, Fals-Borda 1971; on Asia, Inayatullah 1970; and on Africa, Apthc _ - 1970. Eicher and Baker (1982, pp. 204–6) provide a review of African reports on cooperatives. For recent East European views on cooperatives, see FAO 1978a.

counts, for weekly trips to the academy, and for teaching members about cooperative organization, loan arrangements, and agricultural improvement projects. Weekly village meetings of all cooperative members were required, at which time a small savings deposit was to be placed by each member in his account to earn eligibility for a loan. All members of the village cooperative would be jointly responsible for repayment of credit. In addition, the group had to choose a model farmer from among the better farmers, who would go regularly to the academy to learn new agricultural practices; he was then required to try them on his own farm and to provide information about them at village meetings. In this way, an agricultural extension link was established with the village.

The adoption of low-lift water pumps and then tube wells, obtained through the academy from the Department of Agriculture, led to increases in agricultural production in the Comilla District during the 1960s. Considerable amounts of credit extended through the cooperatives increased rice production further. At the end of the decade, as the high-yielding rice varieties became available, the academy and the village cooperatives led in adopting these more productive rice technologies in Bangladesh. By 1970, there were 301 village agricultural cooperatives in Comilla Thana (county), with a membership of about 35 percent of the farm families (Mueller and Anderson 1982). The average loan issued was fifty-three dollars per member, while savings and shares of a member held by the cooperative averaged thirty dollars per member. The cooperative credit system was financially healthy, with only about 2 percent of the loans overdue more than one year. This high performance was achieved in an agricultural area where per capita incomes were estimated in 1970 dollars at about a hundred dollars!

The combined institutional and technological changes in the Comilla program are consistent with the theory of induced development. Institutional change, in the form of village-based credit cooperatives, was seen by the academy leadership as complementary to the flow of more productive technology into these villages. The Comilla cooperatives can be seen in the wider framework of development as a part of the increasing institutional complexity that can be expected to be induced by new economic opportunities. [5]

Cooperatives and Development

Cooperatives have aided farmers in many nations to increase their incomes. Although criticisms of poor performance of cooperatives are often merited, in other cases, criticism is due to unrealistic expectations and to a misunderstanding of cooperative principles (United Nations 1974, pp. 25–36). First, the cooperative institution is only one of a number of possible institutional ar-

5. Other materials on the Comilla cooperatives include A. A. Khan and Solaiman 1978; Stevens 1974, 1976; and Bose 1974; and the standard reference by Raper 1970. Details of cooperative growth and setbacks are found in the continuing series of *Annual Reports* of the Bangladesh Academy for Rural Development.

rangements to provide improved services to farmers. In some cultures, such as those that are more authoritarian, member-controlled cooperatives may not work, so other institutional forms will develop in these areas to provide economic gains to farmers.

Second, criticism of cooperatives is sometimes based on unrealistic and inappropriate goals. Thus, cooperatives "are not welfare or charity organizations whose main interest is to lend money to those who cannot repay or to look after minimum needs of the destitute" (United Nations 1974, p. 30). Other unrealistic goals for member-controlled cooperatives include changing the structure of rural society, assuring equal income to all members, solving the employment and income problems of the landless, and making social and political progress. These examples of unrealistic goals contrast with the specific and modest goals of thousands of successful cooperatives that provide specific economic services to members.

To conclude, cooperatives are economic enterprises. They can succeed only to the extent that they successfully meet or exceed the competitors' economic performance. This may be achieved through reduced transaction costs, joint assurance on unsecured loans, and in other ways. Cooperatives do often enable some reduction in income disparities, by increasing the access by small farmers to credit and by helping them obtain lower prices for inputs and higher prices for products. Independent member-controlled cooperatives, despite their high initial training costs and need for able managers and effective leaders, have contributed and will continue to contribute greatly to the advancement of millions of rural people in areas where economic and social conditions are favorable for their development. In other areas, alternative institutional arrangements will be induced to provide gains.

Changes in Rights to the Use of Land: Land Reforms, Collective Farming, and Communes

Different arrangements of rights to the use of land will be induced by different cultures, under different economic conditions, at different times in history. In the induced innovation model, demand for changes in institutional arrangements are endogenous or exogenous to the economic part of a social system. The two major economic forces endogenous to this model that induce institutional change are changes in the relative prices of resources and changes in technology. Two examples: first, in traditional agricultural areas, increasing rural population pressures often cause increases in the value of land relative to labor; second, new agricultural technologies have increased the productivity of some agricultural lands relative to others—and also their value relative to other inputs. Economic changes that increase the value of land are likely to lead to demands for more security of tenure through land survey and registration and other reforms. Influences external to the economy that affect landholding arrangements include revolutions, invasions, and colonial rule. The establishment of the hacienda system in the New World by the Spanish is an example, as is the collectivization of agriculture by many socialist and communist governments.

Bohannan (1963) provided a useful perspective on the evolution of land tenure concepts in the context of many centuries of human development. "It is not enough to see 'land-tenure' in terms of our own system. We must see it also in terms of the people who are approaching new economic and social horizons" (p. 8). When land is plentiful, the territory controlled by a social group over time often varies, as has been the case of many peoples in history. Under these circumstances, the rights to the use of land are likely to be determined by membership or status in a group, and by use. Bohannan observed that a system of landholding rights may then evolve, so that specific pieces of land and other resources, such as trees and water, can be controlled by individuals. This develops as land becomes scarce and territories become permanently identified with groups of people. These historic systems of rights that control resource use are the focus of many current reforms aimed at enabling greater productivity and better distribution of income.

The Wide Range of Landholding Arrangements

A knowledge of the most important types of landholding arrangements can help identify changes in institutional arrangements that would aid in achieving desired economic and other objectives. Galeski (1977) summarized the wide array of systems of rights to the use of land. Different distributional and productivity outcomes arise from the varied rules for the control of resources. Institutional rules also greatly affect the amount of economic and social independence enjoyed by members of society. Galeski noted two general types of socioeconomic systems: interactive economic systems, in which consumers reward or punish producers through purchase of products; and directive economic systems, in which government agencies and planning groups reward or punish producers. Individual farming is generally associated with interactive economic systems, and collective farming is more likely in directed economic systems. Galeski distinguished five categories of landholding arrangements (see table 10.3).

TRADITIONAL COMMUNAL LAND OWNERSHIP

This arrangement involves social control of the land with periodic, or hereditary, reallocation of land for use by farming families. These traditional landholding arrangements vary widely. Some permit large scope for independent farm decisionmaking, while others exhibit high levels of local group control in production and consumption decisions. In some cases, crops may be produced jointly on communal land and then distributed on the basis of traditional rules implemented by the group leader. In the case of some African groups, social custom prescribes distribution of the products of some plots to persons other than the producer (Dalton 1967).

Table 10.3. Landholding Arrangements Arrayed by Extent of Social Control of Production and Consumption

Landholding Arrangement	Area Where Practiced
Individual Farming	
Traditional communal land ownership, use, rights, and shifting cultivation	Many less developed nations
Owner-operated and tenant farming, often with service cooperatives	Most less-developed and more-developed nations
Group Farming	
Integral collective or cooperative farming	The GAEC, France
Collective farming	Kolkhoz, U.S.S.R.; ejido, Mexico; communes, China (before 1978)
The true commune	Kibbutzin, Israel; agricultural religious monasteries

FAMILY OR INDIVIDUAL FARMING

This arrangement, with full ownership or lifetime tenure rights, or with various forms of short-term tenancy, predominates in a large majority of less developed and more developed nations. In some nations and regions, large ownership units that sublet to tenants predominate, while in many others family farm ownership is more frequent. Different types of independent consumer cooperatives, as well as private businesses, have developed in these agricultural areas to provide family farms with agricultural inputs, equipment, irrigation, marketing, credit, and other needed goods and services.

INTEGRAL OR COOPERATIVE FARMING

These arrangements are not very common. The income from the farm is distributed on the basis of the ownership of the three sets of productive resources: land, capital (including buildings and equipment), and labor. The way in which these resources are valued (priced) influences the distribution of the net farm income.

COLLECTIVE FARMING

This type of farming was established in the belief that greater agricultural productivity, more equal income distribution, and better control of the agricultural sector are achieved by transferring land to collective ownership and operation. The income of the collective is distributed to members based usually on some measure of labor contributed.

The largest concentrations of collective farming are in Eastern Europe, the U.S.S.R., and Vietnam. Considerable collective farming is also present in some less developed nations, including Mexico and Cuba. In Eastern Europe, the importance of collective farming varies greatly. In 1972, more than half the land in five countries (East Germany, Hungary, Bulgaria, Czechoslovakia, and Romania) was farmed collectively. However, in Poland and Yugoslavia, some 80 percent of the agricultural land was farmed under private ownership. In the U.S.S.R., state farms, which operate like factories with hired labor, are most important, controlling more than 60 percent of the farmland (United Nations 1976).

Wong (1979), after reviewing experiences with a wide variety of group farming arrangements in East and Southeast Asia, concluded that relatively little group farming was practiced in these countries. In China, farming used to be organized under a commune system, which is a particular type of collective farm. However, since 1978, increased decentralization and greater use of incentive payments to labor have been implemented. Numbers of group farms are also present in some other less developed nations, where experiments in group farming are being tried.

THE TRUE COMMUNE

This arrangement provides the most social control, with all production under group control and a large amount of goods and services provided on the basis of need, through group-operated central dining halls, nurseries, recreational facilities, and public housing, with small individual cash allowances to members for personal needs. The kibbutzim in Israel provide the most important current example of the commune type of farming system.

From time to time, a few agricultural communes have been established in Europe and the United States. Also, agricultural monasteries sponsored by religious orders have persisted in many parts of the world for many centuries. The history of communes has generally shown that such control of production and consumption is difficult for most people to sustain. Thus, for the true commune to endure, very special conditions are required, especially highly motivated individuals willing to make many sacrifices of individuality (Galeski 1977, pp. 32–35; Arnon 1981, p. 455).

The Great Variability in Farm Size, Tenancy, and Landlessness

In less developed nations, very variable distributions of farm sizes have come about as rural social systems have evolved. Farm size may be measured by land owned, by land operated by a family (including rented land) or by many other measures, such as gross or net income or the value of farm assets.

In some nations, such as Taiwan (Republic of China), where land reform was carried out effectively, disparities in land ownership became small, resulting in a unimodal farm size structure (see figure 10.4). This contrasts with the wider disparities in land area cultivated per farm and the size of the operational units in many less developed nations, as in India and especially, Colombia. Large disparities in size lead to a bimodal farm structure, illustrated by Colombia in figure 10.4. Disparities in farm size can be conveniently compared using a Lorenz curve (see figure 10.5). With highly skewed ownership of farmland, as in Colombia, the top 10 percent of owners control more than 80 percent of total

Figure 10.4. Unimodal and Bimodal Farm-Size Distributions in Taiwan, India, and Colombia

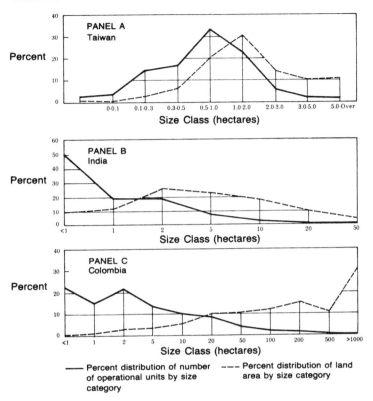

Source: Johnston and Tomich 1985 (p. 9). Reprinted with permission.

farmland, while a large number of farmers hold small amounts of land or are tenants or farm laborers.

The amount of land rented and sharecropped in less developed nations varies greatly, often within the regions of a country. National averages of tenancy for selected countries are given in table 10.4. The distribution of farmland ownership units has important effects on all aspects of agricultural development, especially upon the kinds of agricultural technologies and institutions whose adoption will be induced. As social and economic development proceeds, increasing numbers of citizens may judge that disparities in the ownership of agricultural resources with resulting large income disparities are undesirable, leading to political action to obtain land reform.

Figure 10.5. Lorenz Curves of Agricultural Land Distribution, Seven Nations

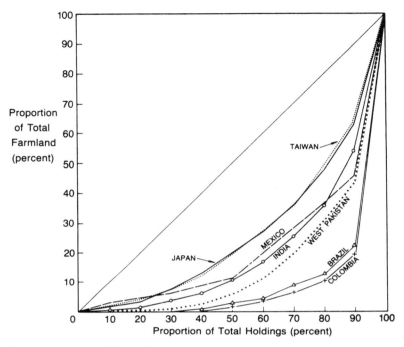

Source: Johnston and Kilby 1975 (p. 16). Reprinted with permission.
Note: This figure shows the proportion of holdings as a proportion of total farmland.

Land Reform, Tenure Reform, and Agricultural Productivity

Institutional changes in agricultural production systems may evolve or undergo rapid change due to land reform, revolution, invasion, or colonial policies. Little agreement exists on the meanings of the terms *land reform* and *tenure reform*. Narrow definitions focus on reforms that change rights to the use of land, while broad definitions include the transformation of the rural socioeconomic structure so that social relations and class composition are also changed (de Janvry 1981, p. 383). Raup (1967) concluded that land reform "must combine redistribution of rights in land and the supporting measures that are necessary to achieve three objectives: social justice, political health, and agricultural output expansion" (p. 270). Raup also emphasized the need for incentives for increased productivity both to the farmer and to the public sector by reforms that strengthen owner-operated farms. Farm owners have a greater incentive to increase investment in the land, such as by digging better irrigation and drainage canals, than a tenant, who may lose control of the land next year. Owner-opera-

Table 10.4. Tenancy and Sharecropping, Thirteen Less Developed Nations

| Region and Country | Renting and Sharecropping as Percent of Total | | Number of Renters and Sharecroppers[a] (thousands) |
	Number of Farms[a]	Farmland	
Asia	33.0	45.7	25,664
India	27.3	n.a.	13,350
Indonesia	35.9	25.9	4,392
Federation of Malaya	31.2	15.7	141
Pakistan and Bangladesh	43.4	57.0	5,271
Philippines	54.3	40.4	1,176
Near East and North Africa	61.1	62.6	2,349
Egypt	62.1	57.2	1,020
Iran	66.7	73.4	1,253
Tunisia	23.3	32.0	76
Latin America and Caribbean	31.4	19.2	776
Dominican Republic	28.9	n.a.	129
Guatemala	22.4	16.6	93
Trinidad and Tobago	49.5	32.8	18
Chile	49.3	24.4	128
Colombia	31.5	13.5	381

Source: Data from World Bank 1974 (p. 59).
Note: Data refer to latest available year in 1960.
[a] Includes holdings (21.8%) operated under more than one tenure form.

tor farms also induce governments to invest in agricultural extension and primary education to accelerate farm development.

Many programs labeled land reform do not involve significant changes in institutional arrangements. These include (1) surveying and granting title to lands currently farmed; (2) land consolidation programs, in which parcels of land are rearranged for more productive use—with the objective that each farmer have the same amount and quality of land that he or she had before; and (3) land settlement programs, in which government land is transferred to settlers.

TENURE REFORMS AND THE NEW LAND TENURE ECONOMICS

Changes in tenure arrangements include modifying rental contracts, increasing the security of tenancy, instituting land-to-the-tiller programs, and shifting to group farms, corporate farms, or state farms, where workers are organized as in factories. We focus here on shifts from share tenancy to fixed rent or ownership.

The theoretical analysis of share tenancy presented in chapter 5 indicates that greater agricultural output would be likely with fixed rent or ownership in place of the usual share rental arrangements. Empirical work in a number of less developed nations, however, has shown little reduction in yield on share rented fields as compared to fields under other tenure arrangements (Berry and Cline 1979, p. 25).

In the last two decades, work on this puzzle in the economics of land tenure arrangements led to explanations of these empirical results. The economics of share tenancy was found to be affected both by the tenant's willingness to bear risk and by the landlord's transaction and supervision costs. In a traditional agricultural environment, where crop practices are unchanging, the landlord can with relatively little cost oversee known farm operations. Also, at very low incomes, many tenants prefer the lesser risk of a share tenure arrangement. These economic realities explain the persistence of share tenancy in many traditional agricultural areas. In these circumstances, premature land reforms may decrease the welfare of the community, as may have happened in some areas of India, for such land reforms can both (1) force tenants to become laborers on the fields they used to operate, as landlords take over control of farm operations; and (2) provide landlords with an increased incentive to adopt labor-displacing farm machinery.

With the arrival of the green revolution and more productive agricultural technology, the landlord's transaction and supervision costs can increase greatly. Without the ability to supervise the changing agricultural technologies effectively, the landlord is more likely to prefer a fixed rent, as this will provide incentive to the tenant to use the land productively, possibly enabling a higher rent next year. The tenant's risk of obtaining minimum subsistance is reduced somewhat also with much higher yields, so the preference for a fixed rent increases (see also p. 105).

Thus, we see in the induced innovation perspective that land reform is not a precondition of productivity growth in agriculture but rather a response to the new economic opportunities provided by technological change and to changes in the relative prices of agricultural inputs and products. However, as is shown below in discussion of land-to-the-tiller programs, the timing of land reforms that transfer ownership rights to those who till the land in relation to the advent of rapid increases in agricultural productivity will greatly affect rural income distribution and rural social development. Hence, the political and cultural endowments of a society may cause a government to act, exogenous to economic forces, to change landholding institutions and land distribution in order to move toward distributional or other social goals.[6]

FARM SIZE AND AGRICULTURAL GROWTH

Many persons assume that large farms are the most productive and increase production more rapidly than small farms. Therefore, they believe land reforms that reduce farm size will decrease agricultural production. Large farms are often more productive in high-income nations. Also, in less developed nations,

---

6. This section draws on Hayami and Ruttan 1985 (pp. 391–96).

Figure 10.6. Adoption Curves of Modern Rice Varieties on Three Sizes of Farms in Thirty Villages in Asia

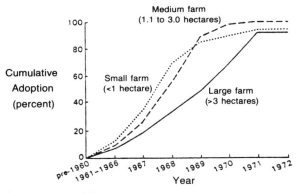

Source: Ruttan 1982 (p. 139). Reprinted with permission.

persons with larger landholdings have greater access to credit and to new technology due to their greater resources and their higher educational levels. Their greater risk-taking ability is also assumed to speed the adoption of more productive agricultural technology. However, the empirical data presented in chapter 4 indicate that in many areas of less developed nations, land productivity is higher on smaller farms (see also Berry and Cline 1979, pp. 186 and 135). Studies of rates of growth in production on different-sized farms in less developed nations reveal varied results. Much of the research reviewed by Berry and Cline indicates that, with reasonable agricultural input availability, the adoption curves for new technology by small farmers are similar to those for large farmers, as are rates of increase in yields (see, for example, figure 10.6).

Therefore, despite the greater resources available to large farms, offsetting factors, such as weaker economic incentives and greater managerial problems on large farms, often result in production increases no greater and sometimes smaller than on small farms. Hence, empirical studies lead to the general conclusion that land tenure reforms that reduce farm size by transferring ownership or increased control to tillers are likely to result in at least equally rapid increases in agricultural production, in the medium and long run. Certainly, reduction in the skewness of income disparities results. Some nations have experienced a temporary slowing of agricultural growth during the transition years of a significant land tenure reform, due to many accompanying changes in rural input and product marketing and in agricultural decisionmaking.

Experiences with Agrarian Reform Programs

LAND-TO-THE-TILLER PROGRAMS

Increasing control of land by the farmer who tills the soil includes a range of possible changes. The more limited steps focus on increasing a tenant's security to continue to farm rented fields. These include measures that encourage written, longer term rental contracts and that make dispossession of tenants more difficult. Larger steps involve changes in tenant contracts, such as a reduction in the share rent or a shift from a share to a fixed rent. Land-to-the-tiller programs go further, transferring land ownership to the cultivator, usually through the purchase of the land from the landlord by the state, with subsequent sale to the tenant.

Koo (1968) estimated the effect on a farmer's income of three different rental contracts in Taiwan over a twelve-year period. Figure 10.7 illustrates the significant gains in gross income of tenants from this land tenure reform. If tenure reforms are not carried out, as farm productivity accelerates, landlords may gain a large proportion of the increases in agricultural production.

The political, social, and economic realities surrounding the implementation of land-to-the-tiller programs, particularly the relative political power of those who would gain and those who would lose, have led in the last four decades to exceedingly varied land reform results, from little real change to very significant amounts of land transferred to farmers, as in the cases of Bolivia, Taiwan, and Japan.

SOCIOECONOMIC EFFECTS OF LAND REFORM

As emphasized in chapter 5, agricultural development involves social and political change. In many rural areas, traditional landholding systems have such a dominant social and political as well as economic role that they determine a farmer's social as well as economic life. Land and other rural reforms, therefore, cannot be viewed as simply another tool of development. For "technological modernization without social reform may frequently turn out to be 'anti-development,' especially if judged from the viewpoint of the large peasant groups adversely affected" (Barraclough 1969, p. 24).

Yang (1970, pp. 467–547) provided insight into the significant social changes likely to accompany effective land reform. Based upon 2,575 interviews in Taiwan in the mid-1960s among all rural groups, he found that in areas where there was a shift to written rental contracts between landlords and tenants personal relations were more businesslike. The contracts tended to eliminate traditional favor seeking and extra payments by tenants, such as gifts and work without pay upon demand. In areas where tenants received ownership of land, a shift from hierarchical to horizontal social relations occurred, as illustrated by changes in village meetings. The meetings used to be conducted by landlords, who sat on high platforms and gave out instructions. After the reform, a circle of chairs was used at the meetings, with participants speaking directly to one another. Local leadership patterns changed also. Previously, landlords had held most of the local positions. After the reform, land ownership was not the primary determinant of local leadership; education, integrity, and other factors became more important. Thus, in Taiwan, a shift from insecure share tenancy to

Figure 10.7. Net Income for the Tenant Under Different Rent Terms in Taiwan, 1948–1960

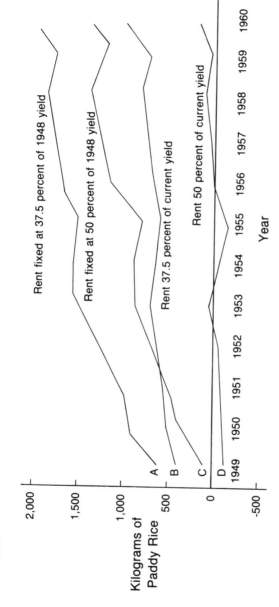

Source: Redrawn from Koo 1968 (p. 53). Copyright © 1968 by Frederick A. Praeger, Inc. Reprinted with permission.

ownership of tilled land was associated with very significant social and political gains for farmers.[7]

ESTABLISHING COLLECTIVE FARMS

In the following brief examination of the large topic of collective and group farming, the focus is on the reasons for collectivization, the usual pattern for its implementation, and the recent shifts toward more liberal policies in nations dominated by collective agriculture.

In authoritarian communist and some socialist societies, arguments for the collectivization of agriculture include the following three. First, Marxist ideology proposes that a society progresses if it moves to "higher forms" of social organization. The shift from individual family farming to collective farm organization is believed to represent such a move. Second, agricultural productivity is believed to be enhanced by collectivization. This belief is based on the assumption that large-scale, factory type organization in agriculture will lead to rapid productivity gains, such as were achieved in the industrial revolution due to economies of scale and increased specialization of labor. And third, administrative and political control of agriculture are greatly enhanced by the establishment of a limited number of large collective, or state, farm units.

Students of agricultural development should be aware of the series of steps often followed in socialist nations in implementing collective farming.

The first step was radical land reform: then encouragement to join old-style co-operatives (in China "mutual aid teams"): then a gradual process of collectivization, proceeding by stages from "lower" to "higher" forms, i.e. from looser to tighter control. . . . In an elaborate facade of graded forms, the lowest was in law voluntary and peasants were induced to join by pressures of various kinds, backed by incentives in prices, costs, and exemption from taxation; once organized in the lower form, however, they were quickly upgraded into collectives which they could not leave. Though there was not open violence, and the process was gradual, taking about eight years or more to complete, the threat of compulsion was always in the background, as is proved by the speed with which the collectives broke up when it was removed, in 1953 in Yugoslavia, in 1956 in Poland (and in Hungary also for a short period after the 1956 rising). (Warriner 1969, p. 64)

Galeski (1977), a Polish economist, in his review of collective farming, concludes similarly, "Spontaneous transformation of 'simple forms' of cooperation into collective farms has never been observed" (p. 28).

During the last decade, some nations in Eastern Europe and China have taken steps away from rigid, centralized control of their collectivized agricul-

7. Sources of data on land tenure conditions in less developed nations include United Nations 1976 and AID 1970. For work on share tenancy, see Ip and Stahl 1978; Roumasset 1979; and Bardhan 1979. Among the very large literature on land reform and land-to-the-tiller programs, important general materials include Ghai et al. 1979; Walinsky 1977; World Bank 1974; Weitz 1971; Warriner 1969; Dorner and Kanel 1979; FAO 1978b; and Hayami and Ruttan 1985 (pp. 389–98). Marxist perspectives on land reform are provided in de Janvry 1981 and Alier 1977. Land reform research on the Third World includes, for Asia, Herring 1983 and Inayatullah 1980; for Africa, Cohen 1980; and for Latin America, Barchfield 1979; Alier 1977; Alexander 1974; and Barraclough and Collarte 1973.

tures in order to stimulate agricultural productivity. Two important changes are increased reliance on private economic incentives and small private enterprise and increased use of the market to determine prices. These steps have enabled real resource costs and consumer demand to be reflected more accurately and more rapidly, leading to more productive allocation of resources in agriculture. In China since 1978, the introduction of the "responsibility system" has led to a very significant shift toward greater use of the price mechanism and increased opportunities for individual farming for profit (see, for example, Lardy 1984). In the mixed economy of Mexico in the last two decades, there has also been some increase in family-controlled farming, as collective *ejido* members have shifted to individual *ejido* farming and to other enterprises as more beneficial to them (Finkler 1978).

Problems that hamper centralized collective farming systems include the following three. First, centralized decisionmaking for the complicated questions of how to obtain high productivity on the many different farm fields that have different resource and technological conditions generally reduces agricultural production. However, despite the generally negative effects of centralized decisionmaking, in some cases the increased rural organization achieved with collectivized agricultures, such as through the commune system in China, may have increased the total production of goods and services by providing more productive employment for those who would have had little work without intensive rural organization. Collective systems have also usually reduced rural income disparities. These gains, however, appear to have been negated in China over the longer run. In particular, large negative effects on agricultural output have followed from gigantic mistakes in national policy and conduct, including the Great Leap Forward, during which agricultural production declined sharply, and the ten-year-long Cultural Revolution, which virtually destroyed higher education in many fields, including particularly agricultural economics and rural sociology.

Second, wage determination methods for members of collective farms often attenuate incentives. All members, who usually are not at liberty to leave, may receive the same daily wage. This tends to discourage hard work, initiative, and the taking on of additional responsibilities. A more usual payment system uses a graduated point scale and additional perquisites for better workers and managers. Under this system, an hour of labor on each type of farm work earns a certain number of points—the more skilled the labor, the more points per hour. Wages are paid on the basis of work points earned. Annual earnings are determined at the end of the year, when any surplus is divided. Managers sometimes receive very much higher incomes. Under the point system, collective members have tended to view their wages as a salary, as other laborers do, and have attempted to bargain for higher wages (Reed 1977, p. 374). This view tends to attenuate the relation between individual effort and earnings, thereby reducing the incentive for increased productivity.

Third, the ambiguous but important role of private farm plots and other private economic activities in collective agriculture tends to drain resources from the collective. Private plots usually are highly productive and account for significant national agricultural output, particularly of livestock products and perishable fruits and vegetables. As private returns to collective members on private plots can be large, members have a strong incentive to work on their plots, reducing their incentive to work on the collective. The temptation is also present to use supplies and other resources of the collective farm for private purposes. In many socialist countries, governments are thus faced with the dilemma of whether to increase or decrease private economic activity. If increased social control of production is sought, the loss of private plots would result in lower total agricultural output and less variety of agricultural products available. If increased production is sought and more land and other resources are made available for family production, increases in agricultural production are likely but at a loss of direct social control. [8]

Conclusions About Changes in Landholding Arrangements

Five general points can be made about land reform and collective agricultural institutions in relation to agricultural development. First, the theory of socioeconomic change and the induced innovation model indicate that landholding institutions can be expected to change with agricultural development. However, large and rapid changes in landholding and rural institutions should be recognized as usually associated with major socioeconomic change in a society. "Land reforms are major cultural events" (Raup 1967, p. 297).

Second, empirical evidence shows that family farming systems (with or without voluntary cooperatives) and private plots in socialist countries generally exhibit the highest levels of resource productivity and growth. The most important exceptions are large plantations that grow certain capital intensive export crops, such as palm oil, rubber, and sugarcane, that have critical large-scale processing requirements.

Third, the income distribution results of different institutional arrangements for agricultural production can vary greatly. In societies where significant land reforms have been carried out, considerable reduction in income disparities has been achieved. In less developed nations with highly skewed landholding and high tenancy rates, farm income disparities are likely to increase with development. In nations with high proportions of collectivized agriculture, it appears that income distributions are less skewed but are associated with lower productivity because agricultural families are less free to respond to alternative economic opportunities that would more fully employ their talents, initiative, and resources. In areas with highly skewed landholding, a well-executed land-to-the-tiller program is likely to achieve both increased rates of agricultural production and greater equity.

---

8. Additional references that examine group farming, cooperatives. collectives, and communes include Dorner 1977; Hopkins et al. 1979; Bonin 1977; and Jacobs 1982. References to the Chinese experience include Perkins 1984; Griffin 1984; and Macrae 1977.

Fourth, in areas with high proportions of collective and state farms, steps to decentralize decisionmaking and to increase personal incentives for productive work will lead to greater productivity. This can be accomplished through improved labor management systems and by increasing the scope for private income-earning activities. Such steps will enable greater individual satisfaction, although income disparities may increase.

Fifth, as development proceeds, continuing experimentation with alternative institutional arrangements for control of land and other resources will enable agricultural productivity to be further increased and income to be distributed more nearly as desired by society.

Important Concepts

Externalities
Rural financial markets
Informal credit
Fungibility of loans
Costs of lending money
Opportunity cost
Risk premiums
Institutional saving
Financial intermediation
Cooperative principles
Quasi-cooperatives
Land reform
Collective farming

Commune
Interactive economic systems
Directive economic systems
Traditional communal land
 ownership
Cooperative farming
Bimodal distribution of land
 ownership
Tenure reform
New land tenure economics
Land-to-the-tiller programs
Collectivization of agriculture

Sample Questions

1. How is institutional change in agriculture incorporated endogenously in the induced innovation model?

2. Explain why agricultural credit is needed for more rapid agricultural development; include an economic explanation of the circumstances under which a farmer would borrow credit for use in agriculture.

3. Briefly state four usual economic characteristics of rural financial markets in traditional agricultural areas.

4. Explain why a 40 percent interest cost for agricultural credit to small farmers may be a reality in some areas of less developed nations.

5. Explain two ways credit may be expanded for small farms.

6. State, and explain the need for, three policies usually required to improve rural financial markets.

7. What are the operating principles of member-controlled cooperatives?

8. Discuss the potential roles and problems of agricultural cooperatives in agricultural development.

9. Discuss some of the many meanings of "tenure in land" in less developed nations.

10. Explain how decisions are made and farm workers paid in three major types of land tenure systems.

11. Land-to-the-tiller programs often cause changes in input and product marketing. Explain why and indicate activities that may be crucial for the success of these programs.

12. Discuss problems collective farms face in attempting to increase productivity. What changes might improve their performance?

11

Investing in Research, Education, Extension, and Communications

> Knowledge is the most powerful engine of production.
> —Alfred Marshall[1]

> The development of institutions capable of producing a continuous stream of new knowledge is a relatively recent phenomenon. According to Alfred North Whitehead "the great invention of the nineteenth century was the invention of the method of invention."
> —Ruttan 1978, p. 327

The fundamental task of development is to discover how to accelerate social learning. Empirical study and economic analysis of traditional agriculture and of more rapidly developing agricultures have led to the theory of induced innovation presented in chapter 6. We learn from this theory that a successful response to human economic opportunities depends upon investment (1) in research, extension, and communication activities; and (2) in human capital. Such investment will generate productive new technologies and institutional arrangements (see figure 11.1). Investment in education also aids social groups to more easily make the associated cultural changes required for economic growth.

Gaining the knowledge required to make the shift from a natural-resource-based to a science-based agriculture is a fundamental step in a society's social learning. To examine the economics of creating a science-based agriculture, we first place the gains achieved by agricultural science and technology in historical perspective. We then focus on the three most important sources of increased agricultural growth: (1) agricultural and social science research; (2) agricultural and general education; and (3) the ongoing revolution in extension and communication methods.

---

1. As quoted by T. W. Schultz (1980) in his Nobel Prize paper.

Figure 11.1. Relations Between Accelerators of Social Learning and Elements of the Hayami-Ruttan Model of Induced Innovation

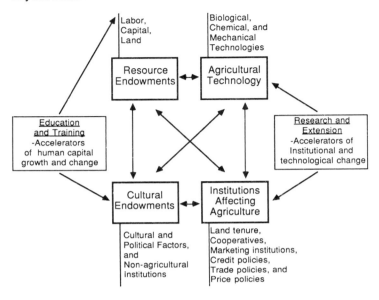

Source: Modified from Hayami and Ruttan 1985 (figure 4-3).

The History of Agricultural Productivity Growth

Slow Increases in Agricultural Productivity in Human History

The increases in population densities achieved by historically important types of agriculture provide a perspective on human success in increasing land productivity (see table 11.1).

HUNTING AND GATHERING

Hunting and gathering enabled homo sapiens to survive for untold centuries, perhaps a half million years. This food system has three important economic characteristics: (1) considerable variability and uncertainty in food supplies due to fluctuations in weather and to natural cycles in wild animal and edible plant populations; (2) the high real cost in family time in obtaining and processing sufficient food, leaving little time for other activities; and (3) the large areas of land per person required for a group to be maintained. Today, anthropologists count about twenty-seven main groups of peoples who live in remote areas and still depend upon hunting and gathering (Boserup 1981, p. 32).

SHIFTING CULTIVATION

Shifting cultivation, or slash and burn agricultural systems, include long periods of fallow in their crop rotations—from five to twenty five or more years

Table 11.1. Population Densities that Can Be Supported by Different Agricultural Systems

Agricultural System	Persons per Square Kilometer
Hunting and gathering (.003–.4 persons/km²)	
Bushmen of Southwest Africa (desert)	0.0033
Australia before European settlement	0.0330
Tasmania before European settlement	0.0590
Pacific Coast of North America (warm and humid)	0.1000
Very best lands	0.4000
Shifting agriculture (2–100 persons/km²)	
Serenje Plateau, Zambia (dry)	2
Ivory Coast, West Africa	10
Iban in Sarawak	5–20
Sumatra	15–40
Hanunoo in the Philippines and Indonesia	39
Sacatepequez Province, Guatemala	120
Village agriculture (50–600 persons/km²)	
Uganda, 1937	48
Uganda, 1955	89
Java, 1950	63
China, 1930	50–200
Egypt	167
Ukara Island, Tanzania	470
Comilla Thana, Bangladesh	600
Modern agriculture[a] (100–1,000 persons/km²)	
United States	107
Michigan, U.S.	116
Poland	200
France	238
West Germany	710
Japan	944

Sources: C. Clark and Haswell 1964; Stevens, 1967; FAO, *Production Yearbook 1967*.
Note: The estimates for modern agriculture do not take into account net trade in agricultural products. If they did, the United States and Michigan figures, for example, would approximately double.
[a] Arable land compared with total population.

on a particular piece of land. First, the forestland is cleared for crops by burning. After a few years of cultivation, weeds increase and soil fertility declines, so the plot is abandoned to forest regrowth, while other areas are cut, burned, and planted to food crops. The regeneration of the forest during the long fallow accumulates plant nutrients and destroys weeds. In Southeast Asia, shifting cultivation has involved some fourteen million square miles and 200 million persons.

The development of shifting cultivation was a significant advance, because it (1) enabled man to periodically draw on plant nutrients accumulated by forest vegetation and soil breakdown for food crop production; (2) considerably increased the security of food supplies through sequential use of the forest plots for crop production; and (3) enabled much greater food yields per hectare compared with the gathering of wild foods. In favorable circumstances, this agriculture has produced more food per unit of labor than continuous cropping in lowlands (C. Clark and Haswell 1964, p. 34). This system enabled much higher population densities (table 11.1). Recent studies have demonstrated the economic rationality of shifting cultivation systems that often appear wasteful to persons from more developed nations. Today, with knowledge of modern science, we still do not know how to achieve lower cost food production in many mountainous areas where shifting cultivation is practiced.

VILLAGE AGRICULTURE

Settled village agriculture involves short rotations and continuous cropping, which enable repeated cultivation of the same fields at productive yield levels. This fundamental advance in agriculture, estimated to have been under way since 8000 B.C., enabled the building of permanent villages. In many areas, these agricultural systems became so productive that a significant part of the population was freed from agricultural labor to do other things. The great civilizations of history were built upon a base of productive agricultural villages, the oldest of which have been dated from about 4500 B.C. in Egypt and 3600 B.C. in Mexico. The population densities supported by village agriculture rise to 600 persons per square kilometer (table 11.1).

The important economic characteristics of village agriculture include (1) greatly increased control over the crop environment through plowing, irrigation, and fertilization with animal manures; (2) greater incentives, due to the establishment of village boundaries, to develop technologies to increase productivity per unit of land; (3) a much increased ability to store food and accumulate wealth; (4) great stability in food production, which has enabled tens of thousands of agricultural villages to survive through many centuries, while empires have expanded and collapsed around them.

Despite the success of village agriculture over the centuries, only very slow productivity increases were achieved. Estimates of historic changes in wheat and rice yields show how slowly (see figure 11.2). In England, beginning in about 1250, five centuries were required for wheat yields to increase 4.3 times, a compound rate of growth in yield of 0.2 percent. In Japan, from about the year 750 to 1885—some eleven centuries—farmers succeeded only in doubling yields, an annual rate of growth of 0.05 percent. The recent annual rates of yield increase, calculated from the data in the figure, are 0.6 percent for wheat from 1850 to 1959 in England and 0.9 percent for rice from 1885 to 1959 in Japan.[2]

---

2. Some useful references to the large literature documenting the historical progress of agriculture include Boserup 1981 (chaps. 4 and 5); Hanks 1972; Dovring 1966; Clark 1967; Slicher van Bath 1963; and T. C. Smith 1959. Other relevant references are given in Hayami and Ruttan 1971, 1985.

Figure 11.2. Historical Trends in Rice and Wheat Yields, 750–1959

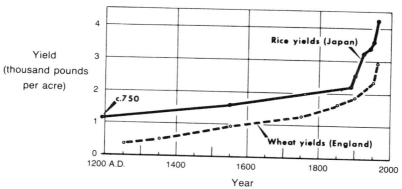

Source: Christensen and Stevens 1962 (p. 162). Reprinted with permission.

The Transition to a Science-Based Agriculture

The induced innovation model of economic development hypothesizes that inventors and entrepreneurs in the private and public sectors will continually attempt to develop more productive technologies and institutions that will economize the use of scarce resources. As physics, biology, chemistry, and the social sciences develop, they open up many more opportunities for inventions and innovations to increase the productivity of agriculture.

The application of scientific knowledge to farming began accelerating in the late eighteenth century in Europe and the United States, as a number of fundamental scientific and technical breakthroughs occurred. In England, Lord Charles Townshend (1674–1738) carried out many experiments to establish improved crop rotations that would increase yields. Robert Bakewell (1725–1795) led in improving the productivity of livestock through systematic breeding programs. In 1840, the German scientist Justus von Liebig discovered that plants were nourished by minerals (nitrogen, phosphorous, potash, and so on). This led Sir John Lawes to develop superphosphate fertilizer in England. Jacob Schleiden and Theodor Schwann proposed the cell theory of biological structure in 1838, and soon afterward, Gregor Mendel made the first discoveries of the laws of genetic inheritance. These advances enabled the later development of the science of plant genetics. Steel technology was first applied to agriculture in the United States in 1837, when John Deere produced the first steel plow. Cyrus McCormick followed in 1840 with the first sale of a mechanical grain reaper pulled by animals. (For more about the history of agricultural technology development, see Hayami and Ruttan 1985, pp. 73–84.)

The application of science and technology to agriculture in the last hundred years has resulted in an agricultural revolution in more developed nations. In the sixty years between 1900 and 1959, both wheat yields in England and rice yields in Japan increased some 75 percent (figure 11.2), a feat which would have required a number of centuries if the art of agriculture had been the only source of new knowledge.

The magnitude of the productivity increases achieved in more developed nations is illustrated by the great reduction in labor required on a farm to produce a bushel (27.2 kilograms) of wheat in the United States. In 1830, a twenty-bushel-per-acre crop of wheat required 50 hours of labor per acre, or about 150 minutes per bushel. A century later, a higher yielding crop took 3.5 hours of labor per acre, or about 10 minutes per bushel. This great increase in labor productivity in agriculture has enabled the large structural changes in the U.S. economy. In 1820, the average farm worker produced only enough agricultural products for four persons, while in 1985 he or she produced enough for seventy-five other persons (USDA, 1987).

High Total Agricultural Productivity Growth Rates in More Developed Nations

The increases in labor and land productivity (yield) cited above are limited measures of economic growth. They do not take account of all the resources used in production, such as machinery and fertilizer. When all the resources, including labor and land, are accounted for, have the agricultural sectors of more developed nations become less productive, as is sometimes alleged? Studies spanning the period 1870–1979 provide the needed information for Japan and the United States (tables 11.2 and 11.3). Although there were periods when total agricultural productivity declined in both nations, during most of the eleven decades, especially during the last three, the total productivity of the agricultural sector has increased at a rate of some 1 percent per year. Note also the high rates of annual labor productivity growth in both countries since the 1950s, averaging some 6 percent. Data from other more developed nations also show that the application of science and technology to agriculture has continued to increase the amount of agricultural products produced per unit of all inputs used. How have such increases been possible? Advances in the basic sciences have continually increased the supply of new principles, new ideas, and new tools in biology, chemistry, physics, and the social sciences. These advances have been drawn upon by those attempting to increase the productivity and profitability of agricultural technologies and institutions, through searches for high-payoff inputs and other means. Without the great advances in the basic sciences in the last two centuries, much slower productivity growth in agriculture would have been achieved.

For less developed nations, data presented in chapters 3 and 8 illustrate the recent extraordinarily rapid increases in land productivity that have been achieved during the green revolution. This advance was based on several decades of scientific and technical research in agriculture, much of it carried out in more developed nations. Today, the application of the knowledge of modern

Table 11.2. Rates of Change in Agricultural Output, Input, and Productivity, Japan, 1880–1975 (percent)

Item	1880–1920	1920–1935	1935–1955	1955–1965	1965–1975
Farm output	1.8	0.9	0.6	3.5	1.5
Total inputs	0.5	0.5	1.2	1.5	0.7
Total productivity	1.3	0.4	− 0.6	2.0	0.8
Labor inputs	− 0.3	− 0.2	0.6	− 2.7	− 4.1
Labor productivity	2.1	1.1	0.0	6.2	5.6
Land inputs	0.6	0.1	− 0.1	0.1	− 0.7
Land productivity	1.2	0.8	0.7	3.4	2.2

Source: Ruttan 1982 (p. 241). Reprinted with permission.

Table 11.3. Rates of Change in Agricultural Output, Input, and Productivity, the United States, 1870–1982 (percent)

Item	1870–1900	1900–1925	1925–1950	1950–1965	1965–1982
Farm output	2.9	0.9	1.6	1.7	2.1
Total inputs	1.9	1.1	0.2	− 0.4	0.2
Total productivity	1.0	− 0.2	1.3	2.2	1.8
Labor inputs	1.6	0.5	− 1.7	− 4.8	− 3.4
Labor productivity	1.3	0.4	3.3	6.6	5.8
Land inputs	3.1	0.8	0.1	− 0.9	0.0
Land productivity	− 0.2	0.0	1.4	2.6	1.8

Source: Ruttan 1982 (p. 241) and updated from Ruttan, personal communication.

science and technology to agriculture in most less developed nations is in its infancy. How can these nations most effectively tap this fundamental source of growth in agricultural productivity? Basic to success in this task are greater investments in agricultural research and education, including nonformal education, extension, and communications activities, the subjects of this chapter.

Accelerating Agricultural Research in Less Developed Nations

Persons with little experience in agriculture are often unaware of the extraordinary range and intricacy of the scientific challenges faced by agricultural and social science researchers in the extremely varied and technically complex physical and social environments of farming systems in less developed nations.

The Complexity of Technological and Socioeconomic Constraints

Two illustrations of the challenges faced by scientists are offered. The first example is the seasonal variability in cropping conditions due to weather and other such factors. This research challenge is shown by data from the Philippines that demonstrate the instability of fertilizer to rice yield relations often found in the wet season in Asia. They contrast with the more stable dry season estimates of the most profitable nitrogen levels for rice (see figure 11.3, panel *B*). In the wet season, highly variable rainfall and sunshine caused large yearly variations in response by both the traditional rice variety (Peta) and a high-yielding variety (IR8). Hence, the economic optimum application of nitrogen each season was exceedingly different, ranging from 8 to 128 kilograms for IR8 (see figure 11.3, panel *A*). What amount of nitrogen should a farmer use under these conditions? How can researchers produce rice varieties with a consistent response to nitrogen in the wet season?

The second illustration comes from the mixed cropping in mounds practiced in Nigeria and other parts of Africa (see figure 11.4). In this example, thirteen different crops may be planted in and around mounds one meter high and three meters in diameter that cover a field. An average of about six different crops per mound is usual, surrounded by rice. How much does modern science know about improving these agricultural practices? What alternative agricultural practices would increase land and labor productivity per unit of land on these farms without increasing the instability of food supplies and income?

The need to identify both technological and socioeconomic constraints to increased production was emphasized by Ruttan (1982). As higher yielding crops and livestock are produced on experiment stations and adopted by farmers, the yields obtained by farmers are often half or less that obtained under the more controlled conditions on experiment stations (see figure 11.5). Researchers at IRRI undertook detailed study of the yield gap to identify the sources of the constraints on yields in farmers' fields. The gap results from (1) nontransferable technology and environmental differences present at experiment stations; (2) biological constraints present on farms, such as disease, soil fertility, or water conditions; and (3) socioeconomic constraints facing farmers, such as the costs of inputs, lack of needed inputs or credit, low prices for agricultural products, product marketing problems, or lack of technological knowledge. In some agricultural regions, technological constraints predominate, while in others, socioeconomic problems constrain the use of more productive technologies.

The Agricultural Research Gap

A large proportion of agriculture in less developed nations is in the tropics or the subtropics. In the past, research in these areas has focused on commercial export crops such as rubber, tea, sugar, and palm oil. Estimates of world agricultural research show that in 1951, 82 percent of the total world expenditures

Figure 11.3. Variability Due to Weather and the Economic Optimum Level of Nitrogen for Two Rice Varieties, Mallgaya, the Philippines

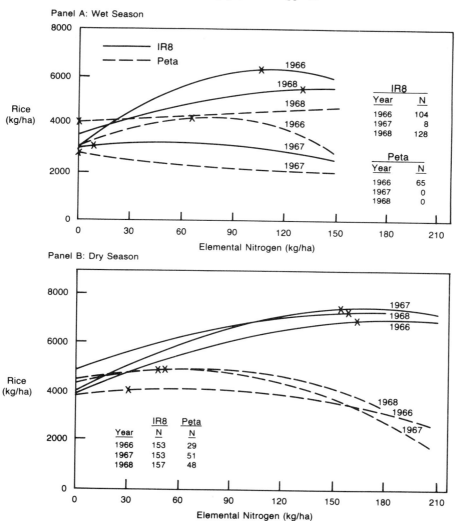

Figure 11.4. Spatial Distribution of Crops Planted in Mounds in a Farmer's Field, Abakaliki, Anambra State, Nigeria

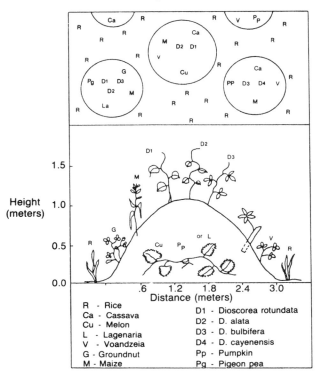

Source: Ruthenberg 1980 (p. 80). Reprinted with permission.

for agricultural research were allocated to the temperate climates of Europe, the U.S.S.R., North America, and Oceania, with the remaining 18 percent to the three largely tropical continents of Asia, Africa, and South America. By 1974, expenditures for agricultural research in the world had increased fivefold, with an increased share—25 percent—devoted to Asia, Africa, and Latin America (Boyce and Evenson 1975, pp. 3–17). After reviewing agricultural research by geoclimatic zones, Boyce and Evenson concluded that agricultural research remained low in the major climate zones of less developed nations, especially in the tropical and desert zones. Agricultural research expenditures were also found to be a smaller percentage of the value of agricultural production in low-income countries, 0.67 percent, as compared with 2.55 percent in more developed countries.

Figure 11.5. Yield Gaps Between Experiment Stations and Farmers' Fields Due to Biological and Socioeconomic Constraints

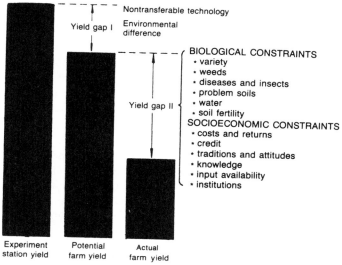

Source: Gomez et al. 1979. Reprinted with permission.

Economics of the Demand and Supply of Agricultural Research

Research is an economic service as it requires resources to produce new technologies and institutional arrangements. Agricultural and social science researchers have to be paid, and they have to be provided with tools, including laboratories, experiment stations, and computers. Under what circumstances will increased demand arise for research services to accelerate agricultural development? What are the economics of supplying research for development?

Both producers and consumers are likely to demand government support of agricultural and social science research (1) in areas where the private sector finds it unprofitable to invest in research because of the nature of the technologies (e.g., unpatentable); (2) when the private sector is constrained from acting by government limitations on the entry of private business; and (3) when government is perceived as more able than the private sector to carry out productive agricultural and social science research.

We now examine the effect of different supply and demand conditions on the demand for agricultural research. When the demand for agricultural products moves more rapidly to the right than the supply of agricultural products, prices increase (see figure 2.3). When food prices increase, there will be increased demand from both urban and rural consumers that government reduce the cost of food by increasing the supply of agricultural products. In most less developed nations, agricultural research, which includes drawing on more productive farming technologies from abroad, is over the longer run a central high-return strategy for both accelerating the growth in agricultural output and reducing the real costs of agricultural production. As governments and private input industries learn this, increased research will be induced in response to the rising prices of agricultural products. However, if governments slow domestic food price increases through price controls and subsidized imports of food, the demand for domestic research and investment in new, more productive technology in agriculture will be dampened as the profitability of farming is reduced.

The Dependency of Research Demand upon Expected Returns

The demand for new agricultural technology and institutions depends upon estimates of the net profit or rate of return expected from investment in research. The perceived potential for high returns usually induces substantial investment in research and development. The greater the rate of advance in the basic sciences, the more likely that more productive technologies and institutions will be developed for agriculture.

Farmers adopt new technologies and institutional arrangements that are profitable. The location of the demand curve for better technologies and institutions is derived from, or dependent upon, the additional returns that the new technologies or institutional arrangements will provide. Farmers will pay a higher price for more productive new inputs if these inputs will provide a higher return for the investment. Thus the demand curve for more productive technologies will be further to the right. Even when agricultural product prices are declining, farmers will buy more productive equipment, crop supplies, or other inputs if they increase net farm returns. Researchers in both the public and private sectors have a ready market for more profitable agricultural technologies and institutions.

High Social Returns of Much Agricultural Research

National planners and decisionmakers have the responsibility to invest scarce development resources in activities that provide high rates of return. If agricultural research is very productive, more national development resources should be allocated to it; if not, other projects with higher rates of return should have priority.

What rates of return can be obtained by a nation from agricultural research? During the last twenty five years many analyses of agricultural research have been carried out in both more developed and less developed nations. Most of them have shown very high annual rates of return from agricultural research, ranging from 20 to 60 percent.[3] These are among the highest return investments

---

3. A sample of the large literature on estimates of the productivity of agricultural research includes Ruttan 1982 (pp. 237–61); Evenson 1984; and Norton and Davis 1981.

available to less developed nations. Thus, more investment in agricultural research is being induced by these opportunities, which in turn will accelerate agricultural development. However, as high returns from any investment are not guaranteed, considerable care in managing agricultural research is required. Productive researchers require a flexible and stable administration, attractive salaries, and adequate equipment, libraries, and computer facilities. If the conditions for productive scientific work are not met, little return may be obtained from the resources allocated to agricultural research.

Demand for Social Science Knowledge

Because it is such a difficult area of analysis, no empirical estimates of the returns from social science research or its contribution to increases in agricultural growth are yet available. However, two examples were given by Ruttan (1982, pp. 304–8) that illustrate the contributions that social science research can make and the difficulty of estimating its value. The first is the recent development of powerful economic analysis tools that agricultural research administrators can use to evaluate the returns from alternative agricultural research activities. These tools thus enable better decisions about the use of research resources and hence make possible increases in the average productivity of all agricultural research.

The second example is of the gains provided by economic studies of agricultural commodity supply and demand conditions and relations. With more detailed knowledge of these markets, governments can make better decisions about agricultural price and other programs, leading to more market stability and increased growth. This information also helps private industry identify more easily high-return business opportunities that enable industry to increase its productivity.

An important part of the demand for knowledge in economics and in the other social sciences, as well as in related professions such as law, is derived from the demand for improvements in the operation of institutions and for institutional change. T. W. Schultz (1968) pointed to the rising cost of labor as a major initiator of institutional innovation. Institutions are desired that would provide more services while using fewer resources. In some cases, technological change induces, or increases the demand for, institutional change. In other cases, demands for a change in the rules governing the control of land and other resources originating in national cultural endowments increase the value of research on the probable outcomes of different landholding arrangements and changes in other social rules. "Advances in knowledge in the social sciences . . . offer an opportunity to reduce the costs of institutional innovation, just as advances in knowledge in the biological sciences and in agricultural technology have reduced the costs of technical innovation in agriculture" (Ruttan 1982, p. 306).[4]

4. For more on social science research and development, see Binswanger and Ruttan 1978 (pp. 334–37); Ruttan 1982 (pp. 298–330), 1984; and T. W. Schultz 1968.

Figure 11.6.   Effect of the Elasticity of Demand for an Agricultural Product on
Pressure for Government Agricultural Research

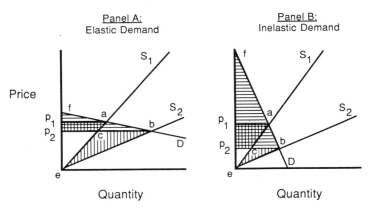

Source: Based on Ruttan and Binswanger 1978 (p. 365).

Price Elasticity of Agricultural Products and the Demand for Research

As those who demand government support for research and development
are likely to influence the direction of agricultural research, it is important to
identify who benefits from agricultural research. To do this, we focus on the
gains and losses of producers and consumers from agricultural research. Ruttan
and Binswanger (1978, pp. 364–71) demonstrated that the economic gain to different groups was dependent upon both (1) the elasticity of the demand curve for
the agricultural products; and (2) the rates at which the supply and demand
curves shift. The concepts of consumer and producer surplus enable us to estimate the magnitudes of these gains.

Consumer surplus equals the area under the demand curve in figure 11.6
above the equilibrium price line, fap_1. Producer surplus, in contrast, is the area
below the equilibrium price line and above the supply curve, aep_1. Changes in
these areas determine the gains and losses to consumers and producers from
supply and demand curve shifts.

Elastic demand for agricultural products leads to farmer pressure for agricultural research. If the demand curve for agricultural goods is relatively elastic
when the supply curve moves to the right, producer surplus is likely to increase
considerably (panel A). In this case, when the supply curve shifts from S_1 to S_2,
the net producer surplus clearly increases. Producers lose only $p_1 acp_2$ but gain a
much larger cbe. The consumer surplus, or the gain to the rest of society, is now
also larger, fbp_2. Hence, with an elastic demand, a shift of supply to the right
due to agricultural research would enable producers to increase their income
significantly. Consumers would also gain from the lower price due to the additional supply generated by the research.

Thus, when producers face elastic demand curves, they are likely to demand increased support by government for agricultural research and development. Producers would even benefit in these circumstances from paying a tax to government or another organization that would conduct agricultural research, education, or communication activities. Such activities would reduce the real costs of production and move the supply curve more rapidly to the right. For example, the tax on rubber producers in Malaysia that supports the Rubber Research Institute has greatly increased foreign exchange earnings for Malaysia and has also increased the income of Malaysian rubber producers.

Inelastic demand with high food prices may lead consumers to demand agricultural research on food crops. Suppose the demand curve for a food crop is fairly inelastic. Then agricultural research that increased food crop production would move the supply curve to the right (see figure 11.6, panel B). In this case, prices would decline greatly, and the consumer surplus, or the net gain to consumers, would increase by the area $p_1 abp_2$. Producer surplus would, however, decline by $p_1 acp_2$ but increase by cbe, for a net change that could be negative if the demand curve were quite inelastic. Then the gross income of producers might decline significantly. However, in this situation, note that producers who are more productive can maintain their net incomes or even increase them through greater volume and reduced unit costs of production. High-cost producers will, of course, have to cease production of unprofitable products and shift to other enterprises or occupations.

To conclude, when demand for agricultural products is relatively inelastic, a large consumer surplus would occur from movement of the supply curve to the right. Hence, consumer demand for government action to support agricultural research and development is more likely in these circumstances. Producers may oppose such research, fearing that their incomes would decline.

The preceding analysis demonstrates that movement of agricultural supply curves to the right relative to the demand curve will always benefit consumers (increase consumer surplus) except in the case of a completely elastic demand curve. Also, note that movement of the staple food supply curve to the right relative to the demand curve has a positive equity effect, for lower food prices increase the real income of lower income groups, since food is a higher proportion of total consumption expenditures (see chapter 3).

CONCLUSIONS ON THE DEMAND FOR RESEARCH

In the preceding discussion, the general categories of consumers and producers were employed. For particular agricultural products, similar analyses could provide estimates of how agricultural research might affect different regions of a country and particular subgroups in the population, such as producers of a particular crop, laborers in particular geographic areas, and large and small farmers. To illustrate this point, in a small region of a nation, farmers selling to a national market often face very elastic demand curves for their agricultural products, even when national demand is inelastic. Such a small competing region has an interest in reducing production costs more rapidly than other regions so that its sales will increase.

The same reasoning applies to a small nation supplying an international market. Thus, nations and subregions of nations that lag in productivity increases are likely to suffer losses in income due to agricultural research that benefits other areas. Hence, new technologies that enable greater reductions in the real costs of production in the better agricultural regions of a nation can increase geographic inequality in farm income. More equal regional income distribution would be attained if greater technological progress could be achieved in the lower income areas. Unfortunately, due to the lower quality of the land and other resources in many of the poorer farming areas of all nations, the returns to investment in agricultural research focused on these areas are often low. Hence, from a national economic growth perspective, it may be difficult to justify the allocation of large amounts of agricultural research resources to these areas.

Although this analysis has focused on the demand for research to increase the productivity of agricultural technology, analytical results are similar for research that produces new institutional arrangements that cause the agricultural supply curve to move to the right. For example, farmers who have experienced increased real costs of agricultural credit and are faced with an elastic demand curve for their products would benefit from government research that helped increase the supply of credit and that reduced the costs of loans through better credit arrangements.

And finally, it is important to recognize that the increases in output from given resources provided by more productive technologies and institutions are not one-time changes due to the initial shift to more productive technologies and institutions. These productivity gains will continue to be enjoyed over many years, until more productive technologies and institutions replace them. Therefore, analyses of the rates of return to agricultural research have to include discounted future benefits. These continuing benefits help explain the high rates of return for agricultural research cited earlier in this chapter.

Increasing the Supply of Agricultural and Institutional Research and Technology Transfer

SUPPLYING PATENTABLE AND UNPATENTABLE TECHNOLOGIES

To carry out research and development tasks in response to the economic opportunities present for the application of modern science and technology to agriculture, two sets of institutional arrangements are induced. Private firms find it profitable to operate in areas where patents on new technologies protect them from easy copying or where technologies cannot easily be copied for other reasons. The expected high returns induce private firms to carry out transfers of technology from more developed nations and provide the local adaptive research needed to produce and deliver the more profitable agricultural technology to farmers. Agricultural machinery is often a good example of such patentable technologies.

Public resources are essential for the development of new technologies that cannot easily be patented, especially in nations where firms have difficulty in securing enforcement of their patent rights, or in other cases where government rules prevent or discourage private research initiatives, as in some socialist nations. Thus, in many technological areas, the acceleration of agricultural technology depends upon government administrative or financial support.

Hayami and Ruttan (1985, p. 250) have emphasized the importance of social support for agricultural research by pointing out that failure to institutionalize effective public sector support for agricultural research can cause serious distortions in national patterns of technological change and resource use. If a nation relies solely on the development of agricultural technologies that can be patented by the private sector, their development and use will be accelerated relative to biological and chemical technologies. Mechanical technologies, however, tend to encourage the development of large farms, leading to more rapid displacement of labor.

THE THREE PHASES OF TECHNOLOGY TRANSFER

Observation of the experiences of less developed nations in obtaining agricultural technology led Hayami and Ruttan (1985, pp. 260–62) to identify three phases of technology transfer—material, design, and capacity—between more developed and less developed nations. Understanding the contributions and the different resource requirements of each phase can enable better use of the scarce agricultural research resources of less developed nations.

Material Transfer. The material transfer phase involves importing more productive agricultural technologies in physical forms, such as high-yielding seeds and plants, animals, machinery, pesticides, and fertilizers, which can be used directly in agricultural production. Material transfer has been a very important source of agricultural growth in world history. Examples include the introduction into the Americas of Asian and European wheat and root crops and the introduction of American maize and potatoes to Europe and Asia. When more productive agricultural inputs can be obtained by material transfer, less developed nations can often achieve rapid increases in production and avoid considerable research and development costs. Once technologies are identified as highly productive locally, domestic production of substitutes is likely to become profitable.

Design Transfer. In the design transfer phase, a particular agricultural input sector attains the scientific and industrial capacity to produce more productive agricultural technologies domestically. It achieves this by training intermediate-level scientists and technicians in the private or public sectors so they can use designs, blueprints, formulas, and books imported from more developed nations to make local versions of technologies. Design research includes a local evaluation and testing of technologies, the multiplication of pure seeds, and research on farmers' fields to determine the productivity of the new inputs. This phase also includes expanded local production of biological, chemical, and mechanical technologies and the strengthening of experiment stations.

Capacity Transfer. The capacity transfer phase involves attaining international status in scientific and technological leadership. It requires large, long-term investments in the education of professionals in the public and private sectors of a less developed nation. To attract and retain top quality scientists and to assure productive research requires sufficiently high salaries, large libraries, laboratories, computers, other essential equipment, and working environments free of political interference. Professionals in this phase of technology development contribute to the expansion of the scientific frontier at the world level.

INVESTING IN TECHNOLOGY TRANSFERS

How should a less developed nation allocate its scarce resources among the three phases of technology transfer? The answer depends upon which phases of technology transfer will provide the highest returns at that particular time in a particular sector. For the next decade or two in many less developed nations, the highest returns from investment in research and development will continue to be obtained primarily from investments in material and design transfers. Over the last thirty years, in less developed nations with open borders, the potential for increased income has induced much material transfer of agricultural technology under both private and public auspices. In other less developed nations, significant barriers have existed to imports of more productive agricultural inputs. In this situation, investment of government resources to facilitate institutional changes could accelerate the importing, testing, and distribution of more productive agricultural technologies. (See the discussion of trade controls in chapter 13).

Design transfer is more likely to provide high returns in less developed nations where material transfers from other nations have been large and relatively free over the last few decades and where extensive distribution systems for agricultural inputs have been developed. A focus on design transfer will facilitate any additional material transfers through careful testing. But more important, it will enable substantial modifications of agricultural technologies and institutions to better fit local economic, technological, institutional, and cultural conditions. Continuous increases in the productivity of agricultural technology and institutions can be achieved in many areas through a combination of material and design transfer.

The more basic, capacity-level, research enhances both the productivity of design transfer research and the development of entirely new technologies. However, in the early years of national development, large allocations of agricultural development resources to the capacity phase of technology transfer are often not productive. The very long invention and development periods and the possibility of poor management and performance of new research institutions often lead to low returns from such premature investments.

To conclude, returns to investment by a nation in the different levels of agricultural technology transfer will be influenced by (1) the current levels of technology transfer; (2) the size of the country; (3) the importance of the particular crop; and (4) the economic, technological, institutional, and cultural conditions. Small less developed nations, for example, are unlikely to find it worthwhile to attempt to achieve a capacity level of scientific ability even for major crops, because the research costs are too great in relation to the additional crop income that would be provided by increases in the relatively small national crop.[5]

APPROPRIATE TECHNOLOGY

Although much agricultural development has been based on successful direct transfer of technology between nations, many technologies used in higher income nations are not profitable in less developed nations because of significant differences in the physical, economic, institutional, and cultural conditions of agriculture. In particular, the low labor costs and high capital costs present in many of these nations often make imported capital intensive technologies unprofitable. This point was made in figure 6.4. In that figure, technologies d and t would be more productive than the traditional technology a. They would be appropriate technologies, as they would provide higher income by reducing capital costs while employing about the same amounts of labor as the traditional technology. Technologies of this kind are of particular importance, because they tend to prevent the widening of income disparities.

This analysis leads to the definition of appropriate technology as production materials or institutional arrangements that provide a higher net income and that fit local resource availabilities, institutions, and culture. The new technologies represented by s and r in figure 6.4 may be either more or less productive than the current local technology a. Technology s, however, would increase unemployment and hence, in most cases would be an inappropriate technology, leading perhaps to serious social problems. Finally, it is important to remind ourselves of the range of economic conditions present in less developed nations. In some oil-exporting nations, for example, the ratio of the cost of labor to capital may be much closer to the ratio in more developed nations. In these nations the transfer of capital intensive labor-saving agricultural technologies from more developed nations may be appropriate and profitable.

THE INTERNATIONAL AGRICULTURAL RESEARCH SYSTEM

International agricultural research institutes have been set up over the last three decades to help fill the research needs of less developed nations. These institutes have placed high priority on research to increase the productivity of

---

5. Additional general material on technology transfer is found in Binswanger and Ruttan 1978 (pp. 164–214); Hayami and Ruttan 1985 (chaps. 9 and 10); and Feder, Just, and Zilberman 1985. Important references to agricultural technology generation and design in less developed nations include Ruttan 1982; Binswanger and Ryan 1977; Valdes, Scobie, and Dillon 1979; and for Latin America, Pineiro et al. 1979 and Pinstrup-Anderson 1982.

tropical and subtropical food crops. The first ones were established under the leadership of the Rockefeller and Ford foundations. The International Rice Research Institute (IRRI) in the Philippines was founded first, in 1959. There are now fifteen international institutes, covering a range of tropical agricultural crops and livestock. The world impact of the rice research at IRRI and of the work at the International Wheat and Maize Institute (CIMMYT) in Mexico has already been immense. These institutes were the source of many of the high-yielding grain varieties, which so greatly increased yields in various parts of the world that the term *green revolution* was coined.

When a less developed nation wants to expand its design and capacity transfer capabilities, technological assistance from universities in more developed nations and from international research institutes can often make important contributions. A considerable literature is available about past technological assistance by U.S. universities and foundations. Assistance includes graduate training of agricultural researchers, building agricultural research institutions, and helping establish local agricultural policy, planning, and research units in government ministries.

FARMING SYSTEMS RESEARCH FOR IMPROVED RESEARCH PERFORMANCE

As design and capacity transfer capabilities are increased on agricultural experiment stations in less developed nations, common problems include (1) the production of technologies that, although they increase production on experiment stations, are not profitable on most farms; (2) the production of technologies that make good reports in international journals but that have little direct relevance to national farm production problems; and (3) great delays in adoption by farmers of profitable technologies because communication is poor between researchers, input suppliers, extension agents, and farmers. These shortcomings of agricultural research and extension cause low returns on investment in experiment station capacity.

Over a hundred years of experience in more developed nations and the recent experience in less developed nations have demonstrated that the production of profitable agricultural and livestock technology requires institutional arrangements that facilitate interaction between farmers and those who develop the new technologies. The four components of effective agricultural technology creation and delivery include (1) research and development organizations, both private and public; (2) on-farm testing, with effective feedback of results to researchers; (3) production of the new technologies by seed programs or companies, agricultural chemical firms, and agricultural machinery factories; and (4) extension and communication of the needed information about the new technologies to farmers. In many less developed nations, there is particular need to strengthen the linkages among farmers, researchers, and commercial producers of agricultural inputs. This is particularly true where agricultural scientists have had little practical farm experience and hence have limited understanding of the complexities of profitable use of the new technologies on farms.

Figure 11.7. Interrelations Between Farm-Level and Experiment-Station-Level Agricultural Research

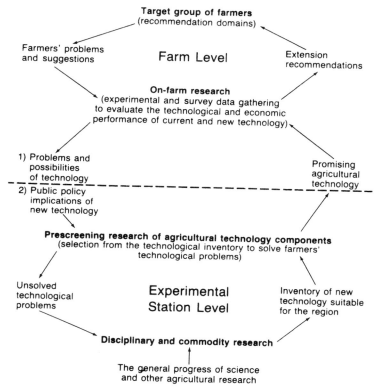

Source: Adapted from Collinson 1982 (p. 5).

The need for integrating tests of new technology on farmers' fields as a regular part of experiment station research has recently been generally accepted. Such testing also enables much better identification of the social and economic problems likely to arise with the use of improved technologies. The important relations between on-farm and experiment station research were identified by Collinson as consisting of three levels of research (see figure 11.7). The first level is disciplinary and commodity research at the capacity level. This research draws on the general progress of science to develop an inventory of new agricultural technologies judged likely to be useful. Less developed nations may obtain these products through material or design transfer, which may include working relations with the specialized international agricultural research institutes and sources in more developed nations.

The technological components developed at this level are then incorporated in the second level, prescreening research, which tests promising technology components on experiment stations in different agricultural areas. The technologies to be screened in this step are selected on the basis of the current problems facing farmers. The third level of research carries out tests on farmers' fields of the most promising prescreened technologies. After technological and economic analysis, the data on the profitable technologies provide the information needed for extension recommendations. Microcomputer and other analytic tools are available to estimate the effect of these new technologies on farm income.[6]

Researchers obtain three important additional kinds of information from tests on farmers' fields. First, feedback about technological and economic results improves the selection of the next set of prescreening experiments on experiment stations. The economic information will also influence disciplinary and commodity research to be locally appropriate. Second, information about local marketing and farm management problems provides better knowledge of institutional, economic, and sometimes cultural barriers to higher returns from the use of the new technologies. And third, such research provides more knowledge about how government agricultural price and other policies are working, including ceiling or floor prices for inputs or farm products and agricultural labor policies. Thus, some farm-level information may point to needed research on institutional changes at national or regional levels. Because of the appreciable professional costs of tests on farmers' fields and the importance of continued disciplinary and prescreening research on experiment stations, on-farm research will necessarily be limited by available research resources.[7]

Future Prospects for Agricultural Research: The New Genetics and Other Breakthroughs

Seldom do farmers have an opportunity to increase their yields 50 to 100 percent, as many did in some areas of Asia and Latin America during the green revolution of the late 1960s and early 1970s. This first shift from traditional crop varieties to modern varieties of wheat, maize, and rice embodied more than fifty years of plant research. If yield increases can be achieved often enough in the future, in repeated increments of 10, 20, and perhaps 30 percent, yields can continue to rise at very high annual rates. The potential for yield increases usually is greater in better farming areas, however.

Looking further ahead, the biological limits on the yields of current important crops have been estimated and compared with maximum yields on experiment stations, where input costs were not a consideration (see figure 11.8). The large differences between current average world yields and experiment station

6. Especially useful material for planning applied research in less developed nations is Andrew and Hildebrand 1982. Perrin et al. (1976) provide valuable tools for the economic analysis of agronomic field trials, as does the MSTAT microcomputer program, Michigan State University 1986.

7. Significant general publications on farming systems research include CIMMYT 1984; Haines 1982; and Shaner, Phillipp, and Schmehl 1982. Useful farm management texts for less developed nations include the following: Dillon and Hardaker 1980; for Africa, Collinson 1972 and Upton 1973; and, for Asia, Thiam and Ong 1979.

Figure 11.8. Average World Yields, Maximum Yields in Selected Tropical Experiment Stations, and Estimated Potential Yields

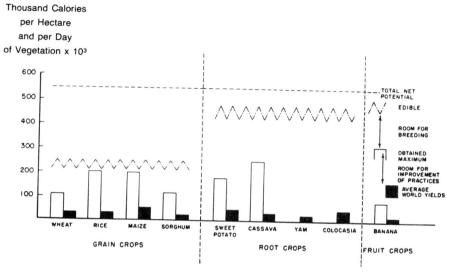

Source: Poleman 1975 (p. 517). Reprinted with permission. Copyright © 1975 by the AAAS.

yields suggest the considerable scope for further increasing yields on farms through plant breeding and other technological developments. We judge that the hundred-year backlog and continuing accumulation of current science and technology in more developed and less developed nations will enable a doubling and quadrupling of many crop yields in the coming decades in good farming areas of less developed nations.

Looking even further ahead, a biotechnological revolution in agriculture is beginning. A proliferation of new technologies is now occurring in laboratories that will enable much more rapid changes in the biological aspects of agriculture. Fishel and Kenney (1986) group the more important sources of this biotechnological revolution as (1) scientists' increasing ability to manipulate and improve plant genetics, particularly through tissue culture and the transfer between plants of selected genes, such as those for resistance to disease and for tolerance to herbicides and such environmental stresses as salts, heavy metals, and drought; (2) new biotechnology products in animal husbandry, including improved vaccines, microbiologically produced animal growth hormones, and methods to rapidly multiply the most productive animals; (3) the development of industrial tissue culture of single plant or animal cells for the production of many plant chemicals; and (4) the increased use by industry of microorganisms to develop products that will displace agricultural commodities, such as the development of fructose corn sweetener to replace sugar and current attempts to convert methanol into a single-cell protein to replace currently used plant proteins in animal feeds. Agricultural researchers and policymakers in less developed nations need to keep informed about these developments. Their potential number and the swiftness of their impacts are likely to greatly affect the agricultural sectors of less developed nations in the decades ahead.

In conclusion, many less developed nations have the opportunity to very rapidly increase the supply of agricultural products through greater investment in research in agricultural technology and institutional development to serve agriculture. The application of science and technology to agriculture through research is a core resource-using process that accelerates agricultural development in all nations. Without more technological and institutional knowledge, a society can increase its land and labor productivity only slowly. Higher-productivity agricultural technologies are increasing exponentially in the different disciplines of agriculture. To continuously capture these breakthroughs, a less developed nation requires high performance in material and design transfer capacities that will enable rapid incorporation into their domestic agriculture of technologies developed throughout the world.

School Education for Increased Agricultural Productivity

What is the role of education in economic and agricultural development? In the most fundamental sense, following Dunn (1971) and Johnston and Clark (1982, chap. 1), we believe that human economic and cultural development is an evolving process of social learning. It includes a range of educational activities and experiences, including the learning by national and local leaders of the theory and practice of agricultural development. In the more specific economic framework of the induced innovation model, education is an attribute of labor, one of the factors in production. Labor, which includes entrepreneurship, is a part of the resource endowments element (see figure 11.1).

Education as an Investment in Human Capital

In the production function methodology presented in chapter 6, the level of education is expressed as a function of the investment of resources (capital) to increase the productivity of labor. Thus, education, or human capital

partakes of most of the classic features of capital formation. Inputs devoted to education, which produces its economic yield only over a long time in the future, must be withdrawn from the production of immediately consumable items. The period of production of human capital is longer than that of most physical plant and equipment, suggesting the need for even more careful long-range planning of human investment than of physical assets. Once produced, human capital continues to yield services over a considerable number of years. However, the stock of human capital does waste and requires replenishment through time. Properly designed, education—investment in human capital—produces a product much more flexible and adaptable than most physical capital. (Millikan 1962, p. 1)

In the last two decades, T. W. Schultz, through his path-breaking studies on human capital, made economists increasingly aware of the fundamental importance of education as an investment. He viewed a farmer's ability to reallocate resources to increase income as subject to change through investment in education. The two effects of education on agricultural output were identified more specifically by Huffman (1974, p. 85) as (1) an allocative effect, enhancing a farmer's ability to acquire, decode, and sort market, technical, and institutional information at less cost; and (2) a worker effect, enabling a farmer to produce more with a given quantity of resources. Although economists generally agree that certain types and amounts of investment in education can provide high social and private returns, little research has been undertaken on the complex questions about the timing and targeting of particular educational investments to the right groups for rapid agricultural and economic growth.

As development requires many changes, there is a need for innovative abilities, especially in the expansion of the capacities of people to solve problems and take inventive, rational approaches to the issues confronting them. Education can reduce the cost of institutional and cultural change. An overemphasis on the transmission of a received body of knowledge through rote learning and study for fixed subject-matter examinations is a weak preparation to deal creatively with the problems of low income and rapid technological and institutional change.

Millikan (1962, p. 4) proposed useful guides for higher performance in education in less developed nations: (1) more economical educational methods, as the costly educational systems in more developed nations have evolved in a different economic environment of high labor and low capital costs; (2) education to change attitudes toward nature, in order to shift thinking from the notion that "natural phenomena are beyond the control of man, are unpredictable, mystical, and subject to the whims of personalized but unseen forces"; (3) increased emphasis on education for problem solving to aid rural people in meeting rapid and unpredictable changes their societies will face; and (4) increases in the search and selection capacity of the educational system so that the students with the best minds are encouraged to remain in school to develop their resources and contribute to national development.

The Demand for School Education

What would induce a change in the demand for school education in agricultural areas? Under what circumstances would more knowledge and a higher level of education become valuable to a farmer, his or her community, or a nation? In traditional agriculture, informal village communications and the father-to-son and mother-to-daughter apprentice system of education is effective in transmitting the existing knowledge about agriculture.

When agricultural technologies and institutions are developed elsewhere that would be more productive locally, it would pay a society, or some of its members, to allocate resources to seek the knowledge needed to incorporate the more productive technologies into their agriculture. If the increases in income achieved from information seeking were greater than the costs of these activities, the net income of the group would increase. As more complex and productive new technologies and institutions that require high levels of verbal and numerical literacy become available to an agricultural area, primary schooling will become a worthwhile private and social investment for farm operators. Thus, as the rate of change in agricultural technology and institutions increases, more education for participants in the agricultural sector is likely to become profitable. However, as there often are significant opportunity costs in sending farm children to school, the advantages of primary education for increasing farm and household income often need to be considerable to induce farm families in good farming areas to educate the children they expect to remain in farming. At some point, however, as agricultural development proceeds, agricultural families will find that schooling provides the literacy and calculating abilities that will enable the children who continue in farming to improve their incomes.

In more developed nations, the contributions of schooling to economic growth have become so great that a large variety of educational activities have been induced. In dynamic economic environments, literacy, calculating ability, and higher levels of education are complementary to the use of other resources, enabling more rapid response and more productive use of the continuing stream of more effective technologies and institutional arrangements in agriculture.

Some empirical evidence on the value of school education in less developed nations is available. In their reanalysis of data in twenty three studies, Lockheed, Jamison, and Lau (1980) concluded that four years of school education was associated with a mean increase of 9.5 percent in agricultural productivity in areas where a significant change in agriculture was taking place. In contrast, in agricultural areas where little change was taking place, an average of only 1.3 percent gain in agricultural productivity was attributable to four years of schooling. Another review of eighteen studies of farmers' education concluded that four years of elementary education increased farm productivity by an average of 7 percent, with some evidence of a threshold number of years of schooling (four to six), at which the effect of education was greater. These results are consistent with T. W. Schultz's (1975) hypothesis "that the ability to deal successfully with economic disequilibria is enhanced by education" (p. 843) and the economic complementarity thesis that technological change enhances the earning capacities obtained from schooling (Welch 1978, p. 277). Thus, in a farming area, as the shift occurs from a static resource-based, traditional agriculture to a dynamic, science-based, agriculture, the value of school education increases.

We should note, however, that rapid increases in agricultural production are possible in some circumstances without additional schooling. The first waves of the green revolution provide many examples, as high-yielding varieties increased output greatly in agricultural areas with low literacy rates. The speed of these adoptions was due in part to the relative simplicity of the innovations, often requiring only the replacement of one seed by another and the addition of chemical fertilizer. Where chemical fertilizer had already been introduced, little change in farming practices was required. Hence, if more productive technologies can be provided in forms that farmers can substitute easily for current practices, the need and therefore the demand for education to obtain literacy and calculating ability may be less. Thus, primary schooling and other types of agricultural investments, such as in locally adaptive agricultural research and extension activities, may be substitutes for each other in achieving increases in agricultural production in an area. Education may be a longer term investment with higher income-increasing potential, while agricultural research and extension activity may produce more rapid increases in farm output. [8]

Supplying School Education for Agricultural Development

What kinds and how much education, and for whom, will provide high social returns by increasing agricultural production? Possible educational activities include formal primary, secondary, and higher education and nonformal education. Among the latter, agricultural extension systems and the print and electronic media may be able to effectively supply needed information and education relevant for farm production and marketing in a very cost effective way. As more resources are used for each type of educational and informational activity, the returns would be expected to decline. Squire (1981, p. 197), in a summary of research on social returns to education in less developed nations, found lower social rates of return for secondary education, averaging 16 percent, than for primary education. However, particular investments in specialized kinds of secondary and higher education for certain persons, including researchers, educational leaders, and persons who will make important decisions affecting agriculture from leadership positions in government, may provide very high social rates of return through greatly improved public decisionmaking. Direct copies of the patterns of education in more developed nations, however, are likely to be less productive than modified forms to fit the cultural, institutional, technological, and economic environments of each less developed country.

PRIMARY SCHOOLING

Investment in primary schools is an almost universal strategy to provide literacy and computational skills. In their analysis of the contribution of primary schooling in Korea, Malaysia, and Thailand, Jamison and Lau (1982) concluded that four years of primary school were associated with a 9 percent increase in farm production and that the rate of return to investment in education in these countries ranged from 7 to 40 percent.

However, the cost effectiveness of primary schools for farm people in less

---

8. Important work on investment in human capital includes Becker 1975; Welch 1978; Hauser 1979; Blaug 1970; Yotopoulos and Nugent 1976, (chap. 11); and Squire 1981 (chap. 16). Useful general references to education and development include Todaro 1981 (chap. 11) and Simmons 1979. References on the contribution of education to farmers' decisionmaking and allocative efficiency include Huffman 1977. Studies of the returns to education are examined in the survey by Lockheed, Jamison, and Lau 1980 and Jamison and Lau 1982.

developed nations is variable; these schools often have curricula and materials irrelevant to rural life because of overcentralization of the school system, urban dominance in determining subject matter, and the desires of rural people that their children be prepared to leave agriculture to obtain higher paying employment elsewhere. Primary schools can alienate rural children from agriculture and thus have a negative effect on agricultural development by excessively influencing the best students to leave rural areas. Thus, although in the long run effective primary schooling is a productive social investment in all less developed nations, much more attention needs to be paid to the cost effectiveness of particular curricula and arrangements. Primary schooling should both be useful to farm and other rural people and provide the educational background required to enable many to leave agriculture.

SECONDARY EDUCATION

The direct contribution of currently available secondary education to agricultural development in many less developed nations remains unclear. First, secondary school curricula often provide few skills and little knowledge of use in agriculture. Second, both families and teachers usually assume that secondary school students will not return to agriculture, views that encourage the exclusion of subjects relevant to agriculture and rural life. However, secondary education for a certain number of rural youths is likely to contribute indirectly to increasing the productivity of agriculture by improving the performance of persons who will work in agricultural input and product marketing firms and who will manage local government.

Alternative secondary schools that provide curricula relevant to agriculture and rural life have been established in a number of nations. Two of the most well known are the Folk Schools of Denmark and Taiwan's technical, agriculturally oriented, secondary schools. A new educational alternative that appears to have considerable potential at the secondary level is distance teaching, in which students meet with a teacher infrequently, sometimes less than once a week. This educational method requires specialized print, radio, or television programs, but requires fewer classrooms and teachers. Alternative types of secondary education and schools face the risk, however, that they may be viewed as providing inferior education.

VOCATIONAL EDUCATION FOR AGRICULTURE

The return to investments is uncertain in formal schooling in agricultural subjects (vocational agriculture) at the secondary level in less developed nations. Detailed studies of vocational agricultural programs are available for only a few less developed nations. Zymelman (1976) pointed out that in order to be productive, vocational training has to be responsive to the labor market its graduates will enter and has to be more cost effective than alternative nonformal and private sector apprentice systems. If graduates do not achieve much higher farm productivity or do not receive appreciably higher salaries, the cost effectiveness of resources devoted to formal vocational education is likely to be low. [9]

Agricultural Extension, Nonformal Education, and Communication Investments

Nonformal education is any organized or deliberate set of educational activities carried on outside a regular school. Agricultural extension and communication activities are forms of nonformal education that can accelerate agricultural development. Adults and out-of-school youth are the usual targets of such education. Its methods include assessing people's needs and interests and motivating and helping them acquire the skills and knowledge to increase their income and well-being. The emphasis is usually on imparting practical skills in community-related projects that are flexibly structured, learner centered, and self-governing (Grandstaff 1979, pp. 179–81). [10] A frustration with the irrelevance to rural life of much school curricula has led to the growth of a nonformal education movement. This movement has also sought particularly to provide relevant technical knowledge and education to the less educated and poorer groups in society.

Demand and Supply of Nonformal Education

Agricultural extension and agricultural communication and other nonformal educational services, including print, radio, and television, are induced as development proceeds. These services enable valuable knowledge to pass from researchers, entrepreneurs, and government officials, who create or obtain the new information about more useful technologies and institutional arrangements, to farmers, marketing personnel, and businessmen, who can use it.

The responsibility of the public sector to support agricultural extension and other agricultural information services is recognized by most governments. The necessity of government support arises because much agricultural information has the characteristics of a public good. A public good has two main attributes: (1) when it is provided to one person, it becomes essentially free to many others; and (2) additional users do not appreciably decrease the value of the good to previous users. Examples of public goods are highway safety activities and police protection, as well as much agricultural, economic, and other technological information. A farmer who receives new useful information about a better tech-

---

9. References to modified high school curricula for farm and rural people include Bertelsen 1961; and on the Danish Folk Schools, Skrubbettrang 1952, 1953. References to vocational agriculture are in an annotated bibliography by Meaders and Gonzalez (1984).

10. A selected bibliography on nonformal education is available in Non-Formal Education Exchange 1982. Important works in this field include Brembeck and Thompson 1973; Coombs 1974; and Dejene 1980. A manual for analysis of costs and outcomes of nonformal education was produced by the Educational Testing Service 1979. The economics of nonformal education have been explored by Ahmed 1975.

nology often passes it on to relatives and neighbors. Hence, the person who initially gave it to the farmer would not be able to charge each farmer for the information to pay for the costs of the service. Thus, information about new technologies and institutional arrangements that have the characteristics of a public good will be undersupplied by the private sector. However, society as a whole benefits through increased production and lower real costs from the provision of such public goods as new agricultural information to farmers. Thus, governments are induced to support agricultural extension and other communication services.

Returns to Investment in Nonformal Education

The social and private returns from agricultural information gathering and distribution depend upon the increased net income that results through the worker and through the allocative effects identified earlier. If a great deal of relevant new technology and better institutional arrangements are being developed somewhere—in more developed countries or in international or domestic research institutes—the likelihood of high returns to nonformal education is greater. Thus, to provide reasonable social returns, the level of activity in agricultural extension and other information services needs to be related to the amounts of information available for transfer that will increase the productivity of agriculture and marketing.

In the early stages of development, overinvestment, and hence low returns to extension and communication services, can occur. These are situations where little new agricultural technology is available to communicate or where the extension and communication services are incapable of effectively communicating the information to farmers due to such factors as erroneous materials, lack of training, and poor incentives. As stressed in chapter 4, the returns to extension work in traditional agriculture are low, as these agricultures have no generators of more productive technology.

However, the costs of an effective extension or agricultural information service can be small compared with the benefits in increased income obtained. Feder and Slade (1984, p. 8) estimated that a gain in crop yield of less than 1 percent per year can generate a sizable rate of return to additional extension effort. Some studies show rates of return to agricultural extension of 15 to 20 percent. Nevertheless, because of the large number of exogenous variables that influence the productivity of agricultural extension and the complementary nature of extension activities with agricultural research and other rural information systems, separating out the contribution of agricultural extension becomes very difficult. [11]

11. Important general references relevant to agricultural extension in less developed nations include Crouch and Chamala 1981; G. E. Jones and Rolls 1982; and Ashby 1979. Huffman (1978) reviewed assessments of the returns to agricultural extension. Perraton et al. (1983) examined the costs, effects, and alternatives in basic education and agricultural extension. This work includes a review of the literature on the impact of agricultural extension by Lamont Orivel (pp. 1–56).

Agricultural Extension: Problems and a Model

The development of agricultural extension institutions has been induced in many less developed nations over the last thirty years to attempt to accelerate agricultural growth. As these systems have been established, many of these nations have had similar problems.

The work program is usually of an ad hoc nature. Little guidance is available on its content, presentation, or means of execution. There is no monitoring of program effectiveness. The extension agent is a ''general agricultural agent'' whose tasks range from promoting new technology, organizing credit schemes, supplying inputs, to performing general administrative duties. This wide-ranging responsibility normally results in little organized work being done. . . .

The task of ''improving the farming community,'' ill-defined in direction and content, is overwhelming for the extension agent, who increasingly falls back on his administrative duties as an excuse for not visiting the field. A vicious circle has thus developed—the lack of response by farmers is blamed on the extension service by research staff and senior government officials, who withdraw support for extension, and extension then achieves even less. (Cernea, Coulter, and Russell 1983, p. 6)

Many approaches have been taken to attempt to solve these and other problems of low performance in extension. In Comilla, Bangladesh, an alternative extension system was devised in which villagers were asked to choose a good farmer, who would obtain training, locally demonstrate, and communicate the new information to the rest of the farmers in his village (Raper 1970). In Taiwan, extension was developed as part of the cooperative system in farmers' associations. More recently a training and visit system for agricultural extension has been developed to increase effectiveness. This model has had considerable success and was by 1982 incorporated in sixty-five projects financed by the World Bank (Benor and Baxter 1984; Moore 1984). An outline of the training and visit system indicates one way the essential resource requirements and important linkages needed for an effective intensive agricultural extension service can be arranged (see figure 11.9).

The essential features of the training and visit system include a single line of command with precise responsibilities, concentration of effort in a carefully set time schedule, regular and continuous training, close linkages to research through subject matter specialists, and no nonextension responsibilities. The instructional system depends upon specific production recommendations for the crops most suitable and economically viable for farmers' conditions. The recommendations, which must be financially feasible and entail minimum risk, are developed by the extension and research staff and can be modified at monthly extension training sessions in the light of additional research or farm experience.

As the training and visit system employs considerable amounts of human and other resources, other models of agricultural extension less demanding of human resources may be more cost effective, particularly in earlier stages of

Figure 11.9. Visit and Training System Model for Agricultural Extension

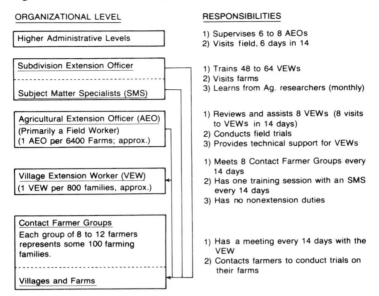

Source: Developed from Benor and Baxter 1984 (p. xii).

agricultural development and in areas with lower densities of farmers. (See also Cernea, Coulter, and Russell 1983; and Feder, Slade, and Sundaram 1984.) The activities of agricultural extension systems should be driven to a considerable extent by the new more productive farming opportunities that have opened up through research or from other sources.

Economics of Communication Services

Recent great reductions in the costs of information transfer over time and space have the potential of providing high returns to society. The economics of better communication in accelerating agricultural growth has been little recognized in the agricultural development literature. Although the print media are heavily used, the value of telecommunications—telephone, radio, ground and satellite television, and the computer—in development is less well understood. The contributions of better telecommunications are both general, through increased performance in the many parts of the agricultural sector, and specific, related to accelerated adoption of more productive agricultural technologies and institutions and the reduction of uncertainty. Radio forums, for example, can both complement and to some extent substitute for agricultural extension activities.

In examining the returns that can be expected from improved telecommunications in less developed nations, especially the telephone, Leff (1984) identified ways to increase productivity and discover why underinvestment is common. The central contribution of telecommunications is through a great reduction in (1) the costs of acquiring information; and (2) negotiating transactions. The lack of information and the misinformation cause many misallocations of resources, resulting in less productive agricultural activities and slower growth. As information and transaction costs are reduced, more input and product markets develop, providing better information to farm and market people about the costs of resources used in production and about likely product prices. This enables better estimates of the likely returns. Although farmers and marketing people in less developed nations gain from improved communications, the society as a whole obtains a significant share of the gains of the resulting increase in the productivity of agriculture. Part of the benefits from communication investments are public goods that require some public investment if they are to be produced at socially optimum levels.

An example of how social conditions and communication activities interact in agricultural areas of less developed nations was provided by a 1983 study in Haryana and Uttar Pradesh states of India. The study compared the information sources of farmers in two areas, where a 35 percent literacy rate prevailed. One area had a training and visit extension system. In both areas, the most important channel for agricultural information for all farmers was advice from other farmers; the second most important was agricultural radio programming. Third in importance, in the training and visit area only, was the extension system (Feder and Slade 1984).

Of particular concern in less developed nations is the observation that some communication processes have widened knowledge gaps between different groups of receivers, especially those of high and low socioeconomic status. This tendency can be controlled to some extent by producing messages whose content is valuable for these lower income groups and by choosing communication channels that reach them.[12]

Complementarities and Substitutions in Agricultural Research, Education, and Communication Investments

The returns to additional investment in agricultural research and education and communication activities will vary in different nations as development proceeds, particularly due to the changing substitutability and complementarity of these investments. Empirical studies have attempted to identify these interactions. A test of a model of diffusion of a new variable-input technology by Feder and Slade (1984, p. 320) found that farmers with better access to information or with more human capital, as indexed by schooling, adopted the inputs earlier and applied them in larger quantities.

12. Important general references about communication activities for development include Jassawalla and Lamberton 1982; Saunders, Warford, and Willenius 1983; McAnany 1979; Feder, Just, and Zilberman 1985; and Feder and Slade 1984. A useful reference about radio use for development is Jamison and McAnany 1978.

The complementarity of different information activities and levels of education in contributing to increased farm productivity adds to the difficulty of making optimum decisions about investments to increase flows of information to farm people. If educational levels are very low, extension activity may not be very productive. Hence primary education can be strongly complementary to extension. Where farmers have attained higher levels of education, much needed agricultural information may be obtained successfully by them from nonextension information channels, such as input suppliers and publications. Some combination of extension, print, radio, and television is likely to be more cost-effective than one channel alone. Thus, attention to the ratio of resources allocated to each channel can enable more cost effective extension, nonformal education and communication activities for agricultural development.

Important Concepts

Hunting and gathering
Shifting cultivation
Demand for agricultural research
Returns of agricultural research
Demand for social science
  knowledge
Consumer surplus
Producer surplus
Public goods
Material technology transfer
Design transfer
Capacity transfer
Farming systems research

Disciplinary research
The new genetics
Allocative effect
Worker effect
Demand for school education
Cost-effectiveness of primary
  schools
Distance teaching
Investment in schooling
Nonformal education
Radio forums
Information costs
Transaction costs

Sample Questions

1. Explain the meaning of "achieving the transition to a science-based agriculture."

2. How do agricultural research and education relate to the theory of induced agricultural development?

3. Using supply and demand curves, explain the circumstances in which producers are likely to demand government aid to support agricultural research.

4. In comparing current farm yields with yields obtained on experiment stations, studies have shown large gaps. Indicate at least three biological and three socioeconomic constraints that help explain the gap.

5. How can the operation of the patent system affect the allocation of resources for agricultural research in a less developed country?

6. Explain the three phases of technology transfer.

7. What is farming systems research? Explain its likely contributions and some possible shortcomings.

8. In what ways does education increase farm productivity? Be specific.

9. Provide an economic explanation for the demand for primary and secondary education.

10. What kinds of school education do you judge would provide high returns in agriculture? Explain why.

11. Agricultural extension and agricultural research can be both economic complements and substitutes. Explain.

IV

National Policies and Programs for Agricultural Development

Introduction to Part IV

In this part of the book, we place primary focus on government policies and programs that can significantly affect the rate of agricultural growth. These actions include changes in the institutions, laws, and operating procedures of government that affect the productivity of the economy, and especially agricultural marketing, farm production, and the prices of agricultural inputs, products, and services. This macroeconomic focus is concerned with understanding the facilitating role government can play in agricultural development through its actions in agricultural marketing and planning, as well as in its trade and price policies.

Government price, trade, and other more direct interventions in an economy often greatly affect performance. Integrated food and agricultural produc-

Figure IV.1. Principal Components in Agricultural Production-Distribution Systems

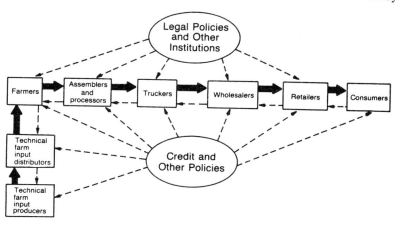

Source: Adapted from Harrison et al. 1974 (p. 7).

tion and marketing systems function in all nations, enabling inputs to flow to farms, farms to produce, and agricultural products to flow to consumers (see figure IV.1). Agricultural and other marketing systems are embedded in the social and government systems they serve. Different cultural groups and kinds of governments have widely different performance goals for their marketing systems and place varied emphasis on productivity, government control, progressiveness, and equity. Marketing systems and complementary government activities provide essential communication systems that enable resource use and consumer purchases. Blundering interventions in an economy can upset the flows of goods and services, leading to reduced performance. Because input supply, farm production, and product-marketing systems are integrated, government intervention in one part of the system often has unexpected effects on other parts of the system. Government planning, price, trade, and other interventions are integral to the economy, as they can greatly slow or increase the productivity of the agricultural sector and the rates of growth in national per capita income and consumption.

12

Transforming Traditional Agricultural Marketing

> *Looked at in this way, the central problem of development is not the gap between rich nations and poor nations; it is the gap between the rich and poor parts of the developing nations themselves. Their critical problem may lie not in the terms of trade in world commerce but in the terms of trade between their industrial and rural areas. The prices paid in the countryside for manufactured goods in these developing nations are too high; while the prices paid by the cities for the output of rural areas and the total resources allocated from the cities for rural development are too low. The operational task is to break down these distortions; to produce self-reinforcing agricultural and industrial expansion; and to create truly national markets within these countries. . . .*
>
> *There are four major jobs that must be done, . . . as part of a conscious national strategy shared by the public and private authority. The four tasks are a revolution in the marketing of agricultural products in the cities; a shift of industry to the production of simple agricultural equipment and consumers' goods for the mass market; and a revolution in marketing methods for such cheap manufactured goods, especially in rural areas. What is involved are two distinct revolutions in marketing and distribution—one urban, the other rural.*
>
> —Rostow 1964, p. 135

Marketing Problems, Functions, and Models

Marketing Problems

Agricultural marketing services in many less developed nations are costly and exhibit relatively low productivity. In many cases, storage losses are high; a large amount of resources, primarily labor, are often required to move a ton of agricultural product short distances; and the few processing activities available use many resources per unit of product processed. A transformation of traditional agricultural marketing is required to achieve high productivity in marketing transactions, storage, transportation, and processing.

In this chapter, agricultural input and product marketing are viewed in the context of a growing economy, where industrialization, specialization, urbanization, and rising incomes place ever-increasing demands on marketing systems. In many less developed nations, marketing problems have been little studied. The "relative neglect of marketing probably reflects a combination of factors, including a general lack of knowledge about the complexities of market processes and the role of the private sector in essential marketing functions; a widely held anti-middleman attitude; and a realization of the politically sensitive nature of price policies and public sector interventions in food marketing" (Riley and Staatz 1981, p. 3). Also, many assume that the marketing system will take care of itself.

In addition, governments may be ambivalent about aiding market people to improve performance, as they are often viewed as "parasites," gaining profit while providing little service.

The Economic Functions of Marketing

Are farmers the sole producers of food and agricultural products and are marketing people parasites who contribute little to the consumer? What do marketing activities produce? Standard marketing texts present the following four economic contributions of marketing. [1]

1. *Storage, or time utility.* As most agricultural crops are produced during a short harvest period but consumed over extended periods of time, often a whole year, storage is undertaken to maintain a product in good condition until needed. Storage uses resources—land, labor, and capital—that the consumer has to pay for.

2. *Movement, or place utility.* The movement of large amounts of agricultural products from farming areas to consumers usually includes some form of packaging, to prevent damage or loss, and transportation. These activities also use scarce resources.

3. *Processing, or form utility.* Processing involves a change in the form of the agricultural product after harvest. Consumers very often will pay a higher price for additional processing by marketing firms to increase food quality and to reduce home-processing costs and preparation time.

---

1. Standard agricultural marketing texts include Shepherd, Futrell, and Strain 1982; Purcell 1979; and Kohls and Uhl 1980. Useful general references on agricultural marketing and development include Timmer, Falcon, and Pearson 1983; Hirschman 1977; Riley and Weber 1983; Abbott 1983; ICRISAT 1985; Shaffer 1985; Abbott and Makeham 1979; Abbott and colleagues 1984; Harper and Kavura 1982; and Breimyer 1973. Useful policy-focused marketing references include Economic Development Institute 1985 and Bates 1981.

4. *Marketing management.* To perform marketing functions, management activities are required. These include (1) gathering information on prices and any government or market regulations; (2) testing product quality; (3) accounting; and (4) making financial arrangements, including those for credit use and risk reduction. Agricultural products available for purchase by consumers are thus produced by both farmers and marketing people. Managing marketing uses resources.

The wide range in costs and margins charged for marketing services in less developed nations raises important questions about the performance levels of marketing systems (see figure 12.1). Are the relatively large rice-marketing costs in India, Pakistan, Papua (New Guinea), and Bolivia due to high transportation and milling costs? Or are they due to rigidities in marketing structure partly or largely caused by government? Are significant monopoly profits present in these systems? Or are cultural traditions and associated traditional marketing systems the cause? In livestock and meat marketing, why are the costs so high in Pakistan, Papua, and Chile? These outcomes result from intricate interactions between the physical, economic, social, and government environments in each nation.

Marketing Models

As relatively little empirical research on the vast number of agricultural marketing activities in less developed nations has been carried out, we are still ignorant of the way many of them perform in these different social and economic environments. In this knowledge vacuum, popular beliefs based on unrepresentative information are often accepted as accurate descriptions.

THE UNPRODUCTIVE AND MONOPOLISTIC MARKETING MODEL

Abolish the evil, parasitic marketing system! Many people believe marketing is exploitative, collusive, unproductive, and highly profitable. With little knowledge of what economic functions marketing performs and how markets operate, these stereotypic beliefs abound. The resulting, often false, diagnoses of marketing problems can lead to well-intended actions that unwittingly reduce marketing performance. For example, some governments have, in attempting to assure low food prices, replaced reasonably effective independent marketing firms with high-cost, low-productivity, overstaffed, state marketing monopolies. In other cases, ideologies prescribe simplistic, uniform marketing answers to all marketing problems or enact complex, sometimes unworkable, regulations to ''control'' the market and marketing people.

After reviewing the marketing research that has been carried out in less developed nations, Elliot Berg (CILSS/Club du Sahel, 1977) concluded that there were very few empirical studies to confirm the stereotypic beliefs about

Figure 12.1. Marketing Margins for Rice and Meat, Selected Countries

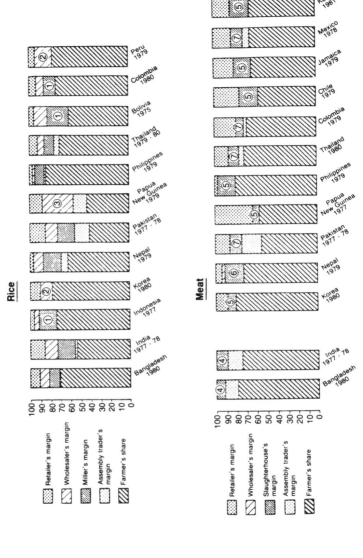

Source: Adapted from Mittendorf and Hertog 1982 (pp. 3 and 5).

328

agricultural marketing. More specifically, he reported that few careful studies of the structure and functioning of grain markets were available, even in India, where there has been much controversy about agricultural marketing for decades. He also judged that Ruttan's earlier comment was generally applicable, that "much of what passes as analysis in the marketing literature represents little more than a repetition of the conventional wisdom regarding middleman behavior with little or no empirical content" (p. 92).

AN ECONOMIC EQUILIBRIUM MODEL OF MARKETING IN TRADITIONAL AREAS

The Schultzian model of economic equilibrium discussed in chapter 4 is an alternative model of the behavior of people who carry out marketing functions in traditional areas of less developed nations. When this model is applied to marketing, it has the following four important theoretical and empirical implications: (1) In many areas, there is likely to have been little change in important technological, institutional, and cultural variables affecting marketing. (2) Local, often largely traditional, marketing activities succeed in large measure in enabling these markets to equilibrate the supplies and demands for agricultural products. (3) As there are usually few barriers to entry into local agricultural marketing in terms of skills or capital, farm families seeking to obtain the most income possible will engage in marketing whenever it promises to provide a greater return to the family than competing activities, such as farming. With much experience in agricultural marketing, rational people can be expected to allocate their resources efficiently in marketing, so that the marginal returns to the different marketing activities will be approximately equal and also equal to alternative economic activities. (4) And finally, as marketing activities compete with farming activities for a rural person's time and other resources, we would expect the returns to marketing activities to be approximately the same as the low returns found in farming; otherwise, a great increase in the number of persons engaged in marketing would occur. (This model does not exclude the existence of some local monopolies and of individual instances of exorbitant returns due to trickery, cheating, or force—actions that unfortunately characterize human behavior everywhere.)

The model of the calculating peasant who also engages in largely competitive agricultural markets is supported by empirical studies that have been carried out in less developed nations. These include the particularly well-known analyses by Lele (1971) in India and W. O. Jones (1972) in African countries. This research found that the marketing of staple food crops is usually competitive, with large numbers of sellers and buyers having easy entry into marketing. Prices of staple food products have also generally been found to reflect transportation costs. Von Oppen, Raju, and Bapna (1979, p. 186) concluded from their research on the marketing of food crops and from review of other empirical studies that agricultural market channels in India are generally competitive.

Hence, rates of returns to investment in marketing can be expected to approximate those in farming.

However, for nonstaple crops, a wide variety of market conditions and performance characteristics might be found. With fewer producers and buyers in the market, opportunities for control of quantities and prices become greater, offering increased possibilities of monopoly profits. Miracle (1969), for example, has reported observing collusive and guild activity to control trade in certain African markets.

A WIDER SOCIOECONOMIC MODEL

A full understanding of marketing activities requires that they be placed in the wider social matrix in which they are embedded. Marketing needs to be viewed in relation to cultural factors and national social objectives. For example, market structure and performance in areas with ethnic groups that are served by marketing people from other cultural and language backgrounds is likely to be very different from areas where farmers and marketing people have the same culture and language. Even in relatively uniform cultural areas, extended family, caste, village political divisions, and farm size can influence the structure and performance of marketing. In some situations, local monopsonistic and even monopolistic agricultural marketing may provide high performance consistent with cultural and community objectives by helping the community maintain its integrity in the face of economic and other pressures. Therefore, conclusions for particular farming areas about the validity of alternative models of marketing require analytic and empirical studies that include understanding the cultural and economic goals of the group and its changing environment. The need for a wider socioeconomic analysis of development was explored in chapter 5. For example, E. D. Smith (1975) concluded that

The issue of free versus controlled market economies is a false one. The real issues . . . are [how] market behaviors [are] to be controlled through collective imposition of market rules, in order to liberate and expand the scope of individual market action, i.e., to develop agricultural markets. . . .

All public policy relating to markets is articulated through and by institutions, including institutions related to nominally private transactions. Adam Smith's "invisible hand" . . . works or fails to work because men have or have not through their customary and formal institutions structured ("controlled") relations among market participants in ways that allow competition to effect a publicly satisfactory result. (p. 2)

Smith also asserted that designs for the development of market institutions must recognize the great differences in political and cultural institutions, both formal and customary, that limit options for workable market institutions. Hence, in responding to economic opportunity, different peoples are likely to develop different institutional arrangements (collective action), consistent with their political and social institutions. Therefore, it is unlikely that direct transfers of marketing institutions from more developed nations will work without modifications in the cultural, institutional, and economic environments of less developed nations, just as direct transfers of much biological, chemical, and mechanical technology often are not productive in these different environments. (For a survey of alternative conceptualizations of marketing, see Breimyer 1973.)

Marketing and Economic Growth

Factors Causing Growth in Marketing

Economic growth causes the following three changes in an economy, thereby greatly increasing the demand for marketing services: (1) increases in regional specialization; (2) increases in the marketing of agricultural inputs and products between farms and the rest of the economy, as the commercialization of agriculture augments agricultural productivity; and (3) the shift of people out of agriculture and into urban areas. We have examined the forces leading to regional specialization in agriculture in a number of chapters, particularly chapters 6 and 13. Here we consider the effects of both the commercialization of farming and urbanization on the demand for marketing services.

THE GREEN REVOLUTION

The transformation of traditional agriculture was shown in chapters 4, 6, 8, and 9 to require the substitution of new high-return, purchased inputs (with more price elastic supply curves) for traditional inputs (with relatively price inelastic supply curves). We also know that increasing purchases of more productive agricultural inputs expand the backward linkages of agriculture to the rest of the economy (see chapters 8 and 9). Backward linkages are concerned with the input supply system of an industry. Hence, as a greatly expanded and more complex farm input supply system develops, agriculture's backward linkages to the economy grow.

On the product side, even in the most traditional agricultural areas some agricultural products are sold outside most communities. As the agricultural transformation proceeds, a greater proportion of farm production is sold in order to pay for a greater amount of agricultural inputs. In this way, forward linkages are increased to the rest of the economy through an expanding agricultural product-marketing system. Thus, the green revolution in farm production also requires a revolution in agricultural input and product marketing.

STRUCTURAL TRANSFORMATION

Increases in consumer incomes and urban population associated with economic growth, as shown in chapter 3, can lead to an explosive increase in the demand for marketing services for agricultural products. Hence, increasing forward and backward linkages between agriculture and the rest of the economy occur with economic growth.

Estimates of rates of increase in demand for marketing services can be obtained by examining the income elasticity of demand for food passing through marketing channels as per capita income increases. This is done by separating the components of national food consumption into six interrelated parts (see figure 12.2). As population migrates to urban areas, the flow of food increases through food-marketing channels, and the proportion of national farm food production consumed on the farm (Subsistence Food Consumption) declines. The fraction of food marketing costs in the Value of Retail Food may remain fairly constant or may change, depending upon the marketing services demanded by consumers and the productivity of the marketing system. The effect of income growth on the marketing services demanded and the speed of the shift of population to urban areas depends upon four variables: (1) the rate of urban population growth relative to the rate of total population growth; (2) the income elasticity of demand for food; (3) the marketing margin; and (4) rate of per capita income changes.

In order to estimate the shift of population to urban areas associated with income growth, ratios of the nonagricultural labor force in seventy countries to these countries' total labor force at different levels of per capita income were analyzed (see figure 12.3). The rate of shift to urban residence was then used to estimate the increase in the flows of food through the wholesale and retail food channels shown in figure 12.2. The long-run income elasticity of demand for total national food consumption, inclusive of marketing services, was demonstrated in chapter 3 to be generally about 0.7. Empirical data from a variety of nations have shown that the overall marketing margin for food does not usually change very rapidly as income increases.

When the four variables are combined with an income elasticity of demand for national food consumption of 0.7, as per capita income increases from $50 to $200 with the associated increase in urban population, the income elasticity of the Value of Retail Food and Food Marketing Costs is 1.2 (see table 12.1). Thus, for every $1 increase in per capita income, both the amount of food sold at retail and marketing costs would increase by $1.20, assuming no change in the marketing margin. Recall from chapter 3 that an income elasticity greater than 1.0 indicates that the sector of the economy is increasing its share. An elasticity larger than 1.0 for retail food and marketing costs due to urbanization and income growth contrasts with the lower 0.7 overall national income elasticity of demand for all food due to income growth alone.

This analysis is particularly interesting, because it demonstrates that many nations in the early stages of development are likely to experience explosive growth rates in the demand for retail food and marketing services, as urbanization accelerates with per capita income growth (see figure 12.4). At higher per capita incomes with the slowing of urbanization, the income elasticity of demand for retail food and marketing services may decline, but the analysis indicates it will remain above the income elasticity for the overall national demand for food. Also observe, if the marketing margin (the share of marketing costs in retail food) increases with income growth, or the overall income elasticity of national food consumption is higher than 0.7, then the marketing sector would

Figure 12.2. Components of National Food Consumption

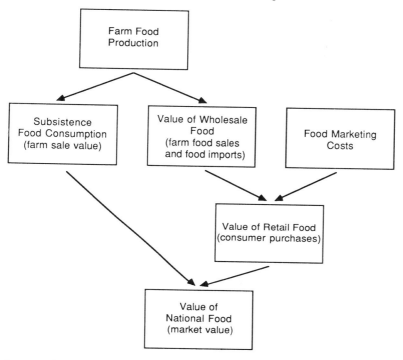

Source: Adapted from Stevens 1965 (p. 9).

Figure 12.3. Retail Food as Percentage of Total Food and per Capita Income

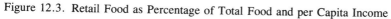

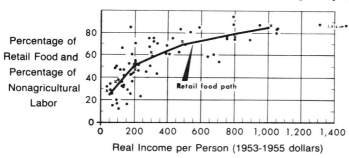

Source: Stevens 1965 (p. 28).
Note: Retail food ratio is estimated by the percentage of the nonagricultural labor force in seventy countries.

Table 12.1. Income Elasticity of Demand for Retail Food and Marketing Services with Increasing per Capita Income

Change in per Capita Income (dollars)[a]	Income Elasticity of the Value of National Food		
	0.9	0.7	0.5
	Retail food and marketing elasticities		
50–200	1.40	1.20	1.00
200–500	1.27	1.07	.87
500–1,000	1.18	.98	.78

Source: Adapted from Stevens 1965 (p. 33).
[a] 1953–55 dollars.

Figure 12.4. Rates of Growth in Retail Food and Marketing Services with Increases in per Capita Income

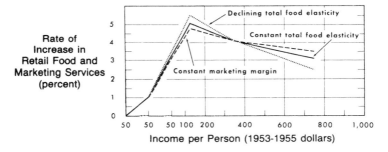

Source: Stevens 1965 (p. 59).

grow more rapidly. Note that the data in figure 12.4 are in 1953–55 dollars. Hence, now, because inflation in the value of the dollar has been about ten times, the peak rate of growth in retail food and marketing services is likely to occur when per capita income in 1986 dollars is in the thousand-dollar range and will occur at varied levels in different nations.

The Role of Marketing in Development

Theories about the role of marketing in development range from the induced development model to Rostow's view that government leadership in market development is crucial for the acceleration of national economic growth. We know generally that with economic development we can expect a long-term shift in marketing structure, from an immense number of small-scale agricultural market participants, who generally allocate their resources efficiently, to smaller numbers of large-scale marketing firms. The larger firms arise because they can take advantage of economies of scale through specialization or vertical integration, thereby reducing costs and enhancing performance.

THE INDUCED DEVELOPMENT MODEL AND MARKETING

The equilibrium and induced innovation approach to marketing development implies that sufficient marketing services will be developed as marketing people respond to changes in economic, technological, and institutional variables. Any of these changes could affect the returns realized in marketing. The potential opportunities for increased returns would be in the four major marketing activities identified earlier: storage, movement, processing, and management. Examples include investment in roads, leading to less costly truck transportation, and improved storage and processing of agricultural products. Also, any reductions in management costs, particularly those spent in acquiring knowledge of prices and product characteristics, will open up new marketing opportunities. These may occur, for example, when telephones and reliable government agricultural price information become available.

THE ROSTOW NATIONAL MARKETING STRATEGY MODEL

A more active view asks what economic, technological and institutional changes might be introduced that would encourage marketing people to respond with additional investment to increase marketing performance. This approach views government action as a major contributor to improved marketing and the acceleration of growth. Rostow, in his national marketing strategy, proposed that four major tasks should be accomplished: (1) a buildup of agricultural productivity; (2) a revolution in the marketing of agricultural products in the cities; (3) a shift of industry to the production of agricultural equipment and consumers' goods for the mass market; and (4) a revolution in marketing methods for such manufactured goods, especially in rural areas. Two of the four tasks concern marketing. Rostow judged that the action by government to use national resources to improve agricultural marketing and the marketing of industrial goods in rural areas would result in high-return investments for a less developed economy and would also contribute to a more desirable economic growth pattern.

AN INTEGRATED MODEL OF MARKETING AND DEVELOPMENT

The two views of the role of marketing in development presented above can be reconciled if we take a wider view of the agricultural production and marketing system. At any time, high returns from investment by government or the private sector in parts of the agricultural production or marketing system may be present. When opportunities for high returns from investment in agriculture are recognized, they may be acted on by either the public or private sector. With high economic complementarity, high returns in marketing may be obtained through carefully sequenced investments by the public and private sectors. The complementarity of public infrastructure investments, such as roads and privately operated trucks, is a good example. The Rostow model can also be seen as part of the induced development model by emphasizing that public sector actors are induced to follow his strategy when they identify productive infrastructure and other investments for public resources. Thus, a variety of patterns of investment of government resources in roads, communications, storage, transportation, and processing, to accelerate growth in less developed nations is observed. Some, of course, especially when viewed with hindsight, have provided low or negative returns to the economy, due to poor planning and judgment, or other reasons. Much infrastructure investment can only be accomplished by government. But assuming a competitive marketing environment, government investments in marketing will often have a lower level of performance than similar investments by the private sector, due primarily to the different incentives for productivity.

Evaluating Market System Performance

Understanding the shortcomings of the perfect competition model of marketing leads to the need for a more comprehensive framework for analysis of market performance. Analysis of marketing is then able to shift from the static economic assumptions required by the theory of a perfect market to a more realistic, dynamic theory, in which changes in marketing performance are weighed against other socially desired objectives.

Limitations of the Perfect Competition Model of Marketing

The neoclassical economic model of a perfect market includes a number of ideal characteristics, which are seldom present. They are (1) a large number of sellers; (2) a large number of buyers; and (3) all buyers and sellers having perfect price and other information. This model tends to focus on the behavior of prices. People using this model assume that if prices are responsive, marketing system performance is good, without looking at marketing costs or other performance indicators, such as the distribution of services among income groups. Critics have pointed out also that researchers using this model often make recommendations for change that would lead to more perfect markets but do not include estimates of the costs of removing the identified market imperfections. In addition, those using the model often assume a static socioeconomic environment and thus accept as given the institutional and technological conditions affecting the market. By not viewing marketing in a developmental context, we miss important opportunities for actions to increase marketing performance.

The Environment-Behavior-Performance Model

The comprehensive environment-behavior-performance framework for analysis of agricultural marketing presented by Shaffer (1980) includes the needed technological, institutional, and cultural variables affecting marketing performance as well as the powerful neoclassical economic tools (see table 12.2). Environmental variables include all the economic and social variables

Table 12.2. Environment-Behavior-Performance Framework for Analysis of Food System Organization and Performance

Environment →	Behavior →	Performance
Physical environment; social, political, and economic environments; including prices and institutions, technology transformation functions, industrial structure, distribution of assets, rights and regulations, including taxes and subsidies, sanctions and constraints, and individual opportunity sets, present and future	Multiple goals, satisficing, bounded rationality, selective perception, adaptive behavior, learning and search processes, strategic techniques and standard operating procedures, perceptions, and preferences	Changes in the social, political, and economic environments; changes in production and employment and the distribution of costs and benefits; changes in perceptions and preferences

Source: Based on Shaffer 1980 (p. 312).

that affect the operation of the marketing industry and individual firms, such as the usual structural elements—the number and size of competitors, input suppliers, and purchasers. Other environmental variables affecting a firm's marketing operations include the system of rights and regulations present in the society, formal and informal, including property rights, enforcement procedures for contracts, taxes and subsidies, perceived social and political pressures, barriers to entry, and cultural values and beliefs (ideologies) about acceptable behavior and possible sanctions. The environment also includes the limited inventory of technologies and institutional arrangements available to the social system for storage, transportation, processing, and other marketing activities.

Specific measures of market environment include seller and buyer concentration ratios. Concentration ratios are the share of total economic activity, as measured by gross sales or other indicators, of the four largest, or the ten largest, firms. Barriers to entry are defined as factors that prevent new firms from competing, including large capital requirements, control of key inputs, product differentiation, established brand name products, patents, and copyrights.

Behavioral variables measure what individuals and organizations do in a given environment. Individuals are assumed to "search narrowly selected portions of the environment and identify patterns of behavior consistent with their perceptions . . . which will satisfy them" (Shaffer 1980, p. 312). These behaviors include nonprice competition, which emphasizes both quality differences and advertising expenditures.

Performance variables include (1) total production (gross sales, value added); (2) the marketing margin; (3) productivity (technical efficiency); (4) pricing efficiency; (5) price level and stability; (6) consistency in regional and vertical pricing; (7) the nutritional quality of foods; (8) profit margins; (9) investment rates; and (10) the amount of research and product development. The meaning of most of these performance measures should be easily understood; however, productivity and pricing efficiency may need clarification.

The productivity of marketing refers to the output to input ratios of the firm or industry, often expressed as sales divided by the value of resources used in storage, transportation, processing, and management. Pricing efficiency measures the extent to which needed adjustments in production methods and the related reallocation of resources in the marketing system are completed with a minimum time lag in response to price signals. Pricing efficiency is often facilitated through the use of standard grades for agricultural products. Pricing efficiency also refers to the relations between the prices for a product in markets separated in time, space, and form. Thus, in a price efficient market, the price for an agricultural product at that time would not exceed the price in a previous period by more than the cost of storage. Markets in different places would exhibit price efficiency if the prices for the same product differed by no more than the cost of transferring the product from one market to another. And similarly, it would be efficient if the price of a processed product differed from the price of the raw product by no more than the cost of processing.

Note that use of the environment-behavior-performance framework enables a flexible analysis of marketing problems, as it does not include predetermined concepts about the desired state of a marketing system by assuming the criterion of the perfect market model. Instead, the model requires that socially set performance objectives be identified to establish evaluation standards. Research is then undertaken to identify factors that prevent desired performance and to find ways in which the system might be improved, along with estimates of the cost of making the changes in the system. Note also that this model of marketing includes learning loops, as structure affects behavior and performance modifies structure and behavior.

Facilitating Agricultural Input Marketing

The challenge of creating entirely new input flows to farmers is often not appreciated. As the stream of new inputs produced in nonagricultural sectors of the economy grows, marketing systems are induced to provide these inputs to farmers. The new inputs complement and replace traditional, locally obtained, lower productivity inputs, such as manures and locally produced agricultural tools and equipment. In traditional areas, agricultural factor markets hardly exist, as marketing people in these areas have had little experience in supplying new agricultural inputs, which usually embody a more complex technology. Thus, the input marketing situation contrasts sharply with product marketing, in which there is much local experience.

Traditional agricultural product marketing units and retail stores are often slow to undertake the marketing of agricultural inputs. This observation led Ruttan (1969, p. 94) to state that, although marketing people in traditional marketing channels in less developed nations are usually effective in transmitting price and quality information about common agricultural products, they may be inexperienced and poor transmitters of the technical knowledge required for productive use of new inputs. Farm productivity is decreased when needed technical information is lost in the marketing channels during the transfer from input producer to farm purchaser. L. P. DeGuzman pointed out other differences between agricultural inputs and many other retail products. He contrasted the product characteristics and technological knowledge demands of a bag of fertilizer and a soft drink. For the soft drink, no new technological knowledge is required to use it successfully; satisfaction is instant, not four to eight months later; the risk of not obtaining satisfaction is very small; and the unit cost is low. Also, sales of a soft drink over the year are fairly constant, not limited to a few weeks. And finally, the benefit of a soft drink is known, whereas the return from the fertilizer, an intermediate input, depends upon weather and uncertain product prices months later (see Ruttan, pp. 94–95).

The unknown and often highly technical nature of the new inputs produced outside of agriculture presents farmers with the need to acquire accurate information about them in order to reduce uncertainty about the returns from their use. A conservative market economy approach would place the responsibility for learning about the new inputs entirely on farmers and private input suppliers. However, with national goals to accelerate agricultural development, governments of both more and less developed nations have undertaken to speed the use of more productive technology and institutional arrangements in agriculture through such means as government-supported public information and agricultural extension systems. Relying solely on a free market in these circumstances can lead to long delays in adoption, especially when significant risk is involved. Free markets can sometimes cause disasters. For example, the performance of new inputs may be reduced through adulteration, as in the case of fertilizers, seeds, and pesticides. When these new inputs provide low returns and farmers suffer, the adoption of more productive inputs by farmers can be set back many years.

Biological Inputs

The complexity of establishing effective input production and marketing systems for biological inputs is illustrated by seeds. Similar issues arise in developing the input supply systems for other modern biological inputs, such as improved animal feed mixes, artificial insemination, and veterinary services. The shift from seeds saved by farmers from crop to crop to the purchase of improved seeds illustrates the input marketing challenge. This change requires the development of an entirely new input production and marketing system. And if hybrid seed is used for cross-pollinated crops, farmers have to buy new seeds each year, because saved hybrid seed yields poorly. To accelerate the availability of more productive seeds and other plant materials, the government may become involved in at least five ways: (1) seed multiplication; (2) seed certification; (3)

seed distribution; (4) quarantine and other seed disease control; and (5) producer subsidies to encourage the production and use of more productive seeds.

Seed multiplication starts with a small amount of breeders' seed, or basic seed, obtained from plant breeders. The initial multiplication steps must be very carefully controlled to obtain highest yields and to assure viability and purity. A foundation seed is then produced, often on a few large private or government farms so that sufficient control can be maintained to assure purity and viability. In the final steps of multiplication for farmers' use, a large number of the better farmers in the different producing regions are organized to produce the seed needed in the next production cycle. The crop acreage required for seed production can be as much as 1 to 2 percent of the total acreage of the crop when nonhybrid and synthetic hybrid seeds are used. When hybrid seeds are used, which have to be purchased every year, up to 4 or 5 percent of the total cropped acreage must be planted for seed production. Thus, seed multiplication alone is a considerable organizational challenge.

Assuring seed purity, germination, and quality at the retail level is an additional challenge. In competitive free market environments, where seed companies have established reputations for high quality, brand name labeling of the seed variety may be sufficient to assure farmers of high quality seed. Where private companies deliver high quality seeds to farmers at reasonable prices and in a timely way, government and quasi-government organizations usually cannot match their performance. In less developed nations, however, where few if any reputable seed companies have been induced as yet, some government involvement in the delivery of high-quality seed to farmers may be necessary. Such involvement may be an inspection, certification, and enforcement system; or the designation of a reliable independent organization for seed supply, such as a crop improvement association. A certification process may involve inspection of growing and processing conditions and testing for germination and purity. Unsealed, uncertified seed containers tempt some sellers to substitute or mix in poorer quality seeds to make a higher profit. However, government subsidies for the production and distribution of seed are likely to make it impossible for other potentially competitive seed producers and distributers to arise. Hence, the use of public funds and public administrative talent to subsidize seed production is in the long run likely to be a low-return use of government resources, except under special circumstances (see also Douglas 1980; Wortman and Cummings 1978, chap. 12). With respect to other policies for biological inputs, quarantine to control the spread of disease is usually an essential government function.

Chemical Inputs

The establishment of input marketing systems that enable farmers to obtain productive pesticides and fertilizers is also a complex process. Pesticides and fertilizers represent high-technology products that, if applied in the right way, at the right time, and in the right location, can bring high returns to farmers. If stored too long or misapplied, they can simply add to costs—or worse, endanger the health of farmers, consumers, and other life.

The marketing of pesticides and herbicides to farmers is particularly complex, as many of these new chemicals require five to ten years to be developed and tested for effectiveness and safety. Therefore, there are usually large economies of scale in development, production, and marketing. Hence the basic chemicals for these products are likely to continue to be produced by large international chemical firms. Thus, in many medium-sized and small less developed nations, the marketing effort will focus on importation, local adaptive research, mixing, and packaging for farmers in different areas with different crops and growing conditions.

THE GOVERNMENT ROLE

Because pesticides can produce such high returns if used correctly but present risks of injury to producers and consumers, governments have an incentive to facilitate their use at acceptable risk levels. In most countries, governments become involved in the control and regulation of pesticides and herbicides, starting at the import level and often reaching to the farm. These considerations suggest that adaptive research and effective extension work by small numbers of highly qualified individuals will be required in each major agricultural area, both to obtain high returns from these chemicals and to keep risks to persons and the environment acceptably low. Wortman and Cummings (1978, p. 354) recommended that government roles should include (1) field testing to develop recommendations for farmers; (2) regulating of manufacture and importation; and (3) supporting the growth of decentralized delivery systems for materials and needed application equipment in order to assure local availability of approved pesticides and herbicides on a timely basis, in packages of appropriate size, with needed information for proper use.

To what extent should government be involved in pesticide and fertilizer markets? Given the highly varied levels of agricultural development and socioeconomic conditions in less developed nations, effective government roles in input supply will vary greatly. Attempts in the 1950s and 1960s in nations such as Pakistan to have government be the sole channel for fertilizer sales to farmers slowed the growth of the fertilizer industry after the initial stage of trials on farmers' fields had been carried out. Independent dealers and storekeepers, who have an economic incentive to sell more fertilizer and are not bound by government working hours and administrative constraints, are likely to outsell government salespersons if they have access to fertilizer supplies at competitive prices.

Some government activities can, however, greatly facilitate input supply systems. Minimum essential government marketing roles include (1) setting quality standards for grades of fertilizer; (2) requiring and enforcing container labeling to indicate contents; (3) requiring inspections of container contents to prevent fraud; (4) setting up an input price and quantity information system; and

(5) developing technically competent government oversight units. These units would have the responsibility of expanding access of agricultural inputs to farmers through such activities as seeking changes in legislation, setting import and production policies and regulations, and monitoring environmental impacts, including water quality.

Government price interventions in fertilizer markets range from setting price ceilings to fixing prices and margins at each stage in the marketing system. Because of the dynamic nature of the development process, the latter approach faces the almost impossible task of continual updating in order to prevent the accumulation of economic disincentives. An intermediate approach to fertilizer price control that has worked at times in a number of nations is to set wholesale prices at a few major distribution points. Such a system can be used to lower fertilizer prices in areas judged to need additional stimulus for increased production and income. Attempts to set different fertilizer prices for crops in the same area usually lead to black markets, as the marginal returns to the use of the fertilizers may be greater on crops that are not supposed to get the low-priced fertilizer.

MARKET DEVELOPMENT

The explosive growth of fertilizer marketing that is likely as agricultural development accelerates was shown in chapter 8. The adoption of fertilizer-responsive seeds can cause profitable fertilizer use to increase from an average 5 to 30 kilograms per hectare to 600 or more kilograms per hectare (see table 8.3). Although chemical fertilizer use has risen rapidly in many less developed nations during the last ten years, it is still at less than 100 kilograms per hectare in many countries. In the next few decades, unless fertilizer prices rise greatly relative to the costs of other inputs, further large increases in the profitable use of chemical fertilizers can be expected, especially in better soil areas that have good moisture availability.

Wierer and Abbott (1978) observed three stages in fertilizer market development: the introductory stage; the rapid expansion stage; and the established, high-volume stage. In the introductory stage, sales strategy has to concentrate on the promotion and provision of technical advice. This strategy aims at creating an effective demand among farmers for fertilizers for crops not previously chemically fertilized. Only low volumes of fertilizer are likely to be purchased initially in any area, and the costs are high to provide information to farmers about fertilizer response and to set up fertilizer trials on farmers' fields. In this stage, public support for the information and demonstration work with farmers may be required before it will be possible for a fertilizer distribution system to operate without loss. The complementary nature of technical information, user learning, and profitable new input use is seen clearly in this case.

Once high returns to the use of fertilizer have been recognized by farmers, fertilizer sales strategies in the rapid expansion stage should include reducing prices and providing other services to cause further increases in volume so that smaller marketing margins are possible. In the high-volume stage, fertilizer marketing requires other strategies as farmers become more particular about input sales performance, including availability, price, and alternative forms.

Providing workable credit arrangements is an important fertilizer marketing activity that can accelerate use. Credit needs can be very large at all levels in the fertilizer production and marketing system as rapid increases in fertilizer flows occur. In a number of instances, low fertilizer marketing capacity—including particularly a shortage of storage and transportation, has forced low fertilizer factory production in relation to capacity, resulting in large losses in investments in fertilizer plants. One reason these problems arise is the ''tendency to overemphasize investments in facilities and to pay little attention to the need for operational credit and almost none to investments in management and know-how. Experience shows that the training of staff, the introduction of advanced management methods, and the availability of credit to purchase fertilizers . . . are as important as the physical facilities'' (Wierer and Abbott 1978, p. 103).

Mechanical Inputs

FROM ARTISANS TO FACTORY SUPPLY

The production and delivery of new high-return mechanical technology to farmers is the task of the farm equipment and machinery supply system. Studies of the development of farm equipment industries in Taiwan, West Pakistan, and India by Johnston and Kilby (1975, pp. 352–88) provide a perspective on the evolution of the mechanical input supply system in less developed nations that is consistent with factor endowments and stage of development.

In traditional agriculture, the village blacksmith and carpenter produced the mechanical equipment for agriculture that could not be produced by the farmer. With growth in demand for more complex equipment, larger scale urban workshops expanded. Through division of labor in casting, forging, machining, assembling, and in the use of power tools, these light engineering workshops developed increased manufacturing capacities. At first, imported equipment was modified (material transfer stage). Then the ability to produce machines from designs was attained (design transfer stage). In Taiwan, workshops were induced to make many modifications of designs. By the mid-1950s, for example, eleven different kinds of harrows were made; one of these had twelve regional variants, based on width, length, material, number of teeth, and shape of the blade, in order to adapt to local farm conditions. Later, larger equipment manufacturers with large financial and technological resources became established, often in collaboration with overseas manufacturers of the same kind of equipment, facilitating the use of patents and technological skills from more developed nations.

Material, Design, and Capacity Transfer. With artisans' production of tools and equipment for agriculture, very few individuals have the ability or resources to participate, unaided, in significant international transfer of material technology or in producing new machines from designs. Hence, at this stage of development, government aid can play a significant role in helping gifted craftsmen and experiment stations adapt mechanical equipment. Once the increased returns from the use of the new tools have been demonstrated on farms, demand will increase to stimulate the production and marketing of the equipment. If the development and testing have been carried out in the public sector, the provision of models of the equipment to local artisans can encourage increased production and local availability.

When significant numbers of light engineering workshops have become established, some research and development in the material and design stages of technology transfer will be undertaken by these firms. Yet their capacities for machine development may remain limited, and the public sector may still need to support machinery transfer, modification, and testing on farmers' fields. Later, when large agricultural machinery firms with strong international linkages have developed and capacity transfer capabilities are present, the public sector can continue to perform useful but more limited functions, such as evaluating machinery performance, setting safety standards, and carrying out farm equipment development that private firms have neglected.

Government Policies. Governments of less developed nations can facilitate the transfer, development, and marketing to farmers of more productive mechanical technologies by actions that encourage the international flow of tools, machinery, and machinery designs. It is particularly important to assure that no more than moderate tariffs apply to tools, equipment, parts, and raw materials needed by domestic equipment producers or farmers. Also, the rapid building of a domestic capacity for the creation of new farm equipment requires support for advanced training at home or abroad in engineering at the postgraduate level. In another arena, if monopolistic conditions develop in the equipment supply industries that prevent progress in agricultural mechanization, government intervention may be required. Governments may need to act, also, if large numbers of laborers are likely to be displaced by new mechanical equipment, because if there is little prospect for alternative employment, serious threats to laborer subsistence and social stability may arise. Under these special circumstances, governments may find it socially desirable to intervene in the market to slow the distribution of certain machines so that the rate of transition is moderated and less suffering occurs.

MARKETING CHOICES FOR INPUT SUPPLY

Alternative channels for input supply in less developed nations range from government systems, to producer-controlled cooperatives, to private distribution systems (see figure 12.5). In many socialist countries and in some less developed nations, governments, for ideological reasons, have set up exclusive input supply systems. Public sector agencies in some cases attempt to reach all the way down to the individual farmer through the use of local government input supply stores, supervised by extension or other personnel. The large involvement of scarce government resources and the usually monopolistic character of

Figure 12.5. Alternative Farm Input Supply Channels

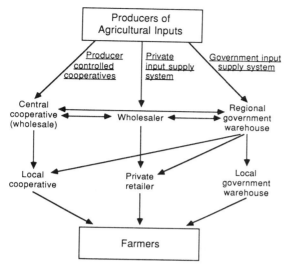

such input distribution systems raise serious questions about productivity and marketing costs in these systems and about alternative use of the social resources absorbed by these systems.

In some instances, producer-controlled cooperatives have provided effective marketing of such inputs as fertilizer and feed supplements. Private market channels provide a range of opportunities for the expansion of input supply systems. In some areas, traditional local product marketing channels may be aided to effectively supply modern agricultural inputs. In other areas, new private organizations with greater technical knowledge may be required to supply these inputs successfully. However, monopolies and collusive practices of private input supply firms also slow the growth of agricultural production.

The varied effects of government intervention in input production and marketing are seen by comparing the way scarce inputs are rationed by different marketing systems. Economic theory indicates that the highest national returns from new, scarce, high-return inputs would be obtained if the inputs were progressively distributed through a competitive marketing system. The initial price for new inputs would be set high by producers and marketing firms to cover development costs and to enable high enough profits to expand production and marketing. Then, as competition increased and production and marketing capacity expanded, the price would decrease. Under this pricing sequence, in the early introduction period only those farmers who could obtain a profit at the initial price would purchase the input.

For various reasons, this theoretically sound pricing and marketing approach for new high-return agricultural inputs is not often followed. For example, a government may fix the price of a new input much below its marginal return on many farms. Then, as the demand is very large relative to the supply, some kind of rationing system arises. Instead of letting the market do the rationing through price, a government may set up an administrative rationing system of quotas and may become the sole distributer of a range of new agricultural inputs, such as chemical fertilizers or pesticides. In these circumstances, non-price rationing arises which almost always leads to black markets and corruption, which divert the low-priced inputs to selected farmers. To conclude, whatever input marketing arrangements are developed, some competition for the farmer's business is needed to encourage better input marketing performance.

Aiding Agricultural Product Marketing

Agricultural product marketing consists of assembling the product from producers, storing and processing as needed, wholesaling, and retailing. When competition is present in product marketing, firms are induced to seek investments that increase their productivity and reduce the costs of operation, or that increase product quality or product differentiation, so that the firm may obtain a higher price to cover the additional costs. If international trade and communications are not limited, a large array of potentially profitable, more productive, marketing technologies are available in other nations for importation and modification.

However, development

involves constant structural transformation of the rural and urban economy which leads to greater interdependencies among agricultural production, distribution and consumption processes. The most important marketing problems related to achieving the desired structural transformation are in the design and promotion of new technologies and new institutional arrangements which may be unprofitable or unavailable to individual market participants, but if adopted by all participants, could yield substantial system improvements. (Riley and Weber 1983, p. 322)

Thus, government may be induced to undertake these technological and institutional changes because net economic and social gains are seen. Examples of such actions include changes in legislation and administrative regulations affecting marketing, dissemination of price information, improved roads, central storage, implementation of standard weights and measures, and enforcement of contracts.

Increasing Marketing Performance

In low-income traditional rural areas, relatively little specialization in agricultural product marketing takes place. Family members often participate in marketing staple and specialized crops. As development proceeds, specialization in marketing occurs that enables reductions in unit costs through an increased scale of operation. Investments in more productive marketing technologies can increase income and, in competitive environments, reduce costs to consumers or provide higher prices to farmers. Economies of scale in marketing cause a shift from a large number of small sellers to a smaller number of larger, often more vertically integrated, marketing firms. Some vertical integration of marketing functions may result in lower costs or, under monopolistic conditions, increased costs and monopoly profits for the government agency or the private firm.

REDUCING STORAGE COSTS

The costs and effectiveness of traditional village crop storage technology are highly variable. In some cases, the cost is low but quality and possible loss due to pests is uncertain. Storage systems built of new construction materials and that use chemical pesticides have the potential of greatly improving storage performance for many agricultural crops, both on the farm and in the larger stores of marketing firms. One can see the range of the potential for increased performance in storage systems in estimates of losses of stored crops from different nations. The following losses were observed in stored crops over a twelve-month period: maize in Zambia, 90–100 percent, compared to a 0.5 percent loss in the United States; rice in Malaysia, at least 17 percent compared to a 0.5 percent loss in Egypt; and wheat in Nigeria, 34 percent and India, 8.3 percent, compared to 3.0 percent in the United States (Pimentel 1978, p. 191).

The challenge is to find new storage technologies that will provide high returns to investment by private or public firms. At any particular time, new, less costly technologies may not be available in a particular developing nation. Thus, Pimentel (1978, p. 156), in a study of storage technologies for millet in Mali, concluded that traditional grain storage costs were very much lower than the alternatives then available in West Africa (see also Pariser 1982).

REDUCING TRANSPORTATION COSTS

The revolution in transportation has been under way in most areas of less developed nations for some time. The shift from the very high costs of human load carrying, to animal, two-wheeled wagon, and finally to motor transport, caused vast changes in domestic comparative advantage among different regions and in international trade. Farm-to-market roads caused much more rapid development in many areas and often great increases in farm income. In traditional marketing in Africa, transportation may be the largest single marketing cost (Whentham 1972). In many low-income nations, all-weather roads still serve only small portions of the rural population. For example, 10 percent of the population of Tanzania was estimated to have access to all-weather roads in 1969 (Eicher and Baker 1982, p. 191).

The range in potential reductions in transportation costs that may be achieved is indicated by a 1974 study in Sierra Leone. Headload costs were estimated at $1.62 per ton-mile when a 150-pound bag of rice was carried six miles per day. On poor dirt roads, the estimated cost by truck was $0.16 per ton-mile, and on all-weather roads, $0.06 per ton-mile, or about 4 percent of the head-loaded transportation cost (Spencer, May-Parker, and Rose 1976, p. 45). A study of the impact of new roads on forty-six communities in the Philippines indicated an increase of 25 to 100 percent in the amount of major agricultural products sold and a decrease in transportation costs of 17 to 60 percent per kilometer. More stores and rice mills were also established following road construction (Santos-Villanueva 1966, p. 775). In another example, a 250-mile trip to market on foot by cattle in Colombia resulted in a loss of 176 pounds per animal. Transport by rail and boat to the same market also resulted in large losses, so that 12 to 20 percent of the beef produced never reached market. In this case air transport for the animals was found profitable (USDA 1970, p. 61).

The rapid growth in transportation of agricultural products that can be expected in many areas are illustrated by the Indian experience. During the ten-year period 1956–1965, rail tonnage of food grains increased 100 percent. Yet in 1965, the railroads were estimated to have handled less than one third of the grains marketed, so immense increases in truck transportation of grains are also likely to have occurred (USAID 1968, p. 6). In Thailand, Conley and Heady (1981) made global estimates of the impact of reductions in transportation costs on income. Using a national linear programming model, they estimated that a 30 percent reduction in transportation costs would increase net income in all five regions of the country an average of 6.4 percent, with an increase of 12 percent in the northeast region, the poorest and most remote area.[2]

TRANSFORMING TRADITIONAL AGRICULTURAL PROCESSING

As development proceeds, the art of traditional agricultural product processing carried out on farms is transferred into more specialized facilities that employ increasing amounts of scientific and technical knowledge. This occurs for two reasons. As per capita income increases, consumers whose opportunity cost increases for the use of their time shift their purchases to agricultural products that include more time-saving services. Thus, many additional processing steps are added by marketing firms, such as cleaning, cutting, canning, freezing, and more convenient packaging. And second, investments in specialized off-farm processing facilities are induced by the opportunity to capture economies of scale (or size) through the use of processing technologies that reduce unit cost.

The economic and income distribution issues that may arise in the transformation of traditional agricultural processing were illustrated by Timmer (1975) in a now classic article. The government of Indonesia was considering purchasing large modern rice mills with annual capacities of some 20 thousand tons of rice per year. At the time, an estimated 80 percent of the rice was processed by hand-pounding on farms; the rest was processed by small, fairly recently introduced, engine-powered rice mills with a capacity of 1,000 to 2,500 tons per

2. Another useful references on rural transportation is Carapetis, Beenhakker, and Howe 1984.

year. Timmer's analysis demonstrated that, given the relative cost of capital and labor in Indonesia, the small-capacity rice mill was the least costly technology even when the interest cost of capital rose to 24 percent. A government decision to construct large, modern rice-processing facilities would have caused an immense loss of employment in rural areas and would have resulted in much higher rice-processing costs.

In Sierra Leone, research was carried out to provide estimates of rice-processing costs that included the transportation costs of consumers associated with the different technologies. This study used a linear programming model (Spencer, May-Parker, and Rose 1976) which included five rice-processing techniques and ten production and consumption regions, as well as imports and exports. The analysis indicated the optimum mix of rice-milling techniques with their associated employment, capital, and foreign exchange implications. It also showed the effects of greater use of large mills, higher interest rates, and reduced rice prices (see table 12.3).

The base run (run 1) under existing price and other conditions showed that, in the early 1970s with transportation costs included, least-cost processing would occur with most rice hand-pounded. When modified costs and prices that reflected international prices were incorporated in the analysis (namely a higher unsubsidized interest cost for capital for the mills, a reduced internal rice price, and an adjustment in the exchange rate to make it more realistic), much hand-pounding continued to be included in the least-cost estimate for processing rice (run 7). The analysis also shows that losses in employment and wage income would be very much greater if subsidized capital were available to make the large capital intensive rice mills profitable (run 3). This analysis of potential major shifts in rice-processing technology, from traditional hand-pounding to powered processes, illustrates the kinds of marketing system changes that can be expected for many crops as the marketing system is induced to adopt larger scale off-farm processing technologies. [3]

Increasing the Productivity of Urban Food Marketing

With the rapid growth of urban populations—and especially the urban poor in the early stages of the economic transformation—reductions in food marketing costs could increase urban real incomes and improve nutrition significantly. Mittendorf (1978) has provided an understanding of the changing importance of different marketing channels and kinds of markets found in urban areas as per capita income increases (see figure 12.6). Public retail markets were found to decline and retail food chains to increase. Also, as incomes increased, separate urban wholesale markets grew in importance until direct shipment in vertically integrated wholesale-retail food marketing chains became more important. Knowledge of these expected changes can aid in decreasing urban food marketing costs.

---

3. Other product marketing references of value are W. O. Jones 1980; Kriesberg 1970; Bohannan and Dalton 1965; and ICRISAT 1985.

Table 12.3. Optimum Rice-Processing Facilities, Employment, and Income: An Example from Sierra Leone

Item	1974 Base	High Milling Percentage of Large Mills	Increased Interest Cost for Capital	Increased Interest, Reduced Rice Price, and Exchange Rate Modification
Run	1	3	4	7
Total costs (minimized; le million)[a]	8.45	6.38	7.40	7.73
Net foreign exchange cost (le million)	2.49	3.64	3.19	1.90
Rice imports (thousand tons)	5.06	5.90	2.07	
Rice exports (thousand tons)				
Hand-pounding (man-years)	40,807		11,615	35,757
Small steel mills (number)	110			
Large disc mills (number)				
Small rubber mills (number)	30	498	508	236
Large rubber mills (number)		36	16	
Total employment (thousand man-days)	12,278	197	3,647	10,789
Rural unskilled (hand-pounding)	12,242		3,484	10,727
Urban unskilled (mills)	1	34	18	2
Urban skilled (mills)	35	163	144	59
Total wages (le thousand)	4,810	216	1,527	4,243
Rural unskilled (hand-pounding)	4,774		1,359	4,185
Urban unskilled (mills)	1	35	16	1
Urban skilled (mills)	35	182	152	57

Source: Adapted from Spencer, May-Parker, and Rose 1976 (p. 57).
[a] Objective function. Processing costs + transport costs + rice import cost − rice export returns (to be minimized).

350

Figure 12.6. Changes in Food Retailing and Wholesaling in Urban Areas of Less Developed Nations During Economic Development

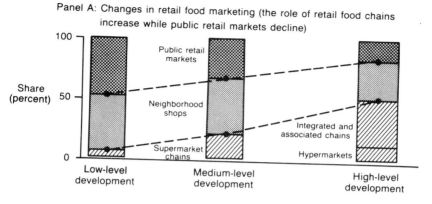

Panel A: Changes in retail food marketing (the role of retail food chains increase while public retail markets decline)

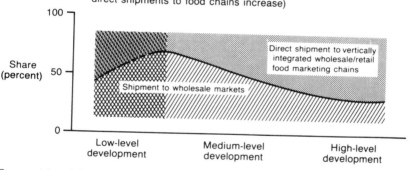

Panel B: Changes in food wholesaling (wholesale markets decline while direct shipments to food chains increase)

Source: Adapted from Mittendorf 1978 (p. 323).

Mittendorf also concluded that obsolete wholesale markets were prevalent in most cities with more than a half million inhabitants in less developed nations. In addition, he found that investments in wholesale markets tended to be wasteful due to inadequate planning, overelaborate buildings, inadequate layout of market stalls, excessive parking space, inadequate maintenance, and poor financial management. Too often, nominal market stall rental fees prevent recovery of capital or even operating costs. The recovery of capital by public bodies for alternative use could be aided by the promotion of wholesale markets that involved considerable financial participation by users.

Food retailing in urban areas of less developed nations includes three general categories: (1) traditional public retail food markets, or bazaars; (2) neighborhood stores; and (3) supermarkets. Traditional food markets tend to specialize in perishable foods and are estimated to sell more than 50 percent of urban food in many cities of less developed nations. Neighborhood stores and grocery shops tend to emphasize staple and dry foods, with the range of foods stocked increasing with neighborhood income. One strategy to decrease the marketing costs of neighborhood stores is group purchasing to improve bargaining for lower prices. Group purchasing may improve vertical coordination and lead to a larger scale of operation through retailer cooperatives or voluntary chains. Supermarkets and self-service shops developed first in higher income neighborhoods in many Latin American and Middle Eastern cities, but as yet they have shown relatively little growth in Africa and Asia.

As business and management skills increase, vertically integrated marketing systems in some commodity areas have considerable potential for increasing marketing performance. Although total vertical integration of marketing systems, whether private or public, makes possible a single management or control center that can issue directives to the different parts of the system, effective centralized management requires great skill and experience to achieve high productivity. Poor central management, especially in monopolistic situations, can lead to high costs and low or negative rates of growth. Lesser degrees of vertical integration can be achieved by other kinds of coordination, such as contractual agreements. More vertically integrated marketing systems may have the potential for high productivity and high social benefits if economies of size are possible, but these systems may also exhibit low productivity and poor social performance, especially if barriers to entry are high. Thus, continuing independent economic analysis of marketing systems, public and private, can provide a nation with the knowledge required to increase marketing performance.[4]

Government Roles and Policies to Increase Marketing Performance

Institutional Arrangements for Market Intervention

This section focuses on government interventions that have as their objective improving marketing services for consumers and producers. Wider political economy, or socioeconomic, analysis of alternative government interventions in agricultural marketing that have other objectives requires broader analysis of the different nations' political and cultural goals. Other government objectives may include, for example, gaining political control of food supplies and of the rural population.

Responsible governments will attempt to invest their resources in marketing interventions that will provide high returns to society. In attempting to identify high-return uses of government resources in marketing, we take the view that most governments in less developed nations have limited management tal-

4. Additional urban wholesale and retail food marketing materials include Harrison et al. 1974; Mittendorf 1976; Bucklin 1977; and FAO 1973, 1974.

ent and other resources and that a wide range of marketing experience, talent, and resources is available in the private sector. Thus, in most nations, the supply of private marketing services is likely to be quite elastic in response to greater demand. In these circumstances, the government should identify areas of intervention where the private supply of marketing services is not likely to be forthcoming. This can mean little government involvement in many areas of the marketing system and deep involvement in a few segments.

State interventions through institutions such as marketing boards and state trading corporations (sometimes collectively called parastatal organizations) take many forms. The kinds of government involvement were usefully classified into six categories by Abbott (1985, pp. 272–73), from least to most involvement.

1. *Advisory and promotional units.* These do not handle commodities. They provide market information and undertake research and promotion.
2. *Regulatory units.* These do not handle commodities. They establish and implement quality grades, packaging standards, quantity limitations on flows to particular markets, and licenses. They also inspect producers and traders to enforce controls.
3. *Price stabilization units.* These do not handle commodities. They negotiate prices for agreed periods with producers, wholesalers, and processors, with the objective of smoothing prices of export commodities through price stabilization funds, which subsidize commodity prices if international prices are lower and tax exporters if the international price is higher than the agreed upon price.
4. *Domestic commodity trading units.* These operate buffer stocks of commodities and buy and sell in the market, attempting to keep the prices of certain agricultural products within a specified range.
5. *Export monopoly trading organizations.* These concentrate export bargaining power, determine market flows, and may use a reserve fund to stabilize prices.
6. *Domestic monopoly trading units.* These implement and administer stabilization and pricing programs and provide large-scale marketing and storage facilities.

Abbott concluded that government buffer stock management tends to be supported by international aid agencies, particularly for food security purposes, but that governments of less developed nations have had difficulty controlling and operating these enterprises successfully. He also found that export monopoly parastatals have generally paid low prices to domestic producers, discouraging agricultural development, and have sometimes done a poor job of marketing. And finally, he commented that domestic marketing monopolies generally experience high marketing costs and cause large market distortions. (For a similar list, see W. O. Jones 1984.)[5]

The possibility that state interventions in agricultural product markets may increase marketing instability and depress food production is illustrated by the effects of government action in some African countries, where parastatal agricultural marketing has proliferated in societies with scarce financial, technological, and trained manpower resources. The instability in structure and functioning of these organizations has led to weak control of resources. Attempts at centralized decisionmaking in complex marketing systems has resulted in less coordination and more confusion, rather than improved performance. In her review of this African experience, Harriss (1979a) concluded that "there is not much evidence that State intervention does anything but accentuate the power of private traders over producers" (p. 279). This is because the interventions have often given private traders at local levels monopolistic powers, through licenses, to assemble products for state trading agencies. In this way, local competition for farmers' products is reduced.

Activities to Increase Marketing Performance

To improve the performance of agricultural marketing, the economic theory presented in this text and the judgment of many international experts on agricultural marketing lead to the conclusion that government actions should focus primarily on (1) supporting technological and institutional change; (2) increasing competition; and (3) improving marketing management. In addition, governments should develop such infrastructure as roads and communications that complement other government and private sector investments. These are summarized under eight headings.

REMOVING REGULATIONS THAT REDUCE PERFORMANCE

Ill-conceived and outmoded government regulations affecting marketing often reduce market performance, forcing consumers to pay higher prices. The removal of regulations that limit competition and provide opportunities for monopolies, or that otherwise inhibit marketing activities, often contribute significantly to improved marketing performance. An example of the value of withdrawing outdated regulations is provided by Indian experience, in which removal of interregional agricultural trade restrictions in 1977 increased agricultural productivity and production an estimated 1 to 15 percent, depending upon the crop. This change caused only minor shifts in regional cropping patterns (Von Oppen, Raju, and Bapna 1979, p. 173).

FACILITATING COMPETITION IN MARKETING

Where monopolistic practices are present, government may judge that encouraging the entry of competing firms would aid consumers and producers.

---

5. Reports examining government organizations involved in agricultural marketing include Abbott and Creupelandt 1966; Hoos 1979; and World Bank *World Development Report 1983* (chap. 8).

Figure 12.7. Potential Economic Gains and Losses from Marketing Monopolies

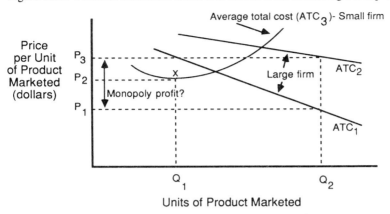

Units of Product Marketed

The usual losses and possible gains to society from large-scale monopolistic marketing firms is shown in figure 12.7. It shows average total cost curves for both large-scale marketing firms (ATC_1 and ATC_2) and small-scale firms (ATC_3).

The value of a large-scale monopolistic firm to society is dependent upon economies of size in production and marketing, the firm's pricing policies, its productivity, and its profits. If, for example, there were significant economies of size in the marketing of an agricultural product, the average total cost curve would continue to decline as the number of units of product marketed increased, as shown by ATC_1. This makes possible low costs and hence prices to consumers of P_1 or less. If, however, technological, institutional, and economic realities prevail that prevent the operation of large monopolistic firms that price their products at less than P_2, a number of smaller firms would be induced to operate at their lowest average total cost, point x, with a price of P_2. This cost is appreciably higher than the potential unit price P_1 that a larger firm could offer.

However, a risk of depending upon large monopolistic firms, private or public, is illustrated by the total cost curve, ATC_2. Without competition, the firm may add unnecessary employees and pay little attention to productivity, so that marketing costs rise and prices to consumers become P_3, much higher than would prevail if the smaller competitive firms were permitted to operate. Also, if the large monopolistic firm were able to keep its costs down to ATC_1, but charged a price of P_3, a large monopoly profit ($P_3 - P_1$ multiplied by the number of units sold) would be obtained by the large firm. If there were low barriers to entry and society's rules permitted private firms or other government units to operate in the same market, the appearance of new firms in a marketing channel would indicate one or more of the following: (1) that new lower-cost marketing technologies and institutional arrangements had been discovered by the new firms; (2) that the costs of the larger firm had drifted up toward P_3; or (3) that the existing firm was earning higher than normal profits.

This analysis leads to the primary policy conclusion that government should help reduce the barriers to entry in marketing channels by (1) facilitating access to credit, so that new firms have an opportunity to challenge the unit marketing costs of established firms; (2) helping establish competitors, which might be other private firms, cooperatives, or government-supported marketing units; and (3) analyzing the subsidies the established firms may be receiving, which provide them with unfair competitive advantages. Where government policy specifically prohibits competition, periodic reviews are needed of the productivity of monopoly units and of possible further reductions in marketing costs. These reviews present many difficulties, however, because alternative cost information is hard to obtain when other operating units have not had opportunities to test alternative marketing technologies and institutional arrangements.

ENFORCING STANDARDIZED WEIGHTS AND MEASURES

If purchasers can be confident that the scales, weights, and containers used for the measurement of agricultural products are accurate, then each partner in the transaction does not have to check measurements. Price is also clarified if it relates to a standard measure. These actions are especially important for price information to be diffused widely among potential buyers and sellers through electronic and other channels.

STANDARDIZING GRADES

Traditional local markets are described by Shepherd, Futrell, and Strain (1976) as places where buyers and sellers congregate:

The buyers and sellers passed from one lot of goods to another, comparing, contrasting, and making up their minds what each lot of goods was worth. An endless amount of time was spent in "haggling and bargaining" and in bringing the goods to the market in the first place and hauling them away afterwards; but since the physical goods, buyers, and sellers were all present . . . the necessary comparisons of goods, bids, and offers could be made without recourse to verbal description. The eye and the hand were adequate for appraising the different lots of goods, and the tongue and the ear were all that were needed to make and receive or reject the price of "this lot" or "that lot." . . . No description other than "this" or "that" was needed. (p. 82)

As development proceeds, transportation costs are reduced and agricultural products are shipped greater distances to markets. With the installation of the telegraph and telephone, information about prices in different markets can be obtained at little cost. At the same time, it becomes increasingly costly for buyers and sellers, whose wages are rising, to travel to the different markets to inspect the products lot by lot. Hence, unless markets are going to remain isolated with different prices, a way has to be found to describe accurately, with standardized grades, the nature of the various lots of agricultural products available. The grades have to be easily communicated in words through modern communication channels.

Standardized grades enable a very important shift in marketing operations, from sale by inspection to sale by description. Sale by description requires a usable and accurate language employing words, numbers, and perhaps other symbols that marketing people find convenient. As thousands of different lots cannot be described individually, they must be classified into a few groups and described by referring to a grade. The acceptance of such grades by market participants is often a slow process, however, and setting the grades used for agricultural products may require considerable research and negotiation with market participants.

Pricing efficiency is increased by grading for the following five reasons. First, grades usually provide a clearer description of products so that the price for the grade provides more information for marketing decisions. Second, grading reduces the costs of sales and enlarges the market area, bringing more sellers and buyers into the market for each product. Third, grades increase competition through improved accuracy of pricing. They also open the market to all, as grades are not privately owned, exclusive descriptions. Fourth, grading improves the allocation of agricultural products to the different buyers, as more buyers have greater access to the whole range of grades at different prices. And fifth, grading facilitates standardization and quality control, which increases sales, for consumers tend to reject products that have high quality variability (Shepherd, Futrell, and Strain 1976, p. 185).

REGULATED MARKETS

Governments may designate marketing areas as "regulated," where certain marketing practices are required, such as standardized weights and measures, fixed marketing charges and traders' commissions, open auctions, and standard methods of payment and grading. Note particularly that prices are not determined by the government in these markets, only the regulations about how transactions in the market should take place. Enforcement is the responsibility of a committee representing market participants, usually including farmers, traders, consumers, and the government. In India, the rapid growth of regulated markets resulted in larger markets replacing many small ones. Larger-scale and increased competition tended to reduce transaction costs and make agricultural prices clearer (Mellor 1970, p. 15).

COLLECTING AND DISSEMINATING TIMELY MARKETING INFORMATION

A significant cause of costly errors in marketing on the part of government and private market participants is a lack of market information. Marketing costs can be reduced by the development of a small group of persons who can accurately gather daily prices and estimates of volumes in major markets and disseminate them through press, radio, television, and government publications.

TRAINING MARKET PARTICIPANTS AND PROFESSIONALS

Although some technical and university training in agricultural marketing has been provided by governments in less developed nations, the usefulness of this training has often been hindered by lack of a practical, business-oriented focus that would include the following: (1) basic budgeting and accounting, needed for improved management of private or government units; (2) teaching materials relevant to marketing the major food and agricultural products in a particular country; and (3) field experience in how local marketing systems actually operate. Without practical training, students often find it difficult to successfully apply the general principles they have learned to specific marketing problems (Riley and Staatz 1981, p. 5).

ESTABLISHING UNITS TO ANALYZE AND PROMOTE MARKETING DEVELOPMENT

Specialists in these units would focus on the diagnosis of marketing problems and the analysis of marketing system performance. Their advisory and training activities would include (1) feasibility studies employing benefit-cost and other project estimates; (2) assistance in pilot operations; (3) aid in implementation of marketing changes and investments; (4) evaluation of marketing performance; and (5) the provision of technical and managerial training to market participants. Topics that generally require regular review by such specialists include (1) laws that may unnecessarily increase costs or reduce the range of foods handled; (2) sanitary regulations; (3) the effects of government marketing units on the economic health of the private sector; (4) price and tax policies; and (5) market fees and margins. Through analysis, specialists can identify and pursue specific higher return marketing infrastructure arrangements and marketing activities for government or private decisionmaking (see Harrison et al. 1974).

Summary

This chapter has drawn on the pioneering research in agricultural marketing in less developed nations which began largely in the 1960s. These studies have provided some basic knowledge of the economics of marketing major agricultural products in these nations. Considerable controversy continues, however, about the methodologies that were used and the interpretation of the results (see for example Harriss 1979b, pp. 197 and 213). The challenge is to develop better marketing research methodologies and to carry out many more studies of different marketing systems, so that poor and good performance may be more clearly identified. With this knowledge, public and private resources could be more sharply targeted on high-return interventions and investments in these marketing systems.

Important Concepts

Time utilities
Place utilities
Form utilities
Marketing management costs
Monopolistic marketer
Backward linkages
Forward linkages
Food marketing costs
Income elasticity of marketing costs
Induced marketing development
Perfect competition model
Environment-behavior-performance
   model

Concentration ratio
Barriers to entry
Performance variables
Pricing efficiency
Urban wholesale markets
Vertical integration
Marketing boards
Standardized grades
Sale by inspection
Regulated markets

Sample Questions

1. Explain the four economic functions carried out in marketing.

2. How would you measure the performance of a marketing system?

3. Outline two views of the role of marketing in economic and agricultural growth.

4. Why is the environment-behavior-performance framework better for evaluating the effectiveness of marketing than the perfect market model?

5. Give examples of three variables that can be used to evaluate each of the following: market environment, market behavior, and market performance.

6. What is pricing efficiency in a marketing system? How would you test for it?

7. Explain the problems facing the development of agricultural input flows to farmers in less developed nations.

8. Discuss two common problems in supplying mechanical inputs, such as tractor services to small farms.

9. What are the usual economic characteristics of staple food markets in less developed nations?

10. How can the productivity of product marketing in less developed nations be increased? Be specific.

11. What actions can government take to encourage reductions in marketing costs?

13

Changing Comparative Advantage and Trade Policies in Agricultural Development

> *Achieving free trade in all products, agricultural as well as non-agricultural, will not bring the millennium; poor countries will not immediately, or even in the longer run, become rich as a result. . . . Achieving free trade is only one of a number of policy measures that governments can undertake to improve the efficiency with which their economies function, and thus increase the national welfare.*
>
> *—Johnson 1973, p. 226*

The complex relation between economic development and international trade has long been examined by development and trade economists. An important aspect of this relation is the role that agricultural trade plays in the process of economic development. Given the importance of agriculture as a major supplier of resources in most less developed countries, some economists have argued that agricultural trade plays a leading role in furthering economic growth by (1) providing the foreign exchange required to import capital goods and other manufactures needed to expand the farm and nonfarm sectors; and (2) stimulating greater efficiency and rapid adoption of more productive technologies within the context of a larger, international market. Others, more pessimistic about the role of trade, have argued that less developed countries' dependence upon agricultural and raw materials exports, products that often have low price and income elasticities of demand, would lead to low growth and economic stagnation. Proponents of this view have urged these countries to implement import substitution industrialization programs, which have discriminated against the (largely agricultural) export sector and encouraged domestic production of industrial goods.

Few countries rely solely on the "free market" to determine their trading opportunities. The import substitution industrialization development strategies followed by many less developed countries after World War II required officials in these countries to adopt trade policies involving government regulation of international trade. Government intervention became necessary to ration foreign exchange earnings and to ensure that the levels of imports and exports were consistent with import substitution goals. To accomplish this, trade policy instruments that alter the domestic prices of goods, or that restrict the amounts that can be traded, have been implemented. However, government officials in countries following a more export-oriented growth path have also intervened in the trade sector to deal with periodic shortages of foreign exchange and to achieve domestic policy objectives, such as assuring low and stable prices to consumers for food and other agricultural products. Government interference with a country's trading opportunities reduces the gains achievable from trade in most cases and, therefore, the contribution that trade can make to the development process.

The Role of Trade in Agricultural Development

An examination of trade data shows that the importance of trade in generating national income (as defined by gross domestic product) varies widely among less developed countries. Exports of goods and services ranged from 95 percent of total income in 1983 in Hong Kong to lows of 8 and 6 percent, respectively, in Brazil and India. Income generated by trade ranges from about 20 to 60 percent in other less developed countries.

What role does trade, and more specifically agricultural trade, play in the economic development process? The positive view of trade, which is attributable to the classical and neoclassical economists in the nineteenth and early twentieth centuries, is that economic growth can be transmitted through trade. This theory of international trade shows that a country can, through trade, increase the level and types of goods available to its citizens and thus raise its real income. The classical model of development is one in which a less developed country produces agricultural and other primary products for an expanding export market and imports manufactured goods.

There were two leading ideas in the classical economic theory about how less developed countries' exports of agricultural and other primary products could lead to economic development. Adam Smith argued that international trade contributed to economic development by providing a market for the output of surplus resources that would otherwise remain unused. This is the vent for surplus theory of international trade. Smith assumed the existence of idle land and labor before trade, and that trade would raise the level of economic activity by using excess resources to obtain imported goods and services. Trade contributed to economic development in this model by raising the level of production and expanding the goods available to a country via imports. Trade was also seen as a dynamic force for development, as it widened the extent of the market, promoted increased specialization of labor, and encouraged technological innovation, which in turn would lead to continuous improvements in worker productivity and income.

Smith's theory was modified by the theory of comparative advantage, which explained not only the benefits of trade but the fundamental reasons for trade, as well. This doctrine, which is examined in the following section, emphasized not the use of surplus resources but the benefits of specialization in production and the international exchange of goods. The gains from trade that emerge from this model stem from a more efficient allocation of a given set of productive resources. Hence, with trade and no increase in resources and employment, output, consumption, and real income are higher than in the absence of trade.

Based upon the experience of the nineteenth century, economists considered trade based upon exports of agricultural and other primary products to be an engine of growth for less developed countries. The classical and neoclassical economists recognized that international trade, which increased in volume tenfold between 1850 and 1913, was also important in fueling economic growth in the industrial countries during the nineteenth century. They considered that the expansion of Western Europe's, and in particular Great Britain's, demand for food and raw materials during this period provided the impetus for development in the United States and in other temperate zone countries. Trade induced growth through an expanding demand for primary products, a demand fueled by economic growth in the more advanced industrial countries. This engine of growth concept was restated more recently by the Nobel Prize-winning economist W. Arthur Lewis (1980): "The rate of growth of output in the developing world has depended on the rate of growth of output in the developed world. . . . The principal link through which the former control the growth rate of the latter is trade. As MDCs [more developed countries] grow faster, the rate of growth of their imports accelerates, and LDCs [less developed countries] export more" (p. 555).

This mechanistic link between less developed country exports and the rate of growth in the more developed countries has been disputed by Riedel (1984), at least for more recent periods. Riedel's research showed that in the 1960s and 1970s there was no stable statistical relation between real income in more developed countries and the volume of less developed country exports. The absence of a strong link between income growth and less developed country exports is attributed to the changing structure of less developed country trade. According to Riedel, changing comparative advantage has led less developed countries to diversify their exports from primary products to manufactured goods that compete with goods produced in more developed countries. This has meant that access to a wide range of more developed country markets, and not just raw material markets, is now a more important determinant of less developed country export growth than economic growth in more developed countries alone.

The Theory of Comparative Advantage

The comparative advantage principle states that mutually beneficial trade may be possible between two countries whenever there are differences in the relative costs (prices) of goods in the two countries. Trade allows a country to specialize in the production of the goods in which it is a relatively low-cost pro-

Table 13.1. Production Possibilities for Two-Country Trade Example[a]

Production Possibility	Less Developed Nation		More Developed Nation	
	Coffee Units	Steel Units	Coffee Units	Steel Units
a	0	10	0	30
b	10	8	2	28
c	18	6	4	24
d	24	4	6	18
e	28	2	8	10
f	30	0	10	0

[a] Note changing internal price ratio.

ducer and to import the products for which the country is a relatively high-cost producer. Specialization in production and trade permits higher real income in both nations than would be possible without trade.

These benefits of trade and its potential contribution to economic development are illustrated in the following example. Two countries, a less developed country and a more developed country, are compared. Production costs for two goods produced in these countries, coffee and steel, differ between the two countries for various reasons, including climate, labor costs, and the manufacturing skills of labor. We assume that resource availability and input costs are fixed.

The production possibilities open to the two countries before trade are shown in table 13.1. Each country could choose to produce any of the production mixes, as shown by production possibilities *a* to *f*. Assuming consumers in each country demand some of both goods, an intermediate production possibility, for example possibilities *b* through *e*, might be chosen in each nation. If, for example, the less developed country chooses production possibility *c*, and the more developed country also chooses production possibility *c*, the total output of both countries together would be twenty-two coffee and thirty steel units before trade.

If each country were to specialize in its comparatively more advantageous product, both countries could gain from trade. In this case to gain one additional unit of steel, the less developed country has to give up four units of coffee (movement from production possibility *c* toward *b*). In contrast, the more developed country would have to sacrifice three units of steel to get one more unit of coffee (movement from possibility *c* toward *d*). Thus, the less developed country could gain if it could buy a unit of steel for anything less than four units of coffee; and the more developed country would gain if it could buy a unit of coffee at anything less than three units of steel. Therefore, for voluntary trade to take place, the terms of trade, or the exchange ratio between coffee and steel,

Figure 13.1. Comparative Advantage and Gains from Trade in Less Developed Nations

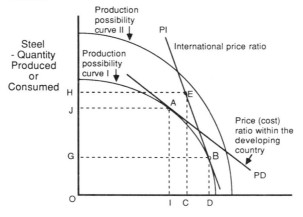

Coffee - Quantity Produced or Consumed

must fall somewhere between these two extremes. At an exchange ratio of say, one unit of steel for one unit of coffee, the less developed country produces one unit of steel indirectly at a domestic resource cost equal to a quarter of the pretrade domestic cost of making a unit of steel. Similarly, the more developed country gains because it can obtain coffee at one-third the pretrade domestic cost of producing a unit of coffee. If, for example, the less developed country moved to production possibility *d* and the more developed country moved to production possibility *b*, and they traded four units of coffee for four units of steel, the less developed country would have two additional units of coffee and two more of steel compared with production possibility *c* and no trade; while the more developed country would get two more units of coffee and the same amount of steel. Total production in both countries would then be twenty-six units of coffee and thirty-two units of steel, greater than before.

The gains from trade and the principle of comparative advantage are illustrated in figure 13.1. The less developed country's production possibilities frontier is now represented by production possibility curve *I*. This frontier is made continuous by filling in all the intermediate production possibility positions. It shows changing internal relative costs as one moves along the frontier. Line *PD* represents the pretrade domestic price ratio of four units of coffee per unit of steel faced by consumers and producers in the less developed country. The equilibrium pretrade position is at *A*, where production and consumption of coffee is *OI*, and of steel, *OJ*. Now assume trade can take place at a price ratio of one unit of coffee per one unit of steel, as represented by the international price ratio *PI*. *PI* is steeper than the domestic price line, *PD*, because steel can be produced more cheaply than coffee in other countries. Thus, the less developed country has a comparative advantage in the export of coffee and in the import of steel.

Table 13.2. Absolute Advantage in the Cost of Producing Wheat and Steel

| Product | Man-Days Required to Make One Ton | |
	Less Developed Nation	More Developed Nation
Wheat	5	3
Steel	20	1

Assume additionally that the less developed country is a small trading country, so that its volume of trade does not affect the international price ratio, PI (the relative price of coffee to steel). If there is no net foreign capital inflow, the value of its exports must equal its imports. In figure 13.1, an assumed volume of coffee exports, *CD*, times the international price of steel in terms of coffee establishes the volume of steel, *GH*, which can be imported. At production point *B*, *CD* units of coffee can be exchanged for *GH* of steel, thus permitting consumption at point *E* in figure 13.1. Real income, an aggregate measure of the country's consumption possibilities, is higher after trade, since its citizens can consume more of both coffee and steel at point *E* as compared to the pretrade equilibrium consumption point *A*. The gains from trade for the country's trading partners can also be demonstrated in a similar way.

Even if a country is at an absolute disadvantage compared to another country in the production of a number of commodities, trade may still increase the income of both. This is illustrated by the example of two goods, wheat and steel, that the more developed country can produce more cheaply (with fewer resources) than the less developed country (see table 13.2). The reason trade still benefits both is that the relative cost of producing the goods in each country is different. In this example, if the less developed country wants an additional ton of steel, it has to give up four tons of wheat to release the twenty days of labor required to produce the steel. The more developed country has to give up three tons of steel to get the three days of labor required for an additional ton of wheat. Thus, despite the fact that the more developed country has an absolute advantage (requires less labor) in producing both goods, it would be better off if it could obtain one ton of wheat at a cost of less than three tons of steel by trading, say, one ton of steel for one ton of wheat. The less developed country would gain at this price ratio also, because it could obtain one ton of steel at a cost of only one ton of wheat, instead of at the domestic cost of four tons of wheat.

Since both countries benefit from trade, an important question relates to how the gains are shared. The greater the divergence between a country's before-trade domestic prices and the international prices realized with trade, the greater is the likely benefit from trade to that country. A large country (in terms of population, income, or production and use) is more likely to influence world market prices and thus cause the world price structure to be more in line with its pretrade prices. For this reason, the benefits of international trade to a large country might be relatively small. On the other hand, most less developed countries are small and can usually benefit from trade at prevailing world prices. Under certain circumstances, a country or group of countries may be able to influence posttrade prices in their favor and thereby capture the gains from trade at the expense of trading partners. (Trade intervention is examined later in this chapter.)

Note also that the principle of comparative advantage applies to regions of a nation. Thus, whenever the ratios of the cost of production are different among regions, there may be an opportunity, depending upon marketing costs, for interregional trade and an associated increase in income in both regions. The greater the differences in production costs, the more likely are the benefits from trade.

Changing Comparative Advantage

We have examined the economic benefits from specialization and trade due to comparative advantage using an example of the gains to two economies with given static production possibilities. The benefits from trade can also change or modify a country's internal cost structure over time and, thereby, expand its production possibilities frontier. The new production possibility curve *II* in figure 13.1 illustrates these benefits by its outward shift from the original production possibility curve *I*.

Classical economists also concluded that there were two indirect effects from trade, which could cause a dynamic process of continued development and change in production structure. First, by widening the extent of the market, trade would promote the specialization of labor and the adoption of improved production processes. Second, by allowing countries to obtain high-payoff inputs and capital equipment from other nations, trade also contributed to increased worker productivity. These cumulative productivity improvements would enable movement to higher national production possibility curves and cause continuing income growth.

Although the comparative advantage model is sometimes criticized as static, economists (for example, Abbott and Thompson 1987) emphasize that cumulative productivity changes and economic growth induced by trade, as well as other factors, can lead to changes in a country's production structure and, therefore, its comparative advantage. In the early stages of development, a country's comparative advantage is primarily determined by its endowment of land, unskilled labor, and traditional technologies. In the long run, a country's comparative advantage has little resemblance to that determined by the original factor endowment, as illustrated in the extreme by Hong Kong and Singapore. As a country imports high-payoff goods and invests its scarce resources among competing sectors and projects, its stock of human and physical capital changes, altering its factor endowment. The accumulated pattern of investment becomes the main determinant of comparative advantage.

The changing pattern of comparative advantage has been investigated by Balassa (1979) and Anderson (1986). Their studies show that, as a country develops, its export structure will change as its relative factor endowment changes. Balassa's research, which deals with manufactures, supports the stages approach to comparative advantage. His research shows that intercountry differences in comparative advantage, as defined in terms of relative export performance, are explained by differences in physical and human capital endowments. He found that the pattern of comparative advantage proceeds over time more or less continuously from unskilled, labor intensive products to skill intensive and physical capital intensive products. Thus, as an economy develops, the production possibilities frontier not only shifts outward to the right, it also becomes skewed toward the production of goods that were more costly to produce in the early stages of development. This is shown in figure 13.1 by the greater shift from curve *I* to curve *II* along the steel axis in relation to the shift on the coffee axis.

Anderson (1986) shows that, while agriculture may employ a declining share of the work force and eventually a declining absolute number of workers as economic growth proceeds, a country's comparative advantage in agriculture does not necessarily decline over time. He illustrates this using a trade model with three factor inputs—land, labor, and capital—between two countries, in which the pattern of comparative advantage between agriculture and manufacturing is determined by the relative endowment of land and capital in the two countries. As income grows and capital is accumulated, labor will be attracted to the manufacturing sector, which will expand relative to the agricultural sector. For any given rate of capital accumulation per worker, the speed of the adjustment toward manufacturing will be greater the lower the agricultural land endowment per worker. As the per worker endowment of capital increases, the comparative advantage within the manufacturing sector will shift toward more capital intensive activities.

With this model, Anderson explains the patterns of trade and growth among the more advanced less developed countries (Singapore, Hong Kong, Taiwan, and the Republic of Korea), other less developed countries located in Southeast Asia (Thailand, Malaysia, the Philippines, and Indonesia), and the United States, Canada, Australia, New Zealand, and Japan. Changing comparative advantage explained the fall in the share of agricultural and other natural-resource-based exports from Japan and the four advanced less developed countries. For Australia, Canada, the United States, and New Zealand, resource-rich countries, this share declined much more slowly. Primary export shares in the Philippines and Thailand, the most densely populated countries in the sample,

Table 13.3. Less Developed Countries' Exports and Share Imported by More
Developed Countries, 1955–1980 (percent)

Commodity	1955	1960	1970	1980
Share of Exports from less developed nations				
Food	36.5	33.6	26.5	11.3
Agricultural raw materials	20.5	18.3	10.0	3.6
Mineral ores	9.9	10.6	12.3	5.1
Fuels	25.2	27.9	32.9	62.0
Manufactures	7.7	9.2	17.1	18.0
Share imported by more developed nations				
Nonfuel exports	76.3	74.3	71.9	61.0
Food	79.0	77.7	74.0	59.2
Agricultural raw materials	74.3	67.8	64.4	59.0
Mineral ores	94.5	92.0	89.2	73.2
Manufactures	45.9	54.0	61.2	58.6

Sources: Riedel 1984 and United Nations 1983.

declined the fastest, as the share of labor intensive manufactured exports, such
as textiles, clothes, and footwear, grew rapidly.

The Trade Experiences and Opportunities of Less Developed Countries

Prior to and immediately following World War II, less developed countries' international trade largely followed the classical pattern. Agricultural and
raw material products were their principal exports, while manufactured goods
accounted for over 50 percent of imports. Many of these countries were also
dependent upon a single agricultural or other primary product export for generating foreign exchange. However, during the 1960s and 1970s, changes occurred in the structure of less developed countries' exports and imports that have
significantly altered this traditional pattern of trade.

The Changing Structure of Trade

The changes in the structure of less developed countries' exports, illustrated in table 13.3, reflect the shifts in comparative advantage of less developed
countries from the export of primary agricultural and mineral products toward
the export of industrialized products. From 1955 to 1960, food and agricultural
raw materials, minerals, and fuels accounted for over 90 percent of these countries' exports. The more developed countries were their major markets, accounting for over 70 percent.

During the sixties and seventies, exports of industrial products from the
less developed countries grew faster than their agricultural exports, resulting in
a decline in the relative importance of agricultural exports in these countries'

Table 13.4. Less Developed Countries' Imports and Share Exported by More Developed Countries, 1955–1980 (percent)

Commodity	1955	1960	1970	1980
Share of Imports by less developed nations				
Food	16.6	17.0	13.7	12.0
Agricultural raw materials	6.2	4.5	4.2	2.9
Mineral ores	7.1	7.6	8.1	7.0
Fuels	11.7	8.6	8.0	18.4
Manufactures	52.6	58.7	61.8	57.2
Share exported by more developed nations				
Food	54.1	58.7	62.1	63.1
Agricultural raw materials	31.0	45.0	44.8	49.9
Mineral ores	90.0	80.2	78.3	78.0
Fuels	18.7	12.8	13.4	8.2
Manufactures	90.2	84.2	84.2	81.1

Source: Riedel 1984 and United Nations 1983.

trade. Manufactures exports increased from approximately 8 percent of exports to 18 percent by 1980. Demand in the more developed countries played an important role in this export growth, as their share in the less developed countries' manufactures exports increased from 46 percent in 1955 to about 60 percent by 1980.

According to Riedel (1984), the doubling of the share of fuels in less developed country exports from 25 percent in 1955 to over 60 percent in 1980 largely reflects the Organization of Petroleum Exporting Countries' (OPEC's) administered oil price rises of the 1970s. However, the increased export share of manufactures reflects changing comparative advantage and three decades of industrialization. Four countries in East Asia—South Korea, Taiwan, Hong Kong, and Singapore—accounted for more than 60 percent of manufactured exports from the less developed countries in 1980.

When less developed countries' imports are examined throughout the 1955–1980 period, manufactured goods have remained the largest category, illustrating the importance of these goods for the development process (see table 13.4). Less developed countries' imports of manufactures have been overwhelmingly supplied by the more developed countries. The share of fuels in less developed countries' imports also increased in 1980, a reflection of the increase in oil prices during the 1970–80 period.

Shares of Different Products in Less Developed Countries' Agricultural Exports and Imports

Less developed countries' comparative advantage in production and export of tropical agricultural products is illustrated in table 13.5. For example, they are the major exporters of coffee, cocoa, tea, bananas, rubber, and jute. They

Table 13.5. Less Developed Countries' Shares of World Exports and Imports of Basic Agricultural Commodities, 1960 and 1981 (percent)

Commodity	Share of Exports		Share of Imports	
	1960	1981	1960	1981
Coffee	97	95	5	12
Cocoa	97	95	3	10
Tea	93	92	22	42
Sugar	78	40	22	43
Beef	19	19	6	19
Bananas	95	96	6	13
Fresh citrus fruits	41	73	4	16
Rice	73	59	70	74
Coarse grains	27	21	7	35
Wheat	8	5	43	56
Soybeans	1	17	9	39
Cotton	47	47	14	48
Jute	98	96	18	56
Rubber	95	98	22	27
Tobacco	35	41	9	17

Source: FAO, *Production Yearbook* and *Trade Yearbook, 1960* and *1981.*

supply over 90 percent of world exports of these products. Despite some less developed countries' successes in increasing exports of manufactures, a few countries are still dependent on a single agricultural export commodity (Colombia, coffee; Ghana, cocoa; and Mauritius, sugar) which account for over 60 percent of these countries' export earnings. Increases in less developed countries' export shares for tobacco, soybeans, and fresh citrus fruits during the 1960s and 1970s reflect the investments in agricultural production undertaken by these countries and their changing agricultural comparative advantage. Duncan and Lutz (1983) noted that less developed countries are also important exporters of some processed agricultural commodities, particularly grain mill products, refined sugars, animal oils and fats, wine, canned and preserved fruits and vegetables, and cocoa and chocolate confectioneries.

Dramatic increases in the less developed countries' import shares for sugar, beef, coarse grains, soybeans, cotton, and jute also occurred in the sixties and seventies. Higher incomes and changing dietary patterns in less developed countries have greatly increased their demand for these products. Increased agricultural raw material imports, such as cotton, jute, and tobacco, reflect the development of manufacturing and processing industries in many less developed countries.

Conditions Under Which International Trade Contributes to Economic Growth

While we have seen the economic gains achievable from trade, it is necessary to consider also the conditions under which trade can make an actual contribution to economic development. According to Myint (1984, pp. 227-28), the opportunity to trade provides potential gains that can promote economic growth only under certain circumstances. For instance, while trade enables a less developed country to import goods from others, the impact of trade on development depends on whether or not the country imports goods that are economically suitable for the development of the country. If the "wrong" goods are imported—that is, capital goods that produce final products not in accordance with a country's comparative advantage, or luxury goods that benefit only a few—then the potential gain from the availability of foreign exchange is reduced. The resulting imports will produce a lower than feasible national income, and economic growth will be slowed.

Others have argued that technological innovations and improved worker skills in the export sector will make a greater contribution to development if the export sector has strong linkages to the rest of the economy (Meier 1984, pp. 503-09). In some instances, exports from enclave sectors, such as from plantation farming or mining industries, have contributed little growth stimulus, because these sectors were isolated from other sectors of the economy. If the export sector has strong linkages, productivity gains will result in increases in employment and income-earning opportunities spreading to the entire economy.

The stimulating effect of trade on development depends on the extent to which foreign demand for less developed countries' exports is expanding, since increased export earnings enable these countries to purchase a larger quantity of critical imports. Growth in demand for these countries' exports could occur as a result of income growth in trading partners or through productivity increases that allow these countries to lower export prices and capitalize on elastic demand. Success in developing new exports and export markets through investments that result in changing comparative advantage can also lead to increased export opportunities and earnings from trade.

Critics of the classical development model have argued that slow growth in primary product demand would result in an export-led development strategy yielding insufficient foreign exchange for rapid development. They argued that, in the extreme, export dependence could lead to a situation of immiserizing growth, whereby a country becomes worse off after trade. This situation is more likely to occur (1) the lower the price elasticity of demand for less developed countries' exports; (2) the higher the income elasticity of demand for imports; and (3) the more the growth process is biased toward exports.

The immiserizing growth case is illustrated in figure 13.2. Production possibility curve *I* is the original pregrowth frontier for producing coffee and steel,

Figure 13.2. Immiserizing Growth with Free Trade

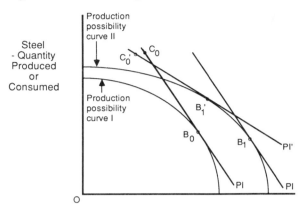

Coffee - Quantity Produced or Consumed

B_0 is the posttrade production point, and C_0 is the posttrade consumption point. At the international exchange ratio of coffee for steel, PI, the country exports coffee in exchange for imports of steel. Now suppose growth, from an increase in resource endowment or productivity, occurs and is biased toward the coffee sector, as represented by the outward shift to production possibility curve II. At unchanged international prices, this growth will result in more coffee and less steel being produced, as shown by the new production point B_1. However, at unchanged prices, an excess supply of coffee and an excess demand for steel will occur. Therefore, the international price of coffee must fall relative to the price of steel until a new production equilibrium is reached at B_1' on the new price line PI', which represents a decline in the price of coffee relative to steel. If PI' cuts above C_0, so that the country is able to consume more coffee and steel, the country is made better off by trade and growth. If PI' cuts below C_0, so that consumption might occur at C_0' (less consumption), the country is made worse off through growth and trade.

The immiserizing growth situation occurs because growth results in the less developed country's demand for the imported good, steel, increasing at a faster rate than its trading partners' demand for coffee. Thus, the price of coffee will fall relative to steel. If demand for coffee is also price inelastic, the decline in the coffee price will result in lower export earnings, since exports do not increase sufficiently to offset the price decline. The lower relative price received for coffee and the reduced foreign exchange earnings cause the consumption of coffee and steel to decline.

Empirical research has not supported the conclusion that export-led growth based on primary product exports leads to less developed countries becoming worse off through trade. For instance, Porter (1970) found that agricultural commodities in the post–World War II period behaved as if they were either price or income inelastic, but not both. Belassa's research also showed that trade can result in less developed countries' growth being skewed toward the products that are imported or more expensive to produce. In addition, the immiserizing growth scenario assumes that a less developed country is a large trading country, whose volume of trade influences the international price of its imports relative to its exports. In a later section it will be shown that under certain circumstances less developed countries could avoid this immiserizing growth situation by implementing trade policies that raise export prices relative to import prices. Nonetheless, in the following section we will see that pessimism about the export earnings of primary products has been a prominent feature in less developed countries' trade policies.

Managing Agricultural Input and Product Trade

Despite the apparent benefits of free trade, many less developed countries employ numerous measures to control the volume and composition of both agricultural and nonagricultural trade. Under a free trade policy, there are no artificial impediments to trade, and international prices translate into domestic prices. Trade intervention instruments place a wedge between the domestic and international prices of traded goods. There are several reasons for extensive trade intervention by less developed countries. Trade measures have been used on a temporary or permanent basis to (1) help implement import substitution development strategies; (2) alleviate shortages of foreign exchange; (3) help control inflation; and (4) raise government revenues.

Import Substitution

Following World War II, pessimism about the potential of agricultural and other primary products to generate foreign exchange, as discussed in the previous section, led a number of less developed countries to adopt strategies for import substitution industrialization. The aim of this policy was to substitute domestic products for manufactured imports by protecting, through trade and other policies, domestic industries that produced finished manufactured goods. In the view of the export earnings pessimists, it was believed that this policy would reduce foreign exchange requirements by substituting domestic products for imports.

To implement this policy, trade policy instruments were used to protect import-substituting industries by outright prohibitions on certain imports or by prohibitively high import tariffs. To subsidize imported intermediate capital goods and raw materials destined for use by the industrial sector, many less developed countries also maintained overvalued exchange rates. Under such a policy, the government sets the exchange rate for foreign currency in a way that enables domestic importers to pay a lower price (use fewer units of their own currency) for imported goods than would have to be paid if the exchange rate were free floating and thus adjusted to world supply and demand. For example, with an overvalued exchange rate, importers who want to buy foreign goods sold in dollars might have to exchange only ten units of local currency at a bank to obtain a dollar, instead of the fifteen units on the free market. An overvalued currency fosters an excess demand for foreign exchange, which is held in check by a licensing process for imports or for foreign exchange.

While subsidizing imports for the industrial sector, an overvalued exchange rate acts as an implicit tax on exports by decreasing the profitability of export industries relative to other opportunities. For instance, in the hypothetical example given above, agricultural exporters who sold their goods overseas for dollars would receive only ten units of local currency for their dollars instead of the fifteen units they might have received on the open market. Thus, an overvalued exchange rate lowers the amount of domestic currency earnings from exports. Since agricultural products have been a major source of exports from developing countries, overvalued exchange rates have taxed agricultural export producers in many of these countries.

Balance of Payments Controls

The General Agreement on Tariffs and Trade (GATT), the multilateral agreement that establishes the rules for international trade, explicitly recognizes that temporary balance of payments crises may require less developed countries to use temporary trade controls. Shortages of foreign exchange can arise from a sudden drop in export earnings, from a sudden increase in the cost of a key import such as food or petroleum, or from overspending by governments in the course of purchasing inputs required for fulfilling development plans and projects. For example, due to the decline in foreign exchange earnings from petroleum, in 1985 Nigeria subjected all of its imports to an import license, which was granted depending upon foreign exchange availability. In a different example, with the fall in its oil revenues in 1982, Mexico introduced a common trade management tool, the multiple exchange rate system. Under this policy, a lower rate of exchange was offered when Mexican pesos were converted to dollars for the imports the government wanted to encourage, and an exchange rate of many more pesos per dollar was used when the import goods were considered nonessential. The problem with many of these temporary trade controls is that, once instituted, they tend to remain long after the crisis has passed—and are even increased in later years.

Inflation Controls

Less developed countries often use trade measures to keep the prices of traded goods low or to prevent them from increasing. A country may wish to do this to assure the availability of sufficient supplies at low prices of essential foodstuffs or raw materials used by domestic industries. Consider the following examples. In the past, Brazil established a system of differential export taxes, which favored exports of soybean products (soybean oil and meal) over soybeans, to give traders the incentive to supply the local soybean-processing industry first before selling soybeans on the export market. In times of shortages, Brazil has also used export quotas, or export prohibitions on soybeans to ensure that the soybeans would be sold to the domestic industry rather that exported. Thailand, a major exporter of rice, has also taxed its rice exports and placed other encumbrances on exporters in times of short supplies, to provide lower rice prices to domestic consumers and to prevent prices from increasing suddenly due to reduced supplies. Export restrictions aimed at keeping domestic prices from rising and at reducing domestic shortages have not been limited to less developed countries, as is illustrated by the embargo placed on soybean exports by the United States in 1973.

Government Revenues

Export taxes on agricultural and other exports, as well as tariffs and other taxes imposed on imports, have been a common source of government revenue in less developed countries. A study by Goode (1984) showed that the importance of trade taxes in providing national revenue is inversely related to both a country's income and its degree of industrialization. For instance, in 1983 taxes on international transactions provided 46 percent of national revenues in Ghana and 29 percent in Zaire (down from around 44 percent in the late 1970s). In contrast, trade taxes provided only about 19 percent of revenues to the Republic of Korea, a more advanced less developed country, and less than 1 percent of revenues in the United States. The poorest countries tend to rely more on trade taxes than on income or sales taxes for raising revenue, because these taxes provide a convenient ''tax handle'' and are more easily administered.

Measures for Trade Intervention

Trade policy instruments used by less developed countries can be classified into two categories, price and nonprice measures (Balassa 1975).

Price Measures

Price measures influence the demand for traded goods by raising or lowering the prices that importers pay or that exporters receive for these goods. That is, importers and exporters might have to pay additional charges if the objective of the controls is to keep the domestic price of export goods low or to discourage imports. If, however, the intent of the controls is to increase exports or lower the prices of imports, they might have to pay less than the equivalent world price in terms of domestic currency or receive a payment to lower the foreign exchange cost of a traded good. The following three price measures are commonly used.

First, tariffs, taxes and other fees require traders to pay additional amounts to the government on exports or imports above the world price. Import tariffs raise domestic prices of imported goods. Export taxes tend to raise the prices of goods sold to foreign consumers and to lower the prices received for exported products by domestic producers.

Second, multiple and overvalued exchange rates require importers and exporters to change domestic currency for foreign currency at rates different from the market rate. An overvalued exchange rate subsidizes imports and taxes exports by requiring traders to exchange domestic currency for foreign currency at less than the market rate. Under a multiple exchange rate policy, the exchange rate may vary according to the use of the foreign exchange. For instance, exporters of a specific good may be required to exchange foreign for domestic currency at a lower than market rate, as has been required of exporters of cotton in Mexico and Egypt, for the purpose of keeping prices low to the domestic processing industry.

And third, export subsidies provide a direct payment to an exporter to encourage lower export prices and expanded export sales. Many countries use export subsidies to sell high-cost products on the world market at prices lower than equivalent domestic prices. Another example is a country that has an import substitution industrialization policy and whose industries have developed with import protection. These industries usually require subsidies to sell their goods on the international market even at world market prices.

Nonprice Measures

Nonprice measures establish permissible quantities of traded goods that, in most cases, are below what would be traded without the control. Nonprice measures that limit imports enable domestic producers (and importers) to raise domestic prices of the imported good. Nonprice measures that limit exports increase the supplies to the domestic market and force producers to lower domestic prices. Nonprice measures include the following five. (1) Export and import quotas are set that establish quantity limits within a certain period of time on the amount of a product that can be imported or exported. (2) Import or export prohibitions are decreed that make import or export of a product illegal. (3) Government permission may be required to import or export. In this case traders would be required to obtain import or export licenses. (4) The government may control access to foreign exchange. This is done by making distinctions among the prospective buyers and the foreign goods and services they wish to buy and giving foreign exchange only to some for certain purposes. Exchange control is usually associated with policies that create excess demand for foreign exchange, such as an overvalued exchange rate. With foreign exchange controls, the incentive for graft and political influence is great in decisions about who obtains the scarce foreign exchange. (5) Governments establish commodity marketing boards, which often have the sole authority to purchase goods from producers and to export and import.

Most less developed countries use a combination of the aforementioned measures to manage their international trade. However, each measure varies by the ease with which it can be administered by the government, its efficacy for regulating trade, and the impact on government revenue. Nonprice measures tend to be the primary means of regulating international trade in less developed countries, because they directly affect the quantity traded, in contrast to price measures, which affect trade through the price mechanism (Balassa 1975; Little 1982). Thus, nonprice measures are more effective for responding to balance of payments crises or other emergencies.

Government officials in many less developed countries have been reluctant to apply high tariffs and thus raise domestic prices of essential agricultural imports. For instance, tariffs on commodities such as wheat, rice, feed grains, and cotton tend to be nonexistent or quite low in less developed countries where imports play a large role in meeting consumer and industrial demand. Imports of these products, particularly wheat and rice, tend to be channeled through commodity marketing boards. On the other hand, tariffs on luxury or processed goods, such as processed tobacco, wine, and vegetable oils, tend to be much higher. Such tariffs serve both to raise revenues and to protect domestic processing industries.

Except in the rare instances when quota rights are sold to traders, quotas and other nonprice measures usually yield no revenue to the government. These measures yield "quota profits" to those traders granted import or export privileges. Quota profits accrue to importers who buy at world prices and are able to resell at higher domestic prices and to exporters who can buy at low domestic prices and resell at higher world prices. In some instances, however, traders must pay fees or bribe government officials to obtain import or export privileges, with the result that quota profits are captured by the government or by dishonest government officials.

Economics of Trade Intervention

Government intervention in international trade is criticized by economists because, in most instances, it reduces a country's ability to use its productive resources in ways that take advantage of trading opportunities. Economic arguments that justify government regulation of trade seek to demonstrate that such intervention is a means of achieving a higher real income than would be achieved under free trade. Most of these arguments are justified on the basis that private exporters and importers acting independently do not realize the same benefits or costs from their actions as are realized by the economy as a whole. (This is the market failure argument, discussed in more detail in chapter 14.)

Arguments Against Trade Intervention

The inefficiencies in resource allocation introduced by trade restrictions are illustrated in figure 13.3. An import tariff is the assumed instrument chosen for intervention. However, the effects of other instruments, such as an import quota or a tax on the export good, could be shown under certain circumstances to have identical effects.

Assume that, with trade, the less developed country is operating at equilibrium point *B* on the production possibilities curve, with the price ratio between

Figure 13.3. Impact of a Tariff on Income and Trade

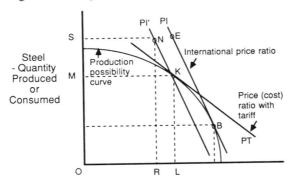

Coffee - Quantity Produced or Consumed

coffee and steel indicted by line *PI* and consumption by point *E*. *PI* is also the world price ratio, since we assume initially no constraints on trade. A tariff on steel is then introduced, which increases the domestic price of steel relative to coffee, as indicated by the new price line *PT*. Since the price of steel is now higher to home producers, a new production equilibrium is established at *K*, with more steel production (*OM*) and less coffee production (*OL*). The tariff does not change the world price ratio, *PI*, due to the assumption that a small country cannot influence the world price. However, since the domestic price of steel is now higher, national consumption and trade possibilities are limited by the new price line, *PI'*. So national consumption and trade can take place at, for example, point *N*, where *RL* of coffee is exported in exchange for *MS* of steel. The real income loss to society from the tariff is illustrated by the lower steel and coffee consumption at point *N*, as compared to the consumption levels achievable under free trade at point *E*.

Another important effect of the tariff is its impact on the export industry, coffee. As steel production expands, the prices of inputs used in both industries, like labor, rise. Since coffee is sold at the world price, exporters have no choice but to absorb any input cost increases. Thus, exporters as well as steel consumers bear the cost of the tariff (Clements and Sjaastad 1984). The effect of the tariff is to displace a lower cost foreign source of steel with higher cost domestic steel and to reduce both imports and exports.

Arguments for Trade Intervention

Arguments for trade intervention include the optimum tariff argument and the infant industry argument.

OPTIMUM TARIFFS

The proponents of optimum tariffs claim that a country can reap greater gains than those possible under free trade if it imposes the right export tax or import tariff. These gains are to be made at the expense of other trading countries by turning the terms of trade in favor of the tariff- or tax-imposing country. This argument pertains to a country (or group of countries acting together) who are sufficiently important in a market to affect the international price of a good. For this to occur, the foreign supply of imports or the foreign demand for exports must be less than infinitely elastic, and the potential for new entrants into the market must be limited. Under these assumptions, an import tariff would result in the tariff-imposing country reducing its imports, causing a fall in the world price of the import relative to the export good (measured net of the tariff) and thus turning the terms of trade in favor of the importing country. Similarly, an export tax would cause a drop in export supply, raising the world price of the export good relative to imports, and turning the terms of trade in favor of the exporting country. Although the volume of trade might be reduced by the imposition of the tariff or tax, the gain to the country per unit of trade would be increased, since both of these actions raise export prices relative to import prices.

There have been a number of instances in which less developed countries acting separately or together have used an export tax for the purpose of increasing their international terms of trade. For example, both Brazil and Ghana have used overvalued exchange rates that act as implicit export taxes to exploit their positions as dominant suppliers of coffee and cocoa, respectively. Facing inelastic export demand, these countries were able to shift the incidence of the tax to foreign buyers as international prices for coffee and cocoa rose in response to reduced production and exports. It should be noted that, while the country as a whole can be made better off, producers of the export commodities may be made worse off by such policies. Since less developed country governments usually pocket the extra revenues earned from the export tax, as has been the case in both of these countries, export producers often receive lower prices and sell less under the optimal tax policy.

Less developed countries have also attempted to increase their export prices and to reduce period-to-period export price variation by negotiating international commodity agreements. The usual approach to these agreements is for the exporting and importing countries to agree to maintain export prices at a certain level or in a specified range by controlling the quantity of the commodity coming onto the world market during a set time (Behrman 1984). In 1985, six international commodity agreements were officially in operation for agricultural products (coffee, cocoa, sugar, wheat, jute, and natural rubber). The coffee agreement assigned export quotas to member countries to maintain prices within a given range, whereas the cocoa and rubber agreements involved buffer stock purchases and sales to stabilize prices. The primary purpose of the sugar, wheat, and jute agreements was to exchange information, since they did not contain any economic provisions for restricting supplies.

International commodity agreements with economic provisions are criticized in principle for distorting international market prices. In reality, they have been rather ineffective in controlling world market prices. The coffee agreement has been the most successful in raising export prices, but this has been due more to Brazil's policy of restricting output than to the workings of the agreement. The histories of commodity agreements show that they have been relatively unsuccessful in raising prices both because they are difficult to police and because they have not been sufficiently flexible to allow for increased market shares for new or lower cost producers.

The optimum tariff argument has also been extended under certain circumstances to a small country that cannot affect international prices. Jabara and Thompson (1982) argued that, if government officials in a less developed country dislike risk and if the prices for a country's exports or imports are highly variable, the optimal trade policy is to raise the price of the import good relative to the export good and thereby reduce the country's dependence on trade. Policymakers may dislike the uncertainty associated with international prices, because sharp swings in foreign exchange earnings or import costs may cause problems in meeting goals for economywide investment or in providing basic food commodities at reasonable and stable prices to consumers. In addition, unexpectedly high import costs or low export revenues might have an adverse impact by reducing domestic savings, tax revenues, and the country's capacity to import and repay foreign debt. The optimal trade control instrument is shown by Jabara and Thompson to be a variable tariff levy, continuously adjusted to stabilize internal prices.

Less developed countries often cite international price instability and uncertain availability of food imports as reasons for increasing their own food production and for reducing or eliminating food imports. For example, following the sharp upswing in commodity prices that occurred in the early 1970s, a number of these countries instituted policies that increased incentives for domestic food production in order to promote food self-sufficiency and to reduce food imports (USDA 1983). Recognizing that the trade and price distortions suggested by Jabara and Thompson impose costs on the economy in terms of sacrificed economic growth, many economists have recommended that less developed countries implement policies that increase food security in order to reduce the uncertainty associated with the prices and availability of food imports. Food security policies are more concerned with stabilizing available food supplies from a variety of sources, rather than from increased domestic food production alone, as a means to reduce the effects of import supply disruptions on prices and food consumption. Food security policies also recognize that shortfalls in domestic food production can also result in increased import volumes and, thus, higher import costs.

One food security policy involves a country holding food security or buffer stocks, which can be released to reduce import demand in the event of a production shortfall or an increase in import cost (Lele and Candler 1984). These stocks might be supplied to a country's stockholding agency from imports or from domestic purchases made during a good harvest. Another food security policy involves providing producer subsidies, such as investments in irrigation or pest control, which increase domestic production while reducing its variability. As will be discussed in more detail in chapter 14, these policies are also not costless to the economy. For instance, purchasing and holding buffer stocks that might not be used in any given year can be very expensive, even if the stocks are ultimately sold at a price higher than the original purchase price. And subsidization of producer inputs and technologies can result in overuse of such inputs by farmers and adoption of inappropriate production technologies.

It has also been argued that an international fund, such as the Compensatory Financing Facility currently operated by the International Monetary Fund, can reduce uncertainty in less developed countries' ability to finance food imports by enabling them to borrow from the facility in the event that declines in export earnings or increases in the cost of food grain imports make it difficult to finance food imports (Siamwalla and Valdes 1984). By reducing the uncertainty associated with imports, the existence of such a fund should permit a country to rely more on international trade to supply its food requirements at a lower national cost as compared to other food security policies. [1]

INFANT INDUSTRIES

The infant industry argument has been recognized in principle by economists as a justification for market intervention. For example, a country might have a potential comparative advantage in a certain industry, but this industry might never develop because its more efficient foreign competitors have had a head start. It follows that temporary protection would let the infant industry find a wide enough market to support economical production. After a sufficient time to allow the industry to become competitive, the temporary protection should be removed.

Two basic assumptions support this argument. First, the infant industry must be a declining-cost industry that would become more competitive as the market expands. Second, there must be external benefits to the economy from allowing the infant industry to develop. Otherwise, the country would still be better off importing from countries with a comparative advantage and channeling development resources elsewhere. These external benefits often exist because of backward and forward linkages with other industries and because of technological gains and management improvements that could be obtained and passed on to other industries. These external benefits make the gains to private investors from the development of the infant industry less than what these gains are to the country as a whole.

Less developed countries have long used the infant industry argument to justify using high tariffs or other measures to protect their industrial sectors. However, it does not follow that infant industry protection should be through tariffs or other measures that raise the prices of infant industry goods. Incentives

---

1. For a thorough summary of the literature related to food security and international trade see Adams 1983 and World Bank 1986.

given to the infant industry impose less of a burden on the economy if provided through a production subsidy aimed at increasing the profitability of producers in the infant industry. Under such a policy, general revenues raised from taxes are transferred to producers in the industry directly. This policy inflicts less distortion on the economy compared to a tariff, because the prices paid by consumers are unchanged.

A common problem with infant industry protection is that industries that develop under high-cost conditions are often reluctant to lose their protection in later years. Continuing protection usually adds to pressures for the proliferation of measures against freer international trade.

Alternative Trade Strategies for Economic and Agricultural Development

Gains from specialization and trade play an important role in improving the growth performance of most nations. The theoretical and empirical evidence suggests that less developed countries are best served through trade policies that allow international market mechanisms to work and that facilitate trade along the lines of comparative advantage.

The high economic costs of import substitution programs have become apparent to many less developed countries. Low growth rates and periodic balance of payments crises have often resulted from these policies. The export promotion strategy, in contrast, has used trade policies to encourage the development of export industries and export-led growth. Countries for which an export promotion policy has been particularly successful in expanding trade and increasing economic growth include Brazil, Hong Kong, the Republic of Korea, Singapore, and Taiwan. Studies that have examined growth under both types of policies show that an export-led strategy, which allows the gains from specialization and trade to contribute to development, has been associated with faster growth of less developed countries (Krueger 1980).[2]

Important Concepts

Import substitution

Export-oriented growth

Comparative advantage

Terms of trade

Absolute disadvantage

Changing comparative advantage

Structure of trade

Immiserizing growth

Trade intervention

Overvalued exchange rate

Implicit tax on exports

Multiple exchange rates

Export quotas

Nonprice measures for trade intervention

Export subsidies

Optimum tariffs

Infant industries

2. Additional useful reading on trade and agricultural development includes Yeager and Tuerck 1969; B. F. Jones and Thompson 1978; Little 1982; and Thompson 1983.

Sample Questions

1. Does a policy in which a less developed country produces everything at home lead to or detract from economic growth? Why?

2. Some very large countries, such as India, Brazil, and the United States, rely very little on international trade. However, in many smaller countries international trade plays a very important role in supplying goods and markets. What explanation can you give for this?

3. What is the classical pattern of trade and development? Is this model still valid today? Discuss.

4. It is often argued that less developed countries should become self-sufficient in food production; that is, they should produce all of their food at home. Does this idea conflict with the theory of comparative advantage? Explain.

5. Explain why a region within a country with an absolute disadvantage in the production of two agricultural products might specialize in the production of one of them to increase its income.

6. Some economists believe the terms of trade between agricultural and manufactured products have a long-run tendency to decline. How has this view affected the trade policies of less developed countries?

7. How does an overvalued exchange rate affect a country's trade? How have less developed countries' agricultural exports been affected by this policy?

8. List some of the arguments less developed countries use to justify intervention in trade. How valid are these arguments in your view?

9. What are the economic costs associated with a country's restrictions on foreign trade?

14

Price Policies and Planning for Agricultural Development

Getting prices right is not the end of economic development. But getting prices wrong frequently is.

—Timmer 1984, p. 288

The Role of Government in Planning for Agricultural Development

Introduction

The prices of the goods, services, and resources available to a society are determined by resource availabilities, the valuation placed on them by individuals in the society, the rules or institutional arrangements that regulate the processes of exchange, and the production technologies employed. Every market includes previously determined social decisions about the property rights of individuals, the agreed upon rules of contracts and transactions, whether in written form or not, and the mechanisms to enforce these social decisions. Without agreement in society about these matters, there is no way to distinguish between a legitimate sale and a theft.

The environment-behavior-performance framework for analysis of markets presented in chapter 12 aids focus on the institutional and cultural environment of a market and the behavior of people in the market as factors affecting market performance, as well as on the prices and quantities of goods and services sold. In every market there is some kind of social or government intervention either through tacit, cultural group agreement about what is or is not done or, in more formally organized societies, through government regulation and enforcement procedures. This intervention ranges from the delineation of rules or laws that establish the conditions for market behavior to direct government involvement in price setting and in the ownership and operation of marketing organizations. A central issue in agricultural pricing policy and planning is what kinds of government intervention—direct, with many detailed rules and formal government control, or indirect, with loose regulation of private behavior—are more effective in achieving identified development goals. Another continuing debate concerns how social and government institutions, property rights, and contractual arrangements might be changed in order to improve market and economic performance. Any change may benefit or hurt particular participants in the economic system (see for example Shaffer 1979).

Many less developed countries subscribe to the idea that governments should play a large, direct role in the economy. This role is often formalized through national "plans," which state the development objectives of government over a specified period of time, and the actions that government intends to undertake to achieve these goals. The governments of less developed countries sometimes implement these plans through public ownership of important economic enterprises but more often through the manipulation of the pricing and marketing of goods and services produced in the private sector. In these countries, intervention takes place at all stages of the economy—in production, marketing, and consumption of agricultural products and inputs. The prices most often affected by planning and agricultural pricing policies include (1) product prices for crops such as wheat, rice, and sugar; (2) the prices of inputs specific to agriculture, such as agricultural machinery, fertilizers, seeds, and pesticides; and (3) what Timmer, Falcon, and Pearson (1983, p. 228) call macro prices—interest rates, wage rates, and the exchange rate—which are determined by economywide, general economic policies but which nevertheless have an important impact on production and investment in the agricultural sector.

Less developed countries' agricultural price policies, whether direct or indirect, have an important influence on the prices received by farmers and paid by consumers. Product and input price levels affect profitability and, therefore, the amounts invested by producers among competing agricultural enterprises. When compared to economic opportunities in the nonfarm sector, these prices also affect decisions to invest in agriculture as opposed to other sectors of the economy. Thus, price policies strongly influence the performance of agriculture, overall economic growth, and the well-being of consumers.

The Economic Functions of Markets and Prices

Before further discussion of the role of government in the economic system, it is useful to recapitulate the economic functions of markets and prices in organizing an economy. In a diagram containing a supply and demand curve, a market equilibrium solution is one in which market supply and demand determine the position of the curves and thus the equilibrium price for a good or service. At this price, the amount supplied equals the amount demanded, and there is no upward or downward pressure on the price. The market is in equilibrium.

Markets also function to allocate society's scarce resources and to determine the distribution of income based upon both consumers' willingness to pay and maximum profit. For instance, if any consumers thought they could get greater utility or producers thought they could get a greater profit, they would not have bought or sold at the equilibrium price.

Using the criterion of maximum profit, the market also allocates the different factors of production among their various uses according to which use pays most for the factor. In so doing, it directs quantities of different types of labor and capital equipment to different uses. And since the costs paid out by business firms are the incomes received by factors of production, including labor, the market distributes income among individuals. The market mechanism also provides incentives for economic growth through the desires of individuals to accumulate both personal capital (in the form of skill and education) and material capital, since both kinds of capital enable individuals to increase a market-determined income.

Note that in a market there is no true value for any good or service. The cost or price of any good or service is influenced by the market's structure, the relevant social rules affecting the production and distribution of the product, and the assets, income, and desires of the market participants. For example, the price in the market for maize (corn) depends upon society's rules about whether farmers have to pay for any reduction in water quality in lakes and rivers due to fertilizers, pesticides, or other chemicals used in maize production. Farmers may have to contribute to the cost of cleaning up these wastes by paying taxes on the polluting inputs or through other means. Competitive markets, through price formation, perform the crucial economic function of indicating to producers their comparative advantage in the production of different products and, hence, whether they should increase or decrease the resources allocated for the production of any good or service.

The Causes and Range of Government Intervention

Private and Social Valuation and the Role of Government

The distinction between private valuation and social valuation of economic activities is also crucial to understanding why governments intervene in economic systems. According to Adam Smith's invisible hand, society is best served (in the sense that both individual and societal income is maximized) when individuals react to price signals in such a way as to earn the greatest possible profit or income. In such a model, the value or worth of an economic activity is the same to society as to the private individual—private valuation equals social valuation. However, in some instances, voters, legislators, or members of the executive branch, including planners, may perceive a divergence between the private profitability of certain activities and their social profitability. This could occur if (1) market-determined prices do not reflect scarcity values, because the markets for products, inputs, or financial services do not function well (market failure); or (2) market prices do not reflect scarcity values that are consistent with society's or government's development objectives and social goals.

To be more specific, market failure could occur when (1) there are externalities (external effects of the activity that benefit or cost others) associated with the activity, such as the pollution example cited above; (2) a firm cannot fully capture the benefits of its productive activity (for example, in the provision of public goods such as defense, research, or basic education; or in the provision of storage, which is a common government activity due to the divergence between the low private return on long-term storage and the potential return to the economy from reduced price fluctuations); and (3) only one buyer or one seller is present in a market, so that the monopoly profits earned by the buyer or the seller in the absence of government intervention would distort prices away from competitive levels. Note that some government interventions that seek to correct for the price distortions that arise from these market failures can improve the efficiency of the economic system.

Goals may be established by the government based upon criteria other than maximizing personal gain (whether accurately reflecting the preferences of society or not). Such goals include improving income distribution and achieving a government-determined growth rate or a particular production strategy, such as rapid industrialization or food self-sufficiency. In many cases, these goals could not be achieved without significant government intervention in markets. If improving income distribution is the most important goal, the efficiency of the market solution may in theory be preserved with government intervention by a neutral income transfer via the government budget to the target populations (Timmer, Falcon, and Pearson 1983, p. 157). However, governments in less developed countries tend instead to change the prices that significantly affect real incomes, because these governments have more control over short-run prices than they do over incomes.

A common theme in the work of the structuralist school of economists in the 1940s and 1950s was that shortcomings in markets and in the price system prevented steady economic growth and an acceptable distribution of income (see Chenery 1975). These economists contended that the price system existed in only a rudimentary form in most less developed countries and that market forces would be too weak to accomplish the changes required for accelerated development. These views supported industrial fundamentalism and the argument for rapid change in economic structure (see chapter 6). Specifically, they argued that agriculture should be forced to provide through savings and taxes a surplus to support investment in the nonfarm, particularly the industrial, sector. These economists believed that to leave economic development to market forces in light of such large required structural changes would mean stagnation or unnecessarily slow economic development, for they assumed that socially desirable investment opportunities would not be taken up by the private sector. Therefore, they concluded that considerable government intervention was required in many sectors, because the market mechanism was too unreliable to achieve economic development.

The Range of Government Intervention

Government involvement in an economy can take many forms. At one hypothetical extreme is the perfect free market economy, in which societal rules allow all economic decisions to be made by private individuals based upon prices determined by supply and demand in markets and without any specific government role. At the other extreme is the totally planned economy, characterized by government ownership of raw materials and factories, the allocation of labor by command, and the management of production by officials who seek to fulfill production quotas set in an economywide plan. In reality, all economies have some mixture of government interventions and market functions. Even so-called market economies have an important public sector, whose role is to assure that the private sector operates in an orderly fashion and to provide public goods and services, such as roads, water, and sewers, that would not be supplied by private firms. And the Soviet economy has some elements of a market economy, for example, in the labor market, in agriculture, and in the setting of production targets that respond in some degree to consumer demand (for more on different economic systems, see Halm 1968).

When less developed countries have attempted deep involvement in the economy, planning and plan implementation have usually included the following major activities: (1) the specification of public expenditures for different purposes over one or several years; (2) the setting of economywide and sector-specific production targets; and (3) a continuing effort to enforce the planning targets through direct or indirect intervention in the economy. Planning in some instances is further supported by the development of econometric models and programming techniques, which are used to determine the relations between desired social objectives and the policy instruments intended to achieve them. In these models, the econometric estimates provide information on the behavior of key elements of the economy, such as the response of agricultural producers to changes in prices, the rate of savings, and the input requirements of each sector. Planning models also show relations between the goals of society and the instruments (resources, etc.) available to achieve them. Because of the great complexity of all economies, these models have to incorporate many simplifying assumptions, such as that input-output relations in production are fixed. Hence, any model may or may not provide valid additional information for making better government decisions to aid development.

The excesses and inefficiencies of too much poorly executed government involvement, which became evident by the early 1960s, led to a resurgence of the neoclassical vision, which stressed the advantages of relying on markets rather than on deep government intervention. The planning experience of the 1950s and 1960s demonstrated that government manipulation of industries, exchange rates, and so on could result in inconsistent and confusing policies, large wastage of scarce resources, and corruption by government officials and citizens. The social learning from these experiences has shown that, even though there are distortions in markets, many work reasonably well and often better than what can be achieved by government price setting, quotas, and other regulations. Thus, the disadvantages of detailed planning are now viewed in many quarters as far more serious than the deficiencies of the markets. Hence, there is a growing consensus that scarce government administrative talent is more productively employed improving and strengthening the market system than in attempting to supplant it with whole new systems of detailed administrative policies and controls.

Because of the central role played by agriculture in the development process, agricultural commodity prices, as well as other prices affecting the agricultural sector, have been deeply involved in this debate over planning. Low farm prices arising from government intervention have been widely cited as a major factor in the poor performance of agriculture in many less developed countries over the past thirty years. Important questions are, What price strategies have less developed countries followed for agriculture? And why have many of these countries maintained low agricultural prices when this sector plays such a key role in development?

The Role of Agricultural Prices in Economic Development

The different views of the role of government in markets, discussed above, have also led to two very different views about how actions to control agricultural prices will affect economic development. The first view, following the thinking of the structural economists, is that agricultural prices should be kept low in order to promote rapid industrialization. It was argued that food prices, in particular, should be kept low to prevent urban unrest and to prevent wages in the industrial sector from rising in response to increasing food costs. The alternative view, following the thinking of the neoclassical economists, holds that agricultural prices should not be kept below their market equilibrium levels, as they are critical in generating increased agricultural production, especially to meet the growing demand for food by urban consumers. The policy advice of the neoclassical economists is "to get the prices right"—that is, to allow prices to reflect their market-determined valuation.

These two views of agricultural prices obviously have different implications for growth and investment in the agricultural sector. When agricultural prices reflect the alternative opportunities for the use of the resources employed in agriculture, the sector will grow or diminish based upon market demand and the associated investment opportunities. On the other hand, when prices are kept artificially low, slower growth or net disinvestment and increased migration of resources out of agriculture will occur, as has happened in countries that have followed this policy.

The import substitution industrialization strategy, largely adopted by economists and policy makers of the structuralist school, has had important negative impacts on agricultural development. As discussed in chapter 13, this strategy is one in which the government distorts prices and other economic incentives away from the market equilibrium in order to promote production of import-substituting, manufactured goods. However, any policy that distorts incentives toward one sector must discriminate or reduce the incentives for production in another sector. Thus, the import substitution policies adopted by many less developed countries have in effect taxed agriculture, since they raised the prices of industrial goods compared to agricultural goods, as well as the prices of protected farm inputs. Taxation of agriculture refers to any policy that results in a net outflow of resources from the agricultural sector.

Government tax revenue collected from agriculture that enables more rapid increases in agricultural income is not a taxation of agriculture. For instance, taxes may be used to develop rural infrastructure, such as roads and communications, or low-cost domestic industries that provide inputs for agriculture, such as fertilizers and farm machinery. In such cases, reinvesting the tax revenue in activities that contribute to agriculture's growth lessens the net tax on agriculture. Of course, if the agricultural sector receives more tax dollars than it pays, so that there is a net inflow of resources into the sector, it is subsidized by tax policy.

Several examples of less developed countries where prices were distorted in order to tax agriculture in favor of the manufacturing sector during the 1960s have been cited by Little, Scitovsky, and Scott (1970). For instance, they noted that the prices of manufactured goods in relation to farm prices in Pakistan were twice as high on the average as they would have been if world market prices had prevailed during that period. In consequence, this distortion of price incentives was estimated to have resulted in an effective tax on agricultural income of 11 to 13 percent. In Argentina, they found that taxes on agriculture reduced the income of agricultural producers by 30 to 40 percent of what it would have been in the absence of government intervention.

In addition to the above examples, a World Bank study found that, during the 1960s, economic policies in countries such as India, Tanzania, Chile, Uruguay, Peru, and Argentina significantly taxed their agricultural sectors (Agarwala 1983). A study of agricultural prices in different nations in the 1968–70 period by Peterson (1979) showed that real farm prices (defined in terms of the amount of fertilizer that could be purchased with 100 kilograms of wheat) were more favorable to farmers in the more developed countries than to farmers in less developed countries. Peterson's data showed that real prices received by farmers in the top ten countries averaged 3.7 times greater than those of the lowest ten countries. He found the same general pattern of prices in 1962–64, although there appeared to be some narrowing of price differences between countries during the 1960s.

Beginning about 1960, many more development economists began to recognize that underpricing agricultural output slows agricultural growth and that this slowdown also adversely affects national economic growth. Hence, greater stress was placed on a more balanced approach to economic development, for industrialization could be impeded by lagging agricultural production, inadequate food and agricultural raw material supplies, and critical shortages of foreign exchange. According to Little (1982), the argument that less developed countries should devote more attention to agriculture requires two propositions: (1) that agricultural output and farmers' marketings will rise in response to increased price incentives, due to technological and institutional changes that increase agricultural productivity and reduce unit costs; and (2) that without such changes, economic growth would be slowed. These propositions were supported by T. W. Schultz who argued in his landmark work *Transforming Traditional Agriculture* (1964b) that farmers in less developed countries maximized profits within the confines of a traditional production function and that, to increase agricultural production, more productive opportunities had to be opened up through public action in research and extension (see chapter 4).

During the late 1960s, several countries, including India and Pakistan, switched to policies that reduced their taxation of agriculture. In East Asia, Taiwan and the Republic of Korea moved even further, significantly subsidizing agricultural producers at the expense of other sectors. Anderson (1983) found that the average nominal protection of agricultural producers, as measured by the percentage difference of domestic prices from world prices, increased from − 15 percent in South Korea and − 21 percent in Taiwan in 1955–59 to 166 percent in South Korea and 55 percent in Taiwan in 1980–82. According to Anderson, these high rates of protection were due to the strong political influence of farmers in these countries and to development objectives that promoted increased rural incomes and greater food self-sufficiency.

During the late seventies and early eighties, many less developed countries raised producer prices for cereals relative to the prices of other, competing opportunities, thus increasing incentives for food production. A study by Jabara (1985) in Kenya showed that real producer prices (output prices deflated by input prices) for food and other crops increased substantially from 1979 to the early 1980s and that these price increases were associated with increases in marketed agricultural production. In a major study on pricing policy in less developed countries, the United Nations Food and Agriculture Organization (FAO 1985a) noted that, while international cereal prices fell 18 percent from 1978–80 to 1980–82, developing countries' domestic producer prices rose an average of 5 percent over the same period. Byerlee and Sain (1986) analyzed the prices received by farmers for wheat relative to world wheat prices and the prices of inputs in a sample of thirty one countries and found no consistent evidence of price disincentives for wheat producers in less developed countries. Many of these countries continue to keep prices low to wheat consumers, according to Byerlee and Sain, but they do so with policies that do not directly tax wheat producers.

Despite increases in agricultural prices in the last decade in many less developed countries, price distortions against agricultural producers are still quite common. Major problems of economic growth and development in the countries of sub-Saharan Africa are believed to be often due to low price incentives and ineffective or counterproductive government interventions in the economy (World Bank 1981). However, the World Bank's *World Development Report 1986* (pp. 63–65) shows that price distortions are often crop specific and that many less developed countries tax some agricultural producers but subsidize others. The tax or subsidy depends on the pricing objectives of the government and whether a crop is used primarily for export, food, or industrial uses. For instance, in the late 1970s and early 1980s, producers of export crops continued to be heavily taxed, particularly producers of cocoa, coffee, cotton, and rubber. On the other hand, producers of food crops, such as wheat, rice, corn, and sugar, were subsidized by some less developed countries and producer prices were higher than what they would have been in the absence of intervention. In countries where industrial crops like cotton and tobacco have been promoted as part of import substitution schemes, production of such crops was also subsidized.

Methods of Agricultural Price Intervention

The Objectives of Pricing Policy

Agricultural pricing policy in less developed countries encompasses a wide range of objectives and measures. Governments use a number of policies and programs to attempt to alter the allocation of resources to meet their objectives. A review of the pricing policies in thirty-seven less developed countries by the FAO (1985a, p. 80) revealed the following objectives: (1) stabilizing or reducing consumer food prices; (2) maintaining uninterrupted food supplies (food security); (3) stabilizing or maintaining producer prices to guarantee incentives for production; (4) reaching food self-sufficiency (reducing imports); (5) providing government revenue through taxation; (6) increasing foreign exchange earnings; and (7) promoting industrialization.

According to this study, stabilizing agricultural prices in order to help farmers in production planning and to ensure the availability of food supplies to consumers at stable and reasonable prices has been a major influence on the design of less developed countries' agricultural policies. When the government guarantees farmers or consumers a certain price, it absorbs risk and eliminates some of the uncertainty that would otherwise be faced in the agricultural sector. Pure stabilization policies are more concerned with the speed of price changes over short periods rather than with the level of prices over time.

In addition to assuring stable prices, some governments have raised producer prices above market equilibrium for the purpose of increasing agricultural production. Governments might do this in order to increase the domestic supplies available for food security stocks or to achieve food self-sufficiency. This policy raises the incomes of the producers receiving the high prices but taxes consumers, who have to pay more for agricultural products. Alternatively, governments have maintained producer prices below market equilibrium for the purpose of keeping agricultural prices, particularly prices of food and domestic raw materials, low to processors and consumers.

As noted by the FAO review, raising the relative incomes of the rural sector was not a prominent goal among the less developed countries surveyed with the exception of seven medium or higher income countries. The objective of increasing agricultural incomes tends to be dominant in more developed countries, such as the United States, Japan, and the European Community, and in the Republic of Korea and Taiwan, whose agricultural policies are designed to maintain rural incomes roughly in line with incomes in the nonagricultural sector.

Government objectives and pricing policies that are inconsistent in the short run may give rise to conflicts in the long run. For instance, low agricultural prices that benefit consumers immediately will eventually have an adverse impact on agricultural production, reducing food supplies and raising consumer prices. A central thesis of this text is that long-run policies that increase productivity by encouraging the adoption of more productive technologies or that improve the performance of the agricultural marketing system will be of greater benefit both to consumers and producers. Such policies will increase agricultural production and lower long-run agricultural prices to consumers and result in more rapid economic growth. Both less developed and more developed nations continually face the challenge of getting prices right—achieving agricultural prices that will best balance the development objectives of the different groups in society. [1]

The Instruments of Price Intervention

Less developed countries implement their agricultural objectives with several policy measures, including price and taxation policies specific to the agricultural sector and general economic policies that affect all sectors. The following five most widely used measures were set out by Reca (1983), and Timmer, Falcon, and Pearson (1983): (1) administered product prices; (2) agricultural input pricing; (3) export taxes; (4) marketing boards; and (5) administered macroprices—exchange rates, interest rates, and wage rates.

ADMINISTERED PRODUCT PRICES
Governments often intervene directly to increase or decrease prices in markets. The prices obtained by such actions are called administered prices. Government-determined prices can be fixed either above or below the levels that would be reached in the absence of the intervention. Administered prices that raise the average price received by farmers above the price that would otherwise prevail encourage agricultural production above its long-run equilibrium,

1. For greater depth in analysis of food policies for less developed nations see Timmer, Falcon, and Pearson 1983 and Timmer 1986.

whereas prices set below equilibrium discourage agricultural production. However, administered prices do not need to raise the average yearly farm price to have a positive effect on production. A positive effect can be obtained in two ways: (1) by reducing producers' uncertainty about the lowest price that will be received; and (2) by ensuring greater competition at harvest time, when prices tend to be depressed (Tolley, Thomas, and Wong 1982, p. 54).

Administered prices are often advocated by less developed countries to remove uncertainty in prices. One of the most common ways in which governments intervene in product markets is through ceiling prices. A ceiling price is the highest price that can be legally offered to producers. Farmers often sell all or practically all of their product to a government marketing agency at this price. This kind of program is used for marketing staple food crops in many African countries as well as for marketing wheat and rice in India and Bangladesh.

When a government wants to encourage farmers to sell to it at the ceiling price, programs are often enforced by marketing rules that prohibit private purchase and transport of the designated commodities. However, the difficulty in enforcing a ceiling price depends on whether this price is set above or below market equilibrium. If the ceiling price is below market equilibrium, farmers will have incentive to try to get a higher price by selling their crop illegally on the black market. A ceiling price at or above market equilibrium can more easily be enforced, since the private market will not have the incentive to offer a higher price.

Government intervention in product markets can also involve floor or support prices, which provide a guaranteed minimum price to producers. Floor prices that are set below the equilibrium price usually involve limited purchases by the government, and marketing is primarily by the private sector, which can pay the producer the higher market price. The government serves as the buyer of last resort should the market prices markets drop to the floor level. For example, due to a lack of storage capacity or farmers' financial constraints that require selling all of a crop at the start of the season, farm prices are often depressed at harvest. Floor prices reduce the risk of even lower prices during this period and encourage agricultural investment. Floor prices are often established in less developed countries for food crops of minor importance in the diet or for traditional food crops consumed primarily in rural areas, such as millet, sorghum, cowpeas, cassava, and even soybeans.

Of course, the government can also set a floor price to producers above market equilibrium, as is done for wheat in Brazil, Nigeria, and Mexico, for soybeans in Indonesia, and for many agricultural commodities in the European Community. In this case, the floor price induces farmers to produce more of the crop than they would without intervention, and the government may collect through stocks the amount not sold or utilized within the year.

There are several variations in administered price programs. One variation is the two-price program, in which an above-market-equilibrium floor price is established for producers and lower ceiling prices are maintained for con-

Figure 14.1. Economics of Administered Prices

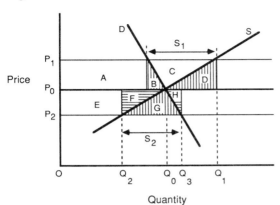

sumers. This type of program is operated for wheat prices in, for example, Brazil, Nigeria, Mexico, and for wheat and rice in Japan. Another variation is Indonesia's buffer stock program for rice, the staple food. Under this program, floor and ceiling prices are set, and the government purchases and sells rice from buffer stocks in order to stabilize farm prices within a price band. An intermediate situation in terms of government control is the pricing policy for rice and wheat in Egypt, where farmers are required to sell a fixed proportion of these crops to the government at the administered price and then are allowed to sell the remainder on the open market at a higher price.

When governments administer prices, their actions usually affect the distribution of income among producers and consumers as well as resource allocation in the economy. Systems set up to administer prices are often more costly to society than allowing market supply and demand to determine prices. This is illustrated in figure 14.1. Without government intervention, the market-determined equilibrium price for a commodity is at P_0 with quantity Q_0 supplied in a given time period in the less developed country. P_0 is also the world price at which the commodity could be either imported or exported. In this example, the less developed country is self-sufficient at P_0, and the commodity is neither imported nor exported.

If the objective of government policy is to raise farm prices above the equilibrium price, then the government could set an above-equilibrium floor price at P_1, and domestic supply would increase to Q_1. A commodity surplus equal to S_1 also develops at P_1, which must be purchased by the government. If the objective behind setting such high prices is to increase food security, then this surplus may be used by the government as food security stocks. Farm income is raised from $(OP_0)(OQ_0)$ to $(OP_1)(OQ_1)$, of which an amount represented by area A is a windfall transfer from consumers to producers due to higher prices. In addition, the government must spend $(OP_1)(S_1)$ to purchase and store the surplus production. Alternatively, the less developed country could export S_1 at price P_0 and incur a lower cost of only $(P_1 P_0)(S_1)$. This occurred in Kenya in 1983, when the government raised the prices of beans above market equilibrium, with the result that it had to export surplus beans at world prices below the domestic support price.

If, instead, the objective of the government is to subsidize consumer prices, the government could set a price ceiling below the equilibrium price, at P_2. Domestic supply would decline to Q_2 in this case, and demand would increase to Q_3. Farm income is now lowered to $(OP_2)(OQ_2)$. An amount represented by area E is transferred directly from producers to consumers through lower commodity prices. At P_2, a shortfall in production equal to S_2 is realized, which must be made up, either through imports or through rationing. If there are imports, the net cost to the government from purchasing S_2 imports at world price P_0 to sell to consumers at P_2 is $(P_0 P_2)(S_2)$, or areas $F + G + H$. If the government decides not to import, then shortages will occur, and the producers will have the incentive to sell on the black market in the hopes of obtaining a higher price for their output.

The government could also implement a two-price policy, which establishes both a floor price to producers at P_0 and a ceiling price to consumers at P_2. With this policy, supply and demand are at Q_0 and Q_3, respectively. The government now must spend $(P_0 P_2)(OQ_3)$ in order to subsidize consumer sales of Q_3 at P_2, with production and imports purchased at P_0. This type of consumer subsidy involves larger government expenditures than when only the ceiling price at P_2 is imposed. This is because the subsidy to consumers in the two-price example is financed only through general tax revenues, whereas the ceiling price subsidizes consumers at the expense of producer income as well.

In addition to the government budgetary resources needed to purchase and sell agricultural commodities, when governments administer prices, they must also devote administrative resources to this activity. A specific person or agency must be responsible for determining and announcing the prices, and a method for price determination must be adopted. In some countries, prices are determined jointly by the different government agencies having an interest in the production and marketing of the crop, such as agriculture, finance, or planning ministries, and marketing boards. In some instances, a single agency is responsible, as in India, where the Agricultural Prices Commission sets the administered prices. Prices can also be set by a marketing agency or by presidential decree.

Criteria used for setting producer support prices are varied. We consider two common ones. Estimates of the cost of production is one criterion adopted in less developed, as well as more developed, countries. This method attempts to set farm prices so as to guarantee farmers a fixed return over their cost of production, based upon average yields, costs, and technology. A fundamental problem with this method is that yields, costs, and technology are not uniform; thus, it is very difficult to determine which data, based on what sampling theory, should be used in the calculations. Moreover, as prices based upon estimated production costs are often high and seldom include adjustments for increasing farm productivity, these prices provide little incentive to farmers to use inputs more efficiently and to use cost-saving technologies that could lead to lower farm product prices. Hence, administered product prices based on production costs tend to creep further and further above international and domestic market prices, leading farmers to rely more and more on the government to purchase the product.

An alternative criterion for the administered price is one based upon domestic and world market demand and prices. In contrast to the cost of production method, the prices used in this method are based upon trying to assure that domestic prices are about the same as import and export prices. This method takes into account marketing opportunities, such as how domestic prices would be affected in competition with imports and how export prices would affect internal export crop prices. If prices are to be administratively determined, this method is generally preferred by economists, because it keeps farm prices more or less in line with market opportunities and encourages the adoption of new technologies to lower production costs over time (see Jabara 1985).

AGRICULTURAL INPUT PRICING

Input subsidies are used in many less developed countries to lower the cost of the modern inputs used in agriculture. The purpose of such subsidies is to encourage increased use of improved production technologies. According to economic theory, farmers should use inputs until the marginal value product from the input equals the price of the input. However, due to several factors—farmers' lack of knowledge about how to use or obtain improved inputs, financial constraints, risk aversion, or general economic policies that artificially raise the prices of inputs—there may be a large gap between actual use and the optimal level in less developed countries.

In analyzing the manner in which input subsidies help to increase agricultural production, it is useful to distinguish different types of input subsidies and their short-run and long-run effects. For example, policies that lower the prices of modern inputs encourage farmers to use more known technologies so as to move along a given production function (Barker and Hayami 1976). As input prices decline, the number of units of input that can be purchased with one unit of output increases, and the quantity used increases (see figure 8.3). Increased agricultural production can also be achieved through investments in new technology and institutional arrangements, as in irrigation projects, better financial markets, and research and extension. These investments shift the agricultural production function outward, but they often require large investments and long gestation periods. Thus governments tend to focus on shorter run policies and programs such as direct output or input price subsidies that will increase output with current production functions.

Temporary input subsidies are often helpful in the early stages of adoption of new inputs and technologies to accelerate their use. If a profitable input does not find acceptance due to ignorance, a subsidy could stimulate its use. For instance, in India, in addition to a fertilizer subsidy available to all farmers, production packages including improved seeds, fertilizer, and pesticides have been provided free to small, marginal farmers. However, a long-run problem of many subsidy policies is that they remain long after farmers have become acquainted with the new production package, and the overuse of these inputs is encouraged.

Because it increases farmers' demand for the subsidized input, an input subsidy could be used to achieve the same increase in output as a floor price policy that maintains producer prices above the equilibrium price (Tolley, Thomas, and Wong 1982, p. 142). An input price subsidy can entail less cost to society and the government budget than an administered floor price to achieve the same output, since it can be limited to the increased use of specific underutilized modern inputs. In contrast, agricultural product price supports encourage not only the use of modern inputs, but increased use of lower productivity, traditional inputs as well.

It is important to observe also that in some countries what appears to be a subsidy on the purchase price of an input may not be when international prices are considered. Some governments protect fertilizer production or mixing industries under import substitution regimes. In this case, a subsidy on the fertilizer price may merely offset the high price farmers would otherwise have had to pay for the protected domestically produced fertilizer.

EXPORT TAXES

Trade policy instruments used by less developed countries were described in detail in chapter 13. Because of the importance of agricultural exports to many of these countries, export taxes have played a primary role in government efforts to transfer resources from agriculture to the rest of the economy. Many less developed countries tax export crops, sometimes at very high rates, and thus force the domestic price of these crops to lower levels. According to the World Bank, farm prices for export crops such as coffee, cotton, groundnuts, and cocoa have ranged from only a third to a half of the export price in countries such as Togo, Mali, Cameroon, and Ghana (*World Development Report 1986*, p. 64). In Ghana, taxes on all exports provided over 35 percent of total government revenues in 1984. However, exports can also be taxed through measures that do not directly contribute revenues to the government, such as through policies that hold down the prices received by farmers and that allow marketing boards to earn greater profits from sales of export goods.

As noted in chapter 13, an overvalued exchange rate can play a role comparable to that of an export tax. However, it does not provide revenue directly to the government except in cases where the government charges importers fees for access to the cheap foreign exchange.

The tax incidence, or who bears the cost of the tax, is important in analyzing the potential costs and benefits of an export tax. In some situations, a tax on agricultural exports can cause foreign consumers to contribute some of their income to the developing country if the exporting country faces an inelastic demand curve (as has been argued for Brazil's coffee exports). Then the quantity exported would decrease only a small amount, and the earnings of the less developed country would increase. Otherwise, with a completely elastic demand curve, the internal price is forced down, and the incidence of the tax falls on the less developed country's agricultural sector.

Some countries, for instance the Ivory Coast for coffee and cocoa exports and Mali for cotton exports, have used export taxes for price stabilization. When export prices are high, export tax funds go to the government treasury or to a price stabilization fund; when export prices are low, funds may be transferred back to farmers to support prices internally. In this case, farmers are alternatively taxed and subsidized in order to maintain more stable domestic prices.

MARKETING BOARDS

Marketing boards are public agencies established by governments to assist in marketing agricultural commodities. A list of the kinds of of marketing boards and their responsibilities was given toward the end of chapter 12. At one extreme, they are limited to advisory and promotional functions that provide market information, promote sales, and do technical work on product quality (for example, the Sisal Board of Kenya). The activities of this type of board may be financed by levies and taxes on farmers, merchants, and processors. At the other extreme are boards with (1) a statutory monopoly control over the foreign and domestic marketing of crops; and (2) the power to fix domestic buying and selling prices and to control foreign trade.

Many less developed countries established marketing boards because they feared that the private market was inefficient and that marketing margins charged by the private sector would be too high, resulting in farm prices that are too low and retail prices that are too high.[2] In some countries, however, marketing boards were inherited from colonial governments upon independence. For instance, in Kenya, marketing boards had been established and operated by the British colonial government for the benefit of expatriate farmers. These institutions were continued by the newly independent Kenyan government.

Although some marketing boards have a monopoly over all marketing operations, marketing boards often coexist with the private sector. When governments maintain a floor or support price below the equilibrium price, farmers will often sell to the marketing board at the low price only as a last resort. For instance, Nigerian farmers sell soybeans primarily to private traders, and any residual is sold to the Nigerian Groundnut Corporation at a guaranteed floor price. In other situations, a marketing board might use private traders to carry

2. See also W. O. Jones 1984. There are other arguments for the establishment of marketing boards. For instance, Ellis (1982) has argued that food marketing boards have been instigated in order to strengthen the power of the state.

out certain marketing functions, such as in Indonesia, where the marketing board, BULOG, uses the private sector to purchase and distribute soybeans.

It is generally argued that marketing boards are costly and inefficient as marketing channels. A marketing board operating as a monopoly is more likely to become less productive and to have higher marketing costs than a system that enables competitive trading. Monopoly control can easily lead to a situation where corruption and a bloated bureaucracy result in high handling and distribution costs, lower prices for producers, and higher prices for consumers.

In many instances, however, a marketing board's inefficiencies may be due to constraints placed on it by the government. Often, marketing boards do not set prices but merely act as marketing agents at prices determined by other units of government. If the price for a certain crop does not allow a sufficient margin to pay for marketing operations, then the board runs up large debts and may not be able to pay farmers for their produce on time. In this situation, the board might be forced to tax producers of other crops in order to make up the shortfall. Marketing boards are also often required to carry out expensive food security policies. Such tasks may require them to carry burdensome stocks and thus raise their marketing costs in comparison to the private sector. Some relatively autonomous marketing boards—for instance, the Kenya Tea Development Authority, which regulates the production and marketing of smallholder tea in Kenya— have been praised for their efficiency and effectiveness.

ADMINISTERED MACRO PRICES

In the absence of government policy intervention, exchange rates, interest rates, and wage rates are determined by the economywide supply and demand for, respectively, foreign exchange, capital, and labor. These macro prices have significant impacts on agricultural investment decisions and production, and intervention in these markets is particularly important in influencing the capital intensity of technologies used in agricultural production.

Government interventions aimed at administering these macro prices can result in the adoption of technologies that are inappropriate to a country's resource endowments. Consequently, there is a loss of both agricultural and other output due to overuse or underuse of factors that would be more profitably used elsewhere. For example, countries often fix a minimum wage for unskilled labor. If this wage rate is above the equilibrium value consistent with resource supplies and labor demand, less labor will be employed, and production techniques, whether in agriculture or in other sectors, will be more capital intensive.

Similarly, low interest rates charged for agricultural or other credit channel money into these uses and sectors at the expense of other uses and sectors. Subsidized credit policies often result in a more capital intensive production technique than if interest rates reflected the cost of capital for a specific use. An overvalued exchange rate, which lowers the local currency cost of imported agricultural machinery, will result in agricultural producers adopting production techniques that tend to be more capital intensive or to substitute crops that can be grown more profitably with capital intensive techniques.

As a country may be simultaneously intervening in all of these markets at once, it may not be clear what the net effect on input use in agriculture is. However, significant distortions in one or more of these macro prices can lower the rate of economic growth by encouraging inappropriate input use in agriculture and other sectors of the economy.

The Effects of Price Interventions on Agricultural Development

Government intervention in agricultural pricing is designed to alter resource allocation, income distribution, and the pattern of economic growth that would otherwise occur with free markets. In some situations, government price intervention can provide a net benefit to a country by compensating for existing market distortions. However, in many instances, price interventions impose extra costs on the economy and waste valuable economic resources. Price distortions encourage resources to shift to opportunities that become privately profitable with government intervention at the expense of economic opportunities that would be more profitable for the nation if prices more nearly reflected resource costs. A World Bank study (Agarwala 1983) of less developed countries found a significant relation between the extent of price distortion and economic growth. The countries that distorted prices away from market equilibrium least were found to have higher rates of growth than countries that intervened more in their economies.

Price intervention affects economic growth in two ways. First, the prices of farm products relative to the prices that can potentially be received in other economic opportunities influence farmers' decisions (1) to shift resources among competing crops or livestock enterprises; and (2) to shift resources into or out of the agricultural sector. For instance, a policy that raises the price of food crops relative to the price of export crops transfers income to food crop producers at the expense of consumers and other producers, including export crop producers. If this income transfer is neutral—that is, the income gains received by the food crop producers offset the losses of other groups—it does not necessarily affect the rate of economic growth. However, assuming that producers and consumers are price responsive, the policy will result in a decline in export crop production, as resources shift to the more profitable food crops, as well as in a decline in food consumption. Such a policy entails real costs to the country because, if the resources were employed in export crop production, the value of the additional exports produced would be greater than the value of the additional food produced when measured at the equilibrium price. In this case, the economic cost to the country is this loss in export crop production and the reduced food consumption by consumers.

In figure 14.1, the economic costs of a policy that raises food prices above equilibrium can be shown to equal triangles $B + D$.[3] Area B represents the loss to consumers in food consumption forgone due to higher prices. Area D represents the efficiency loss to the economy as resources are pulled into food production at the expense of exports. It should also be noted that income transfers such as the one described are often not neutral in their income effects, thus imposing further losses on the economy. The loss of real income by food consumers (especially the poor, whose valuation of marginal income might be higher than the valuation of producers) may result in a net decline in total welfare. Food stamps or other policies to lower food prices or to transfer income to poor consumers could in principle compensate consumers, but at additional government expense.

A second effect of government intervention, as shown in figure 14.1, is that it often involves large government outlays (the areas $[OP_1][S_1]$ or $F + G + H$) in order to subsidize producers, to pay for marketing board operations, or to assure low prices to consumers. These outlays divert scarce savings and capital from important national investment projects as well as from private sector investments that may increase national economic growth much more. In some situations, governments are forced to increase taxes on other producers and sectors to finance these operations, which further increases the economic distortions in the economy. Additionally, high government involvement, especially in marketing systems, hinders the development of private marketing systems in rural areas. Private marketing units will create, in most cases, more employment and income in rural areas than centralized government marketing organizations.[4]

Conclusions

In part IV of this text we have found that slow growth is usually associated with deep government involvement in marketing, trade, and prices. Hence, many governments in less developed nations are finding that activities that support the development of increasing numbers of competitive marketing organizations and markets are a better use of government resources in achieving development goals. Government distortions of prices and exchange rates and the heavy budget costs often associated with subsidies generally slow national economic growth. Governments can often have a greater positive effect on economic and agricultural development if they focus on facilitating further development of competitive production and marketing units than if they attempt to direct, control, or monopolize production and marketing. A remarkable example of

3. This example illustrates the partial equilibrium effects of government price intervention. The effects on other markets could also be shown as in the two-sector model used in chapter 13. Similarly to the tariff example shown in figure 13.3, government intervention that raises the price of a particular product above market equilibrium distorts resource allocation across sectors and results in a less than feasible national income.

4. Additional suggested readings on price policies and planning for agricultural development include Schultz 1978; Waterston 1979; Johnson and Schuh 1983; USDA 1983; and Meier 1976, 1984.

this point is the People's Republic of China, which significantly raised producer incentives and reduced the level of government intervention in agricultural production and marketing in the late 1970s and which saw agricultural production soar by the early 1980s. However, the optimum level of government intervention in marketing, trade, and pricing will vary over time and by country.

Important Concepts

Social valuation of economic activities	Administered prices
Market failure	Ceiling prices
Externalities	Floor prices
Structuralist school of economists	Buffer stocks
Planning models	Self-sufficiency
Underpricing agricultural output	Export taxes
Nominal protection	Tax incidence
Pure stabilization policies	Macro prices

Sample Questions

1. Give two reasons why less developed countries often intervene in their economies. What school of economists supported a relatively large role for government in the economic development process? Why?

2. What roles do agricultural prices play in agricultural development according to the neoclassical school of thought? Do these economists support a development strategy biased in favor of the agricultural sector? Why or why not?

3. It is often argued that less developed countries tax the agricultural sector and subsidize their industrial sectors. Discuss. How have less developed countries' views on agricultural prices changed in recent years?

4. Name two ways in which less developed countries' objectives with respect to the agricultural sector differ from those of the more developed countries. How has this resulted in different agricultural policies between the two groups of countries?

5. When a country intervenes in the economy to attempt to achieve its development objectives, some participants gain from this action and some lose. Why? Give two development objectives, and show how participants might benefit or lose.

6. Give three specific types of price interventions commonly implemented by less developed countries. Discuss their possible impacts on agricultural production and food consumption.

7. Describe the effects on agricultural development and economic growth of two types of price interventions commonly implemented by less developed

countries. Include the effects on economic efficiency, income distribution, and government expenditures.

8. Development goals can often be reached by different strategies. How does a development strategy that relies upon markets operate, as compared to a strategy that involves a planned and controlled economy. What, in your opinion, is a proper role for the governments of less developed countries in economic and agricultural development?

V

Accelerating Agricultural Development

Introduction to Part V

We have sought in this work an internally consistent theory of social and economic development that would aid in identifying high-return investment programs and government policies to accelerate agricultural development. It has been exciting to discover that many of the puzzles of agricultural development are illuminated through the use of neoclassical economic theory. Few problems of agricultural development will not yield to an insightful application of currently available social and economic theory tools. A careful analysis of agricultural development problems clarifies alternative actions and can provide estimates of their benefits and costs to different groups in society. It has been discouraging, however, to be faced with the immense complexity and difficulty of shifting from a resource-based to a science-based farming. It is also discouraging to see that the reality of agricultural development in many areas of less developed nations involves a long time frame of more than a generation, relatively slow rates of growth, continually changing economic conditions, and, in some areas with poor agricultural resources, absolute declines in agricultural output and income.

In this part of the text, we bring together the general policy conclusions obtained from the previous chapters in order to set out examples of alternative strategies for agricultural development. These strategies are based upon the assessment of the problems facing agricultural development presented in part I, the economic and social theory of agricultural development examined in part II, the exploration of ways to increase the productivity of investments in agriculture through the acceleration of change in technology, institutions, and human capital in part III, and the examination of alternative national marketing, trade, and price policies for agricultural development in part IV. The social learning obtained through the economic theory and empirical research illustrated in these chapters, and through observing the implementation of government policies and programs, enables nations to identify and carry out more effective agricultural development strategies.

A wider perspective may help. In this half century, one of the most fundamental global changes has been the greatly increasing interdependence of all nations—economically, politically, and culturally. This is part of the second great transition in human history that Kahn judged will be completed by the year 2200, when most persons in the world will be affluent, barring a catastrophe (see table 1.1). The current scientific-industrial transition enables increased economic growth and greatly reduces world transportation and communication costs, leading to greater gains from comparative advantage and increased interdependence among nations and national subregions. This process also involves continually changing comparative advantage among regions, both internationally and within nations. Hence, in some areas and agricultural sectors, crops will be induced to grow rapidly, due to high rates of return. At the same time, other regions and nations will experience declines in the production of particular crops due to lower returns. Thus, development is associated with both gains and losses, in different regions and countries.

As many nations have experienced increases in real per capita income and in per capita agricultural production, the gains in the more prosperous agricultural regions and economic sectors must have more than offset the declines in other regions and sectors. Thus, for example, the working out of changing comparative advantage through trade adjustments as economic opportunities change may require reductions in the production of some basic foodstuffs, such as potatoes and food grains. But these changes are often associated with increases in the production of other agricultural products, such as vegetables, fruits, livestock, and animal feeds. These changes are due both to changing trade opportunities and to changes in domestic demand patterns for agricultural products as per capita income grows (see chapter 3).

15

Agricultural Development Strategies

> *The predispositions of the leaders of new nations to see development as factory smokestacks and super highways and steel mills has generated hunger among their peoples. Their preoccupation with cheap food for urban masses . . . has destroyed the incentives for their farmers and has left their nations bereft of a strong dynamic rural economy.*
>
> *—Hopper 1981, p. 53*

> *Pigou taught economists that the market was imperfect, but that points of imperfection could usually be eliminated by handing the problem over to the government for tax or subsidy. Such an assumption is not valid for all LDCs [less developed countries]. Here it is often the case that the imperfect solution of the market could be better than that of the government. The government needs to be modernized just as much as the market. Also the assumption that the government "represents" the people may not hold. Political scientists offer us many different models of government—military (with generals), military (with sergeants), technocratic, aristocratic, popular front, peasant, kleptocratic—which react differently to similar stimuli.*
>
> *To sum up . . . Development Economics marches most of the way with the economics of developed market economies, except that there are more special cases; and except that sociological implications cannot be brushed aside, or be assumed to be held constant while decisions are reached on the basis of "economic" considerations alone.*
>
> *—Lewis 1984, p. 4*

Before proceeding to strategies for agricultural development, we need to remind ourselves how the agricultural and economic development of less developed nations fits into the broader perspective of world economic growth. In particular, how does the economic growth of these nations affect the economies of more developed nations? Some assume that gains in agricultural production in the less developed nations reduce income in more developed nations; that is, that there is a fixed economic and trade pie to be divided among the nations.

409

In examining this question, we need to keep in mind the economic and other objectives of the more developed nations for less developed nations. These objectives include, first, to improve the economic and social welfare of people in less developed nations and, second, to do it in ways that will contribute to economic growth in all nations. The second objective follows from the generally accepted belief that economically healthy and growing less developed economies are good for economic progress in more developed nations.

Much evidence indicates that aid programs have contributed greatly to the first goal, despite the fact that some assistance has been used much less productively than aid givers and citizens of receiving nations had hoped. [1]

Evidence about the soundness of the second goal of more developed nations is also plentiful. Economic research indicates that the levels of trade between more developed and less developed nations are directly related to the levels of real per capita income in the less developed nations. Hence, earnings from trade in the more developed nations grow with increases in per capita incomes in less developed nations. There are many examples of greatly expanded U.S. agricultural exports to less developed nations, particularly South Korea and Taiwan, as their incomes have increased. Changing technological, institutional, and human capital in less developed nations eventually lead to a changing comparative advantage in the production of agricultural products and in the total demand for agricultural exports from more developed nations. Thus sales of agricultural products to some less developed nations may decline, but increases in nonagricultural exports to these nations usually more than offset the decline in agricultural exports. Economic theory and empirical research have demonstrated that more developed nations benefit economically from economic and agricultural growth in less developed nations. We must recognize, however, that from time to time rapid shifts in agricultural trade between nations may cause significant temporary economic problems in one of them. The resulting adjustments in agricultural production in some nations may be difficult. [2]

Accelerating the Economic and Social Transformation of Agriculture

To achieve the needed annual rates of growth in agricultural production of 3 to 5 percent in many less developed nations, a full socioeconomic transformation of agriculture is required, an evolutionary task of decades. Increasing theoretical and empirical knowledge of economic and social development has identified the three prime sources of increased income: technological change,

1. Work showing the gains of less developed nations from aid include Falcon 1984 (pp. 176–88); Morss and Gow 1984; and Cassen 1986. U.S. voluntary aid was reviewed by Sommer 1977. Examples of international aid in agriculture provided by U.S. universities are provided by Scoville (1979) and Read (1974).

2. Materials that have examined the impact of economic and agricultural development in less developed nations on the more developed nations include Christiansen 1987; Schuh, Kellogg, and Paarlberg 1987; Wennergren et al. 1986; Cassen 1982; Curry Foundation 1986; and World Food Institute 1982.

institutional change, and investment in human capital. Research is the fundamental accelerator of agricultural and economic development, because it increases the availability of more productive technologies and institutions. These technologies and institutions are used by entrepreneurs in the public and private sectors to continuously upset the existing economic equilibria that markets tend toward. Research has shown that investments that apply knowledge of biology, chemistry, physics, and the social sciences to agriculture can provide high social returns in both the public and private sectors. Hence, investment in research is a core high-return strategy to increase the rate of agricultural growth in most less developed nations. Complementary forms of education to enhance human capital will increase the rate of agricultural growth.

Due to agricultural research and investment in human capital, the most fundamental and rapid transformation of agriculture and rural life in world history is now under way in less developed nations. This century-long economic and social transformation, or agricultural revolution, which began in the 1950s in many of these countries, is as fundamental and far-reaching for less developed nations as was the industrial revolution of the last three centuries for more developed nations. This transformation of rural life is far advanced in only some less developed nations. The immense changes in the rural socioeconomic systems involve myriad interactions among the four major elements of the induced innovation model: (1) technology; (2) institutions; (3) resource endowments; and (4) cultural endowments (see figure 11.1). This process involves a fundamental shift from an inflexible resource-based agriculture, often with rigid rural institutional arrangements, to a flexible science-based agriculture, with rural institutions more responsive to changing needs. The response of a government to the following four requirements of rapid socioeconomic change will affect its rate of progress.

The Need for a National Consensus on the Goals of Development

Nations, both more developed and less developed, consist of many social and ethnic groups, often located in different regions. In some nations, leaders and government administrators have not been able to forge a consensus on national agricultural goals or development policy, with the result that programs and policies often work against each other. In other cases, price, trade, and investment policies have been focused narrowly for the benefit of certain interest groups. Both confusion in agricultural development objectives and narrowly focused agricultural development programs slow national economic development.

The importance of developing agreed upon goals and consistent, balanced policies is illustrated by the dilemma of price policies for basic food and agricultural products, with their different short-run and long-run outcomes and different effects on producers and consumers. In the short run, low food prices are good for consumers, especially for low-income consumers, for they spend a high proportion of their budget on food. In the long run, however, low food and agricultural prices seriously slow agricultural growth, income, and employment, on which broad-based development depends. Two other examples of agricultural policies that often appear attractive but lead to counterproductive outcomes in the longer run are (1) government rules and controls that encourage concentration and monopoly in input and product markets; and (2) subsidized agricultural credit that reaches mostly larger farmers, leading to excess mechanization, greater rural unemployment, and a worse income distribution. Increasing national agreement and accommodating different legitimate interests in setting agricultural goals, with appropriate consideration of likely income distribution impacts on groups and regions, will enable more rapid agricultural development through more consistent price, trade, and investment policies for agriculture.

The Importance of Understanding How Economic and Social Systems Can Be Changed

Theoretical and empirical knowledge of how the operation of economic and social systems can be modified has increased slowly over the last few centuries. It was only in the nineteenth century that a continuous method of invention, through the creation of research institutions, was developed. Social knowledge now includes many powerful theoretical and analytic tools for technological, economic, and social analysis. They can be used to identify technological and institutional changes in production and marketing that will increase incomes and reach desired income distributions. In this volume, we have provided some of these tools. Policymakers who have little understanding of how economic systems grow are likely to make decisions that will slow growth or that will waste development resources.

Recent social learning about agricultural development has included an important paradigm shift from the classical economists' production function, in which agricultural output was viewed as dependent upon the quantities of land, labor, and capital, to a production function, in which output is viewed as primarily dependent upon capital investments in more productive technology, institutions, and human capital to augment the productivity of land and labor (chapters 6 and 11). Therefore, investments in higher yielding seeds, more productive animals, better chemical inputs, and better irrigation or drainage increase land productivity; and investments in tractor mechanization and the education and training of farmers and laborers increase labor productivity. With greater scientific knowledge of how agricultural development is achieved, the identification of the most important problems and possible solutions facing an agricultural area is possible. A particular focus of this volume has been to understand how technological and institutional change is achieved in agriculture (chapters 8, 9, 10, 11, and 12).

The general steps required to increase the incomes of farmers' families, who compose the largest proportion of people in the low-income world, were set out by T. W. Schultz (1980) in his Nobel Prize lecture on the economics of poverty. He advised that land is overrated as a source and limiter of increases in farm incomes. The quality of land resources explains only a small part of the productivity differences in world agriculture, while the quality of human agents is an underrated source of economic growth.

But governments in less developed nations, instead of encouraging and facilitating farmers in their many difficult decisions, frequently have imposed low and uncertain prices on staple crops through procedures that often become very political. In socialist-oriented societies, attempts are made to displace local decisionmaking by centralized decisions on prices, quantities, products, services, and technologies. Such aggregated decisionmaking makes little use of local knowledge about the technological and economic relations that enable productive use of local farm resources. Hence, central directives to farmers generally reduce the returns from farm resources in crop and livestock production.

The Central Role of Agriculture in Economic Growth

Both empirical and theoretical research have demonstrated the critical importance of strong agricultural growth to the general economic growth of less developed nations. This is due both to the importance of the agricultural sector in the economy and to the essential linkages between the agricultural and nonagricultural sectors required for strong economic growth, as demonstrated in chapter 3. Because the agricultural sector produces such a large share of gross national product in many less developed nations, its rate of growth greatly influences national economic growth rates. Essential for the achievement of high rates of national economic growth is meeting the challenge of high rates of growth in demand for food and agricultural products and the even higher rates of growth in marketing services, rates that will continue for many decades (chapters 3 and 12). The agricultural sectors of less developed nations are often particularly valuable, as they can earn large amounts of foreign exchange by reducing the need for food imports or by increasing exports.

The possible high returns from investment in agriculture are an often unrecognized potential in national economic growth. These higher returns will cause nations to make greater investments in agriculture. Advances in the biological, chemical, and mechanical technologies explored in chapters 8 and 9 illustrate the many high productivity farm technologies that may be obtained through the material, design, and capacity transfers examined in chapter 11.

The Government as Facilitator of Development

The history and traditions of different countries lead to different approaches to the role of government and its effects on economic development. Perhaps the most prevalent experience in less developed nations is that of an overambitious, smothering government that seeks to direct and control a large part of the national economy. This role may arise from the view that government is the primary source of economic growth, wisdom, and change, or from the fact that an ideal model for a socioeconomic system has been set forth by leaders and is to be forced into place.

The dominance of government in economic activities may also be reinforced in some countries by the fact that a high proportion of educated and politically dominant individuals are in government service. Domineering and authoritarian approaches to development may also fit with traditional cultural patterns and thus may be viewed as normal—the way government systems should operate. Once in place, government bureaucracies are very uncomfortable loosening control of economic activities. If these cultural traits and attitudes toward government are present, it is almost inevitable that too much will be attempted by government in relation to the limited human and other resources available to it. Hence, overambitious and overdominant governments usually slow economic growth through unnecessary rules and regulations that discourage high-return investments in agriculture and the other sectors of the economy. In agriculture, these governments often greatly hamper the procurement of inputs domestically or from abroad, decisionmaking by farmers, and the creation of more effective farm product marketing systems.

At the other extreme, some less developed nations have experienced a lack of essential government functions that would aid economic growth. A government may be weak because of a suspicion of central government, low government resources from taxation, or an extreme laissez-faire belief about economic activities. In these circumstances, government infrastructure and institutions, such as banking, postal services, communications, and roads, are so poor that agricultural and economic growth are slowed. Additional government activity under these conditions would provide high economic returns.

The goal of government, no matter what kind, is to obtain high social returns from the use of public resources. Thus governments should allocate limited personnel and other resources to activities that will contribute the most to social progress, including desired distributional outcomes. We believe, therefore, that the relation between the amount of public sector activity and the rate of social and economic development is an inverted U-shape. In some less developed nations, particularly in poorer areas, the lack of complementary public sector activity often results in slower social and economic development, while in other cases, wholesale attempts to control or incorporate much of agriculture into the public sector through nationalization and collectivization almost always results in slower rates of social and economic development. In each nation, at each stage in development, there are optimum levels of government activity, which can be identified only through experience as the particular social, political, and economic variables are included in decisions.

A cooperative approach to relations between the public and private sectors is the most productive, for it recognizes the catalytic potential of appropriate government action and the possible economic complementarities between the sectors. It focuses upon facilitating entrepreneurial activity in both sectors. We refer here to public sector entrepreneurial activity that is in the public interest, not to activities of government officials that are focused upon private gain through bribes and other income-increasing strategies that increase the cost of government to society. In particular, government activity that aids the formation of domestic and foreign input and product prices that reflect real resource costs will improve economic performance, as shown in chapters 13 and 14.

Core Strategic Elements for Rapid Growth in Agriculture

The following eight conclusions are core elements of an agricultural development strategy based upon the economics of induced innovation explored earlier.

Investment in High-Return Activities

In traditional agriculture, with little change in relative prices, technology, or institutions, there seldom are opportunities for investment in agricultural activities that provide returns above the low equilibrium level prevailing in the society. Now, in a world of rapid change in relative prices, agricultural technology, and institutions, less developed nations have many new opportunities to invest in more productive agricultural activities.

The modern agricultural production function examined in the first part of chapter 6 emphasizes that production is usefully viewed as a result of investments that either (1) increase the productivity of land and other physical resources; or (2) increase the productivity of labor. With the rapid growth in the biological, chemical, physical, and social sciences over the last three centuries and the recent increasing application of this knowledge to agricultural production and marketing, immense new opportunities for high-return investments in the agricultural sector of less developed nations have opened up. These opportunities are mostly obtained through material, design, and capacity transfer of agricultural technology and scientific knowledge from other nations.

Investment in Applied Research

The development of productive national research on agricultural technology and institutional change in the public and private sectors is a fundamental requirement for accelerating the rate of agricultural development. The location-specific nature of agricultural production almost always requires some adaptive research, for technological, institutional, and economic reasons, to more rapidly identify new profitable technologies. Technological issues requiring research relate to the often different conditions of the growing environment, especially the soils, the climate, and pests. The economic issues concern the ratio of the cost of labor relative to capital, which is lower in most less developed nations. Due to the different relative prices of agricultural inputs and products in less developed nations, many technologies from more developed nations are unprofitable in these nations.

The following sequence of the three phases of technology transfer is likely to be most productive in less developed nations (see also chapter 11). In the first phase, direct transfers, testing, and wide distribution of profitable technologies from abroad would occur. Such material transfers include plant and animal materials, mechanical equipment, and pesticides. In the second phase, the nation would develop the capacity to design and manufacture new technologies through the use of blueprints, textbooks, and other research materials obtained from abroad. This phase requires significant investments in laboratories, libraries, computers, researchers, extension personnel, and local production capacity.

At some point, in some less developed nations—especially the larger ones, such as India and China—the capacity-level phase of technology transfer will be highly productive for agriculture in the longer run in some or many science specialties. This third phase requires large investments in laboratories and long periods of costly training for scientists. If successful, such research capacity will create entirely new, more productive agricultural technologies and institutions not available in more developed nations. These researchers will work on the frontiers of world science.

Investment in Human Capital

Strategic investments in human capital for agricultural development include the following two. First, primary education is needed for farmers and their families to attain verbal and mathematical literacy and, as soon as possible, relevant secondary formal or nonformal education. This education would include especially (1) the basic principles of biology, chemistry, and physics as they apply to agriculture; (2) production economics and farm accounting; and (3) an understanding of rural, national, and international economic and social development. This investment would enable farmers to provide leadership in agriculture and rural areas and to respond to new economic opportunities, increasing both their allocative efficiency and the rate at which they adopt more productive technologies and institutions.

And second, for selected individuals, programs are needed at the university level to train researchers and administrators who would continuously create economic opportunities for increased productivity in agriculture through the development of more productive technology, institutions, and government policy. The education needed varies from increasing abilities to operate a marketing organization to training for postgraduate degrees, as the nation shifts from largely material transfers of agricultural technologies to design transfer to capacity research capabilities in appropriate subsectors of agriculture.

Complementary investments in extension and communication systems are also needed to strengthen the links between researchers and government administrators, on the one hand, and farmers, on the other, so that productivity increases on farms can be accelerated. These investments should increase communication skills and the knowledge of how to design and evaluate more productive extension and other communication activities.

Complementarity Among Investments

A wide range of investments becomes available in all less developed nations for the growth of agriculture. Farmers and private decisionmakers seek investments that will increase income most rapidly. To achieve such growth, government decisionmakers need to invest in those projects with the highest rates of return, based on benefit-cost or other economic analysis. A particular challenge to governments is to increase the average productivity of investments of public resources through careful attention to complementarities in investment projects. Investment complementarities arise in (1) agricultural areas; (2) time sequences; and (3) backward and forward marketing linkages to farming.

The economic theory of complementarity of inputs in production demonstrates that careful attention to these relations can lead to much higher rates of growth and higher rates of return on investments in agriculture (see chapter 8). Examples of complementary investments include (1) relating land ownership surveys, land leveling, and the rationalization of farm boundaries to irrigation investments; (2) relating plantation development and forest clearing to investments in plantation crop technology or market development; and (3) relating investments in rural infrastructure (transportation and communication) to farm needs so that farm costs are reduced, enabling expansion of agricultural production.

Complementary production relations in an agricultural area are incorporated in many package programs for input supply. When farmers receive the most profitable mix of inputs, higher private and social returns may be obtained from the use of limited development resources. The investment of government resources in such package programs has been widespread in less developed nations, including the Indian package program of the 1960s, the BIMAS program in Indonesia, which began in 1965, the Masagna 99 program in the Philippines, the minimum package program in Ethiopia in the 1970s, and the Puebla project in Mexico.[3] Bad experiences with package programs have also occurred when they were poorly designed or executed and were hence unproductive.

The economic complementarities that arise from sequences of investments are illustrated by the following four points drawn from Mosher (1981, p. 30). (1) New agricultural technology should be available before investment is made to increase credit availability. (2) Improved roads may often be required before more productive inputs, such as fertilizer, can be used profitably and paid for through farm marketings. (3) Adaptive research on farmers' fields to identify productive technologies should precede increases in extension and communica-

---

3. Material on the intensive agricultural districts program is provided in Mohar and Evenson 1974. The BIMAS package program in Indonesia was examined by Birowo (1975). The Masagna 99 package program in the Philippines was reviewed by Wortman and Cummings (1978, pp. 216–19).

tion. (4) Irrigation investments will usually be more productive if research on irrigated crops and effective irrigation management has already been carried out. Government planning and investment decisions that ignore these sequences will slow growth.

The economic complementarity of backward and forward linkages also deserves careful attention. Agricultural development can be viewed as the process of encouraging the evolution of a more productive agricultural system. Activities in the different parts of the system are often to some extent complementary, so that the rates at which the various parts of the system increase productivity will affect the whole system. Thus, appropriate balance in investments in both backward linkages to agriculture (input production and marketing) and forward linkages of product marketing can have large effects on the rate of agricultural growth. Improving these linkages very often requires considerable investment in infrastructure (which includes not only roads but communications and government agricultural policy and administrative personnel).

Domestic Prices that Reflect Resource Costs

The economic reason for reducing constraints on prices is the law of comparative advantage, examined in chapter 13. It demonstrates that per capita incomes and rates of growth will generally be higher with more flexible prices and trade, both internationally and in regions of a nation. Thus, constraints on trade, including those caused by significantly overvalued or undervalued exchange rates, slow growth.

The importance of economic flexibility reflects both the need to respond to changing international markets and the need for domestic economic growth. Hence, governments should focus on ways to facilitate rapid responses by the agricultural and other sectors to internal and external price changes. However, a common government response to changes in prices, especially in important agricultural products, is to attempt to control the change. Such control may be useful in preventing shocks and in easing adjustments in an economy over the short run. However, once put in place, controls often remain too long, increasing the cost of food and agricultural products. Distorted prices will reduce growth by causing both overinvestment in agricultural activities that produce low social returns and underinvestment in those farming and marketing activities that would increase growth more rapidly. Also, control mechanisms often increase marketing costs. If, however, price-controlling mechanisms have little influence on market prices, then resources expended in the controlling activities are wasted.

Maximizing the Limited Contributions of International Aid

In most less developed nations, international aid can potentially provide complementary resources that could greatly accelerate growth. These possibilities range widely, depending upon the needs and agricultural development conditions in a particular nation. In the early stages of development, international aid activities that facilitate the material transfer of technologies to the agriculture of a less developed nation could provide very high returns. Over the longer run, aid can make strategic contributions of complementary training and institution building. Examples include (1) improving experiment stations, agricultural colleges and universities, and agricultural extension and communication systems; and (2) augmenting economic and other social science research capabilities to improve the performance of agricultural policy, project planning, and institutional change.

However, international aid generally increases by only a small percentage the investment resources available to the nation. Thus, national agricultural growth will depend primarily on how productively these resources are invested. Aid that is poorly invested may have little effect on growth. Low aid impact can result from poor performance in identifying and formulating productive agricultural investment projects due to a lack of professional capacity domestically or poor performance by the international personnel involved in project design. At worst, dealing with an excess of international aid activities can absorb too large a proportion of the scarce professional and managerial talent available in a less developed nation, preventing it from focusing on activities that would have more impact on development.

Moderating Undesirable Income Distribution Effects

The package of policies and investments that the governments of less developed nations implement in agriculture will often greatly influence income distribution. In the short run, income distribution is affected by taxes, price controls, and subsidies, and in the longer run it is affected by changes in the productive assets controlled by individuals. To take two examples, subsidies for fertilizers and for machinery, if derived from taxes on other sectors, increase the income of farmers who use these inputs. But when the prices of food grains are held below market prices, farmers are taxed by reducing their incomes in order to increase the real income of urban dwellers through low food prices. Although the income transfers achieved through such policies may be desired by a government, economic theory demonstrates that both subsidies and taxes usually distort the growth of the industries affected, causing them to be less productive than they could be and thus slowing national economic growth (see chapter 14).

The kinds of agricultural investments made by governments, and to a lesser extent by the private sector, can greatly influence the productive assets controlled by different individuals and groups in society and hence the distribution of income. Grabowski (1981) pointed out that there is often a direct link between the pattern of government investment in technological and institutional change and political influence. Thus, for example, changes in these investments may "require an increase in the power and influence of farmers with small farms, relative to those with large farms, on government decisions concerning rural research and credit priorities. This could possibly be accomplished through land reforms or, a less radical solution, the organization of small farmers into groups which could put pressure on government agencies to recognize and respond to the interest of small farmers'' (p. 180).

Two investment strategies illustrate differing impacts on income distribution. In one, an aristocratic government interested primarily in the growth of large farms and thus in increasing the bimodal nature of agriculture might invest in the following: (1) importing and producing those biological, chemical, and mechanical technologies that increase the productivity of crops and livestock grown on large farms; (2) increasing the availability of large tractors and machinery at low cost in order to reduce labor costs; (3) increasing the availability of subsidized irrigation water for large farms through irrigation projects that provide water below cost to these farmers; (4) improving institutional arrangements for input and product marketing and for credit that serve large farms; and (5) designing extension services and formal education relevant to agriculture, accessible primarily to the families who work large farms. This portfolio of agricultural investments would increase the productivity, comparative advantage, and income of persons on large farms relative to those on small farms and to rural laborers. It also is likely to cause slower national economic growth than other investment patterns.

An alternative investment strategy would lead to more rapid productivity increases on small and medium-sized farms, hence a reduction in income distribution disparities and greater income for laborers. These investments would (1) accelerate the import and local production of more productive agricultural technologies for the crops and livestock grown by these farmers; (2) augment extension or other communication systems that reach small and medium-sized farms; (3) improve input and product marketing and credit institutions so that they serve small and medium-sized farms; (4) expand primary and secondary education for rural people, accessible to the families who work small and medium-sized farms, including scholarship arrangements to aid the best students from these farms; and (5) redistribute land, if necessary. These investments would both reduce income disparities and accelerate the growth of agricultural productivity, as was so clearly demonstrated by the experience in Taiwan and some other land reforms. This strategy assumes that large farmers have enough entrepreneurial talent and resources to increase their farm productivity with limited direct government help. Much evidence in the development literature indicates that, in those farming areas with large disparities in agricultural holdings, policies and investments that decrease resource and income disparities are usually associated with more rapid agricultural development, especially over the longer run, assuming that supporting programs for small farm development are provided.

There are real dangers in some development strategies if all the gains from development go to a small group:

if technical progress is slower for the small farmers than it is for the large farmers, the relative income gains for small farmers are reduced. . . . A real danger will arise if new technology is monopolized by a small number of large commercial farms with no significant shift in the aggregate supply schedule. In such a case, the large farms could capture the whole gain of technical progress. (Hayami and Herdt 1978, p. 301)

Regional growth disparities can be addressed with two specific strategies: (1) support for migration; and (2) compensatory allocation of government resources to disadvantaged areas. Migration from low-income areas has been a universal strategy of peoples throughout history. Migrations between the different regions of a less developed nation are often a concern; in recent years, overly rapid migration to urban areas may have slowed economic growth in some of these nations. Thus, policies, such as higher agricultural prices, that increase incomes in rural areas could make a positive contribution to development by slowing migration and its costs to society. In other situations, aid for selective migration may contribute to increasing the incomes of people in poor resource regions and, hence, national income.

Compensatory investment in regions with poor agricultural resources could moderate poverty in these regions by facilitating shifts to other economic activities that would increase income. Specific kinds of investments include (1) support for education and other human capital development, which could be later employed locally or in other parts of the country; (2) the development of industries based on natural resources and tourism; and (3) higher levels of social services than in other regions. Overinvestment in compensatory activities of low productivity would, of course, slow national economic development.

Enhancing Government Performance

Governments of less developed nations have immense opportunities to respond creatively to the problems and opportunities of development by increasing performance. Low capabilities in government may greatly slow development. Governments of whatever political persuasion have the opportunity to provide effective leadership, improved management, and education for their citizens, to help them deal with the social and economic changes ahead. Whether the legislative, executive, and judicial branches will facilitate goal identification and change or will impede change depends to a considerable extent upon the human capital investments made by government in its personnel. This investment includes in-service training and the recruiting and support of capable civil servants. It also involves continual review of government performance to determine if government activities do facilitate desired social and economic development. A government also will identify and aid those groups that lose relative to the rest of society during its historic national economic transformation.

Specifically, government development requires improved performance in the political, research, planning, and executive functions. Progress in the political area would include changes that enable a government to better respond to the needs and desires of the different regions and social groups in the nation. This could include (1) changes in electoral processes, so that people could better express their preferences for leadership; (2) a more representative legislature, with more power; and (3) administrative changes that allow effective responses to the needs of the various persons and groups in the society.

In the past, with slowly changing social and economic environments, nations have had little need for economic analysis and planning of possible activities and investments, for the most profitable investments would usually be the same as before. In contrast, in the dynamic world environment of today, governments of less developed nations must greatly increase their ability to explore the economic and social implications of changes in relative prices and new investment opportunities in technology, institutions, and human capital, in order to use their national resources most effectively. Hence, the availability to government of highly trained researchers and policy analysts can increase the returns to development investments and the extent to which government policies facilitate or slow desired development. And finally, the performance of all personnel in carrying out government activities greatly affects the productivity of all government functions and, hence, the overhead costs of development.

Many government activities reduce economic performance, thereby increasing the cost of government to society.

For example, it is common to observe that government market interventions such as licenses, quotas, rationing, and price controls are promoted by interest groups seeking "institutional rents" or monopoly profits. Rent seeking by interest groups does not contribute to the creation of new income streams in society, but it does entail social costs. These costs result in losses in market efficiency that government interventions produce and the waste of resources used to obtain them, such as lobbying and bribery. (Hayami and Ruttan 1985, p. 108)

Three Strategies for Agricultural Development

Offering general strategies for agricultural development is risky, as the economic and agricultural conditions in different areas of less developed nations are so varied. Hence, better strategies can usually be developed for an area or a country by those who know the economics of agricultural development, local prices, and the resource, technological, institutional, and cultural conditions. However, the following summaries of three general strategies may aid in setting out strategies for a particular less developed nation or area. These strategies are all concerned with how best to further upset current production equilibrium to achieve more productive use of national resources.

The High-Payoff Input Strategy

The Asian Development Bank (1969) offered an important general strategy for agricultural development based upon the Schultz high-payoff input model. Four assumptions underlie this strategy: (1) food has first priority; (2) the expansion of output has priority over equity considerations; (3) modern agriculture based on science and technology is sought; and (4) prices of agricultural products influence farmers' decisions.

The strategy identified four conditions as essential for growth: (1) a minimal infrastructure for rural transportation; (2) market facilities; (3) an assured water supply for crops, and (4) a method for providing a flow of new technology to farmers. Given these conditions, the strategy consisted of three steps: (1) begin with improved seeds and fertilizer; (2) undertake plant protection activities; and (3) increase water control, mechanization, and infrastructure activities.

The Improved-Income-Distribution-with-Growth Strategy

A strategy that places emphasis on improved income distribution was offered by Mellor (1976, pp. 281–94). This employment-oriented growth strategy was based on experience with the development problems of India and South Asia and focused on medium- and small-sized farms. Four realities about economic development were set out as underlying the strategy: (1) the economic development problem is not only one of mobilizing resources to produce capital goods (machinery, etc.) but also one of producing consumer goods; (2) with the availability of methods of producing technological change, fixed coefficients of production should not be assumed, and emphasis should be placed on inducing technological advance; (3) with an employment-oriented strategy, increases in consumer income will stimulate consumer goods industries; and (4) greater involvement in international trade requires an increased flexibility in production.

This strategy has three priorities. The first priority is to accelerate the growth of the agricultural sector through a focus on (1) ensuring ample fertilizer supplies; (2) investing massively in water control, especially small-scale, well-controlled projects, including rural electrification, especially in areas with high population densities; (3) expanding research; and (4) expanding the supply of trained rural manpower to staff programs to assist small farmers.

The second priority is the expansion of small-scale industry, particularly through investment in transportation and power.

Investment in these categories interacts with the agricultural strategy, first, in producing commodities with a comparative advantage in export and thereby providing foreign exchange for importation of capital intensive intermediate products and raw materials; second by enlarging the base for the development of institutions to support both agriculture and small scale industry; and third, in providing the increased employment so necessary to expanding consumer markets for increased agricultural production. (Mellor 1976, p. 285)

The third priority is the expansion of exports to pay for capital imports.

The Regional, Total-Resource-Focused Strategy

The third general agricultural development strategy was presented in similar forms by Wortman and Cummings (1978, pp. 233–70) and Mosher (1981). The three parts of this strategic approach are (1) commodity production programs; (2) farming district projects; and (3) improved efficiency of regular agricultural agencies. The core activities in the commodity production part of the strategy are (1) on-farm testing; (2) technological assistance to farmers by production specialists; (3) adaptive research; and in Mosher's exposition, (4) integrated research and extension for the target commodities.

The farming district project part of the strategy attempts to exploit the total resources of a rural area. The strategy requires identifying areas with varied agricultural potentials, because they will provide different rates of return on the investment of different sets of government resources and therefore require different development activities to maximize total return on social investment. They propose that, in areas with immediate agricultural growth potential, on-farm testing, agricultural support activities, and improved local roads will usually provide high returns. Those areas with future agricultural growth potential are likely to require longer term investments in irrigation, roads, or research. Areas with low agricultural growth potential are likely to provide low or negative returns to the investment of scarce national resources in agriculture. However, strategic nonagricultural investments in some of these areas can sometimes be productive.

The second part of this strategy—projects for farming districts—seeks to make opportunities available to all farmers, with the focus upon the total farm system. It aims to bring all land and other resources into the most effective use. However, due to scarce development resources, activities have to be selective and will therefore often include program activities focused on one or a few core crops or livestock. Mosher emphasized that farming district projects have dual organizational needs, which consist of both (1) productive vertical ties between local, regional, and national organizations involved in the same activity, such as veterinarian and soil-testing services; and (2) effective horizontal coordination at the regional and local levels among agricultural support activities (see figure 15.1).

The third part of this strategy focuses on improving the efficiency of regular agricultural agencies. If a high proportion of the highly educated and technically trained persons in a nation are in government service, and if government controls a considerable proportion of national economic activity and investments, better performance by government agencies would have considerable impact on economic growth. Mosher identifies six means for improving agency performance: (1) promote the staff's professional growth; (2) provide incentives for more efficient staff performance; (3) create more appropriate patterns of organization; (4) improve agricultural planning; (5) adopt more efficient operating procedures; and (6) use appropriate styles of administration—"total commitment to improving regular agricultural agencies, and gradual implementation of the various steps to be taken lie at the heart of successful application of this approach" (Mosher 1981, p. 58).

Figure 15.1. Dual Organizational Needs of Each Agricultural Support Activity

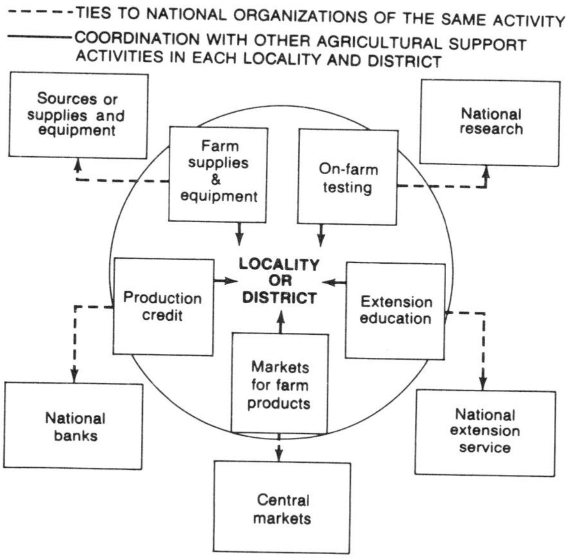

Source: Mosher 1981 (p. 34). Reprinted with permission.

Summary

The reader, while examining the preceding agricultural development strategies, may have noted that, although the emphasis in each one is different, all are based upon sound economic reasoning and are consistent with the induced development model. Each country and region needs a strategy that fits its social, institutional, technological, and resource conditions so that it will contribute to the social objectives of the area. By employing the economic analysis tools provided in this and other sources and by examining the empirical realities in a particular place and time higher return agricultural development policies, programs, and projects can be identified.[4]

The Different Paths of Agricultural Development in the Twenty-first Century

The changing world economic and political environment will provide a large variety of challenges and opportunities for agricultural development in

4. Oshima (1977) provided a review of development strategies. Other significant works that set out agricultural development and food strategies include Hunter 1978; Asian Development Bank 1977; and Timmer 1984. Materials concerned with Africa include World Bank 1981, 1984a; Eicher 1984; Lele 1979, 1984; Mellor, Delgado, and Blackie 1987; and Berg and Whitaker 1986. For an examination of nutritional strategies, see part V in Gittinger, Leslie, and Hoisington 1987.

each less developed nation as it moves into the twenty-first century. Strong markets in more developed nations for some tropical products, such as palm oil and coffee, will enable some less developed nations to earn much foreign exchange from agricultural exports. Other nations will be challenged to increase the growth and productivity of their agricultures in order to reduce dependence on food imports and hence increase food security. With increasing supplies of agricultural products worldwide, all nations will have to reduce unit costs in agriculture by increasing productivity in order to remain competitive internationally. Still other less developed nations, those with poor natural resources for agriculture, face the task of identifying and supporting the development of those agricultural activities that can be profitable, while shifting rural resources into activities that can produce competitively for either local or foreign markets.

Some less developed nations may follow a path leading to the immiserization of rural people, as predicted long ago by Ricardo. This is occurring in some areas with rapid rates of population increase. Common causes of decreasing real incomes are the following: (1) lack of attention to increasing the productivity of agriculture, so that food supply fails to keep up with growing demand, causing increased food prices and a decline in real income; and (2) an overemphasis on large farms and labor-saving technologies that increase unemployment and decrease the real income of the many small farm and laboring families.

Economic and social forces will induce each nation and national subregion to follow a different path of agricultural development, due to great differences in physical, technological, institutional, and human resources. Some paths may be labor intensive for many decades, while others have already become quite capital intensive. Some will involve many complex government actions and changes in institutional arrangements with the objective of achieving more nearly certain economic, distributional, and political goals. Others will involve much less government activity and place reliance on markets. In all nations in the decades ahead, the levels and productivity of the investments in technological and institutional change and in human capital will greatly affect the rate of economic growth and, more specifically, the performance of agriculture. Gradually accumulated social learning will enable each nation to understand better and to capitalize more on core sources of development.

Important Concepts

Compensatory investment	Improved-income-distribution-
Government performance levels	with-growth strategy
Core elements of rapid growth	Total-resource-focused strategy
strategies	Future agricultural growth potential
High-payoff input strategy	

Sample Questions

1. How can a lack of a national consensus on development goals hamper agricultural development? Be specific, and give an example.

2. What alternative roles can government take in relation to the economic system? Illustrate your answer with two specific examples from agriculture.

3. In what ways can high-return investments for agriculture be obtained by a less developed nation?

4. How does human capital investment affect agricultural development? Be specific.

5. Why should attention be paid to economic complementarity in planning investments in agricultural development? Explain. Offer two examples.

6. Explain what comparative advantage has to do with regional growth within a less developed nation.

7. Outline two agricultural development strategies, one that would be likely to increase, and another that would be likely to decrease, income disparities.

8. Summarize two general strategies for agricultural development. Identify a particular less developed nation and explain why one of them would be best for that nation.

References

Abbott, J. C. 1983. "Building Marketing Infrastructure for Development." In *World Food Marketing Systems,* ed. E. E. Kaynek. London: Butterworth.

————. 1985. "Agricultural Marketing Mechanisms and Institutions." In *Agricultural Marketing Policy.* 2 vols. Washington, D.C.: World Bank, Economic Development Institute.

Abbott, J. C., and Creupelandt, H. C. 1966. *Agricultural Marketing Boards—Their Establishment and Operation.* Rome: Food and Agriculture Organization.

Abbott, J. C., and Makeham, L. P. 1979. *Agricultural Economics and Marketing in the Tropics.* London: Longman.

Abbott, J. C., and colleagues. 1984. *Marketing Improvement in the Developing World—What Happens and What We Have Learned.* Agricultural Services Bulletin 58. Rome: Food and Agriculture Organization.

Abbott, P. C., and Thompson, R. L. 1987. "Changing Agricultural Comparative Advantage." *Agricultural Economics* 1:97–112.

Adams, D. 1978. "Mobilizing Household Savings Through Rural Financial Markets." *Economic Development and Cultural Change* 28:547–60.

Adams, D. W., and Graham, D. 1984. "A Critique of Traditional Agricultural Credit Projects and Policies." In *Agricultural Development in the Third World,* ed. C. K. Eicher and J. M. Staatz. Baltimore: Johns Hopkins University Press.

Adams, D. W.; Graham, D. H.; and Von Pischke, J. D., eds. 1984. *Undermining Rural Development with Cheap Credit.* Boulder, Colo.: Westview.

Adams, R. H. 1983. "The Role of Research in Policy Development: The Creation of the IMF Cereal Import Facility." *World Development* 11:549–64.

Adelman, I., and Morris, C. T. 1973. *Economic Growth and Social Equity in Developing Countries.* Palo Alto, Calif.: Stanford University Press.

Agarwala, R. 1983. *Price Distortions and Growth in Developing Countries.* Staff Working Paper 575. Washington, D.C.: World Bank.

Ahammed, C. S., and R. W. Herdt. 1983. "Farm Mechanization in a Semiclosed Input-Output Model: The Philippines." *American Journal of Agricultural Economics* 65:516–24.

Ahmed, M. 1975. *The Economics of Non-Formal Education: Resources, Costs and Benefits.* New York: Praeger.

AID (Agency for International Development). 1970. *Spring Review of Land Reform.* 12 vols. Washington, D.C.: AID.

Alexander, R. J. 1974. *Agrarian Reform in Latin America.* New York: Macmillan.

Alier, J. M. 1977. *Haciendas, Plantations and Collective Farms.* London: Frank Cass.

Alviar, N. G. 1979. "An Economic Comparison Between Tractor Operated and Carabao Cultivated Rice Farms." In *Readings in Asian Farm Management,* ed. T. B. Thiam and S. Ong. Singapore: Singapore University Press.

Amin, S. 1974. *Accumulation on a World Scale: A Critique of the Theory of Underdevelopment.* New York: Monthly Review Press.

————. 1976. *Unequal Development: An Essay on the Social Formations of Peripheral Capitalism.* New York: Monthly Review Press.

————. 1977a. *Imperialism and Unequal Development.* New York: Monthly Review Press.

————. 1977b. "Self-Reliance and the New International Economic Order." *Monthly Review* 29:1-21.

Amsden, A. H., ed. 1980. *The Economics of Women and Work.* New York: St. Martin's.

Anand Milk Cooperative. 1982. *Annual Report.* Anand, India: National Diary Production Board.

Anderson, K. 1986. "Economic Growth, Comparative Advantage, and Agricultural Trade of Pacific Basin Countries." In *Food, Agriculture, and Development in the Pacific Basin,* ed. G. Edward Schuh and Jennifer L. McCoy. Boulder: Westview Press.

————. 1983. "Growth of Agricultural Protection in East Asia." *Food Policy* 8:327-36.

Anderson, R. S., ed. 1982. *Science, Politics, and the Agricultural Revolution in Asia.* Boulder, Colo.: Westview.

Andreae, B. 1981. *Farming, Development and Space: A World Agricultural Geography.* Berlin: Walter de Gruyter.

Andrew, C. O., and Hildebrand, P. E. 1982. *Planning and Conducting Applied Agricultural Research.* Boulder, Colo.: Westview.

Anthony, K. R. M.; Johnston, B. F.; Jones, W. O.; and Uchendu, V. C. 1979. *Agricultural Change in Tropical Africa.* Ithaca, N.Y.: Cornell University Press.

Apthorpe, R. 1970. *Rural Cooperatives and Planned Change in Africa: Case Materials.* Geneva, Switzerland: U.N. Research Institute for Social Development.

Arnon, I. 1981. *Modernization of Agriculture in Developing Countries.* New York: Wiley.

Ashby, J. A. 1979. *New Models for Agricultural Research and Extension: The Need to Integrate Women.* Ithaca, N.Y.: Cornell University Press.

Asian Development Bank. 1969. *Asian Agricultural Survey.* Tokyo: University of Tokyo.

————. 1977. *Rural Asia—Challenge and Opportunity. Report of the Second Asian Agricultural Survey.* Manila: Asian Development Bank.

Asian Productivity Organization. 1983. *Farm Mechanization in Asia.* Tokyo: Asian Productivity Organization.

————. 1984. *Farm Credit Situation in Asia.* Tokyo: Asian Productivity Organization.

Askari, H., and Cummings, J. T. 1976. *Agricultural Supply Response.* New York: Praeger.

Babbie, E. R. 1980. *Sociology: An Introduction.* 2d ed. Belmont, Calif.: Wadsworth.

Balassa, B. 1975. "Reforming the System of Incentives in Developing Countries." *World Development* 3:365–82.

————. 1979. "A 'Stages' Approach to Comparative Advantage." In *Economic Growth and Resources.* Vol. 4. National and International Issues, ed. I. Adelman. New York: St. Martin's.

Baldwin, R. L., ed. 1980. *Animals, Feed, Food and People—An Analysis of the Role of Animals in Food Production.* Boulder, Colo.: Westview.

Baran, P. A. 1975. *The Political Economy of Growth.* New York: Modern Reader Paperbacks.

Barchfield, J. W. 1979. *Land Tenure and Social Productivity in Mexico.* LTC Paper 121. Madison: University of Wisconsin, Land Tenure Center.

Bardhan, P. K. 1979. "Agricultural Development and Land Tenancy in a Peasant Economy: A Theoretical and Empirical Analysis." *American Journal of Agricultural Economics* 61:48–57.

————. 1984. *Land, Labor and Rural Poverty.* Delhi, India: Oxford University Press.

Barker, R. 1978. "Barriers to Efficient Capital Investment in Agriculture." In *Distortions in Agricultural Incentives,* ed. T. W. Schultz. Bloomington: Indiana University Press.

Barker, R.; Bennagen, E.; and Hayami, Y. 1978. "New Rice Technology and Policy Alternatives for Food Self-Sufficiency." In *Economic Consequences of the New Rice Technology.* Los Banos, Laguna, Philippines: International Rice Research Institute.

Barker, R., and Cordova, V. G. 1978. "Labor Utilization in Rice Production." In *Economic Consequences of the New Rice Technology.* Los Banos, Laguna, Philippines: International Rice Research Institute.

Barker, R., and Hayami, Y. 1976. "Price Support Versus Input Subsidy for Food Self-Sufficiency in Developing Countries." *American Journal of Agricultural Economics* 58:617–28.

Barker, R.; Herdt, R.; and Rose, B. 1985. *The Asian Rice Economy.* Baltimore: Johns Hopkins University Press.

Barlett, P. F. 1980. *Agricultural Decision Making: Anthropological Contributions to Rural Development.* New York: Academic.

Barnett, H. J., and Morse, C. 1963. *Scarcity and Growth.* Baltimore: Johns Hopkins Press.

Barnum, H. N., and Squire, L. 1979. *A Model of an Agricultural Household: Theory and Evidence.* World Bank Staff Occasional Paper 27. Baltimore: Johns Hopkins University Press.

Barraclough, S. L. 1969. "Why Land Reform?" *Ceres* 2:21–24.

Barraclough, S., and Collarte, J. C. 1973. *Agrarian Structure in Latin America.* New York: Heath.

Barrett, V.; Lassiter, G.; Wilcock, D.; Baker, D.; and Crawford, E. 1982. *Animal Traction in Eastern Upper Volta: A Technical, Economic and Institutional Analysis.* MSU International Development Paper 4. East Lansing: Michigan State University, Department of Agricultural Economics.

Bates, R. H. 1981. *Markets and States in Tropical Africa—The Political Basis of Agricultural Policies.* Berkeley and Los Angeles: University of California Press.

Bathrick, D. D. 1981. *Agricultural Credit for Small Farm Development—Policies and Practices.* Boulder, Colo.: Westview.

Bayliss-Smith, T., and Wanmali, S., eds. 1984. *Understanding Green Revolutions: Agrarian Change and Development Planning in South Asia.* Cambridge: Cambridge University Press.

Becker, G. S. 1975. *Human Capital.* 2d ed. New York: Columbia University Press.

————. 1976. *The Economic Approach to Human Behavior.* Chicago: University of Chicago Press.

————. 1981. *A Treatise on the Family.* Cambridge, Mass.: Harvard University Press.

Beckford, G. L. 1972. *Persistent Poverty: Underdevelopment in Plantation Economies of the Third World.* New York: Oxford University Press.

————. 1984. "Strategies for Agricultural Development: Comment." In *Agricultural Development in the Third World,* ed. C. K. Eicher and J. M. Staatz. Baltimore: Johns Hopkins University Press.

Behrman, J. R. 1968. *Supply Response in Underdeveloped Agriculture: A Case Study of Four Major Annual Crops in Thailand, 1937–1963.* Amsterdam: North-Holland.

————. 1984. "The Analytics of International Commodity Agreements." In *Agricultural Development in the Third World,* ed. C. K. Eicher and J. M. Staatz. Baltimore: Johns Hopkins University Press.

Benerid, L., ed. 1982. *Women and Development: The Sexual Division of Labor in Rural Societies.* New York: Praeger.

Benor, D., and Baxter, M. 1984. *Training and Visit Extension.* Washington, D.C.: World Bank.

Berg, A. 1981. *Malnourished People: A Policy View.* Poverty and Basic Needs Series. Washington, D.C.: World Bank.

Berg, E. *See* CILSS.

Berg, R. J., and Whitaker, J. S., eds. 1986. *Strategies for African Development.* Washington, D.C.: Overseas Development Council.

Bergmann, H., and Boussard, J. M. 1976. *Guide to the Economic Evaluation of Irrigation Projects.* Rev. ed. Paris: Organisation for Economic Cooperation and Development.

Bernsten, R. H.; Siwi, B. H.; and Beachell, H. M. 1982. *The Development and Diffusion of Rice Varieties in Indonesia.* Research Paper Series 71. Los Banos, Laguna, Philippines: International Rice Research Institute.

Berry, A. R., and Cline, W. R. 1979. *Agrarian Structure and Productivity in Developing Countries.* Baltimore: Johns Hopkins University Press.

Berry, A. R., and Sabot, R. H. 1978. "Labour Market Performance in Developing Countries: A Survey." *World Development* 6:1199–242.

Bertelsen, P. H. 1961. "Folk High Schools for West Africa." *International Development Review* 3:28–31.

Bhuiyan, S. I. 1980. "Irrigation and Agricultural Development in Bangladesh." *Agricultural Mechanization in Asia* 11:55–62.

Binswanger, H. P. 1978. *The Economics of Tractors in the Indian Subcontinent: An Analytical Review.* Hyderabad, India: International Crops Research Institute for the Semi-Arid Tropics.

――――――. 1980. "Attitudes Toward Risk: Experimental Measurement in Rural India." *American Journal of Agricultural Economics* 62:395–407.

――――――. 1984. *Agricultural Mechanization: A Comparative Historical Perspective.* Agricultural and Rural Development Working Paper 673. Washington, D.C.: World Bank.

Binswanger, H. P., and Rosenzweig, M. R., eds. 1984. *Contractual Arrangements, Employment, and Wages in Rural Labor Markets in Asia.* New Haven, Conn.: Yale University Press.

Binswanger, H. P., and Ruttan, V. W. 1978. *Induced Innovation: Technology, Institutions and Development.* Baltimore: Johns Hopkins University Press.

Binswanger, H. P., and Ryan, J. G. 1977. "Efficiency and Equity Issues in Ex Ante Allocation of Research Resources." *Indian Journal of Agricultural Economics* 32:217–31.

Binswanger, H., et al. 1979. "Socio-Economics of Improved Animal-Drawn Implements and Mechanization." In *Socioeconomic Constraints to Development of Semi-Arid Tropical Agriculture.* Patancheru, India: International Crops Research Institute for the Semi-Arid Tropics.

Birowo, A. T. 1975. *BIMAS: A Package Program for Intensification of Food Crop Production in Indonesia.* Seadag Paper 75-4. New York: Asia Society.

Blase, M. G. 1971. *Institutions in Agricultural Development.* Ames: Iowa State University Press.

Blaug, M. 1970. *An Introduction to the Economics of Education.* London, Penguin.

Bliss, C. T., and Stern, N. H. 1982. *Palanpur: The Economy of an Indian Village.* Oxford: Clarenden.

Bohannan, P. 1963. "Land, Tenure and Land Tenure." In *African Agrarian Systems,* ed. D. Biebuyck. London: Oxford University Press.

Bohannan, P., and Dalton, G., eds. 1965. *Markets in Africa.* New York: Doubleday.

Bonin, J. P. 1977. "Work Incentives and Uncertainty on a Collective Farm." *Journal of Comparative Economics* 1:77–97.

Bose, S. 1974. "The Comilla Cooperative Approach and the Prospects for Broad-Based Green Revolution in Bangladesh." *World Development* 2:21–28.

Boserup, E. 1965. *The Conditions of Agricultural Growth: The Economics of Agrarian Change Under Population Pressure.* Chicago: Aldine.

――――――. 1970. *Woman's Role in Economic Development.* New York: St. Martin's.

――――――. 1981. *Population and Technological Change: A Study of Long-Term Trends.* Chicago: University of Chicago Press.

Bottomley, A. 1975. "Interest Rate Determination in Underdeveloped Rural Areas." *American Journal of Agricultural Economics* 57:279–91.

Boulding, K. E. 1967. "The Legitimacy of Economics." *Western Economic Journal* 4:299-307.

Boyce, J. K., and Evenson, R. E. 1975. *National and International Agricultural Research and Extension Programs.* New York: Agricultural Development Council.

Breimyer, H. 1973. "The Economics of Agricultural Marketing: A Survey." *Review of Marketing and Agricultural Economics* 41:115-65.

Brembeck, C. S., and Thompson, T. J., eds. 1973. *New Strategies for Educational Development: The Cross-Cultural Search for Non-Formal Alternatives.* Lexington, Mass.: Heath.

Brewster, J. M. 1967. "Traditional Social Structures as Barriers to Change." In *Agricultural Development and Economic Growth,* ed. H. M. Southworth and B. F. Johnston. Ithaca, N.Y.: Cornell University Press.

Bromley, D. W. 1982a. *Improving Irrigated Agriculture: Institutional Reform and the Small Farmer.* Staff Paper 531. Washington, D. C.: World Bank.

―――. 1982b. "Land and Water Problems: An Institutional Perspective." *American Journal of Agricultural Economics* 64:834-44.

Brush, S. B. 1977. *Mountain, Field and Family: The Economy and Human Ecology of an Andean Valley.* Philadelphia: University of Pennsylvania Press.

Buchanan, N. S., and Ellis, H. S. 1955. *Approaches to Economic Development.* New York: Twentieth Century Fund.

Buck, P. 1949. *The Good Earth.* New York: John Day.

Bucklin, L. P. 1977. "Improving Food Retailing in Developing Asian Countries." *Food Policy* 2:114-22.

Bunting, A. H. 1979. *Science and Technology for Human Needs, Rural Development and Relief of Poverty.* Occasional Paper. New York: International Agricultural Development Service.

Buvinic, M.; Lycette, M. A.; and McGreevey, W. P., eds. 1983. *Women and Poverty in the Third World.* Baltimore: Johns Hopkins University Press.

Byerlee, D., and Sain, G. 1986. "Food Pricing Policy in Developing Countries: Bias Against Agriculture or for Urban Consumers." *American Journal of Agricultural Economics* 68:961-69.

Carapetis, S.; Beenhakker, H. L.; and Howe, J. D. F. 1984. *The Supply and Quality of Rural Transportation Services in Developing Countries.* Working Paper 654. Washington, D.C.: World Bank.

Carruthers, I., and Clark, C. 1981. *The Economics of Irrigation.* Liverpool, U.K.: Liverpool University Press.

Cassen, R. 1982. *Rich Country Interests in Third World Development.* New York: St. Martin's.

―――. 1986. *Does Aid Work? Report to an Intergovernmental Task Force.* New York: Clarendon.

Castillo, G. T.; de Guzman, A. M.; Pahud, S. L.; and Paje, L. 1973. "The Green Revolution at the Village Level: A Philippine Case Study, 1963-1970." In *Technical Change in Asian Agriculture,* ed. R. T. Shand. Canberra: Australian National University Press.

Cernea, M. M. 1986. *Putting People First—Sociological Variables in Rural Development.* New York: Oxford University Press.

Cernea, M. M.; Coulter, J. K.; and Russell, J. F. A. D., eds. 1983. *Agricultural Extension by Training and Visit: The Asian Experience.* Washington, D.C.: World Bank.

Chambers, R. 1969. *Settlement Schemes in Tropical Africa.* New York: Praeger.

Chancellor, W. T. 1978. "Custom Tractor Operations in the Far East." In *Agricultural Technology for Developing Nations.* Urbana: University of Illinois Printing Service.

Charlton, S. E. M. 1984. *Women in Third World Development.* Boulder, Colo.: Westview.

Cheetham, R. J.; Kelley, A. C.; and Williamson, J. G. 1974. "Demand, Structural Change and the Process of Economic Growth." In *Nations and Households in Economic Growth,* ed. M. Abramovitz. New York: Academic.

Chenery, H. B. 1975. "The Structuralist Approach to Development Policy." *American Economic Review* 65:310–15.

Chenery H. B., and Syrquin, M. 1975. *Patterns of Development, 1950–1970.* New York: Oxford University Press.

Chenery, H. B., et al. 1979. *Structural Change and Development Policy.* New York: Oxford University Press.

Chodak, S. 1973. *Societal Development for Comparative Analysis.* New York: Oxford University Press.

Chou, M.; Harmon, D. P., Jr.; Kahn, H.; and Wittwer, S. H. 1977. *World Food Prospects and Agricultural Potential.* New York: Praeger.

Christensen, R. P. 1968. *Taiwan's Agricultural Development: Its Relevance for Developing Countries Today.* Foreign Agriculture Report 39. Washington, D.C.: U.S. Department of Agriculture.

Christensen, R. P., and Stevens, R. D. 1962. "Putting Science to Work to Improve World Agriculture." In *Food—One Tool in International Economic Development,* ed. E. O. Haroldsen. Ames: Iowa State University Press.

Christiansen, R. E. 1987. *The Impact of Economic Development on Agricultural Trade Patterns.* Economic Research Service Staff Report AGES861118. Washington, D.C.: U.S. Department of Agriculture.

Chuta, E., and Liedholm, C. 1984. "Rural Small-Scale Industry: Empirical Evidence and Policy Issues." In *Agricultural Development in the Third World,* ed. C. K. Eicher and J. M. Staatz. Baltimore: Johns Hopkins University Press.

CILSS/Club du Sahel (Working Group on Marketing, Price Policy, and Storage). 1977. *Marketing, Price Policy and Storage of Food Grains in the Sahel: A Survey.* Vol. 1. Ann Arbor: Center for Research on Economic Development, University of Michigan.

CIMMYT. Economics Staff. 1984. "The Farming Systems Perspective and Farmer Participation in the Development of Appropriate Technology." In *Agricultural Development in the Third World,* ed. C. K. Eicher and J. M. Staatz. Baltimore: Johns Hopkins University Press.

Clark, C., and Haswell, M. R. 1964. *Economics of Subsistence Agriculture.* New York: Macmillan.

Clark, G. 1967. *World Prehistory, An Outline.* Cambridge: Cambridge University Press.

Clay, E. 1975. "Equity and Productivity Effects of a Package of Technical Innovations and Changes in Social Institutions." *Indian Journal of Agricultural Economics* 30:74-87.

Cleave, J. H. 1974. *African Farmers: Labor Use in the Development of Smallholder Agriculture.* New York: Praeger.

————. 1977. "Decision Making on the African Farm." In *Contributed Papers Read at the 16th International Conference of Agricultural Economics.* Oxford, U.K.: Oxford University, Institute of Agricultural Economics.

Cleave, M. B., and White, H. P. 1969. "Population Density and Agricultural Systems in West Africa." In *Environment and Land Use in Africa,* ed. M. F. Thomas and G. W. Whittington. London: Methuen.

Clements, K. W., and Sjaastad, L. A. 1984. *How Protection Taxes Exporters.* Thames Essay 39. London: Trade Policy Research Centre.

Cline, W. R. 1975. "Distribution and Development: A Survey of the Literature." *Journal of Development Economics* 1:359-400.

Cloud, G. S. 1986. *Agricultural Mechanization in the Third World: A Selective Bibliography, 1975-1985.* Monticello, Ill.: Vance Bibliographies.

Cohen, J. M. 1980. "Land Tenure and Rural Development in Africa." In *Agricultural Development in Africa: Issues of Public Policy,* ed. R. A. Bates and M. F. Lofchie. New York: Praeger.

Cohen, S. I. 1978. *Agrarian Structures and Agrarian Reform.* Leiden, Holland: M. Nijhoff.

Collinson, M. P. 1972. *Farm Management in Peasant Agriculture—A Handbook for Rural Development Planning in Africa.* New York: Praeger.

————. 1982. *Farming Systems Research in Eastern Africa: The Experience of CIMMYT and Some National Agricultural Research Services 1976-1981.* International Development Paper 3. East Lansing: Michigan State University, Department of Agricultural Economics.

Commons, J. R. 1950. *The Economics of Collective Action.* New York: Macmillan.

————. 1961. *Institutional Economics.* Madison: University of Wisconsin Press.

Conley, D. M., and Heady, E. O. 1981. "The Interregional Impacts of Improved Truck Transportation on Farm Income from Rice in Thailand." *Journal of Developing Areas* 15:549-60.

Coombs, P. H. 1974. *Attacking Rural Poverty: How Non-Formal Education Can Help.* Baltimore: Johns Hopkins University Press.

Council on Environmental Quality. 1980. *The Global 2000 Report to the President.* 3 vols. New York: Pergamon.

————. 1982. *The Global 2000 Report to the President.* New York: Penguin.

Courtenay, P. P. 1980. *Plantation Agriculture.* 2d rev. ed. London: Bell and Hyman.

Coward, E. W. J., ed. 1980. *Irrigation and Agricultural Development in Asia: Perspectives from the Social Sciences.* Ithaca, N.Y.: Cornell University Press.

Crawford, E. W.; Ting-Ing, H.; and Schmid, A. A. 1983. *Users Guide to BENCOS—A Supercalc Template for Benefit-Cost Analysis.* International Development Working Paper 14. East Lansing: Michigan State University, Department of Agricultural Economics.

Crossley, P., and Kilgour, J. 1984. *Small Farm Mechanization for Developing Countries.* New York: Wiley.

Crotty, R. 1980. *Cattle, Economics and Development.* Farnham Royal, Slough, U.K.: Commonwealth Agricultural Bureau.

Crouch, B. R., and Chamala, S. 1981. *Extension Education and Rural Development: Experience in Strategies for Planned Change.* 2 vols. New York: Wiley.

Cummings, R. W. 1968. "Technological Change in Agriculture." In *Development and Change in Traditional Agriculture: Focus on South Asia.* E. Lansing: Asian Studies Center, Michigan State University.

Curry Foundation. 1986. *United States Agricultural Exports and Third World Development: The Critical Linkage.* Washington, D.C.: Curry Foundation.

Dalrymple, D. G. 1986a. *Development and Spread of High-Yielding Rice Varieties in Developing Countries.* Washington, D.C.: Agency for International Development, Bureau for Science and Technology.

―――. 1986b. *Development and Spread of High-Yielding Wheat Varieties in Developing Countries.* Washington, D.C.: Agency for International Development, Bureau for Science and Technology.

Dalton, G., ed. 1967. *Tribal and Peasant Economies: Readings in Economic Anthropology.* Garden City, N.Y.: Natural History Press.

―――. 1971. *Economic Development and Social Change.* Garden City, N.Y.: Natural History Press.

David, C. C., and Barker, R. 1978. "Modern Rice Varieties and Fertilizer Consumption." In *Economic Consequences of the New Rice Technology.* Los Banos, Laguna, Philippines: International Rice Research Institute.

Davis, J. S. 1945. "Standards and Content of Living." *American Economic Review* 35:1-15.

DeBoer, A. J., and Welsch, D. E. 1977. "Constraints on Cattle and Buffalo Production in a Northeastern Thai Village." In *Tradition and Dynamics in Small-Farm Agriculture,* ed. R. D. Stevens. Ames: Iowa State University Press.

Deere, C. D., and de Janvry, A. 1979. "A Conceptual Framework for the Empirical Analysis of Peasants." *American Journal of Agricultural Economics* 61:601-11.

de Janvry, A. 1973. "A Socioeconomic Model of Induced Innovation for Argentine Agricultural Development." *Quarterly Journal of Economics* 87:410-35.

―――. 1978. "Social Structure and Biased Technical Change in Argentine Agriculture." In *Induced Innovation: Technology, Institutions and Development,* ed. P. Binswanger and V. W. Ruttan. Baltimore: Johns Hopkins University Press.

―――. 1981. *The Agrarian Question and Reformism in Latin America.* Baltimore: Johns Hopkins University Press.

―――. 1984. "The Political Economy of Rural Development in Latin America: An Interpretation." In *Agricultural Development in the Third World,* ed. C. K. Eicher and J. M. Staatz. Baltimore: Johns Hopkins University Press.

Dejene, A. 1980. *Non-Formal Education as a Strategy in Development: Comparative Analysis of Rural Development Projects.* Lanham, Md.: University Press of America.

De Kant, E. 1980. "Some Basic Questions on Human Rights and Development." *World Development* 8:97-105.

Dillon, J. L., and Anderson, J. R. 1971. "Allocative Efficiency, Traditional Agriculture, and Risk." *American Journal of Agricultural Economics* 53:26-32.

Dillon, J. L., and Hardaker, J. B. 1980. *Farm Management Research for Small Farm Development.* Agricultural Service Bulletin 41. Rome: Food and Agriculture Organization.

Dixon, R. B. 1978. *Women's Cooperatives and Rural Development.* Baltimore: Johns Hopkins University Press.

Dixon-Mueller, R. 1985. *Women's Work in Third World Agriculture.* Women, Work and Development Series 9. Geneva, Switzerland: International Labour Organisation.

Dobyns, H. F.; Doughty, P. L.; and Lasswell, H. D., eds. 1971. *Peasants, Power, and Applied Social Change: Vicos as a Model.* Beverly Hills, Cal.: Sage.

Donald, G. 1978. *Credit for Small Farms in Developing Countries.* Boulder, Colo.: Praeger.

Doran, M. H.; Low, A. R. C.; and Kemp, R. L. 1979. "Cattle as a Store of Wealth in Swaziland: Implications for Livestock Development and Overgrazing in Eastern and Southern Africa." *American Journal of Agricultural Economics* 61:41–47.

Dorner, P. 1972. *Land Reform and Economic Development.* London: Penguin.

—————, ed. 1977. *Cooperative and Commune: Group Farming in the Economic Development of Agriculture.* Madison: University of Wisconsin Press.

Dorner, P., and Kanel, D. 1979. "The Economic Case for Land Reform: Employment, Income Distribution and Productivity." In *The Political Economy of Development and Underdevelopment,* ed. C. K. Wilber, 2d. ed. New York: Random.

Dos Santos, T. 1970. "The Structure of Dependence." *American Economic Review* 60:231–36.

Douglas, J. E., ed. 1980. *Successful Seed Programs: A Planning and Management Guide.* Boulder, Colo.: Westview.

Dovring, F. 1959. "The Share of Agriculture in a Growing Population." *Monthly Bulletin of Agricultural Economics and Statistics* 8:1–11.

—————. 1966. "The Transformation of European Agriculture." In *The Cambridge Economic History of Europe.* Vol. 6, *The Industrial Revolution and After,* pt. 2. Cambridge, U.K.: Cambridge University Press.

Duff, B. 1978a. "Economics of Small Farm Mechanization in Asia." *Agricultural Mechanization in Asia* 9:11–23.

—————. 1978b. "Mechanization and Use of Modern Rice Varieties." In *Economic Consequences of the New Rice Technology,* ed. R. Barker and Y. Hayami. Los Banos, Laguna, Philippines: International Rice Research Institute.

Dulfer, E. 1980. *Guide to Evaluation of Cooperative Organizations in Developing Countries.* Rome: Food and Agriculture Organization.

Duncan, R., and Lutz, E. 1983. "Penetration of Industrial Country Markets by Agricultural Products from Developing Countries." *World Development* 11:771–86.

Dunn, E. S., Jr. 1954. *The Location of Agricultural Production.* Gainesville: University of Florida Press.

—————. 1971. *Economic and Social Development—A Process of Social Learning.* Baltimore: Johns Hopkins University Press.

Eckert, J. B. 1977. "Farmer Response to High-Yielding Wheat in Pakistan's Punjab." In *Tradition and Dynamics in Small Farm Agriculture: Economic Studies in*

Asia, Africa, and Latin America, ed. R. D. Stevens. Ames: Iowa State University Press.

Economic Development Institute. 1985. *Agricultural Marketing Policy: Background Readings.* 2 vols. Washington, D.C.: World Bank.

Educational Testing Service. 1979. *A Manual for the Analysis of Costs and Outcomes in Non-Formal Education.* Princeton, N.J.: ETS.

Edwards, E. O. 1974. "Employment in Developing Countries." In *Employment in Developing Nations,* ed. E. O. Edwards. New York: Columbia University Press.

Eicher, C. K. 1984. "Facing Up to Africa's Food Crisis." In *Agricultural Development in the Third World,* ed. C. K. Eicher and J. M. Staatz. Baltimore: Johns Hopkins University Press.

Eicher, C. K., and Baker, D. C., eds. 1982. *Research on Agricultural Development in Sub-Saharan Africa: A Critical Survey.* MSU International Development Paper 1. East Lansing: Michigan State University, Department of Agricultural Economics.

Eicher, C. K., and Staatz, J. M, eds. 1984. *Agricultural Development in the Third World.* Baltimore: Johns Hopkins University Press.

Eisenstadt, S. N. 1963. "The Need for Achievement." *Economic Development and Cultural Change* 11:420–31.

———. 1966. *Modernization: Protest and Change.* Englewood Cliffs, N.J.: Prentice-Hall.

Elder, J. W. 1968. "Cultural and Social Factors in Agricultural Development." In *Development and Change in Traditional Agriculture: Focus on South Asia.* South Asia Series Occasional Paper 7. East Lansing: Michigan State University, Asian Studies Center.

Ellis, F. 1982. "Agricultural Price Policy in Tanzania." *World Development* 10:263–84.

Ellis, G. 1981. "The Backward-bending Supply Curve of Labor in Africa: Models, Evidence, and Interpretation—and Why It Makes a Difference." *Journal of Developing Areas* 15:251–74.

Epstein, T. S., and Watts, R. A., eds. 1981. *The Endless Day: Some Case Material On Asian Rural Women.* New York: Pergamon.

Esman, M. J., and Uphoff, N. T. 1984. *Local Organizations—Intermediaries in Rural Development.* Ithaca, N.Y.: Cornell University Press.

Esmay, M. L., and Hall, C. W., eds. 1973. *Agricultural Mechanization in Developing Countries.* Tokyo: Shin-Norinsha.

Evangelou, P. 1984. *Livestock Development in Kenya's Maasailand.* Boulder, Colo.: Westview.

Evenson, R. E. 1984. "Benefits and Obstacles in Developing Appropriate Agricultural Technology." In *Agricultural Development in the Third World,* ed. C. K. Eicher and J. M. Staatz. Baltimore: Johns Hopkins University Press.

Falcon, W. P. 1970. "The Green Revolution: Generations of Problems." *American Journal of Agricultural Economics* 52:698–712.

———. 1984. "Recent Food Policy Lessons from Developing Countries." *American Journal of Agricultural Economics* 66:180–85.

Fals-Borda, O. 1971. *Cooperatives and Rural Development in Latin America: An Analytic Report.* Geneva, Switzerland: U.N. Research Institute for Social Development.

FAO (Food and Agriculture Organization). 1973. *Development of Food Marketing Systems for Large Urban Areas—Latin America.* Rome: FAO.

―――. 1974. *Development of Food Marketing Systems for Large Urban Areas—Asia and Far East.* Rome: FAO.

―――. 1975. *Effects of Farm Mechanization on Production and Employment.* Rome: FAO.

―――. 1978a. *Experiences and Models of Cooperatives and Other Rural Organizations Engaged in Agricultural Production.* Rome: FAO.

―――. 1978b. *Review and Analysis of Agrarian Reform and Rural Development in the Developing Countries Since the Mid-1960s.* Report of a Conference on Agrarian Reform. Rome: FAO.

―――. 1979. *Agriculture: Toward 2000.* Rome: FAO.

―――. 1984. *Land, Food, and People.* Rome: FAO.

―――. 1985a. *Agricultural Price Policies.* Rome: FAO.

―――. 1985b. *World Food Survey.* Rome: FAO.

―――. *Monthly Bulletin of Statistics.* Rome: FAO.

―――. *Production Yearbook.* Rome: FAO.

―――. *State of Food and Agriculture.* Rome: FAO.

―――. *Trade Yearbook.* Rome: FAO.

Farmer, B. H., ed. 1977. *Green Revolution? Technology and Change in Rice-growing Areas of Tamil Nadu and Sri Lanka.* Boulder, Colo.: Westview.

Feder, G.; Just, R.; and Zilberman, D. 1985. "Adoption of Agricultural Innovations in Developing Countries: A Survey." *Economic Development and Cultural Change* 33:255–98.

Feder, G., and Slade, R. 1984. *The Role of Public Policy in the Diffusion of New Agricultural Technology. Agricultural and Rural Development Department Report 26.* Washington, D.C.: World Bank.

Feder, G.; Slade, R.; and Sundaram, A. K. 1984. *The Training and Visit Extension System: An Analysis of Operations and Effects.* Agricultural and Rural Development Department Report 25. Washington, D.C.: World Bank.

Feeny, D. 1982. *The Political Economy of Productivity: Thai Agricultural Development 1880–1975.* Vancouver: University of British Columbia Press.

Fei, J. C. H., and Ranis, G. 1964. *Development of the Labor Surplus Economy: Theory and Policy.* Homewood, Ill.: Irwin.

Fei, J. C. H.; Ranis, G.; and Kuo, S. W. T. 1979. *Growth with Equity: The Taiwan Case.* New York: Oxford University Press.

Finkler, K. 1978. "From Sharecroppers to Entrepreneurs: Peasant Household Production Strategies Under the Ejido System of Mexico." *Economic Development and Cultural Change* 27:103–20.

Fishel, W. L., and Kenney, M. 1986. "Challenge to Studies of Biotechnology Impacts in the Social Sciences." In *Agriculture in a Turbulent World Economy: Proceedings of the 19th International Conference of Agricultural Economists,* ed. A. Maunder and U. Renborg. Aldershot, Hampshire, U.K.: Gower.

Fisk, E. K. 1975. "The Response of Nonmonetary Production Units to Contact with the Exchange Economies." In *Agriculture in Development Theory,* ed. L. G. Reynolds. New Haven, Conn.: Yale University Press.

Foster, G. M. 1967. *Tzintzuntzan: Mexican Peasants in a Changing World.* Boston: Little, Brown.

Frank, A. G. 1975. *On Capitalist Underdevelopment.* London: Oxford University Press.

Galeski, B. 1977. "The Models of Collective Farming." In *Cooperative and Commune,* ed. P. Donner. Madison: University of Wisconsin Press.

Galli, R. E., ed. 1981. *The Political Economy of Rural Development: Peasants, Institutional Capital and the State.* Albany: State University of New York Press.

Geertz, C. 1964. *Agricultural Involution.* Berkeley and Los Angeles: University of California Press.

Ghai, D.; Khan, A. R.; Lee, E.; and Rodwan, S., eds. 1979. *Agrarian Systems and Rural Development.* New York: Holmes and Meier.

Ghatak, S., and Ingersent, K. 1984. *Agricultural and Economic Development.* Baltimore: Johns Hopkins University Press.

Gittinger, J. P. 1982. *Economic Analysis of Agricultural Projects.* 2d ed. Baltimore: Johns Hopkins University Press.

Gittinger, J. P.; Leslie, J.; and Hoisington, C., eds. 1987. *Food Policy: Integrating Supply, Distribution and Consumption.* Baltimore: Johns Hopkins University Press.

Glasser, W. R. 1981. *Survey of Irrigation in Eight Asian Nations: India, Pakistan, Indonesia, Thailand, Bangladesh, S. Korea, Philippines and Sri Lanka.* Foreign Agricultural Economic Report 165. Washington, D.C.: U.S. Department of Agriculture.

Goe, M. R., and McDowell, R. E. 1980. *Animal Traction: Guidelines for Utilization.* International Agriculture Monograph 81. Ithaca, N.Y.: Cornell University Press.

Goldthorpe, J. E. 1975. *Sociology of the Third World.* London: Cambridge University Press.

Gomez, K. A.; Herdt, R. W.; Barker, R.; De Katta, S. K. 1979. "A Methodology for Identifying Constraints to High Rice Yields on Farmers' Fields." In *Farm Level Constraints to High Rice Yields in Asia: 1974–77.* Los Banos, Laguna, Philippines: International Rice Research Institute.

Gonzalez-Vega, C. 1977. "Interest Rate Restrictions and Income Distribution." *American Journal of Agricultural Economics* 59:973–76.

Goode, R. 1984. *Government Finance in Developing Countries.* Washington, D.C.: Brookings.

Goodwin, J. B.; Sanders, J.; and De Hollanda, A. D. 1980. "Ex-Ante Appraisal of New Technology: Sorghum in Northeast Brazil." *American Journal of Agricultural Economics* 62:737–41.

Gotsch, C. H., and Falcon, W. P. 1975. "The Green Revolution and the Economics of Punjab Agriculture." *Food Research Institute Studies* 14:27–46.

Grabowski, R. 1981. "Induced Innovation, Green Revolution, and Income Distribution: Reply." *Economic Development and Cultural Change* 30:180–81.

Grandstaff, M. 1979. "Non-Formal Education as a Concept." *Prospects: Quarterly Review of Education* 9:179–81.

Griffin, K. 1974a. *Political Economy of Agrarian Change—An Essay on the Green Revolution.* London: Macmillan.

————. 1974b. "Rural Development: The Policy Options." In *Employment in Developing Nations,* ed. O. Edwards. New York: Columbia University Press.

————. 1978. *International Inequality and National Poverty.* New York: Holmes and Meier.

————. 1984. *Institutional Reform and Economic Development in the Chinese Countryside.* Armonk, N.Y.: Sharpe.

Griffin, K., and Gurley, J. 1985. "Radical Analysis of Imperialism, The Third World and the Transition to Socialism: A Survey Article." *Journal of Economic Literature* 23:1089–143.

Grigg, D. 1979. "Boserup's Theory of Agrarian Change: A Critical Review." *Progress in Human Geography* 3:64–84.

Griliches, Z. 1957. "Hybrid Corn: An Exploration in the Economics of Technical Change." *Econometrica* 25:501–22.

————. 1960. "Hybrid Corn and the Economics of Innovation." *Science* 132:275–80.

Hagen, E. E. 1962. *On the Theory of Social Change—How Economic Growth Begins.* Homewood, Ill.: Dorsey.

————. 1980. *The Economics of Development.* 3d ed. Homewood, Ill.: Irwin.

Haines, M. 1982. *Introduction to Farming Systems.* New York: Longman.

Hall, A. E.; Cannel, G. H.; and Lawton, H. W., eds. 1979. *Agriculture in Semi-Arid Environments.* New York: Springer-Verlag.

Halm, G. N. 1968. *Economic Systems: A Comparative Analysis.* New York: Holt, Rinehart, and Winston.

Halperin, R., and Dow, J., eds. 1977. *Peasant Livelihood: Studies in Economic Anthropology and Cultural Ecology.* New York: St. Martin's.

Hanks, L. M. 1972. *Rice and Man: Agricultural Ecology in Southeast Asia.* Chicago: Aldine-Atherton.

Hanrahan, C. E.; Urban, F. S.; and Deaton, J. L. 1984. *Longrun Changes in World Food Supply and Demand: Implications for Development Assistance Policy.* Washington, D.C.: U.S. Department of Agriculture, Economic Research Service.

Haroldsen, E. O., ed. 1962. *Food: One Tool in International Economic Development.* Ames: Iowa State University Press.

Harper, M., and Kavura, R., eds. 1982. *The Private Marketing Entrepreneur and Rural Development—Case Studies and Commentary.* Agricultural Service Bulletin 51. Rome: Food and Agriculture Organization.

Harrison, K.; Henley, D.; Riley, H.; and Shaffer, J. 1974. *Improving Food Marketing Systems in Developing Countries: Experiences from Latin America.* Research Report 6. East Lansing: Michigan State University, Latin American Studies Center.

Harriss, B. 1979a. "Going Against the Grain." In *Proceedings: International Workshop on Socio-economic Constraints to Development of Semi-Arid Tropical Agriculture.* Hyderabad, India: International Crops Research Institute for the Semi-Arid Tropics.

————. 1979b. "There Is Method in My Madness: Or Is It Vice Versa? Measuring Agricultural Market Performance." *Food Research Institute Studies* 17:197–218.

————. 1983. "Money and Commodities: Their Interaction in a Rural Indian Setting." In *Rural Financial Markets in Developing Countries: Their Use and*

Abuse, ed. J. D. Von Pischke, D. W. Adams, and G. Donald. Baltimore: Johns Hopkins University Press.

Harsh, S. B.; Connor, L. J.; and Schwab, G. D. 1981. *Managing the Farm Business.* Englewood Cliffs, N.J.: Prentice-Hall.

Harwood, R. R. 1979. *Understanding and Improving Farming Systems in the Humid Tropics.* Boulder, Colo.: Westview.

Hauser, P. M. 1979. "Investment in Population Throughout Low-Income Countries." In *World Population and Development: Challenges and Prospects,* ed. P. M. Hauser. Syracuse, N.Y.: Syracuse University Press.

Hayami, Y. 1983. "Growth and Equity: Is There a Trade Off?" In *Growth and Equity in Agricultural Development: Proceedings,* 18th International Conference of Agricultural Economists, ed. A. Maunder and K. Ohkawa. Aldershot, Hampshire, U.K.: Gower.

————. 1984. "Assessment of the Green Revolution." In *Agricultural Development in the Third World,* ed. C. K. Eicher and J. M. Staatz. Baltimore: Johns Hopkins University Press.

Hayami, Y., and Herdt, R. W. 1977. "Market Price Effects of Technological Change on Income Distribution in Semisubsistence Agriculture." *American Journal of Agricultural Economics* 59:245–56.

————. 1978. "Market Price Effects of New Rice Technology on Income Distribution." In *Economic Consequences of the New Rice Technology.* Los Banos, Laguna, Philippines: International Rice Research Institute.

Hayami, Y., and Kikuchi, M. 1982. *Asian Village Economy at the Crossroads—An Economic Approach to Institutional Change.* Baltimore: Johns Hopkins University Press.

Hayami, Y., and Ruttan, V. W. 1971. *Agricultural Development: An International Perspective.* 1st ed. Baltimore: Johns Hopkins University Press.

————. 1972. "Strategies for Agricultural Development." *Food Research Institute Studies* 11:129–48.

————. 1985. *Agricultural Development: An International Perspective.* Rev. ed. Baltimore: Johns Hopkins University Press.

Hayami, Y., et. al. 1978. *Anatomy of a Peasant Economy: A Rice Village in the Philippines.* Los Banos, Laguna, Philippines: International Rice Research Institute.

Heady, E. O., and Jensen, H. R. 1954. *Farm Management Economics.* New York: Prentice-Hall.

Held, R. B., and Clawson, M. 1965. *Soil Conservation in Perspective.* Baltimore: Johns Hopkins University Press.

Helleiner, G. K. 1975. "Smallholder Decision Making: Tropical African Evidence." In *Agriculture in Development Theory,* ed. G. Reynolds. New Haven, Conn.: Yale University Press.

Herdt, R. W. 1970. "A Disaggregate Approach to Aggregate Supply." *American Journal of Agricultural Economics* 52:518–19.

Herdt, R. W., and Capule, C. C. 1983. *Adoption, Spread, and Production Impact of Modern Rice Varieties in Asia.* Los Banos, Laguna, Philippines: International Rice Research Institute.

Herdt, R. W., and Mellor, J. W. 1964. "The Contrasting Response of Rice to Nitrogen—India and United States." *Journal of Farm Economics* 46:150–60.

Herring, R. J., 1983. *Land to the Tillers: Agrarian Reform in South Asia.* New Haven, Conn: Yale University Press.

Herring, R. J., and Kennedy, C. R. J. 1979. "The Political Economy of Farm Mechanization Policy: Tractors in Pakistan." In *Food, Politics and Agricultural Development,* ed. R. F. Hopkins, D. J. Puchala, and R. B. Talbot. Boulder, Colo.: Westview.

Heyer, J.; Roberts, P.; and Williams, G. 1981. *Rural Development in Tropical Africa.* New York: St. Martin's.

Hill, P. 1966. "A Plea for Indigenous Economics: The West African Example." *Economic Development and Cultural Change* 15:10-20.

––––––. 1977. *Rural Hausa: Population, Prosperity and Poverty.* Cambridge: Cambridge University Press.

Hirschman, A. O. 1977. "A Generalized Linkage Approach to Development with Special Reference to Staples." *Economic Development and Cultural Change* 22:67-98.

Holdcroft, L. E. 1984. "The Rise and Fall of Community Development: A Critical Assessment." In *Agricultural Development in the Third World,* ed. C. K. Eicher and J. M. Staatz. Baltimore: Johns Hopkins University Press.

Holmberg, A. R. 1952. "The Wells that Failed." In *Human Problems in Technological Change,* ed. E. H. Spicer. New York: Russell Sage.

Hoogvelt, A. 1976. *Sociology of Developing Societies.* London: Macmillan.

Hoos, S. 1979. *Agricultural Marketing Boards—An International Perspective.* Cambridge, Mass.: Ballinger.

Hopkins. R.; Puchala, D. J.; and Talbot, R. B., eds. 1979. *Food, Politics and Agricultural Development.* Boulder, Col.: Westview.

Hopper, W. D. 1981. "Recent Trends in World Food and Population." In *Future Dimensions of World Food and Population,* ed. R. G. Woods. Boulder, Colo.: Westview.

Hoselitz, R. F. 1960. *Sociological Aspects of Economic Growth.* Glencoe, Ill.: Free Press.

Howell, J., ed. 1980. *Borrowers and Lenders—Rural Financial Markets and Institutions in Developing Countries.* London: Overseas Development Institute.

Howes, M. 1979. "Appropriate Technologies: A Critical Evaluation of the Concept and Movement." *Development and Change* 10:115-24.

Hsieh, S. C., and Ruttan, V. W. 1967. "Environmental, Technological, and Institutional Factors in the Growth of Rice Production: Philippines, Thailand, and Taiwan." *Food Research Institute Studies* 7:307-41.

Huffman, W. E. 1974. "Decision Making: The Role of Education." *American Journal of Agricultural Economics* 56:85-97.

––––––. 1977. "Allocative Efficiency: The Role of Human Capital." *Quarterly Journal of Economics* 91:59-80.

––––––. 1978. "Assessing Returns to Agricultural Extension." *American Journal of Agricultural Economics* 60:969-75.

Humphreys, C. P., and Pearson, S. R. 1979. "Choice of Technique in Sahalian Rice Production." *Food Research Institute Studies* 17:235-77.

Hunter, G. 1978. *Agricultural Development and the Rural Poor: Declaration of Policy and Guidelines for Action.* London: Overseas Development Institute.

Hunter, J. M.; Rey. L.; and Scott, D. 1982. "Man-Made Lakes and Man-Made Diseases." *Social Science and Medicine* 16:1127–45.

Huntington, S. P. 1969. *Political Order in Changing Societies.* 2d ed. New Haven, Conn.: Yale University Press.

ICRISAT (International Crops Research Institute for the Semi-Arid Tropics). 1979a. *Socio-Economic Constraints to Development of Semi-Arid Tropical Agriculture.* Andhra Pradesh, India: ICRISAT.

————. 1979b. *Economic Constraints to Development of Semi-Arid Tropical Agriculture.* Andhra Pradesh, India: ICRISAT.

————. 1985. *Agricultural Markets in the Semi-Arid Tropics: Proceedings of a Workshop.* Patancheru, Andrah Pradesh, India: ICRISAT.

ILO (International Labour Organisation). 1977. *Poverty and Landlessness in Rural Asia.* Geneva, Switzerland: ILO.

IMF (International Monetary Fund). *International Financial Statistics.* Washington, D.C.: IMF.

Inayatullah, ed. 1970. *Cooperatives and Planned Change in Asian Rural Communities.* Geneva, Switzerland: U.N. Research Institute for Social Development.

————. 1980. *Land Reform: Some Asian Experiences.* Kuala Lumpur, Malaysia: Asian and Pacific Development Administration Centre.

Ip, P. C., and Stahl, C. W. 1978. "Systems of Land Tenure, Allocative Efficiency, and Economic Development." *American Journal of Agricultural Economics* 60:19–28.

IRRI (International Rice Research Institute). 1970–72. *Agricultural Economics Annual Report.* Los Banos, Laguna, Philippines: IRRI.

————. 1976. *Bibliography on Socio-Economic Aspects of Asian Irrigation.* Los Banos, Laguna, Philippines: IRRI.

————. 1978a. *International Agricultural Machinery Workshop.* Los Banos, Laguna, Philippines: IRRI.

————. 1978b. *Interpretive Analysis of Selected Papers from Changes in Rice Farming in Selected Areas of Asia.* Los Banos, Laguna, Philippines: IRRI.

————. 1978c. *Irrigation Policy and Management in Southeast Asia.* Los Banos, Laguna, Philippines: IRRI.

————. 1980. *Irrigation Water Management.* Los Banos, Laguna, Philippines: IRRI.

————. 1984. *Consequences of Small Farm Mechanization.* Los Banos, Laguna, Philippines: IRRI.

Islam, M. S. 1980. "Comparative Performance of Different Types of Manual Pumps." *Agricultural Mechanization in Asia* 12:47–53.

Jabara, C. L. 1985. "Agricultural Pricing Policy in Kenya." *World Development* 13:611–26.

Jabara, C. L., and Thompson, R. L. 1982. "The Optimum Tariff for a Small Country Under International Price Uncertainty." *Oxford Economic Papers* 34:326–31.

Jacobs, E. M., ed. 1982. *Agrarian Policies in Communist Europe.* Totowa, N.J.: Allanheld.

Jamison, D. T., and Lau, L. J. 1982. *Farmer Education and Farm Efficiency.* Baltimore: Johns Hopkins University Press.

Jamison, D. T., and McAnany, E. G. 1978. *Radio for Education and Development.* Beverly Hills, Calif.: Sage.

Jarvis, L. S. 1980. "Cattle as a Store of Wealth in Swaziland: Comment." *American Journal of Agricultural Economics* 62:606–13.

————. 1986. *Livestock Development in Latin America.* Washington, D.C.: World Bank.

Jassawalla, M., and Lamberton, D. M., eds. 1982. *Communication Economics and Development.* New York: Pergamon.

Johnson, D. G. 1973. *World Agriculture in Disarray.* New York: St. Martin's.

Johnson, D. G., and Schuh, G. E., eds. 1983. *The Role of Markets in the World Food Economy.* Boulder, Colo.: Westview.

Johnston, B. F., and Clark, W. C. 1982. *Redesigning Rural Development—A Strategic Perspective.* Baltimore: Johns Hopkins University Press.

Johnston, B. F., and Kilby, P., eds. 1975. *Agriculture and Structural Transformation.* New York: Oxford University Press.

Johnston, B. F., and Mellor, J. W. 1961. "The Role of Agriculture in Economic Development." *American Economic Review* 51:566–93.

Johnston, B. F., and Tomich, T. P. 1985. "Agrarian Strategies and Agrarian Structure." *Asian Development Review* 3:1–37.

Jones, B. F., and Thompson, R. L. 1978. "Interrelationships of Domestic Agricultural Policies and Trade Policies." In *Speaking of Trade: Its Effect on Agriculture.* Special Report 72. Minneapolis: University of Minnesota, Agricultural Extension Service.

Jones, G. E., and Rolls, M. J., eds. 1982. *Progress in Rural Extension and Community Development: Extension and Relative Advantage in Rural Development.* New York: Wiley.

Jones, W. O. 1972. *Marketing Staple Foods in Tropical Africa.* Ithaca, N.Y.: Cornell University Press.

————. 1980. "Agricultural Trade Within Tropical Africa: Historical Background." In *Agricultural Development in Africa: Issues of Public Policy,* ed. R. H. Bates and M. F. Lofchie. New York: Praeger.

————. 1984. "Economic Tasks for Food Marketing Boards in Tropical Africa." *Food Research Institute Studies* 19:114–38.

Jorgenson, D. W. 1961. "The Development of a Dual Economy." *Economic Journal* 71:309–34.

Joy, L. 1967. "One Economist's View of the Relationship Between Economics and Anthropology." In *Themes in Economic Anthropology.,* ed. R. Firth. London: Tavistock.

Kahn, H. 1979. *World Economic Development, 1979 and Beyond.* Boulder, Colo.: Westview.

Kao, C.; Kurt, H. C.; Anschel, R.; and Eicher, C. K. 1964. "Disguised Unemployment in Agriculture: A Survey." In *Agriculture in Economic Development,* ed. C. K. Eicher and L. W. Witt. New York: McGraw-Hill.

Kennedy, E. T., and Pinstrup-Andersen, P. 1983. *Nutritional-Related Policies and Programs: Past Performances and Research Needs.* Washington, D.C.: International Food Policy Research Institute.

Khan, A. A., and Solaiman, M. 1978. *The Academy at Comilla.* Comilla, Bangladesh: Academy for Rural Development.

Khan, A. U. 1974. "Appropriate Technologies: Do We Transfer, Adapt or Develop?"

In *Employment in Developing Nations,* ed. E. O. Edwards. New York: Columbia University Press.

—————. 1977. "Mechanization Toward Self-Sufficiency in Food." In *Proceedings: The World Food Conference of 1976.* Ames: Iowa State University Press.

Kikuchi, M., and Hayami, Y. 1978. "New Rice Technology and National Irrigation Development Policy." In *Economic Consequences of the New Rice Technology.* Los Banos, Laguna, Philippines: International Rice Research Institute.

Kohls, R. L., and Uhl, J. N. 1980. *Marketing of Agricultural Products.* 5th ed. New York: Macmillan.

Koo, A. Y. C. 1968. *The Role of Land Reform in Economic Development: A Case Study of Taiwan.* New York: Praeger.

Korten, F. F. 1982. *Building National Capacity to Develop Water Users' Associations: Experience from the Philippines.* Staff Working Paper 528. Washington, D.C.: World Bank.

Kriesberg, M. ed. 1970. *The Marketing Challenge. Foreign Economic Development.* Report 7. Washington, D.C.: USDA.

Krishna, R. 1967. "Agricultural Price Policy and Economic Development." In *Agricultural Development and Economic Growth,* ed. H. M. Southworth and B. F. Johnston. Ithaca, N.Y.: Cornell University Press.

—————. 1973. "Unemployment in India." *Indian Journal of Agricultural Economics* 28:1–23.

—————. 1974. "Measurement of the Direct and Indirect Employment Effects of Agricultural Growth with Technical Change." In *Employment in Developing Nations,* ed. E. O. Edwards. New York: Columbia University Press.

—————. 1980. "Rural Unemployment in India: Measurement, Policy Issues and Lessons of the 1970's." *Scientific American* 243:166–78.

Krueger, A. O. 1980. "Trade Policy as an Input to Development." *American Economic Review* 70:288–92.

Kunkel, J. H. 1970. *Society and Economic Growth: A Behavioral Perspective of Social Change.* New York: Oxford University Press.

—————. 1976. "Review Article: Psychological Approaches to Development." *Economic Development and Cultural Change* 24:649–57.

Kuznets, S. 1962. "Quantitative Aspects of the Economic Growth of Nations: Part VII, The Share and Structure of Consumption." *Economic Development and Cultural Change* 10:1–92.

—————. 1963. "Quantitative Aspects of the Economic Growth of Nations: Part VIII, Distribution of Income by Size." *Economic Development and Cultural Change* 11:1–80.

—————. 1966. *Modern Economic Growth: Rate, Structure, and Spread.* New Haven, Conn.: Yale University Press.

—————. 1971. *Economic Growth of Nations.* Cambridge, Mass.: Harvard University Press.

Ladejinsky, W. 1970. "The Ironies of India's Green Revolution." *Foreign Affairs* 48:759–68.

Langham, M. R. 1979. "An Introduction to Economic Principles of Production." In *Readings in Asian Farm Management,* ed. T. B. Thiam and S. Ong. Singapore: Singapore University Press.

Lardy, N. R. 1984. "Prices, Markets and the Chinese Peasant." In *Agricultural Development in the Third World*, ed. C. K. Eicher and J. M. Staatz. Baltimore: Johns Hopkins University Press.

Larson, A. 1969. "Universalities of Cooperation." In *Agricultural Cooperatives and Markets in Developing Countries,* ed. K. R. Anschel, R. H. Brannon, and E. D. Smith. New York: Praeger.

Lau, L. J., and Yotopoulos, P. A. 1971. "A Test for Relative Efficiency and Application to Indian Agriculture." *American Economic Review* 61:94–109.

Lauterback, A. 1974. *Psychological Challenges to Modernization.* New York: Elsevier Scientific.

Leagans, J. P., and Loomis, C. P., eds. 1971. *Behavioral Change in Agriculture: Concepts and Strategies for Influencing Transition.* Ithaca, N.Y.: Cornell University Press.

Lee, T. H. 1971. *Intersectoral Capital Flows in the Economic Development of Taiwan, 1895–1960.* Ithaca, N.Y.: Cornell University Press.

Lee, T. Y.; Kim, D. H.; and Adams, D. W. 1983. "Savings Deposits and Agricultural Cooperatives in Korea." In *Rural Financial Markets in Developing Countries: Their Use and Abuse,* ed. J. D. Von Pischke, D. W. Adams, and G. Donald. Baltimore: Johns Hopkins University Press.

Leff, N. H. 1984. "Externalities, Information Costs and Social Benefit-Cost Analysis for Economic Development: An Example from Telecommunications." *Economic Development and Cultural Change* 32:255–76.

Lele, U. J. 1971. *Food Grain Marketing in India: Private Performance and Public Policy.* Ithaca, N.Y.: Cornell University Press.

————. 1979. *The Design of Development: Lessons from Africa.* 2d ed. Baltimore: Johns Hopkins University Press.

————. 1984. "Rural Africa: Modernization, Equity, and Long-Term Development." In *Agricultural Development in the Third World,* ed. C. K. Eicher and J. M. Staatz. Baltimore: Johns Hopkins University Press.

Lele, U. J. and Candler, W. 1984. "Food Security in Developing Countries: National Issues." In *Agricultural Development in the Third World,* ed. C. K. Eicher and J. M. Staatz. Baltimore: Johns Hopkins University Press.

Le Moigne, M. 1980. "Animal Draft Cultivation in French-Speaking Africa." In *Proceedings of the International Workshop on Socioeconomic Constraints to Development of Semi-Arid Tropical Agriculture.* Patancheru, Andhra Pradesh, India: International Crops Research Institute for the Semi-Arid Tropics.

Lenski, G., and Lenski, J. 1978. *Human Societies: An Introduction to Macrosociology.* New York: McGraw-Hill.

Lerner, D. 1958. *The Passing of Traditional Society: Modernizing the Middle East.* New York: Free Press.

Lewis, W. A. 1964. "Thoughts on Land Settlement." In *Agriculture in Economic Development,* ed. C. K. Eicher and L. W. Witt. New York: McGraw-Hill.

————. 1978. *Evolution of the International Economic Order.* Princeton, N.J.: Princeton University Press.

————. 1980. "The Slowing Down of the Engine of Growth." *American Economic Review* 70:555–64.

————. 1984. "The State of Development Theory." *American Economic Review* 74:1–10.

Lipton, M. 1968. "The Theory of the Optimizing Peasant." *Journal of Development Studies* 4:327–51.

Little, I. M. D. 1982. *Economic Development: Theory, Policy, and International Relations*. New York: Basic Books.

Little, I. M. D.; Scitovsky, T.; and Scott, M. 1970. *Industry and Trade in Some Developing Countries*. London: Oxford University Press.

Lockheed, M. E.; Jamison, D. T.; and Lau, L. J. 1980. "Farmer Education and Farm Efficiency: A Survey." *Economic Development and Cultural Change* 29:37–75.

Long, N. 1977. *Introduction to the Sociology of Rural Development*. London: Tavistock.

Loomis, R., and Barton, G. T. 1961. *Productivity of Agriculture, United States, 1870–1958*. Technical Bulletin 1238. Washington, D.C.: U.S. Department of Agriculture, Agricultural Research Service.

Lynd, R., and Lynd. H. 1937. *Middletown in Transition*. New York: Harcourt, Brace.

McAnany, E. G., ed. 1979. *Communications in the Rural Third World*. New York: Praeger.

MacAndrews, C., and Sien, C. L. 1982. *Too Rapid Rural Development: Perceptions and Perspectives from South East Asia*. Athens: Ohio University Press.

McClelland, D. C. 1961. *The Achieving Society*. New York: Van Nostrand.

McClelland, D. C., et al. 1969. *Motivating Economic Achievement*. New York: Free Press.

McDowell, R. E., and Hildebrand, P. E. 1980. *Integrated Crop and Animal Production: Making the Most of Resources Available to Small Farmers in Developing Countries*. Working Paper. New York: Rockefeller Foundation.

McGranahan, D. V.; Proust-Richard, C.; Sovani, N. V.; and Subramanian, M. 1972. *Contents and Measurement of Socioeconomic Development*. New York: Praeger.

McGrath, M. J., ed. 1971. *Guidelines for Cooperatives in Developing Economies*. Madison: University of Wisconsin, International Cooperatives Training Center.

———. 1978. *Cooperatives, Small Farmers and Rural Development. Report on a Seminar*. New York: Agricultural Development Council.

McHale, T. R. 1962. "Econocological Analysis and Differential Economic Growth Rates." *Human Organization* 21:30–35.

McLoughlin, P. F. M., ed. 1970. *African Food Production Systems: Cases and Theory*. Baltimore: Johns Hopkins University Press.

McMeeken, C. P. 1970. "Science and World Animal Production: Achievement and Failure." *Finance and Development* 7:2–6.

Macrae, J. 1977. "Production, Distribution and Economic Organization: Income Distribution and Resource Allocation at the Team Level in China." *Journal of Development Economics* 4:365–85.

Magdoff, H. 1969. *The Age of Imperialism*. New York: Monthly Review Press.

Mahler, H. 1980. "People." *Scientific American* 243:67–77.

Malthus, T. R. 1933. *Essay on Population*. New York: Dutton.

Maunder, A., and Ohkawa, K. 1983. *Growth and Equity in Agricultural Development—Proceedings*, 18th International Conference of Agricultural Economists. Aldershot, Hampshire, U.K.: Gower.

Meaders, O. D., and Gonzales, C. 1984. *Agricultural Education in Developing Countries: An Annotated Bibliography of Research Reports.* East Lansing: Michigan State University, Department of Agricultural and Extension Education.

Meier, G. M. 1976, 1984. *Leading Issues in Economic Development.* 3d and 4th eds. London: Oxford University Press.

Mellor, J. W. 1962. "Increasing Agricultural Production in Early Stages of Economic Development: Relationships, Problems and Properties." *Indian Journal of Agricultural Economics* 17:29–46.

—————. 1966. *The Economics of Agricultural Development.* Ithaca, N.Y.: Cornell University Press.

—————. 1967. "Toward a Theory of Agricultural Development." In *Agricultural Development and Economic Growth,* ed. H. M. Southworth and B. F. Johnston. Ithaca, N.Y.: Cornell University Press.

—————. 1970. "Elements of a Food Marketing Policy for Low Income Countries." In *The Marketing Challenge.* Washington, D.C.: U.S. Department of Agriculture.

—————. 1976. *The New Economics of Growth—A Strategy for India and the Developing World.* Ithaca, N.Y.: Cornell University Press.

—————. 1982. "Third World Development: Food, Employment, and Growth Interactions." *American Journal of Agricultural Economics* 64:304–11.

—————. 1984. "Agricultural Development and Intersectional Transfer of Resources." In *Agricultural Development in the Third World,* ed. C. K. Eicher and J. M. Staatz. Baltimore: Johns Hopkins University Press.

Mellor, J. W.; Delgado, C. L.; and Blackie, M. J., eds. 1987. *Accelerating Food Production in Sub-Saharan Africa.* Baltimore: Johns Hopkins University Press.

Mellor, J. W., and Stevens, R. D. 1956. "The Average and Marginal Product of Farm Labor in Underdeveloped Economies." *Journal of Farm Economics* 38:780–91.

Michigan State University. 1986. *MSTAT—A Microcomputer Program for the Design, Management, and Analysis of Agronomic Experiments.* East Lansing: Michigan State University, Department of Crop and Soil Science.

Millikan, M. F. 1962. *Education for Innovation in Restless Nations: A Study of World Tensions and Development.* New York: Dodd, Mead.

Mills, C. W. 1956. *The Power Elite.* New York: Oxford University Press.

Miracle, M. P. 1969. "Market Structures in the Tribal Economies of West Africa." In *Agricultural Cooperatives and Markets in Developing Countries,* ed. K. R. Anschel, R. H. Brannon, and E. D. Smith. New York: Praeger.

Miracle, M. P., and Fetter, B. 1970. "Backward-Sloping Labor-Supply Functions and African Economic Behavior." *Economic Development and Cultural Change* 18:240–51.

Mitra, G. N., and Das, N. B. 1971. "Protein Quality of the High Yielding Varieties of Rice." *Journal of Agricultural Food Chemistry* 19:927–29.

Mittendorf, H. J. 1976. *Planning of Urban Wholesale Markets for Perishable Food with Particular Reference to Developing Countries.* Rome: Food and Agriculture Organization.

—————. 1978. "The Challenge of Organizing City Food Marketing Systems in Developing Countries." *Zeitschrift fur Auslandische Landwirtschaft* 17:323–41.

Mittendorf, H. J., and Hertog, O. 1982. *Marketing Costs and Margins for Major*

Food Items in Developing Countries. Document W/P7369. Rome: Food and Agriculture Organization.

Mohar, R., and Evenson, R. E. 1974. "The Intensive Agricultural Districts Programme in India: A New Evaluation." *Journal of Development Studies* 11:135–54.

Money, D. C. 1976. *Climate, Soils and Vegetation.* London: University Tutorial Press.

Moore, M. 1984. "Institutional Development, The World Bank and India's New Agricultural Extension Programme." *Journal of Development Studies* 20:303–17.

Morawetz, D. 1977. *Twenty-Five Years of Economic Development, 1950 to 1975.* Baltimore: Johns Hopkins University Press.

Morgan, W. B. 1977. *Agriculture in the Third World, A Spatial Analysis.* Boulder, Colo.: Westview.

Morris, M. D. 1979. *Measuring the Condition of the World's Poor—The Physical Quality of Life Index.* New York: Pergamon.

Morris, R. A., and Anwar, A. 1978. "Comments on Mechanization and Use of Modern Rice Varieties." In *Economic Consequences of the New Rice Technology,* ed. R. Barker and Y. Hayami. Los Banos, Philippines: International Rice Research Institute.

Morss, E. R., and Gow, D. D., eds. 1984. *Implementing Rural Development Projects: Lessons from AID and World Bank Experiences.* Boulder, Colo.: Westview.

Mosher, A. T. 1971. *To Create a Modern Agriculture: Organization and Planning.* New York: Agricultural Development Council.

————. 1981. *Three Ways to Spur Agricultural Growth.* New York: International Agricultural Development Service.

Moss, M. 1973. *The Measurement of Economic and Social Performance.* Studies in Income and Wealth 38. New York: Columbia University Press.

Mueller, E., and Anderson, J. 1982. "The Economic and Demographic Factors." In *Case Studies in the Demographic Impact of Asian Development Projects,* ed. R. Barlow. Ann Arbor: University of Michigan, Center for Research on Economic Development.

Mundlak, Y. 1979. *Intersectoral Factor Mobility and Agricultural Growth.* Report 6. Washington, D.C.: International Food Policy Research Institute.

Myint, H. 1984. "Exports and Economic Development of Less Developed Countries." In *Agricultural Development in the Third World,* ed. C. K. Eicher and J. M. Staatz. Baltimore: Johns Hopkins University Press.

Myrdal, G. 1968. *Asian Drama.* 3 vols. New York: Pantheon.

Nair, K. 1962. *Blossoms in the Dust: The Human Factor in Indian Development.* New York: Praeger.

Nash, M. 1966. *Primitive and Peasant Economic Systems.* San Francisco: Chandler.

National Research Council. 1981. *Workshop on Energy and Agriculture in Developing Countries.* Washington, D.C.: National Academy Press.

Nelson, M. 1973. *The Development of Tropical Lands.* Baltimore: Johns Hopkins University Press.

Nelson, R. R.; Peck, M. J.; and Kalachek, E. D. 1967. *Technology, Economic Growth and Public Policy*. Washington, D.C.: Brookings.

Nelson, W., and Mach, L. 1986. *Production Economics: Computer Aided Instruction Module*. Fargo: North Dakota State University Press.

Nicholls, W. H. 1964. "The Place of Agriculture in Economic Development." In *Agriculture in Economic Development*, ed. C. K. Eicher and L. W. Witt. New York: McGraw-Hill.

Nisbet, C. 1967. "Interest Rates and Imperfect Competition in the Informal Credit Market of Rural Chile." *Economic Development and Cultural Change* 16:73–90.

Non-Formal Education Exchange. 1982. "Select Bibliography: Non-Formal Education and Development." In *The NFE Exchange*. East Lansing: Michigan State University, College of Education.

Norman, D. W. 1977. "Economic Rationality of Traditional Housa Dryland Farmers in the North of Nigeria." In *Tradition and Dynamics in Small Farm Agriculture: Economic Studies in Asia, Africa, and Latin America*, ed. R. D. Stevens. Ames: Iowa State University Press.

North, D. C. and Thomas. R. P. 1970. "An Economic Theory of the Growth of the Western World." *Economic History Review* 23:1–17.

Norton, G. W. and Davis, J. S. 1981. "Evaluation Returns to Agricultural Research: A Review." *American Journal of Agricultural Economics* 63:685–99.

Ohkawa, K. 1956. "Economic Growth and Agriculture." *Annals Hitotsubashi Academy* 7:46–70.

Olson, M. 1982. *The Rise and Decline of Nations: Economic Growth, Stagflation, and Social Rigidities*. New Haven, Conn.: Yale University Press.

Osburn, D. D., and Schneeberger, K. C. 1983. *Modern Agricultural Management*. Reston, Va.: Reston Publishers.

Oshima, H. T. 1977. "Review Article: New Directions in Development Strategies." *Economic Development and Cultural Change* 25:555–79.

Pagot, J. R. 1977. "Constraints in the Introduction of Animal Technology." In *Proceedings: The World Food Conference of 1976*. Ames: Iowa State University Press.

Pariser, E. R. 1982. "Post-Harvest Food Losses in Developing Countries—A Survey." In *Nutrition Policy Implementation*, ed. N. S. Scrimshaw and M. B. Wallenstein. New York: Plenum.

Parsons, T., ed. 1966. *Societies*. Englewood Cliffs, N.J.: Prentice-Hall.

Parsons, T., and Shils, E. A., eds. 1951. *Toward a General Theory of Action*. Cambridge, Mass.: Harvard University Press.

Paulino, L. A. 1986. *Food in the Third World: Past Trends and Projections to 2000*. Research Report 52. Washington, D.C.: International Food Policy Research Institute.

Peacock, F. 1981. "Rural Poverty and Development in West Malaysia (1957–1970)." *Journal of Developing Areas* 15:639–54.

Pearse, A. 1980. *Seeds of Plenty, Seeds of Want: Social and Economic Implications of the Green Revolution*. Oxford: Clarendon.

Perkins, D. H. 1984. *Rural Development in China*. Baltimore: Johns Hopkins University Press.

Perraton, H., et al. 1983. *Basic Education and Agricultural Extension: Costs,*

Effects and Alternatives. Staff Working Paper 56. Washington, D. C.: World Bank.

Perrin, R. K.; Winkelman, D. L.; Moscardi, E. R.; and Anderson, J. R. 1976. *From Agronomic Data to Farmers' Recommendations—An Economic Training Manual.* El Batan, Mexico: International Center for the Improvement of Maize and Wheat.

Peterson, W. L. 1979. "International Farm Prices and the Social Cost of Cheap Food Policies." *American Journal of Agricultural Economics* 61:12–21.

Pimentel, D., ed. 1978. *World Food, Pest Losses, and the Environment.* Boulder, Colo.: Westview.

Pineiro, M., et al. 1979. "Technical Change and the Role of the State in Latin American Development." *Food Policy* 4:169–77.

Pingali, P. L.; Bigot, Y.; and Binswanger, H. 1986. *Agricultural Mechanization and the Evolution of Farming Systems in Sub-Saharan Africa.* Baltimore: Johns Hopkins University Press.

Pinstrup-Andersen, P. 1982. *Agricultural Research and Technology in Economic Development.* New York: Longman.

Pinstrup-Andersen, P., and Hazell, P. B. R. 1987. "The Impact of the Green Revolution and Prospects for the Future." In *Food Policy: Integrating Supply, Distribution and Consumption,* ed. J. P. Gittinger, J. Leslie, and C. Hoisington. Baltimore: Johns Hopkins University Press.

Plusquellec, H. L., and Wickham, T. 1985. *Irrigation Design and Management— Experience in Thailand and Its General Applicability.* Technical Paper 40. Washington, D.C.: World Bank.

Poleman. T. T. 1975. "World Food: A Perspective." *Science* 188:510–18.

Pope, R. 1981. "Supply Response and the Dispersion of Price Expectations." *American Journal of Agricultural Economics* 63:161–63.

Popkin, S. L. 1979. *The Rational Peasant.* Berkeley and Los Angeles: University of California Press.

Population Reference Bureau. 1979. "Our Population Predicament: A New Look." *Population Bulletin* 34:1–39.

Porter, R. C. 1970. "Some Implications of Postwar Primary-Product Trends." *Journal of Political Economy* 78:586–97.

Presidential Commission on World Hunger. 1980. *Overcoming World Hunger: The Challenge Ahead.* Washington, D.C.: Government Printing Office.

President's Science Advisory Committee. 1967. *The World Food Problem.* Vol. 2. *Report of the Panel on the World Food Supply.* Washington, D.C.: Government Printing Office.

Presvelan, C., and Spijkers-Zwart, S., eds. 1980. *The Household, Women and Agricultural Development.* Wageningen, The Netherlands: H. Veenman and Zonen, B. V.

Pryor, F. L. 1977. *The Origins of the Economy: A Comparative Study of Distribution in Primitive and Peasant Economies.* New York: Academic.

Purcell, W. 1979. *Agricultural Marketing: Systems, Coordination, Cash and Future Prices.* Reston, Va.: Reston Publishing.

Radosevich, G. E. 1974. "Water Use Organizations for Small Farmers." In *Small*

Farm Agricultural Development, ed. H. H. Biggs and R. L. Tinnermeier. Fort Collins, Colo.: Colorado State University.

Randhawa, M. S. 1974. *The Green Revolution.* New York: Wiley.

Ranis, G., and Fei, J. C. H. 1961. "A Theory of Economic Development." *American Economic Review.* 51:533–65.

Rao, V. V. B. 1981. "Measurement of Deprivation and Poverty Based on the Proportion Spent on Food: An Exploratory Exercise." *World Development* 9:337–53.

Raper, A. F. 1970. *Rural Development in Action—The Comprehensive Experiment at Comilla, East Pakistan.* Ithaca, N.Y.: Cornell University Press.

Raup, P. M. 1967. "Land Reform and Agricultural Development." In *Agricultural and Economic Development,* ed. H. Southworth and B. F. Johnston. Ithaca, N.Y.: Cornell University Press.

Read, H. 1974. *Partners with India: Building Agricultural Universities.* Urbana: University of Illinois.

Reca, L. G. 1983. "Price Policies in Developing Countries." In *The Role of Markets in the World Food Economy,* ed. D. G. Johnson and G. E. Schuh. Boulder, Colo.: Westview.

Reed, E. P. 1977. "Introducing Group Farming in Less Developed Countries: Some Issues." In *Cooperative and Commune,* ed. P. Dorner. Madison: University of Wisconsin Press.

Reutlinger, S., and Selowski, M. 1976. *Malnutrition and Poverty: Magnitude and Policy Options.* Baltimore: Johns Hopkins University Press.

Reynolds, L. 1971. *The Three Worlds of Economics.* New Haven, Conn.: Yale University Press.

Riedel, J. 1984. "Trade as the Engine of Growth in Developing Countries, Revisited." *Economic Journal* 94:56–73,

Rihani, M. 1978. *Development as if Women Mattered: An Annotated Bibliography with a Third World Focus.* Washington, D.C.: Overseas Development Council.

Riley, H. M., and Staatz, J. 1981. *Food Systems Organization and Problems in Developing Countries.* Report 23. New York: Agricultural Development Council.

Riley, H. M., and Weber, M. T. 1983. "Marketing in Developing Countries." In *Future Frontiers in Agricultural Marketing Research,* ed. P. L. Farris. Ames: Iowa State University Press.

Robinson, W., and Schutjer, W. 1984. "Agricultural Development and Demographic Change: A Generalization of the Boserup Model." *Economic Development and Cultural Change* 32:355–66.

Rogers, E. M. 1971. *Communication of Innovations.* 2d ed. New York: Free Press.

Rostow, W. W. 1960. *The Stages of Economic Growth: A Non-Communist Manifesto.* London: Cambridge University Press.

————. 1964. *View from the Seventh Floor.* New York: Harper and Row.

————. 1980. *Why the Poor Get Richer and the Rich Slow Down.* Austin: University of Texas Press.

Roumasset, J. A. 1976. *Rice and Risk: Decision Making Among Low Income Farmers.* Amsterdam: North-Holland.

————. 1979. "Sharecropping, Production Externalities and the Theory of Contracts." *American Journal of Agricultural Economics* 61:640–47.

Roxborough, I. 1979. *Theories of Underdevelopment.* Atlantic Highlands, N.J.: Humanities Press.

Roy, E. P. 1964. *Cooperatives: Today and Tomorrow.* Danville, Ill.: Interstate.

Ruthenberg, H. 1980. *Farming Systems in the Tropics.* 3d ed. New York: Oxford University Press.

Ruttan, V. W. 1965. "Growth Stage Theories, Dual Economy Models, and Agricultural Development Policy." *Australian Journal of Agricultural Economics* 9:17–32.

—————. 1969. "Agricultural Product and Factor Markets in Southeast Asia." In *Agricultural Cooperatives and Markets in Developing Countries,* ed. K. R. Anschel, R. H. Brannon, and E. D. Smith. New York: Praeger.

—————. 1977. "The Green Revolution: Seven Generalizations." *International Development Review* 19:16–23.

—————. 1978. "Induced Institutional Change." In *Induced Innovation: Technology, Institutions and Development,* H. P. Binswanger and V. W. Ruttan. Baltimore: Johns Hopkins University Press.

—————. 1981. "Three Cases of Induced Institutional Innovation." In *Public Choice and Rural Development,* ed. C. S. Russell and N. K. Nicholson. Research Paper R-21. Washington, D.C.: Resources for the Future.

—————. 1982. *Agricultural Research Policy.* Minneapolis: University of Minnesota Press.

—————. 1984. "Social Science Knowledge and Institutional Change." *American Journal of Agricultural Economics* 66:549–59.

Ruttan, V. W., and Binswanger, H. P. 1978. "Induced Innovation and the Green Revolution." In *Induced Innovation: Technology, Institutions and Development,* ed. H. P. Binswanger and V. W. Ruttan. Baltimore: Johns Hopkins University Press.

Ryan, J. G.; Ghodake, R. D.; and Sarin, R. 1979. "Labor Use and Labor Markets in Semi-Arid Tropical Rural Villages of Peninsular India." In *Socioeconomic Constraints to Development of Semi-Arid Tropical Agriculture.* Hyderabad, India: International Crops Research Institute for the Semi-Arid Tropics.

Sahlins, M. 1972. *Stone Age Economics.* Chicago: Aldine.

Sanders, J. H., and De Hollanda, A. D. 1979. "Technology Design for Semi-Arid Northeast Brazil." In *Economics and the Design of Small-Farmer Technology,* ed. A. Valdes, G. M. Scobie, and J. L. Dillon. Ames: Iowa State University Press.

Sanford, S. 1983. *Management of Pastoral Development in the Third World.* New York: Wiley.

Santon-Villanueva, P. 1966. "The Value of Rural Roads." In *Selected Readings to Accompany Getting Agriculture Moving,* ed. R. E. Borton. New York: Agricultural Development Council.

Sargent, M.; Lichte, J.; Malton, P.; and Bloom, R. 1981. *An Assessment of Animal Traction in Francophone West Africa.* African Rural Economy Working Paper 34. East Lansing: Michigan State University, Department of Agricultural Economics.

Sarker, R. I. 1981. "Energy Input-Output Relationships in Traditional and Mechanized Rice Cultivation in Bangladesh." *Agricultural Mechanization in Asia* 12:30–32.

Sauer, C. O. 1969. *The Domestication of Animals and Foodstuffs.* 2d ed. Cambridge, Mass.: MIT Press.

Saunders, R. J.; Warford, J. J.; and Willenius, B. 1983. *Telecommunications and Economic Development.* Baltimore: Johns Hopkins University Press.

Schaefer-Kehnert, W. 1983. "Success with Group Lending in Malawi." In *Rural Financial Markets in Developing Countries: Their Use and Abuse,* ed. J. D. Von Pischke, D. W. Adams, and G. Donald. Baltimore: Johns Hopkins University Press.

Schmid, A. A. 1965. "Property, Power and Progress." *Land Economics* 41:275–79.

Schmid, L. 1969. "Relation of Size of Farm to Productivity." *Annual Report, 1968,* app. 3, pp. 1–33. Madison: University of Wisconsin, Land Tenure Center.

Schultz, T. P. 1981. *Economics of Population.* Reading, Mass.: Addison-Wesley.

————. 1982. *Women and Economics of the Family: Some Concepts and Issues.* New Haven, Conn.: Yale University Press.

Schultz, T. W. 1953. *The Economic Organization of Agriculture.* New York: McGraw-Hill.

————. 1956. "Reflections on Agricultural Production, Output, and Supply." *Journal of Farm Economics* 38:748–62.

————. 1964a. *Economic Crisis in World Agriculture.* Ann Arbor: University of Michigan Press.

————. 1964b. *Transforming Traditional Agriculture.* New Haven, Conn.: Yale University Press.

————. 1968. "Institutions and the Rising Economic Value of Man." *American Journal of Agricultural Economics* 48:1113–22.

————. 1975. "The Value of the Ability to Deal with Disequilibria." *Journal of Economic Literature* 8:827–46.

————, ed. 1978. *Distortions of Agricultural Incentives.* Bloomington: Indiana University Press.

————. 1980. "Nobel Lecture: The Economics of Being Poor." *Journal of Political Economy* 88:639–51.

Schumpeter, J. A. 1954. *History of Economic Analysis.* New York: Oxford University Press.

Schwarzweller, H. K., ed. 1984. *Research in Rural Sociology and Development.* Greenwich, Conn.: JAI.

Scobie, G. M., and Posada, T. R. 1984. "The Impact of Technological Change on Income Distribution: The Case of Rice in Colombia." In *Agricultural Development in the Third World,* ed. C. K. Eicher and J. M. Staatz. Baltimore: Johns Hopkins University Press.

Scott, J. C. 1976. *The Moral Economy of the Peasant: Rebellion and Subsistence in Southeast Asia.* New Haven, Conn.: Yale University Press.

Scott, W.; McGranahan, D. V.; and Argalias, H. 1973. *The Measurement of Real Progress at the Local Level: Examples from the Literature and a Pilot Study.* UNRISD Report 73.3. Geneva, Switzerland: U. N. Research Institute for Social Development.

Scoville, O. J. 1979. *World Hunger and the Land-Grant Universities.* Association of United States University Directors of International Agricultural Programs. (AUSU-DIAP Publication No. 3.)

Seddon, D., ed. 1978. *Relations of Production: Marxist Approaches to Economic Anthropology.* London: Frank Cass.

Seers, D. 1972. "What Are We Trying to Measure?" In *Measuring Development,* ed. N. Baster. London: Frank Cass.

————. 1977. "The New Meaning of Development." *International Development Review* 19:27.

Sen, A. K. 1980. *Levels of Poverty: Policy and Change.* Staff Working Paper WP-0401. Washington, D.C.: World Bank.

Schaffer, J. D. 1979. "Observations on the Political Economy of Regulations." *American Journal of Agricultural Economics* 61:721–31.

————. 1980. "Food System Organization and Performance: Toward a Conceptual Framework." *American Journal of Agricultural Economics* 62:310–18.

————. 1985. "Designing Market Systems to Promote Development in the Third World Countries." In *Agricultural Markets in the Semi-Arid Tropics: Proceedings of a Workshop.* Patancheru, Andhra Pradesh, India: International Crops Research Institute for the Semi-Arid Tropics.

Schuh, G. E.; Kellogg, E. D.; and Paarlberg, R. L. 1987. *Assistance to Developing Countries' Agriculture and U.S. Agricultural Exports: Three Perspectives.* Washington, D.C.: Consortium for Institutional Cooperation in Higher Education..

Shaner, W. W.; Phillip, P. F.; and Schmehl, W. R. 1982. *Farming Systems Research and Development—Guidelines for Developing Countries.* Boulder, Colo.: Westview.

Shepherd, G. S., and Futrell, G. A., and Strain. 1976 and 1982. *Marketing Farm Products.* 6th and 7th eds. Ames: Iowa State University Press.

Siamwalla, A., and Valdes, A. 1984. "Food Security in Developing Countries: International Issues." In *Agricultural Development in the Third World,* ed. C. K. Eicher and J. M. Staatz. Baltimore: Johns Hopkins University Press.

Simmons, J. 1979. "Education for Development Reconsidered." *World Development* 7:1005–16.

Simon, J. L., and Kahn, H. 1984. *The Resourceful Earth.* Oxford, U.K.: Basil Blackwell.

Simpson, J. R., and Evangelou, P. 1984. *Livestock Development in Subsaharan Africa.* Boulder, Colo.: Westview.

Singh, I. 1985. *Small Farmers and the Landless in South Asia.* World Bank Working Paper 320. Baltimore: Johns Hopkins University Press.

Singh, I. J., and Day, R. H. 1975. "A Micro-Economic Chronicle of the Green Revolution." *Economic Development and Cultural Change* 23:661–86.

Singh, K. 1983. "Structure of Interest Rates on Consumption Loans in an Indian Village." In *Rural Financial Markets in Developing Countries: Their Use and Abuse,* ed. J. D. Von Pischke, D. W. Adams, and G. Donald. Baltimore: Johns Hopkins University Press.

Skrubbettrang, F. 1952. *The Danish Folk High Schools.* 2d ed. Copenhagen: Det Danske Selskab.

————. 1953. *Agricultural Development and Rural Reform in Denmark.* Rome: Food and Agriculture Organization.

Slater, L., and Levin, S., eds. 1981. *Climate Impact on Food Supplies: Strategies and Technologies for Climate-Defensive Food Production.* Boulder, Colo.: Westview.

Slicher van Bath, B. H. 1963. *The Agrarian History of Western Europe, A.D. 500–1850.* London: Edward Arnold.

Smelser, N. J. 1963. *The Sociology of Economic Life.* Englewood Cliffs, N.J.: Prentice-Hall.

————. 1968. *Essays in Sociological Explanation.* Englewood Cliffs, N.J.: Prentice-Hall.

Smith, E.D. 1975. *A Seminar Report—Marketing Institutions and Services for Developing Agriculture.* RTN Seminar Report. New York: Agricultural Development Council.

Smith, J. A., and Hays, V. W. 1982. *Proceedings of the XIV International Grassland Congress.* Lexington: University of Kentucky.

Smith, S. 1980. "The Ideas of Samir Amin: Theory or Tautology." *Journal of Development Studies* 17:5–21.

Smith, T. 1979. "The Underdevelopment of Development Literature: The Case of Dependency Theory." *World Politics* 31:247–88.

Smith, T. C. 1959. *The Agrarian Origins of Modern Japan.* Stanford, Calif.: Stanford University Press.

Sommer, J. G. 1977. *Beyond Charity—U.S. Voluntary Aid for a Changing Third World.* Washington, D.C.: Overseas Development Council.

Spaeth, D. H. 1969. "Quasi-Cooperative Arrangements: The Japanese and Taiwanese Experience." In *Agricultural Cooperatives and Markets in Developing Countries,* ed. K. R. Anschel, R. H. Brannon, and E. D. Smith. New York: Praeger.

Spedding, C. R. W. 1979. *Agricultural Systems.* Barking, Essex, U.K.: Applied Science Publishers.

Spencer, D. S. C.; May-Parker, I. I.; and Rose, F. S. 1976. *Employment Efficiency and Income in the Rice Processing Industry of Sierra Leone.* African Rural Economy Paper 15. East Lansing: Michigan State University, Department of Agricultural Economics.

Spencer, J. E. 1966. *Shifting Cultivation in Southeastern Asia.* Berkeley and Los Angeles: University of California Press.

Spengler, J. J., ed. 1961. *Natural Resources and Economic Growth.* Baltimore: Johns Hopkins University Press.

Spicer, E.H., ed. 1952. *Human Problems in Technological Change.* New York: Russell Sage.

Squire, L. 1981. *Employment Policy in Developing Countries: A Survey of Issues and Evidence.* London: Oxford University Press.

Srinivasan, T. N. 1977. "Development, Poverty and Basic Human Needs: Some Issues." *Food Research Institute Studies* 16:11–28.

Stavenhagen, R. 1975. *Social Classes in Agrarian Societies.* New York: Doubleday.

Stevens, R. D. 1959. "Capital Formation and Agriculture in Some Lebanese Villages." Ph.D. diss. Cornell University, 1959.

————. 1965. *Elasticity of Food Consumption Associated with Economic Growth.* Foreign Agricultural Economics Report 23. Washington, D.C.: U.S. Department of Agriculture Economic Research Service.

————. 1967. *Institutional Change and Agricultural Development*. Agricultural Economics Report 64. East Lansing: Michigan State University.

————. 1974. "Three Rural Development Models for Small-Farm Agricultural Areas in Low-Income Nations." *Journal of Developing Areas* 8:409–20.

————. 1976. "Comilla Rural Development Programs to 1971." In *Rural Development in Bangladesh and Pakistan*, ed. R. D. Stevens, H. Alavi, and P. J. Bertocci. Honolulu: University Press of Hawaii.

————, ed. 1977. *Tradition and Dynamics in Small Farm Agriculture: Economic Studies in Asia, Africa, and Latin America*. Ames: Iowa State University Press.

Streeten, P. 1980. "Basic Needs and Human Rights." *World Development* 8:107–11.

Taiwan Agricultural Yearbook. Annual. Taipei: Republic of China.

Taylor, D. C., and Wickham, T. H., eds. 1979. *Irrigation Policy and the Management of Irrigation Systems in Southeast Asia*. Bangkok: Agricultural Development Council.

Thiam, T. B., and Ong, S. eds. 1979. *Readings in Asian Farm Management*. Singapore: Singapore University Press.

Thomas, J. W. 1974. "Employment Creating Public Works Programs: Observations on Political and Social Dimensions." In *Employment in Developing Nations*, ed. E. O. Edwards. New York: Columbia University Press.

Thompson, R. L. 1983. "The Role of Trade in Food Security and Agricultural Development." In *The Role of Markets in the World Food Economy*, ed. D. G. Johnson and G. E. Schuh. Boulder, Colo.: Westview.

Thorbecke, E., ed. 1979. *The Role of Agriculture in Economic Development*. New York: Columbia University Press.

Timmer. C. P. 1975. "The Political Economy of Rice in Asia: Lessons and Implications." *Food Research Institute Studies* 14:191–96.

————. 1984. "Choice of Technique in Rice Milling on Java." In *Agricultural Development in the Third World*, ed. C. K. Eicher and J. M. Staatz. Baltimore: Johns Hopkins University Press.

————. 1986. *Getting Prices Right: The Scope and Limits of Agricultural Price Policy*. Ithaca: Cornell University Press.

Timmer, C. P.; Falcon, W. P.; and Pearson, S. R. 1983. *Food Policy Analysis*. Baltimore: Johns Hopkins University Press.

Tinker, I. 1979. *New Technologies for Food Chain Activities: The Imperative of Equity for Women*. Washington, D.C.: Agency for International Development, Office of Women in Development.

Tinker, I., and Bramsen, M. B., eds. 1977. *Women and World Development*. Washington, D.C.: Overseas Development Council.

Todaro, M. P. 1976. *International Migration in Developing Countries: A Review of Theory, Evidence, Methodology and Research Priorities*. Geneva, Switzerland: International Labour Organisation.

————. 1981. *Economic Development in the Third World*. 2d ed. New York: Longman.

Tolley, G. S.; Thomas, V.; and Wong, C. M. 1982. *Agricultural Price Policy and the Developing Countries*. Baltimore: Johns Hopkins University Press.

Toquero, A.; Ebron, L.; Maranon, C.; and Duff, B. 1977. "Assessing Qualitative and

Quantitative Losses in Rice Production Systems.'' *Agricultural Mechanization in Asia* 8:31–40.

Turnham, D. 1976. *The Employment Problem in Less-Developed Countries: A Review of Evidence*. Paris: Organisation for European Cooperation and Development, Developing Center.

United Nations. 1974. *Rural Cooperatives as Agents of Change: A Research Report and a Debate*. Report 74.3. Geneva, Switzerland: United Nations, Research Institute for Social Development.

————. 1976. *Progress in Land Reform*. 6th Report. New York: United Nations.

————. 1980. *Handbook of International Trade and Development Statistics*. New York: United Nations, Conference on Trade and Development.

————. 1983. *Handbook of International Trade and Development Statistics*. New York: United Nations, Conference on Trade and Development.

————. 1985. *World Population Prospects—Estimates and Projections as Assessed in 1982*. Population Studies 86. New York: United Nations, Department of International Economic and Social Affairs.

————. *National Accounts Statistics*. New York: United Nations.

University of Illinois. 1978. *Agricultural Technology for Developing Nations: Farm Mechanization Alternatives for 1–10 Hectare Farms*. Urbana: University of Illinois Printing Service.

Uphoff, N. T., and Ilchman, W. F. 1972. *The Political Economy of Development*. Berkeley and Los Angeles: University of California Press.

Upton, M. 1973. *Farm Management in Africa—Principles of Production and Planning*. London: Oxford University Press.

USAID (United States Agency for International Development). 1968. *War on Hunger*. Washington, D.C.: U.S.A.I.D.

USDA (United States Department of Agriculture). 1970. *The Marketing Challenge: Distributing Increased Production in Developing Nations*. Washington, D.C.: USDA, Foreign Economic Development Service.

————. 1983. *Food Policies in Developing Countries*. Foreign Agricultural Economic Report 194. Washington, D. C.: USDA, Economic Research Service.

————. 1985. *1985 Agricultural Chart Book*. Agricultural Handbook 652. Washington, D.C.: USDA.

————. 1986. *National Food Review*. Fall. Washington, D.C.: USDA.

————. 1987. *Economic Indicators of the Farm Sector: Production and Efficiency Statistics 1985*. ECIFS 5.5. Washington, D.C.: USDA, Economic Research Service.

————. *Agricultural Statistics*. Annual. Washington, D.C.: USDA.

————. *World Agriculture: Outlook and Situation Report*. Quarterly. Washington, D.C.: USDA, Economic Research Service.

Valdes, A.; Scobie, G. M.; and Dillon, J. L., eds. 1979. *Economics and the Design of Small-Farmer Technology*. Ames: Iowa State University Press.

Von Oppen, M.; Raju, V. T.; and Bapna, S. L. 1979. ''Foodgrain Marketing and Agricultural Development in India.'' In *International Workshop on Socioeconomic Constraints to Development of Semi-Arid Tropical Agriculture*. Patancheru, Andhra Pradesh, India: International Crops Research Institute for the Semi-Arid Tropics.

Von Pischke, J. D. 1983. "Toward an Operational Approach to Savings for Rural Developers." In *Rural Financial Markets in Developing Countries: Their Use and Abuse,* ed. J. D. Von Pischke, D. W. Adams, and G. Donald. Baltimore: Johns Hopkins University Press.

Von Pischke, J. D.; Adams, D. W.; and Donald, G., eds. 1983. *Rural Financial Markets in Developing Countries: Their Use and Abuse.* New York: Johns Hopkins University Press.

Walinsky, L. J., ed. 1977. *The Selected Papers of Wolf Ladejinsky—Agrarian Reform as Unfinished Business.* New York: Oxford University Press.

Wallerstein, I. M. 1979. *The Capitalist World Economy.* New York: Cambridge University Press.

Wang, J. and Hagan, R. E. 1981. *Irrigated Rice Production Systems—Design Procedures.* Boulder, Colo.: Westview.

Warriner, D. 1969. *Land Reform in Principle and Practice.* London: Oxford University Press.

Waterston, A. 1979. *Development Planning: Lessons of Experience.* Baltimore: Johns Hopkins University Press.

Weber, M. 1956. *The Protestant Ethic and the Spirit of Capitalism.* New York: Scribner's.

Weitz, R. 1971. *From Peasant to Farmer: A Revolutionary Strategy for Development.* New York: Columbia University Press.

Welch, F. 1978. "The Role of Investments in Human Capital." In *Distortions in Agricultural Incentives,* ed. T. W. Schultz. Bloomington: Indiana University Press.

Wells, R. J. G. 1983. "An Input Credit Program for Small Farmers in West Malaysia." In *Rural Financial Markets in Developing Countries: Their Use and Abuse,* ed. J. D. Von Pischke, D. W. Adams, and G. Donald. Baltimore: Johns Hopkins University Press.

Wennergren, E. B., et al., eds. 1986. *Solving World Hunger: The United States Stake.* Cabin John, Md.: Seven Locks.

Wharton, C. R., Jr. 1963. "Research on Agricultural Development in Southeast Asia." *Journal of Farm Economics* 45:1161–74.

Whentham, E. H. 1972. *Agricultural Marketing in Africa.* London: Oxford University Press.

Wierer, K., and Abbott, J. C. 1978. *Fertilizer Marketing.* Marketing Guide 7. Rome: Food and Agriculture Organization.

Wijewardene, R. 1980. "Energy-Conserving Farming Systems for the Humid Tropics." *Agricultural Mechanization in Asia* 11:47–53.

Wilber, C. K., ed. 1984. *The Political Economy of Development and Underdevelopment.* New York: Random.

Wilber, C. K., and Jameson, K. P. 1983. *An Enquiry into the Poverty of Economics.* Notre Dame, Ind.: University of Notre Dame Press.

Williamson, G., and Payne, W. J. A. 1978. *An Introduction to Animal Husbandry in the Tropics.* 3d ed. London: Longman.

Winrock International. 1983. *World Agriculture: Review and Prospects into the 1990's (A Summary).* Morrilton, Ark.: Winrock International.

Wolf, C. J. 1955. "Institutions and Economic Development." *American Economic Review* 45:867–83.

Wolf, E. R., and Mintz, S. W. 1957, "Haciendas and Plantations in Middle America and the Antilles." *Social and Economic Studies* 6:386–412.

Wong, J. C., ed. 1979. *Group Farming in Asia.* Singapore: Singapore University Press.

Woods, R. G., ed. 1981. *Future Dimensions of World Food and Population.* Boulder, Colo.: Westview.

World Bank. 1970. *Trends in Developing Countries.* Washington, D.C.: World Bank.

―――――. 1974. *Land Reform.* Sector Policy Paper. Washington, D.C.: World Bank.

―――――. 1981. *Accelerated Development in Sub-Saharan Africa: An Agenda for Action.* Washington, D.C.: World Bank.

―――――. 1984a. *Toward Sustained Development in Sub-Saharan Africa.* Washington, D.C.: World Bank.

―――――. 1984b. *World Tables.* 2 vol. Baltimore: Johns Hopkins University Press.

―――――. 1986. *Poverty and Hunger: Options for Food Security in Developing Countries.* Washington, D.C.: World Bank.

―――――. *World Development Report.* Annual. New York: Oxford University Press.

World Food Institute. 1982. *World Food Trade and United States Agriculture, 1960–1981.* Ames: Iowa State University, World Food Institute.

Wortman, S., and Cummings, R. W., Jr. 1978. *To Feed This World—The Challenge and the Strategy.* Baltimore: Johns Hopkins University Press.

Yang, M. M. C. 1970. *Socio-Economic Results of Land Reform in Taiwan.* Honolulu, Hawaii: East-West Center Press.

Yeager, L. B., and Tuerck, D. G. 1969. *Trade Policy and the Price System.* Scranton, Pa.: International Textbook.

Yotopoulos, P. A., and Nugent, J. B. 1976. *Economics of Development—Empirical Investigations.* New York: Harper and Row.

Zymelman, M. 1976. *The Economic Evaluation of Vocational Training Programs.* Baltimore: Johns Hopkins University Press.

Index

Absolute advantage, 366
Absolute disadvantage, 365
Access to markets, and trade, 362
Achievement motivation, 94
Administered prices, 394–95; macro-, 400–401; product, 393–97
Administrative costs of credit, 259
Administrative procedures. *See* Government
Administrators, 416
Adoption of new technology, 209; animal-powered mechanization, 232–34; free market and, 339
Advisory units, 353
Aggregate production function, reformulation, 118
Agricultural development: measured, 21–26; paths of, 425; in world history, 2–4
Agricultural development theory. *See* Theory
Agricultural experiment stations. *See* Experiment stations; Research
Agricultural practices: package programs, 214; technological and socioeconomic constraints, 292. *See also* Cropping practices; Traditional agriculture
Agricultural production. *See* Production; Productivity; Productivity change
Agricultural products. *See* Food demand
Agricultural stage model, 130–32
Agricultural transition, 2, 3. *See also* Structural transformation
Aid organizations: cost-benefit analysis, requirements for, 166; international aid, 418–19. *See also* Programs
Allocation of resources. *See* Labor, allocation of, in household; Resource allocation
Allocative effect, of educational investments, 309
Allocative efficiency, 75–77
All-technology isoquant frontier, 228–29

Alternative extension system, 315
Alternative input supply channels, 345
Alternative uses of land, 120
Analysis, economic. *See* Benefit-cost analysis; Economic analysis
Animal manure, 206
Animal-powered machinery, 226–27, 231–34; irrigation, 239–40; land preparation, comparative costs, 233; policy issues, 244–45
Animal productivity: biotechnology and, 307; draft animals, 219, 227, 231–34; increasing, 219–23
Annual cycle of labor demand, 190–191
Appropriate technology, 226, 303
Arable land. *See* Land availability
Arc elasticities, income, 47, 48
Artifacts, defined, 100
Artisans, 343–44
Authoritarian societies, 414; collective farms, establishment of, 280–82; cooperatives in, 266–67; traditional societies as, 94
Average productivity, labor, 191

Backward linkages, 331, 418
Balance of payments controls, 374
Banks, 32. *See also* Credit
Barriers to entry, 337, 342
Barter, 66
Behavioral variables: environment-behavior-performance model of marketing, 337; social change theories emphasizing, 96–97. *See also* Cultural variables
Beliefs: defined, 99; environment-behavior-performance model of marketing, 337; and tenure arrangements, 105–6; theories emphasizing, 93. *See also* Cultural variables

463

Benefit-cost analysis, 164–67; government settlement projects, 172; information services, 317; irrigation, 240; land development, 164
BIMAS program, 417
Bimodal farm structure, 272–73
Biological constraints, 292
Biological inputs: animal, 219–23, 232; genetics, new, 306–8; marketing, 339–40. *See also* Seed varieties, new; Seed varieties, traditional
Biotechnological revolution, 306–8
Birth rates. *See* Population growth
Black markets, 342
Boards, marketing, 376, 399–400
Borrower groups, 261–62
Buffer stock program, 395

Calories, new crop varieties and, 210
Capacity level, research at, 305–6
Capacity transfer of research, 302, 343–44
Capital: contributions of agriculture, 53; cooperative farming, 271; increasing labor productivity and equity, 194–95; investment concepts, 114–15; macro prices, administered, 400; measures of economic growth, 32, 33; neoclassical model of growth, 79; policy areas for increased employment, equity, and productivity, 194–95; quality of, 118; trade and, 366–67; traditional, 81–82
Capital costs: irrigation, 240; mechanization, economics of, 228–29, 233
Capital intensity, of technological change, 153
Capitalist nations, 6
Capital quality, 118
Capital services. *See* Credit
Cash crops, 172. *See also* Export crops
Caste, 330
Ceiling prices, 394, 395, 396
Centralized decisionmaking, 413
Cereals. *See* Grains; Rice; Seed varieties, new
Change: in economic structure, measurement of, 49; institutional, 101–2; in traditional agriculture, 70–73. *See also* Structural transformation
Chemical inputs, 340–43; mechanization of application, 236. *See also* Fertilizers, chemical; Pesticides
Chemicals, plant, 307
Chicken factories, 221
Civil rights, 32
Classical economic theory, 361, 362–66. *See also* Neoclassical models of economic growth
Climate, 18–19, 221

Clothing, 35, 42–43, 44
Collateral, for informal credit, 256
Collective action, 100
Collective farmers, 281; government role in marketing, 354; political systems and, 6
Collective farming, 271–72, 280–82
Colonialism, 169
Colonization, spontaneous, 173–74
Comilla Village cooperatives, 267–68; extension system, 315–16
Commodity agreements, 379–80
Commodity marketing boards, 376
Commodity research, 305
Common law, 250–51
Communal land ownership, 270
Communes, 272
Communications, 316–17; economic complementarities, 317–18; institutional arrangements and, 107; marketing technologies, 346; strategic investments, 416
Community development movement, 125–27
Comparative advantage: changing, 366–68; shifts in, 368–69; theory of, 362–66
Compensatory investment, 421
Competition, 354–56, 357
Complementarities. *See* Economic complementarities
Computers, 306, 316–17
Concentration ratios, 337
Conflict theories of development. *See* Marxist/neo-Marxist theory
Conservationists, concerns of, 120
Conservation model, 119–21
Conservatism, in traditional agriculture, 72
Conservative market economy, new input marketing, 339
Construction costs, irrigation, 240
Consumer demand: consumption patterns, 41–43; contributions of agriculture, 53; for food, 43–45; personal savings, 41–42; structural transformation, 50
Consumption: economic growth and, 41–43; government pricing policy and, 401–2; income allocation, 115; measures of development, 34, 35; measures of economic growth, 32, 33; structural transformation, 50. *See also* Food consumption
Consumption model, household labor allocation, 177
Contracts, tenure, 278
Cooperation, in traditional society, 93
Cooperative farming, 271
Cooperative institutions: at Comilla, Bangladesh, 267–68; family farmer, 271; financial, savings, 261; mechanization, economic issues in, 243;

member-controlled, 266–67; performance of, 268–69; principles of, 266–67; for traditional farmers, 83

Copyright institutions, 106

Corporate ownership of land, plantations, 170

Corruption, 414

Cost-benefit analysis. *See* Benefit-cost analysis

Cost effectiveness of primary schools, 311–12

Costs: of animal power, 231, 232; of credit, 252, 259, 264, 265; of food (*see* Food costs); food production, 26, 27; government settlement programs, 172; and induced innovation, 136–37; of information, 317; of irrigation, 240; of labor (*see* Labor costs); of lending (*see* Costs, of credit); monopoly and, 355; resource allocation, 73–77; of tractors, 237–38. *See also* Benefit-cost analysis; Pricing policy

Credit: cooperatives, 268; counterproductive policies, 412–13; current practices, 254–59; demand for financial services, 253–54; diffusion model, 124; empirical studies, 254–59; existing supply, 254–57; expansion of, 263–64; improvement strategies, 252–65; informal credit market, 254, 256; input marketing, 343; macro prices, administered, 400; and rural financial markets, 252–65; savings, increasing, 260–61; sources of, 261–62; strategic investment, 417; for traditional farmers, 83

Criteria for land development, 175

Cropping practices: animal-powered mechanization, 232; cost of mechanical technology, 233–34; tractor mechanization and, 236–37, 238; and variability in yields, 292. *See also* Land preparation

Crop productivity, 203–7, 287–90. *See also* Yields

Crop varieties, 207; economic complementarities, 217–18. *See also* Seed varieties, new; Seed varieties, traditional

Cultivation. *See* Cropping practices

Cultural-change-first model, 125–27

Cultural systems, components, 99–100

Cultural variables, 89–90, 93, 99–100; and agricultural development, 99–109; and cooperatives, 266–67; environment-behavior-performance model of marketing, 337; goals for development, 5; induced innovation

model, 135 (*see also* Induced innovation model); marketing institutions, 330–31; nonpecuniary elements, 90–91; and social factors, 89–90; in traditional agriculture, 71, 72–73

Current income, changes in, 23

Current inputs, defined, 78

Currently farmed areas, development problem in, 204

Custom, 100. *See also* Cultural variables

Day length, 22–23

Death rates. *See* Population growth

Debt, cultural beliefs, 90. *See also* Credit

Decisionmaking: aggregated, 413; collective farming systems, 281; cost-benefit analysis, 166; government role in marketing, 354, 358; and institutional change, 251; political systems and, 6; price responsiveness of traditional farmer, 65; social structures and, 102–3; in traditional agriculture, 79

Default rates, government credit programs, 262

Demand: for complementary inputs, 216–18; for food (*see* Food demand); for labor (*see* Labor demand); for new crop varieties, 211–12; for school education, 309–11; for social science knowledge, 297–98; structural transformation, 50; in traditional agriculture, 71, 72–73

Demand, consumer. *See* Consumer demand

Demand and supply relationships, 72–73; for credit, 253–54; and income distribution, 155–58; for research, 296, 299; in traditional agriculture, 72–73. *See also* Elasticity of demand; Inelasticity of demand

Demographic transition model, 14–16

Dependency models, 127–29

Depreciation, 114; investment, increasing, 115, 116; measures of economic growth, 32, 33

Design technology transfer, 301–2; levels of research, 305; mechanical systems, 343–44

Development, economic. *See* Economic development; Strategies for development; Structural transformation; *specific policy areas*

Development of technology. *See* Research

Diffusion model, 123–25

Directive economic systems, 270

Disadvantage, absolute, 365

Disciplinary research, 305. *See also* Research

Discounting, cost-benefit analysis of land development, 165–66

Disease control, 222–23
Diseconomies of scale, 243
Diseconomies of size, 68
Disposable personal income, 32, 33, 41–42
Distance teaching, 312
Distribution: input supply, 344–46; institutional arrangements and, 106. *See also* Marketing
Division of labor, 50
Domestic commodity trading units, 353
Domestic prices: strategies for development, 418; trade and, 365. *See also* Pricing policy
Dual-sector models, 176

Econometric models, 388
Economic analysis: cost-benefit, 166; of institutional arrangements, 104; of marketing systems, 358, 384; mechanization, 227–30. *See also* Benefit-cost analysis
Economic change: land development and, 167–69; measurement of, 33–36, 49; in traditional agricultures, 71–72. *See also* Economic development; Structural transformation
Economic complementarities: animal production, 220; education and communication investments, 317–18; among investments, 417–18; irrigation, 240; labor, 216; pesticides, 217–18; seed-fertilizer, 212; strategic investment, 417; water control, 218
Economic development: concepts of, 31–32; measures of, 33–36, 49; mechanization policy issues, 245–46; neo-Marxist theory, 129; role of agriculture in, 52–53; trade, role of, 361–68. *See also* Economic change; *specific variables*
Economic efficiency, in traditional agriculture, 74
Economic environments, marketing institutions, 330–31
Economic equilibrium model of traditional agriculture, 84; in marketing, 329–30; resource allocation, 73–77; return on investment, 77–79; and stability, 70–72; supply and demand, 72–73
Economic functions, of marketing, 326–27
Economic growth: vs. development, 31–32; and government intervention in markets, 387; and income equity, 152; and income levels, 36–41; investment and, 115–17; labor force, 184; marketing, 331–36; measures of, 32–33; price intervention and, 401–2; rates of, 4; role of agriculture in, 413; trade and, 371–73
Economic incentives. *See* Incentives

Economic indexes of development, 34, 35, 36
Economic information, and disciplinary and commodity research, 306
Economic performance, government and, 422
Economic theory: in agricultural development, 113–14; crop productivity increases, 204–6. *See also* Theory; *specific theories*
Economies of scale, plantations and, 169
Economies of size: retail food marketing, 352; traditional farms, size of, 67–69
Education: community, 126; complementarity of, 318; economic complementarities, 317–18; extension services, 315–16; increasing labor productivity and equity, 194–95; and labor supply, 182–83, 184; measures of development, 32; nonformal, 313–18; and quality of labor, 118; schooling, 308–13; strategic investments, 416
Efficient resource allocation, 73–77
Egg factories, 221
Ejido farming, 281
Elasticity of demand: for credit, 253–54; and demand for research, 298–300; income, 47–48; price, 48
Elastic supply schedules, 205–6, 214–16
Embargoes, 375
Employment: gains in, 218; goals for development, 5; and income equity, 158–59; mechanization and, 246, 247; policies for increasing, 194–95; unemployment, 32, 193
Engel curve, 42, 44
Entrepreneurship, theories emphasizing, 94
Environment, biological, 18–19, 120; animal productivity, increasing, 221, 222–23; breeding goals, 307
Environment-behavior-performance model, 336–38, 384
Equilibrium model of traditional agriculture, 70–73, 84, 93
Equipment. *See also* Mechanical technologies
Equity, income. *See* Income distribution
Erosion, 120
Evaluation of land development, 164–67
Evolutionary modernization theories, 92–97
Exchange rates, 363–64, 373–74, 385, 400
Exchange ratio, 363–64
Experiment stations, 246; and farm level research, 304, 305–6; vs. on-farm conditions, 292, 293, 295
Export crops: grain, 27–28; land tenure arrangement and, 282; plantations and, 169; production of, government pricing

policy and, 401. *See also* Trade policy
Export-led development strategy, 371–73
Export monopoly trading organizations, 353
Export-oriented growth, 361
Export quotas, 375, 376
Export restrictions, 375
Export subsidies, 376
Export taxes, 398–99
Extended families, 106, 330
Extension programs: problems of, 315–16; strategic investments, 416; for traditional farmers, 83
Externalities, 250–51, 387

Factories, animal production, 221
Factor shares, inputs, 206–7
Family farming, 21; food consumption, 210; land tenure, 271; marketing, 330; productivity in, 282. *See also* Traditional agriculture
Famines, 16, 25, 35
Farmer performance, 69–70
Farm expenses, defined, 78
Farming systems research, 304–6
Farm inputs. *See* Inputs
Farm-level research, 304–6
Farm problem, 23
Farm productivity. *See* Productivity
Farm size, 21; cultural factors, 89–90; and marketing, 330; policy issues, 246; and productivity, 276–77; and tractor costs, 238; traditional agriculture, 67–69; variability, 272–74
Feeding practices, and animal productivity, 222–23
Females. *See* Women
Fertility, soil, 208. *See also* Soil
Fertilizers, chemical: application with tractor, 236; costs of, changes in, 141; decline in relative costs of, 205; demand, increased, 211–12; economic complementarities, 212–14; government marketing roles, 341–42; history of developments, 289; market development, 342–43; marketing, 340–43; strategic investment, 417; supply curves, 206; variability in response, 292, 293. *See also* Green revolution; Inputs
Fertilizers, manure, 206, 231
Field size, cultural factors, 89–90
Financial analysis, 166. *See also* Benefit-cost analysis
Financial intermediation, 265
Financial markets, improving, 252–65; demand for services, 253–54; increasing savings, 260–61; policies for, 263–65; studies of credit conditions, 254–59. *See also* Credit

Financing, cooperatives, 266
Fish raising, 220
Fixed-capital investment, 228
Fixed costs, tractors, 237–38
Floor prices, 394–95, 396
Flow of capital services, 81–82
Flow of knowledge, 107
Food consumption: government pricing policy and, 401; livestock contributions to, 219; national, 332–34; new crop varieties and, 210; per capita income and, 42–43, 44, 46
Food costs: demand and, 26; government pricing policies and, 402
Food demand: and food costs, 26; and the demand for research, 298–300; income and, 41, 47–48; national, structural transformation and, 332, 333, 334; nutritional need, 43–45, 46; population growth and, 45–47; rate of growth in, 48–49
Food marketing. *See* Marketing
Food marketing costs, 349–52; national food consumption, 332, 333, 334; in value of retail food, 332
Food prices. *See* Pricing policy
Food problem, 22
Food production: demand and supply framework, 21–23; and population growth, 13; price and income changes, real vs. nominal, 23; total and per capita, 24–26
Food security policy, 5, 380–81
Food stocks, world, 26
Foreign exchange, 373, 376. *See also* Exchange rates; Trade
Foreign investment: neo-Marxist theory, 129; plantations and, 170
Forest clearing, 120
Form utility, 326
Forward linkages: economic complementarity of, 418; and marketing, 331
Fraud, 341–42
Free markets, 6; input marketing, 339; trading in, 360
Fungibility of loans, 253, 256

Genetics, 222–23, 306–8
Gini concentration ratio, 40–41
GNP per capita, 32, 33
Goals of development, 5–6, 387, 411
Going concerns, 100, 101
Good, limited, 93
Government: cooperatives, 266–67; credit institutions, 262; development planning, 52; enhancing performance, 421–22; input marketing, 341–42; input supply

marketing, 344–45; and institutional change, 250; institutional saving and, 261; interest rate fixing, 263; managing marketing, 327; marketing input supply, 344–45; marketing models, 335–36; marketing performance improvement, 352–58; measures of economic growth, 32, 33; mechanization, economic issues in, 243; mechanization, policy issues in, 243–47; organizations serving agriculture, 108; performance, improving, 421–22, 424; and production functions, 118; research supply-demand conditions, 295; revenues, trade and, 375; settlement projects, 171–73; strategies for development, 413–15; trade intervention, 377; traditional farmers programs for, 83. *See also* Taxes

Government policies: credit expansion, 263, 264; fertilizer policies, 214–15; land and tenure reforms, 274–77; marketing mechanical inputs, 344; mechanization, 243–47. *See also* Pricing policy; Trade policy

Grading, standardized, 356, 357

Graft, 376

Grains, 218; fertilizer-responsive, high-yielding varieties, 207–8; historical trends in yields, 289; production increases, 170–71; stocks of, 26–27. *See also* Rice; Seed varieties, new

Grain trade, world, 28

Gravity-flow irrigation, 240–42

Green revolution, 16, 123, 204; farm level effects, 207–9; future prospects, 211–16; and marketing, 331; national effects, 209–11

Gross investment: increasing, 115, 116; measures of economic growth, 32, 33

Gross national product, 32, 33

Group farming, 271–72

Group lending, 261–62

Group purchasing, 352

Growing conditions: economic complementarities, 217, 218; and tractor use, 238

Growth: in food production per capita, 24–25; in marketing, 331–34; Marxist model, 128; in traditional agriculture, 79–82. *See also* Economic growth; Population growth

Growth-stage theories, 126, 130–32

Hand-carried motorized machinery, 234–35

Hand hoe cultivation, 227

Hand-powered tools: innovations in, 230–31; land preparation, comparative costs, 233;

new, 230–31; policy issues, 244. *See also* Human-powered devices

Hayami-Ruttan model, 89, 134–51

Health services, 32, 43

Herbicides, 236, 307

Herdsmen, 219

High-payoff input model, 132–34, 422–23

High-return activities, investment in, 132–34, 415

High-technology land investment projects, 169–71

History, 2–4, 286–91

Household consumption decisions, 177

Household income distribution, 39–40

Household labor, 191

Household labor allocation, 176–78

Housing: government settlement projects, 171; measures of development, 32, 35

Human capital: investment in, 134, 308–9; sources of economic growth, 413; strategic investments, 416; trade and, 366–67; in traditional agriculture, 81. *See also* Labor

Human-powered devices: innovations in, 230–31; irrigation, 239–40. *See also* Hand-powered tools

Hunting and gathering, 286

Ideologies, 337

Immiserizing growth, 371–73

Implicit tax on exports, 373–74

Import controls, mechanization policy issues, 246

Import quotas, 376

Import substitution, 361, 373–74

Import substitution industrialization strategy, 361, 373–74, 389–90, 392, 398

Improved-income-distribution-with-growth strategy, 423

Incentives: food production, pricing policy and, 391; goals for development, 5; high-yielding seeds, 209; traditional farmers and, 61

Income: annual cycle of labor demand, 191; and food demand, 47–48; goals for development, 5; institutional arrangements and, 103–6; livestock contributions to, 219; measures of development, 32, 35; measures of economic growth, 32, 33; real vs. nominal, 23; resource allocation, 73–77

Income, farm: high-yielding seeds and, 209; and nutrition, 210; structural transformation and, 52

Income, producer: institutional arrangements and, 103–6; support prices and, 396

Income distribution, 38–41; and agricultural

development, 151–59; collective farming and, 281; counterproductive policies, 412–13; economic factors influencing, 152–58; economic and social theory, 151–52; goals for development, 5; and government intervention in markets, 387; government strategies to reduce disparities, 158–59; industry-first models and, 122; land tenure arrangement and, 273, 282; measures of development, 32, 35; mechanization policy issues, 247; policy areas, 194–95, 196, 246; strategies for development, 419–21; world concentration of resources, 37–38

Income elasticity of demand, 47, 332, 333, 334

Income growth: and consumer demand, 41–45; structural changes, 50

Income transfer strategy, 159

Indexes of development, 34, 35, 36

Induced development model: cooperatives, 268; and marketing, 335; policy areas, 194–95

Induced innovation model, 1, 89, 134–51; central concepts, 136–43; conclusions, 150–51; criticisms, 148–50; crop productivity increases, 204–6; education in, 308; elements in, 135; endogenous and exogenous development, 142–43; high-yielding seeds and, 209; inducement mechanism, 136–37; institutional, 143–46; land ownership, 282–83; land reform, 276; long-run path of, 140, 142; mechanization policy issues, 246; productivity changes, 139–40; in public sector, 146–48; relative factor costs, 138–39, 141; strategies for development, 411; technology development, 138, 139

Industrial fundamentalism model, 121–23, 176, 387

Industrialization: economic growth, 52; and exchange rates, 373; farm input production, 53; and government intervention in markets, 387; income distribution, household, 39; and labor supply, 182–83, 184; and land per agricultural laborer, 162, 163

Industrial market economies. *See* Market economies

Industrial stage, urban-industrial impact model, 123

Inelasticity of demand: credit, 253–54; for food, and demand for research, 299; and income distribution, 155–58

Inelastic supply: credit, 253–54; economic complementarities, 217, 218; inputs, 205–6

Inequality, income, 32, 35. *See also* Income distribution

Infant industries, 381–82

Inferior goods and services, 48

Inflation, 373, 374–75

Informal credit, 252, 253–54

Information: complementarity of, 318; costs of, 317; diffusion model, 124; institutional arrangements and, 107; marketing, 357

Infrastructure, 53; goal of government, 414; government role in marketing, 358; projects, 195; strategic investment, 417

Innovation: Hayami-Ruttan model, 89, 134–51; in traditional agriculture, 72. *See also* Induced innovation model

Innovation possibility isoquant, 136, 137, 138, 139

Input marketing, 338–46; alternative supply channels, 344–46; biological, 339–40; chemical, 340–43; mechanical, 343–46

Inputs, 118; backward linkages, 331, 418; complementarities in (*see* Economic complementarities); crop productivity increases, 204–6; current, 78, 82; elastic vs. inelastic supply, 205–6; factor shares, changes in, 206–7; high-payoff input model, 422–23; improved, 118; marketing (*see* Input marketing); nontraditional, 118; one-variable, 75–76; package programs, 214; pricing policies, 385, 397–98; seed-fertilizer complementarities, 212–14; strategic investment, 417; subsidies, 397–98; substitution, 217, 218; transformation to scientific agriculture, 199; two-variable, 76–77. *See also* Capital; Labor

Input suppliers, credit from, 262

Input supply: elastic vs. inelastic, 205–6; and marketing, 331, 338–46

Inspections, government marketing roles, 341–42

Institutional arrangements: and agricultural development, 102–3; concepts and definitions, 100–102; diffusion model, 124; and economic behavior, 102–7; effects on production and distribution, 106; goal of government, 414; induced innovation model, 135; irrigation systems, 241–42; marketing systems, 330–31; for market intervention, 352–54; mechanization, 243; monopoly and, 355–56; in traditional agriculture, 71. *See also* Induced innovation model; *specific institutions*

Institutional change, 101–2; cooperatives, 265–69; credit and financial markets,

improvement of, 252–65; credit conditions, 254–59; credit sources, 261–62; demand for financial services, 253–54; externalities, 250–51; farm size, tenancy, and landlessness, 272–74; financial markets, 254–59, 263–65; government, role of, 250; for improved input, 118; and income equity, 158–59; induced innovation, 143–46; land development and, 167–69; landholding arrangements, types of, 270–72; land reform, 274–77; land use, changes in, 269–83; marketing institutions, 330–31; savings, increasing, 260–61; social sciences and, 251; technology and, 251; tenure reform, 274–77. *See also* Land reform; Structural transformation
Integral farming, 271
Integrated model of marketing and development, 335–36
Interactive economic systems, 270
Interest rates, 257–59, 385; ceilings on, 264; cost-benefit analysis of land development, 165–66; informal credit market, 254; macro prices, administered, 400; policies for improving financial markets, 263–64; transaction costs and, 265
Internal rate of return, 166
International aid, 418–19
International commodity agreements, 379–80
International Maize and Wheat Improvement Center (CIMMYT), 203
International markets. *See* Trade
International research system, 303–4
Inverted U-shape curve, 414
Investment, 5; and agricultural development, 61; concepts, 114–15; conservation model, 120–21; contributions of agriculture, 53; government pricing policies and, 402; and income equity, 158–59; land development, cost-benefit analysis, 164–67; measures of economic growth, 32, 33; and production functions, 118; in schooling, 308–13; strategic elements for, 415–18; in technology (*see* Technology); in traditional agriculture, 77–79. *See also* Research, investment in
Irrigation, 218, 239–40
Isocost curves, 76, 77, 139, 143, 228–29
Isoquant framework, 76–77; innovation possibility, 136, 137, 228–29; mechanization, 227–30

Joint ownership arrangements, 243

Labeling, 341–42

Labor: agricultural stage models, 131; allocation of, in household, 176–78; contributions to agriculture, 53; cooperative farming, 271; demand, 185–93; economic complementarities, 216–17; economic theory, 176; education (*see* Education); female, 178–82; land development, land-labor relationships, 162–63, 165; macro prices, administered, 400; mechanization policy issues, 246, 247; neoclassical model of growth, 79; plantation, 169–70; policy areas, 194–95; production function, 118; productivity changes, 163; productivity increases, 290; traditional agriculture, 79–80. *See also* Human capital; Settlement/resettlement programs
Labor costs: agricultural stage models, 131; and animal power profitability, 231, 233, 234; induced innovation model, 141, 204–5; mechanization, economics of, 228–29, 233
Labor demand, 185–93, 218; annual cycle of, 190; labor, 185–93
Labor-intensive technologies, 136, 137
Labor productivity, 162–63, 190–94; increase in, 290; traditional agriculture, 65
Labor quality: investments in, 134; as production factors, 118
Labor-saving technology, 154
Labor supply, 176, 182–85; factors affecting, 182–83; technological change and, 153–55
Labor use, 218
Land: as capital, 81; in conservation model, 120; cooperative farming, 271; and economic growth, 412–13; neoclassical model of growth, 79; ownership and control, 163–64; production function, 118; as security, 256; sources of economic growth, 413; in traditional agriculture, 80–81
Land area: agricultural stage models, 131; world grain production increases, 170–71
Land availability, 19–20
Land costs, 141, 204–5
Land development, 204 cost- benefit analysis, 164–67; criteria and policies for, 175; economic evaluation of, 164–67; evaluation of three types of, 174; government settlement projects, 171–73; improvement of currently farmed land, 167; plantations and high-technology projects, 169–71; spontaneous, 173–74; technological, institutional, and economic change, 167–69

Land farmed, changes in selected nations, 121
Landlessness, 272–74
Landlords, 276–77, 278
Land ownership, 105, 163–64, 256; strategic investment, 417. *See also* Land reform; Land tenure
Land per laborer, productivity changes, 163
Land preparation: animal-powered mechanization, 232; costs of mechanical technology, 233–34; economic complementarities, 217, 218; tractors, 235
Land productivity, 162–63; growth rates, 290; traditional agriculture, 63–65
Land reform: conclusions, 282–83; experiences with, 277–82; and productivity, 274–77; socioeconomic effects of, 278–80; strategies for development, 419
Land tenure, 105, 145, 269–83; collective farming, 280–92; communes, 270, 271, 272; conclusions, 282–83; land reform, 274–82; and productivity, 104–5; types of landholding arrangements, 270–72; variability in, 272–74
Land-to-the-tiller programs, 103, 277–78
Leasing, land, 145
Legislation, 145–46
Less developed nations: animal production in, 219–21; land development, 163; mechanization, 226–27; organizations serving agriculture, 108; returns to investment in land, 167; structural transformation, 49–52
Levels of consumption, 32, 33
Levels of living, 32, 33, 35, 191
Licensing, trade, 376
Life expectancy, 35
Limited good, theory of, 93
Linkages, 413; economic complementarity of, 418; and indirect labor demand, 188–89; and marketing, 331
Literacy, 35, 310
Livestock, 65, 219–23, 289
Living standards: measures of development, 33, 34; plantation workers, 169–70
Loans: default rates, 262; fungibility of, 253; losses, risk premium needed, 259; transaction costs, and interest rates, 265. *See also* Credit
Location-specific agricultural technology, 125
Lorenz curves, 40, 272–73, 274
Luxury goods, 48, 377

Machinery. *See* Mechanical technologies
Macro prices, 385, 400–401

Maize. *See* Grains
Malthusian model, 13–14, 75
Management, 327; diffusion model, 124; input marketing, 343; retail food marketing, 352
Management practices: animal production, 223; farming systems research, 306; machinery, 242–43
Manufactures. *See* Inputs
Marginal productivity, labor, 191
Marginal returns, 120, 177
Marginal soil conditions, 208
Margins, marketing, 327, 328
Market access, and trade, 362
Market demand, and income distribution, 155–58
Market development, 342–43
Market economies: cost-benefit analysis, 166; income distribution, household, 39; measures of economic growth, 32, 33; per capita food production, 24, 25
Market equilibrium, 394–95
Market failure, 386–87
Market forces, 21–23
Marketing, 211; biological inputs, 339–40; chemical inputs, 340–43; and comparative advantage, 365–66; economic function of, 326–27; and economic growth, 331–36; evaluating performance, 336–38; fertilizer, 214–15; food, 349–52; government roles and policies, 352–58, 402; growth in, 331–34; increasing performance, 346–49, 350; input, 339–46; institutional arrangement, 352–54; mechanical inputs, 343–46; mechanization policy issues, 246; models of, 327–31; plantations and, 169; problems of, 325–26; product, 346–52; and production functions, 118; role of, in development, 334–36; by traditional farmers, 67; urban food, 349, 351–52
Marketing boards, 353, 399–400
Marketing management, 327
Marketing organizations, credit from, 262
Market prices, 23, 26
Markets, economic functions of, 385–86
Markets, international. *See* Trade
Marxist/neo-Marxist theory, 92, 97–98, 127–29; institutional change, 143–44; wages, 176
Marxist states, collectivization in, 280–82
Material technology transfer, 301, 305
Maximum profit criterion, 386, 387
Measurement: development, 33–36; economic growth, 32–33; economic structure changes, 49
Mechanical technologies: agricultural stage

models, 131; analysis, isoquant framework, 227–30; animal-powered mechanization, 231–34; costs of, changes in, 141, 205; irrigation and drainage, 239–42; managing and servicing, economic issues in, 242–43; marketing, 343–46; mechanization in less developed nations, 226–27; motorized power, stationary and wheeled, 234–35; new hand tools, 230–31; policy issues, 243–47; tractor-powered machinery, 235–39
Mechanization, and household labor, 191
Media, 316–17
Member-controlled cooperatives, 266–67
Microcomputer, 306
Microorganisms, 307
Migration, 421; and labor supply, 182–83, 184; and marketing, 332
Minimum level of consumption, 35
Minimum level of living, 35
Minimum wage, 400
Mixed cropping in mounds, 292
Models: of development (*see* Theory); marketing, 327, 329–31
Modern agricultural production function, 117–19
Money, traditional people, 66
Moneylenders, 252, 257
Monopolies: counterproductive policies, 412–13; and government intervention in pricing, 387; government role in marketing, 354–56; input distribution, 345; marketing boards, 399–402; trading units, government role in marketing, 353
Monopolistic marketing model, 327, 329
Monopsonistic marketing, 330
More developed nations: concentration of income, 37; grain exports, 27; organizations serving agriculture, 108; productivity growth rates in, 290–91
Motivation, theories emphasizing, 94–95
Motorized power, 233, 234–39
Mound cropping, 292, 294, 295
Multinational corporations, 374, 376
Multiple exchange rate, 374, 376

National consensus, on development, 411–12
National demand for food, 332
National economic growth, 32, 33; agriculture in, 52–53, 413; new crop varieties and, 209–11; per capita income and, 36–37; structural transformations, 49–52. *See also* Economic growth
National fertilizer policies, 214
National food consumption, 332–34
National income: allocation of, 115; trade and, 361–68

National income elasticity of demand, 47–48, 332, 333, 334
National market, elastic demand curves for products, 299
National policies. *See* Government; Strategies for development; *specific policy areas*
National resources, marketing, 335
Natural resources, 21
Negative impacts, on women, 181
Negative sanctions, 100
Neoclassical models of economic growth, 79; comparative advantage, 361, 362–66 and wages, 176
Neo-Marxist theory. *See* Marxist/neo-Marxist theory
Net annual investment, increasing, 115, 116
Net farm income, indebtedness and, 257
Net national product, measures of economic growth, 32, 33
New genetics, 306–8
Nitrogen fertilizer. *See* Fertilizers, chemical
Nomadic herding, 219
Nominal income, changes in, 23
Nominal prices, changes in, 23
Nominal protection of agricultural producers, 391
Nonagricultural sectors: labor demand in, 189–90. *See also* Migration
Nonformal education: demand and supply of, 313–14; returns to investment, 314–15
Nonpecuniary elements of utility, 90–91
Nonprice measures, trade intervention, 376–77
Nontraditional inputs, 118
Norfolk crop rotation, 119
Norms, defined, 99–102
Nutrition: and demand for food, 43–45, 46; measures of development, 32; new crop varieties and, 210

Off-farm employment, 177, 218
Oil-exporting nations, 25, 37
One-variable input, 75–76
On-farm research, 304–6
Opportunity costs, 259; animal-powered mechanization, 231–34; labor, 192
Optimum tariffs, 378–81
Organization, concept of, 101
Organizational structures: cooperatives, 266; farming district projects, 424, 425
Organization of small farmers, 419–20
Organizations, in agriculture, 107–9. *See also* Institutional arrangements
Outmigration. *See* Migration
Output: high-payoff input model, 133; productivity of marketing, 338

Overgrazing, 219
Overvalued exchange rate, 373–74, 400
Owner-operator farms, 274–75
Ownership of land. *See* Land ownership;
    Land reform; Land tenure

Package programs, 213–14, 417
Packaging, food, 353, 356, 357
Parastatal organizations, 353
Participation rates of labor, 182
Pastoralists, 219
Patent laws, 106
Paths of productivity change, 139–43
Peak labor demand, 190–91
Pecuniary variables, 90–91
Per capita agricultural production, 24–26
Per capita income: and food demand, 47;
    growth rates, 36–37; measures of
    economic growth, 32, 33; structural
    transformation, 50
Perfect market model, 336, 338
Performance, economic, 69–70;
    environment-behavior-performance model
    of marketing, 337–38; government and,
    422; marketing, 346–49; per capita
    income growth, 36
Personal assets, 153
Personal consumption. *See* Consumption
Personal income, 32
Personal savings, 41–42
Personal utility function, 90–91
Pesticides: application of, 236; economic
    complementarities, 217–18; government
    marketing roles, 341–42; marketing,
    340–43; with traditional crop varieties,
    217. *See also* Inputs
Phosphate fertilizer. *See* Fertilizers,
    chemical
Physical capital, 366–67
Physical environment. *See* Climate
Physical quality of life index (PQLI), 35–36
Physical resources, 18–21
Place utility, 326
Planned economies, 24, 25
Planning, 384–86, 388. *See also* Strategies
    for development
Plantations, 169–71, 282
Plant materials, 219; future prospects,
    306–8. *See also* Seed varieties, new;
    Seed varieties, traditional
Point elasticities, income, 47, 48
Policy issues: land development, 175; in
    mechanization, 243–47. *See also*
    Government; Pricing policy; Strategies
    for development; Trade policy
Political economy, 95–96
Political factors: cooperatives, 267; land and
    tenure reforms, 274–77; marketing

institutions, 330–31; mechanization
    policy issues, 247; strategies for
    development, 419–20; theories
    emphasizing, 95–96
Political influence: of plantation operators,
    170; trade controls, 376
Political systems, 6
Pollution, 250
Population densities, supported by
    agricultural systems, 287
Population growth: agricultural, 185;
    demand and supply framework, 22;
    demographic transition model, 14–16;
    and food demand, 45–47; and labor
    supply, 182–83, 184; land availability
    and, 19; land per agricultural laborer,
    162, 163; Malthusian model, 13–14;
    prospects for, 16–18; rates, 18; world,
    3–4
Population shifts. *See* Migration
Positive sanctions, 100
Positive view of trade, 361
Postindustrial economy, 3
Postproduction operations, 236
Poultry production, 221–22
Poverty: goals for development, 5; labor
    productivity and, 175; measures of
    development, 32, 34, 35
Power in agriculture, kinds of, 227
Poverty level of consumption, 35
Price ceilings, 342
Price changes, and the induced innovation
    model, 204–5
Price distortions, 246, 391–92
Price elasticity of demand, 48, 66; and
    demand for research, 298–300; and
    income distribution, 155–58; traditional
    farming, 66
Price responsiveness of traditional farmers,
    65–67, 84
Prices: demand and supply framework, 22;
    economic functions of, 385–86; food
    production costs and, 26; grains, 26–27;
    international commodity agreements,
    379; measures of development, 35;
    methods of price intervention, 392–401;
    monopoly and, 355; real vs. nominal,
    23; role of, 389–92; strategies for
    development, 418; trade and, 365
Price stabilization, 353
Price supports, 229, 342
Pricing efficiency, 337–38, 358
Pricing policy, 246; administered macro
    prices, 400–401; administered product
    prices, 393–97; and agricultural
    development, 401–2; cause and range of
    government intervention, 386, 387, 389;
    economic functions of markets and

prices, 385–86; effects on development, 401–2; export taxes, 398–99; government role in marketing, 330, 342, 353, 356, 357, 358; input marketing, 342, 345; input pricing, 397–98; instruments of intervention, 393–401; international commodity agreements, 379; marketing boards, 399–400; new technology assessment, 229; objectives of, 392–93; planning, government role in, 384–86; role of prices in development, 389–92; strategies for development, 411; for trade intervention, 373, 375–77

Primary schooling, 311–12, 416
Private economic activities, 281–82
Private profitability, 386–87
Private sector: in government credit programs, 262; government role in marketing, 358; marketing boards with, 399; research supply-demand conditions, 295
Processing, transforming traditional, 348–49, 350
Processing costs, for small loans, 259
Production: costs of, and comparative advantage, 365–66; government involvement in, 387, 388; institutional arrangements and, 106; land-labor relationships, 162–63; measures of economic growth, 32, 33; mechanization policy issues, 246; national, 209–10; price responsiveness of traditional farmers, 65–67; total and per capita food, 24–26; trade and, 363–66; in traditional agriculture, 79–82. *See also* Food production; Structural transformation
Production function analysis, 74–75, 87, 133, 155, 168, 192, 208, 217, 293; education in, 308–9; fertilizer use, 211
Production functions: classical and modern agricultural, 117–19; high-payoff input model, 133
Production possibility curve, 364, 372, 378
Productivity, 23; animal, 219–23; of animal-powered mechanization, 232; collectivization and, 280, 281; in conservation model, 120; crop, 203–7 (*see also* Yields); farm, increases in, 219; goals for development, 5; grain exports, 27–28; induced innovation model, 139–40; institutional arrangements and, 103; of irrigation projects, 242; of labor, 190–93; land reform and, 274–77; of marketing, 338; monopoly and, 355; policies for increasing, 194–95; rates of change, 163;

seed-fertilizer complementarities, 212–14; structural transformation, 50–52; world concentration of, 37–38. *See also* Food production
Productivity, traditional agriculture, 62, 63–65 farm size, 67–69; labor, 65; land, 63–65; livestock, 65
Productivity change: history of, 286–91; paths of, 139–40
Product market demand, 155–58
Profitability: and price policies, 385; social, 386
Profits: calculation of resource allocation, 87; quotas and, 377; resource allocation, 73–77, 87
Programs: failures in traditional agriculture, 82–83; package, 213–14
Project cost-benefit analysis, 166
Promotional units, government, 353
Protection, nominal, 391
Protein quality in crops, 210
Psychological variables: community development movement, 126; theories emphasizing, 94–95. *See also* Behavioral variables; Cultural variables
Public good, 313
Public retail markets, 349, 351
Public sector, 313; capitalist vs. socialist systems, 6; goal of government, 414; induced innovation in, 146–48; and institutional change, 250–51. *See also* Government; *specific policy areas*
Puebla project, 417
Pump irrigation projects, 240–42
Pure stabilization policies, 392

Quality standards, 341–42, 353, 356–57
Quasi-cooperatives, 266
Quotas, 375, 376, 377

Radio programming, 316–17, 318
Rate of growth in food demand, 48–49
Rate of return, cost benefit analysis criteria, 166
Rate of return on investment, 77–79
Real price and income changes, 23, 26, 27
Regional development, 423–25
Regional growth, 50–52, 421
Regulated markets, 357
Regulation, 327; input marketing, 341; government role, 353, 354. *See also* Government; *specific policy areas*
Relative price changes, 205
Rental arrangements: land, 105, 145, 273; machinery, 238, 243
Research: animal-powered mechanization, 232; animal production, 223; at capacity level, 305;

environment-behavior-performance model of marketing, 338; mechanization, 228, 232, 245–46; strategic investment, 417; strategies for development, 415–16

Research, investment in, 291–95; deficiencies in less developed nations, 292, 294–95; demand for social science research, 297; economics of demand and supply, 295–308; farming systems, 303–6; increasing supply of, 300–306; international system, 303–4; price elasticity of demand for food, 298–300; social returns of, 296–97; technological and socioeconomic constraints, 292, 293

Research gap, 292, 294–95

Resettlement programs. *See* Settlement-resettlement programs

Resource allocation: compensatory investment, 421; credit and, 252; government pricing policies, 395, 401; household, 176–78; market functions, 385–86; mechanization, economic issues in, 243; by traditional farmers, 73–77, 84. *See also* Labor, allocation of, in household; Land allocation

Resource-based agriculture, strategies for development, 411

Resource endowments: and innovation, 135, 144; neoclassical model of growth, 79. *See also* Induced innovation model

Retail markets, urban, 349, 351–52

Returns to investment, 77–79; in agriculture, 413; in currently farmed land, 167; in education, nonformal, 314–15; investments in labor, 134; research, 296; in traditional agriculture, 77–79, 84

Returns to labor, 191

Rice: new varieties, 211; real cost of, 26, 27; yields, 90, 289. *See also* Grains; Seed varieties, new

Risk, monopoly and, 355

Risk premium, 259

Roads, strategic investments in, 417

Role, defined, 99

Rostow five-stage growth model, 130

Rostow national marketing strategy model, 335

Ruminants, 219

Sale by description, 357

Salinity, 120

Sanctions, defined, 100

Savings, 260–64; government pricing policies and, 402; measures of economic growth, 32, 33; personal, 41–42;

Scarce resources: investment, optimizing, 117; markets and, 385–86

Scarcity values, 386

Schooling, investment in, 308–13

Schultz high-payoff input model, 132–34, 422

Schultz model. *See* Economic equilibrium model of traditional agriculture

Science-based agriculture: strategies for development, 411; transition to, 199, 289–90

Scientific-industrial transition, 2, 3

Scientific method, 4–5

Seasonal variability in yields, 292

Secondary education, 312

Seed varieties, new: economic complementarities, 212–14, 216–18; future prospects, 306–8; irrigation and, 240; local conditions and, 292; marketing, 339–40. *See also* Green revolution; Inputs

Seed varieties, traditional, 217, 292

Segmented credit supply curve, 264

Self-sufficiency, food, 387, 392–93

Sensitivity analysis, 166

Service sector, 52

Servicing, agricultural machinery, 237, 242–43

Settlement/resettlement programs: government, 171–73; spontaneous, 173–74

Sexual division of labor, 102

Share tenancy, 104–5, 145, 273, 276

Shifting cultivation, 286–88

Shortages, 373, 375

Single-variable production functions, 133. *See also* Production function analysis

Size of farm. *See* Farm size

Slash and burn agricultural systems, 286–88

Social action, 126

Social change: evolutionary modernization theories, 92; government settlement programs, 172; in traditional societies, 71. *See also* Structural transformation

Social conflict theories, 92

Social costs: irrigation, 240; new technology assessment, 229

Social environment: and animal-power adoption, 234; changes in, 88–90; and communications, 317; community development movement, 126; evolutionary modernization theories, 92; goals for development, 5; land reform and, 278–80; and livestock, 219; measures of development, 32; mechanization policy issues, 247; monopoly and, 355; plantation workers, 169–70; population control, 16; research, returns of, 296–97; research challenges, 292; in traditional agriculture, 71. *See also* Cultural variables; Social structure

Social evolution, thresholds, 4–5
Social institutions. *See* Institutional
  arrangements; Institutional change
Socialist states, 6; collective farming in,
  271–72; cooperatives, 266–67;
  cost-benefit analysis, 166
Social learning, 4–5, 96–97, 388
Social norms, 93
Social sciences, 251, 297
Social structure, 94; development theories
  emphasizing, 96; institutions, 102–3; and
  organizations, 101. *See also* Social
  environment
Social valuation of economic activities,
  386–87
Socioeconomic development theories, 91–98;
  evolutionary modernization, 92–97;
  Marxist, 97–98; social learning, 96
Socioeconomic model, marketing, 330–31
Socioeconomic transformation. *See*
  Strategies for development; Structural
  transformation
Soil, 18–19; productivity of as dependent
  variable, 120; structural transformation
  and soil areas, 52; traditional seed
  varieties and, 208
Spare parts, 243
Specialization: structural transformation,
  50–52; trade and, 361, 362
Spontaneous family settlements, 173–74
Stabilization, pricing policy objectives, 392
Stage models of agricultural development,
  130–32
Standardization, marketing, 341–42, 353,
  356, 357
Standard of consumption, 34
Standard of living, 34
State of preferences, 71
State of the arts, 70, 71
State trading units, 353
Status: and animal-power adoption, 234;
  defined, 99; and tenure arrangements,
  105–6; in traditional agriculture, 72
Storage, 326, 347
Strategic elements for growth, 415–22
Strategies for development: future prospects,
  425–26; goals, 410, 411–12;
  governmental role, 413–15; government
  performance, 421–22; high-payoff
  inputs, 422–23;
  improved-income-distribution-with-growth,
  423; income distribution effects, 419–21;
  international aid, 418–19; investment
  areas, 415–18; land vs. labor in, 412–13;
  need for consensus on goals, 411–12;
  prices, domestic, 418; regional
  total-resource-focused, 423–25; role of

agriculture in economic growth, 413;
  traditional agriculture and, 83–84
Structural-functional social theory, 92–97
Structuralist school, 389–90
Structural transformation: forces causing
  change, 49–50; and income equity,
  158–59; and labor supply, 182–83, 184;
  and marketing, 331–34; measurement of,
  49; specialization and growth with,
  50–52. *See also* Strategies for
  development
Structure of production, 366
Structure of trade, 368–69
Subsidies, 412–13; consumer prices, 396;
  counterproductive policies, 412–13;
  credit, 264; fertilizer, 215; government
  pricing policies, 391, 392, 402; input,
  397–98; mechanization policy issues,
  246; new technology assessment, 229;
  overvalued exchange rates as, 373
Subtenancy, 145
Superphosphate fertilizer, 289
Suppliers, credit from, 262
Supply: cereal stocks, levels of, 26–27;
  credit, 264; demand and supply
  framework, 21–23; food, 26, 28–29;
  input, 205–6, 214–16; institutional
  innovation, 146; labor (*see* Labor
  supply); mechanization policy issues,
  245–46; and research, demand for,
  298–300; in traditional agriculture,
  72–73
Supply elasticity, 205–6; of plant materials
  and fertilizers, 214–16; traditional
  farming, 66
Support prices, 394–95, 396
Surpluses, food, 28–29
Symbols, defined, 99

Tariffs, 375, 377, 378–81
Taxes: agricultural income, 390, 391;
  export, 398–99; government role in
  marketing, 358; on imports, 374, 375;
  and income equity, 159; measures of
  economic growth, 32, 33; mechanization
  policy issues, 246
Technical assistance, diffusion model, 124
Technological advantages, plantation,
  169–70
Technological change: capital intensity of,
  153–55; land development and, 167–69;
  as production factor, 118; trade and,
  361, 362
Technology, 21, 131; agricultural stage
  models, 131; biotechnology, 306–8; and
  credit demand, 254; diffusion model,
  124; high-payoff input model, 132–34;

increasing labor productivity and equity, 194–95; and institutional change, 251; investments in development, 133–34; and labor demand, 186–88; marketing, 346; monopoly and, 355–56; policy areas, 194–95; research challenges, 292, 293, 294, 295; strategic investment, 417; supplying, 300–301; in traditional agriculture, 71. *See also* Induced innovation model; Mechanical technologies

Technology transfer: animal production, 223; investing in, 302–3; strategies for development, 415–6; three phases of, 301–2

Telecommunications, 316–17

Television, 316–17, 318

Tenancy, 105, 272–74

Tenure arrangements. *See* Land tenure

Tenure contracts, 105

Tenure reform, 274–77

Theory, 113–60; community development movement, 125–27; conservation model, 119–21; cultural change first model, 125–27; diffusion model, 123–25; economic theory, value of, 113–14; growth-stage theories, 130–32; high-payoff input model, 132–34; income distribution and, 151–59; induced innovation model, 134–51; industrial fundamentalism model, 121–23; investment concepts, 114–17; neo-Marxist and dependency models, 127–29; production functions, 117–19; traditional agriculture, 70; urban-industrial impact model, 123. *See also specific models and theories*

Theory of comparative advantage, 360–68

Theory of limited good, 93

Threshing, mechanical, 236

Thresholds in social evolution, 4–5

Tillage. *See* Land preparation

Time discount rate, 165–66

Time period, loans, 256

Time utility, 326

Titles to land, 256

Total cost curve, monopoly and, 87, 355

Total national consumption, 32, 33

Total-resource-focused strategy, 423–25

Traction, animal-powered, 232

Tractor-powered machinery: economic complementarities, 217, 218; economies of, 237–39; policy issues, 246; potential contributions, 235–37

Trade: contributions of agriculture, 53; economics of trade intervention, 377–82; experiences, 368–73; government pricing policy and, 401; government role in marketing, 353; grain exports, 27; managing, 373–75; marketing technologies, 346; mechanization policy issues, 246; measures for trade intervention, 375–77; monopoly arrangements, 330; neo-Marxist theory, 129; plantations and, 170

Trade policy: alternative strategies, 382; balance of payments, controls, 374; changing structure of, 368; comparative advantage, changing, 366–68; comparative advantage, theory of, 362–66; and economic growth, 371–73; government intervention in, 377–82; government revenues, 375; import substitution, 373–74; infant industries, 381–82; inflation controls, 374–75; managing, 373–75; nonprice measures, 376–77; price measures, 375–76; role of, in development, 361–68; shares of products in LDC, 369–70; taxes, export, 398–99

Traditional agriculture: allocation of resources, 73–77; definitions and hypotheses, 59–61; development strategies, 83–84; diffusion model limitations, 125; economic equilibrium model, 70–79; economic theory, 82–83; empirical findings, 62–70; farm size, 67–69; growth in, 79–82; hypotheses, 61–62; importance of study, 61, 62; labor productivity, 65; land ownership, communal, 270; land productivity, 63–65; livestock productivity, 65; marketing models, 329–30; performance, farmer, 69–70; price responsiveness, 65–67; program failures, 82–83; rate of change in, 70–72; resource input calculations, 87; return on investment in, 77–79; returns to investment in land, 167; supply and demand equilibrium, 72–73; yields, 63–65, 69, 208

Traditional crop varieties, 208, 212

Traditional food markets, 351–52

Traditional societies: and government systems, 414; labor productivity, 175. *See also* Cultural variables; Socioeconomic development theories

Training: in marketing, 343, 358. *See also* Education

Training and visit system, 315–16

Transaction costs, 317; credit, 256; institutional saving and, 261; and interest rates, 265

Transfer of technology. *See* Technology transfer

Transportation: consumption pattern, 43; and fertilizer prices, 214–15; reducing costs,

347–48; structural transformation and, 52
Trial-and-error learning process, 4
Tropical nations, 124
Two-price policy, 396
Two-variable inputs, analysis of, 76–77

Uncertainty, 106–7
Uncultivated land. *See* Land development
Underemployment, 193
Underpricing agricultural output, 390–91
Unemployment, 32, 193
University education, 416
Urban areas: marketing in, 349, 351–52; mechanization policy issues, 247
Urban-industrial impact model, 123
Urbanization. *See* Migration
Utility function, 90–91

Valuation of economic activities, 386–87
Value of retail food, 332, 333, 334
Values: land ownership, 163; and tenure arrangements, 105–6; theories emphasizing, 93. *See also* Cultural variables
Vertically integrated marketing systems, 352
Veterinary services, 222–23
Village agriculture, 288–89
Village-level community development, 126
Visit and training system model, 315–16
Vocational education, 312–13

Wages, 176, 190–94, 385; collective farming and, 281; macro prices, administered, 400; policy areas, 195, 196; women, 179–80
Water, 18–19, 218. *See also* Irrigation
Weeding, 232, 236
Weights and measures, 356, 357
Wheat. *See* Grains; Seed varieties, new
Wholesale markets, urban, 349, 351
Women: contribution to production, 178–79; cultural beliefs, 89–90; household labor allocation, 177; labor supply, 182; wage discrimination, 179–80
Work effect, of educational investments, 309
World Bank, 166, 172
World grain production, 170–71
World income, 36–41
World market prices, trade and, 365

Yields: animal-powered equipment and, 232, 233; livestock production systems, 220; new crop varieties, 209, 306; pesticide use, economics of, 217–18; postharvest operations and, 236; productivity changes, 163; rice, 90; tractors and, 236; with traditional agriculture, 63–65, 69, 208
Yield gaps, 292, 293, 295

Zero marginal productivity, labor, 191–92

ABOUT THE AUTHORS   *Robert D. Stevens* is professor of agricultural economics in the College of Agricultural and Natural Resources at Michigan State University. *Cathy L. Jabara* is an economist with the U.S. Department of the Treasury.